THE  CB SOLUTION

Print

CB delivers all the key terms and all the content for the **Consumer Behaviour** course through a visually engaging and easy-to-review print experience.

Digital

MindTap enables you to stay organized and study efficiently by providing a single location for all your course materials and study aids. Built-in apps leverage social media and the latest learning technology to help you succeed.

1 Open the Access Card included with this text.

2 Follow the steps on the card.

3 Study.

Student Resources

- Interactive eBook
- Flashcards
- Practice Quiz Generator
- Trackable Activities:
  — Graded Quizzing
  — Media Quizzing
- Chapter Videos
- Online Glossary
- Part Videos
- Case Studies
- Chapter Review Cards

Instructor Resources

- Access to All Student Resources
- Engagement Tracker
- Instructor Companion Site
- PowerPoint® Slides
- Updated Test Bank
- LMS Integration

Students: **www.nelson.com/student**

Instructors: **www.nelson.com/instructor**

NELSON EDUCATION

CB, Second Canadian Edition

by Barry J. Babin, Eric G. Harris, and
Kyle B. Murray

**VP, Product and Partnership
Solutions:**
Anne Williams

Publisher, Digital and Print Content:
Amie Plourde

**Senior Marketing
Manager:**
Alexis Hood

Content Development Manager:
Toula Di Leo

Photo and Permissions Researcher:
Karen Hunter

Production Project Manager:
Jaime Smith

Production Service:
MPS Limited

Copy Editor:
Laurel Sparrow/Top Copy
Communications

Proofreader:
MPS Limited

Indexer:
Ever Olano

Design Director:
Ken Phipps

Managing Designer:
Franca Amore

Interior Design:
Trinh Truong

Cover Design:
Trinh Truong

Cover Image:
crossroadcreative

Compositor:
MPS Limited

**Library and Archives Canada
Cataloguing in Publication**

Babin, Barry J., author
    CB / Barry J. Babin, Eric G. Harris,
Kyle B. Murray. — Second Canadian
edition.

Includes index.
ISBN 978-0-17-657038-5 (paperback)

    1. Consumer behavior—Textbooks.
I. Harris, Eric G., author II. Murray,
Kyle B. (Kyle Bayne), 1973–, author
III. Title.

HF5415.32.B33 2016
658.8'342   C2015-906619-0

ISBN-13: 978-0-17-657038-5
ISBN-10: 0-17-657038-1

BRIEF CONTENTS

© Vladgrin

CONTENTS

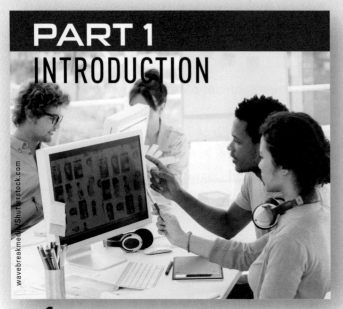
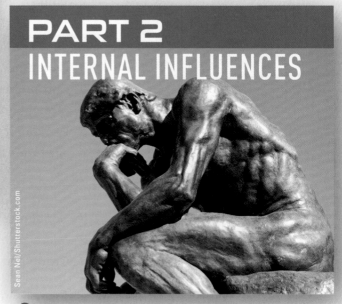

PART 3
EXTERNAL INFLUENCES

AP Photo/Jennifer Szymaszek

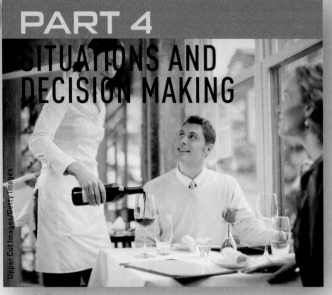

PART 4
SITUATIONS AND DECISION MAKING

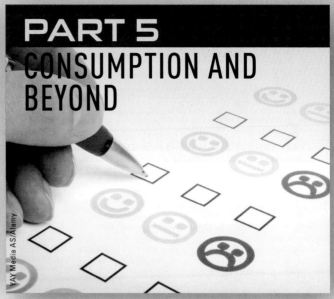

PART 5
CONSUMPTION AND BEYOND

For my family and my mentors, especially Bill and Joe.
—Barry Babin

To my family, Tara, Christian, and Sydney.
—Eric Harris

To my family.
—Kyle B. Murray

1 | What Is CB, and Why Should I Care?

wavebreakmedia/Shutterstock.com

LEARNING OBJECTIVES

After studying this chapter, the student should be able to:

1-1 Understand the meaning of *consumption* and *consumer behaviour*.

1-2 Describe how consumers get treated differently in various types of exchange environments.

1-3 Explain the role of consumer behaviour in business and society.

1-4 Be familiar with basic approaches to studying consumer behaviour.

1-5 Describe why consumer behaviour is so dynamic and how recent trends affect consumers.

INTRODUCTION

How many times a day does the typical university student act like a consumer? If we stop to think about it, we find that the entire day is filled with consumption and consumption decisions. *What should I wear? What will I eat for breakfast? What music should I listen to? Will I go to class today? What am I going to do this weekend?* Many questions like these are routinely answered within the first few moments of every day, with the answers ultimately turning the wheels of the economy and shaping the quality of life for the individual consumer.

How can simple decisions be so important to society? The answer to this question is one of the key points of this chapter and of this text. Indeed, the consumer answers these questions by choosing the options that offer the most value. Thus, consumer behaviour is really all about value.

When consumers buy things, a chain reaction is set in motion that has the potential to enhance value for many people, both directly and indirectly. When a consumer purchases an electronic device such as an Apple iPad, the store will have to replace the item in inventory. The manufacturer will have to replenish the stock. This means that the manufacturer purchases raw materials from suppliers. The raw materials and finished products all need to be shipped by companies such as United Parcel Service (UPS), FedEx, or Canada Post. But that isn't all. The consumer will need a new service plan to take advantage of the device, and companies such as Rogers, Telus, and Bell will kindly oblige with a variety of pricing options. The chain doesn't stop here, as the consumer has yet to accessorize the iPad or add apps to keep the product useful and entertaining. Just think of how something like an iPad can be so meaningful for so many people. Most importantly, assuming all goes well, the consumer improves his or her quality of life!

Although some may call a course like this one "buyer behaviour," the iPad example illustrates that there is much more to *consuming* than simply *buying*. This does not diminish the importance of the buying process. But consumption goes on long after purchase, and the story of consumption ultimately determines how much value is created.

Our behaviour as consumers is critically important not just to ourselves, but also to many other people. This is why so many people are interested in learning

about consumer behaviour. The marketer who understands consumers will be able to design products that provide more value and, through this process, enhance the well-being of both the company and its customers. Policy makers who understand consumer behaviour can make more effective public policy decisions. Last but not least, consumers who understand consumer behaviour can make better decisions concerning how they allocate scarce resources. Thus, an understanding of consumer behaviour can mean better business for companies, better public policy for governments, and a better life for individuals and households.

1-1 CONSUMPTION AND CONSUMER BEHAVIOUR

Consumer behaviour (CB) can be defined from two different perspectives. This is because the term refers to both

1. **human thought and action, and**
2. **a field of study (human inquiry) that is developing an accumulated body of knowledge.**

If we think of a consumer considering the purchase of a new phone, consumer behaviour can be thought of as the actions, reactions, and consequences that take place as the consumer goes through a decision-making process, reaches a decision, and then puts the product to use. Alternatively, if we consider the body of knowledge that researchers accumulate as they attempt to explain these actions, reactions, and consequences, we are approaching consumer behaviour as a field of study. Thus, rather than choosing between the two alternative approaches, we will consider both approaches to gain an understanding of the way the term *consumer behaviour* is used.

1-1a Consumer Behaviour as Human Behaviour

First, **consumer behaviour** is the set of value-seeking activities that take place as people go about addressing needs. In other words, when a consumer comes to realize that something is needed, a chain reaction begins as the consumer sets out to find desirable ways to fill this need. The

consumer behaviour
set of value-seeking activities that take place as people go about addressing needs

CHAPTER 1: What Is CB, and Why Should I Care?   3

Exhibit 1.1

The Basic Consumption Process

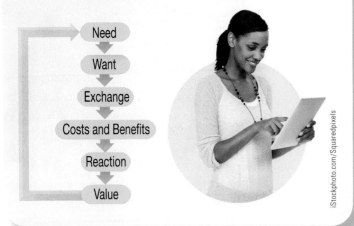

Need
↓
Want
↓
Exchange
↓
Costs and Benefits
↓
Reaction
↓
Value

iStockphoto.com/Squaredpixels

chain reaction involves multiple psychological processes, including thoughts, feelings, and behaviour, and the entire process culminates in value.

THE BASIC CB PROCESS

Exhibit 1.1 illustrates the basic consumption process. Each step is discussed in detail in later chapters. However, the process is briefly illustrated here in the context of a new phone purchase. At some point, the consumer realizes a need for better communication with other people and access to outside media, including the Internet. This realization may be motivated by a desire to do better on the job or to have better access to friends and family. A **want** is simply a specific desire that spells out a way a consumer can go about addressing a recognized need. A consumer feels a need to belong and socialize, and this creates a desire for communication devices.

After weighing some options, the consumer decides to visit a Telus store where communications devices are sold. After looking at several alternative devices, the consumer chooses the latest iPhone. Next, the consumer participates in an exchange in which he or she gives up economic resources in return for receiving the product. An **exchange** is the acting out of a decision to give something up in return for something of greater value. Here, the consumer decides the phone will be worth at least the price of the product and the service plan needed to make the device functional.

The consumer then uses the product and experiences all the associated benefits and costs. **Costs** are the negative results of consumption. The costs involve more than just the price of the product. Consumers spend time both shopping for and learning how to use a phone. Physical effort also is needed if consumers visit retail stores during the process. The time, money, and effort spent acquiring a phone cannot be allocated toward other activities or processes, resulting in high opportunity costs for the consumer. **Benefits** are positive results of consumption. The benefits are multifaceted, ranging from better job performance to more entertainment from the MP3 feature.

Over time, the consumer evaluates the costs and benefits and reacts to the purchase in some way. These reactions involve thoughts and feelings. The thoughts may involve reactions to features such as the ease of use. The feelings may sometimes include frustration if the features do not work correctly or conveniently. Ultimately, the process results in a perception of value. We will discuss value in more detail in Chapter 2.

CONSUMPTION

Another way to look at the basic consumer behaviour process is to consider the steps that occur when consumption takes place. Obviously, a consumer consumes! Interestingly, very few consumer behaviour books define consumption itself. **Consumption** represents the process by which goods, services, or ideas are used and transformed into value. Thus, the actions involved in acquiring and using a mobile communications device like an iPhone create value for a consumer. If the product performs well, a great deal of value may result. If the consumer is unhappy with the product, very little value or even a negative amount of value may result. Eventually, this outcome affects consumer well-being by affecting quality of life.

1-1b Consumer Behaviour as a Field of Study

Consumer behaviour as a field of study represents the study of consumers as they go about the

---

want way a consumer goes about addressing a recognized need

exchange acting out of the decision to give something up in return for something of greater value

costs negative results of consumption

benefits positive results of consumption

consumption process by which goods, services, or ideas are used and transformed into value

consumer behaviour as a field of study study of consumers as they go about the consumption process; the science of studying how consumers seek value in an effort to address needs

---

consumption process. In this sense, consumer behaviour is the science of studying how consumers seek value in an effort to address real needs. This book represents a collection of knowledge resulting as consumer behaviour researchers go about studying consumers.

Consumer behaviour, as a field of study, is a very young field. The first books that discuss consumer behaviour or buyer behaviour date from the 1960s.[1] Thus, compared with older disciplines, researchers have had less time to develop the body of knowledge, and each decade, the accumulated body of knowledge grows significantly. Much uncertainty remains, however, and the body of theory that is generally accepted by researchers and practitioners is relatively small. One reason why consumer behaviour is so exciting to study is that consumer behaviour research is quickly expanding the knowledge base.

Consumer behaviour has ties to other disciplines, some of which are listed in Exhibit 1.2, as research on various subjects produced knowledge relevant to marketers seeking to understand consumers. The genesis of the CB field lies in business and the growing body of academic research produced by business schools in the late 20th and early 21st centuries.[2] Exhibit 1.2 displays the overlapping nature of CB and marketing, as well as other fields. CB shares particularly strong interdisciplinary connections with economics, psychology, marketing, and anthropology, as we discuss below.[3]

Exhibit 1.2

Relationships of CB With Other Disciplines

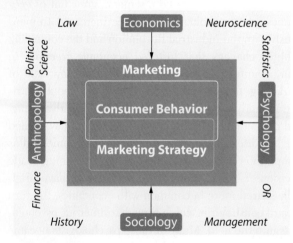

Source: Based on D. J. MacInnis and V. S. Folkes, "The Disciplinary Status of Consumer Behavior: A Sociology of Science Perspective on Key Controversies," *Journal of Consumer Research* 36 (April 2010): 899–914.

ECONOMICS AND CONSUMER BEHAVIOUR

Economics is often defined as the study of production and consumption.[4] Accordingly, it is easy to see that marketing has its origins in economics, particularly with respect to the production and distribution of goods. As the definition implies, economics also involves consumption. Therefore, consumer behaviour and economics also have much in common. In general, economists study consumer behaviour from a broad, or macro, perspective. For example, economics studies often involve things like commodity consumption of nations over time. This may even involve tracking changes in consumption, with different price levels enabling price elasticity to be determined. The economist finds data for a study like this in historical sales records.

To illustrate a macro perspective, we note that researchers and marketing managers are very interested in emerging markets such as China and India. Although these places may seem like very distant lands with little relevance to most business students, of course nothing could be further from the truth. Estimates suggest that, within a decade, China will surpass the United States as the leading country in terms of total consumer purchasing power. To a large extent this explains Prime Minister Stephen Harper's emphasis on the Chinese market, including trips to China aimed at enhancing the opportunities for Canadian companies.

Thus, economists might be very interested in estimating the demand for consumer products such as Canadian wine in an emerging market like China's. One study shows that Chinese consumers display greater price elasticity for wine coolers and wine than they do for beer.[5] In other words, changes in price do not affect overall beer consumption as much as they do consumption of wine or wine coolers. This pattern suggests that beer is more of a staple good to Chinese consumers; thus, beer consumption should remain relatively stable compared to other beverages.

CB researchers tend to focus on a more micro level of behaviour. As such, consumer research often employs experiments or interviews with responses from individual consumers. For example, consumer researchers examined the extent to which exposure to advertisements promoting alcoholic drink specials influences university student drinking. The study was based on responses to such ads from individual consumers. Results suggest that students had a more positive attitude toward the bar running the specials and intended to buy more because of the specials when exposed to the ad.[6]

economics study of production and consumption

Behavioural economics uses traditional econometric models and techniques in combination with psychological theory and methods to better understand the choices of consumers, managers, citizens, and other individuals. Behavioural economists study what happens in markets when the decision makers are influenced by psychological biases and cognitive limitations that are not easily accounted for in the standard economic model.[7] As a result, this field of economics is a close cousin of consumer research and there is a great deal the two can learn from each other. In fact, rise of interest in behavioural economic research is a good example of the integration of knowledge from multiple disciplines to improve our overall understanding of human behaviour.

PSYCHOLOGY AND SOCIAL PSYCHOLOGY

Psychology is the study of human reactions to their environment, including behaviour and mental processes.[8] Psychologists seek to explain the thoughts, feelings, and behaviours that represent human reaction. Psychology itself can be divided into several subdisciplines, of which social psychology, cognitive psychology, and neuroscience in particular are highly relevant to consumer behaviour.[9] **Social psychology** focuses on the thoughts, feelings, and behaviours that people have as they interact with other people (group behaviour). Consumer behaviour most often takes place in some type of social setting; thus, social psychology and consumer behaviour overlap significantly. **Cognitive psychology** deals with the intricacies of mental reactions involved in information processing. Every time a consumer evaluates a product, sees an advertisement, or reacts to product consumption, information is processed. Thus, cognitive psychology is also very relevant to consumer behaviour.

Neuroscience, the study of the central nervous system including brain mechanisms associated with emotion, offers potential for understanding CB by charting a consumer's physiological brain functions during the consumption process. Neuroscience researchers use sophisticated brain imaging equipment to monitor brain activity. One finding suggests that when consumers think about enjoying some of their favourite foods, their brains become more active than when they actually eat the food.[10] The number of neuroscience applications in CB is growing at a rapid rate.

MARKETING

One doesn't have to look very hard to find different definitions of marketing.[11] Many of the older definitions focused heavily on physical products and profitability. Even though products and profits are very important aspects of marketing, these definitions are relatively narrow. **Marketing** involves the multitude of value-producing seller activities that facilitate *exchanges* between buyers and sellers. These activities include the production, promotion, pricing, distribution, and retailing of goods, services, ideas, and experiences that provide value for consumers and other stakeholders.

Consumer behaviour and marketing are very closely related. Exchange is intimately involved in marketing and, as can be seen from Exhibit 1.2, exchange is central to consumer behaviour too. In fact, in some ways, consumer behaviour involves "inverse" marketing as consumers operate at the other end of the exchange. Marketing actions are targeted at and affect consumers, while consumer actions affect marketers. A marketer without customers won't be a marketer very long! In fact, without consumers, marketing is unnecessary.

CONSUMER BEHAVIOUR AND OTHER DISCIPLINES

Marketing, as a recognized discipline, grew out of economics and psychology. Commerce increased tremendously with the Industrial Revolution and the coinciding political changes that fostered economic freedom in many countries. Businesses looked to the new field of marketing for practical advice—initially about distribution, and later about pricing, packaging, advertising, and communication. Eventually, what some have called the "subdiscipline" of consumer behaviour emerged as competition focused marketers on how consumers made decisions.[12] Thus, although marketing may have originally shared more in common with economics, the turn toward consumer research brought numerous psychologists into the field. Many of these psychologists became the first consumer researchers.

Today, consumer behaviour and marketing remain closely tied. Consumer behaviour research and marketing

---

behavioural economics study of what happens in markets with decision makers who display human limitations and complications

psychology study of human reactions to environments, including behaviour and mental processes

social psychology study that focuses on the thoughts, feelings, and behaviours that people have as they interact with other people

cognitive psychology study of the intricacies of mental reactions involved in information processing

neuroscience study of the central nervous system including brain mechanisms associated with thoughts, emotion, and behaviour

marketing multitude of value-producing seller activities that facilitate exchanges between buyers and sellers research overlap with each other more than they do with any other discipline. Thus, the arrow connecting the two disciplines in Exhibit 1.2 represents the fact that marketing and consumer research contribute strongly to each other. After marketing, consumer behaviour research is most closely intertwined with psychology research.[13] Consumer research is based largely on psychology, and to some extent, psychology draws from consumer behaviour research.

Other disciplines share things in common with consumer behaviour. **Sociology** focuses on the study of groups of people within a society. This has relevance for consumer behaviour because consumption often takes place within group settings or is in one way or another affected by group behaviour.

Anthropology has contributed to consumer behaviour research by allowing researchers to interpret the relationships between consumers and the things they purchase, the products they own, and the activities in which they participate. Other disciplines such as geography and the medical sciences overlap with consumer behaviour in that they draw from some of the same theories and/or research approaches. Consumer behaviour shares the strongest interdisciplinary connections with economics, psychology, sociology, marketing, and anthropology.[14]

1-2 THE WAYS IN WHICH CONSUMERS ARE TREATED

The customer isn't always "king." Look at this list of familiar service environments:

▸ **A typical passport office**

▸ **A university registrar's office**

▸ **The line for cashing a cheque at a bank**

▸ **A university health clinic**

▸ **Cable television service**

▸ **A hair salon**

▸ **A fine dining establishment in Toronto**

Think about the following questions: *Does a consumer receive the same amount of service at each of these places? What is the waiting environment like at each of these places? Is there a clean, comfortable waiting area with pleasant music? How dedicated are the employees to delivering a high-quality service experience? How likely are employees to view the customer as a nuisance?*

If you don't see the point of these questions yet, contrast the waiting area at a passport office with the elaborate lounge where customers wait while sipping a cocktail or aperitif before dining in a fine dining establishment in Toronto.

Some organizations can survive while treating customers very poorly, while others need to pamper customers just to have a chance of surviving. Consider these two questions in order to understand how important serving customers well should be to any given organization:

1. **How competitive is the marketing environment?**

2. **How dependent is the marketer on repeat business?**

1-2a Competition and Consumer Orientation

Where do consumers go if they don't like the service at the local passport office? If the choice comes down to visiting that office or not travelling, nearly all consumers will put up with the less-than-immaculate surroundings, long waits, and poor service that all too typically go along with getting a passport. Put yourself into the shoes of the service providers at a typical passport office. Is there a deep concern about doing something that would make a customer want to return to do business again? Is there any real incentive to provide a pleasant and valuable experience?

In essence, the passport office typifies a service organization that operates in a market with little or no competition and a captive audience. No matter how poor the service is, they know consumers will return to do more business the next time they need a passport. The incentive for better customer treatment remains small.

Contrast this with the restaurant. A dining consumer in Toronto has more than 8,000 restaurants from which to choose. Customers do not have to tolerate poor treatment; they can simply go next door. With few exceptions, a highly competitive marketplace in which consumers have many alternatives ensures good customer service.

Unfortunately, government institutions can often be notorious for poor public service.[15]

sociology the study of groups of people within a society, with relevance for consumer behaviour because a great deal of consumption takes place within group settings or is affected by group behaviour

anthropology study in which researchers interpret relationships between consumers and the things they purchase, the products they own, and the activities in which they participate

Why are you treated better in some environments than in others? Perhaps competition is a clue.

better customer service because they are competing with similar firms for the consumer's business. If the service at any one registry is poor or the wait times are too long, consumers can simply take their business down the street.

Governments have recognized that competition is important to protecting consumers. Industry Canada and the Competition Bureau regulate practices such as price fixing, secret rebates, and customer coercion in accordance with federal laws. For example, when Bell Aliant purchased Ontera, the Competition Bureau was concerned about the level of competition in telecommunication services for 16 Northern Ontario communities. The Bureau worked with Bell Aliant to address these concerns and, ultimately, a significant portion of the network was leased to a third-party telecommunications provider.[16]

Competition eventually drives companies toward a high degree of consumer orientation. **Consumer (customer) orientation** is a way of doing business in which the actions and decision making of the institution prioritize consumer value and satisfaction above all other concerns. A consumer orientation is a key component of a firm with a market-oriented culture. **Market orientation** is an organizational culture that embodies the importance of creating value for customers among all employees. In addition to understanding customers, a market orientation stresses the need to monitor and understand competitor actions in the marketplace and the need to communicate information about customers and competitors throughout the organization.[17] Profitable firms are usually market oriented, with a few exceptions that will be discussed later.[18]

1-2b Relationship Marketing and Consumer Behaviour

Let's go back to the list of service environments. Certainly, apparel retailers and restaurants are generally in very intense competition with rival businesses. Businesses are challenged to get consumers to repeatedly purchase the goods or services offered. Even in a city with a population as great as that of Toronto, without repeat business, each restaurant would have fewer than five customers per night. In addition, repeat customers are considered less costly to serve.[19] For instance, while a lot of advertising may be needed for every new customer to learn about a restaurant, old customers already know the place.

Thus, **relationship marketing** is based on the belief that firm performance is enhanced through repeat

consumer (customer) orientation way of doing business in which the actions and decision making of the institution prioritize consumer value and satisfaction above all other concerns

market orientation organizational culture that embodies the importance of creating value for customers among all employees

relationship marketing activities based on the belief that the firm's performance is enhanced through repeat business

Unlike a restaurant, Service Canada management may not be compelled to adjust workloads to demand. Service Canada passport *customers* can face long lines (sometimes more than 100 people in some areas) and wait times counted in hours, not minutes. However, we can compare the federal Service Canada passport application process to motor vehicle licensing in Alberta, where the registry offices have been privatized. In Alberta, consumers are free to choose the firm that they visit to renew their licence. These companies tend to provide business. Relationship marketing is the recognition that customer desires are recurring and that a single purchase act may be only one touchpoint in an ongoing series of interactions with a customer. **Touchpoints** are direct contacts between the firm and a customer. Increasingly, multiple channels (or ways of making this contact) are available, including phone, email, text messaging, and face-to-face contact.[20] Every touchpoint, no matter the channel, should be considered as an opportunity to create value for the customer. As with any type of relationship, a customer–marketer relationship will continue only as long as both parties see the partnership as valuable.

Marketers are increasingly realizing the value of relationship marketing. Wait staff sometimes provide business cards to customers, so that they can ask for this server again on the next visit or recommend the restaurant and server to a friend. Notice that with relationship marketing, the firm and its employees are very motivated to provide an outstanding overall experience. In sum, both a competitive marketplace and a relationship marketing orientation create exchange environments where firms truly treat customers as "king."

Andrea Chu/Digital Vision/Jupiterimages

Every touchpoint is a way to build a relationship with a customer in a competitive environment

1-3 CONSUMER BEHAVIOUR'S ROLE IN BUSINESS AND SOCIETY

Why study consumer behaviour? Many students find studying consumer behaviour interesting relative to other university courses. Why might consumer behaviour be more interesting than, say, calculus? The answer lies in the student's ability to relate to the content. After all, everyone reading this book has years and years of experience as a consumer. Thus, students should come into the course with a better sense of familiarity and an ability to relate to the subject matter. Not only is the subject interesting, but consumer behaviour is also an important topic to understand from multiple perspectives. Consumer behaviour (CB) is important in at least three ways:

1. **CB provides an input to business/marketing strategy.**

2. **CB provides a force that shapes society.**

3. **CB provides an input to making responsible decisions as a consumer.**

1-3a Consumer Behaviour and Marketing Strategy

The ultimate hallmark of success for a business is long-term survival. One hundred years is not a long time in the course of history, but very few companies have survived for 100 years. Exhibit 1.3 lists some famous international companies, the products they are known for, and their age.

The Hudson's Bay Company (HBC) is extremely rare in that it has survived multiple centuries. The vast majority of the world's leading corporations are much less than 100 years old. All of the companies listed in Exhibit 1.3 have beaten the odds, and even though we may think about them as lasting forever, chances are some of these "giants" will not be around 100 years from now. So, surviving is not a trivial goal, and the companies that do survive in the long term do so by obtaining resources from consumers in return for the value they create.

In contrast to the companies listed in Exhibit 1.3, consider Zellers Inc., which was a discount retailer of general merchandise, founded

touchpoints direct contacts between the firm and a customer

Exhibit 1.3

How Old Are These Companies?

Company[22]	Core Products	Year of "Birth"	Place
Hudson's Bay Company	Mass Merchandising	1670	Ontario
Tesco	Food Retailing	1919	London, UK
Toyota	Motor Cars	1937	Japan
McDonald's	Fast Food	1956	Illinois
Walmart	Mass Merchandising	1962	Arkansas
Samsung	Electronics	1969	Seoul, South Korea
Microsoft	Computer Software	1975	New Mexico
Apple	Computers, Communication Devices	1976	California
Home Depot	Building Supply and Retailing	1979	Georgia
lululemon	Specialty Apparel	1998	British Columbia

All dates taken from company websites. Samsung was originally founded in 1938 but as a Korean food exporter. In 1969, Samsung Electronics was created.

in 1931, with more than 250 stores across Canada. The company was a dominant player in the lower price point for apparel and other mass merchandise until Walmart arrived in Canada and Loblaws expanded aggressively into clothing sales. As customers' tastes changed and competition intensified, Zellers found it more and more difficult to remain profitable and deliver the value that consumers were demanding. In response, Zellers' parent company, HBC, sold many of the retail chain's store leases to the U.S.-based retailer Target in 2011. Target opened its first stores in Canada in March 2013 and, after losing more than $2 billion in Canada, announced it was closing all 133 of its Canadian stores in January 2015.[21] Target Canada lasted less than two years (for more detail, see the case at the end of Chapter 3).

WHAT DO PEOPLE BUY?

When a consumer buys something, he or she gives up resources in the form of time, money, and energy in return for whatever is being sold. Consider a customer who purchases a pair of Bauer Vapor 1X skates. What does he or she really get? Well, the tangibles include mostly cloth, plastic, and metal; these are the parts that make up the product. No reasonable consumer would trade $900 for cloth, plastic, and steel. A consumer isn't really buying the physical parts of a product.

However, those parts make up the key **attributes**—the boot and blade—that enable this product to function as a hockey skate. Once again, we can ask, is this really what the consumer wants? The fact is that this function enables the consumer to enjoy the benefits of playing Canada's most popular sport. Outcomes like these are valuable—this is what the customer is ultimately buying.

Marketing firms often implement poor strategies when they don't understand what a product truly is because they don't understand exactly what they are selling. A **product** is a potentially valuable bundle of benefits. Theodore Levitt, one of the most famous marketing researchers, understood this. He emphasized the importance of the value a customer receives from a product, rather than the product itself.

One consumer researcher studied why people bought milk shakes. In contrast to expectation, the largest share of milk shakes purchased in the study was bought before noon, many before 10 A.M., and many were consumed in a car. After studying many milk shake drinkers, one theme emerged: A milk shake is a good solution for consumers with long commutes, as they satisfy one's hunger, they are neat, they can be consumed while using one hand, and they take about 20 minutes to finish—the better portion of the commute. The value provided by the milk shake is partly dealing with hunger but also partly dealing with boredom. Thus, the researcher suggested making shakes

attributes product features that deliver a desired consumer benefit

product potentially valuable bundle of benefits

Makeup or Hope?

Theodore Levitt was a leader in the cause of getting managers not to allow their companies to become *myopic*. A myopic business view defines the business in terms of products that are sold and not in terms of the value that consumers receive.

Here are some examples of better ways to look at products.

Consumers Do Not Want:	Consumers Do Want:
¼ inch B&D drill bits	¼ inch holes so they can hang things
Kodak film	Recorded memories
Lawn mowers	Pride that comes with a great looking lawn
Roach spray	Dead roaches
Dry-cleaning service	Clothes that do not stink

What about a customer buying makeup or cosmetics? What is really being purchased? Charles Revson, founder of Revlon, said, "In the factory Revlon manufactures cosmetics, but in the store we sell hope." Revlon considers itself in the hope business! Thus, in Revlon's eyes, the "hope" helps provide the value as much as the cosmetics. Revlon's understanding of the way value is actually provided eliminates myopia and allows the company to see 20/20.

Sources: Christenson, C.M., S. Cook and T. Hall (2005), "Marketing Malpractice: The Cause and the Cure," *Harvard Business Review*, 83, 74–83; *Branding Ad Vice* (2004), "Needful Things," October 13, 2004. http://brandingadvice.typepad.com/my_weblog/2004/10/index.html, accessed January 14, 2007; Kellogg, D. (2006), "Hope and Agility: The Revlon Test," *Mark Logic CEO Blog*, http://marklogic.blogspot.com/2006/07/hope-and-agility-revlon-test.html, accessed December 7, 2007.

even thicker so they took even longer to finish as a way of improving the "product."[23]

INNOVATION

Ultimately, companies need to understand why people buy their products in order to understand what business they are in. This is also how they identify their competitors. Let's look at the companies that produced buggies (horse-drawn carriages from 100 years ago) and slide rules (rulers used to do calculations). They did not go out of business because their products were flawed. The companies that did well producing those products went out of business because they failed to innovate and because they didn't understand that they were actually competing with Ford automobiles and Texas Instruments calculators, respectively.

Newness alone does not make an innovation. An innovation has to produce value for consumers to be successful. Over time, successful innovations exhibit all or some of these characteristics:

1. **Relative advantage—makes things better than before**

2. **Simplicity—all things equal, a simpler innovation is better than a complex innovation**

3. **Observability—things that are observable tend to get adopted faster**

4. **Trialability—things that can be tried with little or no risk get adopted faster**

5. **Consistency—consumers are more likely to adopt things that are congruent with existing values and knowledge**

Consider a consumer with a new smartwatch. His liking of the device will depend on these characteristics, but more importantly for those involved in marketing these devices, these characteristics will ultimately determine if the category as a whole represents a successful innovation.

WAYS OF DOING BUSINESS

Much of the discussion thus far presumes that a company is market oriented. That is, the presumption is that a company has prioritized understanding consumers, as would be the case in a consumer-oriented corporate culture. This isn't always the case. Each company adopts a way of doing business that is epitomized in its corporate culture. Corporate cultures fall roughly into one of several categories representing different ways of doing business.

Exhibit 1.4

Different Ways of Doing Business

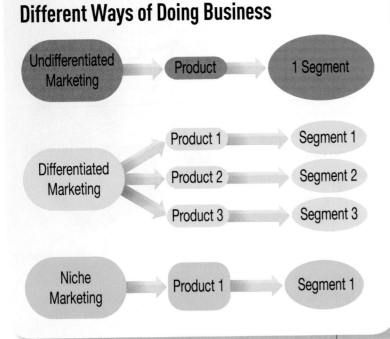

undifferentiated marketing plan wherein the same basic product is offered to all customers

production orientation approach where innovation is geared primarily toward making the production process as efficient and economic as possible

differentiated marketers firms that serve multiple market segments, each with a unique product offering

one-to-one marketing plan wherein a different product is offered for each individual customer so that each customer is treated as a segment of one

niche marketing plan wherein a firm specializes in serving one market segment with particularly unique demand characteristics

Exhibit 1.4 summarizes different business orientations. These orientations often guide a firm's market segmentation practices.

In **undifferentiated marketing**, the same basic product is offered to all customers. Mass merchandisers typify undifferentiated marketers in that they rely on selling high volume to be successful. As such, they focus on serving very large segments in which consumers do not have specific desires (are not picky). Undifferentiated marketers generally adopt a **production orientation**, wherein innovation is geared primarily toward making the production process as efficient and economic as possible. In other words, the emphasis is on serving customers while incurring minimum costs. Walmart typifies this approach with its Supercentres and its state-of-the-art distribution network, which ships massive quantities of products to stores around the world at the lowest possible cost.

Differentiated marketers serve multiple market segments, each with a unique product offering. A market orientation usually serves a differentiated marketer well. The emphasis here is on matching a product with a segment.

Toyota, for example, has three business units targeted toward different automotive segments. Scion appeals to consumers interested in economy cars with a unique sense of style. Toyota operates under the Toyota name itself, of course, offering a more conservative line of autos for consumers seeking a blend of performance and reliability. Finally, Lexus provides luxury cars to those who want the most in performance, style, comfort, and reliability. Taking differentiated marketing even further, each Toyota line offers coupes, sedans, and SUVs. Thus, a Toyota product exists for practically any automobile consumer's taste. Without an understanding of consumers, Toyota would have a difficult time matching products to segments.

Marketers can take differentiated marketing to the extreme with a practice known as **one-to-one marketing**. Here, the company offers a unique product to each individual customer and thereby treats each customer as a segment of one. Companies like Build-A-Bear Workshop allow individual consumers to create and purchase a unique product that is custom-made on a mass scale—that is, a mass customized scale. Computer-aided information processing, design, and production have helped make this a reality on a large scale. Many casinos, for example, develop promotional packages for individual customers based on information collected and stored about that customer's preferences.

Niche marketing is practised by firms that specialize in serving one market segment with particularly unique demand characteristics. Firms that practise niche marketing may be consumer oriented. However, some niche marketers are product oriented and produce a product that has unique appeal within a segment. For example, many companies serve the golf market in one way or another, and some of them are huge differentiated marketers like TaylorMade Golf or Callaway, offering many products aimed at multiple markets. However, the Bobby Grace Putter Company specializes in one product: the putter. It only makes putters and has a very small product offering of accessories beyond that. Bobby Grace markets its putters as highly advanced technologically because all of the company's attention is dedicated to just one club, the putter.

1-3b Consumer Behaviour and Society

The things that people buy and consume end up determining the type of society in which we live. Things like customs, manners, and rituals all involve consumption—value-producing activities. Certainly, not every society around the world is the same. Just think about the ways we eat and the types of food consumed around the world. Additionally, when governments create laws that govern the way we buy and consume products, consumer behaviour is involved. Thus, consumer behaviour creates the society in which we live and serves as an important source of input to public policy in a free society.

For example, how does Canadian society treat smoking today? Interestingly, popular culture used to glamourize smoking as a valued behaviour. On the famous TV classic *The Andy Griffith Show*, produced in the 1960s, the likable Sheriff Andy Taylor casually smoked cigarettes in his living room while talking to his young son, Opie. Cigarette advertisements made up a large chunk of all TV advertising before a U.S. federal ban took effect on January 2, 1971. In the theatre,

James Bond smoked, and his image was certainly not harmed by the behaviour. At home, practically every room in the house included at least one ashtray. "No smoking" sections did not exist, and on airlines, flight attendants (then called stewardesses) walked the aisles of the plane offering passengers "coffee, tea, or cigarettes."

My, how things have changed! Smoking has become nearly taboo in Canada. Smoking inside any public building is practically impossible due either to laws restricting smoking or to rules created by building owners prohibiting smoking. "No smoking" sections in restaurants are now also seen in many parts of Europe and in most cosmopolitan cities around the world. Increasingly, consumers look upon smoking as a non–value-producing activity. Furthermore, politicians realize political advantage in creating more restrictions as consumer opinion continues to turn against the behaviour. Policy makers should make such decisions with a thorough understanding of the consumer behaviour issues involved.

Another current public policy issue concerns the use of mobile devices. Consider how much consumers' widespread adoption of mobile phones and tablets has changed, and continues to change, society. More Canadian households now have a mobile phone (83%) than have a landline (75%).[24] Globally, more than 6 billion people have access to a mobile phone, but only 4.5 billion have access to a flush toilet![25] That's not bad for a product that as we know it did not exist 30 years ago. Certainly, the smartphone has been a discontinuous innovation and has altered our behaviours and communications in many significant ways.

1-3c Consumer Behaviour and Personal Growth

We face many important decisions as consumers, including choices that will affect our professional careers, our quality of life, and the very fibre of our families. By this point in your life, you have already experienced many of these decisions. Some decisions are good; some are not. One hot topic recently has been the rise in Canadian consumers'

Image courtesy of The Advertising Archives. Used with permission of California Department of Public Health.

As this billboard shows, attitudes toward smoking have certainly changed over the last few decades.

Consumers and Their Phones

Today's mobile phones are amazing products that allow us to access vast amounts of information and communicate on-the-go with other people around the world. Mobile devices are also widely adopted in Canada. One recent survey indicated that the majority of Canadian children in grades 4 through 11 have their own mobile phone. In grade 4, about 25% of children have their own phone, which rises to 40% by grade 6 and close to 90% by high school.[26]

But mobile phones can also be a source of aggravation and even a danger to others. Many provinces have enacted distracted driving laws that penalize drivers, with fines and/or demerits, for using a mobile device in their cars. Some restaurants now frown on or even prohibit phone usage. Yet, many airlines are beginning to relax their in-flight restrictions. How much is too much? Consider the following list. In your opinion, do any of these behaviours violate acceptable mobile phone etiquette in Canada?

1. **Having a cellphone conversation at the dinner table**

2. **Using a cellphone while seated on an airplane**

3. **Using profanity on the phone**

4. **Using the phone in a movie theatre**

5. **Using the phone in a public washroom toilet stall**

6. **Speaking so loudly that your phone conversation is easily heard by others three metres or more away from you**

7. **Browsing or texting while involved in a conversation with someone else**

8. **Using a loud and annoying ring tone**

Should public restrictions on mobile usage be created that govern when, where, and how a phone can be used? Studies of consumer behaviour help provide input into public policy decisions on issues like these.

Sources: Krotz, J.L. (2010), "Cell Phone Etiquette: Dos and Don'ts," http://www.microsoft.com/smallbusiness/resources/ArticleReader/website/default.aspx?Print=1&ArticleId=Cellphoneetiquettedosanddonts, accessed June 19, 2010. Cairns, W. (2006), "Child Culture; Kid Consumers and Growing Pains," *Brand Strategy*, December 18, 46; cmch mentors for parents and children, http://www.cmch.tv/mentors/hottopic.asp?id=70, accessed June 19, 2010.

debt load (see Exhibit 1.5). In 1999, Canadian families had $0.78 of debt for every dollar of after-tax income. By 2012, that number had increased to $1.10 of debt for every dollar of after-tax income and more than one-third of families had $2.00 of debt for every dollar of income. However, Canadian household wealth has also increased over that time, and when Statistics Canada looks at how much debt families have relative to their assets, the picture has actually gotten slightly better over time. In 1999, Canadian households had $0.27 of debt for every dollar of assets, and in 2012, they had $0.25 of debt for every dollar of assets. These trends paint a picture of Canadians who are borrowing more, but also have homes and other assets that are worth more.[27]

Possibly more concerning is the rise in credit card debt among particular segments of Canadian consumers. About 46% of Canadians carry credit card debt and, as a result, are paying interest rates of more than 20%. One-quarter of Canadians are caught in a cycle of paying off their credit card debt with available funds and then incurring additional debt to pay for other expenses.[28] In the United States, between 1984 and 2009, real average household debt (including mortgages) more than doubled from $46,000 to $110,000, substantially outpacing income growth over the same period of time.[29] Total American consumer debt exceeded $2 trillion in 2010; that's more than $15,000 per family.[30] In the United Kingdom, the typical young consumer (18–24 years of age) has credit card debt totalling nearly $10,000 USD.[31] Post-secondary students are prime targets for credit cards and, as can be seen on many university and college campuses, students are quite willing to apply for cards in exchange for something as mundane as a new T-shirt. Many consumers continue to have negative net worth years into their professional life because of the debt accumulated in early adulthood.[32]

The decisions that lead to high levels of debt are not always wise as bankruptcy, financial stress, and lower self-esteem often result. Although often overlooked, decisions about budget allocation are very relevant aspects of consumer behaviour. There are many other avenues that can lead consumers to make poor decisions.

Thus, when consumers study consumer behaviour, they should come to make better decisions. Several topics can be particularly helpful in enlightening consumers, including:

1. **Consequences associated with poor budget allocation**

2. **The role of emotions in consumer decision making**

3. **Avenues for seeking redress for unsatisfactory purchases**

4. **Social influences on decision making, including peer pressure**

5. **The effect of the environment on consumer behaviour**

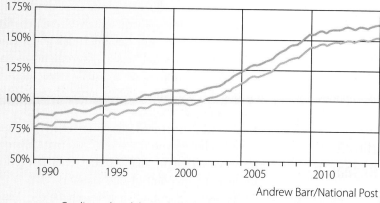

Exhibit 1.5

Canadians' High Consumer Debt Load

Andrew Barr/National Post

—— Credit market debt to disposable income
—— Consumer credit and mortgage liabilities to disposable income

©NATIONAL POST/Andrew Barr

DIFFERENT APPROACHES TO STUDYING CONSUMER BEHAVIOUR

Consumer researchers have many tools and approaches with which to study consumer behaviour, and researchers don't always agree on which approach is best. In reality, the consumer researcher should realize that no single best way of studying consumer behaviour exists. Rather, different types of research settings may call for different approaches and the use of different tools. Thus, we provide a brief overview of three basic approaches for studying consumer behaviour, in order to give the reader an idea of how the knowledge found in this book was obtained. For a more detailed view of the different research approaches, the reader is referred elsewhere.[33]

1-4a Interpretive Research

One consumer's music is just noise to another consumer. What creates value in the musical experience? What does music mean and how much does the meaning shape the value of the experience? These questions evoke very abstract comments and thoughts from consumers, and lend themselves well to interpretive research.[34] **Interpretive research** seeks to explain the inner meanings and motivations associated with specific consumption experiences. Consumer researchers interpret these meanings through the words that consumers use to describe events or through observation of social interactions. With this approach, researchers interpret meaning rather than analyze data.

Interpretive research generally falls into the

interpretive research
approach that seeks to explain the inner meanings and motivations associated with specific consumption experiences

broader category of qualitative research. **Qualitative research tools** include things such as case analyses, clinical interviews, focus group interviews, and other tools in which data are gathered in a relatively unstructured way. In other words, consumer respondents are usually free to respond in their own words or simply through their own behaviour. Data of this type requires the researcher to interpret its meaning.

The roots of interpretive consumer research go back more than 50 years to the earliest days of consumer research. The focus was on identifying the motivations that lie behind all manners of consumer behaviour, including mundane things such as coffee drinking or taking an aspirin, to more elaborate issues such as what "drives" one to buy a Ford versus a Chevy.[35] The motivational research era in consumer research, which lasted through the early 1960s, generally proved disappointing in providing satisfying explanations for consumer behaviour on a large scale. Unfortunately, many interpretive research tools were scarcely applied for years afterward. However, these approaches have made a recent comeback and are now commonly applied to many aspects of the field.

Interpretive researchers adopt one of several orientations. Two common interpretive orientations are phenomenology and ethnography. **Phenomenology** represents the study of consumption as a "lived experience." The phenomenological researcher relies on casual interviews with consumers from whom the researcher has won confidence and trust. This may be supplemented with various other ways that the consumer can tell a story. **Ethnography** has roots in anthropology and often involves analyzing the artifacts associated with consumption. An ethnographer may decide to go through trash or ask to see the inside of a consumer's refrigerator in an effort to learn about the consumer. These approaches represent viable options for consumer researchers.

1-4b Quantitative Consumer Research

Which consumer group is most likely to listen to rap music? Statistical models can be applied to retail sales data to identify clusters of consumers who are more likely to be in the market for specific types of products. For example, these tools can be used to help explain how a 45-year-old consumer who buys Bob Seger music belongs to a segment that is also likely to buy a Faith Hill recording. Similarly, another segment of consumers likes the music of Nirvana and Green Day. These two segments may be differentiated on factors such as age, income, and possibly even education.

Sometimes, the results are so spot-on that they become controversial. For instance, researchers working for Target stores used patterns of purchases to cluster consumers into groups. One such pattern allowed Target to predict which customers are highly likely to be pregnant. Using this data, Target began sending consumers who fell into those groups (coincidentally or not) promotions from the store for baby strollers, diapers, and other maternity-related items. One teen's father went to a Target store to complain when his teenage daughter began receiving the maternity-related promotions, only to have to apologize when his daughter broke the news to him. The fact that individual customer purchases can be recorded and stored by loyalty or credit card numbers makes this type of quantitative modelling possible.

Rather than tracking buying trends, a researcher might ask which consumers are most likely to pirate music via the Internet. This issue illustrates the interplay between ethics and consumer behaviour. The researcher can design a questionnaire and ask consumers to respond, using 10-point scales, to questions about things like the risk of being prosecuted, the extent to which music stars are idolized by the consumer, and the perceived social acceptability of music pirating. Responses can be used to explain how likely a consumer is to illegally pirate music. The researcher may find that one segment of music consumers is more likely to pirate than another segment.

These studies typify quantitative research. **Quantitative research** addresses questions about consumer behaviour using numerical measurement and analysis tools. The measurement is usually structured, meaning that the consumer will simply choose a response from among alternatives supplied by the researcher. In other words, structured questionnaires typically involve multiple-choice-type questions. Alternatively, quantitative research might analyze sales data tracked via the Internet or with point-of-sale scanners.

Typically, quantitative research better enables researchers to test hypotheses as compared to interpretive research, since the data from quantitative research

qualitative research tools means for gathering data in a relatively unstructured way, including case analysis, clinical interviews, and focus group interviews

phenomenology qualitative approach to studying consumers that relies on interpretation of the lived experience associated with some aspect of consumption

ethnography qualitative approach to studying consumers that relies on interpretation of artifacts to draw conclusions about consumption

quantitative research approach that addresses questions about consumer behaviour using numerical measurement and analysis tools

Exhibit 1.6

Comparing Quantitative and Qualitative Research

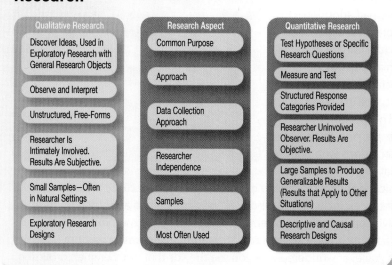

Qualitative Research	Research Aspect	Quantitative Research
Discover Ideas, Used in Exploratory Research with General Research Objects	Common Purpose	Test Hypotheses or Specific Research Questions
Observe and Interpret	Approach	Measure and Test
Unstructured, Free-Forms	Data Collection Approach	Structured Response Categories Provided
Researcher Is Intimately Involved. Results Are Subjective.	Researcher Independence	Researcher Uninvolved Observer. Results Are Objective.
Small Samples—Often in Natural Settings	Samples	Large Samples to Produce Generalizable Results (Results that Apply to Other Situations)
Exploratory Research Designs	Most Often Used	Descriptive and Causal Research Designs

does not require the same type of deep interpretation as qualitative research. For example, if consumers have an average attitude score of 50 for brand A and 75 for brand B, we can objectively say that consumers tend to prefer brand B.

Experimental methodology is also critically important to quantitative consumer research. In particular, experimental research allows us to answer questions like: What causes consumers to hold the attitudes they hold, behave the way that they do, and make the choices that they make? To understand the causes of consumer behaviour, researchers must use experimental methods—both in behavioural laboratories and in field studies—as only experimental research can directly assess cause and effect. As a result, experimental research plays a particularly critical role in testing the causal relationships in theories proposed by interpretive researchers or other quantitative methods. Exhibit 1.6 summarizes some key differences between quantitative and qualitative research.[36]

1-5 CONSUMER BEHAVIOUR IS DYNAMIC

All one has to do is examine the differences in standards of living between today's consumers and the consumers living just 40, 80, or 100 years ago to gain an appreciation of how consumer behaviour has changed over time. As a general statement, we can say that consumers are never completely satisfied. Actually, this is a good thing because as companies strive to meet consumer demands, increasingly innovative products are offered, and companies grow in response to increased sales. As a result, they hire more people and raise the income levels throughout the economy.

The way marketers respond to consumers is changing dramatically. Marketers have historically used advances in technology to provide consumers with greater opportunities to communicate with companies. Today, billions of consumers around the world have 24-hour, seven-day-a-week access to markets via the Internet. Consumers do not need to wait to go to a retail store to purchase music. They can stream music or movies or download a book or a new app while walking down the street. Here are some of the trends that are shaping the value received by consumers today.

1-5a Internationalization

When Chip Wilson opened the first lululemon athletica location in Vancouver in 1998, he could hardly expect the brand to be a global phenomenon in just over a decade (for more on lululemon, see the case at the end of Chapter 6). Similarly, when Tadashi Yanai opened the first Uniqlo store in Hiroshima, Japan, in 1984, it is unlikely he expected the company's basic affordable clothing to have global appeal. Yet, the retailer had more than 1,300 stores worldwide by 2014.[37]

Today, consumers around the world can order up a latte at one of more than 16,000 Starbucks locations in more than 50 countries.[38] Whether in Saskatoon, Canada; Guadalajara, Mexico; Seoul, South Korea; London, England; Shanghai, China; Nantes, France; or Ruston, Louisiana, patrons can relax at a Starbucks. Almost anywhere the modern consumer travels, he or she can find a familiar place to eat or drink. An Outback Steakhouse, McDonald's, or Starbucks never seems far away!

experimental methodology a quantitative approach to research that examines cause-and-effect relationships by measuring changes in one or more key variables, while systematically manipulating and controlling other variables

The Face of the Consumer? Do You "Like" It?

Perhaps no consumer trend is changing consumer behaviour and marketing more than consumers' widespread adoption of Internet social networking sites. Social networking is a global phenomenon and goes beyond Facebook.com (the Canadian, American, and European favourite) to sites such as Gupshup (a Twitter-type site popular in India), Mixi.jp (social networking Japanese-style), and 55tuan (a Groupon-style service in China). Marketers have utilized advancements in social networking technology to reach out to consumers. For example, one company, 33Across, specializes in tracking consumers' interactions with one another via posts and shared messages on social networking sites. 33Across content-analyzes millions of communications. This research is extremely powerful because we discuss so many of our purchases with friends and acquaintances, including Facebook friends, before and after the purchase. In addition, companies can track consumer activity on Twitter and Facebook with the help of the cookies, which are essentially footprints of your online activity. As a result, advertisers can carefully target messages to consumers who should be most receptive to the message. Have you ever wondered why you see the ads that you do when browsing the Internet? Now you may have a clue why so many marketers have a big "like" for Facebook.

Chris Ridley—Internet Stock/Alamy

Sources: Steel, E. (2010), "Marketers Watch as Friends Interact Online," *The Wall Street Journal*, (April 15), B1. Patel, K. (2010), "Profiling the Facebooks of the World," *Advertising Age*, (June 14), 6. Trusov, M., R.E. Bucklin, K. Pauwels (2009), "Effects of Word-of-Mouth Versus Traditional Marketing: Findings from an Internet Social Networking Site", *Journal of Marketing*, 73 (September), 90–102.

Although these chains can be found worldwide, consumers are not alike everywhere these firms operate. Starbucks struggled to compete in Australia when faced with a strong local and independent coffee culture, eventually closing most of its stores in country. The American-based, but Australian themed, Outback Steakhouse operates in 21 countries. The menu, however, is often tailored to local tastes. For example, in Seoul, South Korea, the chain will offer kimchi (fermented cabbage), something that is neither American nor Australian. Companies today deal with cultural distances as well as geographical distances. Globalization places a greater demand on CB research, as every culture's people will interpret products and behaviours differently. The meanings these consumers perceive will determine the success or failure of the product being offered.

1-5b Technological Changes

It is no secret that we are living in an age of ever-increasing technological advances that seem to be coming at a faster pace all the time. Upon reflection, we may realize that technology has influenced business practices since the advent of industry. Certainly, many retailers felt threatened by mail-order technology that was practised through the Sears Roebuck catalogue and the telephone. In 1895, the Sears catalogue contained 532 pages of products that enabled rural consumers to obtain things that would have been otherwise difficult to get.[39] Why would people go to a store when they could simply telephone and have products delivered to their door?

In the mid-20th century, television revolutionized consumer behaviour. Not only did TV change advertising forever, but true home shopping became a possibility. Now, the consumer could actually see a product in use on television and then make a purchase by picking up the phone. Why would someone go to a store?

A consumer now has 24/7 access to purchasing almost any type of product. The Internet has made geographical distance almost a non-issue. Additionally, the consumer can shop on his or her own schedule, not on a schedule determined by store hours. Communication technology has also advanced tremendously. The entire world is now truly the market for consumers in free countries.

What types and amounts of value do consumers seek when shopping online? When a consumer needs an airline ticket, he or she is seeking a solution to a real problem. Buying an airline ticket isn't generally a fun thing to do. Thus, the consumer is primarily seeking "utilitarian" value. (We discuss different types of value in Chapter 2.)

Although technology continues to change, the basic consumer desire for value hasn't changed. In fact, the dot-com failures of the late 1990s illustrated that companies go bust if they do not enhance the value consumers receive from the current ways of doing things. Today, retailers look at web technologies more as complementing traditional retailing than as competing with the bricks-and-mortar option. A pure play (Internet-only) retailer has a difficult time competing with a shopping adventure to West Edmonton Mall or Harrods of London because of the gratification offered by the experience itself.

Shopping online can be a valuable experience, but are virtual shopping and "real" shopping gratifying in the same way?

1-5c Changing Communications

As technology has changed, so have the ways in which people communicate with each other. Once upon a time, consumers' favourite form of communication was face-to-face, but interestingly, many current surveys of preferred communication methods don't even list face-to-face communication. Among other sources, email appears far from dead as consumers rate it as the preferred method for communicating with brands;[40] as a result, marketers continue to invest in email marketing techniques. Customers still express a preference for a phone call (two-way communication) to the company just below one-way communication via email. Sending text messages, Tweeting, or attending a sponsored event come in near the bottom in terms of preferred communication tools. In a later chapter, we'll examine how age influences communication choices. This is not to say that consumers don't get information from other sites. In fact, Facebook is second only to Google in total page views, and both are important sources of information for consumers. One in three of all Internet users in the world use Facebook.[41] In addition, Pinterest has become one of the mostly widely used websites and serves as a commonly used tool for exchanging information, especially among female consumers. Marketers are fast learning how to use these tools to communicate with consumers.

1-5d Big Data

Back in the days of small general stores in small towns, store owners came to know their customers extremely well. They could sometimes predict when a customer would show up, and they could fill his or her order from memory. The business and the customer had an intimate connection. As electronic storage has become simple and cheap, and as more realtime electronic devices are used to record information, the amount of data available for analysis is overwhelming and the flow is not likely to stop any time soon. By the time a current university student finishes his or her degree, more data will have been collected than in all eternity before that time.

The term **big data** has come to be used to represent the massive amounts of information available to companies, which can potentially be used to predict customer behaviours. The data include internal records of customer behaviour like scanner purchase data, survey responses, and web traffic records, as well as data from social network interactions and even Global Positioning System (GPS) tracking.[42] Researchers apply statistical tools to try to discover patterns in the data that will allow better prediction. Although the application of big data in this sense is still in its infancy, one can get an idea about how this works when purchasing something online and getting shown products that "consumers who bought this product also purchased." This is certainly a technological trend that will affect how companies study their customers.

1-5e Changing Demographics

In most of the Western world, notable demographic trends have shaped consumer behaviour patterns greatly over the past quarter-century or so. First, households increasingly include two primary income providers. In contrast to the stereotypical working dad and stay-at-home mom, families today often include two parents with a career orientation. Second, family size is decreasing throughout North America and Europe. As a result, the relative importance of countries as consumer markets is changing. Marketers around the world find it hard to ignore the nearly 2 billion consumers in China or the 1 billion in India. We'll discuss demographic trends more in Chapter 9.

1-5f Changing Economy

Recent years have seen a downturn in the economy in much of the developed world. In parts

big data massive amounts of data available to companies, which can be used to predict customer behaviours of Canada, as well as the United States and much of Western Europe, unemployment numbers have risen sharply in the past few years. Additionally, other consumers are underemployed. Moreover, turmoil in financial markets around the world contributes to an economic picture that leaves consumers uneasy. As a result, consumer spending has changed in several ways. Consumers are more cautious about spending money and react more favourably to price-cutting policies. Private label brands (such as retail store brands like Loblaw's President's Choice) become more attractive alternatives as a way of saving money. Further, consumers perceive themselves as having less discretionary income and one consequence of this is a decrease in charitable giving.[43] If the bad economy continues, consumers will likely continue to be more cautious about spending.

STUDY TOOLS 1

LOCATED AT THE BACK OF THE TEXTBOOK
☐ Rip-out Chapter Review Card

LOCATED AT NELSON.COM/STUDENT
☐ Review Key Terms Flashcards (print or online)

☐ Download audio summaries to review on the go

☐ Complete practice quizzes to prepare for tests

☐ Watch video on Online Marketing@Travelocity for a real company example

Case

The Hudson's Bay Company

The rise of retail in Canada began on May 2, 1670, when the Hudson's Bay Company (HBC) was created as a shareholder organization with a centralized management structure by a royal charter that granted the company exclusive trading rights. In the decades that followed, the company grew its business and played a pivotal role in Canada's economic development. The company's original six stores—in Victoria, Vancouver, Edmonton, Calgary, Saskatoon, and Winnipeg—are an important part of the history of Canadian commerce.

Today, "The Bay" department stores are HBCs flagship retail banner with 92 locations across the country. Over the past 340-plus years, the company has evolved in response to competition and customers' needs. From the early fur trade battles with the North West Company to its current rivalry with competitors like Sears and Walmart, HBC has faced a variety of obstacles and challenges. Most recently, the company has struggled with its identity and what it stands for in the Canadian marketplace.

Realizing that competing on price against the likes of Walmart was likely to be a losing strategy, HBC has undertaken an aggressive revamp of its product lineup to better serve the modern Canadian shopper. Although as a department store the company sells products across a wide variety of categories, its current focus is on introducing more fashionable apparel brands to attract younger shoppers. The company is working hard to focus its position in the marketplace and rebuild "The Bay" brand for new generations of Canadians. This includes bringing banners like Lord & Taylor, Top Shop, and Saks 5th Avenue to the Canadian market. The purchase of Saks, for $2.4 billion, has allowed HBC to dramatically ramp up its online business. Last year, $660 million of the $900 million in ecommerce sales HBC generated came from Saks.

Some pundits still question the extent to which Canadian consumers are willing to buy Hugo Boss and Diesel apparel from the country's oldest retailer. Similarly, some have questioned the ability of the company, which is now

An early Hudson's Bay Company store on Bear Island

owned by the U.S.-based private equity firm NRDC, to continue to retain its loyal older customer segments as it updates its product lines. Competition continues to intensify from specialty apparel retailers, high-end department stores like Holt Renfrew, Nordstrom, and La Maison Simons, and discount chains like Walmart and Target. Critical to its success will be a deep understanding of the consumer segments it is best positioned to serve.

Source: HBC Hudson's Bay Company

QUESTIONS

1 Using the basic consumption process in Exhibit 1.1, discuss how a young Canadian "consumes" clothing.

2 Do you think it makes sense for The Bay to pursue more fashionable apparel brands to attract younger shoppers?

3 Is The Bay a consumer-oriented company?

4 What sort of research will HBC management need to drive its strategic decisions for The Bay in the next few years—interpretive, quantitative, or experimental?

5 Almost any business involves some ethical questions. In this case, do you see any problem with positioning The Bay as Canada's oldest corporation when it is owned by an American private equity firm?

2 | Value and the Consumer Behaviour Value Framework

LEARNING OBJECTIVES

After studying this chapter, the student should be able to:

2-1 Describe the consumer value framework, including its basic components.

2-2 Define consumer value and compare and contrast two key types of value.

2-3 Apply the concepts of marketing strategy and marketing tactics to describe the way firms go about creating value for consumers.

2-4 Explain the way market characteristics such as market segmentation and product differentiation affect marketing strategy.

2-5 Analyze consumer markets using elementary perceptual maps.

2-6 Justify consumers' lifetime value as an effective focus for long-term business success.

NBA Photos/Getty Images

INTRODUCTION

What if you had to get a group of strangers to feel comfortable conversing with each other? Try this. Give each person a name tag that includes his or her first name and just two other things: a favourite thing to eat and a favourite thing to do. All of a sudden, these strangers understand each other much better and have thoughts about these things that they feel compelled to share with each other. Favourites like these are the kinds of things that fill Pinterest boards online; face-to-face they give us something to talk about. Seeing "The Burger's Priest and ice climbing," you feel like you know a little about that person and have some things to talk about.

Consumer behaviour (CB) researchers would love to hear these conversations. They wouldn't be satisfied with knowing only what the favourites were, however; they would also want to know WHY something

is a favourite. People who share favourites also often share common identifiable characteristics. There was a time when Lincoln was an aspirational luxury brand. Then it became more recognizable as a ride home from the airport and not an automobile that most people would want in their garage. That trend was, of course, alarming to Lincoln and its parent company, Ford. The company's customers were getting older, and younger buyers were much more likely to consider a Lexus or BMW. Even as the quality of its automobiles improved, Lincoln struggled to remain relevant in the highly competitive luxury car market. In recent years, the Lincoln brand has seen resurgence. In the fall of 2014, consumers across different demographic groups suddenly started turning up in the showrooms asking about the Lincoln brand and buying Lincoln automobiles. Sales jumped by 25%![1]

Why do consumers' preferences change? Is this a phenomenon related to demographic characteristics

"Consumers are sometimes willing to sacrifice quality and even satisfaction, but consumers never willingly sacrifice value."

such as age or generation? Did the new cars arriving in 2014 have product attributes or design features that were substantially more attractive than previous models? Does advertising play a role in this type of attitude change? Once one considers other factors that are not as observable as demographics, the question of why favourite things change becomes even more complicated. What about psychological factors, cultural factors, and environmental characteristics? All of these can change what consumers like and what they want to buy. This book sheds light on why the things that provide so much value to certain consumers in certain times or certain situations don't really do anything for other consumers, or even for the same consumer at a different time or in a different situation. This chapter introduces the consumer value framework and some of the core concepts that tie all of CB together and make it actionable in marketing.

TalismanPHOTO for the Lincoln Motor Company/AP Images

Did Lincoln's ads featuring Matthew McConaughey change attitudes?

2-1 THE CONSUMER VALUE FRAMEWORK AND ITS COMPONENTS

Consumer behaviour is multifaceted. Not only does the study of consumer behaviour involve multiple disciplines, but anyone who has ever made a major purchase such as a house, automobile, or apartment knows that many factors can affect both the purchase decision and the way one feels after the purchase. This book covers many of these factors.

2-1a The Consumer Value Framework

Given the potential complexity involved in explaining consumption, a framework for studying consumer behaviour is useful. Exhibit 2.1 displays the framework used in this book. The **consumer value framework (CVF)** represents consumer behaviour theory illustrating factors that shape consumption-related behaviours and ultimately determine the value associated with consumption. The different components shown with different colours roughly correspond to the different parts of this book. However, the student of consumer behaviour must recognize and accept the fact that each aspect of the CVF is related in some

way to other components of the model. The arrows connecting the different components typify these connections.

2-1b Value and the CVF Components

Value is at the heart of experiencing and understanding consumer behaviour. Thus, we'll expand more on value throughout this book and will never get too far from value in any of its chapters. In the rest of this section, we present the basic components of the CVF that either contribute to or are outcomes of value.

RELATIONSHIP QUALITY

Over the past two decades or so, **customer relationship management (CRM)** has become a popular catchphrase, not just in marketing but in all of business. A basic CRM premise is that customers form relationships with companies as opposed to companies conducting individual transactions with customers. A CRM system tracks detailed information about customers so marketers can make more customer-oriented decisions that hopefully lead to longer lasting relationships.

---

consumer value framework (CVF) consumer behaviour theory that illustrates factors that shape consumption-related behaviours and ultimately determine the value associated with consumption

customer relationship management (CRM) systematic management information system that collects, maintains, and reports detailed information about customers to enable a more customer-oriented managerial approach

---

Exhibit 2.1

The Consumer Value Framework (CVF)

Internal Influences

Consumer Psychology
- Learning
- Search
- Perception
- Implicit Memory
- Intuition
- Information Processing
- Memory
- Categorization
- Attitudes

Personality of Consumer
- Motivation
- Personal Values
- Personality
- Lifestyle
- Emotional Expressiveness
- Emotional Intelligence

Consumption Process
- Needs
- Wants
- Exchange
- Costs and Benefits
- Reactions

Value
- Utilitarian Value
- Hedonic Value

Relationship Quality
- CS/D
- Switching Behaviour
- Customer Share
- Customer Commitment

External Influences

Social Environment
- Acculturation/ Enculturation
- Culture and Cultural Values
- Reference Groups and Peer Influence
- Social Class
- Family Influence
- Social Media
- Popular Media

Situational Influences
- Environment (Atmosphere)
- Time / Timing
- Conditions

In a CRM orientation, each customer represents a potential stream of resources rather than just a single sale. **Relationship quality** reflects the connectedness between a consumer and a retailer, brand, or service provider.[2] In practice, a consumer who buys the same brand each time a need for that product arises typifies a strong, or high-quality relationship. Businesses see loyal customers as being more profitable than customers who are prone to switching providers each time they make a purchase.

When a consumer realizes high value from an exchange with a company, relationship quality improves. Over time, a consumer who experiences high value with one company may well become a loyal, committed customer. It is worth keeping in mind, however, that high value does not necessarily mean low price. In fact, companies from Starbucks to lululemon to Harley-Davidson have created exceptionally loyal customers with products at relatively high price points. What companies like these have in common is a commitment to ensuring that the value the company offers to consumers is equal to or greater than the price they are asking those customers to pay. Because consumers see greater value in Starbucks coffee, lululemon yoga apparel, and Harley-Davidson motorcycles, they are happy to pay more. In addition, even though they have paid a relatively high price, many of those consumers are happily telling their friends about the value they received. As a result, these companies do not have to spend as much on advertising to attract new customers and can instead invest that money into improving the quality of their customer relationships.

CONSUMPTION PROCESS

Consumers must decide to do something before they can receive value. This process involves deciding what is needed and what options for exchange are available, and includes the inevitable reaction to consumption. The consumption process can involve a great deal of decision making and thus represents a consumer decision-making process. Many factors influence this process, and these factors can be divided into two categories: internal and external influences.

INTERNAL INFLUENCES: THE PSYCHOLOGY AND PERSONALITY OF THE CONSUMER

The Psychology of the Consumer.
Will consumers react in the same way to a price increase from $80 to $100 as they would to a price decrease for the same product? Is there a good reason to sell a product for $69.99 rather than $70? All these questions involve the psychology of the consumer. In other words, these things are **internal influences**, things that are processed inside the mind of the consumer or that can be thought of as part of the consumer.

The psychology of the consumer involves both cognitive and affective processes. **Cognition** refers to the thinking or mental processes that go on as we process and store things that can become knowledge. A child hears parents talk about smoking as a *nasty* thing to do. Smoking becomes associated with nastiness, and the child may develop a dislike for smoking. **Affect** refers to the feelings that are experienced during consumption activities or that are associated with specific objects. If the child continues to receive negative information about smoking, the belief about its being nasty may result in feelings of disgust.

Many people think of these types of things when they think of consumer behaviour. Certainly, our perceptions help shape the desirability of products, which can influence decision processes and the value perceived from consumption. Recall that value is a subjective assessment. Therefore, value is very much a matter of perception.

The Personality of the Consumer.
Every consumer has certain characteristics and traits that help define him or her as an individual. We refer to these traits generally as **individual differences**. Individual differences, which include personality and lifestyle, help determine consumer behaviour. For example, a consumer who is highly health conscious is more likely to be interested in a gym membership and low-fat food products than a consumer who is less health conscious.

Companies have spent vast amounts of money and time trying to harness individual differences in a way that would allow them to predict consumer choices. Individual differences like these include basic human motivations, which trigger consumer desires, and are thus related to product and brand preferences. Also, individual differences shape the value experienced by consumers and the reaction consumers have to consumption.

relationship quality degree of connectedness between a consumer and a retailer, brand, or service provider

internal influences things that go on inside of the mind and heart of the consumer

cognition thinking or mental processes that go on as we process and store things that can become knowledge

affect feelings associated with objects or experienced during events

individual differences characteristic traits of individuals, including personality and lifestyle

Atmospherics: How Mozart Chooses What You Will Drink

The next time you are feeling thirsty, what will determine the beverage you choose to consume? Will it be an energy drink or maybe an iced tea? Is your preference based on taste or the design of the can or the amount of caffeine or some other factor? If you are like most consumers, you probably do not think that your choice of drink depends on the tempo of the music in the store or the scent in the air or the colour of the walls. Yet, atmospheric variables—such as colour, scent, and music—can dramatically affect shoppers' behaviour because they influence their level of arousal or excitement. For example, recent research examined the influence that background music has on consumer choice. The authors found that Mozart played at a slow tempo tends to put people in a pleasant and relaxed mood. Because those consumers wanted to maintain that pleasant mood, more than 70% of them chose iced tea over an energy drink (believing it was the more relaxing beverage). However, when the same Mozart sonata was played at a faster pace, the results reversed—more than 70% of consumers chose the energy drink over the iced tea (believing it would help them maintain the pleasant and exciting mood that they were experiencing). The same research demonstrated that background colours and scents can also substantially change the choices consumers make. Interestingly, the consumers in these studies had no idea that the atmospheric variables were influencing their moods or their decisions.

Source: F. Di Muro & K. B. Murray (2012). "An arousal regulation explanation of mood effects on consumer choice," *Journal of Consumer Research*.

EXTERNAL INFLUENCES

Why do some consumers like foods such as sushi or habañero peppers, while others wouldn't consider eating these things, preferring a hot dog? Why do consumers in different parts of the world have such different tastes for food? In Korea, a typical breakfast often includes a fish soup of some type. In Australia, one might smear a bit of vegemite (a yeast extract paste resembling peanut butter in texture, but not in taste) onto toast in the morning. In the United States, many consumers drink cola as part of their breakfast. In Canada, a bowl of Shreddies with cold milk poured over the top is a common way to start the day. Each of these dishes might be disgusting as a breakfast food to people in certain parts of the world. Even a simple thing like breakfast can cause quite different reactions in different consumers in different places.

These types of events typify external influences on consumers. **External influences** include the social and cultural aspects of life as a consumer. They directly affect the value of activities, although the influence comes from sources outside of the consumer. External influences are critical to a thorough understanding of consumer behaviour.

Social Environment. Any time a consumer chooses to do something in response to another consumer, he or she has been influenced by the **social environment**. The social environment includes the people and groups who help shape a consumer's everyday experiences. Reference group influence is one mechanism through which social influences work. A child's tastes for

external influences
social and cultural aspects of life as a consumer

social environment
elements that specifically deal with the way other people influence consumer decision making and value

External influences determine the value of many things, including what's for breakfast.

breakfast foods are shaped very much by what he or she learns from parents, and by an innate desire to conform to their wishes.

SITUATIONAL INFLUENCES

External influences also include situational influences. **Situational influences** are things unique to a time or place that can affect consumer decision making and the value received from consumption. Situational influences include the effect that the physical environment has on consumer behaviour. Researchers are only beginning to understand the full impact of situational variables on consumer behaviour, but we do know that things like music, colour, scent, physical space, and many other similar factors can have substantial effects on consumer behaviour. Factors like these are discussed further later.

Much of the remainder of the book will be organized around the customer value framework. Because it connects the different theoretical areas of consumer behaviour, the CVF will be a valuable study aid. Additionally, the CVF is a good analysis tool for solving consumer behaviour business problems. Lastly, the CVF is a valuable tool for businesses that are trying to understand the way consumers respond to their product offerings. Thus, the CVF is useful in developing and implementing marketing strategy.

2-2 VALUE AND TWO BASIC TYPES OF VALUE

The heart of the consumer value framework, and *the* core concept of consumer behaviour, is value. **Value** is a personal assessment of the *net worth*—that is, the benefits minus the costs—obtained from an activity. Value is what consumers ultimately pursue because valuable actions address motivations that manifest themselves in needs and desires. In this sense, value captures how much gratification a consumer receives from consumption.

Across all types of restaurants, fast-food chains do not typically offer the highest food quality. When a consumer chooses a fast-food restaurant, chances are lower prices, greater convenience, and faster service are factors that outweigh a need for high food quality. Consumers in fact will repeat behaviour for which they have previously experienced low satisfaction. Walmart stores do not have a relatively high consumer satisfaction index, yet many customers repeatedly visit Walmart. Walmart delivers value, as we will see in a later chapter. In

contrast to these examples, contriving a situation where consumers are not seeking value is virtually impossible. In fact, everything we do in life is done in the pursuit of some type of value.

Consumers develop value perceptions from consumption after considering the costs and benefits associated with a particular activity. In the everyday vernacular, people sometimes use *value* as a synonym for *price*, particularly *low price*, but this view is narrow minded. We do use price to try to reflect value; however, price is in many ways a very poor proxy for value. What kinds of things are of high value to you? How easily can one put a "price" on these most valued things?

2-2a The Value Equation

Exhibit 2.2 reflects some important components of value and how a consumer might put these together to determine the overall worth of something—or its value! Worth to a consumer is actually a function of much more than price. Value can be modelled by playing the "what you get" from dealing with a company against the "what you have to give" to get the product. The "what you get" includes benefits or the positive consequences of consumption. The "what you give" includes sacrifices or the negative consequences of consumption. Nearly all the components in the value equation come into play when a consumer buys a product like a car that requires multiple considerations.

Later in the book, a chapter is devoted to further describing value and other related concepts, including expectations, satisfaction, and quality. Because value is an essential part of consumer behaviour, a basic overview is provided in this chapter.

Value can be understood better by looking at its types. While theoretically one could probably break value down into many very specific types, a very useful value typology can be developed using only two types. Thus, we distinguish utilitarian value from hedonic value.

2-2b Utilitarian Value

Activities and objects that lead to high utilitarian value do so because they help the consumer accomplish some task. **Utilitarian value** is derived from a product that helps the consumer solve problems and accomplish

situational influences things unique to a time or place that can affect consumer decision making and the value received from consumption

value a personal assessment of the net worth obtained from an activity

utilitarian value value derived from a product that helps the consumer with some task

Exhibit 2.2

The Value Equation

Value = What you get — What you give

Benefits such as:
Quality
Convenience
Emotions
Prestige
Experience

Other factors like:
Scarcity
Nostalgia

Sacrifice of:
Time
Money
Effort
Opportunity
Emotions
Image

when a consumer does something to obtain hedonic value, the action can sometimes be very difficult to explain objectively.

Rather than being viewed as opposites, utilitarian and hedonic value are not mutually exclusive. In other words, the same act of consumption can provide both utilitarian value and hedonic value. Dining in a place like the Hard Rock Cafe is an event. One doesn't have to go to a Hard Rock Cafe to eat, but dining there is a lot of fun—an experience! However, a Hard Rock Cafe consumer also accomplishes the task of having something to eat—getting nourished. In fact, the very best consumer experiences are those that provide both high utilitarian value and high hedonic value.

tasks. Consumers usually offer a rational explanation of why something is purchased when utilitarian value is the primary motivation. For instance, when a consumer buys Clorox bleach, he or she undoubtedly will be cleaning something. Quite simply, the bleach enables something to become clean. Having something clean is gratifying to the consumer even if the actual process of cleaning is not. In this sense, one can think of utilitarian value as a means to an end.[3] Value is provided because the object or activity allows something else to happen or be accomplished.

2-2c Hedonic Value

The second type of value is referred to in the consumer behaviour literature as hedonic value. **Hedonic value** is the immediate gratification that comes from experiencing some activity. Seldom does one go to a horror film, ride Disney's Space Mountain, or read fiction in an effort to get a job done. With hedonic value, the value is provided entirely by the actual experience and emotions associated with consumption, not because some other end is or will be accomplished.

Conceptually, hedonic value differs from utilitarian value in several ways. First, hedonic value is an end in and of itself rather than a means to an end. Second, hedonic value is emotional and subjective in nature. Third,

hedonic value value derived from the immediate gratification that comes from some activity

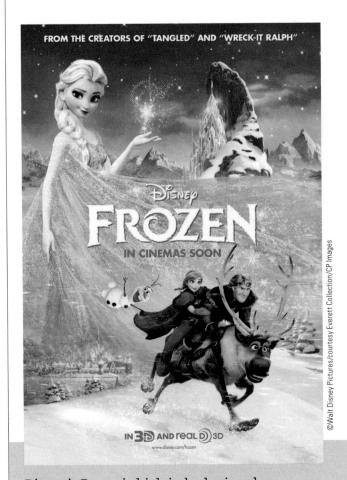

Disney's *Frozen* is high in hedonic value.

Why is Disney's *Frozen* such a huge marketing success? Parents can take the kids to the movie and accomplish the job of keeping the kids happy while at the same time enjoying the movie themselves. In this way, Disney has created a product that provides high value and the value has translated into success.

Exhibit 2.3 illustrates the value possibilities associated with consumption. A marketer who provides low levels of both values is not likely to survive very long. Generally, a consumer goes to a fast-food restaurant to accomplish the task of getting something to eat, and doing this as quickly as possible. Food quality may take a back seat to convenience. When the fast-food experience becomes slow, the consumer receives little value of either type.

In contrast, restaurants can survive by specializing in providing one type of value or the other, as would be the case in a place with a great atmosphere but perhaps less than the best food or service quality. As mentioned earlier, the best experience comes when a restaurant can put everything together—high-quality food and impeccable service in a memorable place with a great atmosphere. These are the types of experiences a consumer is most likely to want to repeat.

Exhibit 2.3

Consumption Activities Can Fall Into Any of These Categories

		Utilitarian Value	
		Low	**High**
Hedonic Value	Low	Bad Positioning: *slow* fast food in an unpleasant environment; can only survive with captive market	Okay Positioning: *fast* fast food; competes well for a market more concerned about time than taste
	High	Okay Positioning: restaurant with nice atmosphere but poor service; competes well for a market wanting to escape to a pleasant place	Superior Positioning: restaurant with great atmosphere, great food, and great service; will compete well in any market

2-3 MARKETING STRATEGY AND CONSUMER VALUE

One way that a company can enhance the chance of long-term survival is to have an effective marketing strategy. Generally, a **strategy** is a planned way of doing something to accomplish some goal.

2-3a Marketing Strategy

In a business environment, a **marketing strategy** is the way a company goes about creating value for customers. The strategy should provide an effective way of dealing with both competition and eventual technological obsolescence by making sure that value is delivered in a way that is not easily duplicated by other companies and not defined only in terms of the tangible product offered.

A complete understanding of the value consumers seek is needed to develop and implement a strategy effectively. Bell may compete directly with Rogers in many Canadian markets, but Bell also competes with companies such as Skype, which provides local, long distance, and even international calling via the Internet, all for prices much lower than traditional telephone services. The consumer who uses Internet calling services like Skype no longer needs a telephone to receive the benefits of talking to friends and family who are far away, and computer-to-computer calls are free. If Bell laid out a marketing strategy that depended on people buying and owning "phones," technological obsolescence would represent a real threat. A better strategic orientation would focus on providing value by enabling and facilitating communication. Bell also sells cellphones that can make Skype calls. To succeed in the long run, telecommunications companies will have to focus on the core benefits they provide, in this case all derived from electronic communication. Without this focus, companies run the risk of developing **marketing myopia**, defined as a company that views itself in a product business rather than in a value, or benefits producing, business.[4] Thus, when technology makes the product obsolete, the myopic company goes out of business. In contrast, the company that

strategy a planned way of doing something to accomplish a goal

marketing strategy way a company goes about creating value for customers

marketing myopia a common condition in which a company views itself in a product business rather than in a value, or benefits producing, business; in this way, it is short sighted

Exhibit 2.4

Business Strategy at Different Levels

Corporate Culture

CORPORATE STRATEGY

MARKETING STRATEGY

TACTICS

focuses on value creation builds solutions around the need, not the physical product.

Strategies exist at several different levels. Exhibit 2.4 demonstrates this point. Basically, **corporate strategy** deals with how the firm will be defined and sets general goals. This strategy is usually associated with a specific corporate culture, which provides an operating orientation for the company. Marketing strategy then follows, and different business units within the firm may have different marketing strategies. In describing how value is created, the strategies tell why customers will choose to buy things from the company.

Strategies must eventually be implemented. Implementation deals with operational management. In marketing, this level includes activities known as tactics. **Marketing tactics**, which involve price, promotion, product, and distribution decisions, are ways marketing management is implemented. Together, marketing strategy and marketing tactics should maximize the total value received by a company's customers.

2-3b Total Value Concept

Products are multifaceted and can provide value in many ways. Even a simple product like a soft drink offers consumers more than a cold drink that addresses one's desire to

corporate strategy way a firm is defined, and its general goals

marketing tactics ways marketing management is implemented; involves price, promotion, product, and distribution decisions

quench a thirst. If a soft drink were a product that provided value only as a thirst quencher, the market share statistics for soft drink brands would certainly be different than they are today. Exhibit 2.5 shows the Canadian market shares for carbonated beverages. Global data also shows Coke and Pepsi as the leading players.[5]

As can be seen, Coke and Diet Coke account for one-quarter of all carbonated beverage sales in Canada. Taken together, Coke, Pepsi, Sprite (owned by Coca-Cola), and 7-Up (owned by Pepsi) make up half of all carbonated beverage sales in Canada. Yet with a quick look around the grocery store, consumers will find competing brands—including private labels from Loblaw, Sobeys, and Walmart—that sell at much lower prices. In addition, many consumers are unable to pick out their favourite brand in a blind taste test. Yet private label colas and other colas that compete with Coke and Pepsi have relatively minuscule market shares. The fact of the matter is that Coke is more than coloured, carbonated, flavoured water. One can look back to the 1980s and see what happened when "old" Coke was pulled from the market in favour of "new" Coke. Consumers revolted and demanded that Coke be restored, even though the "new" Coke was supported by millions of dollars of research that focused on flavour. But flavour explains only one small part of the total value offered by a Coke.

Some products require installation or other types of service before one can enjoy any benefits. The Apple iPhone is a technological marvel. However, without a service plan, the technology offers practically no

Exhibit 2.5

Canadian Carbonated Beverages Market Share Data

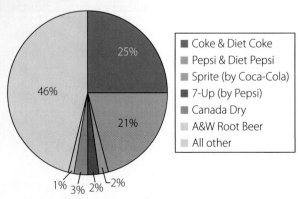

- Coke & Diet Coke — 25%
- Pepsi & Diet Pepsi — 21%
- Sprite (by Coca-Cola)
- 7-Up (by Pepsi)
- Canada Dry
- A&W Root Beer
- All other — 46%

1% 3% 2% 2%

Sources: Adapted from *Euromonitor* (2015), "Carbonates in Canada."

benefits and, therefore, no value. Additionally, the owner will want at least some of the more than a million apps offered by Apple—each offering some new benefit ranging from gaming to scanning bar codes. Going further, a consumer might want to complement an iPhone with an iWatch.

Thus, every product's value is made up of the basic benefits, plus the augmented product, plus the "feel" benefits. A company must try to understand all the ways a product offers value to its customers. The **total value concept** is practised when companies operate with the understanding that products provide value in multiple ways. Many products and brands, for instance, provide some benefits that produce utilitarian value and some that provide hedonic value. This value, in turn, helps provide a brand with meaning in the consumer psyche.

2-3c The Total Value Concept Illustrated

Let's consider a consumer who purchases a 2014 LaFerrari limited production hybrid sports car. Does the consumer buy the car for its gas–electric V12 motor producing over 950 horsepower, seven-speed dual-clutch automatic transmission, carbon-fibre body shell, carbon–ceramic regenerative brakes, bright red colour, or 14 L/100 km fuel efficiency (it is a hybrid after all)? No, consumers buy cars because of the total value offered. How does the LaFerrari offer value?[6] The answer may not be the same for all consumers, but here are some likely value factors:

1. **Transportation.** The LaFerrari solves the job of getting a consumer from point A to point B. This is one way the LaFerrari provides value—utilitarian value, in this case.

2. **The Ferrari service plan.** A LaFerrari needs TLC. Ferrari offers a three-year warranty, which means that for at least three years, the problem of repairing the LaFerrari is solved—utilitarian value is added.

3. **The feelings associated with driving the car.** The car is very fast and handles well. It has a top speed of just over 350 kilometres per hour. Of course, Ferrari owners always obey the speed limit—right?! The excitement that is the LaFerrari driving experience provides hedonic value.

4. **The positive feelings that go along with ownership.** The LaFerrari owner will certainly take pride in the car. A Ferrari jacket and cap help make the statement, "I'm a Ferrari owner." He or she can impress friends with a drive on the 401 or the Coquihalla Highway. He or she may believe that increased social status is a benefit of being a Ferrari owner. The realization of ownership provides hedonic value.

5. **The negative feelings that go along with ownership.** Hopefully, our LaFerrari owner is independently wealthy. At a price tag of more than $1,400,000 USD, the car loan would be a substantial monthly payment, not to mention the insurance. In addition, the LaFerrari requires expensive service upkeep. If the LaFerrari is a financial strain, then worry will result when the owner thinks about the car. Friends may have also suggested that LaFerraris are unreliable. All of these feelings may detract from the hedonic value offered by the car.

Altogether, many readers might be interested in owning the LaFerrari, but it is unlikely that many would care to pay the high price. Thus, the LaFerrari does not offer enough benefits for us to make the necessary sacrifice. A Honda Civic may do the trick, although the hedonic-to-utilitarian value ratio may not be the same as with a LaFerrari.

Automobile marketers sometimes miss the total value equation for their product. In 2005, General Motors began to offer consumers a "total value promise," hoping this would convey the value of extended warranties, more standard equipment, and lower sticker prices to consumers. Was GM missing something if the executives believed total value to be confined to these tangible aspects?

A few years ago, GM created a discount program in which consumers received the employee discount on new car purchases. This program was wildly successful in producing sales. Among other factors, GM's plan was to increase the value equation in the consumer's favour both by lowering the price and by creating positive feelings during the buying process. Consumers perceived themselves as getting a great deal and thus the program added hedonic value.[7] But by 2009, GM had gone through bankruptcy and survived only with drastic government intervention. The reasons for GM's poor performance are many, but some claim that once the drastic discounting began, consumers felt no need to accept any GM products at premium "non-employee" prices, and the company increasingly lost money. This illustrates a danger of deep discounting: It's easy to cut prices to gain a little business, but the gain in business comes at a drop in margin that proves

total value concept
business practice wherein companies operate with the understanding that products provide value in multiple ways

CHAPTER 2: Value and the Consumer Behaviour Value Framework

How does Ferrari provide value?

very difficult to get back. That is, as consumers learned the price at which to buy a GM product, GM could no longer obtain a gross margin from purchases sufficient to sustain profitability.

Innovation is necessary to provide consumers with high value. When a firm practises the total value concept, a full understanding of how value can be created from a product is necessary. In the future, Ferrari might consider rolling routine service into the warranty plan as a way of enhancing value—particularly given the reliability of competitors. Total value is also affected by the technologies and infrastructures that exist. For instance, is Ferrari researching a way to provide value if self-driving cars make traditional automobiles and highways obsolete? What value would a Ferrari offer if you couldn't drive it?[8]

value co-creation the realization that a consumer is necessary and must play a part in order to produce value

marketing mix combination of product, pricing, promotion, and distribution strategies used to implement a marketing strategy

target market identified segment or segments of a market that a company serves

market segmentation separation of a market into groups based on the different demand curves associated with each group

2-3d Value Is Co-Created

A marketer can only propose a way of creating value to consumers. In other words, a marketer alone cannot create value.[9] Rather, the consumer adds resources in the form of knowledge and skills to do his or her own part in the consumption process. Value is not created solely by the marketer's offering; consumption involves **value co-creation**. Rosetta Stone can offer language instruction to consumers via its specialized software. However, the consumer can only realize value from the offer by purchasing the product and applying effort and skills. In many instances, a bad consumption experience is not entirely the fault of the business. The consumer plays a role in the value equation as well.

2-4 MARKET CHARACTERISTICS: MARKET SEGMENTS AND PRODUCT DIFFERENTIATION

Marketing management involves managing the marketing mix and deciding to whom a marketing effort will be directed. The **marketing mix** is simply the combination of product, pricing, promotion, and distribution strategies used to position some product or brand in the marketplace. The marketing mix represents the way a marketing strategy is implemented within a given market or exchange environment. Marketers often use the term **target market** to signify which market segment a company will serve with a specific marketing mix. Thus, target marketing requires that managers identify and understand market segments. But, what exactly is market segmentation?

2-4a Market Segmentation

Market segmentation is the separation of a market into groups based on the different demand curves associated with each group. Market segmentation is a marketplace condition; numerous segments exist in some markets, but very few segments may exist in others. We can think of the total quantity of a product sold as a simple mathematical function (f) like this:[10]

$$Q = f(p, w, x, \ldots z)$$

where Q = total quantity sold, p = price, and w, x, and z are other characteristics or attributes of the particular product. The function means that as price and the other characteristics are varied, the quantity demanded changes.

For example, as the price of 4K televisions decreases, the quantity sold increases; in other words, there is a negative relationship between price and quantity sold. This type of relationship represents the typical price–quantity relationship commonly depicted in basic economics courses. As the length of the warranty increases (w in this case), more 4K TVs are sold. Thus, if we limit the demand equation to two characteristics (in this case, price p and warranty w), the equation representing demand for 4K TVs overall might be

$$Q = -3p + 2w$$

The numbers, or coefficients, preceding p and w, respectively, for each group represent the sensitivity of each segment to each characteristic. The greater the magnitude (absolute value) of the number, the more sensitive a group is to a change in that characteristic. In economics, **elasticity** is a term used to represent market sensitivity to changes in price or other characteristics.[11] This equation suggests that consumers are more sensitive to price than warranty, as indicated by the respective coefficients, -3 for price and $+2$ for warranty in this case.

However, this overall demand "curve" may not accurately reflect any one particular consumer. Instead, the market may really consist of two groups of consumers that produce this particular demand curve when aggregated. In other words, the two groups may be of equal size and be represented by equations that look something like this:

$$q_1 = -1p + 3w$$
$$q_2 = -5p + 1w$$

In this case, q_1 and q_2 represent the quantity that would be sold in groups one and two, respectively. Group one is more sensitive to the warranty ($|3| > |1|$), and group two is more sensitive to price ($|-5| > |1|$). When we put all the segments together, we get total demand once again:

$$Q = q_1 + q_2$$

Thus, a market for any product is really the sum of the demand existing in individual groups or segments of consumers. The fast-food market may consist of many segments, including a group most interested in low price, a group most interested in food quality, a group most interested in convenience, and perhaps a group that is not extremely sensitive to any of these characteristics. Market segmentation is not really a marketing tactic because the segments are created by consumers through their unique preferences. Market segmentation is critically important to effective marketing, though, and part of the marketing researcher's job is to identify segments and describe the segments' members based on characteristics such as age, income, geography, and lifestyle.

Earlier, we discussed the soft drink market in the context of the total value concept, and how higher-priced brands were the best sellers. If we think of the change in price as the difference in price between the bargain brands and Coke, most consumers seem to prefer higher-priced sodas. At the very least, soft drink consumers are insensitive to price. Although this may seem inconsistent with "rational" economics, consumer behaviour theory offers an explanation. Name-brand soft drinks like Coke simply are worth more, meaning they are more valuable, than bargain soft drinks. This is a very important point to understand. Ultimately, consumer segments exist because different consumers do value different alternatives in different ways.[12]

Market segments are associated with unique value equations just as they are associated with unique demand equations. Thus, if each segment is offered a product that closely matches its particular sensitivities, all segments can receive high value. This brings us to product differentiation.

2-4b Product Differentiation

Product differentiation is a marketplace condition in which consumers do not view all competing products as identical to one another. We refer to commodities very often as products that are indistinguishable across brands and/or manufacturers—that is, no matter who produced them or where they were produced. Regular gasoline approaches a commodity status, but even here, a few consumers will regard certain brands as unique. In contrast, consumers do not all consider Internet retailers the same way. Some purchasers consider a third-party seller like eBay inconvenient and only visit if there is something there that they cannot find easily elsewhere. Conversely, other consumers view the eBay shopping and buying process as intrinsically entertaining and a source of high hedonic value. In this case, market segments can be identified based on the way different consumers view Internet shopping and their differing sensitivities to characteristics of Internet transactions. Fortunately, these segments often align with consumer characteristics like age or generation that enable marketers to reach, communicate with, and serve the segments more efficiently.[13]

elasticity reflects how sensitive a consumer is to changes in some product characteristic

product differentiation marketplace condition in which consumers do not view all competing products as identical to one another

2-5 ANALYZING MARKETS WITH PERCEPTUAL MAPS

Product differentiation becomes the basis for **product positioning**. Positioning refers to the way a product is perceived by a consumer and can be represented by the number and types of characteristics that consumers perceive. A standard marketing tool is a perceptual map.

2-5a Perceptual Maps

A **perceptual map** is used to depict graphically the positioning of competing products. When marketing analysts examine perceptual maps, they can identify competitors, identify opportunities for doing more business, and diagnose potential problems in the marketing mix. For instance, the analyst may realize that by changing the amount of some product characteristic, they can "move" closer to some segment's ideal point and thus increase the competitiveness of the product. Alternatively, a new business may choose to position a product in a way that leaves it facing little direct competition. This can be done by "locating" the product as far away from other brands as possible.

The Canadian-founded company Cirque de Soleil followed a marketing strategy that positioned its offering far away from other circuses by eliminating tents and circus animals (moving into arenas and auditoriums), raising prices (a ticket far above the normal circus ticket), reducing the number of acts, and creating themes for acrobatic shows. In doing so, they created what marketing analysts refer to as a blue ocean.[14] A **blue ocean strategy** seeks to position a firm so far away from competitors that, when successful, the firm creates an industry of its own by finding an uncontested market space where, at least for a time, it isolates itself from competitors.

2-5b Illustrating a Perceptual Map

Exhibit 2.6 illustrates a perceptual map. Perceptual mapping is used throughout this book as a way to link differences in consumer behaviour to changes in marketing strategy or tactics. In this case, the perceptual map depicts consumer beliefs about tourist attractions in New Orleans, Louisiana. Each attraction is listed in a small rectangle.

The researcher identified and collected consumer perceptions of the 10 tourist destinations and their **ideal point**, meaning the combination of tourist destination characteristics providing the most value

product positioning
way a product is perceived by a consumer

perceptual map tool used to depict graphically the positioning of competing products

blue ocean strategy positioning a firm far away from competitors' positions so that it creates an industry of its own and, at least for a time, isolates itself from competitors

ideal point combination of product characteristics that provides the most value to an individual consumer or market segment

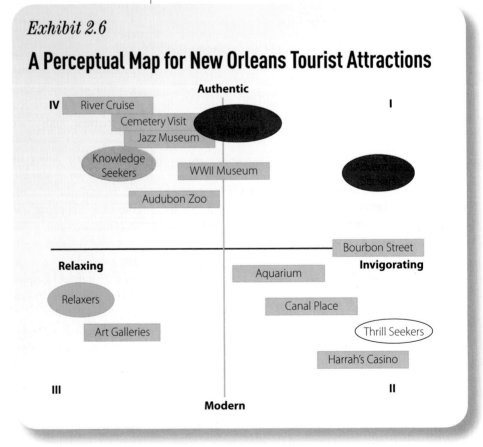

Exhibit 2.6

A Perceptual Map for New Orleans Tourist Attractions

among the five most prominent consumer segments: Adventure Seekers, Culture Explorers, Relaxers, Knowledge Seekers, and Thrill Seekers.[15] Coloured ovals indicate these segments centred on each segment's ideal point. The *x*- and *y*-axes of this plane represent important dimensions that consumers use to separate competitors on specific characteristics. Here, the *x*-axis identifies product offerings based on how relaxing to invigorating consumers view each. The *y*-axis separates product offerings based on how relatively modern versus authentic consumers view each. The perceptual map allows several key observations.

1. **The competition among attractions viewed as highly authentic and relaxing is intense. Consumers regard the Mississippi River Cruise, a visit to the Jazz Museum, a cemetery visit, and the Audubon Zoo as possessing these characteristics as shown in quadrant IV of the perceptual map. The World War II Museum also competes with these attractions, viewed as a moderately authentic, moderately invigorating attraction.**

2. **Two segments, Culture Explorers and Knowledge Seekers, possess ideal points near the five segments mentioned above.**

3. **Harrah's Casino offers an option for the thrill-seeking market with its position as highly invigorating and highly modern.**

4. **The city's numerous art galleries offer the Relaxer segment an attractive option.**

5. **The Adventure Seeker segment appears underserved, with no option prominent in quadrant I.**

The marketing analyst draws several conclusions based on these observations:

1. **The highest demand positioning is in quadrant IV (highly authentic, relaxing). The city's overall image as rich in heritage and relatively laid-back—"The Big Easy" being one of the many nicknames—helps attract consumers looking for these types of experiences. An entrepreneur wishing to open another major tourist attraction positioned in this way may see the large number of potential customers desiring this positioning as an opportunity. However, the downside to this positioning is the large number of entrenched competitors. In general, competing directly with large, entrenched competitors usually requires a large amount of resources.**

2. **An opportunity may exist in quadrant I. Here, major competition for the adventure-seeking market appears absent. The advantage of positioning**

a new business away from the competitors is that it takes fewer resources to get started because the major competitors are not likely to see the new offering as a threat. Here, the opportunity for rustic, overnight stays in the swamplands that surround New Orleans may provide an attractive offering for this segment. The success of such an offering depends on a steady stream of Adventure Seekers coming to New Orleans.

Perceptual maps are widely used to plot the way consumers view competitors in an industry. As illustrated in the example, they are very useful for spotting opportunities in the marketplace, allowing a business to better understand exactly whom they compete with, and identifying what-if situations by examining what would happen if they changed an offering by raising or lowering characteristics. Very commonly, brands analyze themselves on a perceptual map with price and quality as the dimensions. If a firm lowers price or raises quality, its competition may well change. Perceptual mapping is used in practically every competitive industry, including the nonprofit sector.[16] The simple two-dimensional graphics give the user an easy way to analyze a market.

2-5c Using Consumer Behaviour Theory in Marketing Strategy

Businesses are constantly using consumer behaviour to make better strategic and operational marketing decisions. We will focus on using consumer behaviour in business decision making many times throughout this book. Students, and practising managers for that matter, sometimes struggle with the application aspect of consumer behaviour. Essentially, this comes down to effective decision making. Checklists can be a useful aid to decision making as a way to effectively develop marketing strategy and tactics. Exhibit 2.7 displays a consumer behaviour analysis checklist—the CB idea checklist.

2-6 VALUE TODAY AND TOMORROW—CUSTOMER LIFETIME VALUE

We defined marketing earlier as value-producing activities that facilitate exchange. In other words, marketing makes exchange more likely. Exchange is far from a one-way street. Both consumers and companies

Exhibit 2.7

The CB Idea Checklist

Question	Idea
What specific consumer needs and desires are involved?	
▶ Is a specific product(s) involved in this situation?	
▶ Can something else provide the same value or address the same need or desire?	
How is the product positioned (types and amounts of value intended)?	
▶ How is our position superior to competitors'?	
▶ How can we move closer to desirable ideal points?	
▶ How is our position inferior to competitors'?	
▶ How can we isolate ourselves from competition?	
How does the consumer actually receive value from this company?	
▶ In the current situation, has value been diminished? Can value be enhanced?	
▶ Can the product be modified to enhance value?	
▶ Can the company introduce a new product to enhance value?	
▶ Can the company add services to improve value for consumers?	
▶ Can communication be improved?	
▶ Is a competitor in a better position to provide superior value?	
▶ If so, how?	
Where is this product consumed?	
▶ Can value be enhanced by changing the consumption setting?	
Who?	
▶ Is buying the product?	
1. Individual Consumers	
2. Groups of Consumers (Families)	
3. Business Consumers	
▶ Is not buying the product?	
Why should a consumer?	
▶ Buy this product?	
▶ Avoid this product?	
When do consumers?	
▶ Find the product most valuable?	
▶ Find the product least valuable?	
What are the key CVF elements involved in understanding the consumption process in this case?	
Is additional consumer research needed?	
▶ Will the information be worth what it would cost to obtain it?	
▶ What type of research would be required?	

Is It the Real Cheese? Does Anyone Care?

Is it just blue cheese? Well, to some consumers cheese is cheese and, especially, blue cheese is blue cheese. If you are in the cheese business, though, you realize that some consumers recognize the real cheese from the pretenders. When it comes to blue cheese, consumers who find value in, and are therefore sensitive to, the authenticity of cheese are willing to spend more for Stilton cheese. Governments, including the European Union (EU), recognize the uniqueness of certain products with geographical identification, such as Champagne, Parma hams, Dijon mustard, and Stilton cheese, by protecting their names by law. Thus, only the blue-veined cheese produced in three counties in England can legally be called Stilton. Curiously, cheese makers from the town of Stilton, England, cannot call their cheese Stilton. The town lies outside the three-county region legally recognized as producing authentic Stilton cheese. The EU protects more than 800 products with specific regional authenticity. True Champagne comes from the Champagne region of France. A wine producer from any other area that calls its wine Champagne risks legal problems and is potentially misleading customers because its products are not authentic. Authenticity is a potential product characteristic that creates product differentiation. There are segments of consumers sensitive to authenticity and others that are not. Which segment are you in?

Sources: Miller, J. W. (2009), "English Village Tries to Milk a Connection to Its Cheesy Past," *The Wall Street Journal*, (12/8), A1. Beverland, M. B., F. Farrelly and P. G. Quester (2010), "Authentic Subcultural Membership: Antecedents and Consequences of Authenticating Acts and Authoritative Performances," *Psychology & Marketing*, 27 (July), 698–716.

enter exchanges seeking value. The value a company receives from exchange may be slightly easier to explain than the value a consumer receives. Obviously, when a consumer spends money for a product, the company receives economic resources in the form of revenue, which the company can use to pay employees, cover costs, and help the firm grow. The company may also receive additional benefits if the consumer becomes a loyal customer who is an advocate for the firm's products.

Not every customer is equally valuable to a firm. Firms increasingly want to know the customer lifetime value associated with a customer or customer segment.[17] **Customer lifetime value (CLV)** represents the approximate worth of a customer to a company in economic terms. Put another way, CLV is the overall, long-term profitability of an individual consumer. Although there is no generally accepted formula for the CLV, the basic idea is simple. The customer lifetime value is equal to the net present value (NPV) of the stream of profits over a customer's lifetime plus the worth attributed to the equity a good customer can bring in the form of positive referrals and word of mouth. This idea can be represented as follows:

$$CLV = NPV(Sales - Costs) + NPV(Equity)$$

Consider a consumer shopping twice weekly at IKEA. On average, this IKEA customer spends $200 per week, or $10,400 per year. If we assume a 5% operating margin, this customer yields IKEA a *net* $520 per year. Even if any potential positive word of mouth is not considered, the consumer is worth about $9,000 to IKEA today assuming a 30-year lifespan and a 4% annual interest rate.

Interestingly, until recently Walmart did not record customer-level data. Thus, out of more than 500 terabytes of data, Walmart had no data on CLV.[18] In contrast, other firms, from convenience

> **customer lifetime value (CLV)** approximate worth of a customer to a company in economic terms; overall profitability of an individual consumer

Consumers see IKEA as a value provider; in return, each regular customer is highly valuable to IKEA.

British Retail Photography/Alamy

stores to Harrah's Casinos, have elaborate systems for tracking individual customer behaviour and targeting these consumers with individualized promotions and products. This allows them to practise one-to-one marketing in a real sense and to identify segments of consumers containing a high proportion of very valuable customers. For instance, one retailer found that high CLV customers tend to have the following characteristics:[19]

▸ **Female**

▸ **30–50 years of age**

▸ **Married**

▸ **$90,000 income**

▸ **Loyalty card holder**

In contrast, the low CLV customers tend to have quite different characteristics:

▸ **Male**

▸ **24–44 years of age**

▸ **Single**

▸ **Less than $70,000 income**

▸ **Single channel shopper (meaning only Internet or only stores)**

Thus, marketers can maximize the value they receive from exchange by concentrating their marketing efforts on consumers with high CLVs.

STUDY TOOLS 2

LOCATED AT THE BACK OF THE TEXTBOOK
☐ Rip out Chapter Review Card

LOCATED AT NELSON.COM/STUDENT
☐ Review Key Terms Flashcards (print or online)

☐ Download audio summaries to review on the go

☐ Complete practice quizzes to prepare for tests

☐ Watch video on E-Business at Evo for a real company example

Case

Rogers Communications Market Segmentation in Atlantic Canada

Rogers Communications was looking to expand its cable business in Atlantic Canada. The company realized that the industry was at a critical point in its history; some might even call it a revolution. For years, consumers' access to programming had been growing as an ever-increasing number of channels and on-demand content was made available from a wide variety of sources. Traditional competition from satellite, cable, and telephone companies was intensifying at the same time that Canadians were becoming increasingly comfortable accessing and viewing programming online and through their mobile devices.

As a diversified communications and media company, Rogers was well positioned to play a leading role in the new environment through its wholly owned subsidiaries: Rogers Cable, Rogers Wireless, and Rogers Media. However, the company was not convinced that the same marketing strategies that worked in other parts of Canada would be effective in the Atlantic market.

To better understand its Atlantic Canadian customers, Rogers engaged Environics Analytics to help segment the market based on the PRIZM5 segmentation system. The PRIZM5 system captures the diversity of Canada's population using 68 segments based on the most important drivers of consumer behaviour: demographics, lifestyles, and values. The system is built upon a foundation of geographic and demographic data from Statistics Canada's census. It is also enhanced by Environics Analytics's links to national survey data, which adds critical information about Canadians' lifestyles and values.

Using the PRIZM5 system, Environics Analytics was able to develop detailed profiles of Rogers customers in a number of provinces and then compare those customers to Atlantic Canadians based on demographics, lifestyles, and values. That analysis provided Rogers with the insight it needed to customize its communications campaign to Atlantic Canadian consumers. In particular, the company was able to recognize an opportunity to grow its business with unique offers to four target groups: Affluent Families, Middle-Class Families, Francophone Families, and Midscale Older Adults/Seniors.

ValeStock/Shutterstock.com

Building on that knowledge, Rogers launched the "Bringing Value Home" campaign across multiple channels and tailored to the Atlantic market. Direct mail and newspaper advertising, for example, used local imagery, area actors, and a message that reflected the strong family values of the region. For one newspaper ad, this generated a 250% increase in calls inquiring about Rogers products and services. "We know that all the provinces are different," says Dana Gheorghiu, manager of analytics and call forecasting at Rogers Marketing Communications. "But we wanted to understand how different they are so that we could customize ads for different provinces."

Source: Environics Analytics Communications Case Study: Rogers Communications.

QUESTIONS

1 What benefits does Rogers Cable offer Atlantic Canadians? Provide examples of both hedonic and utilitarian value.

2 If the quality of Rogers Cable's offering is defined as $Q = f(p, w, x, \ldots z)$, what are the key characteristics (x, y, and z) that will determine Rogers Cable's success?

3 How might those key characteristics (x, y, and z) differ among the four target groups that Rogers has identified?

4 What might a perceptual map of Rogers Cable versus iTunes look like based on two of these key characteristics?

5 Go to www.environicsanalytics.ca and click on the "PRIZM5 Lifestyle Lookup" link. By entering your postal code, you can see which of Environics Analytics's 68 PRIZM segments you belong to. Does the segment overview accurately describe you and your neighbours?

3 | Consumer Learning Starts Here: Perception

LEARNING OBJECTIVES

After studying this chapter, the student should be able to:

3-1   Define learning and perception and how the two are connected.

3-2   List and define phases of the consumer perception process.

3-3   Apply the concept of the just noticeable difference (JND).

3-4   Contrast the concepts of implicit and explicit memory.

3-5   Know ways to help get a consumer's attention.

3-6   Understand key differences between intentional and unintentional learning.

INTRODUCTION

Marketing strategy represents the way a firm goes about creating a unique and valuable bundle of benefits for the consumer. As such, marketing strategy focuses on value creation. Unfortunately, many firms never fully understand the value they create, and this can lead to major problems. For example, the firm Webvan started amid the dot-com boom in the late 1990s, delivering groceries directly to consumers and seemingly creating great value for them. Webvan attracted tremendous interest among investors but went out of business in 2001, a few years after its creation. Ultimately, Webvan failed to get enough consumers to perceive the value offered by its service. Of course, if a consumer doesn't *think* that a product will deliver the value desired or doesn't understand a product in the intended way, why purchase the product? Today, Amazon owns the Webvan name and offers grocery delivery in just one city, Seattle, through its AmazonFresh website.

learning   change in behaviour resulting from some interaction between a person and a stimulus

perception   consumer's awareness and interpretation of reality

 ## 3-1 DEFINING LEARNING AND PERCEPTION

Value cannot be communicated without involving consumer learning and perception. **Learning** refers to a change in behaviour resulting from the interaction between a person and a stimulus. **Perception** refers to a consumer's awareness and interpretation of reality. Accordingly, perception serves as a foundation upon which consumer learning takes place. Stated simply, value involves learning, and consumer perception plays a key role in learning because consumers change behaviour based on what they perceive. Sometimes, consumers set out to *intentionally* learn marketing-related information. Other times, consumers learn *unintentionally* (or incidentally) by simply being exposed to stimuli and by forming some kind of response to it. Both types of learning rely, to greater or lesser degrees, on perceptual processes.

This chapter focuses on issues that are central to understanding the learning process. Specifically, the chapter details the earliest phases of perception along with a number of issues related to unintentional learning. The chapter closes with a discussion of *conditioning*, which represents a well known approach to unintentional learning. Intentional learning and the cognitive processes associated with it are discussed in a later chapter.

3-1a Consumer Perception

What's more important, perception or reality? This probably seems like a typical "academic" question, but the issue is very important to consumer researchers. Consumer researchers expend a great deal of effort trying to understand consumer perception because the way a consumer perceives something greatly influences learning.

Perception and reality are distinct concepts because the perceptions that consumers develop do not always match the real world. For example, we've probably all listened to a fanatical sports fan boast about a favourite team. The cliché "rose-coloured glasses" might apply if the favoured team is not as good as the fan makes it out to be. Perception simply doesn't always match reality. Perception can also be ambiguous. Exhibit 3.1 illustrates this point.

We treat perception as a consumer's awareness and interpretation of reality. Perception represents a *subjective* reality, whereas what actually exists in the environment determines objective reality. For example, at a restaurant, the objective reality is that a certain amount of food is served on a plate. A chef can weigh the food so that she knows the actual amount. However, equally hungry consumers may disagree that it is enough. How can this be? The answer to this question illustrates the concept of subjective reality. In this case, subjective and objective reality may differ because the size of the plate affects the quantity of food a consumer perceives. Exhibit 3.2 illustrates this effect by showing the same amount of food on three different plates. Placing food on a smaller plate can actually increase the chance that diners are satisfied, not because they have actually had more food, but because they perceive that they are getting more![1]

Exhibit 3.1

What Is the Reality in the Image?

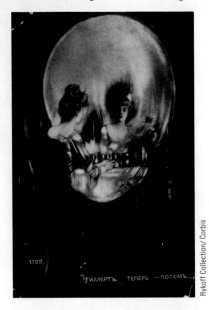

The same amount of food on a larger plate tends to leave a diner wanting more.

3-1b Exposure, Attention, and Comprehension

During the perceptual process, consumers are *exposed* to stimuli, devote *attention* to stimuli, and attempt to *comprehend* stimuli. **Exposure** refers to the process of bringing some stimulus within the proximity of a consumer so that it can be sensed by one of the five human senses (sight, smell, taste, touch, or hearing). The term **sensation** describes a consumer's immediate response to this information.

McDonald's delivers the message "four bucks is **dumb**" on billboards, exposing consumers to a not-so-subtle message about coffee. Marketers can expose consumers to messages like this, but that does not guarantee that the consumer will pay attention. **Attention** is the purposeful allocation of information processing capacity toward developing an understanding of some stimulus. Many times, consumers simply cannot pay attention to all the stimuli to which they are exposed. As such, consumers are selective in the information to which they pay attention. Quite simply, there is just too much stimulation in the environment for consumers to pay attention to everything!

Comprehension occurs when consumers attempt to derive meaning from information they receive. Of course, marketers hope that consumers comprehend and interpret information in the intended way, but this is not always the case. As a simple example, a receptionist tells patients there will be a *short* wait. Will all patients think the wait is short? For example, two consumers who wait 20 minutes may perceive the wait differently. What is short to one may not be so short to another. A professional taking an hour away from a busy day may react differently than a retired person without a hectic daily schedule. A patient's

---

exposure process of bringing some stimulus within proximity of a consumer so that the consumer can sense it with one of the five human senses

sensation consumer's immediate response to a stimulus

attention purposeful allocation of information processing capacity toward developing an understanding of some stimulus

---

Exhibit 3.2

Objective and Subjective Reality Don't Always Match

Enough to Eat?
May look like more than 500 grams

500 grams of food

Not Enough to Eat?
May look like less than 500 grams

Sources: Levinsky, D.L. and T. Youm (2004), "The More Food Young Adults are Served, the More they Overeat," *Journal of Nutrition*, 134, 2546–2549. Rolls, B.J., L.S. Roe and J.S.I Meengs (2006), "Reductions in Portion Size and Energy Density of Foods are Addictive and Lead to Sustained Decreases in Energy Intake," *American Journal of Clinical Nutrition*, 83, 11–17.

When consumers go by a billboard, they are provided with an opportunity to pay attention to the message.

previous experiences will also affect what length of time they associate with *short*. Can something be done to change perceptions of the wait time? The receptionist might update the patient every few minutes, explaining what is going on and why the wait is continuing. Alternatively, pleasant music could be played in the waiting room. In either case, the patient might perceive a shorter wait than if simply left quietly alone.[2]

3-2 CONSUMER PERCEPTION PROCESS

If a friend were to ask, "Do I look good in this outfit?", you would immediately draw upon your perceptions to determine how to respond to the question. (Whether you voice your true opinion is an entirely different subject!) As we have stated, in its most basic form, perception describes how consumers become aware of and interpret the environment. Accordingly, we can view consumer perception as including three phases: *sensing*, *organizing*, and *reacting*. This is shown in Exhibit 3.3.

Notice that the phases of perception overlap with the concepts of exposure, attention, and comprehension. That is, we sense the many stimuli to which we are exposed, we organize the stimuli as we attend and comprehend them, and then we react to various stimuli by developing responses.

3-2a Sensing

A consumer senses stimuli to which he or she is exposed. Sensing is an *immediate* response to stimuli that have come into contact with one of the consumer's five senses (sight, smell, touch, taste, or hearing). Thus, when a consumer enters a store, browses on eBay, reads a tweet, tastes food, encounters an advertisement, or tries on some clothes, the perceptual process goes into action. However, sensing alone does not allow a consumer to make *sense* out of something. This leads to the second stage of the perceptual process.

3-2b Organizing

Imagine being blindfolded and handed an unknown small object. How would you determine what the object might be? Of course, you can feel the object. Is it rough or smooth? Is it soft or hard? These answers may help you decide. A consumer's brain addresses questions like these every time something is sensed, in a process that takes place literally thousands of times each day and so quickly in most cases that we are unaware organization is happening.

Exhibit 3.3

Sensing, Organizing, and Reacting

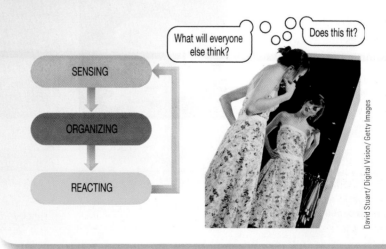

What's the Best Time to Buy?

There is a best time to buy. That time is 10:10! Shop for luxury watches online and you'll start to notice something that seems peculiar at first. Practically all the watches are set to 10:10—that is, 10 minutes after 10. Is this a coincidence? Hardly! The conventional wisdom is that when a consumer senses (sees) a watch showing 10:10, the image is organized in the consumer's mind as a smile (1:50 would smile too). In contrast, a consumer might see a watch showing 8:20 and perceive a frown. According to this theory, when consumers perceive that a product is smiling, it is preferred. Research indicates that, under certain conditions, consumers do indeed demonstrate a preference for smiling products. The effect goes beyond watches and includes cars with a front grill that smiles, or fabrics with certain patterns, among other things. A preference effect occurs particularly when a product can be given some human-like characteristic. A watch smiling at you says "Buy me," right?

Both Photos: iStockphoto.com/Denis Beyeler

Sources: Aggarwal, P., and A. L. McGill (2007), "Is That Car Smiling at Me? Schema Congruity as a Basis for Evaluating Anthropomorphized Products," *Journal of Consumer Research*, 14 (December), 468–479. Labroo, A. A. (2006), "Do Products Smile? When Fluency Confers Liking and Enhances Purchase Intent," *Advances in Consumer Research*, 33, 558–561.

When we speak of **cognitive organization**, we refer to the process by which the human brain assembles the sensory evidence into something recognizable. This is an important part of perception. Exhibit 3.4 may help you visualize this process. The organization that takes place in your brain is analogous to someone performing a sorting task—such as sorting mail. When an object is first handled, the sorter hasn't a clue what slot the object belongs in. However, information allows the sorter to place the object into progressively more specific categories.

When someone tries to decide if an outfit looks right, the perceptual process goes to work. Consider the clothing pictured in Exhibit 3.3. Is this outfit appropriate for Emilia, a professional consultant? At first, we

cognitive organization
process by which the human brain assembles sensory evidence into something recognizable

Exhibit 3.4

"Organizing" Morning Beverages

George Dolgikh/Shutterstock.com

weedezign/Shutterstock.com

Wollertz/Shutterstock.com

Assimilation—Product Characteristics Fit Category Easily

Accommodation—An Adjustment Allows Product to Fit Category—Coffee Can Be Served on the Rocks!

Contrast—The Product Characteristics Are Too Different to Fit Category perceive that the outfit is obviously a woman's dress. However, does the outfit represent proper business attire? If Emilia's brain organizes the outfit into this category, then she becomes likely to buy it and wear it to work as a consultant. Her clients may perceive the outfit differently and react differently. Again, we see the subjectivity of perception.

Consumers develop an interpretation during this stage of the perceptual process and begin to *comprehend* what the stimulus is. This interpretation provides an initial cognitive and affective meaning. The term *cognitive* refers to a mental or thinking process. A reader of this book almost instantly converts a word into meaning as long as the word on the page matches a known English-language word. Sometimes marketers need to know how consumers will react to unknown words when creating the name for a new product or new company. In fact, the actual sound of a name (that is otherwise nonsense) can evoke different meanings and feelings. Consider the following two sounds (say them each out loud):

▶ **Sepfut**

▶ **Sepsop**

Which would make a better name for a new ice cream brand? Actually, when consumers sampled the same new ice cream described with one of these two names, Sepsop was the preferred ice cream. The researchers theorized that consumers evaluate sounds with a repetitive pattern (like sep-sop) more favourably, and prefer things associated with it, than sounds with no repetition.[3] Consumers' moods can even be affected by sending sounds that produce a favourable evaluation.[4]

Consumers cannot organize everything they sense so easily. When a consumer encounters a stimulus that is difficult to categorize, the brain instinctively continues processing as a way of reconciling inconsistencies. When even this extra effort leaves a consumer uncertain, he or she will generally avoid the stimulus.

In general, depending on the extent to which a stimulus can be categorized, three possible reactions may occur.

1. **Assimilation. Assimilation** occurs when a stimulus has characteristics such that individuals readily recognize it as an example of a specific category. A light brown, slightly sticky, sweet, round food with a hole in the middle is easily recognized as a doughnut in nearly every part of the world.

2. **Accommodation. Accommodation** occurs when a stimulus shares some, but not all, of the characteristics that allow it to fit neatly in an existing category. At this point, the consumer will begin processing, which allows exceptions to rules about the category. For example, in New Orleans, a tourist may encounter a *beignet*, which is a type of doughnut. Because the beignet does not have a hole, the tourist's perceptual process may have to make an exception to the rule that all doughnuts have holes. Curiously, research indicates that novel stimuli that are mildly incongruent with expectations are actually preferred.[5] Thus, new products that consumers can categorize through accommodation may produce favourable reactions.

3. **Contrast. Contrast** occurs when a stimulus does not share enough in common with existing categories to allow categorization. For example, consumers in Kyrgyzstan routinely enjoy fermented mountain mare's milk, known as *koumis*. The only similarity to the milk that most Western consumers know is the colour. When a Westerner tastes the milk, particularly if the taster doesn't know what is being consumed, contrast is a nearly certain outcome. People tend not to like things that are so completely unknown. Therefore, contrast is usually associated with negative feelings.

Categorization is discussed in more detail in Chapter 4.

3-2c Reacting

The perceptual process ends with a reaction. If an object is successfully recognized, chances are some nearly automatic reaction takes place. For example, when a driver notices that the car in front of him or her has its brake lights on, the learned response is to apply brakes as well. Here, the reaction occurs as a response or behaviour. Note that reactions can include both physical and mental responses to the stimuli encountered.

APPLICATIONS TO CONSUMER BEHAVIOUR

The perceptual process has many implications for consumer behaviour. For example, think about how the music playing in a store can affect one's perceptions of and reactions to the store. Would a fine watch be perceived the same way with alternating current (AC)

assimilation state that results when a stimulus has characteristics such that consumers readily recognize it as belonging to some specific category

accommodation state that results when a stimulus shares some but not all of the characteristics that would lead it to fit neatly in an existing category, and consumers must process exceptions to rules about the category

contrast state that results when a stimulus does not share enough in common with existing categories to allow categorization

/direct current (DC) or Mozart in the background?[6] Recall Emilia's questions about her outfit. Online retailers often use technology to allow for more realistic visual depictions of clothing in an attempt to improve consumer perceptions and retail performance.[7] If consumers perceive that a piece of clothing will look good and be a good fit, they will be more likely to purchase it.

Even subtle cues influence perception. Take a look at an advertisement for a watch. Chances are, time stands still in watch advertisements. The watch almost certainly had a time of about 10 past 10. Why? A watch with that time appears to be smiling at the consumer, and this subtle difference can cause a watch to be preferred over a frowning watch that says 20 past 8.[8] The term **anthropomorphism** refers to a design that gives humanlike characteristics to inanimate objects. Consumers who attribute humanlike characteristics to their automobiles also have been shown to trust them more and even be less likely to blame them for an accident![9]

3-2d Selective Perception

Consumers encounter thousands of stimuli each day. If all stimuli were consciously processed, they would truly be overloaded. Rather than processing all stimuli, consumers practise selective perception. Selective perception includes selective exposure, selective attention, and selective distortion. That is, consumers are selective in what they expose themselves to, what they attend to, and what (and how) they comprehend. **Selective exposure** involves screening out most stimuli and exposing oneself to only a small portion of stimuli. **Selective attention** involves paying attention to only certain stimuli.

Consider a tourist walking through downtown Seoul, South Korea. How can he or she possibly pay attention to all of the available information? Marketers use the term *clutter* to describe the idea that consumers often are bombarded with too much information in their daily lives. Consumers can't possibly pay attention to all of this. Instead, they will choose something that stands out,

Ed Freeman / The Image Bank/ Getty Images

What would you pay attention to if you saw this?

or is personally relevant, and devote attention to that object.

Selective distortion is a process by which consumers interpret information in ways that are biased by their previously held beliefs. This process can be the result of either a conscious or an unconscious effort. For example, consumers with strong beliefs about a brand tend to comprehend messages about the brand either positively or negatively, depending on their pre-existing attitudes. Sports fans provide good examples of selective distortion. Fans from one team may be enraged when a "bad call" goes against their team. Fans for the other team are unlikely to comprehend the controversial play in the same way. Both sets of fans observe the same thing but comprehend and react differently.

We now discuss the exposure, attention, and comprehension concepts of perception in more detail.

EXPOSURE

Exposure occurs when some stimulus is brought within the proximity of a consumer so that it can be sensed. Obviously, marketers who want to inform consumers about their products must first expose them to information. As such, exposure represents a first step to learning. In fact, exposure is a vital component of both intentional and unintentional learning.

Of course, consumers cannot be expected to learn from information to which they've never been exposed.

anthropomorphism
giving humanlike characteristics to inanimate objects

selective exposure
process of screening out certain stimuli and purposely exposing oneself to other stimuli

selective attention
process of paying attention to only certain stimuli

selective distortion
process by which consumers interpret information in ways that are biased by their previously held beliefs

If someone asked you, "Have you seen the new Power Gig video game?" and you replied "No," then perhaps you haven't been exposed to it! Next, we discuss issues that pertain to exposure, including subliminal processing, the absolute threshold, the just noticeable difference, and the mere exposure effect.

3-2e Subliminal Processing

Subliminal processing refers to the way in which the human brain senses low-strength stimuli, that is, stimuli that occur below the level of conscious awareness. Such stimuli have a strength that is lower than the **absolute threshold** of perception, the minimum strength needed for a consumer to perceive a stimulus. This type of "learning" is unintentional, because the stimuli fall below the absolute threshold. To illustrate effects below the absolute threshold, consider what often happens when a mosquito lands on one's arm. Chances are the mosquito is so small that the person will not be consciously aware of the sensation without seeing it. Likewise, sounds often occur that are below the threshold. Images also can be displayed for such a short period of time, or at such a low level of intensity, that the brain cannot organize the image and develop a meaning.

Subliminal persuasion is behaviour change induced or brought about based on subliminally processing a message. Popular conceptions about subliminal persuasion have fuelled interest in it for many years. For instance, many people believe that:

▶ **Marketers can somehow induce consumers to purchase products by using subliminal advertising.**

▶ **Marketers can subliminally alter products or packages to make them more appealing to consumers.**

▶ **Sexual imagery can be "hidden" in a product itself, in the product packaging, or in product advertising.**

▶ **People's sense of well-being can be enhanced by listening to subliminally embedded recordings of nature sounds and/or music.**[10]

The belief is that communication can influence consumers through mere exposure to subliminal stimuli.

Exhibit 3.5

The Vicary Subliminal Persuasion "Study"

The motion picture *Picnic* is run with a standard projector.

A frame is replaced displaying a subliminal message for 1/2,000 second.

The movie *Picnic* continues while the audience flocks to concession stand.

Source: Gable, M., H. Wilkens, L. Harris and R. Feinbert (1987), "An Evaluation of Subliminally Embedded Sexual Stimuli in Graphics," *Journal of Advertising*, 16, 26–31.

The most famous example of subliminal persuasion involves a researcher for an ad firm who claimed that he had embedded subliminal frames within the movie *Picnic* in a New Jersey movie theatre several years ago. Exhibit 3.5 illustrates the way this process reportedly took place. Very brief embeds of the phrases "Drink Coke" and "Eat Popcorn" were supposedly placed in the movie. The researcher claimed that popcorn sales rose nearly 60% as a result and that Coke sales rose nearly 20%. This experiment is often called the "Vicary experiment."

This story's popularity grew so much that researchers attempted to replicate the study. Interestingly, these scientific replications failed to produce any increase in desire for popcorn or Coke. Consumer researchers also conducted experiments testing the effectiveness of sexual embeds involving air-brushed genitalia, the word *sex*, or provocative nudity in advertisements. Results of these experiments generally indicate that these practices do nothing that would make a consumer more likely to buy the advertised product.[11]

As a general statement, the research examining subliminal processing is conclusive: subliminal persuasion is ineffective as a marketing tool.[12] This is not to dismiss subliminal processing as having no impact whatsoever on what consumers might learn or how they might behave. But any effects appear not to significantly influence consumer attitude or choice.

subliminal processing way that the human brain deals with very low-strength stimuli, so low that the person has no conscious awareness

absolute threshold minimum strength of a stimulus that can be perceived

subliminal persuasion behaviour change induced by subliminal processing

Estimates suggest that more than 60% of Americans believe that advertisers can exert subliminal influences strong enough to cause purchase behaviour.[13]

Despite evidence that subliminal advertising is ineffective, consumers are generally willing to believe that such powerful influences exist.[14] Over the years, books have fuelled the controversy by promoting the idea that advertisers know about, and use, certain "hidden persuaders" to create an irresistible urge to buy.[15]

Consumers are often willing to attribute their own behaviour to some kind of "uncontrollable influence," especially when the consumption involves products like cigarettes or alcoholic beverages.[16] Consumers' willingness to believe that subliminal persuasion tricks them into buying these products may simply be an attempt to downplay their own role in decision making.

The truth is that the Vicary experiment was a *hoax*. Vicary himself never conducted the experiment. Rather, he fabricated the story in an effort to create positive publicity for the advertising firm.[17]

3-3 APPLYING THE JUST NOTICEABLE DIFFERENCE CONCEPT

We have discussed the concept of the absolute threshold as representing a level over which the strength of a stimulus must be greater to activate the perceptual process. A closely related concept deals with changes in the *strength* of stimuli. The **just noticeable difference (JND)** represents how much stronger one stimulus has to be relative to another so that someone can notice that the two are not the same.

The JND concept may be best explained in terms of a physical example. How do people pick out one sound over another? For example, for consumers to be able to physically discern two sounds that originate from the same source, the two sounds must be separated by at least 0.3 second. Separating the sounds by only 0.1 second is likely to produce the perception of one sound. Separating them by 0.3 second or more likely produces the perception of two different sounds.[18]

In general, the ability to detect differences between two levels of a stimulus is affected by the original intensity of the stimulus. This is known as **Weber's Law**. The law states that as the intensity of the initial stimulus increases, a consumer's ability to detect differences between two levels of the stimulus decreases.[19] For example, if the decibel (dB) level at a rock concert decreases from 120 to 115 dB, the change likely won't be noticeable. Marketers need to understand that change made a little at a time may be unnoticed by a consumer; change a lot at once and it will be noticed. The JND has numerous implications for marketers who attempt to provide value for consumers, including:

▸ **Pricing.** Consumers do not perceive very small differences in price as truly different.[20] A price of $19.95 is generally not perceived as being different from a price of $19.99. Thus, marketers may consider increasing prices in small increments to avoid a negative backlash from consumers. Conversely, a price reduction needs to be large enough so that consumers truly perceive the new price as representing significant savings.[21]

▸ **Quantity.** Small differences in quantity are often not perceived as being different. For instance, if a toilet paper roll is reduced from 412 to 407 sheets, consumers are not likely to perceive a difference.

▸ **Quality.** Small improvements in quality may not have any impact on consumers. Thus, if a service provider promotes an improvement such as faster service or better food quality, the difference must be large enough to create a true perceptual difference.

▸ **Add-on Purchases.** A small additional purchase tacked on to a large purchase may not create the perception of increased spending. For instance, a consumer buying a $145 pair of athletic shoes may be receptive to the suggestion of adding a pair of $8 socks to the order. The total for the shoes is not perceived as being really different from the total for the shoes and socks together.

In general, these examples highlight an important idea: when marketers make a "positive" change, they should make sure the difference is large enough to be perceived by consumers. Conversely, when they make a "negative" change, they should think about implementing the change in small increments so that each difference is

just noticeable difference (JND) condition in which one stimulus is sufficiently stronger than another so that someone can actually notice that the two are not the same

Weber's Law law stating that a consumer's ability to detect differences between two levels of the stimulus decreases as the intensity of the initial stimulus increases

Legal Perceptions

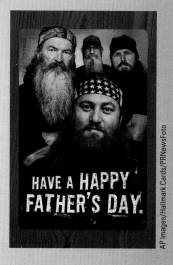

Lawyers often find themselves consumers of CB! That's because a lot of lawsuits involve consumer perceptions in one way or another. Two recent examples illustrate the important role that CB knowledge can play in creating justice.

Duck Dynasty is likely the biggest television hit of all time for the A&E Network. The show also has been a marketing boon as the *Duck Dynasty* brand has been leveraged far beyond duck calls to apparel, books, restaurants, and even *Duck Dynasty* wine. Here, though, the duck commanders ran afoul (no pun intended) of Duckhorn Wine Company, which considered suing for trademark infringement based on the idea that consumers would be confused and unable to tell the products apart.

The FTC recently took issue with a Nissan truck ad in which a Nissan Frontier pickup pushed a stalled dune buggy up a steep hill in the desert. The footage was digitally enhanced to create the commercial, and the FTC argues that the ad may well create the perception among consumers that the truck could do things it is clearly unable to do. In both cases, consumer research into the perceptual process may help resolve the legal disputes.

Sources: Bussewitz, C. (2014), "Duckhorn Files Lawsuit Over *Duck Dynasty* Wines," *The Press Democrat*, (1/10), http://www.pressdemocrat.com/article/20140110/business/140119935, accessed March 9, 2014; Kendall, B. (2014), "Nissan Truck Ad Goes Too Far for FTC," *The Wall Street Journal*, (1/23), B4.

not distinguished from what existed previously. However, marketers should make sure that changes are not perceived as being deceptive. Deliberately deceptive actions are unethical, tend to damage the firm's relationship with the customer, and ultimately reduce profitability.

3-3a Just Meaningful Difference

A topic closely related to the JND is the **just meaningful difference (JMD)**. The JMD represents the smallest amount of change in a stimulus that would influence consumer consumption and choice. For instance, how much of a change in price is really needed to *influence* consumer behaviour and learning? A consumer can surely "notice" an advertisement stating a price drop of a Rolex from $19,999 to $19,499. Clearly, this is a $500.00 difference. However, is this price drop really meaningful? Retailers generally follow a rule that states that effective price drops need to be at least 20%.[22]

How sensitive consumers are to differences also depends on the context and how much attention they are paying to the situation. For example, when Air Canada and WestJet began introducing baggage fees, the $25 increase in travel costs was clearly meaningful and upset many consumers, even though that change in price represented a very small percentage increase in the cost of flying. In contrast, when Tim Hortons raised the price of a cup of coffee by $0.10, people noticed—it was even the subject of dozens of national and local news stories—but it wasn't meaningful enough to change behaviour.[23] A more extreme example comes from the introduction of the Mercedes-Benz C-Class to the Canadian market. For the first time ever, Canadians could buy a Mercedes for under $35,000.[24] The company invested significantly in advertising this new "Baby Benz" at a much lower price that was a fraction of what one would traditionally pay for a Mercedes. Many cars at Benz dealerships were selling for two, three, or four times that price. Nevertheless, it turned out the price was not as meaningful to consumers as the company had hoped and it struggled to sell the new model. Ultimately, for a change in stimulus to be meaningful it has to be noticeable, but just because it is noticed does not mean that it will have a meaningful impact on consumer behaviour.

3-4 IMPLICIT AND EXPLICIT MEMORY

Normally, we associate learning with educational experiences. When we think about learning, we think of people studying and paying close attention, like when you read this book!

> **just meaningful difference (JMD)** smallest amount of change in a stimulus that would influence consumer consumption and choice

The knowledge one obtains from this type of experience is stored in **explicit memory**, that is, memory for information one is exposed to, attends to, and applies effort to remember. However, this is not the only kind of memory we develop. **Implicit memory** represents stored information concerning stimuli one is exposed to but does not pay attention to. Implicit memory creates **pre-attentive effects**, learning that is developed in the absence of attention. The following example illustrates the contrast between implicit and explicit memory.

How effective are banner ads like the ones you see on practically every web page? If a consumer clicks a banner ad to an advertiser's site, that consumer may absorb the resulting advertisement content and develop some explicit memory of the information. However, click-through rates on banner ads are extraordinarily low and continue to decline. Consumers click through fewer than 1 in 100 banners ads to which they are exposed. Do web advertisers waste their resources on the other 99 plus consumers? Perhaps not. It turns out that consumers' implicit memory system addresses these ads. Even when consumers pay no attention to a banner ad on a crowded computer screen, implicit memory for the brand develops. This implicit memory creates more favourable attitudes toward the brand that increase the likelihood that the consumer would consider buying something associated with the brand.[25] Interestingly, unlike explicit memory, implicit memory becomes stronger the more distracted one is from attending to the stimulus.

3-4a Mere Exposure Effect

The **mere exposure effect** represents another way that consumers can learn unintentionally.[26] The mere exposure effect is the idea that consumers will prefer stimuli they have been previously exposed to over stimuli that they have not been exposed to. This effect occurs even when there is no recall of the previous stimulus!

Exhibit 3.6 illustrates a classical approach to studying the mere exposure effect, experiments in which subjects encounter something they do not know. In this case, a group of consumers were shown a list of Norwegian words. Among these words, two were target terms representing potential name brands for a new energy

explicit memory
memory that develops when a person is exposed to, attends, and tries to remember information

implicit memory
memory for things that a person did not try to remember

pre-attentive effects
learning that occurs without attention

mere exposure effect
that which leads consumers to prefer a stimulus to which they've previously been exposed

Exhibit 3.6

The Mere Exposure Effect

January 10	May 10
Agentur	baadsmand
Forfølgelse	prestegård
alderdomssvakhet	prosti
Overære	tidsperiode
brændevinsbrænderi	bryggeri
Amme	tjueseks
Nittiende	mindreårig
Disktriktslege	Forfølgelse
Bagermester	badedrakten

Source: Smith, Gene F. (1982), "Further Evidence of the Mediating Effect of Learning in the Mere Exposure Phenomenon," *Journal of General Psychology*, 197: 175–178; Stang, D.J. (1975), "Effects of "Mere Exposure" on Learning and Affect," *Journal of Personality and Social Psychology*, 31: 7–12.

food. Some of the words even contain letters that do not exist in the English alphabet.

On January 10, subjects were exposed to the list of words on the left. Then, on May 10, the same subjects were exposed to the list on the right. If you look closely, you'll notice that two of the words on the May 10 list were also on the January 10 list.

The results of this type of experiment generally show that the two "familiar" words will be preferred even though subjects have no recall of having ever seen them before. Consumers not only develop preferences for words, but they learn them as well. In fact, the learning process facilitates positive feelings that become associated with the stimuli.[27] The mere exposure effect therefore has applications in both consumer learning and attitude formation.

The mere exposure effect is very resilient. The effect is true for practically any type of content. If the Norwegian words are replaced with faces, names, Chinese characters, brand logos, web pages, or musical samples, the mere exposure effect still holds.[28] Theoretically, an explanation for the increased preference involves familiarity. Even though consumers can't "remember" seeing the stimuli, some degree of familiarity is created.

FAMILIARITY

All things equal, consumers prefer the familiar to the unfamiliar. Once exposed to an object, a consumer exhibits a preference for the familiar object over something unfamiliar. An interesting application involves

Sick of It!

Want to hear something new? What happens when consumers get a chance to listen to music? Two theories make different predictions. (1) Consumers like stimulation. As a result, they will choose new music over music they already know. (2) Consumers like the familiar. In this case, consumers will choose familiar music over novel music. Research into this topic demonstrates how strong the familiarity effect is on music. In fact, when given a chance to choose songs to listen to, consumer familiarity influences choice more than even liking! Consumers will even choose a song that they rate as "sick of" before listening to something unfamiliar. It's funny, but consumers respond more favorably to music that they could hear on their playlist anytime they want!

Sturti/iStockphoto.com

Sources: Ward, M. K., J. K. Goodman, and J. R. Irwin (2014), "The Same Old Song: The Power of Familiarity in Music Choice," *Marketing Letters*, 25: 1–11.

political campaigns. Modern technology allows advertisers to morph one individual's characteristics onto a photograph of another. For instance, a photograph of a political candidate can be modified so that subtle physical characteristics of a particular voter are morphed onto the candidate's appearance. In such a case, the particular voter will express a greater liking of the candidate, even if the changes are too subtle to be noticed.[29] The rationale is that the addition of characteristics, even below the JND, increases the perceived familiarity between the voter and the candidate. Familiarity plays a big role in understanding the way pre-attentive processes can improve attitudes, and the mere exposure effect highlights this.

Several relevant points can be made about the mere exposure effect.

▶ **The mere exposure effect is created in the absence of attention. For this reason, the effect is considered pre-attentive.**

▶ **Preferences associated with the mere exposure effect are easy to elicit. Thus, marketers can use this effect to improve attitudes marginally.**

▶ **The mere exposure effect has the greatest effect on novel (previously unfamiliar) objects.**

▶ **The size of the effect (increased liking) is not very strong relative to an effect created by a strong cohesive argument. For example, an Edmonton Oilers hockey fan might develop a preference for a face to which he's repeatedly been exposed, but if he finds that the face belongs to a Calgary Flames fan, the preference will likely go away based on the strong information!**

▶ **The mere exposure effect works best when the consumer has a low involvement in processing the object, and indeed when a consumer is distracted from processing the focal stimulus. For example, if a small brand logo is displayed on a magazine page across from an involving story, a greater increase in liking would be found than if the consumer were less distracted from the stimulus.**

NOTE ON SUBLIMINAL AND MERE EXPOSURE EFFECTS

Before moving on, we should distinguish the mere exposure effect from subliminal effects. A subliminal message is one presented below the threshold of perception. In other words, if you are aware of the stimulus or message, then the process is not subliminal. With the mere exposure effect, the stimulus is evident and someone could pay attention to it if they wanted to. As with the Norwegian words, no attempt is made to keep someone from seeing it. The stimuli are presented with strength above the threshold of perception.

PRODUCT PLACEMENTS

An interesting application of implicit memory and mere exposure involves brand placements in video games. Video games, quite simply, can be very captivating! The person playing a game will likely not be paying attention to things like embedded brand logos. In a manner similar to the way banner ads are processed, implicit memory is created when the logos are executed within a game and an attitude toward the brand develops.[30] As with other pre-attentive effects, the effect is stronger as the game is more involving!

Product placements represent another way that promotions can impart implicit memory among consumers. **Product placements** involve branded products placed conspicuously in movies or television shows. These placements can result in implicit memory formation. For instance, researchers in the United Kingdom once demonstrated implicit memory learning by exposing children to the movie *Home Alone*. Half of the children saw the movie with a scene in which the actors consumed unbranded drinks. The other half saw the identical scene but with the drinks changed to Pepsi cans. After the movie, the children were given their choice of soft drink. Those who saw the unbranded drink scene chose Coke and Pepsi in similar proportion to the United Kingdom market share. However, those who saw the "branded" scene chose Pepsi over Coke by a wide margin.[31]

3-4b Attention

From the discussion above, it's clear that attention plays a key role in distinguishing implicit and explicit memory. Attention is the purposeful allocation of cognitive capacity toward understanding some stimulus. Intentional learning depends on attentive consumers. However, we don't pay attention only to things we wish to. **Involuntary attention** is attention that is beyond the conscious control of the consumer and that occurs as the result of exposure to surprising or novel stimuli. For example, if you were to cut your finger, you would automatically direct attention to the injury due to its pain. When attention is devoted to a stimulus in this way, an orientation reflex is said to occur. An **orientation reflex** is a natural reflex that occurs as a response to a threat from the environment. In this way, the orientation reflex represents a protective behaviour. When consumers pay attention to something, is it more often voluntary or involuntary?

product placements
products that have been placed conspicuously in movies or television shows

involuntary attention
attention that is beyond the conscious control of a consumer

orientation reflex
natural reflex that occurs as a response to something threatening

involvement
the personal relevance toward, or interest in, a particular product

3-5 ENHANCING CONSUMERS' ATTENTION

Consumers face a difficult challenge in penetrating the clutter to pay attention to an intended message. What's more, consumers today have so many information and entertainment sources (iPods, tablets, and smartphones), creating an entire other layer of clutter. Getting a consumer's attention, voluntarily or involuntarily, is even more difficult in today's multitasking society, but that is the job of effective marketing communication.

3-5a Factors That Get Attention

These factors can help create attention:

▸ **Intensity of Stimuli.** All things equal, a consumer is more likely to pay attention to stronger stimuli than to weaker stimuli. For example, vivid colours can be used to capture a consumer's attention. Loud sounds capture more attention than quieter sounds. A television commercial with a louder volume than the rest of the programming tends to get consumers' attention.

▸ **Contrast.** Contrasting stimuli are extremely effective in getting attention. Contrast occurs in several ways. In days past, a colour photo in a newspaper was extremely effective in getting attention. However, today's newspapers are often filled with colour, so a colour advertisement is less prominent. A black-and-white image in a magazine filled with colour, however, can stand out. A period of silence in an otherwise noisy environment can attract attention.[32] Like loud television commercials, silent commercials also usually work in gaining consumer attention. Nonconformity can also create attention because of the contrast with social norms.[33] Marketers often show consumers who "stand out from the crowd" as a means of capturing attention for an ad.

▸ **Movement.** With electronic billboards or electronic retail shelf tags, marketers attempt to capture consumer attention by the principle of movement. Items in movement simply gain attention. Flashing lights and "pointing" signage are particularly effective tools for gaining consumer attention.

▸ **Surprising Stimuli.** Unexpected stimuli gain consumers' attention. Infomercials often contain surprising scenes. Recent infomercials showed a car running over a man's hand and the strength of Mighty Putty pulling a "fully loaded 18-wheeler."

▸ **Size of Stimuli.** All else equal, larger items garner more attention than smaller ones. Marketers therefore often attempt to have brands appear large in advertisements. This is a reason advertising copy usually features large headlines.

▸ **Involvement.** **Involvement** refers to the personal relevance a consumer feels toward a particular product. In general, the more personally relevant (and thus more involving) an object, the greater the chance that the object will be attended to. We discuss involvement in more detail in the cognitive learning chapter.

Surprising stimuli can get attention.

Gaining consumer attention is an important task for any marketer. Of course, paying attention can be beneficial for consumers as well. Consumers should devote cognitive capacity to comprehend choices that offer the most value for them.

3-5b Comprehension

As stated previously, consumers organize and understand information through comprehension. Comprehension is the interpretation or understanding that a consumer develops about an attended stimulus. Comprehension is an especially important topic for marketers because it allows consumers to interpret messages in the intended way. It is during comprehension that biases enter into perception. A fan of Dodge trucks may comprehend a message from Chevy very differently than would a die-hard Chevy fan. Furthermore, personal factors such as intelligence and motivation affect comprehension. Comprehension is discussed further in the next chapter, focusing on cognitive learning.

3-6 THE DIFFERENCE BETWEEN INTENTIONAL AND UNINTENTIONAL LEARNING

Before moving on to cognitive learning and information processing, let's detail the distinction between the two types of consumer learning—intentional and unintentional learning. Both types of learning concern what cognitive psychologists refer to as perceptual processes; however, with **unintentional learning**, consumers simply sense and react (or respond) to the environment. Here, consumers "learn" without trying to learn. They do not attempt to comprehend the information presented. They are exposed to stimuli and respond in some way. With **intentional learning**, consumers set out specifically to learn information devoted to a certain subject. To better explain intentional and unintentional learning, we examine two major theories in the psychology of learning.

3-6a Behaviourism and Cognitive Learning Theories

Recall that perception and learning are closely related topics. As the pre-eminent behavioural psychologist B. F. Skinner once wrote: "In order to respond effectively to the world around us, we must see, hear, smell, taste and feel it."[34]

Historically, psychologists have generally followed one of two basic theories of learning. One theory focuses on changes in behaviour occurring as conditioned responses to stimuli, without concern for the cognitive mechanics of the process. The other theory focuses on how changes in thought and knowledge precipitate behavioural changes. Those in the first camp follow a **behaviourist approach to learning** (also referred to as the behavioural learning perspective). This approach suggests that because the brain is a "black box," the focus of inquiry should be on the behaviour itself. In fact, Skinner argued that no description of what happens inside the human body can adequately explain human behaviour.[35] Thus, the brain is a black box, and we can't look inside.

From the behaviourist perspective, consumers are exposed to stimuli and directly respond in some way. Thus, the argument is that the marketing focus should be on "stimulus and response." Behaviours do not deny the existence of mental processes; rather, they consider these processes to be behaviours themselves. For example, thinking is an activity in the same way that walking

unintentional learning learning that occurs when behaviour is modified through a consumer–stimulus interaction without any effortful allocation of cognitive processing capacity toward that stimulus

intentional learning process by which consumers set out specifically to learn information devoted to a certain subject

behaviourist approach to learning theory of learning that focuses on changes in behaviour due to association, without great concern for the cognitive mechanics of the learning process

For behaviourists, perception itself is an activity, not a mental process.

is; psychological processes are viewed as actions.[36] Note that the term conditioning is used in behavioural learning, as behaviour becomes conditioned in some way by the external environment.

The second theory of learning involves an **information processing (or cognitive) perspective**. With this approach, the focus is on the cognitive processes associated with comprehension, including those leading to consumer learning. The information processing perspective considers the mind as acting much like a computer. Bits of knowledge are processed electronically to form meaning.

Historically, the behavioural learning and cognitive perspectives competed against each other for theoretical dominance. However, we avoid such debate because on closer inspection, the two theories really share much in common. At the very least, both perspectives focus on changes in behaviour as a person interacts with his or her environment. We adopt an orientation more directly applicable to consumer learning by separating learning mechanisms into the intentional and unintentional groups that we have presented. The next section discusses unintentional learning and how consumers respond to stimuli to which they are exposed.

3-6b Unintentional Learning

Unintentional learning occurs when behaviour is modified through a consumer–stimulus interaction without a cognitive effort to understand a stimulus. With this type of learning, consumers respond to stimuli to which they are exposed without thinking about the information. The focus is on *reacting*, not cognitive processing.

Unintentional learning can be approached from the behavioural learning perspective. Two major approaches found in behavioural learning theory are *classical conditioning* and *instrumental conditioning*.

CLASSICAL CONDITIONING

Classical conditioning refers to a change in behaviour that occurs simply through associating some stimulus with another stimulus that naturally causes a reaction. The most famous classical conditioning experiment was performed by the behavioural psychologist Ivan Pavlov. Pavlov conducted experiments using dogs, meat powder (an **unconditioned stimulus** that naturally led to a salivation response), and a bell (a **conditioned stimulus** that did not lead to the response before it was paired with the powder).[37] The experiment reveals that the bell eventually evokes the same behaviour that the meat powder naturally caused.

In the experiment, Pavlov began ringing the bell every time meat powder was provided to the dogs. Thus, the bell became associated with the meat powder. Eventually, Pavlov rang the bell without providing the meat powder. As predicted, the bell proved enough to increase the amount of saliva the dogs produced. Originally, the dogs would salivate from being exposed to the unconditioned stimulus. The salivation was called an **unconditioned response**, which occurred naturally as a result of exposure to the unconditioned stimulus (the meat powder). The dogs eventually would respond in the same way to the exposure to the bell. This response became known as a **conditioned response**. The response became conditioned by the consistent pairing of the unconditioned and conditioned stimuli. Dogs do not cognitively process in the way we usually think that humans do. So, the dogs learned this response without trying to do so.

To be effective, the conditioned stimulus is presented before the unconditioned stimulus, and the pairing of the two should be done consistently (and with repetition). The advertisement illustrates a popular use of unintentional learning through classical conditioning—the use of sexual, or intimate, imagery.

INSTRUMENTAL CONDITIONING

Much of what we know about instrumental (or operant) conditioning comes from the work of Skinner.

information processing (or cognitive) perspective approach that focuses on changes in thought and knowledge and how these precipitate behavioural changes

classical conditioning change in behaviour that occurs simply through associating some stimulus with another stimulus that naturally causes some reaction; a type of unintentional learning

unconditioned stimulus stimulus with which a behavioural response is already associated

conditioned stimulus object or event that does not cause the desired response naturally but that can be conditioned to do so by pairing with an unconditioned stimulus

unconditioned response response that occurs naturally as a result of exposure to an unconditioned stimulus

conditioned response response that results from exposure to a conditioned stimulus that was originally associated with the unconditioned stimulus

Advertisers try to "condition" brands by pairing branded products with arousing images such as this.

With **instrumental conditioning**, behaviour is conditioned through reinforcement. Reinforcers are stimuli that strengthen a desired response. The focus is on behaviour and behavioural change—not on mental processes that lead to learning. With instrumental conditioning, the likelihood that a behaviour will increase is influenced by the reinforcers (consequences) of the behaviour. The reinforcers are presented after the initial behaviour occurs.

As an example of instrumental conditioning, consider childhood development. When a parent is "potty training" a child, he or she is more concerned with getting the desired result than with teaching the child the benefits of using a toilet over a diaper. All parents know that it is very difficult to rationalize with young children. Therefore, attempting to get them to think about the various reasons to become trained is almost useless. The focus is on changing the behaviour through reinforcement. When a child performs the desired behaviour, he or she receives rewards in the form of hugs, kisses, toys, and so on. These rewards reinforce the desired behaviour.

Positive reinforcers come in many forms in the consumer environment and often take the form of some type of reward. The effects can be seen in marketing efforts that encourage repeat purchase behaviour. For example, many casinos have players' cards that accumulate points the more a customer plays. The casino keeps tracks of these points. As the points accumulate, various offers are provided to the consumer, including free hotel rooms, meals, and other things that could otherwise be expensive. In this case, the points are used to elicit a desired response—repeat purchase behaviour.

DISCRIMINATIVE STIMULI, REINFORCEMENT, AND SHAPING

Discriminative stimuli are stimuli that are differentiated from other stimuli because they signal the presence of a reinforcer. These stimuli essentially signal that a type of reward will occur if a behaviour is performed. Advertisements that feature special promotions represent marketing examples of discriminative stimuli. Here the ad informs consumers that they will receive some type of reward (e.g., 10% off a purchase) if they perform the desirable behaviour (e.g., shop at a store). The stimulus serves as a signal presented before the behaviour occurs, and the behaviour must occur in order for the reinforcement to be delivered. Brand names can be discriminative stimuli because they signal potential customer satisfaction and value. For example, consumers realize that by using FedEx, they can receive overnight delivery with outstanding quality. The reinforcer occurs after the behaviour has been performed. Exhibit 3.7 presents this process. Again we see the importance of exposure to the discriminative stimuli, further highlighting the relationship between perception and behavioural learning.

SHAPING BEHAVIOUR

Shaping is a process through which the desired behaviour is altered over time, in small increments. Here, the focus is on rewarding "small" behaviours that lead to the "big"

instrumental conditioning type of learning in which a behavioural response can be conditioned through reinforcement—either punishment or rewards associated with undesirable or desirable behaviour

positive reinforcers reinforcers that take the form of a reward

discriminative stimuli stimuli that occur solely in the presence of a reinforcer

shaping process through which a desired behaviour is altered over time, in small increments

Exhibit 3.7

Discriminative Stimuli, Behaviour, Reinforcer

DISCRIMINATIVE STIMULI → BEHAVIOUR → REINFORCER

behaviour ultimately desired. For example, a motorcycle shop manager might offer free hot dogs and soft drinks to consumers on a special promotional day. When the consumers come in to the store and receive the food and drinks, the manager may offer them a coupon for free pizza simply for test-driving an ATV. Finally, the manager may offer the consumer a $200 rebate on the purchase of a new ATV. Notice that the behaviour that is ultimately desired is the purchase of an ATV. The small rewards along the way help shape the desired behaviour.

Not all reinforcement is positive. **Punishers** represent stimuli that decrease the likelihood that a behaviour will occur again. When children misbehave, they get punished. The hope is that the behaviour will not occur again. In the same way, when consumers make poor decisions and purchase products that deliver less value than expected, they are punished. Chances are they won't buy those same products again! **Negative reinforcement**, on the other hand, refers to the removal of bad stimuli as a way of encouraging behaviour.

Punishers and negative reinforcers are commonly confused. The concepts are not the same. A punisher is the presence of bad stimuli after an undesirable behaviour has occurred, whereas a negative reinforcer represents the removal of undesirable events. Companies frequently use negative reinforcement techniques. For example, advertisements that focus on the bad outcomes associated with not using a company's products utilize this technique. The message is essentially "If only you had tried us, this bad thing wouldn't have happened!"

punishers stimuli that decrease the likelihood that a behaviour will persist

negative reinforcement removal of harmful stimuli as a way of encouraging behaviour

extinction process through which behaviours cease because of lack of reinforcement

Behaviours often cease when reinforcers are no longer present. This represents the concept of **extinction**. For example, consumers may become accustomed to receiving free doughnuts and coffee at a local service station every time they get their oil changed. If the station decides to stop offering the free food and drink, the consumers may take their business elsewhere.

FINAL THOUGHT ON BEHAVIOURAL CONDITIONING

Conditioning represents a type of learning because it focuses on behavioural change that occurs through a consumer's interaction with the environment. For behaviourists, perception itself is an activity, not a mental process. Through the behavioural approach, consumers are exposed to stimuli and react in some way. Consumer learning through behavioural conditioning occurs without a conscious attempt to learn anything new.

STUDY TOOLS 3

LOCATED AT THE BACK OF THE TEXTBOOK
☐ Rip out Chapter Review Card

LOCATED AT NELSON.COM/STUDENT
☐ Review Key Terms Flashcards (print or online)

☐ Download audio summaries to review on the go

☐ Complete practice quizzes to prepare for tests

☐ Watch video on Culvers for a real company example

Case

Target Misses the Mark in Canada

When Target announced it was buying more than 125 Zellers stores and coming to Canada in 2013, consumers were excited and competitors were nervous. Target was widely regarded as one of the most sophisticated, smart, and competitive retailers in the United States. A survey in British Columbia indicated that 82% of consumers planned to visit a Target store and only 14% disapproved of another American chain entering the Canadian market. As the stores began to open across the country, customers lined up hours before opening to be the first to get a glimpse inside one of the world's most successful retailers.

Yet, almost as soon as the doors opened, the problems began. Customers were not impressed with the products or the prices. The stores still looked a lot like the Zellers outlets that they replaced. There was little customer traffic and no background music, which gave Target an eerie empty feel, made worse by shelves that were chronically out of stock. Canadian customers who loved Target stores they had visited in the United States didn't recognize the retailer that had opened in Canada. Shoppers openly complained that they were unable to find the low prices and unique fashions they had expected.

Nevertheless, Target pushed ahead at a breathtaking pace, expanding to 133 stores from coast to coast in less than two years. The company invested billions of dollars in its Canadian operations and hired more than 17,000 employees.

In the summer of 2014, Brian Cornell joined Target as CEO and promised to take a hard look at the business's performance. The Canadian expansion became a substantial drag on corporate performance, wiping out almost half of the company's global profits in 2013. Internal analysis indicated it would take at least six years to start making money in Canada. The company held out hope that the 2014 holiday season would turn things

Paul McKinnon/Shutterstock.com

around, but when it did not, Cornell announced in early 2015 that Target would leave Canada, closing all of its stores and laying off its employees. Even though the company lost $5.4 billion in the fourth quarter of 2014 and closing the Canadian operations would cost hundreds of millions more, Target's stock jumped 7% when it announced its withdrawal from Canada.

Sources: Mah, Bill (2015), "Target's closure leaves malls scrambling, shoppers shrugging," *Edmonton Journal*, January 16 accessed at http://www.edmontonjournal.com/Target+closure+leaves+malls+scrambling+shoppers+shrugging/10732789/story.html on May 12, 2015.

QUESTIONS

1 Many Canadians were aware of Target long before the company announced its planned expansion into Canada. What was the perception of Target prior to its entry into Canada? How did that perception conflict with the reality?

2 How did consumers react to Target in Canada? If you were leading Target in Canada how would you address consumers' perception of the company?

3 How could Target have taken advantage of instrumental conditioning and introduced positive reinforcers in an effort to win back consumers who were initially disappointed with the retailer?

4 | Comprehension, Memory, and Cognitive Learning

LEARNING OBJECTIVES

After studying this chapter, the student should be able to:

4-1 Identify factors that influence consumer comprehension.

4-2 Explain how knowledge, meaning, and value are inseparable, using the multiple store memory theory.

4-3 Understand how the mental associations that consumers develop are a key to learning.

4-4 Use the concept of associative networks to map relevant consumer knowledge.

4-5 Apply the cognitive schema concept in understanding how consumers react to products, brands, and marketing agents.

INTRODUCTION

The previous chapter discussed the preliminary stages of perception and consumer learning. We defined learning as a change in behaviour resulting from interaction between a person and a stimulus. We also described the behaviourist approach to learning, which focuses on behaviours rather than inner, mental processes. Cognitive learning focuses on *mental* processes occurring as consumers comprehend and elaborate upon information received. The cognitive perspective views learning as an active, mental process wherein information is processed, associations are made, and knowledge is gained.

Cognitive learning takes place through information processing. Exhibit 4.1 shows the basic components of information processing. We have already discussed several of the concepts presented in the exhibit, including exposure, attention, and comprehension. In the current chapter, we look more closely at comprehension and other issues related to cognitive learning, including memory and elaboration.

Consumers are exposed to thousands of stimuli each day. The chances are slim that any one message will be attended to, comprehended, and elaborated upon in a way that will enable the consumer to encode the message accurately in memory. As a result, consumers rarely gain meaningful knowledge from any particular marketing communication in a way they actually can use. In the same way, students also find studying a challenge because one can only pay attention to, comprehend, elaborate upon, and meaningfully encode so much information.

4-1 WHAT INFLUENCES COMPREHENSION?

Consumers can't realize value without knowing the meaning of the things consumed. **Comprehension** refers to the interpretation or understanding a consumer

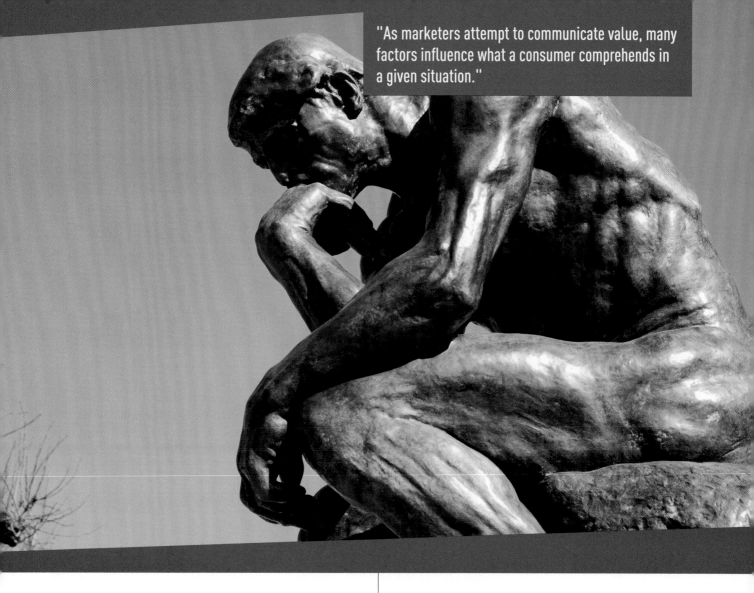

develops about some attended stimulus based on the way meaning is assigned. What happens when a consumer sees a "some assembly required" sticker on a product? Of course, this means that the consumer will likely have to master a set of detailed instructions before consumption can begin. An easy-to-comprehend set of instructions would certainly contribute to the total value equation for the product. However, we all know how frustrating these instructions can be! In this and in many other ways, marketers must teach us things so that we realize the most value from consumption.

Other products contain warning labels that signal specific associated risks. Consider a typical cigarette package. A warning label will be effective only if consumers comprehend the intended message. Consumers don't always comprehend messages as intended, however. A consumer might even see a cigarette warning label as authoritarian, and ignoring it or challenging it as something contributing to smoking's appeal as "rebellion." Other times, consumers may actually overestimate the dangers associated with smoking when they read a warning of "rare" side effects.[1]

Cigarette warning labels actually have only a small effect on consumer behaviour.[2] Thus, warnings are only moderately successful in teaching consumers about potentially dangerous consumer behaviours.

Getting consumers to comprehend messages accurately can be difficult. Here are three important issues regarding comprehension:

1. **Internal factors within the consumer powerfully influence the comprehension process. Recall from a previous chapter that factors influencing consumer behaviour often interact with one another. Numerous components in the consumer value framework alter comprehension.**

2. **Comprehension includes both cognitive and affective elements. That is, the process of comprehension involves both thoughts and feelings. As such, comprehension applies not only to consumer learning but to consumers' attitudes as well.**

> **comprehension** the way people cognitively assign meaning to (i.e., understand) things they encounter

Meaning and value are inseparable, and consumers must comprehend marketing messages to learn the intended value of a product.

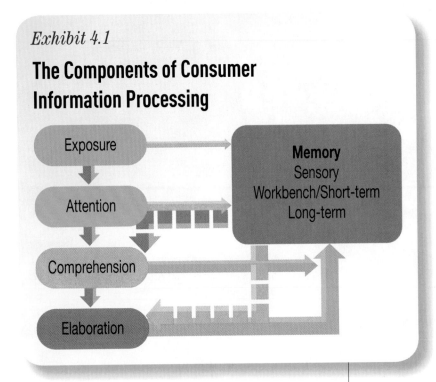

Exhibit 4.1

The Components of Consumer Information Processing

- Exposure
- Attention
- Comprehension
- Elaboration

Memory
Sensory
Workbench/Short-term
Long-term

A number of topics in this chapter apply equally to consumer attitude formation and persuasion (a later chapter is devoted to these topics).

3. Every message sends signals. **Signal theory** tells us that communications provide information in ways beyond the explicit or obvious content. A retailer promises to match competitors' prices (a price-matching guarantee) as a signal to consumers that prices are indeed low.[3] Consumers don't always comprehend messages or get the

signal theory explains ways in which communications convey meaning beyond the explicit or obvious interpretation

desired signal, and to this extent, consumer comprehension is not always "correct." After all, perception is subjective reality, which may or may not equal objective reality! Quite simply, consumers sometimes just don't get it; however, they act on what they get.

4-1a Factors Affecting Consumer Comprehension

Meaning and value are inseparable, and consumers must comprehend marketing messages in order to learn the intended value of a product. As marketers attempt to communicate value, many factors influence what a consumer comprehends in a given situation. While consumer researchers still have a great deal to learn about the factors that influence comprehension, Exhibit 4.2 lists things we do know

Exhibit 4.2

Comprehension Depends on Multiple Factors

Message Characteristics
- Physical Characteristics
- Simplicity-Complexity
- Congruity-Incongruity
- Figure-Ground
- Message Source

Message Receiver Characteristics
- Intelligence
- Prior Knowledge
- Ability
- Involvement
- Familiarity/ Habituation
- Expectations
- Physical Limits
- Brain Dominance

Environmental Characteristics
- Information Intensity
- Framing
- Timing

regarding these factors. These factors can be divided into three categories:

1. **Characteristics of the message**
2. **Characteristics of the message receiver**
3. **Characteristics of the environment (information-processing situation)**

4-1b Characteristics of the Message

Marketers believe that they can affect consumer learning by carefully planning the execution of marketing communications. If you flip through any popular magazine, you will see advertisements with many different execution styles. Here are a few tools marketers use to potentially influence comprehension and control what consumers learn.

PHYSICAL CHARACTERISTICS

The **physical characteristics** of a message refer to the elements of a message that one senses directly. These parts come together to execute a communication of some type. While these elements affect comprehension, you may note that some of these characteristics also affect the likelihood that consumers pay attention. Here are just a few physical characteristics that can contribute to effective communication.

Intensity. Generally speaking, the greater the movement, the larger the picture, or the louder the sound, the more likely a consumer is to attend and comprehend something from a message. Large numbers or letters appear to shout. Signage with large numerals communicates the notion of low prices to consumers more effectively than a smaller font.

Colour. Colour affects the likelihood of gaining a consumer's attention, but it can also have an impact on comprehension. Gold signals quality. Similarly, blue is associated with higher quality and higher price expectations. Warm colours like red and orange get attention but also may lower quality perceptions relative to cool colours. For fresh produce, colours that blend in with the actual fruit (red mesh for red apples) also can enhance quality perceptions.[4]

Font. Consumers derive meaning from both the actual text of a message and the visual presentation of the message. Font styles send meaningful signals. The same brand or store name presented in a block font such as Courier may take on a different meaning if presented in a script font. For instance, research suggests that

In recent years, Black Friday sales have been prevalent in Canada, along with intense price-based advertising.

different fonts signal masculinity, femininity, activity, elegance, softness, or tradition, just to name a few. Consider the two examples below:

ACME BRICK COMPANY
ACME BRICK COMPANY

Which sends the better message for a brick company? One can easily see that the signal the font sends should be consistent with the type of service offered.[5]

Numbers. Many brand managers rely on alphanumeric names, combining letters and numbers, for new products. Automobiles provide an interesting illustrative example of this practice. For example, makes and models include Lexus RC-F, Mercedes CLS-550, and Mazda CX-8. Compare these names with something like Volkswagen Rabbit or Dodge Ram. A consumer expects a car named after a rabbit to possess rabbit-like qualities, which can be both good and bad. In contrast, combinations of numbers and letters have little specific meaning. This gives marketers a better opportunity to shape the intended meaning of a brand. Names with letters and numbers used in combination do tend to signal a "technologically advanced" meaning.

Spacing. All types of communicators, from salespeople to advertisers to teachers, repeat messages as a way of increasing comprehension. If a communicator is going to repeat a message multiple times, is it better to repeat it in sequence or to break up the repetition? Actually,

> **physical characteristics** tangible elements or the parts of a message that can be sensed

The Super 8 image signals low price. Originally, Super 8 hotel rooms were $8.88 per night.

consumers display greater recall of an intended message when information is presented in intervals rather than in sequence.[6] For instance, in media advertising, three 30-second ads spread over three hours achieve better consumer recall of information than a single 90-second advertisement.

SIMPLICITY VERSUS COMPLEXITY

Generally speaking, the simpler the message, the more likely a consumer is to develop meaningful comprehension, which, of course, relies on a consumer's ability to process information. For example, research has helped identify the simplest way to communicate important consumer information. Summary terms like *fat-free* and *low-fat* have replaced more complicated terms that were once linked to specific product attributes.[7] Experts believe the new terminology better allows consumers to comprehend the desired messages.

MESSAGE CONGRUITY

Message congruity represents the extent to which a message is internally consistent and fits surrounding

information. To illustrate, consider this question: "Does a consumer more effectively comprehend information when exposed to three different ads about hair care products in a row, or when exposed to one hair care product ad preceded by a detergent ad and followed by an automobile ad?"

The conventional wisdom is that congruent content would lead to improved comprehension. However, this may not always be the case. Moderate levels of incongruity motivate deeper processing than when everything in a string of messages is highly congruent. The result can be improved comprehension. However, incongruence can have drawbacks. Celebrity spokespeople endorse many brands, some of them congruent with their personas and some not. DeMar DeRozan plays basketball. Thus, his meaning is consistent with sports-related products like energy drinks or athletic shoes, but inconsistent with products like gardening supplies or heart medicine. When consumers pay attention to an ad, an incongruent endorser can hurt the product's image.[8] Thus, if the primary goal is to create a favourable attitude rather than increased comprehension, then marketers should minimize incongruity. If comprehension is the goal, a little incongruity can be appropriate.

The incongruity of a message with surrounding messages works in much the same way.[9] In fact, consumers will comprehend and remember more from an ad that is presented with incongruent material surrounding it. Consider a brand like L'Oréal Preference hair care products. The consumer will comprehend and remember more when presented with only one hair care message in any three-message sequence (see Exhibit 4.3). In this case, frame B offers better comprehension for the L'Oréal Preference brand.

This doesn't mean that incongruent information is always better.[10] An ad with inconsistent background music, such as an ad for Thailand that includes country and western music, will generally be liked less than an ad with consistent music. Therefore, the decision to use highly consistent message content depends on the marketing goal. If the primary goal is conveying meaningful information explicitly, some degree of incongruity is a good idea. If the primary goal is to create a favourable attitude, then marketers should minimize incongruity.

FIGURE AND GROUND

Every message is presented with background, although sometimes the background becomes the message. A photographer usually concentrates on capturing a focal image in a photo frame. The focal image, or the object intended to capture a person's attention, is much the

Exhibit 4.3

Congruent or Incongruent Message Sequences?

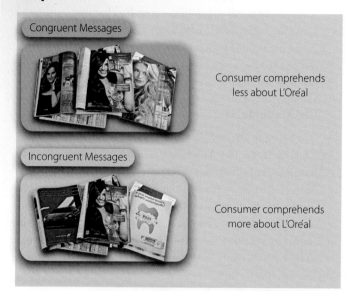

Congruent Messages — Consumer comprehends less about L'Oréal

Incongruent Messages — Consumer comprehends more about L'Oréal

same as a **figure** in a message. In a message, everything besides the figure should be less important and simply represent the **ground** (or background) relative to the central message. The contrast between the two represents the psychological **figure–ground distinction**.

One reason consumers do not always comprehend a message as the sender intended is because the product intended to be the figure becomes the ground. Exhibit 4.4 illustrates how this occurs psychologically. What is this a picture of? If a consumer focuses on the outer rings,

Exhibit 4.4

The Figure and Ground Distinction

it looks something like a funnel. However, focus on the dot in the centre and the rings can actually begin to disappear. What one consumer interprets as the figure may be the background to another.

MESSAGE SOURCE

The source of a message also can influence comprehension. Message sources include a famous celebrity in an advertisement, a salesperson in a sales context, a family member giving advice, a Facebook friend, or even a computer-animated avatar. A source influences comprehension to varying degrees based upon characteristics like these:[11]

1. **Likeability**

2. **Attractiveness**

3. **Expertise**

4. **Trustworthiness**

A likeable source can change the interpretation of a stimulus. For years, consumers have enjoyed the M&M's characters as the most liked spokes-characters for any product. However, younger generations express a preference for the Aflac Duck and the Geico Gecko.[12] Most people would find it difficult to argue with the claim, "15 minutes can save you 15% or more on car insurance" when voiced by the Gecko. In contrast, the Geico Cavemen were not so liked, and if one of them stated the same claim, a consumer might be compelled to disagree. Consumers react much the same way to a source perceived as attractive. The Geico Cavemen lose out here too.

Expertise refers to the amount of knowledge that a source is perceived to have about a subject. **Trustworthiness** refers to how honest and unbiased a source is perceived to be. Consumers associate expertise and trustworthiness with **credibility**. As with likability, credible sources tend to lower the chances that consumers will develop **counterarguments** (thoughts that contradict a message).

figure object that is intended to capture a person's attention; the focal part of any message

ground background in a message

figure–ground distinction notion that each message can be separated into the focal point (figure) and the background (ground)

expertise amount of knowledge that a source is perceived to have about a subject

trustworthiness how honest and unbiased the source is perceived to be

credibility extent to which a source is considered to be both an expert in a given area and trustworthy

counterarguments thoughts that contradict a message

Support arguments are thoughts that further support a message. Brand managers should especially rely on a likeable, attractive, and credible source. BP chief executive Tony Hayward may not have been the best face for messages related to the 2010 oil spill disaster off the coast of Louisiana. His expertise alone proved insufficient to prevent counterarguments to practically anything he said.

In summary, we can say that desirable source characteristics can help convey the desired message through cognitive processes. However, sources can influence consumers in other, more subtle ways. In a later chapter, we focus on how sources affect attitude change.

4-1c Message Receiver Characteristics

INTELLIGENCE/ABILITY

As a general statement, intelligent, well-educated consumers are more likely to accurately comprehend a message than are less intelligent or less educated consumers. With this being said, we offer two caveats. First, a great deal of knowledge is specific to particular product categories. Therefore, a consumer who does not have a high intelligence quotient (IQ) may be able to comprehend certain product information more readily than another consumer with a high IQ. Second, even a highly intelligent consumer would understand a simpler message better than a more complex message. Marketers should communicate information pertaining to product warnings, usage instructions, or assembly directions as simply as possible.[13]

PRIOR KNOWLEDGE

The human brain matches incoming information with pre-existing knowledge. This pre-existing, or prior, knowledge provides resources, or a way through which other stimuli can be comprehended. Even consumers of very high intelligence may lack prior knowledge to comprehend certain consumer messages. This is why parents sometimes need their children to operate the television remote control. Even young kids have more knowledge of handheld electronic devices than many adults—particularly university professors. Consumers display a preference for things that are consistent with their prior knowledge.

Consider the role that superstition can play in comprehending value propositions. Lucky in love? Ritz-Carlton and Walmart each offered promotions encouraging consumers to get married on 7/7/07. Consumers could get a seven-night honeymoon stay at the Ritz for $77,777.[14] The same promotion offered on a Friday the 13th in 2013 would not likely be so successful. Going beyond lucky and unlucky numbers, consumers in some cultures associate certain colours with good or bad fortune, and some associate certain foods with good fortune. Even marketers who are not superstitious would be wise to acknowledge the meanings that such beliefs, examples of prior knowledge, can convey to products.

INVOLVEMENT

Consumers are not equally involved with every message sent their way. As discussed in Chapter 3, highly involved consumers tend to pay more attention to messages. They also exert more effort in comprehending messages.[15] As a result, these consumers show better recall than consumers with lower levels of involvement.[16] Consider the consumer who views a website describing a new product. The highly involved consumer will click through more hyperlinks, explore more pages, and comprehend more information than a less involved consumer.

Consider, for example, two Montrealers watching a Canadiens hockey game on CBC: one is a rabid Habs fan and the other is a much more casual viewer. The highly involved fan is likely to comprehend a lot of information

Youppi, the popular Montreal mascot, began with the Expos and then moved to the Canadiens.

support arguments
thoughts that further support a message

Brands that Stay in Shape

Comprehension depends on message, consumer, and environment characteristics. Which of the three logos do you like best? Psychology theory allows us to predict and explain why one of the three logos may be interpreted more favourably.

Designs with a 1.62 width-to-length ratio (called the golden ratio) are preferred over other types of shapes. The middle logo is quickly eliminated because it does not follow golden ratio principles.

Next, a majority of consumers would prefer the third image to the first. Why? People intuitively interpret boxed designs with sharp edges or corners as potential threats to safety based on the association with things like a thorn, a shark's tooth, or barbed wire. Curved edges are preferred.

In some periods, such as the 1970s, boxy designs for appliances, autos, and furniture became the rule. Some argue that a principle known as *zeitgeist*, taken from the German language and meaning "the spirit of a time," can influence the comprehension of a message and the way a consumer receives that message. Consumer input may help design engineers understand such principles. What do you think of the zeitgeist today and how it influences preferred designs?

Sources: C. C. Carbon, "The Cycle of Preference: Long-Term Dynamics of Aesthetic Appreciation", *Acta Psychologica* 134 (2010): 23344. J. Lander, "Seize the Zeitgeist: How Timing Impacts Success", *Inventor Digest* 26 (March 1, 2010): 40. Lan Luo, "Product Line Design for Consumer Durables: An Integrated Marketing and Engineering Approach", *Journal of Marketing Research* 48 (February 2011): 12839.

during the game—including player statistics, team standings, impact of the salary cap, injuries, line match-ups, and so on. The less involved fan, who is watching the same game and hearing the same commentators, may only remember the final score or a funny stunt by the mascot, Youppi. It is important for marketers to remember that consumers receiving the exact same message may come away with very different levels of knowledge and understanding depending on how involved they are in the topic domain.

FAMILIARITY/HABITUATION

Consumers tend to like the familiar. However, in terms of comprehension, familiarity can *lower* a consumer's motivation to process a message. While some degree of familiarity may improve consumer attitude, high levels of familiarity may actually reduce comprehension.[17]

Consumer habituation is a concept resulting from familiarity. **Habituation** is the process by which continuous exposure to a stimulus affects the comprehension of and response to some stimulus. Consider the following psychological experiment. Subjects in one treatment group immerse their arms in extremely cold water (5°C) for 60 seconds. Obviously, this is an unpleasant task. Another group of subjects is asked to do the very same thing, except after the first immersion, they are asked to immediately immerse their arms in slightly less frigid (10°C) water for 30 additional seconds. At the end of the procedure, both groups rated the task hedonically. Surprisingly, the group that immersed their arms for 90 seconds rated the task more favourably than did the group that immersed their arms for only 60 seconds.

Habituation theory explains this result. The first 60 seconds of exposure to the extremely cold water habituated the subjects and created an **adaptation level**. As a result, when the second group was exposed to water that was still unpleasant, but slightly warmer than the first, a more favourable evaluation was obtained because the entire experience was framed by the relatively more valuable (less painful) last 30 seconds.

To illustrate habituation in a consumer setting, consider that consumers in the United States, Canada, Australia, and throughout Western Europe have long been habituated to fairly pleasant shopping experiences in which many goods and services are readily available. This hardly compares with many parts of the world, including developing nations, where shopping as we know it hardly exists. A decade after the breakup of the Soviet Union, consumer researchers measured the hedonic and

habituation process by which continuous exposure to a stimulus affects the comprehension of, and response to, the stimulus

adaptation level level of a stimulus to which a consumer has become accustomed

Healthiness Can Be Bad for Your Brain?

Comprehending the consequences of consuming various foods is difficult. Just wanting to eat healthy food isn't enough to allow consumers to know what's best. Foods that experts say are healthy today may not be considered so tomorrow. Eggs, for instance, have repeatedly come in and out of vogue as a healthy food. University consumers today frequently down an energy bar as a quick alternative to a full lunch—are these bars good for you? Some contain trans fat. They can also be very high in calories. At the same time, they contain vitamins, protein, and fibre. Do health-conscious consumers always make better decisions about their diet? Sometimes they make mistakes. Two reasons for this are that the consumer lacks the ability to process health-related information and that even when consumers are knowledgeable, prior beliefs strongly influence their comprehension. Once a consumer believes a certain food is healthy, he or she may discount information that contradicts that belief to maintain consistency in knowledge. What about an energy drink before class? Read the label. Is it a healthy choice? In other cases, consumers may not have easy access to nutritional information—for example, on a restaurant dessert menu—and as a result focus their attention on how good it will taste. Research suggests that access to information on foods' fat and caloric content is critically important for consumers on a diet.

Sources: E. Howlett, S. Burton, J. Kozup (2008), "How Modification of the Nutrition Fats Panel Influences Consumers at Risk for Heart Disease: The Case of Trans-Fats," *Journal of Public Policy and Marketing*, 27 (Spring), 83–97. R.W. Naylor, C.M. Droms and K.L. Haws (2009), "Eating with a Purpose: Consumer Response to Functional Food Health Claims in Conflicting Versus Complementary Information Environments," *Journal of Public Policy and Marketing*, 28 (Fall), 221–233.

utilitarian shopping value Russian consumers experienced trying to obtain everyday goods and services.[18] The capitalist reforms had been slow to spread throughout Russia and these consumers still faced shops with empty shelves and long lines to buy things like boots or jackets. A Russian word to describe this experience is *dostats*, which roughly means "acquiring things with great difficulty." The surprising result of the research was that the Russian consumers reported similar amounts of shopping value compared with American shoppers. What is the explanation for this outcome? Even though shopping in Russia was certainly worse than shopping in the United States, shopping was still framed by people's life experiences beyond the familiar reality of dostats. These life experiences provided a frame of reference in which shopping was less unpleasant than were many other routine activities.

EXPECTATIONS

Expectations are beliefs of what will happen in a future situation. They play an important role in many consumer behaviour settings and can affect comprehension. We discuss expectations in more detail later when satisfaction becomes the focus. For now, note that what consumers expect to experience has an impact on their comprehension of the environment.

To illustrate, consider how packaging influences consumers' comprehension of products. Beverage marketers have realized for decades that packaging plays a major role in how beverages are perceived. In fact, studies indicate that consumers cannot even identify their "favourite" brand of beer without the package/label.[19] Removing the label affects consumers' expectations, which affects their comprehension, by blocking brand-specific thoughts.

PHYSICAL LIMITS

A consumer's physical limitations can also influence comprehension. For example, we all have limits in our ability to hear, see, smell, taste, and think. Obviously, if someone can't hear, then they can't comprehend information in an audio message. Also, consumers who are colour blind will have difficulty comprehending information related to colour. For instance, if a caution or warning label is coloured red to signal risk, a colour-blind consumer will not likely comprehend this aspect of the message.[20]

expectations beliefs of what will happen in some future situation

BRAIN DOMINANCE

Brain dominance refers to the phenomenon of *hemispheric lateralization*. Some people tend to be either right-brain or left-brain dominant. This, of course, does not mean that some consumers use only the left or right parts of their brains! Right-brain–dominant consumers tend to be visual processors (tend to favour images for communication), whereas left-brain–dominant consumers tend to deal better with verbal processing (words).

4-1d Environmental Characteristics

INFORMATION INTENSITY

Information intensity refers to the amount of information available for a consumer to process within a given environment. When consumers are overloaded, the overload affects not only their attention but also their comprehension and eventual reaction. For example, evidence suggests that the amount of information presented to consumers participating in online auctions affects their bidding behaviour, with highly intense information environments being associated with lower price sensitivity.[21]

FRAMING

Framing is a phenomenon in which the meaning of something is influenced (perceived differently) by the information environment. Thus, the same event can produce multiple meanings depending on how the information is presented. For example, what does a driver comprehend when the gas gauge shows only a quarter of a tank of gas remaining? If she is driving through the suburbs of her hometown, she probably does not comprehend this as very significant. However, if she is driving through a sparsely populated wilderness, that same information may result in an entirely different comprehension and reaction. The environment has framed the information.

Prospect theory explains that the way in which information is framed differentially affects risk assessments and associated consumer decisions. For example, a consumer may read a message like "save 50%" or "you pay half price!" Or a beef label might read "95% lean" or "5% fat." Which one is better? Are they saying the same thing?

To illustrate prospect theory, consider what you have likely heard about risks associated with prolonged exposure to the sun. The following are two methods of presenting information about those risks:[22]

1. **"Failing to use sunscreen leaves one vulnerable to skin cancer."**

2. **"Using sunscreen helps avoid skin cancer."**

Exhibit 4.5

An Illustration of Framing—What Would You Do?

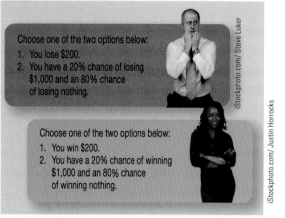

Choose one of the two options below:
1. You lose $200.
2. You have a 20% chance of losing $1,000 and an 80% chance of losing nothing.

Choose one of the two options below:
1. You win $200.
2. You have a 20% chance of winning $1,000 and an 80% chance of winning nothing.

iStockphoto.com/ Steve Luker

iStockphoto.com/ Justin Horrocks

Source: Tversky, A. and D. Kahneman (1981), "The Framing of Decisions and the Psychology of Choice," *Science, 211*, 453–458.

The first statement is negatively framed: "Use this product or get skin cancer!" The second statement is positively framed: "Use this product and stay healthy!"

Priming refers to a cognitive process in which active concepts frame thoughts and therefore affect both value and meaning. Negatively framed information primes losses, which consumers wish to avoid, and encourages consumers to be more willing to take a chance on a product and in this case spend some money on the sunscreen. Also, negatively framed information generally has a greater impact on consumers, and so the perceived value of the sunscreen in the above example may be increased by framing the information negatively. The greater impact of negative information is a key aspect of prospect theory. Exhibit 4.5 illustrates this aspect of framing.

Most consumers faced with the first choice set in Exhibit 4.5 will choose option 2. Notice that the frame is negative.[23] In the second choice set, consumers tend to choose option 1. In the second set, the frame is positive (priming gains—winning

information intensity amount of information available for a consumer to process within a given environment

framing a phenomenon in which the meaning of something is influenced (perceived differently) by the information environment

prospect theory theory that suggests that a decision, or argument, can be framed in different ways and that the framing affects risk assessments consumers make

priming cognitive process in which context or environment activates concepts and frames thoughts and therefore affects both value and meaning

$200 rather than losing $200). This happens even though the expected value ($E(v)$) for each choice is the same ($200). Presenting a negative frame primes thoughts that lead to a consumer being more willing to take risks. In terms of prospect theory, we say that losses weigh more heavily than gains. Losing $200 is certainly a loss and hurts hedonic value more than winning $200 helps create hedonic value.[24] As such, consumers faced with the first choice set are more willing to take a risk.

Priming occurs in many subtle ways beyond positive and negative frames. Brand names and logos can serve as primes, for instance. A recent experiment suggested that the Apple logo primed greater creativity among problem solvers exposed to the logo compared to other problem solvers.[25] The expectations of a bargain can be primed by other prices in the shopping environment. For instance, a consumer may think $200 is a good price for a watch in a counter filled with watches selling for $1,000 or more. Conversely, the same watch at $200 may not seem like a good deal when it is the most expensive watch in the case.[26]

TIMING

Timing also affects comprehension. For our purposes, timing refers to both the *amount of time* a consumer has to process a message and the *point in time* at which the consumer receives the message. For example, consumers who have only a couple of seconds to process a message, such as when driving by a billboard advertisement, cannot possibly comprehend a message in as much depth as a consumer who is not facing a timing issue.

The time of day can also affect the meaning and value of a product. For many consumers, coffee is a morning beverage. Consumers comprehend an advertisement for a brand of coffee quite differently based on the time of day. Most consumers will respond to a coffee advertisement in the morning far more enthusiastically than to the same ad shown before bedtime, because of familiarity effects associating hot coffee with morning consumption.

As you can see, many factors influence how we comprehend marketing messages. Now, we turn our focus to the other major concept in cognitive learning, memory.

A 50 Million Dollar Store

What do people think when they first walk inside your home? Chances are, your living environment changes the way people understand you. This is also true for retail stores. When La Maison Simons began its Canadian expansion, it selected West Edmonton Mall as its first location outside of Quebec. The company understood that first impressions for English Canadian consumers would be formed quickly and to a large extent based on the look and feel of the store.

Simons wanted to make a good impression, not just on local shoppers, but also on the national media and retail observers. According to Peter Simons, the company's CEO, "It was a conscious decision to try to make it an exceptional store. There are people who question whether our concept can survive outside of Quebec … I'm out to prove them

Allan McInnis/Montreal Gazette 2015. Reprinted by permission.

wrong." The store included a canopy of crystalline columns in a glass cube, cone shaped dressing rooms that descended from the ceiling, and digital photo booths that allow customers to share items they are considering on social media for instant feedback. In total, La Maison Simons spent nearly $50 million on the store. The store has a variety of sections that cater to specific segments through unique designs and layouts that aim to attract particular customers. Bright colours and styles highlight athletic apparel, brown and grey tones frame men's business wear, blue frames more casual male clothing and yellow and pink are prevalent in the "twik" section for younger female shoppers. Simons hopes that investing in the store's design will provide the right environment for shoppers at Canada's largest mall.

Source: Strauss, Marina (2012), "Quebec retailer Maison Simons takes its eclectic style west," *The Globe and Mail*, October 30, accessed at http://www.theglobeandmail.com/report-on-business/quebec-retailer-maison-simons-takes-its-eclectic-style-west/article4778740/ on May 13, 2015.

4-2 MULTIPLE STORE THEORY OF ACQUIRING, STORING, AND USING KNOWLEDGE

Memory is the psychological process by which knowledge is recorded. As shown in Exhibit 4.1, all of the elements of the information-processing model are related to memory. In our chapter on perception, we discussed the topics of implicit and explicit memory. Here, we discuss memory from the cognitive learning perspective—the multiple store theory of memory.

4-2a Multiple Store Theory of Memory

The **multiple store theory of memory** views the memory process as utilizing three different storage areas within the human brain. The three areas are sensory memory, working memory, and long-term memory. Exhibit 4.6 illustrates this approach.

SENSORY MEMORY

Sensory memory is the area in memory where we store what we encounter with our five human senses. When we hear something, sensory memory is responsible for storing the sounds. The consumer walking through a movie theatre lobby encounters many sounds, smells, and sights. Sensory memory picks these things out and stores them even though the consumer has not yet allocated attention to any of these sensations. As such, this portion of memory is considered to be pre-attentive.

Sensory memory is truly remarkable. For one thing, it has unlimited capacity. Sensory memory stores everything one is exposed to, taking an exact record of what is encountered. All sights, sounds, smells, tactile sensations, and tastes are recorded as exact replicas in the mind of the consumer.

If this is the case, then why can we recall only a fraction of what we encounter? Another remarkable aspect of sensory memory concerns duration. Sensory memory is very perishable and lasts only a very short time. In most cases, sensory memory begins to fade immediately after the sensation is recorded and lasts less than a second. Thus, the strength of sensory memory is capacity, but the weakness is duration.

Sensory memory can easily be illustrated. Take a quick look at an object and then close your eyes. What happens in the fractions of a second immediately after you shut your eyes? In most instances, your brain will hold the image immediately after you close your eyes—that is, you will be able to see the image mentally. However, very quickly things will start to fall out of the mental picture until eventually only the most central features can be pictured. If you are familiar with a strobe light, you may have noticed that when the light speeds up, images look continuous. This is because sensory memory is able to "hold" the image through the dark portion of the strobe, that is, until the next image is physically sensed.

Although sensory memory is important, its usefulness is limited because images are lost very quickly. Fortunately, sensory memory works in conjunction

---

memory psychological process by which knowledge is recorded

multiple store theory of memory theory that explains memory as utilizing three different storage areas within the human brain: sensory, working, and long-term

sensory memory area in memory where a consumer stores things exposed to one of the five senses

---

Exhibit 4.6

The Multiple Store Approach to Memory

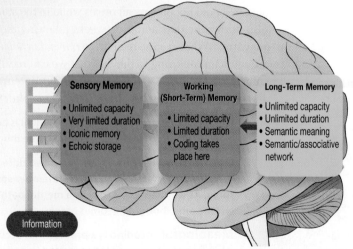

Sensory Memory
- Unlimited capacity
- Very limited duration
- Iconic memory
- Echoic storage

Working (Short-Term) Memory
- Limited capacity
- Limited duration
- Coding takes place here

Long-Term Memory
- Unlimited capacity
- Unlimited duration
- Semantic meaning
- Semantic/associative network

Information

Meaningful encoding takes place with the transfer from workbench to long-term memory.

with other memory functions, allowing a consumer to gain information and knowledge.

WORKING MEMORY

Working memory is the storage area in the memory system where information is stored and encoded for placement in long-term memory and, eventually, retrieved for future use. As we will see, working memory interacts and collaborates very closely with long-term memory. **Encoding** is the process by which information is transferred from working memory to long-term memory for permanent storage. **Retrieval** is the process by which information is transferred back into working memory for additional processing when needed.

To illustrate working memory, imagine a consumer who is walking the aisles of an Auchan hypermart in France. The consumer places several produce items into the cart, including some Camembert, duck liver paté, Morbier, and multiple household items, including paper towels, storage bags, bleach, and toilet tissue. How much do you think all of this is going to cost the consumer? If he doesn't physically write down each item's cost, can we expect that he will be able to know what the total bill will be? To some extent, his accuracy will depend on his ability to hold prices in memory long enough to be able to compute a total upon checkout.

Let's consider a single item. He picks up the paté, checks the price, and puts the item in the cart. The price quickly enters his sensory memory and then moves on to his working memory because he is trying to pay attention to the price. The relevancy of duration, capacity, and involvement quickly come into play.

▸ **Duration.** *Short-term* is often used when describing working memory because this memory storage area, like sensory memory, has limited duration. The duration is not nearly as limited as sensory memory, but stimuli that enter short-term memory may stay there approximately 30 seconds or so without some intervention. Therefore, our consumer can hardly be expected to remember the prices for all items in his cart by the time the checkout counter is reached.

▸ **Capacity.** Unlike sensory memory, working memory has very limited capacity. Generally, the capacity limit for working memory is between three and seven units of information. Think of a physical workbench. If the bench is almost full, we cannot expect to put additional items on it; some items must be removed first. Thus, our consumer cannot be expected to remember all the prices of all items in a shopping cart, especially if he is buying several products. In fact, working memory is taxed even further if the prices contain more syllables. A price of $13.37 is harder to remember than $12.10 because it contains more sounds.[27]

▸ **Involvement.** The capacity of working memory expands and contracts based on the level of a consumer's involvement. The more involved a consumer is with a message, the greater will be the capacity of his working memory. When involvement is very low, working memory capacity contracts to a minimum.

To test your own working memory, try to do the following: Without looking back, name all the items purchased by our French consumer. How many can you remember? Don't feel bad if you can't remember them all. In fact, most people would not be able to recall all of the items. However, most consumers would be able to recall at least two items. For instance, many would recall that toilet tissue was one item. Unless a consumer has some knowledge of French cheeses, the Camembert and Morbier are not likely to be recalled. We recall things better when we can make meaningful associations.

4-3 MAKING ASSOCIATIONS WITH MEANING AS A KEY WAY TO LEARN

So, what kind of work goes on in working memory? The task of a consumer may be to recall things, both over a short time period and over a long time period. The consumer should not only recall prices while in the store, but also during the days and even weeks following the shopping trip.[28] When we use the phrase *remember something*, we often are referring to the fact that we can recall some information or make it active in our minds intentionally. Four mental processes help consumers remember things:

1. **Repetition** is a process in which a thought is held in working memory by mentally repeating the thought.

2. **Dual coding** is a process in which two different sensory "traces" are available to remember something. As we shall see, a trace is a mental path by which some thought becomes active.

3. **Meaningful** encoding is a process that occurs when pre-existing knowledge is used to assist in storing new information.

working memory storage area in the memory system where information is stored while it is being processed and encoded for later recall

encoding process by which information is transferred from working memory to long-term memory for permanent storage

retrieval process by which information is transferred back into working memory for additional processing when needed

4. Chunking is a process of grouping stimuli by meaning so that multiple stimuli can become a single memory unit.

Meaningful encoding and chunking rely heavily on making associations between new information and meaning that is stored in long-term memory.

4-3a Repetition

Repetition is a commonly employed way of trying to remember something. Picture someone trying to remember this licence plate number:

TT867-53-09

One way to remember this number is by thinking it repeatedly. This process is known as *rehearsal*. However, one major problem with this approach is **cognitive interference**, which simply means that other things are vying for processing capacity when a consumer rehearses information. To illustrate, try to count backward from 1,000 by 3. This seems like an easy task. But, if you try to do this while someone is calling out random numbers at the same time, the task becomes much more difficult. All things equal, repetition is the weakest form of learning.

4-3b Dual Coding

Dual coding can be more effective than repetition. To illustrate dual-coding effects, consider Exhibit 4.7, which illustrates the way a scent can improve recall.[29]

CP PHOTO/Don Denton

Boston Pizza opened its first restaurant in Penticton, British Columbia, in 1968.

Researchers tested the extent to which product feature recall might be enhanced by dual encoding using scents. Consumers in the experiment showed greater recall for product features, even a product as innocuous as a pencil, when the product was infused with a scent. In a similar way, associating products with music helps consumers remember information. Why is this? A consumer is able to retrieve the information in two ways—by the content of the message and by the sound of the music. Jingles have lost favour recently in favour of recycled pop songs.[30]

Images also can assist with dual coding.[31] For example, the Boston Pizza logo is a large B and P set inside a pizza-like circle with a pizza-like swirl on the B. This can help consumers easily remember Boston Pizza and the type of product that it sells.

4-3c Meaningful Encoding

Meaningful encoding involves the association of active information in short-term memory with other information recalled from long-term memory. By this process, new information is coded with meaning.

Exhibit 4.7

Dual Coding Illustrated

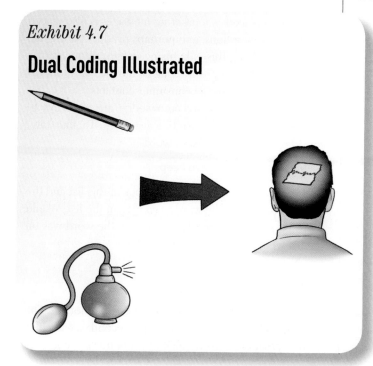

> *Chunking is an important mental activity because better chunking leads to improved recall.*

To illustrate meaningful encoding, let's return to the licence plate example. Consumers often find it difficult to associate anything meaningful with a number. However, a fan of 1980s pop rock would recognize the sequence of digits as the title of a famous hit by the rock artist Tommy Tutone. (The letters *TT* on the plate support this.) If a consumer can retrieve memory of this song and attach it to the licence plate, the plate's number would be much easier to remember. In a way, this example involves both dual and meaningful encoding because the music (also stored in memory) serves as a memory aid itself. For a consumer who knows 1980s music, the numbers 867–5309 can only mean Tommy Tutone. (If you know the song, it's probably going to be stuck in your head now.)

4-3d Chunking

Chunking is the process of grouping stimuli by *meaning* so that multiple stimuli can become one memory unit. Remember that the capacity of working memory is rarely more than seven chunks of information. A chunk is a single memory unit. Here's a simple experiment that helps demonstrate what is meant by a chunk of memory. Show someone the following list of numbers for only a few seconds:

1 8 1 2 1 8 6 7 1 9 8 2

After taking the list away, engage them in conversation for a couple of minutes. Then, ask the person to recall the list. Why is this task so difficult? When someone treats each numeral as a distinct chunk of information, his or her memory capacity is exceeded. After all, 12 numerals, or chunks, are included in the list.

Now, look at the list in this way:

1812   1867   1982

If the person did well in Canadian history class, the task should be considerably easier. A history student should recognize that these are all important dates in Canadian history. The set of 12 numbers can now be stored and recalled as only three pieces of information instead of 12!

Marketers can also use humour to encourage chunking. Consider a coffee advertisement using the following lines spoken by two cartoon-type characters:[32] The first character says, "Other coffee tastes like mud"; then the other character says, "That's because they're ground every morning!" A tagline for the ad could be either "The Taste of Well-Balanced Coffee" or "The Taste of Exquisitely Ground Coffee." The second tagline plays on the idea of ground coffee, related to the ad's humour. Therefore, the second tagline would lead to better encoding and recall. Humour helps to facilitate the process of encoding the message into a meaningful chunk. Marketers designing advertisements or websites, for example, should be careful to group information by meaning in order to assist consumers in encoding chunks of information.

4-3e Retrieval and Working Memory

As we have discussed, a task of working memory is the retrieval of information from long-term memory. When a consumer retrieves information from long-term memory, it is processed once again in working memory. As a part of this process, long-term memory is scanned for relevant information. When trying to remember something, consumers reconstruct memory traces into a formed recollection of the information they are trying to recall.

Marketers can help this process by ensuring that information placed in marketing messages is also placed on in-store promotions, and perhaps product packaging. One way of doing this is by using *integrated marketing communications* to ensure that a unified promotional message is sent across all consumer contacts.

Clearly, meaning and knowledge are the keys to effective coding and cognitive learning. To illustrate, consider the following list of words:

▶ **Weep Sheep Deep Keep Peep**

Suppose a subject is asked to look at this list and the next day is asked if the word *sleep* was on the list. Would there be many false recalls (indicating the word was on the list when it was not or vice versa)?

Now consider another list:

▶ **Night Rest Awake Tired Dream**

Would this list produce fewer false memories? The answer is yes. The key is that the second list enables more meaningful encoding and thus better memory.[33]

chunking process of grouping stimuli by meaning so that multiple stimuli can become one memory unit

long-term memory repository for all information that a person has encountered

LONG-TERM MEMORY

A consumer's long-term memory plays a very important role in learning. **Long-term memory** is a repository for all information that a person has encountered. This portion of memory has unlimited capacity and unlimited duration. Barring some physical incapacity, long-term memory represents permanent information storage.

Why can't consumers always recall information when needed if storage is permanent? The problem is not a storage issue as much as it is a retrieval issue. To illustrate, consider that even things consumers process at very low levels leave some memory trace. A **memory trace** is the mental path by which some thought becomes active. For example, the childhood Christmas memories of French consumers generally include a bûche de Noël. The memory traces from Christmas to the bûche de Noël also spread to branded products associated with these products, such as Hershey's cocoa and Domino powdered sugar.

Psychologically, a memory trace shows how cognitive activation spreads from one concept to another, in a process known as **spreading activation**. Marketers want their brand names to cause cognitive activation to spread to favourable, rather than unfavourable, thoughts. For example, consider the Tabasco brand. Tabasco is most often associated with "hot." Generally, hot things are good. Hot music is good, hot fashions are good, and hot food is good. Therefore, consumers are willing to purchase Tabasco brand clothing (ties, shirts, etc.).

4-3f Mental Tagging

Let's look again at Exhibit 4.1. In psychological terms, a **tag** is a small piece of coded information that helps a particular piece of knowledge get retrieved. The tags function much like the barcoded information on checked luggage. When everything works right, the information on the tag allows the luggage to be located. However, we all realize that not everything always goes right and luggage sometimes ends up in the wrong place. Similarly, if consumers do not tag information in a meaningful way, the encoding process results in errors.

iStockphoto

As adults, most people have recalled some innocuous childhood memory for seemingly no apparent reason. These types of memories illustrate how long-term memory is permanent and how events that were poorly tagged during encoding can emerge at practically any time. Stimuli that consumers pay attention to but do not really comprehend or elaborate upon tend to be poorly tagged.

Nostalgia, a mental yearning to relive the past, produces emotions of longing. Often, nostalgic memories are tagged with product and brand associations. Products from Coca-Cola to the Hudson Bay blanket rely on nostalgia to make them more appealing.

4-4 ASSOCIATIVE NETWORKS AND CONSUMER KNOWLEDGE

4-4a Associative Networks

Knowledge in long-term memory is stored in an **associative network**—a network of mental pathways linking knowledge within memory (and sometimes referred to as a semantic network). These networks are similar to family trees, as they represent known linkages between objects.

4-4b Associative Network Graphics

Exhibit 4.8 illustrates the concept by showing a portion of a consumer's associative network that shows spreading activation from the Mercedes-Benz brand. This illustrates the knowledge that can help identify a Mercedes-Benz within a consumer's long-term memory. The network illustration also shows where cognitive activation flows after the Mercedes concept becomes active.

memory trace mental path by which some thought becomes active

spreading activation way cognitive activation spreads from one concept (or node) to another

tag small piece of coded information that helps with the retrieval of knowledge

nostalgia a mental yearning to relive the past associated with emotions related to longing

associative network network of mental pathways linking all knowledge within memory; sometimes referred to as a semantic network

Exhibit 4.8

A Typical Consumer's Associative Network Associated with Mercedes-Benz

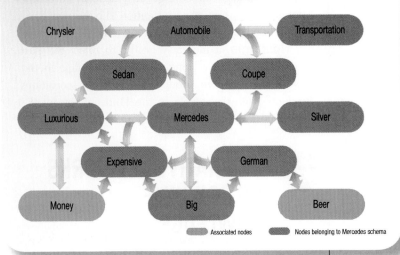

Legend: Associated nodes · Nodes belonging to Mercedes schema

4-4c Declarative Knowledge

Declarative knowledge is a term used in psychology to refer to cognitive components that represent facts. Declarative knowledge is represented in an associative network when two nodes are linked by a path. **Nodes** simply represent concepts in the network, while **paths** show the association between nodes in the network. Consumers' declarative knowledge may not always be correct, but they do act upon the beliefs this knowledge represents. The following are examples of declarative knowledge based on the associative network in Exhibit 4.8:

A Mercedes is an automobile. A Mercedes is expensive. A Mercedes is luxurious. A Mercedes is silver. A Mercedes is a sedan. A sedan is an automobile. A Mercedes is German. Germans drink beer.

In everyday experiences, a consumer compares all of these bits of knowledge with reality. Every time a consumer encounters a supportive instance of declarative knowledge, that knowledge becomes stronger. Consider: "A Mercedes is silver." Not every Mercedes is silver. But

declarative knowledge cognitive components that represent facts

nodes concepts found in an associative network

paths representations of the association between nodes in an associative network

schema cognitive representation of a phenomenon that provides meaning to that entity

when consumers are asked to name the first colour that comes to mind when they think of a Mercedes, they are most likely to say silver (with black coming in second). Every time a consumer sees a silver Mercedes, this belief becomes stronger, and so the association between Mercedes and silver becomes stronger. When a consumer sees a white or blue Mercedes, the rule may diminish slightly in strength. Associative networks contain rules that become more likely to be used as they get stronger. Now consider: "Germans drink beer." If consumers hold this declarative knowledge, they will expect to encounter more Germans who are beer drinkers than, say, Germans who enjoy sipping a Cabernet Sauvignon.

Amazingly, every concept within a consumer's associative network is linked to every other concept. Consider the following request:

List at least 10 snack foods in 60 seconds or less.

A typical consumer would list things like potato chips, an energy bar, Smarties, and a candy bar. Few would argue that these are indeed snack foods. All are linked to the snack concept and are distinct from other food categories—like dinner entrees. A glass of milk may also be a snack, but the association between milk and snack food must first pass through several nodes. By that time, the association is weak. Selling milk as a snack, therefore, is more difficult. However, if a dairy packages milk in a small container reminiscent of a snack food's plastic wrapper and sells it out of a vending machine, the likelihood that consumers would view milk as a snack will increase, and the rule that milk can be a snack would subsequently increase in strength.

4-5 PRODUCT AND BRAND SCHEMAS

A consumer's knowledge for a brand or product is contained in a **schema**—a type of associative network that works as a cognitive representation of a phenomenon that provides meaning to that entity. Exhibit 4.9 illustrates a product schema—snack food—while Exhibit 4.8 illustrates a brand schema—Mercedes-Benz. A brand schema is the smaller part within one's total associative network responsible for defining a particular marketing

Exhibit 4.9

The Knowledge for Snack Foods

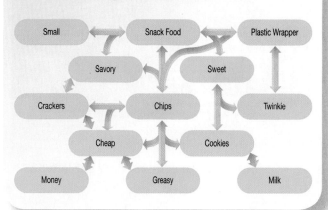

Exhibit 4.10

Category Exemplars

Product Category	Exemplar
Fast Food	McDonald's
Motorcycle	Harley-Davidson
Dollar Store	Dollarama
Supercentre	Walmart
Politician	Stephen Harper
Yoga Apparel	lululemon

entity. Each time a consumer encounters something that could be a Mercedes-Benz, the mind quickly compares all the associations in the schema to see if indeed the thought is correct. Several types of schemata (plural for schema) exist.

4-5a Exemplars

An **exemplar** is a concept within a schema that is the single best representative of some category. Exemplars can be different for different people. In a snack food schema, potato chips may be the exemplar. Taylor Swift may be the category exemplar for a female pop singer. Disney World may be the exemplar for a family vacation destination. Other examples in a category are compared to the exemplar. When a consumer encounters a carrot,

the association with chips (the exemplar of a snack food) may not be close. But if the retailer offers bite-sized carrots enclosed in a small plastic bag, they may be associated with a bag of chips and fit into the snack food category. Exhibit 4.10 illustrates other possible category exemplars.

4-5b Prototypes

Some categories are not well represented by an exemplar. For instance, a "car salesman" category likely does not evoke a specific person who best represents that category. However, an image is associated in one's mind with the category. The image contains the characteristics most associated with a car salesperson. Several characteristics may come to mind. This type of schema is known as a **prototype**. Whether represented by a prototype or an exemplar, consumers compare new and unknown examples to the standard by comparing features with those found in the schema.

4-5c Reaction to New Products/Brands

When consumers encounter new products or brands, they react to them by comparing them to the existing schema. Sometimes new products fail because they are too different or just way ahead of their time. Tablet computer-type devices first appeared in the 1990s but

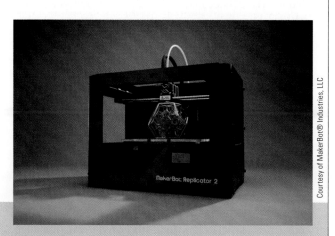

Courtesy of MakerBot® Industries, LLC

3D printers, like those sold by MakerBot, offer much more rapid prototype design than was previously available.

examplar concept within a schema that is the single best representative of some category; schema for something that really exists

prototype schema that is the best representative of some category but that is not represented by an existing entity; conglomeration of the most associated characteristics of a category didn't catch on. Today, wearable technology such as the Apple iWatch and Google Glass are in a similar position with consumers (see the case at the end of this chapter on "Wearables"). Are we ready for being "always on"— having a heads-up web display and engaging in real-time recording of all activities? One way that new products can ease their way into a market is through cobranding. Tim Hortons tried this approach with Stone Cold Creamery when it decided to introduce ice cream into its stores. Google is currently exploring cobranding opportunities for Glass. Ray-Ban and Oakley, both high-end eyewear brands, are partnering with Google to offer more stylish Glass versions.[34]

4-5d Script

A **script** is a schema representing an event. Consumers derive expectations for service encounters from these scripts. For instance, when a consumer dines at a Four Seasons Hotel, the script probably contains things such as valet parking, a greeting by a maitre d' in a nice suit, a table covered with a tablecloth, and so on. Since the script is positive (dining at a Four Seasons Hotel is a good experience), restaurant managers try not to vary too much from expectations or risk confusing, and even frustrating, consumers. Similarly, salespeople employ scripts in performing their jobs. For instance, salespeople who work for charitable appeals use scripts that consist of sequences of actions known to increase consumer compliance.[35] The salesperson develops these scripts over time, facilitating an ability to predict what will happen next.

4-5e Episodic Memory

Episodic memory refers to the memory for past events, or episodes, in one's life. A consumer may have fond memories of childhood holiday celebrations. Another consumer may remember graduating from university or getting a first job. Both of these are episodes and they involve products and brands. Brands associated with positive events stored in episodic memory receive something of a halo, and tend to be preferred by consumers.[36] Episodic memories and scripts both can include knowledge necessary for consumers to use products. Young consumers can probably use Facebook or Twitter to communicate with each other with little problem, while other consumers may not have this script stored in memory and ready for use.

Do you have a social schema for people who drive a Prius?

4-5f Social Schemata

A **social schema**, sometimes called a social stereotype, is the cognitive representation that gives a specific type of person meaning. This type of schema captures the role expectations of a person of a specific type. For instance, consumers generally like when a service provider matches an existing stereotype. Consumers are comforted by a surgeon who looks like a surgeon and acts like a surgeon. However, consumer behaviour may be altered when a service provider does not fit a social schema. A server who does not match the stereotype, in this case by being over- or underweight, may cause consumers to eat more or less than they might otherwise![37]

A social schema can be based on practically any characteristic that can describe a person, including occupation, age, sex, ethnicity, religion, and even product ownership. What kind of person do you think drives a Toyota Prius or a Dodge Ram 3500? A team of researchers sought to identify if drivers were more or less courteous based on what make and model of car they drive. The researchers were surprised, in contrast to their preconceived stereotype, to find that Prius drivers were the least courteous drivers![38]

Consumers also realize that, as consumers, they belong to certain categories of person types. This phenomenon falls under the general heading of *social identity*. Many consumers will try to match the characteristics associated with a stereotype. For instance, male consumers often exhibit characteristics that confirm their fit with the male stereotype. Male consumers' reactions to feminine-based advertising may be less positive when viewed in the presence of another

script schema representing an event

episodic memory memory for past events in one's life

social schema cognitive representation that gives a specific type of person meaning

Value Is Meaning: The Small and Big of It!

The associations we have with brands and activities shape the value we expect and actually receive from these brands and activities. Each time we go to a ballpark and see a brand banner, a memory trace is formed. Run for the Cure is a successful social marketing effort and a brand in itself in the fight against breast cancer. CIBC is the major national sponsor for Run for the Cure, and, as a result, the bank and the event are consistently advertised together. The association connects the two in memory and helps build brand equity. Topics in the news also leave memory traces. In late 2009 and early 2010, the Toyota brand was assailed in the media for auto safety problems that supposedly placed drivers at risk. Because the Toyota brand is associated with reliability, consumer rules (built-in memory) made it difficult for many consumers to assimilate the new knowledge. By mid-2010, stories surfaced that Toyota's problems with unintended acceleration were often due to driver error. Thus, consumers in general, and Toyota owners in particular, generally maintain a very positive schema for Toyota, and owners enjoy continued value from their ownership experience.

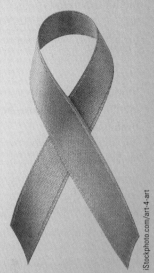

Sources: Lacey, R., A. G. Close and R. Z. Finney (2010), "The Pivotal Roles of Product Knowledge and Corporate Social Responsibility in Event Sponsorship Effectiveness," *Journal of Business Research*, in press. Freeman, D., S. Shapiro and M. Brucks (2009), "Memory Issues Pertaining to Social Marketing Messges about Behavior Enactment versus Non-Enactment," *Journal of Consumer Psychology*, 29, 629–642. Ramsey, M. and K. Linebaugh (2010), "Crash Data Suggest Driver Error in Toyota Accidents," *The Wall Street Journal*, http://online.wsj.com/article/SB10001424052748703834604575364871534435744.html?mod=WSJ_hps_LEFTTopStories, accessed July 13, 2010.

male consumer. This may be the result of trying to protect their male identity.[39] A male consumer may sometimes seek out products that allow him to fit better into this category.

A social schema can be based on practically any characteristic that can describe a person, including occupation, age, sex, ethnicity, religion, and even product ownership. For example, what type of person shops at Whole Foods versus Walmart for groceries? Do these retailers play up those stereotypes in their advertising and promotion? Even children associate certain types of person, like a "cool kid," with specific types of brands and products (e.g., Triple Flip or Ivivva clothing for dancers).[40]

Also, attempts to demarket a product can be implemented by stigmatizing consumption with a negative stereotype. Perhaps no better example exists than the stigmatization of smoking. A "smoker," as opposed to a nonsmoker, is more likely to be attributed with the following characteristics: energetic, interesting, disgusting, offending, and unkempt. Additionally, a person described as a smoker is liked less than a similar person described as a nonsmoker, and interestingly, even smokers are more likely to describe a fellow smoker as disgusting and offensive.[41] Thus, the stereotype seems pervasive. Obviously, a product associated with increasing the belief that

a consumer is disgusting and offensive is more difficult to sell. To the extent that antismoking public policy messages have tried to stigmatize smokers, the messages have been effective.

4-5g Elaboration

Elaboration refers to the extent to which one continues processing a message even after one develops an initial understanding in the comprehension stage.[42] With elaboration, increased information is retrieved from long-term memory and attached to the new information and understanding. This means more and richer tags and a better chance of recall. In particular, **personal elaboration**, in which a person imagines himself or herself associating with a stimulus being processed, provides the deepest comprehension and greatest chance of accurate recall.

In Exhibit 4.1, notice that the information-processing steps linked to memory get more pronounced from exposure

> **elaboration** extent to which a consumer continues processing a message even after an initial understanding is achieved
>
> **personal elaboration** process by which a person imagines himself or herself somehow associating with a stimulus that is being processed

through elaboration. The darker and more pronounced lines linking comprehension and elaboration to memory represent the strength with which incoming information is tagged. Remember, our brains tag information so that we can understand it. Consumers who reach the elaboration stage are most likely to encode information meaningfully so that intentional retrieval is possible later. In a marketing context, therefore, appeals to consumers to associate aspects of their own lives are likely to lead to deeper comprehension and better recall.[43] When an advertisement says, "Have you ever been in this situation?" or, "Imagine yourself in a new Porsche Cayenne," these primes can trigger personal elaboration in a consumer, resulting in better recall. Personal elaboration is highly desirable when influence is expected to take place through cognitive reasoning.

STUDY TOOLS 4

LOCATED AT THE BACK OF THE TEXTBOOK
☐ Rip out Chapter Review Card

LOCATED AT NELSON.COM/STUDENT
☐ Review Key Terms Flashcards (print or online)
☐ Download audio summaries to review on the go
☐ Complete practice quizzes to prepare for tests
☐ Watch video on Cold Stone Creamery for a real company example

Case

Wearables: Can iWatch Succeed Where Glass Failed?

Prince Charles, Jennifer Lawrence, Oprah, Beyoncé, and Bill Murray all wore Google Glass. The new technology had its own 12-page spread in *Vogue* magazine, was the subject of a feature article in *The New Yorker* on its cultural significance, and starred in an entire episode of *The Simpsons*. Glass had a prominent role at Fashion Week in 2012 and was officially announced to the world when a group of skydivers wearing the technology jumped out of a zeppelin above San Francisco. If you believed the hype, it was to be the future not just of mobile devices, but of society itself. Everyone, it seemed, wanted to be one of the select few "Glass Explorers" given the privilege of paying $1,500 for early access to the technology.

Yet, Glass quickly failed as a consumer product. It made people uncomfortable. It was too incongruent with the role that consumers are used to mobile devices playing in their lives. The ability to record anytime anywhere violated expectations of privacy and generated social backlash. Wearers came to be known as "Glassholes." Bars, movie theatres, casinos, and other places banned the technology. Many early adopters found that it was neither useful nor easy to use. Two and a half years after its launch, Google announced it would stop selling Glass. Google hasn't given up on the technology, but it has gone back to the drawing board.

In the meantime, Apple has jumped aggressively into the market for wearables with the long-rumoured iWatch. Other similar devices already existed, but few arrived with the buzz or marketing momentum of Apple's wearable. Unlike Google Glass, the iWatch is a more polished consumer product that estimates suggest was pre-ordered by about 1 million people in North America alone, generating revenue of more than $600 million for Apple. A watch is a more familiar consumer product that is less likely to make people uncomfortable and is easier to comprehend. Most of us already own a watch and a mobile phone, and many people own some type of wearable fitness tracker. The iWatch is being positioned more as an upgrade than a disruptive technology.

Of course, both Google Glass and Apple's iWatch are early entrants into what is likely to be a very large consumer market in the years to come. As the components of mobile devices get smaller, get smarter, and join ever more robust networks, the value of the wearable technology will only increase. What today is quite unfamiliar might one day be commonplace.

AP/Paul Sakuma/The Canadian Press

Sources: Bilton, Nick (2015), "Why Google Glass Broke," *The New York Times*, February 4, accessed at http://www.nytimes.com/2015/02/05/style/why-google-glass-broke.html?WT.mc_id=D-NYT-MKTG-MOD-34830-02-07-HD&WT.mc_ev=click&WT.mc_c=&_r=0 on May 13, 2015. Metz, Rachel (2014), "Google Glass is Dead; Long Live Smart Glasses," *MIT Technology Review*, November 26, accessed at http://www.technologyreview.com/featuredstory/532691/google-glass-is-dead-long-live-smart-glasses/ on May 13, 2015. Sterling, Greg (2015), "How many watches did Apple sell: 1 million, 2 million or more?" *Marketing Land, Mobile Marketing*, April 13, accessed at http://marketingland.com/how-many-watches-did-apple-sell-1-million-2-million-or-more-124985 on May 13, 2015.

QUESTIONS

1 Did Google Glass make the wrong choice in using celebrities as the source of its message about the new product? Did the product garner too much attention?

2 Why did Google Glass fit so poorly into consumers' product schemata? Will the iWatch fare any better?

3 Wearable products are very new. What is your social schema for people who buy these types of products? How do you think that social schema will change over time?

4 What are your expectations for wearable technology? How do your expectations affect the probability that you will be an early adopter?

5 Could you map out your associative network for Google Glass or Apple's iWatch?

6 In the long term, what impact do you think having easy, constant access to vast amounts of information through mobile, even wearable, devices will have on human memory? Sensory memory? Working memory? Long-term memory?

5 | Motivation and Emotion: Driving Consumer Behaviour

LEARNING OBJECTIVES

After studying this chapter, the student should be able to:

5-1 Understand what initiates human behaviour.

5-2 Classify basic consumer motivations.

5-3 Describe consumer emotions and demonstrate how they help shape value.

5-4 Apply different approaches to measuring consumer emotions.

5-5 Understand how different consumers express emotions in different ways.

5-6 Define and apply the concepts of schema-based affect and emotional contagion.

5-1 WHAT DRIVES HUMAN BEHAVIOUR?

How many times do people ask, "Why did I do that?" Sometimes the reason is simple. A consumer might ask, "Why did I eat two whole Big Macs?" The reason may be as simple as "I was hungry." Many consumers may also relate to another familiar question—"Why did I drink so much?"—usually asked the morning after a long night out. The reason here may not be as simple or obvious as "I was hungry" or "I was thirsty." But ultimately, excessive drinking, like all acts, does indeed have an explanation.

The basic consumption process (recall from Chapter 1) is a central component of the CVF and includes consumer needs as the first component. Consumer needs start the process because they kick-start or "motivate" subsequent thoughts, feelings, and behaviour. Simply put, **motivations** are the inner reasons or driving forces behind human actions and drive consumers to address real needs. As the CVF indicates, motivations do not completely determine behaviour. Other sources, including situational factors like the physical environment, influence behaviour. However, motivations do much to provide the intended reason for a consumer's actions.

5-1a Homeostasis

Human motivations are oriented around two key groups of behaviour. The first is behaviour aimed at maintaining one in a current acceptable state. **Homeostasis** refers to the fact that the body naturally reacts in a way so as to maintain a constant, normal bloodstream. Shivering motivates consumers to wear coats to keep their blood from becoming too cold. When one's blood sugar falls

motivations inner reasons or driving forces behind human actions as consumers are driven to address real needs

homeostasis state of equilibrium wherein the body naturally reacts in a way so as to maintain a constant, normal bloodstream

"Marketing success is determined by emotions because actions bring value to a consumer to the extent that desirable emotional states can be created."

below an acceptable state, the physiological reaction is hunger. Hunger then motivates a consumer to eat something and restore the body to an acceptable state. In this way, a consumer comes to want a Big Mac or some other way of restoring a normal state. Thus, consumers act to maintain things the way they are, and their wants are a function of the need driven by homeostasis.

5-1b Self-Improvement

The second group of behaviour results from **self-improvement motivation**. These behaviours are aimed at changing one's current state to a level that is more ideal—not simply maintaining the current state of existence. Consider why one exercises. Beyond some level, consumers exercise not to maintain themselves but to improve their health and well-being. In much the same way, when a consumer upgrades from a Fossil handbag to a Prada handbag, she is not acting out a decision to maintain herself, but she sees Prada as a way

of improving her status in life. Self-improvement leads consumers to perform acts that cause emotions that help create hedonic value.

Basic motivations are relatively simple to understand. As with many psychological concepts, motives can be classified in several ways. We turn now to two related classification schemes—one a general motivational classification, and another aimed more specifically at consumer behaviour.

5-1c Regulatory Focus

Consumer researchers try to capture the manner through which motivation orients consumers through various theories about how we try to control our behaviours. **Regulatory focus theory**, following closely from the contrast between

self-improvement motivation motivation aimed at changing the current state to a level that is more ideal, not at simply maintaining the current state

regulatory focus theory consumers orient their behaviour through either a prevention or a promotion focus homeostasis and self-improvement, puts forward the notion that consumers orient their behaviour through either a prevention focus or a promotion focus. A prevention focus orients consumers toward avoiding negative consequences, while a promotion focus orients consumers toward the opportunistic pursuit of aspirations or ideals. The prevention terminology captures the motivation to maintain homeostasis, and the promotion focus shares similarity with self-improvement goals.

1. **White-Bright:** White-Bright gives you an appealing white smile!

2. **No-Cavities:** No-Cavities is the leader in preventing tooth decay.

White-Bright appeals fit more with a promotion focus and achieving the ideal of a sexy, white smile. No-Cavities fits better with a prevention focus and trying to avoid the pain, discomfort, and inconvenience of tooth decay and related diseases.

Theories like self-regulatory focus try to describe the different motivational approaches that orient us as consumers. We turn now to two related classification schemes—one a classic, general motivational classification and another aimed more specifically at CB and value creation.

5-2 A GENERAL HIERARCHY OF MOTIVATION

Perhaps the most popular theory of human motivation in consumer and organizational behaviour is **Maslow's hierarchy of needs**. This theory describes consumers as addressing a finite set of prioritized needs. The following list displays the set of needs starting with the most basic need.

▸ **Physiological.** Basic survival (food, drink, shelter, etc.)

▸ **Safety and security.** The need to be secure and protected

▸ **Belongingness and love.** The need to feel like a member of a family or community

▸ **Esteem.** The need to be recognized as a person of worth

▸ **Self-actualization.** The need for personal fulfillment

Maslow's hierarchy of needs a theory of human motivation that describes consumers as addressing a finite set of prioritized needs

According to Maslow's theory, consumers first seek value by satisfying the most basic needs. Thus, a starving consumer will risk safety to get something to eat. A consumer whose survival is in doubt would find little value in things that might provide esteem or self-actualization. In contrast, when a successful businessperson retires, he or she may indeed find the most value in things that do not bring esteem, love, or safety, but instead provide self-fulfillment. Several financial firms run advertisements showing retirees leaving high-paying careers to travel to far-off places or go off and work in a mission. This appeal typifies how consumer behaviour can provide value by addressing the self-actualization need.

Further, consider how Maslow's hierarchy may operate differently around the world. In war-torn areas of the world, consumers may indeed risk their lives to buy basic necessities. Clearly, this type of shopping is providing only utilitarian value. In Canada, consumers may find esteem through performing well on the job and owning a large house. In Japan, however, space is so scarce that very few people own large homes. Therefore, esteem may manifest itself more in owning a nice car or in one's manner of dress.

Similarly, the things that address self-actualization needs are likely to vary in different places around the world. Motivations can determine what type and amounts of value that consumers seek. Generally, the most basic needs are addressed with utilitarian value, and as needs become more elaborate, hedonic value is often needed to satiate the need state. Exhibit 5.1 illustrates the hierarchical aspect of needs and includes an example of a consumer behaviour that goes with each need.

Exhibit 5.1

An Illustration of Consumer Motivations According to Maslow's Hierarchy

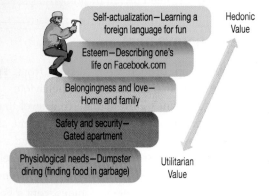

Source: Childers, T. L., C. L. Carr, J. Peck, and S. Carson (2001), "Hedonic and utilitarian motivations for online retail shopping behavior," *Journal of Retailing, 77 (Winter),* 511–535.

5-2a Simpler Classification of Consumer Motivations

The preceding discussion suggests an even simpler classification of consumer motivations. Not surprisingly, the types of motivations match up with the types of needs. A simple but very useful way to understand consumer behaviour is to classify motives based on whether a consumer can best address a particular need by realizing utilitarian or hedonic value.[1]

UTILITARIAN MOTIVATION

Utilitarian motivation is a drive to acquire products that consumers can use to accomplish things. Utilitarian motivation bears much in common with the idea of maintaining behaviour. When the consumer runs out of toothpaste, there will be a strong motivation to do something about this problem and acquire more toothpaste. He or she may want to buy some Crest toothpaste. In the sense that utilitarian motivation helps a consumer maintain his or her state, these motivations work much like homeostasis.

HEDONIC MOTIVATION

Hedonic motivation involves a drive to experience something personally gratifying. These behaviours are usually emotionally satisfying. Interestingly, although sales via the Internet continue to grow, they still account for a small percentage of retail sales (less than 10% in most categories). Perhaps part of the reason is that the process itself is not very rewarding. For people who really love to shop, the Internet may not provide the multisensory experience that a rich shopping environment can deliver. For these consumers, the Internet may be fine for acquiring things but disappointing as a rewarding shopping experience. Exhibit 5.2 illustrates some typical behaviours that are motivated by utilitarian or hedonic shopping motives.

5-2b Consumer Involvement

Two Canadian tourists are seated in a restaurant in Strasbourg, France. A waiter arrives at the table, provides them with English menus, and asks if anyone would like the special "entrée du jour": fois gras d'oie avec marmalade. One customer responds by saying he isn't ready for his entrée, while the other says, "Why, yes, that would be a terrific starter, and please serve it with crusty toast points and sweet pickles." How are these consumers different? Well, many differences may exist, but one big difference is obviously the level of involvement each consumer has in the food category.

Involvement is nearly synonymous with motivation in the sense that a highly involved consumer tends to be strongly motivated to expend effort and resources in consuming that particular thing.[2] **Consumer involvement** represents the degree of personal relevance a consumer finds in pursuing value from a given category of consumption. Thus, when a consumer is highly involved, there is a greater chance that relatively high value can be achieved, as long as things go as expected.

CONSUMER INVOLVEMENT AS A MODERATOR

Consumer researchers often consider involvement a key moderating variable. A **moderating variable** is one that changes the nature of a relationship between two other

---

Exhibit 5.2

Utilitarian and Hedonic Motivations Lead to Consumer Behaviours

Utilitarian Motivations Lead to	Hedonic Motivations Lead to
Choosing the most convenient place to have lunch	Going out to a trendy, new restaurant for dinner
Buying a tank of gas for the car	Driving the car fast on a curvy road even when not rushed
Choosing to shop with retailers that are seen as useful and easy to use	Choosing to shop with retailers that are seen as fun and exciting
Using air freshener to cover up a strange smell in the apartment	Using air freshener because one really enjoys the smell
Going gift shopping out of a sense of obligation to give a gift	Giving a gift to enjoy the giving process and the joy the recipient experiences when opening the gift

utilitarian motivation drive to acquire products that can be used to accomplish something

hedonic motivation drive to experience something emotionally gratifying

consumer involvement degree of personal relevance a consumer finds in pursuing value from a particular category of consumption

moderating variable variable that changes the nature of the relationship between two other variables

---

variables. For example, consider the relationship between the number of alternative brands of a product, perhaps running shoes, and the amount of time and effort a consumer spends choosing a pair of shoes. Logically, one might expect that the larger the selection, the greater the time needed to make a decision. However, would this be the case for all consumers?

A highly involved consumer is likely to take more time because he or she recognizes a greater number of attractive alternatives. He or she is willing (motivated) to spend time evaluating multiple pairs of shoes, trying them on, and comparing their attributes. Value is closely tied to making the right choice. On the other hand, a consumer who lacks motivation to study shoes is quickly overwhelmed by a large selection and falls back to some simple choice decision like "pick the cutest." A consumer needs some degree of involvement to have an ability to evaluate multiple brands effectively. A consumer with low involvement will not spend more time just because there are more types of shoes. A consumer with high involvement, though, is likely to spend more time making a decision as there are more alternatives from which to choose.

DIFFERENT TYPES OF INVOLVEMENT

Involvement can mean different things to different people. However, one way to bring different perspectives together is to realize that there are different types of involvement. In each case, high involvement still means high personal relevance and the importance of receiving high value. Here are some key types of consumer involvement:

▸ **Product involvement** means that some product category has personal relevance. **Product enthusiasts** are consumers with very high involvement in some category. For example, a relatively large segment of product enthusiasts can be found in the fashion market. These consumers find great value in learning about fashions, shopping for fashions, and wearing fashionable clothes. For every consumer, some product categories are much more involving than others. Exhibit 5.3 contrasts products that are generally associated with low and high consumer product involvement.

product involvement
the personal relevance of a particular product category

product enthusiasts
consumers with very high involvement in some product category

shopping involvement
personal relevance of shopping activities

Exhibit 5.3

Typical High and Low Product Involvement

High Product Involvement	Low Product Involvement
Dresses	Detergents
Televisions	Facial soap
Champagne	Toothpaste
Bras	Yogurt

▸ **Shopping involvement** represents the personal relevance of shopping activities. This relevance enhances personal shopping value. From a utilitarian value perspective, highly involved shoppers are more likely to process information about deals and are more likely to react to price reductions and limited offers that create better deals.[3]

High levels of involvement can also be associated with high levels of emotional arousal, which can in turn lead to events like Vancouver's 2011 Stanley Cup riot.

REUTERS/Mike Carlson

- ▶ **Situational involvement** represents the temporary involvement associated with some imminent purchase situation. Situational involvement often comes about when consumers are shopping for something with relatively low involvement but a relatively high price. Things like household and kitchen appliances usually fit this category. For instance, few consumers are highly involved with air conditioners. However, when a consumer is about to purchase an air conditioner, he or she may temporarily learn a lot about air conditioners to avoid paying too much or choosing an inappropriate unit.

- ▶ **Enduring involvement** is not temporary but rather represents a continuing interest in some product or activity. The consumer is always searching for opportunities to consume the product or participate in the activity. Enduring involvement is associated with hedonic value because learning about, shopping for, or consuming a product for which a consumer has high enduring involvement is personally gratifying.

- ▶ **Emotional involvement** represents how emotional a consumer gets during some specific consumption activity. Emotional involvement is closely related to enduring involvement because the things that consumers care most about will eventually create high emotional involvement. Sports fans typify consumers with high emotional involvement, and as we know, sports fans can be rowdy and do wild and crazy things.

AntonioDiaz/Shutterstock.com

Enduring involvement is emotional. Consumers often show passion for activities in which they are enduringly involved.

5-3 CONSUMER EMOTIONS AND VALUE

5-3a Emotion

What is emotion? *Emotion* is a difficult term to define. In fact, some refer to emotion as a "fuzzy" concept, believing that no exact definition exists. According to this view, the best that one can do is list examples of emotions. Love, for example, is a primary example of an emotion, and all readers can relate to the experience of love. Yet, how is *love* defined? Ask someone to put love into words and people will usually provide examples or types of love such as romantic love, brotherly love, maternal love, or love for one's school. Although quite different from love, anger is also a typical emotion and shares something in common with love. Both love and anger are controlling emotions, in that they tend to shape one's behaviour strongly.

While emotions seem a bit "fuzzy," we can offer a simple definition. **Emotions** are specific psychobiological reactions to appraisals. Thus, when a consumer receives bad service in a restaurant, he or she appraises the situation and then reacts emotionally. When a consumer is contemplating a vacation, he or she appraises different sites and thinks about the total vacation experience.[4] A consumer reacts differently to Las Vegas than to, say, Red Deer, Alberta. Emotions are considered **psychobiological** because they involve both psychological processing and physical responses.[5] Indeed, emotions create **visceral responses**, meaning that certain feeling states are tied to behaviour in a very direct way. Exhibit 5.4 lists some typical visceral responses to emotions.

Emotions are extremely important to consumer behaviour and marketing because consumers react most immediately to their feelings. Notice that the word *motivation* and the word *emotion* both contain

situational involvement temporary interest in some imminent purchase situation

enduring involvement ongoing interest in some product or opportunity

emotional involvement type of deep personal interest that evokes strongly felt feelings simply from the thoughts or behaviour associated with some object or activity

emotions specific psychobiological reactions to human appraisals

psychobiological a response involving both psychological and physical human responses

visceral responses certain feeling states that are tied to physical reactions/behaviour in a very direct way

Exhibit 5.4

Visceral Responses to Emotions by Consumers

Type of Appraisal/Situation	Emotion	Behavioural Reaction
Anticipation appraisal—Consumer waits while doctor examines X-rays	Worry	Grim face with turned-down eyebrows and cheeks. Hands likely near face. Consumer would rather avoid situation.
Outcome appraisal—Consumer wins a contest	Joy	Genuine smile, including turned-up cheeks and eyebrows and open hands. The consumer approaches the situation.
Equity appraisal—Consumer sees one customer receive faster and better service than he or she receives	Anger	Turned-down cheeks and eyebrows with clenched fists and hunched back. The consumer seeks to approach an agent of the company.
Agency appraisal—Consumer sees a waiter sneeze near a food preparation area	Disgust	Pinched-in facial expression and turned head. The body naturally withdraws (avoids) the situation.
Outcome appraisal—Consumer shows up at an important party inappropriately dressed	Embarrassment	Face blushes (turns red and feels hot), head cowers, and a strong desire to flee is experienced.

Source: O'Shaughnessy, J. and N. J. O'Shaughnessy (2003). *The Marketing Power of Emotions*. Oxford: Oxford University Press. Slama, M. E. (2003). "Book Review: *Emotions and Life: Perspectives from Psychology, Biology and Evolution,*" *Psychology & Marketing, 22 (January),* 97–101.

"motion" as a root. The fact that emotions are hardwired to behaviour has been explained as follows: "[Emotions are] fuels for drives, for all motion, every performance, and any behavioural act."[6]

Behaviours are closely tied to emotion, creating close links between emotions, consumer behaviour, and value. Thus, to this extent, marketing success is determined by emotions because actions bring value to a consumer to the extent that desirable emotional states can be created.[7] One of the secrets to the success of Starbucks is an environment that creates relaxing feelings. These emotions end up contributing to the overall value of the Starbucks experience. Price discounts also create emotions that drive consumer behaviour. A $200 discount on a $20,000 automobile may not create a lot of emotion, but a $200 discount on a $500 suit creates emotion that can cause consumers to drive out of their way to buy the product.[8]

5-3b Cognitive Appraisal Theory

What gives rise to consumer emotions? Psychologists have debated the different sources of emotions for decades, but **cognitive appraisal theory** represents an increasingly popular school of thought. Cognitive appraisal theory describes how specific types of thoughts can serve as a basis for specific emotions.

cognitive appraisal theory theory proposing that specific types of appraisal thoughts can be linked to specific types of emotions

When a consumer makes an appraisal, he or she is assessing some past, present, or future situation. Four types of cognitive appraisal are especially relevant for consumer behaviour.[9]

1. **Anticipation appraisal.** Focuses on the future and can elicit emotions like hopefulness or anxiety
2. **Agency appraisal.** Reviews responsibility for events and can evoke gratefulness, frustration, guilt, or sadness
3. **Equity appraisal.** Considers how fair some event is and can evoke emotions like warmth or anger
4. **Outcomes appraisal.** Considers how something turned out relative to one's goals and can evoke emotions like joyfulness, satisfaction, sadness, or pride

Exhibit 5.4 illustrates each of these appraisal types. A basic behavioural response is to either approach or avoid. Marketers generally benefit from approach responses and thus, they would like to create appraisals leading to emotions evoking approach behaviours, and avoid appraisals and emotions evoking avoidance.

Appraisals are often complicated enough to involve more than one type of appraisal and sometimes conflicting behavioural responses. Anticipatory appraisals can involve emotions such as hope. A consumer may appraise an ad for a charitable cause in a manner that evokes hope and he or she may become more willing to consider donation to that cause. However, the same ad could cause a consumer to feel guilty if he or she makes an agency appraisal and ends up feeling a sense of responsibility for the problem that the charity addresses. Guilt may be less effective than hope in gaining compliance to an appeal.[10] Consumers also make equity appraisals such as the perception of very unfair treatment. They end up feeling angry and may cope with the anger by seeking revenge.[11] Health services often create situations involving both anticipation and outcome appraisals. A consumer visiting the dentist may be worried about having cavities but feel joyful when the dentist provides a clean bill of health.

5-3c Emotion Terminology

MOOD

Moods can be distinguished from the broader concept of emotion based on specificity and time. Consumer **mood** can be thought of as a transient (temporary and changing) and general feeling state often characterized with simple descriptors such as a "good mood," a "bad mood," or even a "funky mood." Moods are generally considered less intense than many other emotional experiences; nevertheless, moods can influence consumer behaviour. Consumers in good moods tend to make decisions faster and to outspend their bad-mood counterparts. In addition, consumer mood affects satisfaction, with a bad mood being particularly detrimental to consumer satisfaction.[12] In this sense, marketers do not have complete control of the satisfaction they deliver.

Employees' moods can also affect consumption outcomes as they interact with consumer mood. A salesperson in a bad mood can negatively affect a consumer's overall attitude and willingness to buy. Perhaps curiously, consumers who enter a situation in a bad mood react better to service providers who are also in a bad mood than they do to service providers in a good mood. Exhibit 5.5 provides an overview of results from a study investigating this phenomenon. Consumers seem to be most receptive to an employee with a matching mood rather than to an employee who always has a positive mood.[13]

A consumer's mood can serve as a type of frame that can transfer into product value judgments. For example, when consumers are evaluating alternative vacation sites, they tend to rate sites more favourably when they evaluate them in a good mood as opposed to when they are in a bad mood.[14] Consumers make **mood-congruent judgments**, an evaluation in which the value of a target is influenced in a consistent way by one's mood.

Exhibit 5.5

Bad-Mood Consumers Seek Out Employees with Bad Moods

Source: Raghunathan, R. and J. R. Irwin (2001), "Walking the Hedonic Product Treadmill: Default Contrast and Mood-Based Assimilation in Judgments of Predicted Happiness with a Target Product," *Journal of Consumer Research*, 28 (December), 355–368.

As a result, marketers should prefer consumers to buy and consume their products when they are in a good mood. This has some implications for designing the purchase and service environment, as we will see in a later chapter.

Sometimes, consumers act to change their moods. Consumers may purchase a gift for themselves, for instance, as a way of improving their mood. In much the same way, research shows that consumers who are in bad moods can be more likely to be generous to others. The rationale is based on the hedonic value produced when one is generous.[15]

AFFECT

Affect is another term used to represent the feelings a consumer experiences during the consumption process. At times, affect is used as a general term encompassing both emotion and mood. However, in consumer behaviour, **consumer affect** is more often used to represent the feelings a consumer has about a particular product or activity.[16] Thus,

mood transient and general affective state

mood-congruent judgments evaluations in which the value of a target is influenced in a consistent way by one's mood

consumer affect feelings a consumer has about a particular product or activity when consumers like Tim Hortons coffee more than McDonald's coffee, they are expressing their positive affect toward the Tim Hortons brand.

MEASURING EMOTION

Marketing and consumer researchers place a great deal of emphasis on properly measuring consumer emotion because emotions play such a key role in shaping value. However, there is no consensus on the best way to measure consumer emotions.

5-4a Autonomic Measures

Perhaps autonomic measures offer the greatest validity in representing consumer emotions. **Autonomic measures** are those responses that are automatically recorded based on either automatic visceral reactions or neurological brain activity. These include facial reactions, physiological responses such as sweating in a galvanic skin response (GSR) or lie detector test, heart rate monitoring, and brain imaging, which can document activity in areas of the brain responsible for certain specific emotions.[17]

While these measurement approaches have the advantage of assessing emotional activity without requiring a volitional response from the consumer, they have the drawback of being intrusive. The researcher must attach some type of device to the consumer. Imagine a consumer wearing a net stocking cap attached to a computer by wires, in a lab, while a researcher tells him or her to watch some ads and act naturally, as if in his or her own living room. This would be very difficult to do. So, the disadvantage of this approach is the obtrusiveness created by the measuring device. Interestingly however, research suggests that these autonomic responses generally correspond fairly well to introspective self-reports of emotional experience.[18]

5-4b Self-Report Measures

Self-report measures are generally less obtrusive than biological measures because they don't involve physical contraptions. Self-report affect measures usually require consumers to recall their affect state from a recent experience, or to state the affect they are feeling at a given point in time. These paper-and-pencil tests usually involve a questionnaire; the process is not perfect, but generally results are valid enough to be useful to consumer and marketing researchers. However, many different options exist for applying self-report measures, and each option is usually based on a somewhat different perspective of emotion theory.

PANAS

One of the most commonly applied ways to assess one's emotional state is by using the **positive-affect–negative-affect scale (PANAS)**, which allows respondents to self-report the extent to which they feel one of 20 emotional adjectives. Exhibit 5.6 shows an example.

Researchers generally apply the PANAS to capture the relative amount of positive and negative emotion experienced by a consumer at a given point in time. However, this raises several questions about the nature of emotion, including whether positive and negative emotions can coexist.

Look at the items making up the PANAS. Each item represents either a good or a bad feeling. Thus, one might wonder why "inspired" and "upset" would both need to be measured. If a new product inspired a consumer, it would seem that the consumer could not be upset at the same time. If feeling good excludes feeling bad, then wouldn't a researcher need only to measure positive terms or negative terms to account for a consumer's feelings?

This might be an interesting academic question, but the issue also has practical implications if consumers react differently to equal amounts of positive and negative emotions. Does a mad consumer or a glad consumer react more strongly? Considerable attention in psychology and marketing research addresses this question and the evidence isn't crystal clear. The best we can say in addressing whether feeling bad is more influential than feeling good is "sometimes." Take a look at the following situations:

▸ A consumer is rating the feelings experienced when a pop-up box shows up on an electronics retailer website.

▸ A consumer is rating the feelings experienced when planning a wedding.

The first situation is quite simple. In situations like these, positive and negative emotions tend to be opposites. If people have bad feelings during the experience, they are unlikely to have any good feelings. The second situation is more complex and extends over a longer

autonomic measures responses that are automatically recorded based on either automatic visceral reactions or neurological brain activity

positive-affect–negative-affect scale (PANAS) self-report measure that asks respondents to rate the extent to which they feel one of 20 emotional adjectives

Exhibit 5.6

A Short-Form PANAS Application

The scale below lists words that describe the feelings or emotions that you may have experienced while shopping at Hometown Bathshop today. Please use the items to record the way you felt while shopping by indicating the extent to which you felt each of the feelings described. The scale ranges from 1 = very slightly or not at all to 5 = extremely.

	Very Slightly or Not at All	A Little	Moderately	Quite a Bit	Extremely
Upset	☐	☐	☐	☐	☐
Hostile	☐	☐	☐	☐	☐
Alert	☐	☐	☐	☐	☐
Ashamed	☐	☐	☐	☐	☐
Inspired	☐	☐	☐	☐	☐
Nervous	☐	☐	☐	☐	☐
Determined	☐	☐	☐	☐	☐
Attentive	☐	☐	☐	☐	☐
Afraid	☐	☐	☐	☐	☐
Active	☐	☐	☐	☐	☐

Source: Thompson, E.R. (2007), "Development and Validation of an Internationally Reliable Short-Form of the Positive and Negative Affect Schedule (PANAS)," *Journal of Cross-Cultural Psychology* 38, 227. Reprinted by permission of SAGE Publications.

period. In situations such as these, bad and good feelings do not cancel each other out completely, and people can indeed experience some levels of both.

Thus, when consumer researchers are studying highly complex situations, a scale like the PANAS allows them to capture both positive and negative dimensions of emotional experience. The possibility exists that each dimension might explain somewhat unique experiences. For example, positive affect is highly related to increased spending, but negative emotion is not. The more good feelings a consumer has, the more he or she buys. A consumer experiencing negative emotions may still complete the shopping task, but he or she may also be more likely to look for another place to shop next time.

PAD

The **pleasure–arousal–dominance (PAD) scale** asks consumers to rate their feelings using a number of semantic differential (bipolar opposite) items that capture emotions in these three dimensions. The theory behind PAD, unlike PANAS, is that pleasure—the evaluative dimension of emotion—is **bipolar**, meaning that if one feels joyful, one cannot also experience sadness.[19] Arousal, which is the degree to which one feels energized, excited, or interested, is also seen as bipolar, in that a consumer is either aroused or bored. Likewise, dominance, the degree to which one feels in control of a situation, is also bipolar. Thus, researchers have combined the PAD and PANAS approaches and applied adjectives taken from the PAD scale and put them in a format similar to that in Exhibit 5.6, rather than a semantic differential.

pleasure–arousal–dominance (PAD) scale self-report measure that asks respondents to rate feelings using semantic differential items. Acronym stands for pleasure-arousal-dominance

bipolar situation wherein if one feels joy he or she cannot also experience sadness

You Should be Ashamed!?

Some ads have a way of making us feel bad! They can remind us that we sometimes do things that are inconsistent with our physical or moral well-being. These ads may include disturbing images of distressed animals. Do ads for diet and health products make you want to turn away? What about ads that encourage donations to prevent starvation among developing-world children or cruelty to animals? Do images of distressed children and animals evoke the same feelings?

Ads like these typically evoke emotions like shame, guilt, or perhaps disgust. The negative emotions are sometimes counteracted by empathetic feelings that encourage approach behaviours like giving. This is really a tricky business though, because negative reactions create avoidance as the consumer feels distressed by having to see the images. Here are a few things that research suggests about the situation:

1. **If part of a captive audience (as in a movie theatre), consumers who feel personally distressed (ashamed) are likely to react much as those who feel truly sympathetic.**

2. **Consumers feel more empathy and give more when an ad provides a victim's personal identity.**

3. **Empathetic feelings don't always lead to a prosocial response, because consumers are sometimes inundated with charitable appeals.**

4. **Negative emotions experienced repeatedly may cause consumers to give up on a cause.**

Sources: G Usher, K., Park, T., & Foster, K. (2013). "The experience of weight gain as a result of taking second-generation antipsychotic medications: the mental health consumer perspective." *Journal of Psychiatric and Mental Health Nursing*, 20(9), 801–806. E. G. Danit and L. Levontin, "Giving from a Distance: Putting the Charitable Organization at the Center of the Donation Appeal," *Journal of Consumer Psychology*, 23 (April 2013), 197–211.

Many researchers use the PAD or a modified PAD approach to study retail atmospherics across many environments, including museums and parks, and even in advertising contexts.[20] Because the scale captures arousal separately, the approach is advantageous when the degree of activation or excitement is of particular interest. For example, when consumers go to a movie, they may feel pleased but not excited. Similarly, the PAD approach allows a separate accounting for feelings of dominance, sometimes known as control. When consumers feel lower control, situational influences play a greater role in shaping their behaviour.

5-5 DIFFERENCES IN EMOTIONAL BEHAVIOUR

Not all consumers react emotionally or show their emotions to the same extent or in the same way.[21] Two consumers, for instance, may receive the same poor service from a crowded retail store. One might complain furiously to store management, while the other simply walks away to find a more quiet shopping environment. Emotions, as discussed earlier, are deeply tied to personal motivations and traits. Thus, personality

In situations like this, one consumer may become angry and another may become sad. This customer appears to be angry!

One question asked by many who study emotions is whether women are more emotional than men.

characteristics can affect the way consumers respond or demonstrate their emotions. For instance, neuroticism, an important personality trait, is positively related with the amount of negative affect a consumer reports in various service settings.[22]

5-5a Emotional Involvement

Motivation and involvement are closely related, as we discussed earlier in the chapter. The things that tap our deepest emotions have the ability to evoke the greatest value. This brings us to emotional involvement, meaning the type of deep personal interest that evokes strongly felt feelings associated with some object or activity. Emotional involvement drives one to consume generally through relatively strong hedonic motivations. Often, emotional involvement can make a consumer appear irrational. Consider the amount of money and time a hockey fan will spend following his or her favourite team. In addition to spending thousands of dollars for season tickets and possibly spending years on waiting lists to get those tickets, many sports fans also buy team merchandise and special television packages to ensure they are part of the full-season experience. The consumer is deeply and emotionally involved with the team and in many ways becomes one with the team (see the case study at the end of this chapter).

Other consumers may experience deeply held feelings over certain fashion products, automobiles, music, wine, or even social networking via the Internet. A consumer experiencing a fantastic dinner with an exemplary bottle of wine is achieving a total customer experience, a maximum value experience, through a combination of high emotional involvement and products that served as expected or better than expected.[23]

Emotional involvement can be increased by receiving something extra with products purchased. For instance, if someone buys a nice leather backpack, the company might consider adding a premium, which may include a phone holster, calculator, or gift certificate to a local pub. In this way, the consumer may develop an emotional attachment or become emotionally involved with the product and with the brand.[24]

Perhaps there is no better example of how different consumers react emotionally than the responses different consumers get when involved with a motion picture. Some consumers have difficulty getting through any heart-touching scene without tears coming to their eyes—which generally means they like the movie. Other consumers see the same scene and are bored. They would rather be watching a classic slapstick movie like *Caddyshack* or *Dumb and Dumber*, which may bring them to tears through laughter.

FLOW

All consumers can probably relate to the experience of enjoying a good book or a game like Candy Crush so much that one loses awareness of time passing. When this occurs, a consumer has achieved a state of **flow**, meaning extremely high emotional involvement in which a consumer is engrossed in an activity.

A great deal of the work on flow deals with computer-related activities. For instance, consumers can become so involved in video games or social networking that they have little physical awareness of their surroundings.[25] When a parent calls a child for dinner and the child seems to be ignoring him or her, the child may be so caught up in gaming that there is no conscious awareness of being called. Generally, consumers can become addicted when their level of obsession with an activity becomes too high. In the extreme, consumers can become addicted to video game consumption,[26] and similarly, more and more consumers exhibit Facebook addiction symptoms, which can include:[27]

▸ **Spending more than one hour a day on Facebook**

▸ **Ignoring work to stay on Facebook**

▸ **Feeling more attached to the world of Facebook than the real world**

▸ **Replacing sleep with time on Facebook**

▸ **Becoming nervous when facing an extended period away from Facebook (more than a day)**

Addictions like this are driven in part by a desire to achieve the state of flow where one escapes the real world and realizes high hedonic value.[28]

Highly involved shoppers sometimes achieve a flow experience. When this occurs, the consumer is more likely to spend time browsing, spend more money, make repeat purchases, and be more prone to impulse purchasing.[29] Online consumers can pursue a flow state while shopping; however, interruptions in Internet service, poor

flow extremely high emotional involvement in which a consumer is engrossed in an activity

The state of flow is value enhancing, but can it facilitate addiction—such as Facebook addiction?

navigational clues, or slow page load times can inhibit the flow experience and lower both utilitarian and hedonic shopping value.[30] If the consumer achieves hedonic value, positive outcomes can result for both the consumer and the marketer. However, the consumer must be able to maintain control of the situation to avoid compulsive or addictive behaviours.

5-5b Emotional Expressiveness

Not all consumers express their emotions as obviously as others. **Emotional expressiveness** represents the extent to which a consumer shows outward behavioural signs and otherwise reacts obviously to emotional experiences. The consumer with relatively high emotional expressiveness is likely to react in some way to outcomes that are unexpected. A bad poker player, for example, is unable to hide emotions from other players, and, as such, his or her reaction displays high emotional expressiveness.

Many who study emotions ask whether women are more emotional than men. Researchers do not provide a clear answer to this question. For instance, psychologists interested in studying the human experience of, and reaction to, disgust have conducted experiments in which subjects are exposed to films

emotional expressiveness extent to which a consumer shows outward behavioural signs and otherwise reacts obviously to emotional experiences

emotional intelligence awareness of the emotions experienced in a given situation and the ability to control reactions to these emotions

depicting either an actual amputation or a man being swarmed by cockroaches.[31] Male and female subjects report on average the same level of disgust while viewing the films. However, female respondents are more likely than males to react to the disgusting experience by leaving the room before the film is finished. Studies show similar emotional expression by females for other emotions besides disgust, both positive and negative.[32] Research suggests that when male and female consumers react with similar emotions, women express the emotions more noticeably.[33] Because of this, to the extent that a marketer can judge a consumer's emotional reaction, female consumers may prove more valuable in signalling poor or outstanding service than would male consumers.

5-5c Emotional Intelligence

Emotions can be useful in determining the most appropriate reaction to events. **Emotional intelligence** is a term used to capture one's awareness of the emotions experienced in a situation and ability to control reactions to these emotions. This includes awareness of the emotions experienced by the individual as well as an awareness and sympathy for the emotions experienced by others. Emotional intelligence (EI) is a multifaceted concept, and Exhibit 5.7 illustrates EI components. High EI consumers are able to use awareness

Exhibit 5.7

Emotional Intelligence Consists of Multiple Elements

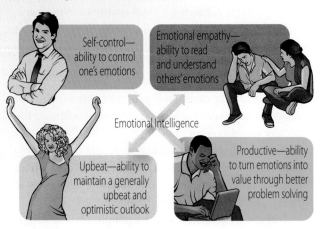

Self-control—ability to control one's emotions

Emotional empathy—ability to read and understand others' emotions

Emotional Intelligence

Upbeat—ability to maintain a generally upbeat and optimistic outlook

Productive—ability to turn emotions into value through better problem solving

Source: Various authors have defined EI with different numbers of emotions and using different terms to capture dimensions. These are a composite of common dimensions. For a review, see Frye, C. M., R. Bennett, and S. Caldwell (2006), "Team Emotional Intelligence and Team Interpersonal Process Effectiveness," *Mid-American Journal of Business, 21,* 49–56.

of emotions in decision making and are better able to manage their own emotions and exhibit self-control.[34]

In a marketing context, salespeople with high emotional intelligence are more effective in closing sales with consumers than are salespeople with low emotional intelligence.[35] Sales companies are increasingly realizing the benefits of employees with high EI. EI training is becoming commonplace as marketers attempt to get consumers to buy more and to be more satisfied with the things they buy.[36]

5-6 EMOTION, MEANING, AND SCHEMA-BASED AFFECT

What is the relation between cognition and emotion? Intuitively, emotion and cognition seem so different that one can easily presume they are completely independent of each other. However, emotion and cognition are actually quite closely related, and this is seen clearly in the role that affect, mood, and emotion can play in signalling and developing meaning. This section focuses on the interplay between emotion and cognitive learning.

5-6a Semantic Wiring

In a previous chapter, we learned that in our memory, a network connects all concepts to other concepts.

A concept such as "toaster" is closely linked with a concept like "breakfast" but very remotely linked with another concept like "hurricane." A consumer's ability to remember things about brands and products can be explained using theory developed around the principles of *semantic or associative* networks. Remember, all concepts are linked to all other concepts, but some are linked strongly and others very weakly. It's difficult to put weak concepts together.

Although the term *semantic* is more closely tied to cognitive thought processes, the active processing and storage of knowledge is significantly influenced by emotions in several ways. The general expression **emotional effect on memory** refers to relatively superior recall for information presented with mild affective content compared with similar information presented in an affectively neutral way.[37]

The implications for marketing are fairly direct. Marketing communications that present product information in a way that evokes mild levels of emotions will tend to be more effective in producing recall than communications that are affectively neutral.[38] Caution is needed in executing such communications because intense emotions are more complicated to deal with and can sometimes even distract consumers from the task of actually processing information. But clearly, emotion and cognition can become closely linked semantically in the mind of a consumer. Exhibit 5.8 illustrates this point.

5-6b Mood-Congruent Recall

Many consumers can remember their first day of school, first airplane trip, or first visit to a theme park. In each case, products and brands are associated with the experience. Likewise, in each case, each event is associated with a fairly specific mood. For many consumers, the first day of school is filled

Exhibit 5.8

Illustration of Emotion Aiding Learning

Courtesy of Roots Canada.

Courtesy of Roots Canada.

emotional effect on memory relatively superior recall for information presented with mild affective content compared with similar information presented in an affectively neutral way with apprehension, the first airplane ride may be a blend of fear and excitement, and a visit to a theme park is associated with joy.

Autobiographical memories are memories of previous, meaningful events in one's life. Consumers are more likely to recall autobiographical memories characterized by specific moods when the same mood occurs again in the future.[39] Simply put, moods tend to match memories.

Mood-congruent recall means that to the extent that consumers' moods can be controlled, their memories and evaluations can be influenced. Music is one tool useful in inducing moods. When music sets a mood, consumers will recall products associated with that mood more readily. In addition, consumers in good moods tend to evaluate products positively compared with consumers in bad moods, and vice versa.[40]

5-6c Nostalgia

Nostalgia affects consumers in a manner similar to that of mood-congruent recall and autobiographical memory. Recall that we introduced nostalgia in an earlier chapter as a yearning for the past motivated by the belief that previous times were somehow more pleasant. Nostalgia can motivate product purchases as consumers attempt to relive the pleasant feelings of the past. Music, toys, magazines, and movies are products that consumers report commonly buying in association with feelings of nostalgia.[41] The large number of advertisements that include popular "oldies" songs illustrates attempts at evoking nostalgic feelings. Further, consumers become more willing to make purchases when a nostalgic ad evokes or recaptures a childhood mood.

5-6d Schema-Based Affect

As we know from consumer information processing theory, knowledge of familiar things becomes organized in a cognitive unit of meaning known as a schema. A schema contains the knowledge of a brand, a product, or any concept. However, a schema is not a purely cognitive entity. Schemata are developed and reinforced through actual experience. For instance, we come to perceive what a car salesperson truly is based on our total experience with that category. Experience involves more than cognition. When we encounter a car salesperson or hear stories that involve car salespeople, we also experience some type of affect or emotion. These emotions become part of the meaning for a category in the form of **schema-based affect**.

Schema-based affect helps provide meaning and thus is another example of how affect and cognition are wired together. However, a consumer can actually experience schema-based affect once a schema becomes active. For example, a consumer who fears going to a dentist can actually experience true nervousness and apprehension simply by thinking about a visit to the dentist. This makes the dentist visit schema active.

Exhibit 5.9 displays a typical schema for a car salesperson, including the schema-based affect.[42] The exhibit displays schema-based affect in yellow. When managers realize that a category is associated with negative affect,

autobiographical memories cognitive representation of meaningful events in one's life

mood-congruent recall consumers will remember information better when the mood they are currently in matches the mood they were in when originally exposed to the information

schema-based affect emotions that become stored as part of the meaning for a category (a schema)

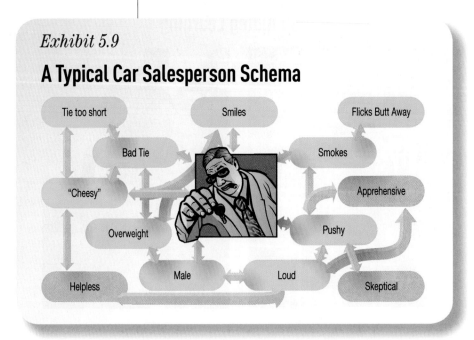

Exhibit 5.9

A Typical Car Salesperson Schema

Tie too short

Smiles

Flicks Butt Away

Bad Tie

Smokes

"Cheesy"

Apprehensive

Overweight

Pushy

Helpless

Male

Loud

Skeptical

as in this case, they may be wise either to change the characteristic attributes (in this case, of the car salesperson) to prevent the schema from becoming or remaining active, or to activate an entirely different schema (i.e., team member). Further, negative schema-based emotions of this type can interfere with the consumer's ability to process information about the product. In recent years, many car dealerships have changed the appearance of their salespeople to avoid activating this schema. More females perform the job and the staff attire is more casual, generally sporting a brand logo.

Exhibit 5.10 displays examples of schema-based affect that can influence consumers' reactions to consumption experiences.

AESTHETIC LABOUR

Aesthetic labour deals specifically with employees who must carefully manage their own personal appearance as a requisite to performing their job well and fitting what managers see as the stereotype for their particular company's service. Many service employees perform aesthetic labour, including cosmetic representatives, fashion models, and flight attendants and table servers for such companies as Air Korea and Hooters. The belief is that a specific appearance is needed to generate the appropriate emotional reaction in the consumer. These emotions promote behaviour that can ultimately lead to loyalty.

Courtesy of Quit Victoria, Australia. Used with permission

Many ads evoke negative self-conscious emotions. This powerful anti-smoking ad's tag line says: "If this is how a child feels when they lose you for a minute, just imagine how he'd feel if he lost you for life."

5-6e Self-Conscious Emotions

Getting laughed at can be painful. Marketers sometimes execute communications designed to take advantage of consumers' natural tendency to avoid ridicule. Apple introduced a campaign in the late 2000s in which a *cool dude* using an Apple product pokes fun at a *nerdy dude* using a Windows product.

aesthetic labour effort put forth by employees in carefully managing their appearance as a requisite for performing their job well

---

Exhibit 5.10

Examples of Schema-Based Affect

Schema	Affect	Typical Consumer Reaction
Disney	Joyfulness, fun	Consumers have increased brand equity and lower price sensitivity for Disney products.
Individual countries (the United Kingdom, France, the United States, Japan, Israel, China)	Consumers may have slightly different affect associated with each country	Consumers are less favourable toward products manufactured in countries for which that consumer's schema evokes negative affect.
Telemarketing	Aggravation	Consumers often hang up quickly as a built-in avoidance response.
Baby	Tenderness, warmth	Products associated with babies are viewed more favourably.
Sports star	Excitement	Consumers may generalize excitement to products and services endorsed by the star.
Stereotypes	Each stereotype evokes slightly different affect	The affect associated with the stereotype can cause consumers to be more or less willing to approach and may alter information processing.

Bad Hair Days—Bad Times!

Procter and Gamble (P&G) probably won't win a Nobel Peace Prize for its research, but some consumers may feel it deserves one for its efforts to stamp out bad hair days. P&G research relies on the PANAS to help identify just how bad a bad hair day can make a girl feel.

Bad hair days can really bring a consumer down—they make women feel more hostile, ashamed, nervous, and even guilty! Many of these feelings fall into the category of self-conscious emotions, and have a moral element when a consumer perceives that he or she has violated some personal or societal norm ("I shouldn't be seen with hair like this! It's embarrassing!!"). P&G's Pantene brand offers help by designing shampoos aimed at keeping hair healthy. When they feel good about their hair, consumers can face the day feeling excited, proud, and confident instead of angry, embarrassed, or ashamed. That's good for the consumer and everyone around her!

Consumers will act to avoid negative feelings, but negative feelings also motivate a consumer to find a solution. Think about the ways negative feelings cause you to realize the need to act!

iStockphoto.com/tderden

Sources: Byron, E. (2010), "Wash Away Bad Hair Days," *The Wall Street Journal*, 255 (June 30), D1–D3; Honea, H. (2005), "Investigating the Impact of Negative Self-Conscious Emotions on Consumer Memory, Processing and Purchase," *Advances in Consumer Research*, 32, 189–192; Chun, H., V. M. Patrick, and D. J. MacInnis (2007), "Making Prudent vs. Impulsive Choices: The Role of Anticipated Shame and Guilt on Consumer Self-Control," *Advances in Consumer Research*, 34, 715–719.

Other brands emphasize how embarrassed one should feel for having less than pearly white teeth, body odour (BO), bad hair, a less than beautiful golf swing, too big a waist, cankles, and on and on. These appeals work because they cause consumers to appraise themselves in some way and play on any resulting negative self-conscious emotions.[43] **Self-conscious emotions** result from some evaluation or reflection of one's own behaviour—which can include both actions and failures to act. Self-conscious emotions include pride, embarrassment, guilt, regret, shame, and hope. Consumers experiencing negative self-conscious emotions can perceive not only the need to rectify some problem, but also the need to restore their self-esteem.

self-conscious emotions specific emotions that result from some evaluation or reflection of one's own behaviour, including pride, shame, guilt, and embarrassment

STUDY TOOLS 5

LOCATED AT THE BACK OF THE TEXTBOOK
☐ Rip out Chapter Review Card

LOCATED AT NELSON.COM/STUDENT
☐ Review Key Terms Flashcards (print or online)

☐ Download audio summaries to review on the go

☐ Complete practice quizzes to prepare for tests

☐ Watch video on Marketing at Jordan's Furniture for a real company example

CASE STUDY

Case

The Most Valuable Team in Hockey

At the end of 2014, the average professional hockey team was worth about $490 million—more than double the average team's value of $240 million in 2011. That is not a bad return on investment over three years! Three teams were valued at $1 billion or more: Toronto Maple Leafs ($1.3 billion), New York Rangers ($1.1 billion) and Montreal Canadiens ($1 billion).

The sport's popularity has been growing. Sponsorships and merchandise sales have also increased. Yet many teams—such as the Carolina Hurricanes, Columbus Blue Jackets and Phoenix Coyotes—are in relatively poor financial shape and are worth significantly less than the average NHL franchise.

In contrast, Toronto's team is the league's most valuable at $1.3 billion, with an operating income of more than $70.6 million. Although the Leafs played their last playoff hockey game on May 4, 2004, and they have not won the Stanley Cup since 1967, a Leafs ticket is coveted and games are sold out.

How can an underperforming product be the most valuable? Relatively good teams like the St. Louis Blues, Nashville Predators, and Tampa Bay Lightning are worth $235 million, $250 million, and $230 million, respectively, and they are all losing money.

One consolation for Maple Leafs fans is that at least the team is not the Edmonton Oilers. The Oilers won the draft lottery three years in a row—that is, they were the worst team in 2009–10 and 2010–11 and the second worst team in 2011–12. In recent years, losing has become as much a tradition as winning was for the Oilers during their dynasty years in the 1980s. However, like the Maple Leafs, the Oilers are profitable and more valuable (at $475 million) than many of the other teams in the NHL. It is worth noting that the valuation for Edmonton's team was set before they were again incredibly lucky in the 2015 draft, winning the number one pick for the fourth time in the past six years, which allows them to draft highly touted Conor McDavid!

While strong teams are wondering what they can do to make money selling hockey in markets like St. Louis and Nashville, weak teams like the Toronto Maple Leafs

Michael Matthews/Alamy

and the Edmonton Oilers are able to sell out their arenas while putting a relatively poor product on the ice. Consumers seem to be getting something from being hockey fans that is uncorrelated with a winning team. From the perspective of the NHL, it is important that the league can survive and thrive across all 30 teams. Team presidents and general managers are left to wonder what the true value of hockey is for its fans. At the same time, other businesses dream of building the high levels of emotional involvement and blind loyalty that the Leafs and Oilers seem to enjoy.

Sources: Zeisberger, Mike (2015), "Oilers Euphoric, Sabres Not So Much With Draft Lottery," *Toronto Sun* (April 18) accessed at http://www.torontosun.com/2015/04/18/edmonton-oilers-win-first-overall-nhl-draft-pick-yet-again on June 1, 2015. The Canadian Press (2015), "Babcock Aims to Put Maple Leafs 'Back on the Map,'" *The Toronto Star* (May 21), http://www.theglobeandmail.com/sports/hockey/maple-leafs-introduce-babcock-as-new-coach/article24542388/, accessed June 1, 2015. Orzanian, Mike (2014), "The Most Value Teams in the NHL," *Forbes* (November 25), http://www.forbes.com/sites/mikeozanian/2014/11/25/the-most-valuable-teams-in-the-nhl/, accessed June 1, 2015.

QUESTIONS

1 According to Maslow's hierarchy of needs, what value do the Toronto Maple Leafs provide to their fans?

2 Beyond the team's performance on the ice, do franchises like the Toronto Maple Leafs and Edmonton Oilers do anything else to facilitate emotional involvement?

3 What type of appraisal might Maple Leafs fans engage in? What emotional and behavioural reaction is that appraisal likely to generate?

4 Does nostalgia affect how fans feel about underperforming products, such as the Toronto Maple Leafs or the Edmonton Oilers? If so, how?

6 Personality, Lifestyles, and the Self-Concept

LEARNING OBJECTIVES

After studying this chapter, the student should be able to:

6-1 Define personality and know how various approaches to studying personality can be applied to consumer behaviour.

6-2 Discuss major traits that have been examined in consumer research.

6-3 Understand why lifestyles and psychographics are important to the study of consumer behaviour.

6-4 Comprehend the role of the self-concept in consumer behaviour.

6-5 Understand the concept of self-congruency and how it applies to consumer behaviour issues.

INTRODUCTION

This chapter focuses on consumer personality, lifestyles, and self-concept. As such, the chapter deals with what are known as **individual difference variables**, which are descriptions of how individual consumers differ according to specific traits or patterns of behaviour.[1] These concepts have several applications to both consumer research and marketing practice. Marketing managers are especially interested in identifying consumer characteristics that are associated with the likelihood of purchasing products. Concepts like personality, lifestyle, and self-concept help describe these differences.

individual difference variables descriptions of how individual consumers differ according to specific traits or patterns of behaviour

personality totality of thoughts, emotions, intentions, and behaviours that a person exhibits consistently as he or she adapts to the environment

6-1 PERSONALITY AND CONSUMER BEHAVIOUR

Personality has been studied for many years, and the term has been defined in a number of different ways. We define **personality** as the totality of thoughts, emotions, intentions, and behaviours that a person exhibits consistently as he or she adapts to the environment.[2] This definition highlights the *cognitive* (thoughts), *affective* (emotions), *motivational* (intentions), and *behavioural* (behaviours) aspects that are central to the study of personality. Personality is but one characteristic that helps explain why a particular behaviour—for example, listening to the

"Although all consumers ultimately seek value, some are more highly focused on value than others".

band Mumford and Sons—provides great value to one consumer but none to another.

Personality exhibits a number of distinct qualities, including:

1. *Personality is unique to an individual.* Personality helps distinguish consumers based on the specific characteristics each exhibits. Consumers differ in personalities, although some characteristics, or traits, may be shared across individuals.

2. *Personality can be conceptualized as a combination of specific traits or characteristics.* Like all consumers, your overall personality is really a combination of many stable characteristics, or traits. In fact, for many psychologists, personality psychology deals exclusively with the study of human traits.[3]

3. *Personality traits are relatively stable and interact with situations to influence behaviour.* Personality traits are expected to remain consistent across situations. However, consumer researchers realize the importance of situational influencers, and the combined influence of situations and traits greatly influences specific behaviours (this is referred to as an interaction between the person and the situation).[4] To illustrate, imagine how an impatient person acts in a crowded restaurant.

4. *Specific behaviours can vary across time.* One major issue in personality research is that simply knowing a consumer possesses a specific trait does not allow us to predict a specific behaviour. For example, knowing that a consumer is "materialistic" does not allow the researcher to predict the exact type of product the person may buy. For this reason, personality researchers often advocate an **aggregation approach** in which behaviours are measured over time, rather

aggregation approach
approach to studying personality in which behaviour is assessed at a number of points in time

than relying on a single measure of behaviour at one point in time.

As we have mentioned, marketing managers are particularly interested in how consumers differ according to their personalities. Consistent patterns of thoughts, emotions, intentions, and behaviours can signal the need for individualized marketing campaigns, and today's marketers are becoming quite adept at individualizing messages. To understand how personalities differ across consumers, it is important to begin with a description of the various approaches to studying the concept. There are a number of ways to explore the human personality; however, here we focus on two popular approaches: the psychoanalytic approach and the trait approach. These approaches have received considerable consumer research attention.

6-1a Psychoanalytic Approach to Personality

According to famous psychologist Sigmund Freud, human behaviour is influenced by an inner struggle between various systems within the personality system.[5] His approach, commonly referred to as the **psychoanalytic approach to personality**, is applicable to both motivation and personality inquiry. Freud's approach highlights the importance of unconscious mental processes in influencing behaviour.

For Freud, the human personality consists of three important components: the *id*, the *superego*, and the *ego*. The **id** focuses on pleasure-seeking and immediate gratification. It operates on a **pleasure principle** that motivates a person to focus on maximizing pleasure and minimizing pain. One's id, therefore, focuses on hedonic value. Indeed, a key concept in the id is the *libido*.

The libido represents a drive for sexual pleasure, although some researchers view it in slightly different ways. The **superego** works against the id by motivating behaviour that matches societal norms and expectations. The superego can be conceptualized as being similar to a consumer's conscience. The ego focuses on resolving the conflicts between the id and the superego. The **ego** works largely in accordance with the **reality principle**. Under this principle, the ego seeks to satisfy the id within the constraints of society. As such, the ego attempts to balance the desires of the id with the constraints of, and expectations found in, the superego.

PSYCHOANALYTIC APPROACH AND MOTIVATION RESEARCH

In the early days of consumer research, researchers applied psychoanalytic tools to try to identify explanations for behaviour. This was known as the **motivational research era**. Consumer researchers in this era utilized tools such as *depth interviews* and *focus groups* to improve their understanding of inner motives and needs.[6] Researchers applying depth interviews try to explore deep-seated motivations by asking consumers to describe an activity through a series of probing questions. As discussed in our motivation chapter, motivations are the reasons or driving forces behind actions.

Suppose a researcher is studying a consumer who has a strong preference for rhythm and blues (R&B) music. The researcher might ask the following probing questions:

▶ "How do you feel when you hear R&B?"

▶ "What does it mean to you to feel this way?"

▶ "What kinds of things do you think about when you listen to R&B?"

▶ "What would you do if you could no longer listen to R&B?"

Although motivational research has been popular, in general, the motivational research era proved disappointing because it did not spawn any compelling, practical consumer behaviour theories or guidelines for marketing actions. Nonetheless, Freud clearly influenced the study of personality and consumer behaviour.[7] To this day, for instance, consumer researchers remain interested in discovering consumer motivations below the level of conscious awareness.

As an example of the influence of deeply held motivations influencing behaviour, consider the id. Although the use of sexual imagery in advertising is often criticized, overtly sexual advertisements are

psychoanalytic approach to personality approach to personality research, advocated by Sigmund Freud, that suggests personality results from a struggle between inner motives and societal pressures to follow rules and expectations

id the personality component in psychoanalytic theory that focuses on pleasure-seeking motives and immediate gratification

pleasure principle principle found in psychoanalytic theory that describes the factor that motivates pleasure-seeking behaviour within the id

superego component in psychoanalytic theory that works against the id by motivating behaviour that matches the expectations and norms of society

ego component in psychoanalytic theory that attempts to balance the struggle between the superego and the id

reality principle the principle in psychoanalytic theory under which the ego attempts to satisfy the id within societal constraints

motivational research era era in consumer research that focused heavily on psychoanalytic approaches rather common. In fact, the old adage that "Sex sells!" may be directly tied to the Freudian approach. The use of phallic and ovarian symbols in advertising may be traced to a belief that such messages appeal to, and provide value for, the id.

6-1b Trait Approach to Personality

While the psychoanalytic approach helped set the groundwork for much of consumer personality research, the **trait approach to personality** has received significant attention over the past few decades. A **trait** is defined as a distinguishable characteristic that describes one's tendency to act in a relatively consistent manner.

Not surprisingly, there are multiple approaches available for consumer researchers. Here, we discuss the differences between nomothetic and idiographic approaches, and between single- versus multi-trait approaches.

NOMOTHETIC VERSUS IDIOGRAPHIC APPROACHES

The nomothetic perspective and the idiographic perspective can be distinguished as follows.[8] The **nomothetic perspective** is a "variable-centred" approach that focuses on particular variables, or traits, that exist across a number of consumers. The goal of this perspective is to find common personality traits that can be studied across people.

An example helps explain the nomothetic approach. Consider university student Tia. Tia's friends notice that she is very conscientious with her work. That is, she's

Does this ad appeal to some deeply held motivation?

very organized, efficient, and precise in everything that she does. Of course, many other people can be described in this way. Here, the focus is on the conscientiousness trait, and it is used to help describe the characteristics of a number of consumers.

The **idiographic perspective** focuses on the total person and the uniqueness of his or her psychological makeup. Attention is not placed on individual traits or how they can be studied across multiple consumers. Rather, the focus is on understanding the complexity of each individual consumer.

The trait approach takes a nomothetic approach to personality. That is, the trait approach assumes that the human personality can be described as a combination of traits that can be studied across consumers. From this perspective, individuals can be described by using various trait descriptors.

SINGLE-TRAIT AND MULTIPLE-TRAIT APPROACHES

We can further distinguish between single-trait and multi-trait approaches to consumer research. With the **single-trait approach**, the focus of the researcher is on one particular trait. Here, researchers can learn more about the trait and how it affects behaviour. For example, a researcher may want to investigate the competitiveness trait and how it affects the selection of athletic wear. Perhaps highly competitive consumers will prefer one brand of athletic clothing over another.

With the **multiple-trait approach**, combinations of traits are examined and the total effect of the collection of traits is considered. Here, the researcher is interested in trait scores on numerous traits as potential predictors of consumer behaviour. The prediction of individual behaviour tends to be stronger with the multiple-trait approach.[9] However, both the single- and multiple-trait approaches have been used extensively in consumer research.

trait approach to personality approaches in personality research that focus on specific consumer traits as motivators of various consumer behaviours

trait distinguishable characteristic that describes one's tendency to act in a relatively consistent manner

nomothetic perspective variable-centred approach to personality that focuses on particular traits that exist across a number of people

idiographic perspective approach to personality that focuses on understanding the complexity of each individual consumer

single-trait approach approach in trait research wherein the focus is on one particular trait

multiple-trait approach approach in trait research wherein the focus remains on combinations of traits

Athletic consumers are often very competitive.

Courtesy Pro Hockey Life

6-2 SPECIFIC TRAITS EXAMINED IN CONSUMER RESEARCH

To say that there are many traits that can be studied would be a serious understatement! To illustrate, researchers Gordon Allport and Henry Odbert identified nearly 18,000 names for human characteristics found in *Webster's New International Dictionary*. And that was in 1936![10] Although numerous traits have received attention, we will discuss only a handful of important traits found in consumer research, including value consciousness, materialism, innovativeness, need for cognition, competitiveness, productivity orientation, and others.

6-2a Value Consciousness

As we have stated throughout this text, value is at the heart of consumer behaviour. Although all consumers ultimately seek value, some consumers are more highly focused on value than are others. As such, value consciousness is often studied as a trait. **Value consciousness** represents the tendency for consumers to focus on maximizing what is received from a transaction as compared to what is given.

Research reveals that value consciousness is an important concept in consumer behaviour. For example, value consciousness underlies tendencies to perform behaviours such as redeeming coupons.[11] Value-conscious consumers can be expected to pay close attention to the resources that they devote to transactions and

value consciousness the extent to which consumers tend to maximize what they receive from a transaction as compared to what they give

materialism extent to which material goods have importance in a consumer's life

to the benefits that they receive. In today's turbulent economy, value consciousness is an important trait to study.

MATERIALISM

Materialism refers to the extent to which material goods are important in a consumer's life. Most Western cultures, including Canadian culture, are generally thought of as being relatively materialistic. However, within each culture, the degree to which each individual is materialistic varies. Studying this trait has been very popular among consumer researchers, and numerous studies have examined the impact of materialism on various consumer behaviours.

Materialism is seen as consisting of three separate dimensions:[12]

▸ *Possessiveness.* A tendency to retain control and ownership over possessions

▸ *Non-generosity.* An unwillingness to share with others

▸ *Envy.* Resentment that arises as a result of another's belongings and a desire to acquire similar possessions

Highly materialistic consumers tend to be possessive, non-generous, and envious of others' possessions. Not surprisingly, these consumers view possessions as a means of achieving happiness and they tend to hold on to possessions as long as possible.[13] What's more, research even indicates that materialistic people establish strong bonds with products in order to ease fears regarding their own mortality![14] Products can be a real source of comfort for materialistic consumers.

Interestingly, consumers today commonly bring many of their favourite material possessions into the workplace. Personal possessions in the workplace can produce calm feelings and stabilize an employee's sense of self.[15] In this way, material possessions play an important part in self-expression. That is, material possessions help consumers express who they think they are, and even who they would like to be.[16] These issues are discussed later in the chapter.

Materialism tends to differ among generations, with lower materialism scores typically found among older consumers.[17] Indeed, younger consumers have long been thought of as relatively materialistic. A change in the prevalence of materialism does appear to be occurring, however. Although Canadian culture is widely viewed as materialistic, research suggests that consumers are beginning to "downshift." Downshifting refers to a conscious decision to reduce one's material consumption. This may be a positive development as high levels of materialism can adversely affect debt levels and personal relationships.[18]

INNOVATIVENESS

Consumer **innovativeness** refers to the degree to which a consumer is open to new ideas and quick to adopt buying new products, services, or experiences early in their introduction.[19] Innovative consumers are generally dynamic and curious, and they are often young, educated, and relatively affluent.[20] Obviously, consumer innovativeness is an important trait for marketers to consider when introducing new products.

Although researchers do not necessarily agree on the extent to which innovativeness is exhibited across product categories, a consumer with a strong degree of innovativeness may be expected to be innovative in a number of situations. For example, innovativeness has been shown to relate to a number of behaviours, including new product adoption, novelty seeking, information seeking, and online shopping.[21]

NEED FOR COGNITION

Need for cognition refers to the degree to which consumers tend to engage in effortful cognitive information processing.[22] Consumers who have a high degree of this trait tend to think carefully about products, problems, and even marketing messages. For example, research has shown that consumers with a high need for cognition tend to be influenced heavily by the quality of the arguments in an advertisement. Conversely, consumers with a low need for cognition tend to be more influenced by things like an endorser's physical attractiveness and other cues that are not central to a message.[23]

Research also indicates that the effect of humorous advertising is influenced by need for cognition. Humorous ads tend to lead to more positive consumer attitudes and purchase intentions for consumers who have a low degree of need for cognition.[24] Studies also indicate that the need for cognition trait influences consumers' reactions to ads with sexual content. For example, consumers with a low degree of need for cognition have exhibited more positive attitudes and purchase intentions toward brands that are advertised using sexual imagery than consumers with a high degree of need for cognition.[25]

COMPETITIVENESS

The **competitiveness** trait may be defined as an enduring tendency to strive to be better than others. The predominance of competitiveness in consumer society is easy to see, and the use of competitive themes in marketing messages is widespread.

A competitive person is generally easy to identify, and research reveals that the trait often emerges in the following ways:[26]

▶ *When a consumer is directly competing with others.* Thanks to the Internet, many sports and games are now "played" online. A great example is fantasy sports leagues. The sports network ESPN has even promoted fantasy football, baseball, basketball, and hockey contests with the winners receiving valuable prizes. The growth of online video gaming highlights consumer competitiveness in a technologically advanced environment.

▶ *When a consumer enjoys winning vicariously through the efforts of others* (as when we enjoy seeing "our team" win). Sports fans often *bask in reflected glory* (BIRG) when "their" team wins. This means that they will wear team apparel and display team merchandise when their team is successful. By attempting to show an association between themselves and the team, consumers vicariously live through their team and make proclamations like, "We're number one!" (As researchers point out, you hardly ever hear them say, "They're number one!"[27]) BIRGing has been tied directly to consumer ego and self-esteem. Interestingly, fans may also CORF—that is, they *cut off reflected failure* by hiding their association with losing teams. These fans are often called "fair-weather" fans. Obviously, sports marketers love fan BIRGing behaviour and hope to minimize CORFing.[28]

▶ *When a consumer attempts to display superiority over others* by openly flaunting exclusive products (as when we flaunt a nice car in front of others). The term *conspicuous consumption* describes a tendency of the wealthy to flaunt their material possessions as a way of displaying their social class. Numerous product categories, ranging from automobiles to jewellery, help to signal a consumer's status and can be used to convey images of consumer "superiority." By buying and displaying the correct products, consumers often feel that they can send the message, "I'm better than you are!"

PRODUCTIVITY ORIENTATION

Productivity orientation represents the tendency for consumers to focus on

innovativeness degree to which an individual is open to new ideas and tends to be relatively early in adopting new products, services, or experiences

need for cognition the degree to which consumers enjoy engaging in effortful cognitive information processing

competitiveness enduring tendency to strive to be better than others

productivity orientation represents the tendency for consumers to focus on being productive, making progress, and accomplishing more in less time

Trait Superstition

Do you feel uneasy if a black cat crosses your path? Do you avoid walking under ladders or opening umbrellas indoors? Have you ever noticed baseball players jumping over the foul line rather than stepping on it? Although a lot of people laugh off superstitions and superstitious rituals, to other people they are very real. Being superstitious can be thought of as a trait because it represents a consumer's tendency to act in relatively consistent ways.

Although consumer research in the area is relatively scarce, some interesting findings have been revealed. For instance, the superstition trait has been shown to influence decisions to gamble, to participate in sweepstakes, to forward emails, and to invest in the stock market. Superstitious consumers have also been shown to be risk averse when negative cues are present.

Decisions based on superstition can have significant effects on business. An example of this was found in the dramatic jump in weddings on the date *07/07/07*. The number of weddings on that day nearly tripled due to consumer belief in the lucky 7s. The industry was busy that day!! While 07/07/07 was important for these consumers, dates like 10/10/10 and 11/11/11 hold significance as well. Even though the origins of many superstitions are difficult to determine, it is clear that trait superstition is a relevant topic for consumer researchers.

Sources: Based on online content retrieved at http://www.time.com/time/business/article/0,8599,1630320,00.html, accessed May 24, 2010. Mowen, John C. and Brad D. Carlson (2003), "Exploring the Antecedents and Consumer Behavior Consequences of the Trait of Superstition," *Psychology & Marketing*, 20 (12), 1045–1065. Carlson, Brad D., John C. Mowen, and Xiang Fang (2009), "Trait Superstition and Consumer Behavior: Re-Conceptualization, Measurement, and Initial Investigations," *Psychology & Marketing* 26 (8), 689–713. Kramer, Thomas, and Lauren Block (2008), "Conscious and Nonconscious Components of Superstitious Beliefs in Judgment and Decision Making," *Journal of Consumer Research*, 34 (6), 783–793.

being productive, making progress, and accomplishing more in less time. The pressure on consumers to be productive in their everyday life seems to be ever increasing. Consumers with a high degree of productivity orientation are able to be productive even when pursuing leisure activities. For example, researchers have found that this trait influences the tendency for consumers to pursue collectable experiences before dying, such as compiling a list of places to visit or sampling a list of food or beers from around the world. Having a strong productivity orientation affects one's bucket list!

OTHER TRAITS FOUND IN CONSUMER RESEARCH

It should be emphasized that the preceding traits represent only a small fraction of the many traits that have been investigated in consumer research. Exhibit 6.1 highlights other traits that are often studied. Again, we emphasize that there are many more!

THE FIVE-FACTOR MODEL APPROACH

One of the most popular multiple-trait approaches found in both personality psychology and consumer research

Exhibit 6.1

Examples of Other Traits in Consumer Research

Frugality	The tendency of a consumer to exhibit restraint when facing purchases and using resources.
Impulsiveness	The tendency for consumers to make impulsive, unintended purchases.
Trait Anxiety	A tendency to respond with anxiety when facing threatening events.
Bargaining Proneness	The tendency for a consumer to engage in bargaining behaviours when making purchases.
Trait Vanity	The tendency for consumers to take excessive pride in themselves, including their appearance and accomplishments.

is the **five-factor model** (FFM) approach.[29] Numerous studies have examined the influence of the traits in the FFM on a wide range of behaviours, both inside and outside of the field of consumer research. The FFM proposes that the following five dominant traits are found in the human personality:

1. **Extroversion**

2. **Agreeableness**

3. **Openness to experience (also referred to as "creativity")**

4. **Stability (or instability; sometimes referred to clinically as "neuroticism")**

5. **Conscientiousness**

Extroverted consumers are outgoing and talkative with others. Agreeable consumers are kind-hearted to others and sympathetic. Creative consumers are imaginative and enjoy new ideas. Stable consumers tend to be able to control their emotions and avoid mood swings. Conscientious consumers are careful, orderly, and precise. These traits are presented in Exhibit 6.2.

As we have stated, the FFM approach is a multiple-trait approach, meaning that a consumer's personality is conceptualized as a *combination* of these traits and that each consumer will vary on the respective traits. For example, Corbin might possess relatively strong degrees of extroversion, agreeableness, and openness, but he may not be very stable or conscientious. By examining consumers across the five dimensions of the FFM, we gain an expanded view of how multiple traits influence specific consumer behaviours.

The FFM approach is indeed popular with consumer researchers, and the traits found in the FFM have been shown to affect consumer behaviours such as complaining, bargaining, banking, compulsive shopping, mass media consumption, and commitment to buying environmentally friendly products.[30]

Even though the FFM has proven useful for presenting an integrative approach to personality, the model is not universally accepted by all researchers. In fact, there have been some lively debates regarding its usefulness.

HIERARCHICAL APPROACHES TO PERSONALITY TRAITS

If you are beginning to think that there are so many different approaches to trait psychology theory that it is hard to keep them all straight, you are not alone! Organizing all of these traits is one of the goals of what are known as **hierarchical approaches to personality**.

Hierarchical approaches begin with the assumption that personality traits exist at varying levels of abstraction. That is, some traits are specific (bargaining proneness), and others are more broad (extroversion). Specific traits refer to tendencies to behave in very well defined situations. For example, a bargaining-prone consumer will bargain when shopping for products. Here, the situation is very specific. Broad traits refer to tendencies to behave across many different situations. For example, an extroverted consumer may be very outgoing when with friends, when in a restaurant, or when discussing a group project with classmates. As a general statement, specific traits tend to be better predictors of individual behaviours than

Exhibit 6.2

Five-Factor Model

Personality Trait	Description
Extroversion	Talkative, outgoing
Agreeableness	Kindhearted, sympathetic
Openness to Experience	Creative, open to new ideas, imaginative
Stability	Even-keeled, avoids mood swings
Conscientiousness	Precise, efficient, organized

Source: Based on McCrae R. R. and P. T. Costa (2005), *Personality in Adulthood: A Five-Factor Theory Perspective*, 2nd edition. New York; Guilford.

five-factor model multiple-trait perspective that proposes that the human personality consists of five traits: agreeableness, extroversion, openness to experience (or creativity), conscientiousness, and neuroticism (or stability)

hierarchical approaches to personality approaches to personality inquiry that assume that personality traits exist at varying levels of abstraction

Exhibit 6.3

Criticisms of the Trait Approach

▸ Personality traits have not traditionally been shown to be strong predictors of consumer behaviour relative to other explanatory variables.

▸ So many personality traits exist that researchers often select traits for study without any logical theoretical basis.

▸ Personality traits are sometimes hard to measure, and researchers often use measures with questionable validity.

▸ Personality inventories used to measure traits are often meant for use on specific populations, but they are frequently applied to practically any consumer group.

▸ Researchers often measure and use traits in ways not originally intended.

▸ Consumer traits generally do not predict specific brand selections.

Source: Baumgartner, Hans (2002), "Toward a Personology of the Consumer," *Journal of Consumer Research*, (September), 286–292; also McAdams, Dan P. (1996), "Personality, Modernity, and the Storied Self: A Contemporary Framework for Studying Persons," *Psychological Inquiry*, (7), 295–321.

broad traits. A number of researchers have argued for the existence of these hierarchies, with many suggesting that abstract traits influence more specific traits in a hierarchical fashion.[31]

FINAL THOUGHTS ON THE TRAIT APPROACH

The trait approach in consumer research is very popular today in large part due to its ability to objectively assign a personality trait score, from a survey for example, to a consumer. In this way, the approach has an advantage over the psychoanalytic approach in which personality dimensions are assigned based on the psychologist's subjective interpretation. We should emphasize, however, that the trait approach is not without criticism. Exhibit 6.3 reveals a number of criticisms that have been levelled against trait research.[32]

6-2b Brand Personality

We know that people have personalities, but do brands have personalities? Does your favourite brand of soft drink have a personality? Does the personality of the drink match your personality? These questions may sound a bit strange at first, but upon reflection, consumers do describe

brand personality
collection of human characteristics that can be associated with a brand

brands with humanlike qualities. How would you describe the personality of the CBC? What qualities are associated with lululemon apparel? How is Holt Renfrew different from Dollarama?

Marketing managers and consumer researchers alike are very interested in the "personalities" of products. **Brand personality** refers to human characteristics that can be associated with a brand.[33] Brand personalities can be described across five dimensions, including competence, excitement, ruggedness, sincerity, and sophistication. These dimensions are described in Exhibit 6.4.

Brand personalities represent opportunities for companies to differentiate their products. Accordingly, a brand's personality may be viewed as a part of its overall image.[34] Brand personalities also provide marketers with opportunities to build strong brand relationships with consumers, especially when they have an understanding of their customer's personality.[35] A well-known LG marketing campaign says "Life's Good," signifying how its products relate to this overall belief. Hallmark cards are seen as sincere and trustworthy. Guess is considered to be sophisticated clothing compared with the more rugged Wrangler brand.[36]

Wrangler has a rugged brand personality.

Exhibit 6.4

Brand Personality Dimensions

Personality Trait	Description	Example
Competence	Responsible, reliable, dependable	Maytag—"Depend on Us"
Excitement	Daring, spirited	Mountain Dew—"Do the Dew!"
Ruggedness	Tough, strong	Ford Trucks—"Built Ford Tough"
Sincerity	Honest, genuine	Wrangler Jeans—"Genuine. Wrangler"
Sophistication	Glamorous, charming	Cartier jewellery—"Brilliance, Elegance, Exuberance"

Source: Based on Aaker, Jennifer (1997), "Dimensions of Brand Personality," *Journal of Marketing Research*, (August), pp. 347–356; permission conveyed through Copyright Clearance Center, Inc.

FORMATION OF BRAND PERSONALITY

Many factors contribute to the development of a brand's personality.[37] A product's category can infer certain qualities. For example, if you hear the name *Sampson, Whitten,* and *Taylor* and find out that it is a law firm, you may develop an idea that the firm is serious, professional, and competent. If, however, you hear of a new brand of athletic wear called *Activesport*, you might expect the brand to be adventurous and outdoorsy. Other factors that contribute to the development of a brand's personality include packaging, price, sponsorships, symbols, and celebrity endorsements.

PERSONALITY AND BRAND RELATIONSHIPS

The brand personality concept is especially important when one considers that consumers, to a certain extent, have relationships with brands, and that personality traits are important in the formation and maintenance of these relationships.[38] To illustrate, Coca-Cola's sincere and traditional personality enables the Coca-Cola Company to easily remind consumers that the brand has always been and will always be a part of their life. In fact, "Always Coca-Cola" is one of Coke's best-known advertising campaigns.

The concept of consumer–brand relationships has received considerable research attention, and several factors help indicate the level of relationship between a consumer and a brand. Consumer researcher Susan Fournier proposes that the overall quality of the relationship between consumer and brand can be described in terms of the following:[39]

Love and Passion. A consumer may have such strong feelings about a brand that they actually describe it with the term *love*. A consumer may say, "I love my Apple MacBook Pro" or "I love Axe cologne."

Self-Connection. Brands may help express some central component of a consumer's identity. Research indicates that the correct match between a customer's personality and a perceived brand personality leads to higher overall satisfaction.[40]

Commitment. In a strong consumer–brand relationship, consumers are very committed to their brands and feel very loyal to them. Harley-Davidson owners are well known for their commitment to their bikes. In fact, the Harley Owners Group (H.O.G.) is the largest factory-sponsored group in the world, with more than 1 million members![41]

Interdependence. Consumer–brand relationships may be marked by interdependence between the product and the consumer. This can be described in terms of the frequency of use, the diversity of brand-related situations, and the intensity of product usage. For example, consumers are often reminded that "Like a good neighbour, State Farm is there."

Intimacy. Strong relationships between consumers and brands can be described as intimate. Deep-seated needs and desires of consumers can be tied directly to specific brands. For example, a need for intimacy and passion can be directly tied to a specific brand of perfume, like Obsession. A need for excitement or status can be related to a sporty automobile, like Porsche.

Brand Partner Quality. In general, brands that are perceived to be of high quality contribute to the formation of consumer–brand relationships. In this sense, consumers develop feelings of trust regarding specific brands, and these feelings of trust foster

Demographics Today

The study of demographics is known as *demography*. Demographic variables include age, ethnicity, income, family size, and occupation.

▸ **Age.** Age is important not only because of its descriptive nature, but also because consumers who experience significant life events at approximately the same age are influenced greatly by the events. This is the "cohort effect." Groups such as "Generation Y" or "Millennials" (born between 1981 and 1995), "Generation X" (born between 1966 and 1980), and "Baby Boomers" (born between 1946 and 1965) and "The Greatest Generation" (born prior to 1946) are identifiable segments. Baby Boomers receive a lot of attention because of the group's size and spending power. Younger consumers, like pre-teens, also receive attention.

▸ **Ethnicity.** Ethnocultural diversity is increasing in Canada. South Asian and Chinese immigrants continue to be the two largest visible minority groups, but West Asians, Koreans, and Arabs are likely to be the fastest-growing populations between now and 2017. Statistics Canada predicts that, by 2017, one in five Canadians is likely to be foreign-born.

▸ **Income.** Income is another important variable. Engel's Law states that as income increases, a smaller percentage of expenditure is devoted to food, and the percentage devoted to consumption rises more slowly than the rise in income.

Demographics can be used to help locate and understand lifestyle segments. This is why demographic information is often combined with psychographics. Failing to consider psychographic measures leads to the trap of assuming that all consumers of a certain demographic have the exact same tastes. An example is found in the concept of "psychological age." A person's actual age and his or her psychological age can be very different. As some have said, "Today's 60 is yesterday's 40." The demographics topic is discussed again in a later chapter.

Source: Statistics Canada Report on Demographics: http://www.statcan.gc.ca/pub/91-209-x/91-209-x2011001-eng.htm

consumer–brand relationships. Research reveals that brand personality traits also affect customer–brand relationship quality when service problems occur, with sincere brands suffering more than exciting brands when service breakdowns occur.[42]

6-3 CONSUMER LIFESTYLES AND PSYCHOGRAPHICS

The term *lifestyle* is used commonly in everyday life. For example, we often speak of "healthy lifestyles," "unhealthy lifestyles," "alternative lifestyles," and even "dangerous lifestyles." The word has also been used in many ways in consumer research. Stated simply, consumer **lifestyles** refer to the ways consumers live and spend their time and money.

Personality and lifestyles are closely related topics. In fact, lifestyles have been referred to as context-specific personality traits.[43] This has implications for how the concepts are measured. That is, instead of asking consumers if they are "outdoor types," a lifestyle approach will ask the consumers about the amount of time they spend outdoors and what they do when they are outdoors. Importantly, lifestyles aren't completely determined by personality. Instead, they emerge from the influence of culture, groups, and individual processes, including personality.[44] Not surprisingly, consumer lifestyles vary considerably across cultures.

Lifestyles have proven extremely valuable to marketers and others interested in predicting behaviour. Purchase patterns are often influenced by consumer lifestyles, and numerous lifestyle categories can be identified. It shouldn't be surprising, therefore, that marketers often target consumers based on lifestyles. For example, Pepsi's Code Red has been aimed at active, young male consumers, while Dasani water appeals to the more health-conscious consumer. Because lifestyle can be directly tied to product purchase and consumption, consumer lifestyles are considered an important manifestation of social stratification.[45] In other words, they are very useful in identifying viable market segments. Appealing to a consumer's lifestyle is so important

lifestyles distinctive modes of living, including how people spend their time and money that it's not uncommon to see advertisements focusing as much on lifestyle as on the actual product itself.

6-3a Psychographics

The term **psychographics** refers to the way consumer lifestyles are measured. Psychographic techniques use quantitative methods that can be used in developing lifestyle profiles. Notice that this is not the same thing as demographics. **Demographics** refers to observable, statistical aspects of populations, including such factors as age, gender, or income. Lifestyles, although also observable, refer to how consumers live.

Although psychographic research has been used to investigate lifestyles for many years, advances in technology have helped psychographics become even more popular with consumer researchers and marketing managers today. Psychographic analysis involves surveying consumers using **AIO statements**, which are used to gain an understanding of consumers' *activities*, *interests*, and *opinions*. These measurements can be narrowly defined (as relating to a specific product or product category) or broadly defined (as pertaining to general activities that the consumer enjoys).

Consumer segments very often contain consumers with similar lifestyles. Although the categorization of segments is rarely based on consumer behaviour theory, the process can be very helpful in identifying marketing opportunities. As an example, one recent effort to identify segments in the European tourism industry resulted in the following lifestyle segment profiles:[46]

▶ **Home Loving.** Fundamentally focused on the family, this segment values product quality. These consumers enjoy cultural activities such as visiting art exhibits and monuments. The home-loving group takes the greatest number of long, family-oriented travel vacations.

▶ **Idealistic.** These responsible consumers believe that the road to success is based on bettering the world. They enjoy classical music and theatre. Travel destinations for this group are primarily rural locations and country villages.

▶ **Autonomous.** These independent-thinking consumers strive to be upwardly mobile. They enjoy the nightlife and read few newspapers. This segment enjoys weekend travel.

▶ **Hedonistic.** The hedonistic segment values human relationships and work. They are interested in new product offerings and enjoy listening to music. These consumers enjoy visiting large cities.

▶ **Conservative.** Like the home-loving segment, this segment focuses largely on the family. These consumers tend to view success simply in terms of their work careers. This group dislikes nightlife and modern music and instead focuses on issues related to religion, law, and order. These consumers take few weekend trips, but they do enjoy visiting seaside destinations.

Psychographic profiles of various other consumer groups have resulted in lifestyle segments identified for Harley-Davidson owners (including "cocky misfits" and "classy capitalists"),[47] wine drinkers (including "conservatives," "experimenters," and "image oriented"),[48] Porsche owners (including "top guns," "elitists," and "fantasists"),[49] and health, wellness, and sustainability focused consumers (including "lifestyle of health and sustainability").[50] As you can see from these examples, there are numerous ways in which to segment consumers based on lifestyles.

SPECIFICITY OF LIFESTYLE SEGMENTS

The lifestyle approaches that we have discussed here can be categorized in terms of specificity—either narrowly defined or more broadly defined. Generally, lifestyles are indeed quite specific. The magazine industry is particularly efficient at identifying consumer lifestyles and developing products around lifestyle segments. For example, consumers who skateboard can read magazines such as *Thrasher*, while those who enjoy paintball can read *PaintballX3*. Exhibit 6.5 presents sample measures used for psychographic analysis for the leisure curling segment.

6-3b VALS

When using lifestyle segmentation, a marketer can either identify his or her own segments or use established methods that are already available. One popular method in consumer research is the **VALS** approach.[51] Developed and marketed by Strategic Business Insights, VALS is a very successful segmentation approach that has been adopted by several companies. VALS originally stood for "Values and Lifestyles," and was based on social

psychographics
quantitative investigation of consumer lifestyles

demographics
observable, statistical aspects of populations such as age, gender, or income

AIO statements activity, interest, and opinion statements that are used in lifestyle studies

VALS popular psychographic method in consumer research that divides consumers into groups based on resources and psychological consumer behaviour motivations

Exhibit 6.5

Sample Psychographic Items for Segmenting the Curling Market

TYPE OF ITEM	EXAMPLE	Strongly Disagree	Disagree	Neutral	Agree	Strongly Agree
Activity	I spend much of my free time curling.	☐	☐	☐	☐	☐
Interest	I am very interested in the latest developments in curling equipment technology.	☐	☐	☐	☐	☐
Opinion	Curling is truly "Canada's favourite sport."	☐	☐	☐	☐	☐

Robbie Shone/Alamy

values. The current approach, also known as VALS, classifies consumers into eight distinct segments based on resources available to the consumer (including financial, educational, and intellectual resources), as well as three primary motivations (ideals motivation, achievement motivation, and self-expression motivation).

As seen in Exhibit 6.6, VALS includes eight groups:

1. **Innovators.** Innovators are successful, sophisticated people who have high self-esteem. They are motivated by achievement, ideals, and self-expression. Image is important to these consumers.

2. **Thinkers.** Thinkers are motivated by ideals. They are mature, reflective people who value order and knowledge. They have relatively high income and are conservative, practical consumers.

3. **Achievers.** Achievers have an achievement motivation. Their lives largely centre around church, family, and career. Image is important to this group, and they prefer to purchase prestige products.

4. **Experiencers.** Experiences are self-expressive consumers who tend to be young, impulsive, and enthusiastic. These consumers value novelty and excitement.

5. **Believers.** In some ways, believers are like thinkers. They are ideal motivated and conservative. They follow routines, and their lives largely centre around home, family, and church. They do not have the amount of resources that thinkers have, however.

Exhibit 6.6

The VALS™ Framework

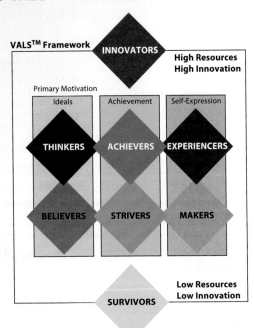

Source: Strategic Business Insights (SBI): www.strategicbusinessinsights.com/vals.

6. **Strivers.** Strivers are achievement motivated, but they do not have the amount of resources that are available to achievers. For strivers, shopping is a way to demonstrate to others their ability to buy.

7. **Makers.** Makers are like experiencers in that they are motivated by self-expression. They have fewer

resources than experiencers. They tend to express themselves through their activities such as raising children, fixing cars, and building houses.

8. **Survivors.** Survivors are very low on resources and are constricted by this lack of resources. They tend to be elderly consumers who are concerned with health issues and who believe that the world is changing too quickly. They are not active in the marketplace, as their primary concerns centre around safety, family, and security.

6-3c PRIZM5

Another popular tool for lifestyle analysis is a geodemographic procedure known as Environics Analytics's PRIZM5.[52] **Geodemographic techniques** combine data on consumer expenditures and socioeconomic variables with geographic information in order to identify commonalities in consumption patterns of households in various regions. **PRIZM5** is a popular lifestyle analysis technique that was developed by Environics Analytics. PRIZM5 is based on the premise that people with similar backgrounds and means tend to live close to one another and emulate each other's behaviours and lifestyles. PRIZM5 recognizes the changing geodemographic nature of Canadian society (discussed in greater detail in Chapter 9). Jan Kestle, the founder and president of Environics Analytics, explains: "PRIZM5 paints a vivid picture of the changing face of Canada; because

Courtesy of Environics Analytics

You can explore PRIZM5 segments at the Environics website (www.environicsanalytics .ca). Check out your favourite Canadian postal codes.

changes happen gradually over time, they may not always be noticeable. However, when we analyzed the data for PRIZM5 at the neighbourhood level, the differences became apparent in the new 68 lifestyle types."[53] Interestingly, some PRIZM5 segments indicate exceptional diversity in household languages and cultural backgrounds. The segment labelled "New World Symphony," for example, includes 49 different languages spoken at home, and in the "Newcomers Rising" segment (a group of younger, downscale city immigrants), 70 languages are spoken at twice the national average.

PRIZM5 also reflects interesting changes in demographic groups. For example, many segments include empty-nesting couples living in households beside families with middle-aged couples and older children. Millennial children are also remaining in their Boomer parents' home, which led to the creation of a segment Environics has labelled "Boomerang City." In this group, nearly a third of the children at home are over the age of 20.

A great way to better understand how this type of segmentation works is to find your own segment or those of your friends and family using the online "Lifestyle Lookup" tool offered by Environics Analytics (http:// www.environicsanalytics.ca/prizm5). Does your segment describe you? Does it describe your neighbours? Take a moment to consider why this type of segmentation scheme may or may not accurately portray a specific household in one of its segments.

PRIZM combines demographic and behavioural information in a manner that enables marketers to better understand and target their customers. The technique uses 68 different segments as descriptors of individual households, which are ranked according to socioeconomic variables. Segments found using the PRIZM technique include "Arts & Affluence," "Street Scenes," "Vieille École," "Grads & Pads," and "Kids & Careers."

There are other geodemographic techniques available as well, including Psyte HD Canada, which separates Canadians into 59 unique segments (http://www.utahbluemedia. com/pbbi/psyte/psyteCanada. html). The Psyte system touts its household level data, especially as it relates to buying behaviour, as a key advantage of this approach.

geodemographic techniques techniques that combine data on consumer expenditures and socioeconomic variables with geographic information in order to identify commonalities in consumption patterns of households in various regions

PRIZM5 popular geodemographic segmentation system developed by Environics Analytics

The Cyber Self

It will probably come as no surprise that estimates indicate that nearly three-quarters of online teens and young adults use social networking sites, with millions of young consumers updating their profiles several times per day. Popular websites such as Facebook, Pinterest, and Twitter allow users to post various aspects of their lives and present themselves in almost limitless ways. Connecting with your peeps is, of course, very important.

Unfortunately, some social website users feel that almost any detail of their life is fair game. In many cases, improper information is posted to websites. Young consumers seem to think that posting explicit information related to sexual behaviour, drugs, or violence is not a problem, often because they feel in some way distinct from their cyberpersonalities. Of course, the downside is when too much information is given out and bad things happen. This is becoming all too common. From employers reviewing online profiles to websites like pleaserobme.com, which highlights the dangers of revealing when consumers are (and are not) at home, the implications of social networking are far-reaching. This brings a whole new perspective to the ideal social self! Although the Internet allows consumers to post all kinds of material about themselves, common sense should still apply.

Sources: Based on Gordon, Serena (2009), "Teens Divulge Risky Behavior on Social Networking Sites," *Washington Post online edition*, January 6, 2009, online content retrieved at http://www.washingtonpost.com/wp-dyn/content/article/2009/01/05/AR2009010502588.html, accessed May 25, 2010. Lenhart, Amanda, Kristen Purcell, Aaron Smith, and Kathryn Zickuh (2010), "Social Media and Young Adults," *Pew Internet & American Life Project*, online content retrieved at http://pewinternet.org/Reports/2010/Social-Media-and-Young-Adults.aspx, accessed May 25, 2010.; Fletcher, Dan (2010), "Please Rob Me: The Dangers of Online Oversharing," *Time*, online edition, online content retrieved at http://www.time.com/time/business/article/0,8599,1964873,00.html, accessed May 25, 2010.

6-4 THE ROLE OF SELF-CONCEPT IN CONSUMER BEHAVIOUR

Another important topic in consumer behaviour is the **self-concept**—the totality of thoughts and feelings that an individual has about him- or herself. Self-concept can also be thought of as the way a person defines or gives meaning to his or her own identity, as in a type of self-schema. It can include self-esteem, but also specific attributes or traits that one assigns to oneself. For example, a consumer may think of him- or herself as environmentally conscious, studious, fashionable, thrifty, competitive and/or technologically savvy. Does how you think about yourself affect the decisions you make? Does seeing yourself as fashionable or environmentally conscious affect the consumption decisions you are likely to make? These are the types of questions that are of interest to consumer researchers and have led to a strong interest in better understanding self-concepts in CB.

In general, consumers are motivated to act in accordance with their self-concepts. As such, consumers often use products as ways of revealing their self-concepts to others. According to a **symbolic interactionism** perspective, consumers agree on the shared meaning of products and symbols.[54] These symbols can become part of the self-concept if the consumer identifies with them strongly.

An important field of study that relates to the symbolic interactionism approach is **semiotics**—the study of symbols and their meanings. As we have stated, consumers use products as symbols to convey their self-concepts to others. In this sense, products are an essential part of self-expression.[55] Popular websites like Pinterest, Facebook, and Twitter give consumers easy ways of expressing themselves.[56]

Let's first explore various dimensions of the "self" before examining how a consumer's self-concept influences

self-concept totality of thoughts and feelings that an individual has about himself or herself

symbolic interactionism perspective that proposes that consumers live in a symbolic environment and interpret the myriad of symbols around them, and that members of a society agree on the meanings of symbols

semiotics study of symbols and their meanings

various behaviours. First, we note that a consumer will have a number of "concepts" about him- or herself that may emerge over time and surface in different social situations.[57] A few of the different "self-concepts" that may emerge include the actual self, the ideal self, the social self, the ideal social self, the possible self, and the extended self.[58]

The *actual self* refers to how a consumer currently perceives him- or herself (i.e., who I am). The *ideal self* refers to how a consumer would like to perceive himself (i.e., who I would like to be in the future). *The social self* refers to the beliefs that a consumer has about how he or she is seen by others. The social self is also called the "looking-glass" self because it denotes the image that a consumer has when he or she looks into the mirror and imagines how others see him or her. The *ideal social self* represents the image that a consumer would like others to have about him or her. The *possible self*, much like the ideal self, presents an image of what the consumer could become, whereas the extended self represents the various possessions that a consumer owns that helps him form perceptions about himself.

The relationship between consumer self-concept and product consumption is a two-way street. That is, consumers express their self-concepts by purchasing and displaying various products, while products help define how the consumer sees himself or herself.[59] Note that the relationship between the self-concept and consumption is not limited to adult consumers only, as consumer–brand connections have been shown to form as early as childhood![60]

6-4a Self-Concept and Body Presentation

The issue of self-concept in consumer behaviour has several practical implications. For example, the cosmetics and weight-loss industries are well known for offering products that purportedly help improve one's self-image. The term **self-esteem** refers to the positivity of an individual's self-concept. The effect of advertising on consumers' self-esteem is an important topic in this area.

The fashion industry is constantly under fire for promoting overly thin models and body types. In fact, research confirms that consumers compare their bodies with those of models found in advertisements, and that these comparisons often have harmful effects. This is particularly the case for young females.[61]

In response to growing public concern regarding this issue, the Council of Fashion Designers of America (CFDA) updated guidelines to encourage healthy eating

Daniele Schiavello/Catwalking/Getty Images

Unrealistic body images affect consumers' self-esteem.

habits and to discourage the use of overly thin models in advertisements. "The fashion business should be sensitive to the fact that we do have a responsibility in affecting young girls and their self-image," CFDA president Diane von Furstenberg commented.[62] The problem is not solely for women, however, as evidence suggests that male consumers are also affected by unrealistic body imagery in advertising.[63] Although the industry has received much negative publicity, note that not all model effects are negative. Consumers can sometimes feel better about themselves when they find similarities between their bodies and those of models.[64]

Unilever Corp. recently addressed the issue of unrealistic body types with its Real Beauty campaign for the Dove brand of personal care products. The campaign seeks to provide more realistic views of beauty and to improve the self-esteem of both women and young girls.

COSMETIC SURGERY AND BODY MODIFICATION

Because of the many ways in which consumers compare themselves with others, it is easy to understand why many medical procedures that promise to improve a consumer's perception of his or her body are now being offered. According to a 2007 survey of Canadian female consumers, approximately one in five has had some type of cosmetic surgery and one in

self-esteem positivity of the self-concept that one holds three has had a nonsurgical cosmetic enhancement. Breast augmentation, lipoplasty, and eyelid surgery are common procedures for female patients, while liposuction and rhinoplasty are popular among men. The majority of procedures were found among consumers aged 35–50.[65]

BODY PIERCINGS AND TATTOOS

Body piercings and other forms of body decorations, such as tattoos, represent other methods of promoting one's self-concept. The growth of piercing among university-aged students is particularly noteworthy. Estimates vary widely, with one recent study revealing that as many as 51% of teenagers and young adults have some form of body piercing. The same estimates reveal that up to 14% of the general population has body piercings. Interestingly, piercings tend to be more popular with female consumers than with male consumers.[66] The growth in popularity of body art suggests that new attitudes about the body and its role in self-presentation are emerging.[67]

While body piercings are popular forms of self-expression and are frequently used as innocent methods of self-expression, research also indicates that the use of piercings can sometimes be associated with increased levels of drug and alcohol use, unprotected sexual activity, trait anxiety, and depression.[68] Consumers also form impressions of employees who have tattoos and piercings, and these perceptions may affect how they view organizations with such employees.[69] For consumers, body piercings and tattoos have become more popular than ever.

6-5 SELF-CONGRUENCY THEORY AND CONSUMER BEHAVIOUR

Reference group members share similar symbolic meanings. This is an important assumption of **self-congruency theory**. This theory proposes that much of consumer behaviour can be explained by the congruence (match) between a consumer's self-concept and the image of typical users of a focal product.[70] For example, one study found that store loyalty is largely influenced by the degree of congruency

self-congruency theory theory that proposes that much of consumer behaviour can be explained by the congruence of a consumer's self-concept with the image of typical users of a focal product

between self-image and store image.[71] How would you describe shoppers of popular Canadian apparel stores like Roots? Aritzia? Harry Rosen? Do you possess any of these characteristics?

6-5a Segmentation and Self-Congruency

Marketers can use congruency theory by segmenting markets into groups of consumers who perceive high self-concept congruence with product-user image. Imagine a consumer who sees himself as being a stylish person. If he believes that people who drive BMWs are stylish, then he will be motivated to drive a BMW. In this way, brands become vehicles for self-expression.[72]

As discussed earlier, there are several types of self-concepts, and different products may relate to each concept. That is, one product may relate quite well to the actual self-concept, but not as strongly to the ideal self-concept. One study found that the purchase of privately consumable items (such as frozen dinners or suntan lotion) is heavily influenced by the actual self-concept, while the purchase of publicly visible products (like clothing) is more strongly related to the ideal self-concept.[73]

A recent advertising campaign for Ford trucks illustrates the role of self-congruency theory in marketing. The successful ad campaign, which centres on the "Built Ford Tough" theme, sends the message that if you are a hardworking man you need a hardworking truck like Ford. Rolex has a long history of positioning its watches

Matching the image of a user to the image of a product is a popular marketing tactic.

as the watch for the successful consumer who pursues excellence. Rolex is well known for being the watch for people who have either "arrived" or who soon will be "arriving."

FINAL THOUGHT ON PERSONALITY, LIFESTYLES, AND THE SELF-CONCEPT

Personality, lifestyles, and the self-concept are all important topics in the study of consumer behaviour. Consumers differ across each of these concepts, and these differences help signal the need for targeted marketing communications. As technological advancements continue to develop, it can be expected that marketing managers and consumer researchers alike will continue to be interested in these topics.

STUDY TOOLS 6

LOCATED AT THE BACK OF THE TEXTBOOK
☐ Rip out Chapter Review Card

LOCATED AT NELSON.COM/STUDENT
☐ Review Key Terms Flashcards (print or online)
☐ Download audio summaries to review on the go
☐ Complete practice quizzes to prepare for tests
☐ Watch video on Wheelworks for a real company example

Case

Lululemon Athletica

Lululemon athletica opened its first location in Vancouver in 1998. By 2012, the company was operating 174 stores in Canada, the United States, Australia, and New Zealand. Its sales were more than $1 billion, and it had stock market value of more than $10 billion. The company had quickly become one of Canada's great retail success stories.

The idea for the business grew out of what founder Chip Wilson saw as key trends in the apparel market. First, athletic apparel for women was not particularly comfortable or attractive. Second, female consumers were driving retail sales in Canada and throughout North America. Third, yoga was rapidly rising in popularity. Wilson believed that the time was right for the launch of a female-focused yoga apparel company.

Consumers agreed, and lululemon grew rapidly as it soon became apparent that the comfortable and attractive clothing was a wardrobe staple both in and out of the yoga studio. The company, the clothing, and the focus on health and fitness resonated with consumers and the way they wanted to live their lives.

From the beginning, lululemon has taken a grassroots approach to marketing. When opening a new store, the company develops word of mouth by giving clothing samples to local yoga studios, athletes, and fitness instructors. Similarly, it is very careful in hiring people who are a good fit with the company's message of health, fitness, and well-being. Those employees are trained to be educators and ambassadors for lululemon in the local community. The company is also constantly collecting and analyzing feedback from its customers and using that information to improve its products. This strong emphasis on corporate values and culture is important to lululemon and may provide it with a strong point of competitive differentiation relative to many other companies that have followed lululemon's lead and launched similar lines of female athletic apparel.

In March of 2013, however, lululemon became embroiled in what many have since dubbed the "Sheer

Bloomberg via Getty Images

Pants Scandal." The company was forced to recall 17% of its Luon pants after customers complained that they were see-through. This was made worse by asking some customers to prove the pants were sheer by putting them on and then bending over in the store. Initially Cristine Day, lululemon's CEO at the time, responded by firing the company's chief product officer. A few months later, in June, Day resigned. A few months after that, Chip Wilson appeared on Bloomberg TV and seemed to blame women for the problems with the pants, saying, "Some women's bodies just actually don't work for [the pants]."

While lululemon has struggled with its public relations in recent years, its competitors from Lole to Gap's Athleta to Nike have slowly gained market share. This has led some pundits to question the Canadian company's ability to continue to thrive, or even survive, in the yoga pant market that it created and once dominated.

Sources: Bouw, Brenda (2007), "Zen and the Art of Retailing," *The Globe and Mail, Report on Business* (November 30), http://www.theglobeandmail.com/report-on-business/zen-and-the-art-of-retailing/article1090270/?page=all, accessed August 15, 2012. Caplinger, Dan (2012), "Has lululemon athletica Become the Perfect Stock?" *The Motley Fool* (fool.com) (March 30), http://www.dailyfinance.com/2012/03/30/has-lululemon-athletica-become-the-perfect-stock, accessed August 15, 2012. Reuters (2010), "Lululemon Shares End at a Record High after Oprah's Blessing," *Reuters News* (November 22), http://ca.reuters.com/article/domesticNews/idCATRE6AL5YH20101122, accessed August 15, 2012. lululemon athletica Press Release (March 22, 2012), "lululemon athletica inc. Announces Fourth Quarter and Full Year Fiscal Results, 2011," http://www.lululemon.com/media/index.php?id=219, accessed July 5, 2012.

QUESTIONS

1 What are the personality traits that lululemon is looking for in its customers? Are those the same traits the company looks for in its employees?

2 Does lululemon have a brand personality? How might the sheer pants scandal affect that personality?

3 How would you describe the relationship between consumers and the lululemon brand? Before and after the sheer pants scandal?

4 What demographic segments does lululemon serve?

5 What psychographic segments does lululemon serve?

6 What impact might wearing lululemon have on consumers' self-concept?

7 In light of lululemon's early success and its recent struggles, how do you think the company will perform over the next five years?

PART 2

7 | Attitudes and Attitude Change

LEARNING OBJECTIVES

After studying this chapter, the student should be able to:

7-1 Define attitudes and describe attitude components.

7-2 Describe the functions of attitudes.

7-3 Understand how the hierarchy of effects concept applies to attitude theory.

7-4 Comprehend the major consumer attitude models.

7-5 Describe attitude change theories and their role in persuasion.

7-6 Understand how message and source effects influence persuasion.

INTRODUCTION

Keiton recently bought a new Apple iPad. He always liked his iPhone and he figured that the iPad would be the next logical purchase. As it turns out, he really likes it a lot and he thinks it is well worth the price that he paid. He even joined an iPad fan page on Facebook and follows tweets about the iPad on Twitter.

Getting consumers to feel strongly about a product is something that marketers constantly try to achieve. When consumers have positive attitudes toward products, they often promote them to others. This is a win–win situation for both the customer and the company. Conversely, negative attitudes can have a profound impact as well. Some people become so upset with a company and its products that they boycott everything the company sells—and tell others that they should do the same.

Understanding the factors that influence consumer attitudes is very important for marketers. This may seem obvious for companies, but the importance of consumer attitudes

attitudes relatively enduring overall evaluations of objects, products, services, issues, or people

is found in nontraditional settings as well. For example, politicians want to know how voters *feel* about candidates. City managers want to know if citizens will approve of some new construction project. Musicians want to know if consumers will *like* their new songs. In each of these examples, consumer attitudes are very important.

7-1 ATTITUDES AND ATTITUDE COMPONENTS

The term *attitude* has been used in many ways. **Attitudes** are relatively enduring overall evaluations of objects, products, services, issues, or people.[1] Attitudes play a critical role in consumer behaviour, and they are especially important because they motivate people to behave in relatively consistent ways. It is therefore not surprising that the attitude concept is one of the most researched topics in the entire field of consumer research. In fact, attitude is one of the most popular concepts in all of the social sciences.

Attitudes and value are closely related. Recall from our opening example that Keiton is very pleased with the

value that his iPad provides. In general, consumers have positive attitudes toward products that deliver value. Likewise, when products deliver poor value, consumer attitudes are usually negative. In order to appreciate how attitudes influence consumer behaviour, we need to distinguish between the various components of attitudes and the functions that attitudes perform.

7-1a Components of Attitude

According to the **ABC approach to attitudes**, attitudes possess three important components: **a**ffect, **b**ehaviour, and **c**ognitions (or beliefs). To understand these components, consider the following statements:

▶ "I really like my new iPad."

▶ "I always buy Apple products."

▶ "My iPad helps me study."

These statements reflect the three components of a consumer's attitude found in the ABC approach. "I really like my new iPad" is a statement of affect because the feelings, or affection, a consumer has about the product is captured in the concept of liking. "I always buy Apple products" refers to one's behaviour

regarding Apple products. "My iPad helps me study" is a cognitive statement that expresses the owner's view of the usefulness of the new product.

7-2 FUNCTIONS OF ATTITUDES

Knowing that attitudes represent relatively enduring evaluations of products and that attitudes can be broken into three components is valuable. But what's the big deal about attitudes? What do they do for the consumer? Understanding the answer to these questions gives marketers an opportunity to develop better promotional messages.

According to the **functional theory of attitudes**, attitudes perform four functions:[2] the *utilitarian* function, the *knowledge* function, the *value-expressive* function, and the *ego-defensive* function. These functions are summarized in Exhibit 7.1.

ABC approach to attitudes approach that suggests that attitudes encompass one's affect, behaviour, and cognitions toward an object

functional theory of attitudes theory that attitudes perform four basic functions

Exhibit 7.1

Functions of Consumer Attitudes

Attitude Function	Description	Example
Utilitarian	Attitudes are used as a method to obtain rewards and to minimize punishment.	High school boys wear cool brands so they fit in.
Knowledge	The knowledge function of attitudes allows consumers to simplify their decision-making processes.	A consumer will only consider HP computers because she believes that HP is the best brand on the market.
Value-expressive	This function of attitudes enables consumers to express their core values, self-concept, and beliefs to others.	A consumer supports Greenpeace because he places much value on environmentalism.
Ego-defensive	The ego-defensive function of attitudes works as a defence mechanism for consumers to avoid facts or to defend themselves from their own low self-concept.	Smokers discount information that suggests that smoking is bad for their health.

Source: Based on Katz, Daniel (1960), "The Functional Approach to the Study of Attitudes," *Public Opinion Quarterly*.

UTILITARIAN FUNCTION

The **utilitarian function of attitudes** is based on the concept of reward and punishment. This means that consumers learn to use attitudes as ways to maximize rewards and minimize punishment. Buying, and liking, a product because it delivers a specific benefit is one example of the utilitarian function of attitudes. The consumer is rewarded through a desired product benefit. For example, the iPhone delivers many benefits in the form of apps, and millions of consumers enjoy the apps. These consumers therefore develop positive attitudes toward the iPhone. Another way in which consumers maximize rewards through expressing attitudes is by gaining acceptance from others. Consumers often express their attitudes in order to develop and maintain relationships. A study of sports fans presents an example. In the study, football fans revealed that one of the many reasons they wear their team's apparel is to help fans make and enjoy connections with new friends.[3] In other words, the outward behaviour of wearing the apparel leads to the desired consequence of making friends and having fun.

KNOWLEDGE FUNCTION

The **knowledge function of attitudes** allows consumers to simplify decision-making processes. For example, consumers may not like credit card offers because they want to stay out of debt. The decision to shred the offers would then be easy. Attitudes perform the important function of helping consumers avoid undesirable situations and approach more desirable situations. They also help consumers select objects that they do like. Brand loyalty is important here. It is usually much easier to repurchase a product that you know you like than it is to try a new one. Attitude components become stored in the associated network in consumers' long-term memory and become linked together to form rules that guide behaviour. Here, we can see again that attitudes are linked to comprehension and knowledge.

VALUE-EXPRESSIVE FUNCTION

The **value-expressive function of attitudes** is found in a number of consumer settings. This function enables a consumer to express his or her core values, self-concept, and beliefs to others. Accordingly, this function of attitudes provides a positive expression of the type of person a consumer perceives himself or herself to be. Satisfaction comes from the expression of attitudes that reflect the self-image. For example, consumers who believe in the protection of animals and animal rights may join and promote the actions of a group like People for the Ethical Treatment of Animals (PETA). The behaviour of joining the group allows consumers to express core dimensions of their self-image. Another vehicle for the value-expressive

utilitarian function of attitudes function of attitudes in which consumers use attitudes as ways to maximize rewards and minimize punishment

knowledge function of attitudes function of attitudes whereby attitudes allow consumers to simplify decision-making processes

value-expressive function of attitudes function of attitudes whereby attitudes allow consumers to express their core values, self-concept, and beliefs to others function is products such as bumper stickers, posters, or T-shirts. Joining specific groups on Facebook is another example of the value-expressive function of attitudes at work. Ultimately, the expression of attitudes becomes a mechanism by which consumers can make statements about closely held values.

EGO-DEFENSIVE FUNCTION

Finally, the **ego-defensive function of attitudes** works as a defence mechanism for consumers. There are a couple of ways in which this function works. First, the ego-defensive function enables a consumer to protect himself or herself from information that may be threatening. For example, people who like to smoke may discount any evidence that smoking is bad for their health. In this case, the attitude works as a defence mechanism that protects the individual from the reality that smoking isn't healthy.

Another example of the ego-defensive function is when a consumer develops positive attitudes toward products that enhance his or her self-image. Consider April, a first-year university student. April likes to wear expensive brand-name clothing because she is concerned about how people perceive her physical attractiveness. April's positive attitude toward expensive brands helps her project a positive image.

7-3 HIERARCHY OF EFFECTS

As discussed earlier, the ABC approach to consumer attitudes suggests that there are three components to attitudes: affect, behaviour, and cognition. Research indicates that these components may be formed in a sequential pattern. This attitude formation process is known as the **hierarchy of effects** approach.[4] According to this approach, affect, behaviour, and cognitions form by following one of the four following hierarchies:

1. **High-involvement (or standard learning) hierarchy**

2. **Low-involvement hierarchy**

3. **Experiential hierarchy**

4. **Behavioural influence hierarchy**

These hierarchies are discussed in the next section and are presented in Exhibit 7.2.

7-3a High-Involvement Hierarchy

The high-involvement, or standard learning, hierarchy of effects occurs when a consumer faces a high-involvement

Exhibit 7.2

Hierarchy of Effects

Purchase Context	Low Involvement
High involvement	Cognition–affect–behaviour
Low involvement	Cognition–behaviour–affect
Experiential	Affect–behaviour–cognition
Behavioural influence	Behaviour–cognition–affect

decision. High-involvement decisions are important to a consumer and often contain significant risk. In this hierarchy, cognitions (or beliefs) about products are formed first. The consumer carefully considers various product features and develops cognitions about each feature. Next, feelings, or evaluations, about the product are formed. The consumer may begin to think the product is good and will suit his or her needs based on the beliefs that have been formed. Finally, after beliefs and feelings are formed, the consumer decides to act in some way toward the product. Here, a purchase decision is made. The consumer may decide to buy (or not buy) the product.

Imagine the process that Matt went through when he bought a new gaming system. Matt knew that it would be a significant purchase, and he was therefore careful about his selection. He first considered the various attributes of each system and began to develop favourable evaluations toward a few of the brands. Realizing that he felt best about the Xbox One, he decided that this would be the one to buy.

7-3b Low-Involvement Hierarchy

The standard learning approach was once considered the best approach to take in order to understand consumer attitude formation. Marketers began to realize, however, that consumer purchases are often neither risky nor involving. In fact, many purchases are routine and boring.[5]

When low-involvement purchases are made, consumers often have some basic beliefs about products without necessarily having strong

ego-defensive function of attitudes function of attitudes whereby attitudes work as a defence mechanism for consumers

hierarchy of effects attitude approach that suggests that affect, behaviour, and cognitions form in a sequential order

I Like This Store!

Retail managers are well aware of the powerful effects that music has on consumer behaviour. In general, consumers tend to walk faster through a store when fast music is played, and they tend to slow down (and buy more!) when slower music is played. Music can even affect consumers' perceptions of wait time.

What is equally important for managers, however, is that the wrong choice of music may actually drive customers away. Of course, different segments of consumers like different types of music, and consumers can quickly become turned off if the wrong kind of music is played. In fact, companies like DMX Music and Muzak know that the tendency to leave a store if unappealing music is played cuts across demographic segments. Quite simply, no one likes to be bombarded with bad music! The right choice of background music can be a critical factor in retail success. Managers should pay close attention. Background music is very important!

Sources: Online content retrieved at *DMX* website, www.dmx.com, accessed May 28, 2010; Online content retrieved at *Muzak* website, www.muzak.com, accessed May 28, 2010; Ebenkamp, Becky (2004), "Songs in the Key of Flee," *Brandweek* (February 16) 17; Morrison, Michael, and Michael Beverland (2003), "In Search of the Right In-Store Music," *Business Horizons*, 46 (November–December), 77; Milliman, R. E. (1986), "Using Background Music to Affect the Behavior of Supermarket Shoppers," *Journal of Marketing*, 46, 86–91.

feelings toward them. Marianne, a self-proclaimed hardcore videogamer, may not carefully consider the feelings that she has toward a brand of paper towels. In fact, she probably doesn't think much about paper towels at all. She may just think, "Bounty is a popular brand, so I'll buy it." Only after she buys and uses the product will she develop any type of feeling, or evaluation, of the towel. At first, she thinks, "Bounty is popular" (cognition) and she decides to buy it (behaviour). Only later does she say, "I like Bounty" (affect). Chances are, however, that she would carefully consider videogame features first, develop an overall like or dislike for each brand, and then buy one type of game or another. As such, it is easy to see that the purchase of an expensive gaming system is much more involving for Marianne than a $2 roll of paper towels.

7-3c Experiential Hierarchy

Many purchases are based on feelings. That is, consumers purchase products or perform behaviours simply because it "feels good" or "feels right." For example, when a student decides to visit a new dance club, he makes the decision simply because it sounds like a fun thing to do.

Impulse purchases can be explained from the experiential perspective. These purchases are often motivated by feelings. Impulse purchasing means that a consumer buys a product spontaneously and with little concern for consequences. Dessert items are often purchased on impulse. When the waiter brings the tray by, the chocoholic feels strongly about one of the desserts and simply buys it on impulse. Here, he or she feels strongly and acts on those feelings. A great deal of research focuses on the experiential perspective, exploring the feelings and pleasures that accompany consumer purchases and behaviours.[6]

7-3d Behavioural Influence Hierarchy

The behavioural influence hierarchy suggests that some behaviours occur without either beliefs or affect being strongly formed beforehand. Strong environmental pressures lead to behaviours without belief or affect formation. An example of this may be found when a consumer eats at a restaurant that is playing soft, slow music. Restaurant managers know that one way to get people to relax and order more drinks is to play soft, soothing music. Consumers have been conditioned to slow down and relax when slow music is played. Canada Safeway introduced Starbucks kiosks into the company's grocery stores for much the same reason. As such, behaviour is influenced by environmental cues. This means that there are times when behaviours may be performed in the absence of strong beliefs or feelings.

7-4 CONSUMER ATTITUDE MODELS

As you can see, understanding consumer attitudes is very important for understanding consumer behaviour. This leads to the question of how to measure attitudes. As noted earlier, the study of attitudes has a long-established research tradition. It shouldn't be surprising, therefore, that several methods for measuring attitudes have been used. In this section, some of the major approaches to measuring consumer attitudes are presented, beginning with a well-known approach advanced by Martin Fishbein and Icek Ajzen, the attitude-toward-the-object model.[7]

7-4a Attitude-Toward-the-Object Model

The **attitude-toward-the-object (ATO) model** (sometimes simply referred to as the *Fishbein model*) proposes that three key elements must be assessed to understand and predict a consumer's attitude. The first element consists of the *beliefs* a consumer has about a salient attribute, or feature, that the consumer thinks the product should possess. The second element is the *strength of the belief* that a certain brand does indeed have the feature. The third element is an *evaluation of the attribute* in question. These elements are combined to form the overall attitude toward the object (referred to as A_o, or attitude toward the object). This approach is known as a *multiattribute* approach because consumers consider a number of attributes when forming attitudes in this way. The formula for predicting attitudes with this approach is

$$A_o = \sum_{I=1}^{N} (b_i)(e_i)$$

where A_o = attitude toward the object in question (or A_{brand}), b_i = strength of belief that the object possesses attribute i, e_i = evaluation of the attractiveness or goodness of attribute i, and N = number of attributes and beliefs.

The formula states that belief (b) and evaluative ratings (e) for product attributes are combined (multiplied) and the resulting product terms are added together to give a numerical expression of a consumer's attitude toward a product. This model can be used both for predicting a consumer's attitude and for understanding how salient attributes, beliefs, and evaluations influence attitude formation.

USING THE ATO APPROACH

To understand this model, first consider how the various elements are measured. To begin, note that belief ratings (b) can be measured on a 10-point scale such as:

How likely is it that the Sony television will give you a clear picture?

1   2   3   4   5   6   7   8   9   10

Extremely unlikely   Extremely likely

The evaluative (e) rating can then be measured on a −3 to +3 scale such as:

How bad/good is it that a television has a clear picture?

−3   −2   −1   0   +1   +2   +3

Very bad   Very good

The consumer would rate the Sony television and any other brand being considered on each relevant attribute. They would also consider their evaluations of the attributes, and ultimately combine the information.

An example may help clarify the use of this formula. Think of the situation that Jamal faces selecting a new apartment. Jamal recently graduated from college and received a job offer in a large city. He is now considering three different apartment complexes that currently have vacancies. How could we predict his attitude toward each one? This information is presented in Exhibit 7.3.

Jamal is evaluating the following three complexes: *City Pointe, Crown View,* and *Kings Landing.* He first thinks of the attributes, or features, that come to mind when he thinks of apartment complexes. He decides that the following attributes are relevant: location, high rent/fees, security, fitness centre, and pet friendliness. It is important to emphasize that the attributes need to really be relevant to the product under consideration. After identifying the relevant attributes, Jamal thinks of how likely it is that each apartment will perform well on the various attributes, or how likely it is that

> **attitude-toward-the-object (ATO) model**
> attitude model that considers three key elements, including beliefs consumers have about salient attributes, the strength of the belief that an object possesses the attribute, and evaluation of the particular attribute

Exhibit 7.3

Attitude-Toward-the-Object Model Applied to Apartment Complexes

Attribute	e	City Pointe b	City Pointe (b)(e)	Crown View b	Crown View (b)(e)	Kings Landing b	Kings Landing (b)(e)
Location	3	7	21	9	27	6	18
High rent/fees	−2	8	−16	9	−18	7	−14
Security	3	7	21	8	24	6	18
Fitness center	1	5	5	7	7	10	10
Pet friendliness	−3	5	−15	2	−6	9	−27
A_o			16		34		5

Note: e = evaluative ratings. These ratings are generally scaled from −3 to +3, with −3 being very negative and +3 being very positive. b = strength of belief that the object possesses the attribute in question. Beliefs are generally scaled from 1 to 10, with 1 meaning "highly unlikely" and 10 meaning "highly likely." $(b)(e)$ is the product term that is derived by multiplying the evaluative ratings (e) by belief strength (b). A_o is the overall attitude toward the object. This is determined by adding the $(b)(e)$ product terms for each object.

the complexes have these attributes. Jamal would be answering questions such as:

How likely is it that City Pointe is pet-friendly?

1   2   3   4   5   6   7   8   9   10

Extremely unlikely   Extremely likely

Jamal rates each apartment across all relevant attributes. His belief (b) ratings for the apartments are shown in Exhibit 7.3. From his belief ratings, we can see that he thinks that Kings Landing is most pet-friendly. This complex allows dogs of any size. City Pointe allows dogs under 50 pounds with a large damage deposit, and Crown View does not allow any pet over 20 pounds.

Next, Jamal considers how he *feels* about the relevant attributes, or how good (or bad) the attributes are. An example from the model would be:

How good/bad is it that an apartment complex is pet-friendly?

−3   −2   −1   0   +1   +2   +3

Very bad   Very good

Jamal has a number of pet allergies and would prefer to stay away from complexes that he considers to be overly pet-friendly ($e = -3$). Unfortunately all three complexes that have vacancies allow pets. Most complexes require some fee for pets, and they also limit the size of pets that are allowed. He evaluates the other attributes as well. He highly values a location that is close to the downtown entertainment district ($e = +3$) and

a complex with its own security force ($e = +3$). Jamal knows that the fees and limitations can vary greatly and he really doesn't want to have problems with his allergies. He also values a fitness centre but realizes that these centres usually raise the overall costs associated with a lease ($e = +1$). He would naturally like to pay as little as possible in rent. He does believe in the old adage "you get what you pay for," however, so he thinks that higher rent probably signals higher quality ($e = -2$). As such, he doesn't view higher rent as a completely bad thing. *It is important to emphasize that the evaluative ratings (e) do not vary across the brands under consideration, while the belief ratings do.* That is, consumers know what attributes they like regardless of which product they are considering.

Using this model, Jamal's attitude would be calculated by multiplying each belief rating (b) by the corresponding evaluation (e). For example, the belief rating of 7 for City Pointe (security) would be multiplied by the evaluation of 3 to arrive at 21. Similarly, the belief rating of 2 for Crown View (pet-friendliness) would be multiplied by the evaluation of 23 to arrive at 26. This is performed for all belief ratings and evaluations. Finally, the product terms are added together to arrive at a predicted attitude score. From Exhibit 7.3, we see that his most positive attitude is toward Crown View ($A_o = 34$), followed by City Pointe ($A_o = 16$), and finally Kings Landing ($A_o = 5$).

What was it that led to the higher attitude toward Crown View versus the other complexes? An examination of Exhibit 7.3 reveals that Crown View was rated higher than the other two complexes on the two highly valued attributes, location and security. Kings Landing has an excellent fitness centre, but it is also the most pet-friendly of the three complexes, with practically no limitations on pets. He also views City Pointe as relatively pet-friendly. Notice that Crown View was considered to be the most expensive complex ($b = 9$), but this is still the complex to which Jamal holds the most positive attitude. How could this be? The higher ratings on other attributes compensated for the belief that Crown View would be the most expensive complex. Accordingly, the ATO approach is known as a **compensatory model**. With compensatory models, attitudes are formed holistically across a number of attributes, with poor ratings on one attribute being compensated for by higher ratings on another attribute.

IMPLICATIONS OF THE ATO APPROACH

Information obtained from this model has important marketing implications. First, we note that attitude research is most often performed on entire market segments rather than on individuals. Marketing researchers would generally want to understand how an entire segment of consumers feel about apartment complexes. Information would be gathered from a sample of several consumers in the segment.

An equally important issue for managers would be learning if consumers believe that products offer relevant attributes. Does the target segment know that Crown View offers excellent security? Do they know that Kings Landing offers a high-quality fitness centre? If targeted segments do not know these things, then they could be emphasized in advertising campaigns. This would particularly be the case if the attribute was highly valued by the consumers. Therefore, both belief (b) and evaluative (e) ratings have important implications.

As a general statement, it would be easier for managers to convince a targeted segment that they do offer a specific feature (like an excellent fitness centre) than it would be to attempt to change how consumers evaluate the attribute (in other words, how people feel about fitness centres). This is why marketers need to perform extensive research up front to gain a clear understanding of attributes that are highly valued, and then develop their products and services around these features.

A couple of questions commonly arise regarding this approach. "Do consumers really form attitudes in this way?" Most consumer researchers would respond "Yes." Think of a person considering the purchase of a new cellphone. Chances are that they will first think of the features that are relevant. Next, they will rate each

brand on how well it performs on those features. They will also consider how they feel about each of the features. Finally, they will combine their beliefs with the evaluations and make a decision. Granted, *they probably won't write down the formula when they evaluate different cellphones*, but consumers think about relevant features of products, how much they value the features, and how each product rates on the features.

The next question that is commonly asked is, "Do consumer researchers really do this?" Again, the answer is yes. Researchers are very interested in how attitudes are formed, and the approach presented here can easily be performed through consumer surveys. The resultant information can have a significant impact on marketing strategy. As the apartment example reveals, this type of research can affect both product development and promotional strategy. For example, managers could decide that they should improve features that are desired by the targeted segment. Or they could focus on improving customer awareness that a complex actually does have the features that the targeted consumers want. Managers could also do both of these things.

Overall, the attitude-toward-the-object model has value from both an academic and a practical viewpoint. We do note, however, that one difficulty with the model is that the weights that are associated with the various attributes do not necessarily remain constant over time, and the list of relevant attributes may indeed change. For this reason, managers should try to stay current on these issues.

DO ATTITUDES ALWAYS PREDICT BEHAVIOUR?

Marketing managers and researchers alike realize that just because a consumer has a positive attitude toward a product, this doesn't mean that he or she will always purchase the product. In fact, there would be little need for sales promotion if this were the case. **Attitude–behaviour consistency** refers to the extent to which a strong relationship exists between attitudes and actual behaviour. A number of situations may keep a consumer from selecting a product for which a positive attitude is held.[8] In general, attitudes are stronger predictors of behaviour when the decision to be made is classified as high involvement, when situational factors do not impede the product selection (e.g., the product is out of stock or the consumer doesn't

compensatory model attitudinal model wherein low ratings for one attribute are compensated for by higher ratings on another

attitude-behaviour consistency extent to which a strong relationship exists between attitudes and actual behaviour

Hey Girl, Don't Be Trashy

Internet memes are ideas propagated through the World Wide Web. Memes can come in a variety of forms but are often pictures or video. One of the most popular in recent years is the Ryan Gosling "Hey Girl" meme. The basic template for the meme is text inserted onto a picture of Ryan Gosling—ranging from "Hey Girl, Paris just isn't the same without you" to "Hey Girl, If you queried #mylove, the only result would be you."

Marketers have started to pile on to popular memes in an attempt to get their message out to a large group of people at a relatively low cost. The hope is that if the meme is prevalent enough, the advertising message will be able to piggyback on its popularity and "go viral"—that is, be quickly passed from consumer to consumer in the virtual world, much like a virus might in the real world.

DoSomething.org did exactly that with the "Hey Girl, Don't Be Trashy" campaign, which leveraged the Ryan Gosling meme to distribute a message about the importance of recycling (the same website also piled on to the LOLCats meme). The extent to which this approach to attitude change can be effective remains to be seen. Has your attitude toward recycling changed after exposure to this meme?

Allstar Picture Library / Alamy

Sources: Jennifer Leggio, (2011). "Hey Girl: Introducing Silicon Valley Ryan Gosling's meme goddess, Lian Amaris," *Forbes Online*, Dec. 28, 2011, found at: http://www.theglobeandmail.com/news/arts/hey-girl-time-to-catch-up-on-your-ryan-gosling-memes/article2221206/; Sarah Lilleyman, "Hey girl, time to catch up on your Ryan Gosling memes," *The Globe and Mail Update*, Nov. 1, 2011. Found at: http://www.forbes.com/sites/jenniferleggio/2011/12/28/hey-girl-introducing-silicon-valley-ryan-goslings-meme-goddess-lian-amaris/; Andrew Pulver, "Everbody loves Ryan Gosling: How Hey Girl Wooed the Web," *The Guardian*, Jan. 13, 2012. Found at http://www.guardian.co.uk/film/filmblog/ 2012/jan/13/everybody-loves-ryan-gosling-hey-girl; DoSomething.org (2012). "Don't Be Trashy. Recycling Matters. Help Pass It ON." Found at http://www.dosomething.org /trashy /project-ideas.

have enough money), and when attitudes toward the product are very strong. Because attitudes don't always predict behaviour, other approaches, including the behavioural intentions model, have been developed to improve upon the ATO approach.

7-4b Behavioural Intentions Model

The **behavioural intentions model**, sometimes referred to as the *theory of reasoned action*, has been offered as an improvement over the attitude-toward-the-object model. This model differs from the attitude-toward-the-object model in a number of important ways.[9] First, rather than focusing explicitly on attitudes, the model focuses on intentions to act in some way. Second, the model adds a component that assesses the consumer's perceptions of what other people think they should do. This is referred to as the *subjective norm*. Finally, the model explicitly focuses on the consumer's attitude toward the behaviour of buying rather than the attitude toward the object.

> **behavioural intentions model** model, developed to improve on the ATO model, that focuses on behavioural intentions, subjective norms, and attitude toward a particular behaviour

The formula for the behavioural intentions model is as follows:[10]

$$B \approx BI = w_1(A_{\text{behaviour}}) + w_2(SN)$$

where B = behaviour, BI = behavioural intention, $A_{\text{behaviour}}$ = attitude toward performing the behaviour (or, A_{act}), SN = subjective norm, and w_1, w_2 = empirical weights.

This model states that a consumer's behaviour is influenced by the intention to perform that behaviour (BI), and that this intention is determined by the attitude toward performing the behaviour ($A_{\text{behaviour}}$) and *subjective norms* (SN).

From our apartment complex example, the $A_{\text{behaviour}}$ component includes the belief that the behaviour will lead to a consequence (e.g., "If I rent from Crown View, I'll be safe") and an evaluation of the consequence (e.g., "Being safe is a good thing"). The SN component includes a consumer's belief that a reference group thinks that he or she should (or should not) perform the behaviour (e.g., Jamal's friends think he should choose Kings Landing because of its excellent fitness centre) and the extent to which the consumer wants to comply with the suggestions of others (e.g., will Jamal follow his friends' recommendations?).

Exhibit 7.4

Behavioural Intentions Model (a.k.a. The Theory of Reasoned Action)

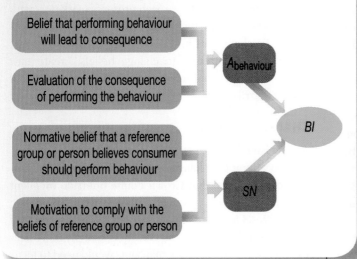

The aspects of the behavioural intentions model are presented in Exhibit 7.4. The behavioural intentions model was introduced as an improvement to the ATO model.

Again, two major differences are found in the attitude toward the behaviour and subjective norm components. For marketers, a clear understanding of the perceived consequences of product selection is crucial. Researchers must determine the consequences that are highly valued by their targeted consumer segments. Consumers don't always select products for the most predictable reason. Losing weight isn't the only reason people join a fitness centre. Consumers may join simply to meet people and make friends.

Marketing managers should also pay close attention to the subjective norm component of the model. Word-of-mouth communications are becoming critical for marketers. What do referent others think that the consumer should do? To what extent are they motivated to comply with the input of these people? The answers to these questions are quite valuable.

FACTORS THAT WEAKEN ATTITUDE–BEHAVIOUR RELATIONSHIP

Although consumer attitude models are very popular in consumer research, researchers note that a number of factors can detract from the accuracy of this approach. For example, as the length of time between attitude measurement and overt behaviour grows, the predictive ability of attitudinal models weakens. The specificity with which attitudes are measured also has an impact on accuracy. For example, measuring the intentions of buying a new Sony television would be more appropriate for Sony managers than would measuring one's intentions to buy a new "television" in the next month.

Strong environmental pressures can also keep consumers from performing intended behaviours. For example, when consumers feel rushed, decisions are often made in haste. Finally, attitude–behaviour models tend not to perform very well in impulse-buying situations. As discussed earlier, these behaviours are quite common in a number of consumer contexts.

ALTERNATIVE APPROACHES TO ATTITUDE

One small variation of this theory is the **theory of planned action**, which expands upon the behavioural intentions model by including a *perceived control* component. This component assesses the difficulty involved in performing the behaviour and the extent to which the consumer perceives that he or she is in control of the product selection.[11] Products can be difficult to purchase, especially if they are in short supply.

EXPANDING THE ATTITUDE OBJECT

The definition of attitudes presented earlier states that attitudes are relatively enduring evaluations of objects, products, services, issues, or people. For this reason, consumer researchers often study attitudes toward several different entities, not just brands or products.

One area that has received considerable consumer research attention is *attitude toward the advertisement*. Research has shown that there is generally a positive relationship between a consumer's attitude toward an advertisement and his or her attitude toward a particular product.[12] We note, however, that several factors have been shown to affect this relationship, including the overall liking of the television program in which the ad is embedded, the vividness of the imagery in the ad, the ad context, and the mood of the consumer.[13]

A growing area of research interest has also focused on attitude toward the company. What consumers know or believe about a company (sometimes referred to as *corporate*

> **theory of planned action** attitudinal measurement approach that expands upon the behavioural intentions model by including a perceived control component

associations) can influence the attitude they have toward its products.[14] The study of consumer beliefs toward companies is therefore gaining considerable attention from consumer researchers. Of particular importance for many consumers is the question of how responsible companies are with their business practices. In general, consumers who feel positively about a company's business practices are likely to react more favourably toward the brands that the company markets.[15]

ATTITUDE TRACKING

Assessing one's attitude toward a specific product, brand, purchase act, advertisement, or company at only one specific point in time can also limit the accuracy of attitudinal models. Researchers therefore track how attitudes change over time. Because attitudes toward a brand can be influenced by several things, including attitude toward advertisements and companies, it is especially important to study changes in consumer attitudes. **Attitude tracking** refers to the extent to which a company actively monitors its customers' attitudes over time. What is important to understand is that even though attitudes are relatively enduring evaluations of objects, products, services, issues, or people, these attitudes should be monitored over time to gauge changes that may occur.

7-5 ATTITUDE CHANGE THEORIES AND PERSUASION

An important issue in the study of consumer behaviour is how attitudes are changed. Marketers frequently want to change consumer attitudes about their products, and they focus their efforts on developing persuasive messages. Advertising obviously plays a major role in this effort. The term **persuasion** refers to specific attempts to change attitudes. Usually, the hope is that by changing beliefs or feelings, marketers can also change behaviour.

There are many different persuasive techniques, and the following discussion presents the theoretical mechanisms through which persuasion may occur. These include the ATO approach, the behavioural influence approach, the schema-based affect approach, the elaboration likelihood model, the balance theory approach, and the social judgment theory approach.

attitude tracking effort of a marketer or researcher to track changes in consumer attitudes over time

persuasion attempt to change attitudes

7-5a Attitude-Toward-the-Object Approach

According to the ATO model, both beliefs about product attributes and evaluations of those attributes play important roles in attitude formation. By focusing on these components, the ATO approach presents marketers with a number of alternatives for changing consumer attitudes. To change attitudes according to this approach, marketers can attempt to change beliefs, create new beliefs about product features, or change evaluations of product attributes.

CHANGING BELIEFS

As discussed in our apartment complex example, marketers may attempt to change consumers' beliefs. If consumers do not believe that Crown Pointe offers an excellent fitness centre, then managers could focus on improving its facilities. Or, let's assume that the complex already does have an excellent centre, but consumers simply don't realize that it does. In this case, managers would need to focus more on this attribute in advertisements. With each effort, the focus is on improving the belief rating for an attribute that is evaluated positively (here, fitness centre).

Another approach would be to focus on decreasing the strength of belief regarding a negatively evaluated attribute. For example, since pet-friendliness is evaluated negatively in this case (23), managers might decide to promote the idea that the walls of the apartments are quite thick and pet allergies shouldn't be a problem in their apartments. Here, the focus is on decreasing the belief rating of a negatively evaluated attribute. As we have discussed throughout this text, communicating value is an important marketing task. A good example of changing beliefs about a product is orange juice manufacturers attempting to convince consumers that the juice can be consumed all day instead of only at breakfast time.

ADDING BELIEFS ABOUT NEW ATTRIBUTES

Another strategy for changing attitudes under the ATO approach is adding a salient attribute to the product or service. Like the changing beliefs approach, this may require a physical change to the product itself. For example, an apartment complex might add basic cable TV service to all units. Here, a new attribute that is likely to be evaluated positively by consumers is added. When a valued attribute that was not previously considered is added, the overall attitude toward the complex may be improved.

At other times, the new beliefs may not be exactly tied to a "new" attribute. Rather, they may simply emphasize something that consumers had previously not considered. To illustrate, consider what has

"À votre santé! To your health!" The belief that wine is healthy can lead people to like it even more.

is associated with a reduced risk of heart disease and cancer, and this information has now been widely promoted. Thus, although the health-related benefits of red wine are nothing new, only in the last few years has the belief become prominently known and accepted. By adding a new belief, wine marketers have increased the market share of wine relative to beer and spirits.

CHANGING EVALUATIONS

As noted earlier, marketers may also attempt to change the evaluation of an attribute. Here, the marketer tries to convince consumers that an attribute is not as positive (or negative) as they may think. For example, an apartment complex may attempt to persuade consumers that a downtown location is not necessarily a good thing and that living in the suburbs is better. As discussed previously, changing evaluations of an attribute is usually more difficult than changing the strength of a belief regarding that attribute. Quite simply, consumers know what they like, and they make selections accordingly.

happened with the marketing of red wine. In the 1980s, an American winery, Robert Mondavi Winery, added labelling to its wines that referred to the health benefits of drinking wine. Initially, the U.S. Food and Drug Administration stopped this practice, based on the notion that the label was misleading and detrimental to consumers. However, after years of research, the health-giving properties of wine are widely accepted. Red wine

7-5b Behavioural Influence Approach

Another strategy commonly applied by marketers is directly changing behaviours without first attempting

The Canadian Census 2011

Under the authority of the Statistics Act, Statistics Canada collects data through a national census every five years. The most recent census was conducted in 2011, with prior data collections in 2006, 2001, and so on. Citizens are required by law to complete the short-form questionnaire which for 2011 included 10 questions—such as who lives at the address, languages spoken in the house, and information on each individual at that address (e.g., age, sex, and marital status). In previous data collections, a percentage of the households responding to the census were also selected to complete a long-form questionnaire that asked many additional questions. For the 2011 Census, the long-form questionnaire was no longer mandatory for any households and that data was instead collected as part of a voluntary National Household Survey (NHS). The details on the type of data collected from the NHS can be found online at: www.statcan .gc.ca/survey-enquete/household-menages/5178-eng.htm. Statistics Canada planned to include approximately 4.5 million households in the NHS.

The initial results from the 2011 Census provided a snapshot of a nation that was growing rapidly between 2006 and 2011. In fact, Canada's population grew by 5.9%, which was the highest rate of growth among G8 countries. Every province and most territories saw population increases between 2006 and 2011.

National census data is an extremely valuable resource for many different types of researchers from public policy analysts to genealogists to marketers. Therefore, creating more positive consumer attitudes toward the census was an important first step in collecting the information.

Sources: Statistics Canada, 2011 Census publications, http://www12.statcan.gc.ca/census-recensement/index-eng.cfm, http://www12.statcan.gc.ca/census-recensement/2011/ref/gazette-eng.cfm, and http://www.gazette.gc.ca/rp-pr/p1/2010/2010-08-21/html/order-decret-eng.html, all accessed August 15, 2012.

to change either beliefs or feelings. According to the behavioural influence hierarchy, behaviour change can precede belief and attitude change. Changing a retail store's design or atmospherics can have a direct influence on behaviour. In fact, an entire industry called scent marketing (using scents to influence behaviour) is emerging.

You may remember from our discussion on conditioning in an earlier chapter that behavioural conditioning can be very effective. Consumers respond to marketing stimuli in certain ways, and behaviours frequently result without either beliefs or affect occurring prior.

7-5c Changing Schema-Based Affect

We introduced the notion of schema-based affect in a previous chapter. From an attitude perspective, schema-based affect refers to the idea that schemas contain affective and emotional meanings. If the affect found in a schema can be changed, then the attitude toward a brand or product will change as well.

To illustrate, consider what happened when Domino's Pizza first entered Japan. Initially, the company had to deal with a commonly held belief that tomatoes were unhealthy, and that delivery food was not clean. Rather than trying to change these beliefs directly, Domino's created funny delivery carts and advertisements that attempted to attach positive feelings to the product schema and its brand. Thus, a positive attitude was shaped by this feeling found within the schema. This attitude-change technique can be effective if performed properly.

7-5d The Elaboration Likelihood Model

Another popular approach for conceptualizing attitude change is found in the **elaboration likelihood model** (ELM),[16] which illustrates how attitudes are changed based on differing levels of consumer involvement. Numerous research studies have examined the usefulness of the ELM in explaining the attitude change process. This model is shown in Exhibit 7.5.

According to the ELM, a consumer begins to process a message as soon as it is received. Depending on the level of involvement and a consumer's ability and motivation to process a message, the persuasion process then follows one of two routes: a *central route* or a *peripheral route.*[17]

THE CENTRAL ROUTE

If the consumer finds that the incoming message is particularly relevant to his or her situation (and thus highly involved), then he or she will likely expend considerable effort in comprehending the message. In this case, high-involvement processing occurs, and the **central route to persuasion** is activated. Here, the consumer develops a number of thoughts (or cognitive responses) regarding the incoming message that may either support or contradict the information. Contradicting thoughts are known as counterarguments. Thoughts that support the main argument presented are known as support arguments.

In the central route, the consumer relies on **central cues**. Central cues refer specifically to information found in the message that pertains directly to the product, its attributes, its advantages, or the consequences of its use.

elaboration likelihood model attitudinal change model that shows attitudes are changed based on differing levels of consumer involvement through either central or peripheral processing

central route to persuasion path to persuasion found in ELM where the consumer has high involvement, motivation, and/or ability to process a message

central cues information presented in a message about the product itself, its attributes, or the consequences of its use

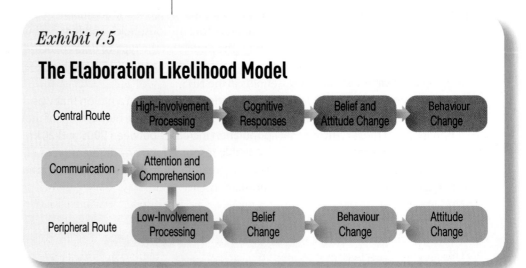

Exhibit 7.5

The Elaboration Likelihood Model

To illustrate this process, imagine an experienced photographer who sees an advertisement for Sony cameras. Because she knows a lot about cameras and is highly interested in them, she will likely think carefully about the message she sees and the arguments presented as to why Sony cameras are the best cameras on the market. The arguments presented in the ad are critical. The photographer will consider the arguments and compare them to her current beliefs. She may even form counter-arguments against the ad. For example, she may think, "Canons are better." Or, she may think, "Sony cameras really are better than Canons after all." (It is important to note that responses can be either negative or positive.)

If the consumer's beliefs are changed as a result of message exposure, attitude and behaviour change will follow. Because the consumer is highly involved, and because she has made an effort to carefully attend to the message, it is likely that the attitude change will be relatively enduring. This is an important aspect of the central route to persuasion: *Attitude change tends to be relatively enduring when it occurs in the central route.*

THE PERIPHERAL ROUTE

If a consumer is not involved with a message or lacks either the motivation or ability to process information, the **peripheral route to persuasion** will be followed. In this route, the consumer is unlikely to develop cognitive responses to the message (either supporting arguments or counterarguments), and he is more likely to pay attention to things like the attractiveness of the person delivering the message, the number of arguments presented, the expertise of the spokesperson, and the imagery or music presented along with the message. These elements of the message (i.e., non-product related information) are referred to as **peripheral cues**.

If the consumer is influenced more by peripheral cues than by central cues, any resulting belief or attitude change will likely be only temporary. That is, because the consumer is not highly engaged in the process, it is unlikely that attitude change will be enduring.

A popular ad campaign for Corona beer illustrates peripheral processing. The campaign includes a series of advertisements that show a man and woman relaxing on a beach. In the ads, there is no ad copy at all, other than the tagline "Corona—Find Your Beach." While there is little ad copy, the ads are full of peripheral cues—from the soothing sound of the waves hitting the sand to the beautiful imagery of the ocean. These cues play a major role in persuasion even if the consumer isn't presented with a list of reasons of why they should buy Corona, or why Corona is the best beer available on the market.

iStockphoto.com/Mattia Pelizzari

Beer advertisements tend to rely heavily on peripheral cues.

LOW-INVOLVEMENT PROCESSING IN THE CONSUMER ENVIRONMENT

It is important to note that the vast majority of advertisements to which consumers are exposed are processed with low-involvement processing. Consumers are simply not motivated to carefully attend to the thousands of ads that they are exposed to each day! Therefore, advertisers tend to rely heavily on the use of peripheral cues—attractive models, enticing imagery, upbeat music—when developing advertisements.

7-5e Balance Theory

Another way to conceptualize attitude change processes is through balance theory. The **balance theory** approach was introduced by social psychologist Fritz Heider.[18] The

peripheral route to persuasion path to persuasion found in ELM where the consumer has low involvement, motivation, and/or ability to process a message

peripheral cues non-product related information presented in a message

balance theory theory that states that consumers are motivated to maintain perceived consistency in the relations found in a system

Exhibit 7.6

Balance Theory

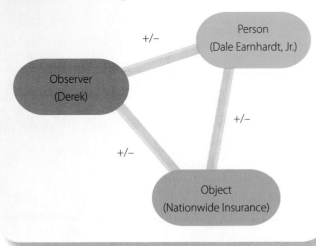

To illustrate, look carefully at Exhibit 7.6. Assume that Derek, a big NASCAR fan, really likes his favourite driver, Dale Earnhardt, Jr. That is, there is a positive (+) sentiment connection between Derek and the star. If Derek sees that Dale is endorsing a service like Nationwide Insurance (an attitudinal object), he would perceive a positive unit relation (+) between Dale and Nationwide. That is, Derek assumes that Dale endorses Nationwide because he really likes it. How would Derek feel about Nationwide? Well, in order to maintain balance in this triad, he would develop positive feelings toward Nationwide, resulting in a positive sentiment connection between himself and the brand.

This example illustrates a key premise of balance theory: Consistency in the triad is maintained when the multiplication of the signs in the sentiment and unit relations results in a positive value. When the resulting value is negative, consumers are motivated to change the signs (feelings) associated with one of the relations.

Suppose Derek doesn't like Dale Earnhardt, Jr. That is, suppose there is a negative (−) sentiment relation between Derek and the star. Because he perceives a positive unit relation between Dale and Nationwide,

basic premise of balance theory is that consumers are motivated to maintain perceived consistency in the relations found in mental systems. Accordingly, this approach is based on the **consistency principle**. This principle states that human beings prefer consistency among their beliefs, attitudes, and behaviours.

Balance theory focuses on the associations, or relations, that are perceived among a person (or observer), another person, and an attitudinal object. The relations among these elements may be perceived as being either positive or negative. An example is shown in Exhibit 7.6.

Note that the system (composed of observer, person, and object) is referred to as a *triad* because it consists of a set of three elements. The relations between the elements are referred to either as sentiment relations or as unit relations. *Sentiment relations* are the relations between the observer (consumer) and the other elements in the system. In Exhibit 7.6, the observer–person relation and the observer–object relation are referred to as sentiment relations. The object–person relation is referred to as a *unit relation*. Unit relations are based on the idea that two elements are in some way connected to each other.

Again, the basic premise of balance theory is that consumers are motivated to maintain perceived consistency in the relations found in the triad. Importantly, the perceived relations between the cognitive elements in the balance theory system may be changed when inconsistency occurs.

consistency principle
principle that states that human beings prefer consistency among their beliefs, attitudes, and behaviours

Balance theory influences celebrity endorsement decisions.

he will be motivated to form a negative sentiment relation between himself and the brand (note that $[-] \times [+] \times [-] = +$). According to the theory, weak perceived relations are generally changed, while stronger relations remain unchanged. Here, Derek would be turned off by the advertisement and would develop a negative sentiment relation between himself and the brand. We note that while balance theory is often used to explain endorser effectiveness, the theory has also been applied in several other contexts, including product placements in television shows,[19] goal-oriented behaviour,[20] and consumer–brand relationships.[21]

It should also be noted that marketers who rely on this approach should be careful to monitor any changes that occur in how a target market perceives an endorser. As we have seen, public attitudes toward celebrities can change nearly overnight. In this case, the sentiment connection between the endorser and the consumer can become negative, leading to trouble for the brand advertised!

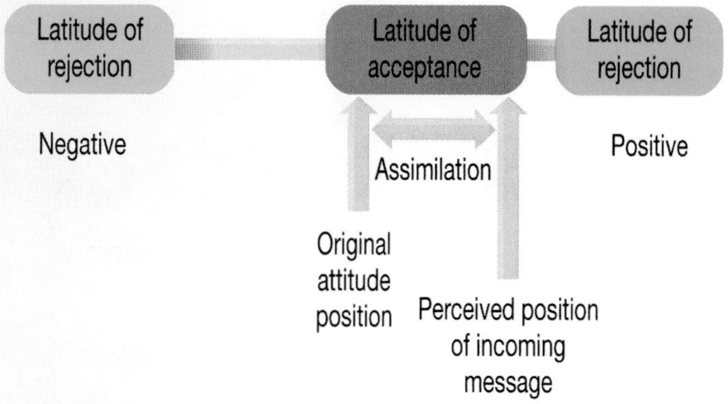

7-5f Social Judgment Theory

Social judgment theory is yet another theory for explaining attitude change.[22] This theory proposes that consumers compare incoming information to their existing attitudes about a particular object or issue. The initial attitude acts as a frame of reference, or standard, against which the incoming message is compared. Around these initial reference points are *latitudes of acceptance* and *latitudes of rejection*. For a message to fall within the latitude of acceptance, the information presented must be perceived as being close to the original attitude position. A message that is perceived as being far away from, or opposed to, the original attitude position will fall within the latitude of rejection. These aspects of the theory are presented in Exhibit 7.7.

According to the theory, when an incoming message falls within the latitude of acceptance, *assimilation* occurs. This means that the message is viewed as being congruent with the initial attitudinal position, and the message is received favourably. In fact, the message may be viewed as being even more congruent with the initial attitudinal position than it really is. As a result, the consumer is likely to agree with the content of a message falling within the latitude of acceptance, and the attitude would change in the direction of the message.

If the message is perceived as falling in the latitude of rejection, an opposite effect occurs. In fact, the

Exhibit 7.7

Social Judgment Theory

message will be viewed as being even more opposed to the original attitude than it really is and the message will be rejected. In this way, a *contrast effect* is said to occur.

The implication for marketers is that messages should be constructed so that they fall within the latitude of acceptance of the targeted consumer. An important finding in this line of research is that when the original attitude is strongly held (either positive or negative), the latitude of acceptance is quite small and the latitude of rejection is large. On the contrary, when the original attitude is weak (either positive or negative), the latitude of acceptance is large and the latitude of rejection is small. This finding helps explain why it is difficult to change a person's attitude when his or her attitude is very strong.

7-6 MESSAGE AND SOURCE EFFECTS AND PERSUASION

An important part of understanding persuasion is comprehending the many ways in which communication occurs. Marketing messages come to consumers in a variety of ways. As we have discussed, consumers are exposed to literally thousands of messages every day. Many of these messages come directly from marketers. Other messages come from other consumers. In both cases, the message being sent and the source delivering the

social judgment theory theory that proposes that consumers compare incoming information to their existing attitudes about a particular object or issue and that attitude change depends upon how consistent the information is with the initial attitude

Exhibit 7.8

Basic Communication Model

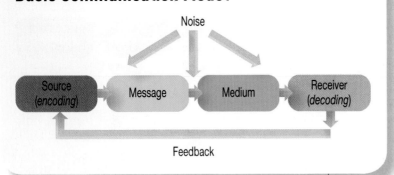

message influence persuasiveness. For this reason, it is important to consider the roles of message effects and source effects in persuasion.

Message effects describe how the appeal of a message and its construction affect persuasion. **Source effects** refer to the characteristics of the person or character delivering a message that influence persuasion. To understand how message and source effects work, we must begin by introducing a simple communication model in Exhibit 7.8.

According to this model, a source encodes a message and delivers the message through some medium. The medium could be personal (e.g., when one consumer talks to another, or when a salesperson speaks with a customer) or impersonal (e.g., when a company places an ad on television, radio, or a web page). The receiver (consumer) decodes the message and responds to it in some way. Feedback consists of the responses that the receiver sends back to the source. For example, a consumer might voice an objection to a sales pitch or decide to call a 1-800 number to receive additional product information.

The *noise* concept is very important to this model. Noise represents all the stimuli in the environment that disrupt the communication process. In today's environment, noise comes in many different forms. For example, the popularity of online pop-up blockers is evidence of the number of distractions found on the web. From a traditional advertising perspective, the basic communication model is referred to as a "one-to-many" approach because

message effects how the appeal of a message and its construction affects persuasiveness

source effects characteristics of a source that affect the persuasiveness of a message

it illustrates how a marketer may attempt to communicate with numerous consumers.[23]

7-6a Interactive Communications

The one-to-many communications model works well when examining personal communications or traditional advertising media such as television, newspapers, or radio. However, interactive communications have radically changed the communication paradigm. In fact, recent estimates reveal that over 39% of the world's population (approximately 2.4 billion consumers) now use the Internet; 80% of those consumers live in developed countries.[24] Due to the continued proliferation of the Internet and smartphone technologies, we must consider its effect on the communication process.

Importantly, information flow is no longer considered a "one-way street," in which consumers passively receive messages from marketers. Rather, communication is seen as an interactive process that enables a flow of information among consumers and/or firms in what might be referred to as a many-to-many approach.[25] Senders can place content (web pages, blogs, interactive TV ads) into a medium and communicate directly with receivers through social networking sites, apps, and text messages. Satellite and cable television programming has also become much more interactive. This dramatically changes the communication model, with a newer conceptualization being presented in Exhibit 7.9. Research confirms that social media significantly influence consumer loyalty and word-of-mouth (WOM) today.[26]

Exhibit 7.9

Communication in a Computer-Mediated Environment

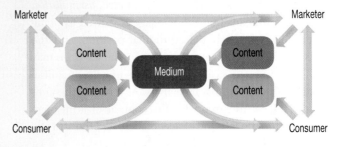

Source: Adapted from Hoffman, Donna L., and Thomas P. Novak (1996), "Marketing in Hypermedia Computer-Mediated Environments: Conceptual Foundations," *Journal of Marketing* 60, no. 3, 50–68.

As we have discussed, both the message itself and the person delivering the message have an impact on the overall effectiveness of an advertisement. For this reason, marketers must consider both elements when developing communication strategies. This section discusses a number of findings regarding message and source effects. As you may remember, some of these topics were first introduced in our chapter on comprehension.

7-6b Message Appeal

There are several ways to conceptualize how a message may affect the persuasiveness of an advertisement. Here, we focus on the appeal (or general content) of an advertisement. A number of appeals are used by advertisers, including sex appeals, humour appeals, fear appeals, and violence appeals.

SEX APPEALS

A popular saying in marketing is that "Sex sells!" Using sexual imagery in advertisements certainly is popular in many parts of the world. In fact, European media usually contain stronger and more explicit sexual appeals than do North American media. As we discussed in Chapter 6, the rationale for this approach is found within the psychoanalytic approach, which assumes that behaviour is influenced by deep-seated desires for pleasure.

Does Sex Sell American Apparel?

Gregory Holmgren / Alamy

Dov Charney—the Montreal-born founder and CEO of American Apparel, who got his start in the fashion business selling T-shirts on Montreal's Sainte-Catherine Street—had two important insights into casual fashion. First, girls liked wearing tight boy-style T-shirts. Second, while everyone else was going offshore to manufacture apparel, there was a large segment of the market willing to support an American-made clothing company. He opened up his first American Apparel factory in downtown Los Angeles, and he paid his workers double the minimum wage. Charney then built the company's reputation on attractive, fashionable, and socially conscious casual clothing.

But when the company began to expand rapidly, its brand became more about its advertising imagery and less about its social conscience. American Apparel's new approach to reaching consumers could easily be described as "Sex Sells!" (recall Freud's influence on consumer research in Chapter 6).

Charney took many of the ad photos himself in the bedroom of his home, using young employees, interns, or people he picked off the street as his models. That approach made the images unique and distinctive in the casual apparel industry. Rather than professional models airbrushed to glossy perfection in carefully designed settings, American Apparel ads have an amateur and personal feel. However, the advertisements have also been very controversial for depicting young girls in poses that are often described as inappropriately sexual or even semi-pornographic. This has led to many of the print ads and website images (http://store.americanapparel.ca) being criticized by the mainstream media and banned by the Advertising Standards Authority (ASA).

However, the real problems for the company have been financial. American Apparel has been losing money and accumulating debt, always seeming to be on the edge of bankruptcy. In 2013, the company lost $106 million and saw interest rates on its loans spike to 20%. Its stock price dropped from a high of $15 in 2007 to less than $0.50 in 2014. Charney's "Sex Sells!" approach was no longer appealing to the customers. On June 18, 2014, Dov Charney was fired as CEO and removed from the company that he founded.

Sources: Baker, Rosie (2012), "Pornographic American Apparel Ads Banned," *Marketing Week* (April). Lipke, David (2012), "American Apparel Faces Crunch of Debt, Losses," *Women's Wear Daily* 203, 54. Kirby, Jason, and MacDonald, Nancy (2008), "Dov Charney's Antics Helped Build a Retail Empire. Now They May be Destroying It," *Maclean's Magazine* 121(17), 36-38. Hess, Amanda (2014), "Dov Charney was Fired for Losing Money, Not Sexual Harassment," *Slate.com* (June 27) http://www.slate.com/ blogs/xx_factor/2014/06/27/dov_charney_firing_american_apparel_ceo_was_fired _for_financial_reasons.html., accessed on April 29, 2015.

Interestingly, consumers often find sexually appealing ads to be persuasive, even when they consider them to be exploitative or offensive![27] However, consumers' reactions to the strategy depend on a number of factors. Moderate levels of nudity appear to be most preferred, as highly explicit content tends to direct attention away from the product.

Gender plays a role in advertising effectiveness regarding nudity. For example, one study found that women react negatively to the use of female nudity in advertising, but that men respond favourably toward the practice.[28] Conversely, a later study revealed men react negatively toward the use of male nudity in ads and that women responded favourably. The type of product being advertised also plays an important role. That is, the use of nudity is most effective for products that have some level of intimate appeal.[29]

Finally, research also reveals that including a romantic theme (rather than focusing on the explicit pleasure of sex) may have positive benefits for marketers. This is good news for fragrance marketers, who often focus their ads on romantic situations and settings.[30]

HUMOUR APPEALS

Marketers also frequently use humorous ads. In today's age of intense advertising clutter, ads that are humorous can be effective. One recent study confirmed that humorous ads can attract attention, create a positive mood, and enhance both attitude toward a brand and purchase intentions. However, humour appeals can also decrease the credibility of a message source.[31] Research also suggests that the use of humour should relate to the product being advertised.[32]

The overall effectiveness of a humorous ad depends, in part, on the characteristics of both the individual consumer and the advertisement. As discussed in another chapter, research indicates that humour is more effective when a consumer's need for cognition is low rather than high,[33] and also when a consumer has a high need for humour.[34] Furthermore, the initial attitude that a consumer has regarding the product plays an important role, as humorous ads appear to be most effective when the consumer's attitudes are initially positive rather than negative.[35]

The amount of humour to place in an advertisement is another issue. High levels of humour can cause consumers to fail to pay attention to the product being advertised, and high levels can also limit information processing.[36] Obviously, marketers don't want to spend millions of dollars on ad campaigns simply for entertainment purposes.

Cats everywhere are having a hard time smelling their litter boxes.   freshstep.com

Humorous ads can attract attention and create a positive mood.

FEAR APPEALS

In addition to using sexual and humour appeals, advertisers also frequently attempt to evoke some level of fear in their target audiences, as a means of changing attitudes and behaviours. These ads often rely on the relationship between a threat (an undesirable consequence of behaviour) and fear (an emotional response).[37] The product being advertised is often promoted as a type of "hero" that will remove the threat.

For example, an insurance company might try to evoke fear in consumers by suggesting that their loved ones may fall into financial hardship if the consumer doesn't carry enough life insurance. Public service announcements may attempt to evoke fear in consumers by highlighting the tragic consequences of unsafe sexual practices (e.g., HIV). Security monitoring services may use fear appeals to draw attention to the frightening consequences of home invasions.

Numerous research studies have addressed the effectiveness of fear appeals in marketing. As a general statement, research suggests that the use of fear appeals can be effective. However, the level of fear that results is very important. Overly high levels of fear may lead consumers to focus on the threat so much that they lose focus on the proposed solution.[38] Also, different consumers are likely to react in different ways to the exact same fear appeal, complicating the issue further.[39] As a result, it is very difficult to predict how an individual consumer will react to any fear appeal. The context in which fear appeals are placed can also influence their effectiveness. For example, attitudes toward a fear-inducing ad have been found to be less positive when the ad is embedded in a sad television program than when the ad is placed in a happy (comedic) program.[40] As an overall statement, fear appeals appear to be effective when they (1) introduce the severity of a threat, (2) present the probability of occurrence, (3) explain the effectiveness of a coping strategy, and (4) show how easy it is to implement the desired response.[41]

Although the use of fear appeals is popular among advertisers, it is important to note that there is an ethical question regarding their use. Critics often argue that the use of fear appeals in advertising is essentially a means of unfair manipulation.[42]

VIOLENCE APPEALS

One trend that has been growing over the last few decades is the use of violent scenes in advertisements. There is much variety in violent themes, from the seemingly innocent to the downright shocking. The effects on viewers often go beyond marketing-related reactions. For example, children who view violent ads are more likely to develop aggressive thoughts, which can eventually lead to aggressive behaviour.[43] Evidence has also shown that women are less receptive to violence in advertisements regardless of the level of severity of the violence, and that younger consumers are generally more receptive to violence in advertising.[44] It is interesting to note that many violent ads also use elements of humour, seemingly in an attempt to lessen the degree to which the ad is disturbing. In fact, many popular commercials have a combination of violence and humour, and a recent study found that the most popular Super Bowl ads include both humour and violence.[45] This area is likely to continue to gain research attention in CB.

7-6c Message Construction

The way that the message is constructed also affects its persuasiveness. Advertisers must consider a number of issues when constructing a message, including both message and source effects. Here, we present a number of questions that marketers must answer.

▸ *Should an ad present a conclusion, or should the consumer be allowed to reach his own conclusion?*

Advertisements that allow consumers to arrive at their own conclusions tend to be more persuasive when the audience has a high level of involvement with the product. Conversely, when the audience is not engaged with the message, it is generally better to draw the conclusion for consumers.[46]

▸ *Should comparative ads that directly compare one brand against another be developed?*

Advertisers generally have three alternatives when developing an ad. First, they can promote their brands without mentioning competing brands. Second, advertisers can promote their brands and compare them generically to "the competition." Third, they can actively compare their products against specific competitors by explicitly naming the competing brands in the advertisement.

Directly comparing one brand against specific competitors can be effective—especially when the brand being promoted is not already the market leader.[47] Promoting a brand as being "superior to all competition" can also be very persuasive when a firm hopes to court users away from all competing brands.[48]

▸ *Where should important information be placed?*

The placement of information in a specific message at the beginning, middle, or end of the message affects the recall of the information. This is a basic tenet of what is known as the **serial position effect**.[49] When material presented early in a message is most influential, a **primacy effect** is said to occur. When material presented later in the message has the most impact, a **recency effect** is said to occur.[50]

Research suggests that primacy effects are likely to occur when the audience is highly engaged (highly involved) and when verbal (versus pictorial) content is present.[51] If marketers are attempting to reach a highly involved audience, important information should be placed early in the message. Marketers can also attempt to gain the consumer's attention as early as possible and encourage careful processing of information by using

serial position effect occurs when the placement of information in a message affects recall of the information

primacy effect occurs when the information placed early in a message has the most impact

recency effect occurs when the information placed late in a message has the most impact statements such as "an important message" or "listen carefully." For audiences with lower levels of involvement, important information can be placed late in the message. These effects also occur in series of messages and can affect the recall of commercials placed in any particular block of commercials. For example, research has revealed that primacy effects prevail for the recall of Super Bowl commercials. That is, commercials placed at the beginning of a block resulted in higher levels of consumer recall.[52]

▶ *Should the message be straightforward and simple, or complex?*

In general, complex ads take more effort on the part of the consumer and require deep information processing. Overly complex messages can cause frustration within consumers and lead to unfavourable reactions. As presented earlier in the section on the ELM, the number of arguments presented in an ad is considered a peripheral cue. Highly involved consumers are more motivated to attend to a larger number of arguments than are less motivated consumers.

As you can see, a marketer must consider numerous message-related issues.

7-6d Source Effects

Another important issue in the study of persuasion is how the source of a message (a spokesperson or model, for example) influences consumers' attitudes. Source effects include issues such as credibility, attractiveness, likeability, and meaningfulness.

SOURCE CREDIBILITY

Source credibility plays an important role in advertising effectiveness. In general, credible sources tend to be more persuasive than less credible sources. This effect tends to be highest when consumers lack the ability or motivation to expend effort attending to the details of an ad (low involvement).[53] However, credible sources also influence highly involved consumers, especially if their credentials are clearly communicated early in a message.[54] The credibility of sources also affects the certainty with which consumer attitudes are held, with lower levels of credibility leading to higher levels of certainty.[55]

As we discussed in our comprehension chapter, credibility consists of two elements: expertise and trustworthiness. *Expertise* refers to the amount of knowledge that a spokesperson is perceived to have about the product or issue in question. You may remember from our presentation on the ELM that source expertise represents a peripheral cue in advertising. Expertise can be an

Source credibility is important in advertising.

important quality for a spokesperson to possess. In fact, a major review of source effects has revealed that source expertise has the biggest influence of all source effects on consumer responses to advertisements.[56]

Trustworthiness refers to a perception of the extent to which a spokesperson is presenting a message that he or she truly believes, with no reason to present false information. Interestingly, expertise and trustworthiness can independently influence persuasion. That is, trustworthy sources can be persuasive even if they're not experts, and expert sources can be persuasive even if they're perceived as being untrustworthy.[57]

Finally, we note that source credibility, although generally conceptualized as pertaining to a spokesperson or model, also applies to the sponsoring company. In fact, research reveals that the credibility of both the spokesperson and the company influences the effectiveness of an advertisement, with the credibility of the spokesperson having a stronger influence than the credibility of the company.[58]

SOURCE ATTRACTIVENESS

Source attractiveness is another quality that has received a great deal of attention. Attractive models are often thought to possess desirable qualities and personalities. They also tend to be more persuasive than unattractive spokespeople.[59] However, the type of product plays an important role in the process. Much like the research regarding the use of sex appeals, research into attractiveness reveals that attractive models are more effective when promoting products that have an intimate appeal, whereas unattractive models are more effective when promoting products that have no intimate appeal.[60] This is particularly the case when consumers have the ability and motivation to process the message being presented.[61]

SOURCE LIKEABILITY

Source likeability also affects a spokesperson's effectiveness. Likeable sources tend to be persuasive. Of course, individuals differ in terms of which celebrities they like and dislike, and marketers are very interested in finding the best possible spokesperson for a given market segment. The advertising industry relies heavily on a Q-score rating provided by Marketing Evaluations, Inc., as an indication of the overall appeal of celebrities.[62] Interestingly, it has been found that source likeability affects persuasion more for consumers with low need for cognition than for those with a high degree of this trait. This again highlights the importance of individual difference variables in persuasion.[63]

SOURCE MEANINGFULNESS

Celebrities have images and cultural meanings that resonate with consumers. For example, a famous athlete like LeBron James embodies the image of hard work and success. Pairing LeBron with athletic apparel or footwear simply makes sense. You should recall that research on the use of sexual imagery and source attractiveness suggests that these characteristics should be matched with the type of product being advertised. This is true for source meaningfulness as well. That is, the dominant characteristics of a source should match the characteristics of the product. This is a key concept that is found in the **matchup hypothesis**, which states that a source feature is most effective when it is matched with relevant products.[64] As such, we should expect LeBron James to be an effective spokesperson for footwear and less effective when promoting a product that has no athletic qualities at all.

matchup hypothesis
hypothesis that states that a source feature is most effective when it is matched with relevant products

STUDY TOOLS 7

LOCATED AT THE BACK OF THE TEXTBOOK

☐ Rip out Chapter Review Card

LOCATED AT NELSON.COM/STUDENT

☐ Review Key Terms Flashcards (print or online)

☐ Download audio summaries to review on the go

☐ Complete practice quizzes to prepare for tests

☐ Watch video on Southwest Airlines for a real company example

Case

Find Your Greatness

For Adidas, the 2012 London Olympics were an opportunity to build its brand, gain market share and, maybe most importantly, outperform Nike. As a "tier one" sponsor, Adidas paid about £40 million (approximately $65 million Canadian) to be the Games' official clothing licensee.[65] In exchange the company was given the exclusive rights to Olympic branded clothing and the opportunity to outfit the athletes and the 70,000 volunteers. Adidas opened 100 temporary Olympic-themed "AdiZones" in England and advertised heavily around the Games. The company aimed to leverage its sponsorship to affect consumers' attitudes toward the brand. Adidas's CEO described the Olympics as "the ideal platform to show the world that we are one of the greatest sports brands in the world."[66]

The Adidas sponsorship meant that competitors, such as Nike, were not allowed even to mention the Olympics or London, England, in their advertising. Nike was also struggling with its traditional marketing model in the face of substantial negative publicity surrounding celebrity endorsers like Tiger Woods and Lance Armstrong.

Unable to focus on the Olympics directly and reluctant to rely on celebrity endorsements, Nike decided to take a different approach and launched a guerrilla marketing campaign with the hashtag #findyourgreatness. The voice-over on the company's television commercial told us that *"Greatness is not in one special place, and it is not one special person. Greatness is wherever somebody is trying to find it."* Nike went on to profile everyday people in "other Londons" in Ohio, Jamaica, Nigeria, and Norway, as well as Canada's own London, Ontario. The YouTube videos became a viral sensation and Twitter users posted about Nike together with the Olympics in more than 16,000 tweets using #findyourgreatness. As a result, Nike grew its Twitter following by 11% or 57,000 followers during the games, while Adidas attracted only 12,000 new followers (4% growth). As the Games kicked off on July 27, survey results

Joe Toth/BPI/Corbis

indicated that 37% of consumers thought that Nike was an Olympic sponsor, compared to only 24% who correctly identified Adidas.[67]

The YouTube videos can be viewed here: https://www.youtube.com/watch?v=WYP9AGtLvRg).

Sources: *BoxUK* (2013), "Analysis: Nike #findyourgreatness," BoxUK.com (April 5), accessed at http://www.boxuk.com/blog/analysis-nike-findyourgreatness/ on April 30, 2015. Gianatasio, David (2012), "Nike Looking for Greatness in Ordinary People and Places: Olympic-timed work, for once, is celeb-free," *Adweek* (July 26), accessed at http://www.adweek.com/adfreak/nike-looking-greatness-ordinary-people-and-places-142207 on April 30, 2015. Sweney, Mark (2012), "Olympics 2012: Nike plots ambush ad campaign," *The Guardian* (July 25), accessed at http://www.theguardian.com/media/2012/jul/25/olympics-2012-nike-ambush-ad on April 20, 2015.

QUESTIONS

1 Take a few minutes to view some of the Nike Greatness videos on YouTube. Do the protagonists in these videos have source credibility? Why or why not?

2 How would you explain Nike's success using a computer-mediated model of communication versus the more basic communication model used by Adidas?

3 What values or aspect of one's self-concept might a consumer be expressing with a positive attitude toward the Nike Greatness videos?

4 From a hierarchy of effects perspective, how would you describe the process that a consumer might go through when purchasing and using Nike products?

5 Is Nike advertising trying to influence the evaluation ratings or the belief ratings in the ATO model of consumers' attitude toward Nike? What "attribute" of the product is the focus of Nike's attempt to affect consumers' attitude toward Nike?

6 Based on the elaboration likelihood model, what level of involvement does Nike's advertising expect from the target consumers?

8 | Consumer Culture

AP Photo/Jennifer Szymaszek

LEARNING OBJECTIVES

After studying this chapter, the student should be able to:

8-1 Understand how culture provides the true meaning of objects and activities.

8-2 Use the key dimensions of core societal values to apply the concept of cultural distance.

8-3 Define acculturation and enculturation.

8-4 List fundamental elements of verbal and nonverbal communication.

8-5 Discuss current emerging consumer markets and scan for opportunities.

 ## 8-1 CULTURE AND MEANING ARE INSEPARABLE

"Grande doppio latte, please!" What language is this? A consumer can use this expression in 50 countries and get exactly what he or she wants, with no translation. The popularity of Starbucks has led to a universal language describing coffee consumption.

Canadians do not really have a deep history as gourmet coffee lovers. In fact, historically, the typical Canadian coffee was cheap, weak, and nondescript at best. Yet, in Canada, coffee is the first choice for a morning beverage. In parts of Asia, coffee consumption is relatively rare, as tea is preferred in the morning and throughout the day.

With all of these different coffee-drinking habits and orientations, how could a single coffee company succeed, with the same basic formula, in so many different places around the world? In fact, this chapter's feature, "The World *Is* Their Cup," describes how Starbucks defied the odds in expanding in new and different cultures, like China. In North America,

consumer culture
commonly held societal beliefs that define what is socially gratifying

a $2 cup of coffee may seem relatively costly compared with traditional convenience store prices, but $2 is within reach of nearly all Canadians. However, consider how a $2 price tag might compare in countries such as Poland, Mexico, or China. For Starbucks to succeed globally, it has to offer an experience that adds value to consumers who come from many different backgrounds and many different orientations. Thus, Starbucks's success depends on being accepted by the local culture and somehow creating a meaning that conveys value in the coffee shop experience.

8-1a What Is Culture?

Consumers make very simple decisions involving things like coffee drinking, and very important and meaningful decisions involving things like religious affiliations. In all cases, what a person consumes helps determine how accepted one is by other consumers in society. Likewise, the consumption act itself generally has no absolute meaning, only meaning relative to the environment in which the act takes place. Culture, therefore, embodies meaning.

Consumer culture can be thought of as commonly held societal beliefs that define what is socially

gratifying. Culture shapes value by framing everyday life in terms of these commonly held beliefs. The fact that the average price for a cup of coffee in Canada has risen indicates that the beliefs that people have about the coffee-drinking experience have certainly changed and define a more valuable experience than in decades past. Culture ultimately determines what consumption behaviours are acceptable.

Although Canadian adults enjoy coffee, some consumers believe that providing coffee to a child is unacceptable. In other areas, however, consumers may see this behaviour as quite normal. Culture shapes the value of beverages, just as it does with other products. Exhibit 8.1 lists some consumption behaviours that vary in meaning, value, and acceptability from culture to culture.

8-1b Culture, Meaning, and Value

The focus of this chapter is on culture. This focus acknowledges that the marketplace today truly is

Exhibit 8.1

Culture, Meaning, and Value

Behaviour	Meaning in Canada	Alternative Meaning
People aged 14–18 consuming beer or wine in a restaurant.	Unacceptable or even illegal in most areas.	Wine is part of a nice family meal in other areas, including much of Western Europe.
People gathering to eat barbecue pork ribs.	This menu is part of a pleasant social event.	Pork is not an acceptable food item among Jews and Muslims.
Supervisors and employees socializing together.	Supervisors and co-workers can be friendly with one another.	Employees and supervisors should keep their distance away from work. An employee who acts too casually with a "senior" could incur a sanction.
Kissing.	Purely a family or romantic activity.	In many nations, kissing is common when making a new acquaintance or greeting a friend.

The World *Is* Their Cup!

Starbucks has more than 21,000 stores in practically every corner of the world. Starbucks has even been successful in places like Paris, where "experts" said the concept was too American and inconsistent with the Parisian idea of a coffeehouse. However, can Starbucks succeed in a place where consumers associate drinking coffee with the parched sensation of the Sahara Desert?

This is the challenge that faces Starbucks. China is a tea-drinking country, and one where a $4 grande latte is truly a luxury for many consumers. The average income in this area is under $4,000 per year. Starbucks's strategy in China is to capitalize on the stores as a gathering place. So, the stores are generally bigger with larger sitting areas than in a typical North American Starbucks. The ambiance is clearly Starbucks. Additionally, an emphasis on sweeter products, more food items, and fresh-brewed tea is the recipe the company will follow. Starbucks hopes to deliver a high-hedonic-value experience that will lead to success for most of its more than 400 stores across China.

iStockphoto.com/sapandr

Sources: Adamy, J. (2006), "Eyeing a Billion Tea Drinkers, Starbucks Pours it on in China," *The Wall Street Journal*, (November 29), A1; Chao, L. (2006), "Starbucks Raises Stake in Beijing, Tianjin Stores," *The Wall Street Journal Online*, (October 25), http:online.wsj.com/article/SB116167895560901902.cb.html, accessed 10/25/2006; Adamy, J. (2007), "Starbucks Chairman Says Trouble May be Brewing," *The Wall Street Journal*, (February 24), A4.

global. Modern technology has greatly reduced the geographic barriers that prevented consumers from doing business with marketers in other parts of the world. Without culture, consumers would have little guidance as to the appropriate actions in many common consumer situations. Thus, culture performs important functions for consumers. These functions shape the value of consumer activities and include the following:

▸ **Giving meaning to objects.** Consider how much culture defines the meaning of food, religious objects, and everyday items like furniture. For instance, in Japan, refrigerators are tiny by most Western standards.

▸ **Giving meaning to activities.** Consider, for example, the role of things as simple as recreational activities and even washing (hygiene). A daily shower is not a universally accepted norm.

▸ **Facilitating communication.** The shared meaning of things facilitates communication. When strangers meet, culture indicates whether a handshake, hug, or kiss is most appropriate. Things as simple as making eye contact can take on dramatically different meanings from one culture to another.

8-1c Cultural Norms

Culture, meaning, and value are very closely intertwined. For this reason, culture determines things that are socially rewarding (valuable) or socially unrewarding (not valuable). A consumer who acts inconsistently with cultural expectations risks being socially ostracized. The term **cultural norm** refers to a rule that specifies the appropriate behaviour in a given situation within a specific culture. Most, but not all, cultural norms are unwritten and simply understood by members of a cultural group.

In South Korea, for example, a consumer is not expected to pour a drink for himself or herself when out in a bar or restaurant with friends or family. The cultural norm is that one pours a drink for friends and family. Thus, by pouring drinks for others and waiting for someone else to pour a drink for him or her, the consumer has performed a socially rewarding (valuable) act consistent with the norms of that society.

8-1d Cultural Sanctions

So, what happens to a consumer who performs an act inconsistent with cultural norms? Unfortunately, the consumer is likely to experience a **cultural sanction**—the

cultural norm rule that specifies the appropriate consumer behaviour in a given situation within a specific culture

cultural sanction penalty associated with performing a nongratifying or culturally inconsistent behaviour penalties associated with performing a nongratifying or culturally inconsistent behaviour. Cultural sanctions often are relatively innocuous. For instance, if one were to pour his own drink in Korea, he is likely to get only a curious look or suffer some innocent teasing from members of the group. In other instances, however, a consumer performing a culturally inconsistent act may be shunned or suffer banishment from a group.

Many societies still have strong cultural norms about marrying outside of one's social class, religion, or ethnic group. Violation of this norm can result in isolation from family or worse. Physically or socially harming a family member for fraternizing beyond one's cultural group represents a fairly strong cultural sanction.

POPULAR CULTURE

Popular culture captures cultural trends and shapes norms and sanctions within society. A few decades ago, a male university student might have routinely worn platform shoes, silk shirts, sideburns, and maybe even an Afro hairstyle. For a student in the 1970s, all of these consumer behaviours would have been consistent with popular culture. A student who showed up at class in this fashion today would certainly stand out from his or her classmates and might face at the least one or two curious glances. Pop icons such as Lady Gaga or Kanye West help determine acceptable style for many groups of admirers who desire to fit in with today's popular culture.

Does Lady Gaga set any cultural norms?

ROLE EXPECTATIONS

Every consumer plays various roles within society. Culture expects people to play these roles in a culturally rewarding fashion. In other words, when a consumer interacts with another person, any characteristic upon which that person can be categorized activates certain behavioural expectations. Recall that in a previous chapter we described how social schema (stereotypes) help consumers organize knowledge about people. **Role expectations** are the specific expectations that are associated with each type of person. One's sex, one's occupation, one's social class, and one's age all are relevant bases for forming societal role expectations. Role expectations become a primary basis for cultural norms and sanctions. They define not only the way one should act to play the role, but also the types of products that are appropriate for a person within a role. When a consumer travels to a foreign country, he or she may well find that expectations for a given role are different from at home. As a result, the consumption activities associated with roles can also vary from culture to culture.

In Western Canada, for example, a typical service employee in a restaurant, a department store, or even a hotel plays his or her societal role well by speaking English. However, in Montreal, a consumer expects that a service employee can respond in at least two languages. In many other parts of the world, a service employee will speak multiple languages. Exhibit 8.2 provides some other examples of cultural role expectations. In the next chapter, we focus more specifically on societal roles tied to demographic characteristics.

8-2 USING CORE SOCIETAL VALUES

8-2a Where Does Culture Come From?

Consumer researchers commonly use culture to explain and predict consumer behaviour.[1] Estimates suggest that out of all academic explanations of consumer behaviour, more than 10% of all explanations include culture as a key factor.[2] Cultural beliefs define what religion is acceptable, what types of art and recreation are preferred, what manners are considered polite, the

role expectations the specific expectations that are associated with each type of person within a culture or society

Exhibit 8.2

Societal Role Expectations Vary

Role	Role Expectations in Canada	Role Expectations Outside of Canada
Service employee	Treat customers promptly, courteously, and as a priority.	Russia: Customers not treated quite so promptly or courteously—the worker is prioritized over the customer.
University student	Casual relationship with professors, often on first-name basis. Expected to question professors and challenge ideas.	China: More formal relationship with professors. Less likely to question professors or challenge ideas.
Motorcycle driver	Dress down and generally follow the same driving rules as automobile drivers.	Italy: Dress up (often going to the office) and generally ignore the rules for automobiles—particularly traffic lanes.

roles for different types of individuals, including expectations for men and women in a society, and much more. Distinguishing the unique effects of culture on these more specific things is extremely difficult since as part of culture, these things tend to function together. There is, however, little doubt that culture causes differences in the value consumers perceive from different products and experiences.[3]

How do people in one nation end up with a culture distinct from that of people in another? In other words, what causes culture? The answer to this question involves two important components.

First, ecological factors cause differences in culture because they change the relative value of objects. **Ecological factors** are the physical characteristics that describe the physical environment and habitat of a particular place. Thus, for example, consumers from groups that have traditionally lived in desert areas place a great value on water relative to consumers from areas filled with freshwater lakes. As a result, consumers from a desert area may have different habits when it comes to hygiene, including the frequency and duration of baths or showers. This can affect sales of beauty products, soaps, and toilet water, and also things like hotel room and building design.

Second, over time, tradition develops among groups of peoples, and these traditions carry forward to structure society. **Tradition** in this sense refers to the customs and accepted ways of structuring society. Traditions include things like the family and political structures of a society. In Canada, the United States,

Australia, and much of Europe, families traditionally consist of two generations (parents and children) living in a household, in which a husband and wife share decision making. In other cultures, more than two generations (grandparents, parents, and children) may share a household, and the key decision maker is the oldest male living in the house. Thus, consumer advertising may need to differ based on the traditional family decision-making style associated with a culture. While tradition can be thought of as influencing culture, one can safely say that, in the long run, culture also defines tradition.

FoodPix/ Jupiterimages/Getty Images

Religious traditions shape consumption experiences.

ecological factors
physical characteristics that describe the physical environment and habitat of a particular place

tradition customs and accepted ways of everyday behaviour in a given culture

Exhibit 8.3

Inputs and Outputs of Culture

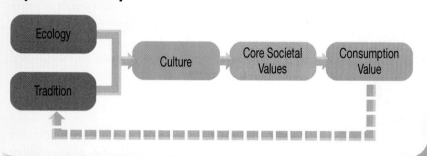

Exhibit 8.3 illustrates how tradition and ecology come together to influence culture, with each culture described by different amounts of core societal values (discussed later in this chapter), and these values driving differences in consumer behaviours and the value derived from them. Over time, traditions become embedded in culture and become relatively stable. However, while stable, they do slowly change, as illustrated by the changes in places where people could traditionally smoke without fear of sanctions. In this sense, not only are the choices and behaviours of consumers influenced by culture, but, in the end, subtle changes in these choices and behaviours also influence culture.

8-2b Dimensions of Cultural Values

Although conflicting views exist on what exactly are the best dimensions to describe differences in cultural values, the most widely applied dimensions are those developed by Geert Hofstede.[4] This theory of value-based differences in cultures is based on five key dimensions, with each dimension representing a core societal value. **Core societal values (CSV) or cultural values** represent a commonly agreed-upon consensus about the most preferable ways of living within a society. Even though not all members of a culture may share precisely the same values to the same degree, a specific cultural group will tend to have common worldviews along these dimensions. Exhibit 8.3 illustrates how core societal values serve as the mechanism by which culture affects value. Cultural values can be classified using multiple dimensions. In some cases, the dimensions overlap with each other or relate to one another.

INDIVIDUALISM

The first core societal value dimension contrasts cultures based on relative amounts of individualism and collectivism.[5] **Individualism** as a CSV means the extent to which people expect each other to take responsibility for themselves and their immediate family. Highly individualistic societies place high value on self-reliance, individual initiative, and personal achievement. In contrast, nations with low individualism are seen as high in **collectivism**, which refers to the extent to which an individual's life is intertwined with a large, cohesive group. Highly collectivistic societies tend to live in extended families, take their identity from the groups to which they belong, and be very loyal to these groups.

Clearly, this dimension has important implications for the way consumers make decisions and the way that consumers extract value from consumption (see Chapter 2 for an illustration). In Canada, marketers often communicate the value of various products by illustrating the extent to which they help one achieve personal freedom. American consumers often see important purchases as an extension of themselves. Advertisements for cigarettes, jeans, ATVs, and even laptop computers commonly use adjectives such as *rugged, tough,* and *dependable*.[6] In contrast, an advertisement for a collective culture may rely more on adjectives such as *honest* or *friendly*.

Generally, Western societies tend to be more individualistic, whereas Eastern nations tend to be more collectivistic. Collectivist societies tend to be more compliant with requests from group members. North American consumers, for instance, once they have made a choice, are more likely to repeat that choice a second time because its value is enhanced by virtue of having been selected originally. In contrast, consumers from Asia do not increase the value of something they chose previously, and are more susceptible to making a choice that someone in their group has chosen previously.[7]

core societal values (CSV) or cultural values commonly agreed-upon consensus about the most preferable ways of living within a society

individualism extent to which people are expected to take care of themselves and their immediate families

collectivism extent to which an individual's life is intertwined with a large cohesive group

New Dove Firming. As tested on real curves.

campaignforrealbeauty.com ➤ Dove

VIACOM

Bill Aron/PhotoEdit

A typical advertisement appealing to individualism as a core societal value.

This generality is just that—a generality! There are, of course, exceptions to this type of rule. Later, we'll discuss specific scores on all dimensions across many countries.

MASCULINITY

The **masculinity** CSV dimension captures distinctions existing in societies based on mannerisms typically associated with Western male traits, such as valuing assertiveness and control, over traditional feminine traits such as caring, conciliation, and community. **Femininity** represents the opposite of masculinity, but in this case, the masculinity–femininity distinction does not refer to a political or social movement, or to the prominence that men and women have within a society. In fact, women's traits tend to vary less from nation to nation than do those of men, so femininity is most clearly obvious within a masculine culture. In other words, in a culture with low masculinity, men also tend to share some *feminine* traits.[8]

Advertisements for laptop computers in a highly masculine nation, such as Japan, may emphasize the computer's ability to help one get ahead. A newer, faster computer with more features can help a man assert himself in the workplace or at school. In contrast, in a more feminine country such as Mexico, an advertisement for the same laptop computer might emphasize the benefit of being able to stay in touch with family and friends through email and web-based communication.

POWER DISTANCE

Power distance is the extent to which authority and privilege are divided among different groups within society and the extent to which people accept these divisions as facts of life within the society. Social class distinctions become a very real issue among consumers in high-power-distance nations. However, the distinctions go beyond just social class and affect relationships between supervisory and subordinate employees, and even between students and teachers.

Low-power-distance nations tend to be more egalitarian. First names are commonly used among people of different social classes, and even between employees and supervisors. In high-power-distance nations, those with less status must show deference to those with greater status; therefore, the lower-status person would not likely call a person of higher status by first name.

In many Asian nations, where power distance is relatively high compared with that in the Canada, the terms *senior* and *junior* are often used to capture status distinctions. A student might be junior to a faculty supervisor or to another student who preceded him or her through a program of study. When one is unclear about whether he or she is junior or senior to another, he or she might well ask the other person, "How old are you?" Age would be a tiebreaker, with older people having more status than younger people. Senior and junior status can affect simple things such as seating arrangements and whether one carries his or her own briefcase. Juniors may need to be careful in what they buy and do so as not to seem superior in any substantive way to a senior. A consumer violating a custom and acting more "senior" than appropriate may well face cultural sanctions for the behaviour.

In high-power-distance nations, certain consumer behaviours are designated exclusively to individuals by class or status. For example, in high-power-distance nations, golf is seen as an activity only for those with very high status. Additionally, authority appeals in marketing are more effective when power distance is high.[9]

masculinity role distinction within a group that values assertiveness and control; core societal value opposite of femininity

femininity sex role distinction within a group that emphasizes the prioritization of relational variables such as caring, conciliation, and community; core societal value opposite of masculinity

power distance extent to which authority and privileges are divided among different groups within society and the extent to which these facts of life are accepted by the people within the society

UNCERTAINTY AVOIDANCE

Uncertainty avoidance is just what the term implies. A culture high in uncertainty avoidance is uncomfortable with things that are ambiguous or unknown. Consumers high in uncertainty avoidance prefer the known, avoid taking risks, and like life to be structured and routine. Uncertainty avoidance has important implications for consumer behaviour because marketing success and improved quality of life often depend on obtaining value from something innovative and, therefore, somewhat unfamiliar. The task becomes making the unfamiliar seem familiar in appealing to consumers high in uncertainty avoidance.

Nations that are high in uncertainty avoidance will be slower to adopt product innovations. Additionally, nations that are relatively high in uncertainty avoidance, such as France, will react differently to basic CB generalizations. For instance, one such generalization is that scarcity affects the perceived value of products. A scarce product is worth more, and consumers are more likely to purchase a product perceived to be scarce. The extent to which scarcity drives actual purchase intentions is more pronounced among cultures high in uncertainty avoidance.[10] In other words, consumers in high-uncertainty-avoidance cultures are quicker to buy something because of perceived scarcity.

Uncertainty avoidance has important implications for consumer behaviour, because marketing success and improved quality of life often depend on obtaining value from something innovative and, therefore, somewhat unfamiliar.

Basic consumer principles such as the price–quality relationship are also affected by differing CSV. For instance, the price–quality relationship is not as strong among cultures with high uncertainty avoidance. These consumers are more skeptical and likely to discern individual features of products separately. Such is the case with Chinese consumers, who are more likely to perceive a price–risk relationship than a price–quality relationship. In other words, higher price means higher risk in conditions of uncertainty.[11] Superstitions and myths also play a bigger role among cultures high in uncertainty avoidance.[12] Consumers in these cultures may even use astrological charts to help plan visits to casinos. Thus, the casinos in these cultures can somewhat predict peak periods of traffic based on these types of beliefs.

Consumers in high-uncertainty-avoidance cultures also demand greater amounts of product information and explanation. Bosch automotive industries, based in Germany, designs different packages for products sold

Photosani/Shutterstock.com

Astrological charts are important ways to predict the future in some cultures high in uncertainty avoidance. Can astrology reduce uncertainty avoidance?

in Europe and products sold in North America. For example, a packet containing replacement windshield wipers might be sold in a simple cellophane package in Canada. In Europe, the same product might require a box, not because the products differ in size but because the box allows more room to include product information about the wipers and how to install them than does a plastic wrapper. As a result, the European customers find more value and experience greater satisfaction with these products.

LONG-TERM ORIENTATION

The final CSV dimension is long-term orientation. **Long-term orientation** reflects values consistent with Confucian philosophy and a prioritization of future rewards over short-term benefits. As such, high long-term orientation means that a consumer values thriftiness and perseverance as well as the maintenance of long-term relationships.[13] Relationships need time to develop and are intended to last for a lifetime. As a result, negotiations between suppliers and buyers are more likely to consider long-term effects for both parties in a high long-term orientation culture such as Japan.[14] At the other end of the spectrum, a short-term orientation is associated more with immediate payoffs and face saving.[15]

uncertainty avoidance
extent to which a culture is uncomfortable with things that are ambiguous or unknown

long-term orientation
values consistent with Confucian philosophy and a prioritization of future rewards over short-term benefits

Guanxi (pronounced *gawn-shi*) is the Chinese term for a way of doing business in which parties must first invest time and resources in getting to know one another, and becoming comfortable with one another, before consummating any important deal. Guanxi is a common mode of operation among cultures with high long-term orientation—as in many nations in the Far East.[16] Western consumers depend on credit cards for everyday purchases, and even in many cases as instant financing for luxury items. Thus, Canadian consumers often have multiple credit cards, each from a different bank or credit company. As the Chinese economy develops, the principles of guanxi and long-term orientation present barriers for credit card companies.[17] The Chinese consumers are loath to take a card from a company they do not know or fully understand. Also, the idea of financing consumer products remains foreign.

Renquing is another phenomenon associated with long-term orientation. **Renquing** is the idea that when someone does a good deed for you, you are expected to return that good deed. The reciprocation need not be immediate, however. In fact, the expectation of reciprocation at some point in the future fosters long-term relationships, as individuals are forever trying to balance the renquing score with one other.[18] Thus, a consumer and personal service provider may end up in a long-term relationship facilitated in part by renquing.

8-2c The CSV Scoreboard

A CSV scoreboard can be put together using historical CSV dimension scores found in many resources, including the Hofstede website (www.geert-hofstede.com). The CSV scores for a given country can be essential information for marketers wishing to appeal to consumers in another country. The more

guanxi (pronounced *gawn-shi*) Chinese term for a way of doing business in which parties must first invest time and resources in getting to know one another and becoming comfortable with one another before consummating any important deal

renquing the idea that favours given to another are reciprocal and must be returned

BRIC acronym that refers to the collective economies of Brazil, Russia, India, and China

Exhibit 8.4

CSV Scoreboard for a Select Group of Nations

	Power Distance	Individualism	Masculinity	Uncertainty Avoidance	Long-Term Orientation
Canada	39	80	52	48	23
United States	40	91	62	46	29
Australia	36	90	61	51	31
United Kingdom	35	89	66	35	25
Brazil	69	38	49	76	65
Russia	93	39	36	95	n/a
India	77	48	56	40	61
Pakistan	55	14	50	70	n/a
China	80	20	66	30	118

Source: Geert Hofstede, Gert Jan Hofstede, Michael Minkov, *Cultures and Organizations, Software of the Mind*, Third Revised Edition, McGrawHill 2010, ISBN 0-07-166418-1. © Geert Hofstede B.V. quoted with permission.

similar the CSV scores, the more likely consumers find value in the same or similar products and experiences.

BRIC

Exhibit 8.4 shows a CSV scoreboard for a few select nations. Brazil, Russia, India, and China represent widely accepted emerging economies. The acronym **BRIC** refers to the collective economies of these nations. These nations are key targets for foreign investment, and the ripple effect is that consumers in these nations are becoming wealthier and better targets for all manner of goods and services. Doing business in these nations is hardly the same, though, as their CSV scores show. In this truly global marketplace, serving consumers in emerging markets can be an important route to business success. Some are now considering where the next emerging nations will be.[19]

CSV LEADERS

Among all nations with CSV scores, Austria has the lowest power-distance scores, and Malaysia has the highest. Canada has relatively low power distance, with only 14 nations reporting lower scores. For individualism, Guatemala reports the lowest score and the United States the highest. Sweden reports the lowest masculinity score and Japan the highest, with the exception of the

Slovak nations. Canada is neither clearly masculine nor clearly feminine. Singapore reports the lowest uncertainty avoidance score and Greece the highest. Canada is relatively low on uncertainty avoidance. Long-term orientation scores are available for only a few nations. But, among those listed in Exhibit 8.4, China has the highest at 118, while Canada has the lowest at 23.

8-2d Cultural Distance

More and more businesses are considering reaching out to markets outside of their own country. Certainly, the Internet has helped reduce the market separations caused by geographic distance. However, consider businesses like Carrefour, Subway, Accor Hotels, and Zara. Each already operates many stores in many countries. How should a company decide where it should expand internationally? In other words, where will it be successful?

Two approaches to this important question can be taken. First, perhaps the most intuitive response is to look to neighbouring countries with which the home country shares a border. This approach is based on geographic distance. Countries are attractive because they are nearby and can be easily reached in terms of both marketing communications and physical distribution. Certainly, many U.S. businesses exist in Canada and vice versa.

The second approach looks more at how similar a target nation's consumers are to the home consumers. This

How should a company decide where it should expand internationally?

approach is based more on **cultural distance**, which represents how disparate one nation is from another in terms of their CSVs. With this approach, consumers can be compared by using scores available in a CSV scoreboard. For example, Exhibit 8.5 shows the difference scores for all nations depicted in the CSV scoreboard compared with those of Canada. These are obtained simply by using Exhibit 8.4 and subtracting the score for each nation on each dimension from the corresponding score for Canadian consumers.

cultural distance
representation of how disparate one nation is from another in terms of their CSVs

Exhibit 8.5

CSV Difference Scores Relative to Canadian Consumers

	Power Distance	Individualism	Masculinity	Uncertainty Avoidance	Long-Term Orientation	Total Distance Scores
United States	1	11	10	−2	6	16.2
Australia	−3	10	9	3	8	16.2
United Kingdom	−4	9	14	−13	2	21.6
Brazil	30	−42	−3	28	42	72.3
Russia	54	−41	−16	47	32	89.9
India	38	−32	4	−8	38	63.2
Pakistan	16	−66	−2	22	−23	75.0
China	41	−60	14	−18	95	121.8

Source: Geert Hofstede, Gert Jan Hofstede, Michael Minkov, *Cultures and Organizations, Software of the Mind*, Third Revised Edition, McGrawHill 2010, ISBN 0-07-166418-1. © Geert Hofstede B.V. quoted with permission.

Notice the small score differences on each dimension between Canada, Australia, the United Kingdom, and the United States compared with the other nations. A simple distance formula can summarize the cultural differences between nations. One might consider simply adding up the difference scores; however, the negative and positive scores could cancel each other out, making two nations that are really quite different appear similar. One way to correct this problem is by using the squared differences, much as would be the case in computing statistical variation. For example, the following formula is used to compute the total cultural distances from Canada for each nation shown in Exhibit 8.5:

$$CD = \sqrt{\sum_{i=1}^{5}(TCSV_i - BCSV_i)^2}$$

where CD = cultural distance, TCSV = target country value score on dimension i, and BCSV = baseline country value score on dimension i.

Thus, for example, the CD for the United States from Canada is 16.2:

$$CD = \sqrt{\begin{array}{c}(40-39)^2 + (91-80)^2 + (62-52)^2 \\ + (46-48)^2 + (29-23)^2\end{array}}$$

$$CD = \sqrt{(262)}$$

$$CD = 16.2$$

Among all comparisons, few would show so little difference as this. Compare these with the CD scores for the BRIC countries. The CD score between any two countries is easily computed for all nations for which CSV scores are available.

Countries with relatively low CD scores are more similar and thus tend to value the same types of consumption experiences. In fact, the term **CANZUS** is sometimes used to refer to the close similarity in values between Canada, Australia, New Zealand, and the United States.[20] Additionally, the U could represent the United Kingdom because this nation too is very similar from a CD perspective. Not surprisingly, common consumer products, retailers, and restaurant chains that are successful in one of these countries tend to be successful in the others as well.

CANZUS acronym that refers to the close similarity in values between Canada, Australia, New Zealand, and the United States

socialization learning through observation of and the active processing of information about lived, everyday experience

enculturation way a person learns his or her native culture

acculturation process by which consumers come to learn a culture other than their natural, native culture

International expansion decisions should consider CD as well as geography.

8-3 HOW IS CULTURE LEARNED?

Culture is a learned process. Consumers learn culture through one of two socialization processes discussed in this section. **Socialization** involves learning through observation and the active processing of information about lived, everyday experience. The process takes place in a sequence something like this:

Social Interaction ↦ Modelling ↦ Reinforcement

As consumers interact, they begin to model (meaning enact) behaviours learned or seen. Reinforcement occurs through the process of rewarding reactions or sanctions. Additionally, learning results in CSVs that are relatively enduring. Societal values are not easily changed, and the clash between peoples with differing CSVs has been around since the beginning of time.

8-3a Enculturation

The most basic way by which consumers learn a culture is through an enculturation process. **Enculturation** represents the way a person learns his or her native culture. In other words, enculturation represents the way in which a consumer learns and develops shared understandings of things with family.

Why do some consumers like wasabi or hot peppers? The answer is enculturation. Consumers are not born liking very pungent food. But, early in life, children observe the diets of their parents and relatives and come to mimic those behaviours. When they do, they receive overt social rewards, thereby reinforcing their dietary choice. In Kyrgyzstan, children grow up drinking fermented mare's milk. Although *koumis*, the Kyrg name for fermented mare's milk, has what can kindly be called a "peculiar" flavour by most standards, the fact that one grows up drinking it creates the acquired taste that makes it palatable or even tasty.

8-3b Acculturation

Acculturation is the process by which consumers come to learn a culture other than their natural, native culture—that is, the culture to which one may adapt when exposed to a new set of CSVs. Acculturation is a learning process. When a consumer becomes acculturated, chances are that old beliefs have been replaced by new beliefs. Children generally become acculturated more quickly than adults because the old rules are not as old and thereby less resistant to change.[21] Retail managers at Sainsbury's supermarkets in the United Kingdom are aiming more lines of food products specifically at children. As a marketing tool, this may attract more shoppers, but as an image tool, the move positions Sainsbury's as a more healthy alternative for children.[22]

Not all consumers who are introduced into a new culture acculturate. Several factors can inhibit acculturation. For example, strong **ethnic identification**, the degree to which consumers feel a sense of belonging to the culture of their ethnic origins, can make consumers feel closed-minded about adopting products from a different culture. When ethnic identification is strong, consumers in a new land may even avoid learning the language of that new land. For instance, pockets of Chinese immigrants in Canada with strong ethnic identification choose to live the majority of their lives interacting with only other Chinese immigrants, purchasing Chinese products nearly exclusively, and primarily paying attention to Chinese language media.[23]

Consumer ethnocentrism is a belief among consumers that their ethnic group is superior to others and that the products that come from their native land are superior to other products. Consumers who are highly ethnocentric believe that it is only right to support workers in their native country by buying products from that country. Ethnocentrism is highly related to the concept of uncertainty avoidance. When ethnocentrism is very high, consumers who are in a foreign land may create their own communities within a larger enclave and display little interaction with the "outside world." Many Turkish neighbourhoods exist in Germany, for instance, and many of these Turks have little contact with people outside their own neighbourhoods.

Exhibit 8.6 illustrates factors that either inhibit or encourage consumer acculturation. Simply put, male consumers who have high ethnic identification, have high ethnocentrism, and are relatively old are the worst targets for adopting products of a different or new culture. Interestingly, from an international marketing perspective, CSV profiles characterized by high uncertainty avoidance and strong masculinity are likely not good targets for imported goods relative to other countries. The inhibitions that consumers have about "foreign" products distract from the value the products offer because

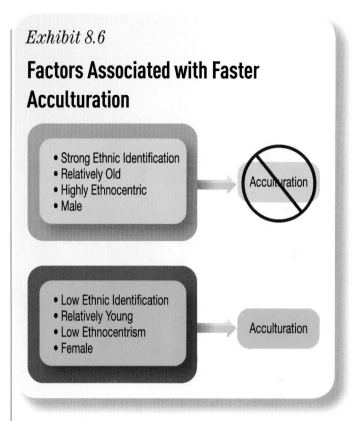

Exhibit 8.6

Factors Associated with Faster Acculturation

- Strong Ethnic Identification
- Relatively Old
- Highly Ethnocentric
- Male

→ Acculturation (crossed out)

- Low Ethnic Identification
- Relatively Young
- Low Ethnocentrism
- Female

→ Acculturation

their very meaning is inconsistent with the consumer's current belief structure.

8-3c Quartet of Institutions

Consumers *get* culture through either enculturation or acculturation. Each of these is a learning process. Consumers learn primarily through the influence of cultural institutions. Previously, consumer behaviour theory suggested that a triad of institutions accounted for much of the cultural learning process. However, more recently a fourth institution has been recognized. Thus, we now recognize a **quartet of institutions** that are responsible for communicating the CSV through both formal and informal processes from one generation to another. As shown in Exhibit 8.7, the four institutions comprised by the quartet are family, school, church, and media.

ethnic identification degree to which consumers feel a sense of belonging to the culture of their ethnic origins

consumer ethnocentrism belief among consumers that their ethnic group is superior to others and that the products that come from their native land are superior to other products

quartet of institutions four groups responsible for communicating the CSV through both formal and informal processes from one generation to another: family, school, church, and media

Exhibit 8.7

The Quartet of Institutions

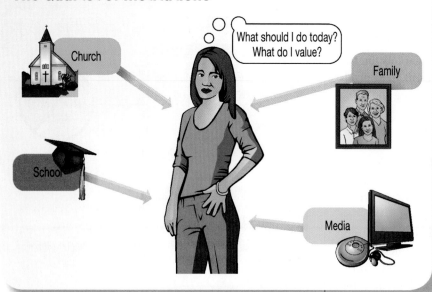

Differences in CSVs may have public policy implications as well. A study of teen consumers in countries such as Italy, Austria, Slovenia, Uzbekistan, Russia, and the United States, among others, found that anti-smoking ads were not equally effective. The results suggest that anti-smoking ads targeted toward countries high in individualism should emphasize the ill effects to individuals of smoking. In contrast, in countries with high collectivism, anti-smoking ads that emphasize the negative effects of smoking to other consumers are more effective.[27]

Studies measuring CSV among consumers still show distinctions consistent with the profiles discussed earlier. Thus, beyond the teen years particularly, differences in tastes, political views, and preferences are expected to remain consistent within cultures.

MODELLING

Modelling is an important way in which consumers are socialized into a specific culture either through acculturation or enculturation. A famous cliché says that imitation is the sincerest form of flattery. Well, **modelling** is precisely a process of imitating others' behaviour.

Young children, for instance, observe their parents and model their behaviour—at least until adolescence. As children become older, they may choose to model the behaviour

Family, school, and church have long been recognized as primary agents for acculturation and enculturation. Each of these is recognized as a vehicle for teaching values to children; therefore, they are agents of enculturation. Consumers become socialized by the behaviours that are affiliated with specific institutions.

More recently the impact of media on culture has been recognized. For instance, many nations actively limit the amount of American media that is allowed in the belief that this will protect their culture from becoming overly Americanized or Westernized. For example, the Canadian Radio-television and Telecommunications Commission (CRTC) requires radio and TV broadcasters to have a certain percentage of content that is contributed by Canadians.

An influx of non-native media can indeed influence the rate of acculturation.[24] In addition, children who watch more television have a more distorted view of reality, and generally presume that the typical family owns more luxury items and is better off materialistically than families in that particular culture really are. Children who watch more television become more acculturated to consumer society and are more materialistic than children who view less television.[25] Therefore, many families try to actively limit the amount of television viewed by their children.[26]

modelling process of imitating others' behaviour; a form of observational learning

Consumers model each other, particularly for novel products like the vuvuzela.

Exhibit 8.8

Modelling and the Quartet

Institution	Behaviour	Description
School	Studying	First-year university students learn study habits from more senior students.
Family	Table manners	Children observe parents to learn how to behave at the table.
Church	Prayer	People observe others in the church to learn the appropriate way to behave when in a church.
Media	Language	Consumers learn slang by repeating terms learned through television, movies, music, and Internet media.

of older peers more than they model that of their parents. Adolescent children's attitudes toward smoking, as well as their actual smoking behaviour, are largely influenced by the activities of peer referents.[28] In other words, adolescents will tend to model the behaviour of those they aspire to be like. The 2010 World Cup created a sensation for the vuvuzela, as young soccer fans across the country modelled the behaviour of World Cup attendees by seeking out the long,

colourful, and obnoxious-sounding horns. A small company in Alabama cashed in by anticipating the craze and selling 30,000 vuvuzelas in a few weeks' time.[29] Exhibit 8.8 displays ways that institutions facilitate modelling.

SHAPING

The instrumental conditioning process of shaping plays a key role in socialization as consumers' behaviour slowly

Somebody's Watching Me

Chris Batson / Alamy

Some governments certainly believe that electronic media can affect the core societal values of consumers. Chinese officials are actively engaged in censoring Internet sites. This censorship has caused problems for companies like Google, Microsoft, and Yahoo!, all of which face scrutiny in Canada and the United States for participating in censorship. Google actually places a disclaimer along with its searches that notifies the Chinese consumer of censorship. Partly as a result, Baidu, a search engine originating in China, has grown tremendously as Chinese consumers see disclaimers from Western search engines as rebellious. Baidu also participates in the censorship but does so without resistance and with no disclaimers.

In June 2013, Edward Snowden released thousands of documents that he acquired while working as a contractor for the United States' National Security Agency. Those documents revealed massive global surveillance programs operated by U.S. agencies, including the National Security Agency (NSA). Some see Snowden as a patriot and a whistleblower, while others see his actions as those of a traitor.

In Canada, the anti-terrorism act Bill C-51 gives new powers of surveillance to government departments, police, and the Canadian Security Intelligence Service. It also gives departments the ability to share private information about any person or group deemed to be a threat to national security. Some see this bill as necessary in the fight against terrorism, while many others see it as an unnecessary infringement on the rights of Canadians.

Culture affects the way consumers view privacy. How do you feel?

Sources: Fletcher, O. (2010), "Baidu's CEO Pursues Long-Term Growth," *The Wall Street Journal*, (August 4), B8. *The Guardian Editorial* (2015), "The Guardian view on surveillance after Snowden: an outlaw rewrites the law," *The Guardian*, (June 1), accessed at http://www.theguardian.com/commentisfree/2015/jun/01/guardian-view-on-surveillance-after-edward-snowden-outlaw-rewrites-law on June 2, 2015. *The Globe and Mail Editorial* (2015), "Bill C-51: Soon to be law, and as murky as ever," *The Globe and Mail*, (May 5), accessed at http://www.theglobeandmail.com/globe-debate/editorials/bill-c-51-soon-to-be-law-and-as-murky-as-ever/article24267240/ on June 2, 2015.

adapts to a culture through a series of rewards and sanctions. Think about how one might modify personal behaviour to win acceptance from a group. A child might decide to wear different clothes to school as a way of trying to fit in. The way that other students react to the new attire can serve to shape the student's future behaviour.

The CSV profile of a culture can influence the effectiveness of cultural shaping. For instance, more individualistic cultures are less susceptible to these types of normative influences.[30] Not all cultures reward complaining in the same way.[31] In collectivistic cultures, complaining can be a sign of disrespect and may be looked at as inappropriate for minor inconveniences. Canadian consumers who complain about their hotel room being slightly too warm are not likely to risk sanction. However, in a more collectivistic culture, complaining about a room that is slightly warm can be looked down upon. The extra added value that comes from group acceptance is greater among cultures where collectivism is stronger than individualism.

8-4 FUNDAMENTAL ELEMENTS OF COMMUNICATION

8-4a Verbal Communication

Obviously, language can sometimes be a problem. Anyone who has ever needed directions to some location in a place where he or she doesn't know the language can appreciate this. Sometimes, even when the correct language is used, communication can still be awkward or difficult.

In this section, **verbal communication** refers to the transfer of information through either the literal spoken or written word. Consumers will have difficulty finding value in things they cannot understand. Marketers have long wrestled with the problem of translating advertisements, research instruments, product labels, and promotional materials into foreign languages for foreign markets. This problem is only made more prevalent in today's truly international marketplace.

Verbal communication can even be difficult within a single language. Almost every language is spoken slightly differently from place to place—or with several unique **dialects**. English in Canada is different from English in England, which is not the same as English in Australia, which is not the same as English in Ireland. Even within Canada there are noticeable differences in how English is spoken from the east coast to the west coast. Thus, translation alone is insufficient to guarantee effective communication. Exhibit 8.9 provides some examples of difficulties in communicating even simple ideas through the spoken or written word. And we are not even considering the complications added by slang!

TRANSLATION EQUIVALENCE

Bilingual speakers realize that there is often more than one way to express the meaning of a word or phrase in one language when speaking in a second language. In some cases, words that exist in one language have no precise equivalent in another language. In other instances, even when the same word may exist, people in other cultures do not use the word the same way. Thus, interpretation errors and blunders occur unless one takes great care.

Translational equivalence exists when two phrases share the same precise meaning in two different cultures. Translation–back translation is a way to try to produce translational equivalence. With this process, one bilingual speaker takes the original phrase and translates it from the original language into the new language. Then, a second, independent bilingual speaker translates the phrase from the new language back into the original language. Assuming the retranslated phrase matches the first, translational equivalence exists. If not, either the phrase needs to be dropped or more work involving other speakers fluent in both languages may be needed to determine if a common meaning can be found by changing the words in one or both languages.

METRIC EQUIVALENCE

Once a common meaning is established, things could still go wrong when consumer researchers compare consumer reactions from one country with those from another. Researchers who apply typical survey techniques, such as Likert scales or semantic differentials, may wish to compare scores from one culture with those from another. This is valid only if the two culture–languages use numbers in a somewhat similar fashion. For example, if a Filipino consumer rated a 5-foot, 3-inch young woman for height, she might be rated quite

verbal communication transfer of information through either the literal spoken or written word

dialects variations of a common language

translational equivalence two phrases share the same precise meaning in two different cultures

Exhibit 8.9

Example Problems with Verbal Communication

Communication	Situation	Intended Communication	Problem
"Yo vi la Papa!"	Spanish-language slogan on T-shirts prior to Pope's visit to Mexico	"I saw the Pope!"	"La Papa" is "the potato." El (or al) Papa is the Pope. So, the T-shirts read, "I saw the potato."
"Boy, am I stuffed!"	English-language restaurant slogan spoken by middle-aged man.	"Boy, am I full!" (meaning had a lot to eat)	Slogan works fine in the United States; however, in Australia, "stuffed" means pregnant. So, slogan depicts middle-aged, slightly overweight man saying, "Boy, am I pregnant!"
"Strawberry Crap Dessert"	English placed on premade, refrigerated pancakes by Japanese firm intending product for Chinese market.	"Strawberry crêpe"	English can convey a quality image to products in much of Asia even if most consumers can't read the words. Here, the phonics are probably just a little off.
"Bite the waxed tadpole"	Chinese label for Coca-Cola	"Coca-Cola"	Coke tried to find the best phonetic way to produce something sounding like "Coca-Cola." In some Chinese dialects, but not all, strange interpretations like this resulted.
"Mist-stick!"	Clairol's name for a new hair care product introduced in Germany	Literally a mist stick that helped tame unmanageable hair.	The English "mist stick" phonetically sounds like "miststueck," which is at best an impolite German word to use as a name for a women's product!

tall. However, if a Norwegian rated the same person, she would be rated as quite short.

Metric equivalence refers to the state in which consumers are shown to use numbers to represent quantities the same way across cultures. Metric equivalence is necessary to draw basic comparisons about consumers from different countries concerning important consumer relationships. Comparing average scores for consumer attitudes from one culture to the next requires another form of equivalence known as scalar equivalence. The procedures for performing tests of metric equivalence are beyond the scope of this text, but students of consumer behaviour and international marketing should be aware of these approaches because comparing quantities across cultures can be tricky.[32]

8-4b Nonverbal Communication

A conductor at a train station in Germany is approached by an American tourist who wants to know how many stops it will be until he reaches his destination. The train is noisy and filled with people, so the conductor holds up his pointer finger in response. When the train stops, the tourist quickly exits. However, he'll soon realize he is not in the right location. Why? In Germany, one would be indicated by holding up the thumb.

Nonverbal communication refers to information passed through some nonverbal act—in other words, communication not involving the literal spoken or written word. This example illustrates intentional nonverbal communication; however, much communication through this means is unintentional or automatic. Many nonverbal communication cues are culturally laden so that the meaning depends on culture.

Exhibit 8.10 depicts several aspects of nonverbal communication and the way they come together to create effective communication. High-context cultures emphasize communication through nonverbal elements. In contrast, low-context cultures, such as Germany,

metric equivalence statistical tests used to validate the way people use numbers to represent quantities across cultures

nonverbal communication information passed through some nonverbal act

What Do You Get When You Cross Chinese and English? Lost!

During the 2008 Olympics, thousands upon thousands of visitors flocked to China. Chinese officials launched a campaign to clean up something they felt was embarrassing, but that others felt was charming. What were they cleaning up? The awkward English translations of simple phrases that exist throughout China. Imagine encountering signs with the following messages:

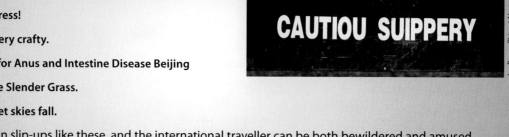

1. **Execution in progress!**

2. **The slippery are very crafty.**

3. **Dongda Hospital for Anus and Intestine Disease Beijing**

4. **Show mercy to the Slender Grass.**

5. **Be careful not to let skies fall.**

China is not alone in slip-ups like these, and the international traveller can be both bewildered and amused. Retailers and service providers operating internationally need to take care that their translations are accurate and send the right message. Obviously, the Chinese government understands that even non-native words can shape a consumer's image of a country or brand.

Okay, here are the intended meanings of the lines above, respectively: (1) Caution—work in progress!; (2) Wet floor; (3) Dongda Proctology Hospital Beijing; (4) Keep off the grass; and (5) Hold on to your skis so they don't fall (from a chair lift)!

Sources: Xinhua (2007), "Ahead of Olympics, Beijing Says Goodbye to 'Chinglish,'" *Yahoo Sports India*, http://in.sports.yahoo.com/070929/43/6lcge.html, accessed 2/20/2008. Fong, Mei (2007), "Tired of Laughter, Beijing Gets Rid of Bad Translations," *The Wall Street Journal*, February 5, A1.

emphasize the spoken word, and what you say is truly what you mean. The elements of nonverbal communication are touched on briefly in the following sections.

Exhibit 8.10

Nonverbal Communication Affects the Message Comprehended

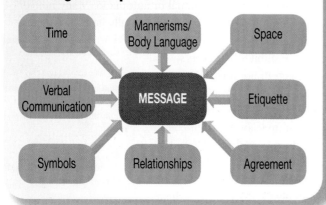

TIME

In Canada, the expression "Time is money" is often used. Canadians typically place a high value on time and timeliness. The high value placed on timeliness may be due to the importance of individualism and achievement as core values. When a Canadian consumer plans a formal dinner meeting for 7:30 P.M., he or she expects everyone to be present at 7:30 P.M.

Consumers from some other cultures do not value timeliness in the same way. For example, in Spain, where individualism is much lower than in Canada, a formal dinner scheduled for 9:00 P.M. will certainly not begin at 9:00 P.M. The exact starting time is uncertain, but dinner will almost certainly not be served until sometime much later than 9:00 P.M.

Consistent with high long-term orientation, Asian cultures exhibit much patience. Thus, while CANZUS and many Western European salespeople will want to close a sale on the first meeting, such an approach with Asian buyers will not come across well. Asian exchange partners need time to get to know one another and are not anxious to either close a sale or be closed until guanxi is established.

MANNERISMS/BODY LANGUAGE

Body language refers to the nonverbal communication cues signalled by somatic (uncontrollable biological) responses. Consumers may use certain mannerisms when discussing issues with other consumers or salespeople. These cues can be more telling than the words that are spoken. The mannerisms that reveal meaning include the following characteristics:

▶ **Facial expressions**

▶ **Posture**

▶ **Arm/leg position**

▶ **Skin conditions**

▶ **Voice**

For most consumers, there are times when they must pretend to be happy. This requires a fake smile. While most people can easily make their mouths produce a grin, true happiness would also be indicated by smiling eyebrows, slightly dilated pupils, and a tilted head (back). Similarly, the posture of a truly happy person generally indicates a willingness to approach the object of the emotion. Salespeople can be trained to detect by close observation of facial expressions and posture if a consumer is truly experiencing pleasant emotion or if they are only pretending.

Service providers may be successful in trying to guess which consumers will complain out of anger long before any negative words are voiced.[33] Thus, if anger is detected, intervention may actually turn the experience into something positive through proactive measures to remedy the situation causing the anger.

In today's virtual marketplace, nonverbal communication extends to virtual employees. Marketers are currently studying the mannerisms of avatars to investigate the way their messages are interpreted. In other words, how do you make an avatar seem agreeable, or disagreeable, or welcoming, or even trustful? Currently, the effects of avatars alone are small; however, the combination of verbal communication and use of an avatar may contribute to higher trust and to increased hedonic value from the shopping experience.[34] So, an interesting question for web retailers is how to get an avatar to communicate a message that will be understood by all consumers.

SPACE

In places like Canada, the United States, and Australia, there is a lot of space! Relative to many parts of the

Lifesize/Brand New Images/Jupiterimages

Body language communicates, as this message illustrates.

world, like Japan or Western Europe, Canada and Australia are sparsely populated. Thus, space varies in importance. The typical consumer in Seoul, South Korea, lives in a large high-rise condominium, in a small apartment identical to that of many neighbours living in the same building. For many Canadians, Americans, or Australians, the fact that so many people would be packed into a tight space may make them uncomfortable. For citizens of Seoul, being very close to other people is a fact of life.

The value that consumers place on space affects communication styles. Generally, CANZUS consumers, for instance, do not like to be too close to each other. When having a conversation, they remain at "arm's length." However, Italian, Armenian, or many Arabian consumers

body language
nonverbal communication cues signalled by somatic responses

Just over 1 billion consumers live in India. Today, the largest group of consumers in India is between 12 and 20 years old.

are comfortable communicating when they are so close to each other that they are physically touching. The CANZUS consumer engaged in a conversation with an Armenian, for instance, will likely automatically try to obtain some space in the conversation by leaning backward at the waist. The differing approaches to space have implications for sales approaches, the way other consumers are depicted in advertising, and the design of retail environments.

ETIQUETTE/MANNERS

When Canadians greet each other, the typical response, particularly if a man is involved, is a handshake. Different handshakes may communicate different impressions. However, Asian consumers would expect a bow as a greeting and show of respect. Many Europeans may plant a kiss or two on the cheek. Greeting a business client with a kiss on the cheek would likely create an awkward situation in Canada; however, in France, a couple of kisses to the cheek could be an appropriate greeting.

Different cultures have different etiquettes for handling various social situations. **Etiquette** represents the customary mannerisms consumers use in common social situations. Dining etiquette varies considerably from one culture to another. In Canada, consumers tend to cut food with the right hand, put the knife down, and then pick up a fork in the right hand to place food into their mouths. In Europe, however, good manners tend to dictate that the knife stays in the right hand and the fork in the other. One cuts with the right hand and uses the left to efficiently scoop food into one's mouth. In any event, violating etiquette can lead to a cultural sanction.

Service providers need to be sensitive to the various differences in etiquette. For example, although no formal airline passenger etiquette exists, there is an informal code, and passengers who break these unwritten rules can actually decrease the satisfaction of other passengers. This situation is exaggerated on airlines carrying multinational groups of passengers. These passengers have different rules about space, privacy, dress, and hygiene. Passengers with body odour or who dress inappropriately (e.g., a man wearing

etiquette customary mannerisms consumers use in common social situations

a tank top is generally considered inappropriate for such close company in Western cultures) can ruin the experience for other consumers. When consumers are unaware of or lack concern for the proper etiquette in a given situation, the result can be awkward and diminish the value of the experience.

RELATIONSHIPS

How do consumers respond to attempts by marketers to build a personal relationship? Earlier, we discussed the Asian principle of guanxi and the different ways that a relationship may develop under this principle as opposed to conventional Western principles. Differing CSVs have other implications for consumer–brand or consumer–service provider relationships.

For example, with high collectivism, the idea of a relationship is no longer personal. Consumers from collectivist nations define relationships in terms of the ties between a brand or service provider and a family or relevant group of consumers. Therefore, marketing appeals aimed at building personal relationships should emphasize the collective preference of this group rather than the individual.[35]

AGREEMENT

How is agreement indicated and what does it mean? An Asian consumer who responds to a sales appeal with "Yes" is not indicating agreement. Instead, this "Yes" is more a way of indicating that he or she understands what is being said. Further, many Asian cultures will avoid strong affirmative or negative responses and instead use expressions like "That is possible" or "That may be difficult" to indicate agreement or lack of agreement.

Additionally, the extent to which a contract is seen as binding varies from place to place. Traditionally, South Koreans are not accustomed to signing contracts. The fact that one would be asked to sign such an agreement might be viewed as an insult. Thus, Western firms may have to adjust their practices to indicate formal agreements when doing business in these cultures.

SYMBOLS

The chapter began by emphasizing the link between culture and meaning. Because different cultures have different value profiles, objects and activities take on different symbolic or semiotic meaning. Perhaps nowhere is this more obvious than in the arena of religious objects. A large wooden cross is a device that has been used to execute people, but to Christians, a cross is an important symbol signifying everlasting life.

The symbolic meaning of objects also affects gift-giving from culture to culture. In some Western cultures, particularly among French cultures, including Quebec and south Louisiana, a knife is regarded as an inappropriate gift because a knife symbolizes cutting a relationship. In China, clocks and watches are inappropriate gift items because they symbolize the finite nature of life—time is running out. Also, in Japan, the term *omiyage* refers to the custom of bringing gifts to friends from foreign trips. In particular, an omiyage gift of a famous brand can help symbolize freedom for the typical female office worker.[36] Marketers need to take care against unintentionally promoting offensive items based on cultural symbolism.

8-5 EMERGING CULTURES

Marketing efforts are largely directed at consumers from developed nations. However, less-developed nations can offer attractive markets and many may represent emerging economies. Even low-income consumers in developing nations can represent attractive markets to serve, particularly if low-priced, basic products can be offered. Market segments in developing nations offer tremendous opportunities, but communicating and delivering value in these segments means that the nuances of culture must be known and understood.

8-5a BRIC Markets

As discussed previously, the acronym BRIC stands for "Brazil, Russia, India, and China." These four nations are often singled out as having economies that are growing very rapidly. In each market, large middle classes are emerging as consumers who formerly would have had little opportunity for a good job benefit from corporate capital investment. As a result, consumers in these nations have rising standards of living, and they have become attractive markets for many goods and services. More recently the dramatic drop in oil prices has dampened the economic outlook for Brazil and Russia. Russia may also represent a political risk for investors and its economy has struggled substantially in recent years. Even India and China face real challenges to their economic growth. Nevertheless, in the longer term these continue to be economies with positive demographic and economic trends.

Consider China relative to the United States, for example, in terms of **purchasing power parity (PPP)**, which estimates the total size of the consumer market in each country in terms of total buying power. By 2020, China is expected to match or exceed the total purchasing power of the United States.

In terms of consumer demographics, India today compares favourably to the United States and Canada in 1970. Just over 1 billion consumers live in India, and today, the largest group of consumers is between 12 and 20 years old. This cohort group is similar to the Baby Boomer generation in Canada and the United States, which was responsible for tremendous economic growth domestically and abroad.

More than 190 million households call India home. Today, millions of those households are considered aspiring consumers, with equivalent household incomes of only a few thousand dollars per year. As Indian incomes rise, the market potential of India expands as well. The market potential for India and China is made clear in the fact that population is assessed in billions rather than millions. Even inexpensive products can mean a lot of revenue for a company selling to the large Chinese and Indian populations.

WHAT'S NEXT?

During the Cold War, consumer markets like those in Russia and China were hardly seen as attractive to marketers in North America and Europe. However, times have changed. The advancement of free market economies has led to increased standards of living in many corners of the globe.

However, the fact is that approximately half the world's consumer population remains illiterate and struggles to maintain anything more than a meagre way of life. As the emerging economies advance today, so will the cost of doing business in those countries. Companies will search for cheaper places to do business and, through this process, new emerging

purchasing power parity (PPP) total size of the consumer market in each country in terms of total buying power economies will develop. Much of Africa, for example, remains without the type of industrial or technological development necessary to create good jobs and the incomes that lead to a higher standard of living. Africa has a total population of nearly 800 million people, and even though parts of South Africa and northern Africa are developed, much of the rest remains destitute. Perhaps this area too will be a new emerging market later in this century.

Like other places, though, the cultural barriers presented there are not trivial. The cultural barriers go beyond dealing with consumers, and are also engrained in the sociopolitical environment. Therefore, changes in government institutions will probably be needed before many companies will feel comfortable doing business there.[37]

STUDY TOOLS 8

LOCATED AT THE BACK OF THE TEXTBOOK
☐ Rip out Chapter Review Card

LOCATED AT NELSON.COM/STUDENT
☐ Review Key Terms Flashcards (print or online)

☐ Download audio summaries to review on the go

☐ Complete practice quizzes to prepare for tests

☐ Watch video on Lonely Planet for a real company example

T&T Supermarket

When the first T&T Supermarket store opened in 1993, it was an ambitious effort to sell Asian groceries in a supermarket format. Traditional Canadian grocery stores sold a limited selection of Asian products, while Asian grocery stores did not typically offer the convenience and amenities of conventional mass-market retailers. T&T Supermarket quickly found its niche by offering a wide selection of high-quality products beautifully presented in a large, modern format.

T&T Supermarket initially targeted Asian Canadians, who had cooking styles and consumption tastes that were not well served by the average grocery store. However, the company soon realized that its stores appealed to other segments of the market as well. Not only were Canadians from a wide variety of ethnic backgrounds interested in Asian food, but the stores also offered a unique, even entertaining, shopping experience, from the broad range of seafood, including choosing from a number of different types of live fish right out of an in-store tank, to unique fresh produce and spices, which offered non-Asian consumers a sense of adventure and discovery.

T&T Supermarket found itself in an enviable position—it was serving the traditional needs of a rapidly growing Asian Canadian population and introducing consumers from different backgrounds to Asian food. As a result, the company grew rapidly to become Canada's largest ethnic grocery supermarket, with more than 20 stores in British Columbia, Alberta, and Ontario.

In 2009, Loblaw Companies Limited—Canada's largest retailer, with more than $30 billion in annual sales—purchased T&T Supermarket. Like many of the more conventional grocers in Canada, Loblaw recognized that the country's population was continuing to evolve and becoming increasingly diverse. Loblaw wanted to learn from what T&T had accomplished, while T&T wanted the financial strength and support it needed to continue to grow its business. T&T Supermarket's CEO, Cindy Lee, believed the sale of her stores would allow the company to sell Asian food to even more Canadian families.

Sources: Canada NewsWire (2009), "Loblaw to Acquire T&T Supermarket, Canada's Largest Asian Food Retailer," *Canada Newswire* (July 24), http://www.newswire.ca/en/story/562169/loblaw-to-acquire-t-t-supermarket-canada-s-largest-asian-food-retailer, accessed August 15, 2012.

Jim Rankin/GetStock.com

Lee-Young, Joanne (2007), "Cindy Lee Takes T&T to New Heights: Asian Supermarket Chain Has 15 Stores across Canada," *The Vancouver Sun* (January 15), http://www.canada.com/topics/finance/story.html?id=6a25e4c7-2cb2-4c87-8a30-f2fd8b92bd4a&k=33112, accessed August 15, 2012. Leung, Wendy (2011), "Kraft Calls on Star Chefs to Capture Immigrant Market, *The Globe and Mail* (April 13), http://www.theglobeandmail.com/life/food-and-wine/food-trends/kraft-calls-on-star-chefs-to-capture-immigrant-market/article576132, accessed August 15, 2012.

QUESTIONS

1 Culture gives meaning to objects and activities, such as food and cooking. How does T&T Supermarket give a different meaning to food and cooking, as compared with a more conventional Loblaw's Superstore?

2 Looking at the core societal values (CSVs) for Canada and China, how is T&T Supermarket's market positioning tapping into differences between the two cultures?

3 What role are enculturation and acculturation playing in T&T Supermarket's success?

4 How does a business like T&T Supermarket affect acculturation? Does it help Canadians learn more about Asian culture? Does it inhibit Asian immigrants learning about Canadian culture?

5 Which of the quartet of institutions influence consumers' choice of grocery stores? What impact does the Canadian media have on consumers' food preferences?

PART 3

9 | Microcultures

LEARNING OBJECTIVES

After studying this chapter, the student should be able to:

9-1 Apply the concept of microculture as it influences consumer behaviour.

9-2 Know the major Canadian microcultural groups.

9-3 Realize that microculture is not a uniquely Canadian phenomenon.

9-4 Perform a demographic analysis.

9-5 Identify major cultural and demographic trends.

Alex Milan Tracy/NurPhoto/NurPhoto/Corbis

9-1 MICROCULTURE AND CONSUMER BEHAVIOUR

The climate is remarkable in many ways. A tourist driving through British Columbia's Okanagan Valley will find the southern area around Osoyoos to be warm and arid with desert-like conditions. Heading north toward Kelowna, that same tourist will soon enter a region that is considerably cooler and wetter. As the tourist heads up into the mountain resorts of Silver Star or Big White, the climate will change yet again. Scientists explain that regional climates contain microclimates within them. Areas like the Okanagan Valley in British Columbia and the Niagara Peninsula in Ontario have become well known for microclimates that are particularly conducive to growing grapes and producing wines.

In a similar way, we can think of a given culture containing multiple smaller and more specific microcultures. A microculture is indeed a culture, only smaller. We define a **microculture** as a group of people who share similar values and tastes that are subsumed within a larger

microculture a group of people who share similar values and tastes that are subsumed within a larger culture

culture. The smaller group can be quite distinct from the larger group or overall culture. The term *subculture* is often used to capture much the same idea as microculture, however, the term *microculture* is used here to portray the idea that the group is smaller but in no way less significant in terms of the potential influence on consumer behaviour. You may notice that the microculture concept is similar in some ways to the group influence topic. Microcultures, however, are generally based on specific variables that we detail in this chapter. How many microcultures do you belong to? Let's take a look.

9-1a Culture Is Hierarchical

Culture is a universal phenomenon. In fact, each consumer belongs to many cultural groups—or more precisely, they move in and out of microcultures. For instance, a student attending McGill University in Montreal is likely part of Canadian culture, but may also be part of Québécois culture, university culture, and possibly Greek culture, should he or she belong to a fraternity or sorority. In this way, culture is hierarchical. A consumer belongs to one large, overall culture and then to many smaller cultural groups—microcultures—existing and interlinking within the overall culture. Exhibit 9.1 illustrates a cultural hierarchy.

Exhibit 9.1

The Hierarchical Nature of Culture and Microculture

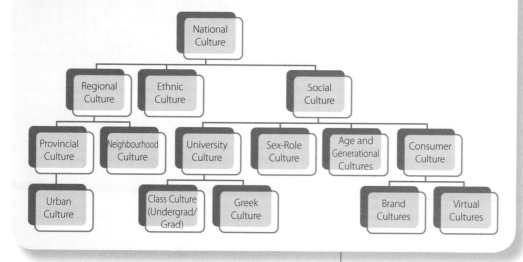

the group.[1] Obviously, some of the roles are inconsistent with each group and the consumer makes a choice to behave in ways more consistent with one group than with another. When a consumer faces a situation involving conflicting expectations based on cultural expectations, he is experiencing **role conflict**. For instance, when students attend a career fair for the first time, they may experi-

Each microculture brings with it role expectations for its members. The role provides a signal as to the behaviours that one should perform to truly belong to the group; or, in other words, what it takes to be an authentic member of ence some conflict over how to dress. College students may see a certain outfit as business attire, but the career-oriented

role conflict a situation involving conflicting expectations based on cultural role expectations woman representing a company at the event may see the same outfit as inappropriate for the office.

Assuming that the McGill student mentioned earlier is Québécois and from Montreal, he or she is part of a unique and identifiable culture. Many Canadians will have a "Québécois" schema in mind that might include being a fan of the Habs and of the fine arts, as well as enjoying fine dining and possibly the occasional dish of poutine. This particular consumer likely also identifies with a specific age-based or generational culture, and makes consumer choices that either reinforce this social identity or send the signal that he or she does not wish to be part of this group. Think about how these decisions explain simple things like music preferences. Polka music may be traditional in Austria, but an Austrian university student is not likely to find being a huge polka fan very gratifying among his peers. Similarly, an authentic Goth may well have to hide a liking of a country music song or two.

9-1b Microcultural Roles and Value

Microculture membership changes the value of things. In Canada, hockey is a popular sport from coast to coast, highly valued as both recreation and entertainment. Some might even call it a national obsession. Yet, globally, hockey is a relatively minor sport. In fact, in many countries you will have to talk about *ice* hockey; otherwise, people are likely to assume you are referring to a very different game played on outdoor soccer-like fields of grass. Cultural groups commonly arise within sports fans, and an extreme soccer fan may even become a *soccer hooligan* who participates in excessive and sometimes violent behaviours as a way of creating a personally meaningful soccer experience. Anthropologists have studied this cultural phenomenon by immersing themselves within the hooligan group. Some hooligans are professional people who find involvement in soccer to be a way to escape other realities and thus they find hedonic value in hooligan activities. However when soccer hooligans took up Burberry caps as preferred headwear, young male British business professionals abandoned the caps so as not to have an overlapping preference that could identify them as a hooligan. We again see how culture is hierarchical in this example. Indeed consumers often choose membership in microcultures in an effort to stand out or define themselves from the crowd. This phenomenon is known as **divergence**.[2]

divergence situation in which consumers choose membership in microcultures in an effort to stand out or define themselves from the crowd

sex roles societal expectations for men and women among members of a cultural group

9-2 MAJOR CANADIAN MICROCULTURES

Marketers can divide the Canadian population into consumer groups along a number of dimensions when engaging in market segmentation. These groupings are particularly effective when microcultures are involved, because the consumers within these groups likely have very similar preferences. There are many types of microcultures in Canada, including regional, sex role, age-based, generation, religious, ethnic, income/social class, and street microcultures.

9-2a Regional Microculture

Some might think of Canada as a nation without a distinct culture, however, many social scientists would disagree. In fact, many different cultural groups can be identified in Canada. Some are geographically determined—for example, distinct cultural groups exist in the Maritimes, Quebec, Ontario, the Prairie provinces, and on the West Coast. Others are mixed in throughout Canada and are driven more by lifestyle and psychographic differences.

In his 1998 book *Sex in the Snow: Canadian Social Values at the End of the Millennium*, Michael Adams argues, "The stereotype of Canadians as respectful and reserved and not that imaginative is fast losing its validity." He identifies 12 "tribes" in Canada that are classified by age but really differ in terms of their values and motivations (outlined in Exhibit 9.2).

Although any system that separates all Canadians into only 12 categories will have some weaknesses, this type of approach can provide marketers with useful insight into the motivations that underlie Canadian behaviour. For example, an offer that is appealing to the more socially conscious "New Aquarians" or "Autonomous Post-Materialists" will likely be very different from one made to "Rational Traditionalists" or "Thrill-Seeking Materialists."

9-2b Sex Roles and Microculture

Sex roles are the societal expectations for men and women among members of a cultural group. Sex roles are ubiquitous in society, and inconsistency with them can be a source of sanctions. The differences between societal expectations of men and women vary less in

Exhibit 9.2

The 12 Tribes of Canada

Social Values Tribe	Percent of Canadian Population	Fundamental Motivation	Key Values
Rational Traditionalists (age 50+)	15%	Financial independence, stability, and security	Religiosity, reason, tradition, respect for authority, deferred gratification
Extroverted Traditionalists (age 50+)	7%	Traditional communities, institutions, social status	Religiosity, family, tradition, respect for institutions, deferred gratification
Cosmopolitan Modernists (age 50+)	6%	Traditional institutions and experience-seeking	Global worldview, respect for education, desire for innovation
Anxious Communitarians (age 30–49)	9%	Traditional communities, institutions, social status	Family, community, need for respect
Connected Enthusiasts (age 30–49)	6%	Traditional and new communities and experience-seeking	Family, community, hedonism, immediate gratification
Disengaged Darwinists (age 30–49)	18%	Financial independence, stability, and security	Fear, nostalgia for the past
Aimless Dependants (age 15–29)	8%	Financial independence, stability, and security	Fear, desire for independence
Autonomous Post-Materialists (age 15–29)	6%	Personal autonomy and self-fulfillment	Freedom and respect for human rights
Social Hedonists (age 15–29)	4%	Experience-seeking and new communities	Aesthetics, hedonism, sexual permissiveness, immediate gratification
New Aquarians (age 15–29)	4%	Experience-seeking and new communities	Egalitarianism, ecologism, hedonism
Thrill Seeking Materialists (age 15–29)		Traditional communities, social status, and experience-seeking	Desire for money and material possessions, recognition, respect, and admiration

Source: Excerpted from *Sex in the Snow* by Michael Adams. Copyright © Michael Adams, 1997. Reprinted by permission of Penguin Canada, a division of Penguin Random House Canada Limited.

Western cultures than they do in Eastern cultures, in which sex-based divisions in roles remain more obvious.[3] For example, recent comparisons of brand personality tend to show greater androgyny—meaning appearing neither clearly male nor clearly female—among U.S. perceptions of brands relative to Korean brands.[4]

INCOME TRENDS AND SPENDING PATTERNS

Women in Canada continue to earn less than men, on average. However, that gender gap has narrowed in recent years. To a large extent, this is because older generations—in which the two genders have very different skills, training, and experience—are leaving the workforce, and younger men and women who have increasingly similar skills, training, and experience are replacing them.[5]

One of the most dramatic changes in Canadian society over the past 50 years has been the transition from primarily single-earner household to dual-income families. In 1967, 67% of families were supported by a single, almost always male-earned, income.[6] Today, about the same percentage of families are dual-income families, and it has become increasingly common for women to be the primary income earners in Canadian households.[7] This trend is also evident in the United States, where some estimates suggest that women make more money than their husbands in approximately 22% of American marriages (up from just 4% in 1970).[8] In the United Kingdom, women in their 20s are now earning more on average than men in their 20s.[9] These demographic trends are likely to continue to have a substantial impact on marketing and consumer behaviour.

Marketers need to be aware of the relative sex roles within societies. Men and women may share purchasing responsibilities differently from culture to culture. In North America, the woman in the family remains the primary purchasing agent for most things. Men are more likely to make purchase decisions for things such as lawn care equipment and home electronics. Men also play a much larger role in the purchase of big-ticket items. Women tend to purchase the majority of clothing for males in North American households. However, in Italy, men place great pride in their business attire and are more likely to want control of these purchase decisions. Marketers therefore need to do research to help identify these roles, or else run the risk of targeting the wrong family member with marketing communications.

MALE AND FEMALE SEGMENTS

A great deal of marketing communication is directed toward either a male or a female market segment. Media are often distinguished easily based on the proportion of male and female customers. SportsNet channels, for example, offer an opportunity to reach out to a predominantly male market. *The Oprah Winfrey TV Network* and *HelloGiggles.com* offer an opportunity to reach a female market. These media clearly contain appeals geared toward the respective sex.

Although role expectations associate certain types of purchases with men or women, marketers sometimes reach out to the opposite sex. Men traditionally are the household buying agent for electronics. However, Best Buy altered its marketing strategy in a special effort to appeal to female shoppers. Consumer research showed that women were not particularly enamoured with the big box format, so Best Buy launched Best Buy Mobile—units that are relatively small and located in shopping centres and malls.[10] Now, female consumers are exposed to electronic gadgets in an environment more suited to their tastes. Marketers outside North America are also taking this approach. Vespa, the world's top name in scooters, redesigned its basic model into the "Indian Vespa" by adding a foot-rest extension to the left side because Indian women, who wear relatively close-fitting foot-length garments, only ride in a sidesaddle style. The effort to provide cheap transportation to relatively low-income women may pay off in a big way in the long run.

Conversely, online fashion retailers like Gilt Groupe and Rue La La have changed their marketing approach to better appeal to men.[11] Currently, only about one in four adult men regularly purchase clothing products online. These retailers seek to entice more men to their sites by offering more sports-oriented merchandise lines, such as golf apparel. The retailers believe that appealing to men will be successful based on the relatively high amount of disposable income of many middle-aged professional men.

9-2c Age-Based Microculture

In an **age-based microculture**, people of the same age end up sharing many of the same values and develop similar consumer preferences. Perhaps no age-based group receives more attention than teens. Nearly 2.2 million Canadians are between 15 and 19 years of age.[12] Teens seem to share many similar behaviours. In fact, some argue that teen behaviour is not just similar within a given country, but similar across countries.

WORLD TEEN CULTURE?

Consumer media involves more than just television. Radio, print publications, music, and web-based communication all can play a role in shaping culture and, therefore, the things that consumers value.[13] The Internet facilitates communication among consumers around the world, contributing to what some believe is a more universally similar **world teen culture**. Evidence of similar tastes among teenaged consumers around the world is obvious if one takes a look at teen purchase and consumption patterns. Many of these tastes are influenced by the Western media's

age-based microculture people of the same age end up sharing many of the same values and develop similar consumer preferences

world teen culture speculation that teenagers around the world are more similar to each other than to people from other generations in the same culture

© Simon Rawles/Alamy

The Perfect Panty for Jacklyn

Courtesy Mark's Work Wearhouse

Market researchers have long recognized that women make the vast majority of retail buying decisions. For many years, grocery stores, furniture retailers, and drug stores have catered to female shoppers. Recently, however, even auto dealers, electronics retailers, and hardware stores, which have traditionally focused on the male customer, are trying to make themselves more attractive to female consumers. Lowes, for example, changed the nature of competition in the hardware business when it introduced wider aisles, better lighting, and improved displays to attract women into its stores.

Maybe the most dramatic example of a retailer that has historically targeted men moving its focus to women is Mark's Work Wearhouse. Mark's built its business on providing blue-collar work clothes for men—jeans, shirts, belts, and other items that are rugged and job-site functional. Nevertheless, the retailer soon realized that many of its customers were actually women buying for their husbands, and once in the store they were willing to pick up an item or two for themselves.

In fact, Mark's created a persona for this target consumer, which the company calls "Jacklyn"—a 40-something working mother interested in clothes that are as functional as they are fashionable. She may have originally walked into a Mark's store to make a purchase on her husband's behalf, but she quickly became a valuable customer in her own right.

As Mark's learned more about Jacklyn, the company had an interesting insight: Jacklyn was very dissatisfied with the choices she had in underwear. In response, Mark's introduced a lingerie section in many of its stores, including the national launch of its new "Perfect Panty" in 2010. This product line might seem counterintuitive for a brand that built its reputation on durable work wear for men, and Mark's does not aim to be a leader in female fashion, but with women's wear making up about 17% of total revenue, it does illustrate the powerful influence of the female shopper in Canada.

Sources: Strauss, Marina (2010), "Brief Encounters: Mark's Has Designs on Panties," *CTV News* (March 22), http://www.ctv.ca/generic/generated/static/business/article1507537.html, accessed May 31, 2012; O'Neill, Katherine (2011), "Mark's Goes Beyond Cool," *The Globe and Mail* (June 13), http://www.theglobeandmail.com/report-on-business/marks-goes-beyond-cool/article1286241/, accessed May 31, 2012. Strauss, Marina (2013), "Apparel retailer Mark's to refocus on men's market," *The Globe and Mail* (September 29, 2013), http://www.theglobeandmail.com/report-on-business/apparel-retailer-marks-to-refocus-on-mens-clothing-market/article14593816/, accessed September 29, 2015.

iStockphoto.com

Coca-Cola is a favourite among teens worldwide.

depiction of celebrities. Thus, fashion and entertainment companies in particular may find segmenting based on age as useful as geography.

Brands listed in Exhibit 9.3 have particular appeal to teens in practically all parts of the globe. CocaCola and McDonald's, for example, are brand names that are listed among teens' favourite brands throughout much of the world.[14] Coca-Cola takes advantage of virtual media to help stay on top. For example, through the website Second Life, Coke offered opportunities for consumers to build a virtual vending machine that dispenses experiences to loyal Coke drinkers.[15] Thus, Coke is attempting to use new media to create virtual experiences that help build loyalty among the teen market segment worldwide.

Exhibit 9.3

Similarities and Differences Among Teen Consumers

Favourite Brands	Similar Activities	Less Similar Choices
Coca-Cola	Listening to Music	Religious Ideas/Activities
McDonald's	Using Mobile Phone	Cosmetic Brands
Nike	Surfing the Internet	Political Ideas
Disney	Video Games	Equality of Sexes
Cadbury	Smoking	
Apple		

Although teens around the world may find value in many of the same types of music and clothing, research suggests that the cultural values of their home nation remain relatively distinct from nation to nation, particularly concerning personal products.[16] American teen consumers, for instance, still rate freedom as the most important core societal value (CSV). In contrast, teens from Arab countries list faith as the most important CSV.[17] These differences translate into different consumption habits. For example, even though McDonald's is popular among teens practically everywhere, preferences for fast-food brands still differ between Asians and North Americans.[18]

9-2d Generation Microculture

Age-based groups can be distinguished from generational groups. Consumers grow out of age groups. When a consumer reaches age 20, she is no longer in the teen microculture. However, that consumer still "belongs" to a group with her peers. Notice that people who age in the same generation still belong to the same cohort. A **cohort** is a group of people who have lived the same major experiences in their life, and the experiences end up shaping their core values. Life experiences have many different effects on a cohort. For instance, while teens tend to share some behaviours in common, such as experimenting with tobacco, their preference for music tends to be much more of a generational effect. Consumers tend to enjoy music from their own generation, and each generation seems to carry its taste for music with

cohort a group of people who have lived the same major experiences in their life

it to a large extent. Here, we briefly introduce some of the main generational groups in Canada.

BABY BOOMER

Although the exact dates for the generational cohorts vary slightly between studies and authors, the Conference Board of Canada categorizes Baby Boomers as those Canadians who were born between 1945 and 1964.[19] Looking at the population pyramid in Exhibit 9.4, it is clear that this generation represents a population explosion much larger than the cohorts that had preceded or were to follow it. The Boomers grew up in post-war economic prosperity of the 1950s and 1960s, during which Canadian society experienced rapid technological change and social progress. As the largest generation, Boomers have had a significant impact on popular and consumer culture in North America.

Relative to other generations, Boomers also have an enormous amount of buying power. They have substantially influenced the economy during their working lives, and they may be the first generation to continue to command significant spending power into their later years. Although it is anticipated that the Boomers' spending will slow somewhat as they enter into retirement, this generation is expected to continue to have a transformative impact on sectors of the economy such as health care, pensions, real estate, and tourism.

GENERATION X

Those consumers born between 1965 and 1979 are generally referred to as Generation X (sometimes called the "Baby Bust" generation because it is considerably smaller than the Baby Boom cohort). This generation grew up in the turbulent economic climate of the 1970s and 1980s, decades characterized by the Cold War and the eventual collapse of the Soviet Union. The careers of Generation X have been marked by recession and recovery. Often labelled as independent and self-reliant, Generation X is also described as cynical and as having a skeptical attitude toward authority. This generation tends to believe in a work–life balance. Although much fewer in number than the Baby Boomers, members of Generation X are now in their 30s to 50s—prime earning and spending years.

Exhibit 9.4

Canadian Population Pyramid

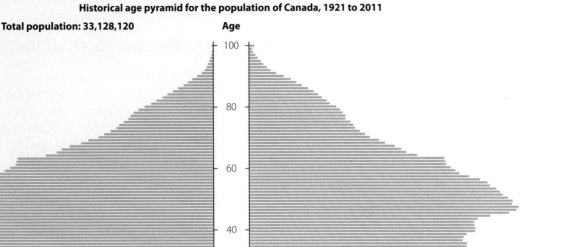

Historical age pyramid for the population of Canada, 1921 to 2011

Total population: 33,128,120

Age

Male population

Year: 2011

Female population

Source: Statistics Canada, census of population and Population Estimates Program, 1921 to 2011. Total population counts originate from the census for census years. Between census years, total population counts were extrapolated using the annual rates of population growth from the Population Estimates Program. For all years included between 1921 and 2011, the age structures are those of the Population Estimates Program.

MILLENNIALS

Sometime referred to as Generation Y or the "Echo Boom", Millennials are consumers born between 1980 and 2000. These teenagers to 30-somethings are of substantial interest to marketers because they represent a larger cohort than Gen X and they have grown up with unprecedented access to personal technologies, ranging from the personal computer to mobile devices, connected together over the World Wide Web. In addition, this generation has grown up in the midst of economic and cultural globalization that is distinct from the postwar Baby Boomers and the Cold War Generation Xers.

Data from Statistics Canada indicate some striking lifestyle differences between Millennials and previous generations. For example, approximately 33% of Millennials is married or living common-law in their 20s, which is much lower than either of the previous generations when they were in their 20s (Gen X, 37%; Baby Boomers, 48%). Correspondingly, Millennials is having children later and staying in school longer. More than half of 20-something Canadian Millennials are living at home with their parents, which is a considerably higher percentage than was the case among Gen X (31%) at the same stage of life. This generation is also the most ethnically and culturally diverse, with almost one in five members having been born outside of Canada.[20]

All of this has marketers both excited by the size of this cohort and confused by the major differences between Millennials and prior generations. Some attribute this to a change in values among Millennials, who have grown up in the media-saturated world of omnipresent branding and marketing. This is a generation of sophisticated consumers who are cynical of companies that try to persuade them through mass marketing.[21] They are very diverse and they expect to be treated as heterogeneous individuals rather than a homogeneous mass. Millennials are used to being asked their opinions by market researchers, and they have grown up with an increasingly customized and customizable consumer experience. This generation has been described as consumers who want—even expect—to co-create value in the products and services that they purchase.

GENERATIONAL INFLUENCE AND MARKETING

Generations provide a good basis for marketing segments because the consumer's age identifies their generation. Not every person who is age 21 right now matches the tastes of all the other millennial generation consumers, but the largest number of people within a generation are similar to some extent. McDonald's recent strategies illustrate the difference between appealing to an age group versus a cohort group. For decades, practically every McDonald's restaurant featured a playground built conspicuously at the front of each restaurant. Not only that, consumers also strongly associated the Happy Meal with McDonald's. Thus, in consumers' long-term memories, McDonald's was strongly defined by the play area, Happy Meals, and children. In the past few years, McDonald's has moved away from that strategy and has even removed the play areas from some of the restaurants. In some cases, they have been replaced with sections called McCafé. The Happy Meal still remains, but the shift in marketing corresponds to the fact that McDonald's is more interested in serving the markets that grew up playing in the playgrounds and eating Happy Meals than they are in directly appealing to children themselves. In a way, McDonald's has shifted from looking at the markets based on their age to capitalizing on a cohort group. Millennial generation consumers won't be found in the play area any longer, but you can still find them at McDonald's.

Generational effects can also explain why country music has changed so dramatically over the years. Have you ever wondered why today's country music doesn't sound like your grandparents' country? The answer lies largely in the fact that many of today's biggest stars grew up listening to classic or even alternative rock music. As you may have noticed, much of country music has a rock-edge sound to it. In some cases, it's even hard to tell the difference between today's country and rock music. Many of today's younger country music stars were just as likely to listen to rock groups such as Van Halen, Aerosmith, or Guns N' Roses when they were growing up as to traditional country legends like Willie Nelson or Johnny Cash. Comparing today's country music star in his 30s with a country music star of the same age in 1950 clearly illustrates how generations change.

9-2e Religious Microculture

Recall that religion represents one of the key institutions that shape consumer culture. Not surprisingly then, religious affiliation provides a basis for microcultures within national or regional cultures. Religion affects all manner of daily life, sometimes even among those who are not devout followers of any religion. For instance, in Canada and throughout the Western world, the weekend occurs on Saturday and Sunday. In Arab lands, however, where Islam is the predominant religion, Friday is the day of prayer, so the weekend occurs on Thursday and Friday. Exhibit 9.5 illustrates the proportion of consumers belonging to the main religions in Canada, other diverse nations, and the world at large.

During the 2001 census, seven out of ten Canadians identified themselves as Christians, and four of those seven identified themselves as Catholic.[22] One can hardly say that all Protestant denominations are the same, but generally speaking, Protestants are relatively conservative in their approach to life, and emphasize hard work and accomplishment as important goals. They also tend to be more comfortable with material acquisitions than are Catholics.[23] Some Protestant denominations are more likely than Catholics to have a moral prohibition against the consumption of beer, wine, and other forms of alcoholic beverages.

Consumer research examines the extent to which an overt Christian appeal influences Christians.[24] For example, an advertisement containing the fish symbol (Christian fish emblem) caused Evangelical Christians to rate the perceived quality of service, and their intention to use that particular service, higher than an ad that was otherwise identical. No such effect was seen among consumers of other religious

Tim Boyle/Getty Images

McCafé products appeal to many consumers who once occupied the play area out front.

Exhibit 9.5

Religious Percentages in the World and Select Nations

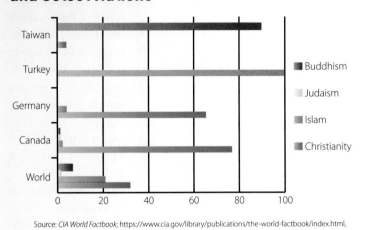

Source: *CIA World Factbook*; https://www.cia.gov/library/publications/the-world-factbook/index.html, accessed December 9, 2010.

affiliations. In fact, the authors of that particular research suggest that the symbol may even backfire and have negative effects on non-Evangelicals.

Religion also affects consumers' diets and the clothing they wear. During Lent each year, fast-food restaurants heavily advertise fish offerings as a way of capitalizing on the Catholic tradition of abstaining from meat during Lent, particularly on Fridays. Jewish consumers often follow a kosher diet, which places a high standard on cleanliness and purity of foods and forbids some common foods like shrimp and bacon. The Islamic religion also places dietary restrictions on its followers, and it strictly prohibits the consumption of pork. The word *halal* describes the dietary restrictions that prohibit alcohol, pork, and meats that are not slaughtered in the prescribed manner. Restaurateurs who serve these markets need to be well aware of the dietary restrictions and the sensitivity of these cultures to violations of the restrictions.

Additionally, various religions have rules and customs about public displays of the body. Muslim women often wear veils, or even cover their entire face. Although this practice may be stigmatized in Western countries, some fashion retailers have offered fashionable veils that may even cross over into the secular market.[25] **Stigmatization** means that the consumer is marked in some way that indicates their place in society. Sometimes the mark is not particularly flattering. In 2010, France's legislature voted to make the public wearing of full veils (those covering the face as well as the head) illegal, arguing that the practice

was demeaning to women. Other European countries are considering adopting similar legislation.[26] In Canada, a Quebec judge refused to hear the case of a woman wearing a hijab.[27] Friction is often inevitable as cultures interact and as consumers of all faiths choose to follow their religious beliefs rather than laws that they perceive to clash with these beliefs. Without question, religion plays a major role in both culture and microculture.

9-2f Ethnic Microculture in Canada

Canada was the first country in the world to officially institute multiculturalism with the adoption of the 1971 Multiculturalism Policy of Canada. This policy formalized the notion that all citizens are equal regardless of their race, ethnic origins, language, or religion. Unlike the American notion of a melting pot that aims to blend together people from a wide range of ethnic backgrounds, multiculturalism encourages people to take pride in their ancestry and aims to establish a culture of mutual respect for different races and ethnic backgrounds. At the same time, multiculturalism in Canada encourages active participation among all of its citizens in the country's social, economic, and political affairs.[28]

A policy of multiculturalism allows ethnic microcultures to thrive in Canada, and those microcultures affect consumer behaviour. Consumers from different ethnic backgrounds tend to have different preferences in products and services in a variety of categories that range from housing to entertainment to food (see, for example, the T&T Supermarket case in Chapter 8).

Early immigrants to Canada were mostly from Western Europe, predominantly from France and the United Kingdom. More recently, the largest numbers of first-generation Canadians have ethnic origins in China and South Asia. However, the fastest-growing visible minorities in Canada are West Asians, Koreans, and Arabs, with their populations increasing by 150%, 120%, and 118%, respectively. In fact, one in five Canadians is expected to be foreign-born by 2017 (see Exhibit 9.6). That proportion of new immigrants in Canada has not been seen since the period from 1911 to 1931, and it differentiates Canada from many other Western countries. By way of comparison, the proportion of foreign-born citizens in

stigmatization a situation in which a consumer is marked in some way that indicates their place in society

Exhibit 9.6

Proportion of Foreign-Born Canadians, 1901 to 2011

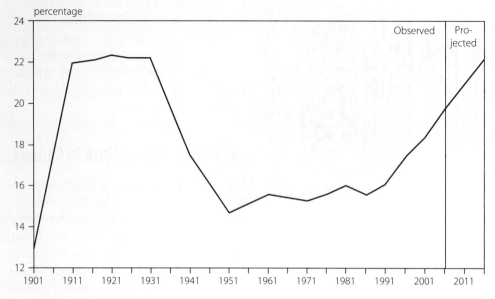

Sources: Chui, T., K. Tran, and H. Maheux, 2007, Immigration in Canada: a portrait of the foreign-born population, 2006 Census: findings, 2006 Census Analysis series, Statistics Canada Catalogue number 97-557XWE2006007; and Bélanger, A., and É. Caron Malenfant, 2005, Population projections of visible minority groups, Canada, provinces and regions, 2001–2017, Statistics Canada Catalogue number 91-541-XIE, reference scenario.

Figure source: Statistics Canada, 2007, Canadian Demographics at a Glance, Statistics Canada Catalogue number 91-003-XWE. http://www.statcan.gc.ca/pub/91-003-x/2007001/figures/4129876-eng.htm, accessed Oct. 21, 2012."

the United States is about 12.5%.[29] This change in the origins of immigrants is illustrated in Exhibit 9.7.

WESTERN EUROPEAN

Most Canadians who are third generation or more identify themselves as simply Canadian (see Exhibit 9.7 and Table 9.1). However, among those who identify a foreign ethnic origin, the largest groups are from France, Ireland, and the United Kingdom. This reflects the historical immigration patterns of a country that was originally settled by pioneers from Western Europe. Second-generation Canadians' ethnic origins reflect a similar composition; however, citizens of German and Italian descent make up a large proportion of the total for this group.

Canadians with Western European ancestry are a majority of the population and, as such, have traditionally had the largest cultural influence on the country. That is changing, however, as Canada's francophone population decreases and new immigrants are increasingly from China and South Asia.

FRANCOPHONE

Immigrants from France have played a major role in founding and shaping Canada and its culture. The impact of French culture may be centred in Quebec, but it is clearly evident across the entire nation. French is one of the country's two official languages, along with English, and the distinctiveness of the French culture has been recognized since the Quebec Act of 1774.[30] The effect of French and Québécois culture on marketing and consumer behaviour has been significant and is clearly the most influential of any minority culture in the country.

However, as illustrated in Exhibit 9.8, in the second half of the 20th century there was a substantial decline in the percentage of Canadians who have French as their mother tongue. In 1951, 29% of Canadians reported that they were francophone, 59.1% reported that English was their first language, and 11.8% reported a different mother tongue. By the 2006 census, those reporting French as their first language fell to 22.1%, while English was at 57.8% and other languages grew to 20.1%. As one might infer from these figures, the decline in the francophone population as a percentage of the Canadian population is primarily the result of immigration from countries where the native language is neither French nor English, which has been compounded by low birthrates among the francophone population. According to the 2006 census, the proportion of Canadians who could conduct a conversation in both French and English was 17%; while 68% could speak only English and 13% knew only French. The non-official languages with the highest numbers of speakers are Chinese (3.9%), Spanish (2.4%), Italian (2.1%), German (2.0%), Punjabi (1.5%), and Arabic (1.2%).[31]

CHINESE AND SOUTH ASIAN

In recent years, the composition of ethnic origins among Canadian immigrants has changed from its traditional

Exhibit 9.7

Top 10 Ethnic Origins for First, Second, Third, and More Generations in Canada*

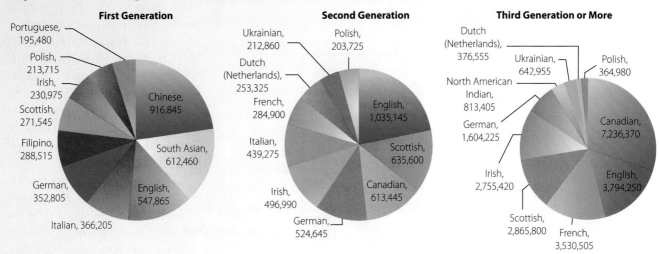

Table 9.1

Top 10 Ethnic Origins by Generational Status for People Aged 15 Years and Over, Canada, 2006

First Generation			Second Generation			Third Generation or More		
Ethnic Origin	Percent	Number	Ethnic Origin	Percent	Number	Ethnic Origin	Percent	Number
Total population	100	6,124,560	Total population	100	4,006,420	Total population	100	15,533,240
Chinese	15	916,845	English	25.8	1,035,145	Canadian	46.6	7,236,370
South Asian	10	612,460	Scottish	15.9	635,600	English	24.4	3,794,250
English	8.9	547,865	Canadian	15.3	613,445	French	22.7	3,530,505
Italian	6	366,205	German	13.1	524,645	Scottish	18.4	2,865,800
German	5.8	352,805	Irish	12.4	496,990	Irish	17.7	2,755,420
Filipino	4.7	288,515	Italian	11	439,275	German	10.3	1,604,225
Scottish	4.4	271,545	French	7.1	284,900	North American Indian	5.2	813,405
Irish	3.8	230,975	Dutch (Netherlands)	6.3	253,325	Ukrainian	4.1	642,955
Polish	3.5	213,715	Ukrainian	5.3	212,860	Dutch (Netherlands)	2.4	376,555
Portuguese	3.2	195,480	Polish	5.1	203,725	Polish	2.3	364,980

Source: Statistics Canada, Census of Population, 2006. Found at: http://www12.statcan.ca/census-recensement/2006/as-sa/97-562/table/t1-eng.cfm

*Note: Table shows total responses. Because some respondents reported more than one ethnic origin, the sum of the total responses is greater than the total population, or 100%. Figures are for Canadians over the age of 15.

Exhibit 9.8

Languages in Canada as a Percentage of the Total Population, 1951 to 2006

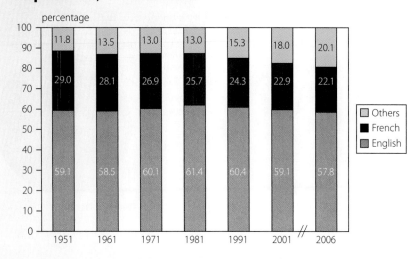

Sources: Marmen, L., and J. P. Corbeil, 2004, Languages in Canada: 2001, Census, Statistical Canada Catalogue number 96-326-XIE, and Statistics Canada, Census of Population, 2006.

Figure source: Statistics Canada, 2007, Canadian Demographics at a Glance, Statistics Canada Catalogue, number 91-003-XWE. http://www.statcan.gc.ca/pub/91-003-x/2007001/figures/4129882-eng.htm, accessed Oct. 21, 2012.

Western European roots. Although England, Scotland, Ireland, Italy, and Germany all rank in the top 10 ethnic origins of first-generation Canadians, the largest groups are Chinese and South Asians. In fact, as illustrated in Exhibit 9.9, the Chinese and South Asian populations in Canada are expected to approximately double in size, with both groups reaching nearly 2 million people. As a result of this growth, by 2017 one in five Canadians is expected to belong to a visible minority.

This trend will have a substantial impact on consumer behaviour in Canada as these microcultures express their unique preferences for a broad variety of consumer products and services in the country. One example is the integration of ethnic food sales into the major grocery chains in Canada, such as Loblaw's purchase of T&T Supermarket. The introduction of products popular among Canada's ethnic microcultures to the broader population means greater choice for all consumers and a unique set of Canadian consumer behaviours that reflect the country's exceptional ethnic diversity.

ABORIGINAL CANADIANS

As illustrated in Exhibit 9.7, a large proportion of Canadians who have lived in Canada for three generations or more identify themselves as First Nations people. Moreover,

while Canada's overall population grew 8% between 1996 and 2006, the country's Aboriginal population—which includes the First Nations people, the Métis, and the Inuit—grew by 45%. During this period, the Métis population doubled, the First Nations population grew by 29%, and the Inuit population increased by 26%. Statistics Canada has predicted that the total Aboriginal population in Canada could be nearing 1.5 million people by 2017.[32]

This rapidly growing population provides both a challenge and an opportunity to marketers in Canada. Clearly, any large segment of the population that is growing at double-digit rates should be of interest to retailers and other consumer-focused organizations. In addition, the Aboriginal population is young, with a median age of 27, as compared with 40 for the non-Aboriginal population. Moreover, in Saskatchewan and Manitoba, Aboriginal children account for a very high percentage of the population under six years old (20% in Saskatchewan and 19% in Manitoba). At the same time, 57% of these families are classified as low income and their parents are much more likely to be struggling with their personal finances and their housing situation, as compared to non-Aboriginal families. The median total income for the Aboriginal population was $22,000, compared with $33,000 for the non-Aborginal population. Nevertheless, given the Aboriginal populations' size and rate of growth, this is an ethnic microculture that demands attention from Canada's policy makers and consumer marketers.[33]

9-2g Income and Social Class Microculture

Two very important topics in consumer behaviour are income and social class. The concepts permeate our everyday life, and it seems that consumers are always trying to better themselves by moving up the income and class ladders. To say that income and social class are variables that marketers track closely would be a huge understatement.

Income level and social class are closely related, but distinct, concepts. Income level is truly a demographic issue, based on the amount of monetary resources a

Exhibit 9.9

Visible Minority Groups in Canada, 2001 to 2017

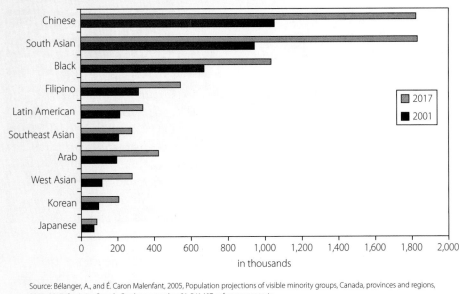

Source: Bélanger, A., and É. Caron Malenfant, 2005, Population projections of visible minority groups, Canada, provinces and regions, 2001–2017, Statistics Canada Catalogue number 91-541-XIE, reference scenario.

Figure source: Statistics Canada, 2007, Canadian Demographics at a Glance, Statistics Canada Catalogue number 91-003-XWE. http://www.statcan.gc.ca/pub/91-003-x/2007001/figures/4129878-eng.htm, accessed Oct. 21, 2012.

person receives. **Social class** is a culturally defined group to which a consumer belongs based on resources like prestige, income, occupation, and education. Income and occupation are two of the most recognizable determinants of social class.

Tastes and preferences are largely determined by social class, a finding that falls under the sociological concept of **habitus**—mental and cognitive structures through which individuals perceive the world based largely on their standing in a social class.[34] Although concrete generalizations regarding the influence of income and social class on purchase behaviour are difficult, it can be said that social class tends to be a better predictor of purchases that involve value and lifestyles, as well as symbolic and highly visible products. Income tends to be a better predictor of purchases that require very substantial expenditures, while both income and social class predict purchases of symbolic, expensive products.[35]

SOCIAL CLASS IN CANADA

At a basic level, social classes can be categorized from low to middle to high. Some studies go further and create finer gradations, such as *upper class, lower upper class, upper middle class, lower middle class, upper lower class,* and *lower lower class*.[36] Many consumers

strive to move up the social ladder throughout their lifetimes, but this is not true of all consumers. Some consumers are simply content with their social standing and do not aspire to move up the social ladder. Some consumers are born into a social class (termed an *ascribed* status), while others work their way into a class (termed an *achieved* status).

Social class is an important concept because a class strongly influences lifestyles, opinions, attitudes, and behaviours. Sayings such as "birds of a feather flock together" and "keeping up with the Joneses" typify the social class conceptualization. That is to say, consumers in a particular class tend to behave similarly in the marketplace. Again, it should be emphasized that this does not mean that *every* consumer in a social class will exhibit the *exact* same behaviours, attitudes, and opinions. However, in general, it is a good rule of thumb that they will act similarly.

Two issues regarding social class that have been discussed here illustrate the difficulties with considering class in consumer behaviour. The facts that (1) not all consumers strive to move up the social ladder and (2) not every consumer in a social class will act similarly highlight the limitations of using the concept in consumer research. Nevertheless, social class is a very important societal and cultural issue that we observe in everyday life. A simple example of the influence of social class on behaviour is the finding that most marriages comprise people from similar classes. In sociology, this is referred to as **homogamy**, or *assortative mating*.[37]

social class a culturally defined group to which a consumer belongs based on resources like prestige, income, occupation, and education

habitus mental and cognitive structures through which individuals perceive the world based largely on their standing in a social class

homogamy the finding that most marriages comprise people from similar classes

Changing Class

According to a recent report in *The New York Times*, Canada's middle class has now surpassed the same segment in the United States to become the world's richest. In 1980, the United States had the highest after-tax income at each level of income except the bottom 5% (where Norway was the leader). By 2010, the United States was still the leader in the 60th, 70th, 80th, and 90th income percentiles, but Canada tied or had a higher income in the 50th, 40th, and 30th percentiles. For the 5th, 10th, and 20th, the Netherlands was leading. Since 2010, the *Times* estimates that Canada's middle class—that is, the 30th, 40th, and 50th income percentiles—has continued to outpace similar groups of Americans.

In the United States, the group typically defined as the middle class has shrunken and more Americans in the middle class find themselves at the lower end of the income range (which the *Times* defined as $35,000 to $100,000 per year). In Canada, the size of this group has been stable. In response to the report in the *Times*, William Robson, president and CEO of the C.D. Howe Institute, commented that, "It's interesting how sometimes we don't pay attention to how well we're doing unless it's somebody outside our borders who reports it. Statistics Canada has been publishing these data for a number of years and they have been telling a relatively positive story, but it's not gotten a lot of attention." Of course, among the highest income earners in the world, the United States continues to lead.

Sources: Gollom, Mark (2014), "Canada vs. U.S. Middle Class: What the New York Times missed," *CBC News*, April 25, accessed at http://www.cbc.ca/news/canada/canada-vs-u-s-middle-class-what-the-new-york-times-missed-1.2621147 on June 19, 2015. Leonhard, David and Kevin Quealy (2014), "Losing the Lead: This Simple Table Summarizes Our Story on American Living Standards," *The New York Times*, April 22, accessed at http://www.nytimes.com/2014/04/23/upshot/this-simple-table-summarizes-our-story-on-american-living-standards.html?abt=0002&abg=0 on June 19, 2015. Stabile, Mark and Lauren Jones (2015), "The Shrinking Middle Class: So Far a U.S. Story," *The Globe and Mail*, February 6, accessed at http://www.theglobeandmail.com/globe-debate/the-shrinking-middle-class-so-far-just-a-us-story/article22828747/ on June 19, 2015

SOCIAL STRATIFICATION

The concept of social stratification underscores the role of social class in society. **Social stratification** can be defined as the division of society into classes that have unequal access to scarce and valuable resources.[38] Of course, the finer things in life are generally enjoyed by the upper or lower upper class. Luxury items and **status symbols** are enjoyed by these groups, while the bare essentials are relegated to the lower lower class.

Of growing concern is the disparity between the upper and lower classes in countries such as Canada and the United States. Consider, for example, the number of homeless people who currently live in the tunnel systems under the city of Las Vegas. Below the very streets where excess is flaunted live some of the poorest and most destitute consumers in North America.[39] The problems of poverty and homelessness are becoming an increasingly important topic for consumer research.

SOCIAL CLASS WORLDWIDE

Social classes obviously exist throughout the world. For example, China, with its enormous population, exhibits a range of social classes. Rapid economic development has led to recent gains in the Chinese middle class, and forecasts reveal that as many as 700 million consumers will be in the Chinese middle class by the year 2020. Middle class consumers occupy a variety of positions in the Chinese workplace, from entrepreneurs to managers of high-tech companies.[40] Japan, on the other hand, has witnessed a gradual widening of the gap between

social stratification
the division of society into classes that have unequal access to scarce and valuable resources

status symbols
products or objects that are used to signal one's place in society

the "haves" and the "have-nots," along with a generally shrinking middle class. India, like China, has a large middle class, estimated at approximately 170 million. Many of these consumers are young, with nearly half of India's billion-plus population younger than 25 years old. Estimates reveal that as much as 40% of the population of India will be middle class in the next two decades.[41]

9-2h Street Microculture

Microcultures can grow around any number of phenomena, not just around ethnic, income/social class, generational, regional, or religious differences. As we have seen, sports can provide a basis for microculture. Music can as well. One way to refer to these microcultures is by using the label *street microcultures.*

The hip-hop microculture illustrates one such group. Obviously, hip-hop culture has influenced consumer tastes outside of its group (consider the pervasiveness of hip-hop apparel). "Gothic" (or "goth") microculture represents another prevalent microculture in North America. Gothic influence can be very strong as group members almost universally wear dark, macabre attire. The goth microculture is a great example of how strong microculture influence can be. In fact, some argue that gothic identification is even more important than gender identification.[42] The "emo" subculture has received a lot of media attention in recent years, though its roots are thought to go back at least a few decades. Most consumers can recognize a goth or emo person easily, further evidence of how microcultures permeate our daily lives and are observed by many consumers.

Microcultures can even grow out of gaming experiences, virtual communities, and practically any other consumer activity that brings together consumers with something in common. The more easily a microculture can be reached, either physically or with various media, the better marketers can connect with them through value-added communications and products. lululemon's success, for example, is associated with the growth in popularity of yoga microculture in Canada and around the world.

How many levels of culture are represented in this scene?

jarvis gray/Shutterstock.com

9-3 MICROCULTURE IS NOT UNIQUELY CANADIAN

We often think of foreign countries with a single stereotype. A Parisian may represent all French people to some consumers. Even a country as diverse as China might be looked at very narrowly, with unfounded stereotypes. Other countries also have many bases around which microcultures are formed.

Although Canada is a highly multicultural country, it is not unique in its diversity of microcultures. Germany, Spain, and South Africa, for instance, are all countries where different languages are spoken in different regions of the country. Bavarians, from the German Alps, feel quite distinct from the typical German population. More than 1,800 languages are spoken on the continent of Africa, across 53 countries. Furthermore, immigration is fast spreading through Europe, and the influx of Muslim microcultures in many European countries is adding to the diversity of these nations.

Many street microcultures—including music, sports, and fashion—exist around the world as well. Punk, goth, and emo microcultures are all good examples. Emo, for example, represents a popular microculture in Japan. Japanese "gothic Lolita" is another popular microculture that can best be illustrated by imagining a gothic China doll. Some Japanese girls also follow the "decora" microculture, which is marked by wearing extremely bright clothing and plastic accessories. Given the pervasiveness of microcultures throughout the world, firms' efforts to market products in virtually any part of the world need to take into account not only culture, but microculture as well.

DEMOGRAPHIC ANALYSIS

Ultimately, any group or microculture has to be reached before a value proposition can be effectively delivered to them. *Demographics* is a term that we have used throughout this text, and it is an important concept for marketers and consumer researchers alike. **Demographics** are relatively tangible human characteristics that describe consumers, including age, ethnicity, sex, occupation, income, region, religion, and gender.

Demographic variables are closely related to microculture. In fact, you may have noticed from previous sections that demographic variables help one describe microcultures. As an example, we previously discussed the fact that age distinctions can be used to describe generational microcultures. Consider the fact that consumers in the Millennial microculture can be described as currently falling between the ages of 15 and 35. As such, the demographic variable "age" helps us better understand and describe this microculture. The combination of demographic and microcultural information is therefore very valuable for today's marketers. This information becomes even more valuable when it is combined with **geodemographics**, because members of many microcultures often live in close proximity to one another. Geodemographic tools such as PRIZM5 assist the consumer researcher with these analyses.

A **demographic analysis** develops a profile of a consumer group based on their demographics. As we have discussed, these analyses often include geodemographic approaches because marketers find it advantageous to know where targeted consumers live. These analyses become important components of a demographic segmentation strategy.

demographics relatively tangible human characteristics that describe consumers

geodemographics study of people based on the fact that people with similar demographics tend to live close to one another

demographic analysis a profile of a consumer group based on their demographics

Exhibit 9.10

Statistics Canada's Website

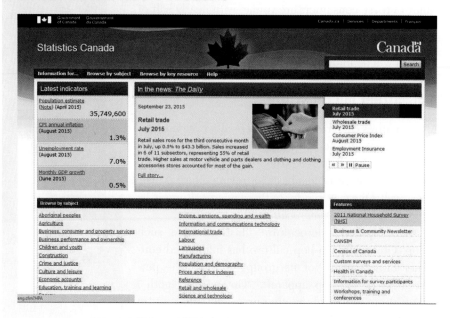

A powerful source of demographic information is the Statistics Canada website.

Source: Statistics Canada, http://www.statcan.gc.ca/start-debut-eng.html

If marketers can identify where their targeted consumers live, they can implement marketing campaigns much more efficiently. Newspapers, radio, television, and even Internet communications can then be geared to specific regions.

One very important source for performing a demographic analysis is Statistics Canada (www.statscan.gc.ca). Exhibit 9.10 shows the interface from Statistics Canada's main page.

The website provides access to a wealth of information from surveys conducted by Statistics Canada and analysis and reports written by both Statistics Canada and third parties. Generally, the search engine can be used to find statistics on a region of interest. Exhibit 9.11 shows the demographic profile for Saskatoon.

9-5 MAJOR CULTURAL AND DEMOGRAPHIC TRENDS

A number of cultural, microcultural, and demographic trends currently affect consumer behaviour and are also greatly influencing marketing practice. Notable trends include declining birth rates, increased consumer affluence, increasing life expectancy, and increasing cultural diversity worldwide.

Exhibit 9.11

Demographic Profile for the Province of Saskatchewan: Selected Trend Data for Saskatchewan, 1996, 2001, and 2006

Characteristic	Saskatoon, CY Saskatchewan (Census subdivision)			Saskatchewan (Province)		
	Total	Male	Female	Total	Male	Female
Marital status						
Total population 15 years and over by marital status	184,385	89,255	95,125	835,525	410,545	424,980
Married or living with a common-law partner	98,485	49,320	49,160	487,980	244,485	243,495
Married (and not separated)	83,585	41,865	41,720	416,355	208,700	207,655
Living common law	14,900	7,460	7,440	71,630	35,785	35,845
Not married and not living with a common-law partner	85,900	39,935	45,970	347,535	166,055	181,480
Single (never legally married)	60,560	32,135	28,420	232,160	128,325	103,835
Separated	4,125	1,760	2,365	18,210	8,220	9,990
Divorced	11,140	4,390	6,755	43,665	19,500	24,170
Widowed	10,070	1,650	8,420	53,500	10,015	43,490
Family characteristics						
Total number of census families in private households	58,630	...	...	285,370	...	...
Size of census family: 2 persons	29,695	...	...	148,805	...	...

Information such as this is very valuable.

Source: Statistics Canada. 2012. Saskatoon, Saskatchewan (Code 4711066) and Saskatchewan (Code 47) (table). Census Profile. 2011 Census. Statistics Canada Catalogue no. 98-316-XWE. Ottawa. Released October 24, 2012. http://www12.statcan.gc.ca/census-recensement/2011/dp-pd/prof/index.cfm?Lang=E (accessed August 10, 2015).

9-5a Trends Affecting Consumer Behaviour

DECLINING BIRTH RATES

One of the biggest trends in Western countries is the declining birth rate. In many European countries, the birth rate has dropped to 0.5 per person. That means that each couple is having at most one child. If this trend continues, these countries will experience declining populations. One particularly important trend in China, thought to be the result of the country's "one child" policy, is a relative imbalance in the number of men compared to women. Estimates reveal that by 2020, China could have as many as 30 million more men than women.[43] Exhibit 9.12 displays select birth rates. While birth rates are relatively low in many Western countries, notice that birth rates remain high in other countries, including Bangladesh, India, and Nigeria. Immigration is especially important to the social and economic well-being of countries like Canada that have a birth rate of less than 2.

INCREASING CONSUMER AFFLUENCE

The combination of working couples and lower birth rates has led to greater levels of consumer affluence. As a result, many consumer segments have become targets for products once considered to be luxuries, such as cruises and high-end automobiles. Furthermore, consumers have generally become less price sensitive in many categories. Families eat out more often and are more likely to own the latest electronic devices than consumers of the past. These trends affect not only Canada and the United States, but other countries as well. As detailed earlier, the rise in the middle class in both China and India is evidence of growing consumer affluence worldwide.

To say that consumer affluence is a trend is not to imply that poverty is not a major problem worldwide. To the contrary, poverty remains a major problem in many nations, as evidenced by the approximately 4 billion "bottom of the pyramid" consumers. Nevertheless, the growth in consumer affluence is an important trend.

INCREASING LIFE EXPECTANCY AND THE AGING CONSUMER

The right pane of Exhibit 9.12 displays the life expectancy for citizens of a number of different countries. Life expectancy is increasing in many, but not all, countries. The most obvious increase is found in developed nations. If we consider life expectancy as a proxy for standard of living, we can see that as the birth rate declines, the standard of living increases. Thus, unfortunately, the countries with the highest birth rates in the world are among the poorest. In developed countries, more wealth is spread over fewer consumers.

The growth trends in population, along with birth rate and life expectancy trends, all affect consumer culture in many ways. One major issue in North America today is the aging Baby Boomer population. This segment of the consumer population is expected to dramatically affect business practices for many years to

Exhibit 9.12

Projected Birth Rates per Couple and Life Expectancies for Countries Around the World (2010)

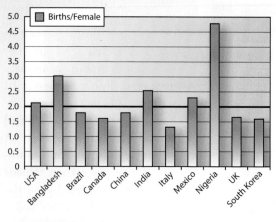

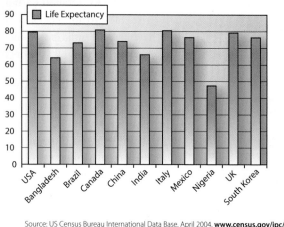

Source: US Census Bureau International Data Base, April 2004, **www.census.gov/ipc/www/idbnew.html.**

come. As discussed earlier, this segment attracts much marketing attention due to its large size and overall spending power.

9-5b Disparate Regional Growth Rates and Urbanization

Ontario remains the largest province in the country by a wide margin, with 38.4% of the population, but its population growth rate is lagging well behind the Western provinces' rates. Alberta, British Columbia, and Saskatchewan are growing at considerably higher rates than the rest of the country (see Exhibit 9.13).

Based on data from the 2011 census, Western Canada now has a larger population than Quebec, the Maritimes, and Newfoundland and Labrador combined for the first time in the country's history. Almost one-third of Canadians now live west of Ontario, as compared to approximately 26% in 1961. The fastest-growing metropolitan areas between 2006 and 2011 were Calgary and Edmonton.

While the demographic shift from east to west is interesting, it is the underlying cause of this shift that is especially noteworthy for marketers: As the traditional manufacturing engine of the eastern economy declines, the resource sector in the west is continuing to grow. That shift in economic strength can have a substantial effect on a broad range of business decisions, from where to open a new store to where to locate a head office, and on government policy decisions, from where new immigrants land in Canada to what type of career training Canadians need.

In addition, Canada's population is increasingly urban, with 35% of Canadians now living in the areas around Canada's three largest cities: Toronto, Montreal, and Vancouver. Smaller towns are growing at a slower rate, and growth in rural areas has stalled. In combination, the shifts in Canada's population from east to west and from rural to urban are significant trends in the country's geodemographic profile.

INCREASING CULTURAL DIVERSITY

Many societies worldwide are becoming increasingly culturally diverse. One way in which cultures become more diverse is through immigration and the growth of microcultures. There are numerous trends that could be discussed, and they range from religious to street microcultural diversity. Regarding religious microcultures, one significant trend in European countries is the growth of the Muslim faith. Islam is rapidly growing in popularity in Europe, and this religious microculture is influencing consumer behaviour throughout the region.

The United Kingdom is also experiencing a general increase in immigration, with many immigrants arriving from the European Union. As such, the United Kingdom is realizing a growth in microcultural diversity, particularly pertaining to ethnic and religious microcultural diversity. The continued expansion of the world teen culture market is expected as many Western brands, such as Coca-Cola, McDonald's, and Starbucks, continue to succeed with foreign expansion. The influence of Western ideals and practice

Exhibit 9.13

Provincial Growth Rates and Population Share

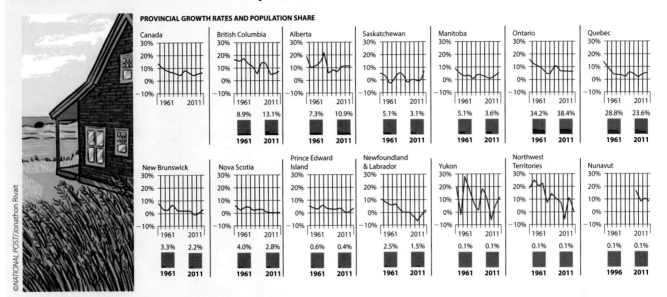

PROVINCIAL GROWTH RATES AND POPULATION SHARE

	1961	2011
British Columbia	8.9%	13.1%
Alberta	7.3%	10.9%
Saskatchewan	5.1%	3.1%
Manitoba	5.1%	3.6%
Ontario	34.2%	38.4%
Quebec	28.8%	23.6%
New Brunswick	3.3%	2.2%
Nova Scotia	4.0%	2.8%
Prince Edward Island	0.6%	0.4%
Newfoundland & Labrador	2.5%	1.5%
Yukon	0.1%	0.1%
Northwest Territories	0.1%	0.1%
Nunavut	0.1% (1996)	0.1%

Source: Jonathon Rivait, "Census Canada 2011 infographic: How the new population stats break down by province and city," *National Post*, Feb. 8, 2012. Found at: **http://news.nationalpost .com/2012/02/08/census-canada-2011-infographic-how-the-new-population-stats-break-down-by-province-and-city/**

©*NATIONAL POST*/Jonathon Rivait

on the world teen culture continues. This is not to say that all young consumers will completely think and act alike. In fact, many Asian teens are carving out new and developing microcultures unlike those found in North America. Some teens worldwide are breaking away from punk, goth, and emo microcultures to focus on more traditional, clean-cut, even conservative styles.[44] As mentioned, there are many ways in which cultural diversity is increasing worldwide.

As we have seen, microcultures influence consumer behaviour throughout the world, and for this reason, the study of microculture is very important for consumer researchers and marketers alike.

STUDY TOOLS 9

LOCATED AT THE BACK OF THE TEXTBOOK

☐ Rip out Chapter Review Card

LOCATED AT NELSON.COM/STUDENT

☐ Review Key Terms Flashcards (print or online)

☐ Download audio summaries to review on the go

☐ Complete practice quizzes to prepare for tests

☐ Watch video on Vans for a real company example

Case

The Ultimate Fighting Championship

Sports provide many different microcultures, ranging from *Hockey Night in Canada* to American tailgate parties prior to football games to soccer fanatics in Europe. In recent years, however, the fastest-growing sport has not been hockey, football, baseball, soccer, or basketball. It has been mixed martial arts (MMA) cage fighting.

Once described by U.S. senator and Republican presidential candidate John McCain as "human cockfighting," the Ultimate Fighting Championship (UFC) has become a popular spectator sport. The UFC began in 1993 as a fighting competition designed to determine which fighting style was the best—it included fighters from boxing, sumo, karate, wrestling, jujitsu, and a number of other backgrounds. There were no weight classes, no rounds, no judges, and few rules. To win, you had to either knock your opponent out or force him or her to quit. The competition had a small group of hardcore fans, but it was not making money, and a decade after it began the company that ran the UFC was on the verge of bankruptcy. It was saved in 2004 when Spike TV aired a reality television program—*The Ultimate Fighter*—that was built around fighters competing for a contract in the UFC. That show introduced a much larger audience to cage fighting and initiated a growth phase for the business that led to regular broadcasts on the Fox network and millions of subscribers to its pay-per-view broadcasts.

Globally, UFC programming is now broadcast in more than 149 countries and territories, reaching a half-billion homes worldwide, in 20 different languages. It is also popular in Canada, where it has hosted events at the Air Canada Centre in Toronto, the Bell Centre in Montreal, Rogers Arena in Vancouver, and the Calgary Saddledome. In 2008, 2009, and 2010, Rogers SportsNet named Canadian UFC fighter and welterweight champion Georges St–Pierre the Canadian Athlete of the Year, ahead of sports stars such as hockey players Sidney Crosby and Jonathan Toews, figure skater Patrick Chan, baseball's national league MVP Joey Votto, tennis star Daniel Nestor, and many other worthy contenders.

Canadian mixed martial artist Georges St-Pierre

Jim Kemper/Zuffa LLC via Getty Images

Fans of the UFC are an interesting consumer microculture that not only watches the cage fighting events but also buys UFC and MMA merchandise, DVDs, video games, and apparel. Nevertheless, MMA is a difficult business. A long list of companies operating MMA events in competition with the UFC have failed financially and either disappeared or been merged with the UFC. The challenges for the UFC going forward are very similar to those faced by many other consumer marketers who hope to take a successful business built within a microculture and expand it to the general population. lululemon was able to successfully leverage the yoga microculture into a thriving mainstream business. West 49 has done well with the skateboard and snowboard microculture. Yet for every lululemon and West 49, there are a number of trends and companies that have not made the jump from micro to mainstream culture. As the UFC continues to expand, many observers have been left to wonder how much further cage fighting can grow.

Sources: Associated Press (2009), "Ultimate Fighting Circuit Reaches a Milestone," *The New York Times* (July 11), http://www.nytimes.com/2009/07/12/sports/12ufc.html, accessed May 31, 2012. Deibert, Dave (2012), "UFC 149 Confirmed for Calgary," Postmedia News (March 21), the *Vancouver Sun* http://www.vancouversun.com/sports/confirmed+Calgary+2012+Canadian+stops+announced+Vancouver/6337552/story.html, accessed May 31, 2012. http://www.ufc.com/discover/ufc, accessed May 31, 2012.

QUESTIONS

1 How would you define the MMA microculture in terms of its audience demographics? Does it make sense to define this microculture in terms of age and gender? How about geography, generation, social class, or ethnic background?

2 What aspects of the UFC make it possible for the company to grow MMA into a mainstream sport, similar in size and scope to hockey, football, baseball, or basketball?

3 What parts of the UFC appeal to the MMA microculture that might not appeal to a more general audience?

4 Has the MMA microculture influenced the mainstream culture in North America? If so, how? If not, why not?

10 | Group and Interpersonal Influence

LEARNING OBJECTIVES

After studying this chapter, the student should be able to:

10-1 Understand the different types of reference groups that influence consumers and how reference groups influence value perceptions.

10-2 Describe the various types of social power that reference groups exert on members.

10-3 Comprehend the difference between informational, utilitarian, and value-expressive reference group influence.

10-4 Understand the importance of word-of-mouth communications in consumer behaviour.

10-5 Comprehend the role of household influence in consumer behaviour.

INTRODUCTION

The motivation to belong is an important part of human life. Consumers are social creatures who desire contact and affiliation with others. As a result, consumers often belong to (or aspire to belong to) a number of formal or informal groups that can exert significant influence on consumer behaviour. Other individual consumers can also influence a consumer's behaviour. In this chapter, we discuss a number of issues relating to the concept of group and interpersonal influence and how these concepts apply to value. We begin by discussing the various types of reference groups that influence consumer behaviour.

reference group
individuals who have significant relevance for a consumer and who have an impact on the consumer's evaluations, aspirations, and behaviour

group influence ways in which group members influence attitudes, behaviour, and opinions of others within the group

10-1 REFERENCE GROUPS

A **reference group** is a group of individuals who have significant relevance for a consumer and who have an impact on the consumer's evaluations, aspirations, and behaviour.[1] This influence affects the ways that consumers seek and receive value from consumption. Most people don't realize all the ways that reference groups influence their behaviour. A good start in realizing how great the influence truly is comes when one takes inventory of all his or her reference groups. Consumers become members of many groups that either meet physically or, thanks to the Internet, meet in cyberspace. In fact, the popularity of social networking websites brings a whole new perspective on the structure and influence of personal reference groups. How many Facebook groups do you belong to? How many do you "like"? How many people or companies do you follow on Twitter? Have you posted a board to Pinterest? How many Instagram followers do you have? All of these examples illustrate how social media shapes group and individual behaviour. To begin a discussion of these issues, we must first define what we mean by "group influence."

10-1a Group Influence

Group influence refers to ways in which group members influence attitudes, opinions, and behaviours of others within the group. Groups are an important part

"Gaining acceptance into a group can provide value for a consumer by satisfying needs for belonging."

of social life, and group processes profoundly affect consumer behaviour by changing the perceived value of things. In fact, gaining acceptance into a group provides value for a consumer directly by satisfying his or her needs for belonging. Consider the following aspects of group life:

▸ Group members share common goals and interests.

▸ Group members communicate with, and influence, one another.

▸ Group members share a set of expectations, rules, and roles.

▸ Group members view themselves as members of a common social unit.[2]

These qualities of group membership are important. Sorority sisters share a common set of expectations that ultimately influences members' decisions about things such as activities, attire, and social involvement. A student marketing club organizes fundraisers for an end-of-the-year field trip, with all members sharing a common goal. An "over 50" student organization meets regularly to discuss the difficulties associated with being a nontraditional student. A Facebook group shares common interests in products and services. When you join

(or like) a Facebook group or page, you share some common interest in the relevant subject.

Group influence does not just affect buying behaviour. Consumer attitudes, opinions, and value perceptions are also heavily influenced by groups, even if a specific purchase does not directly result. This is particularly the case with social networking website groups. Some groups, whether online groups or otherwise, have more influence on consumers than do others.

PRIMARY/SECONDARY GROUPS

A **primary group** includes members who have frequent, direct contact with one another. Primary reference groups generally have the most influence on their members, and *social ties* for these groups are very strong. A social tie is a measure of the strength of connection between group members. An example of a primary reference group is the family unit. Family members generally have much influence on one another, and many times it directly affects behaviour in the marketplace. For example, studies reveal that parental influence on children's shopping

primary group group that includes members who have frequent, direct contact with one another and saving behaviour can be quite strong.[3] Parents who openly discuss financial matters, such as developing savings accounts, can greatly influence these behaviours.

In a **secondary group**, interaction within the group is much less frequent than in a primary group. Professional organizations and social clubs are examples of secondary groups. Usually, the influence of these groups on members is not as strong as the influence of primary groups on their members. Furthermore, social ties are not as strong in secondary groups as they are in primary groups.

One special type of secondary group is a **brand community**. Brand communities are groups of consumers who develop relationships based on shared interests or product usage.[4] A popular example of a brand community is Harley-Davidson's H.O.G. (Harley Owners Group). Fans of Harley-Davidson meet regularly at events that marketers refer to as *brandfests*. Some brand communities are found online in the form of Facebook groups, for example. Canadian clothing company Triple Flip has created its own brand community by promoting its customers' interests and using local tweens in its advertising. Triple Flip believes that real girls who love to wear the company's clothes make the best models and ambassadors for the brand. "Flip girls" not only buy the clothing, but they also see themselves and their friends in the company's marketing both within the stores and online. The company uses its blog to profile and promote local community events that its customers are engaged in and to provide lifestyle advice to girls. For a retailer with a dozen stores, it is very active on social media, including more than 27,400 likes on Facebook and 8,500 followers on Instagram. All of this connects its customers to each other based on their shared interests in tween apparel.

In general, personal connections originating in brand communities lead to positive outcomes for consumers and companies. Consumers learn more about the products they enjoy, and they develop bonds with other users. Companies reap the rewards of positive consumer attitudes. The brand devotion

Dana Pugh Photography

Triple Flip builds a brand community by featuring its customers in its ads.

that community members share helps members strongly identify with each other.[5]

FORMAL/INFORMAL GROUPS

A **formal group** is a group in which a consumer officially becomes a member. For example, a consumer becomes a formal member of a church congregation. Formal groups generally have a set of stated rules, accepted values, and codes of conduct that members are expected to adhere to.

An **informal group** has no membership or application requirements, and codes of conduct may be nonexistent. Examples of informal groups include groups that meet regularly to exercise, have coffee, or go to sporting events. Although informal group influence may not be as strong as formal group influence, these groups can have an impact on consumer behaviour.

ASPIRATIONAL/DISSOCIATIVE GROUPS

An **aspirational group** is a group of which a consumer desires to become a member. Aspirational group membership often appeals to the consumer's *ideal self*. The ideal self is an important part of the consumer's self-concept, and consumers often visualize themselves as belonging to certain groups. For example, a business student may desire to become a member of a professional business association once she earns her degree. Consumers frequently emulate the members of aspirational groups and perform behaviours that they believe will lead to formal acceptance into the group. Getting the first job would be the first step for joining a business organization.

secondary group
group whose members have less frequent contact than that found in a primary group

brand community
group of consumers who develop relationships based on shared interests or product usage

formal group group in which a consumer officially becomes a member

informal group group that has no membership or application requirements and that may have no code of conduct

aspirational group
group of which a consumer desires to become a member

A **dissociative group** is a group to which a consumer does not want to belong. For example, a Conservative might want to avoid being perceived as belonging to a Liberal group (and vice versa). Recent university graduates may want to disassociate themselves from past groups as they take the next step into adulthood.

10-1b Conformity

An important topic in the study of reference group influence is **conformity**, which occurs when an individual yields to the attitudes and behaviours of other consumers. Conformity is very similar to the concept of persuasion, with the key difference that with conformity, the other party does not necessarily defend its position. That is, a group may give no reason for why it expects its group members to act or think a certain way. Persuasion, on the other hand, relies on one party defending its position to another party in an explicit attempt to change attitude or behaviour.[6]

PEER PRESSURE

Peer pressure and conformity are also closely related topics. **Peer pressure** is the pressure an individual feels to behave in accordance with group expectations. Peer pressure can greatly influence behaviour. In fact, peer pressure is often the strongest type of influence a consumer experiences in daily life.

Consumers of all ages feel peer pressure. In fact, very young children often desire to wear the types of clothing and brands that will allow them to feel accepted. One study found that children as young as 10 years old prefer to wear brand-name footwear (e.g., Nike) so that they will fit in with their peers.[7]

NEGATIVE PEER PRESSURE

Peer pressure to wear a certain brand of clothing is not necessarily a bad thing. Unfortunately, negative consumer behaviours are often heavily influenced by peer pressure. Consumers sometimes succumb to group pressures that subtly or not so subtly encourage counterproductive or unethical—perhaps illegal—behaviours.

Experts frequently cite peer pressure as particularly persuasive among young consumers. The media direct a lot of attention to peer pressure and illegal alcohol or tobacco consumption. Binge drinking among underage consumers is a serious societal problem that can have disastrous, and sometimes fatal, effects. Peer pressure often plays a large role in this behaviour. Even virtual group pressure, such as is exerted through social networking sites, is sometimes accused of encouraging underage smoking.[8] Although this form of peer pressure is negative, marketers can harness the power of peer pressure in positive ways. For example, advertisements that encourage young consumers to abstain from negative behaviours (like underage drinking) can be effective when peer group members deliver the message.[9] And consumers who stick together can change together, as illustrated by a Facebook group that encourages friending among those who want to stop smoking.

Adolescents are particularly susceptible to peer pressure and are often compelled to rebel against their families in favour of behaviours that win acceptance from their peers. Teens commonly go against family expectations and parental rules. At this stage in social development, friends begin to take on additional importance and exert greater influence in teens' lives. This can be considered a natural part of a child's development; nevertheless, negative influences, including conflict within the family, can result.

Adults also feel and yield to peer pressure, and sometimes the pressure is directed toward negative behaviours. In fact, one study of adult consumers reveals that respondents reported a greater likelihood to buy an illicit product (counterfeit or stolen merchandise) if their friends did the same.[10] As with influence on children, this form of peer pressure is negative and can affect consumers, marketers, and society as a whole.

10-2 SOCIAL POWER

Another important topic in the study of reference groups and group influence is **social power**—the ability of an individual or a group to alter the actions of others.[11] Consumers often believe that others hold a great deal of power over their own behaviour. As a result, social power can greatly influence the types of products that consumers buy, the attitudes that consumers hold, and the activities in which they participate.

10-2a Types of Social Power

Social power can be classified into five categories:[12] referent

dissociative group group to which a consumer does not want to belong

conformity result of group influence in which an individual yields to the attitudes and behaviours of others

peer pressure extent to which group members feel pressure to behave in accordance with group expectations

social power ability of an individual or a group to alter the actions of others

Exhibit 10.1

Types of Social Power

Type of Power	Description	Example
Referent Power	A consumer admires the qualities of a group and emulates their behaviour as a way to identify with the group.	A new resident desires to join the local Rotary Club.
Legitimate Power	Specific agreements are made regarding group membership and the punishment for nonconformity is understood.	Bosses have legitimate authority over their employees.
Expert Power	Groups possess knowledge that members, or aspirant members, desire to gain.	Consumers seek out groups that have health-related information such as the Canadian Dental Association.
Reward Power	A group has the power to reward members for various behaviours.	Sports teams give MVP honours to a team member.
Coercive Power	A group has the power to sanction members for failing to follow expectations or rules.	A university football player is kicked off a team for using illegal substances.

power, legitimate power, expert power, reward power, and coercive power. These forms of power can be exerted both by referent groups and by other individuals. These power bases are presented in Exhibit 10.1 and then discussed in more detail.

REFERENT POWER

Consumers often imitate the behaviours and attitudes of groups as a means of identifying with the group. For example, a new resident of a city might desire to join the local Rotary Club, or perhaps a country club. In these cases, it is likely that the behaviours of other group members will be imitated. Belonging to such groups often allows consumers to feel as though they are fitting in.

LEGITIMATE POWER

In many situations, social arrangements dictate that differing levels of power are dependent upon one's position in a group. Legitimate power is used to describe this type of power, and it is associated with authority. For example, bosses have legitimate power and authority over their employees. A boss has the authority to fire his employees. Notice that employees are usually very limited in any power that they can exert over a boss.

EXPERT POWER

An important motivation in consumer behaviour is the motivation to understand the environment. Expert power refers to the ability of a group or individual to influence a consumer due to the group's or individual's knowledge of, or experience with, a specific subject matter. For example, consumers often get advice on health issues by consulting groups such as the Heart and Stroke Foundation of Canada or Canadian Diabetes Association. Medical patients also often consult various online discussion groups for information. By consulting these groups for advice and direction relating to specific medical issues, consumers can alter their behaviours based on the perceived expertise of the source of information.

REWARD POWER

Groups frequently have the power to reward members for compliance with expectations. For example, at season's end, sports teams often distribute "most valuable player" awards based on performance. The desirability of the rewards is very important. If the reward isn't valued by the group members, then the motivation to perform the desired behaviour is not overly strong.

COERCIVE POWER

Groups may also exert coercive power over their members. When consumers fail to give in to group expectations or rules, disapproval can be harsh and may even result in loss of membership. For example, university athletes can be kicked off sports teams for using illegal substances like steroids. As mentioned earlier, groups may sanction members based on their legitimate power to do so, or they may revoke the membership of group members who do not comply with group rules.

How does social power originate? Social power actually depends upon a member's agreement to, or acceptance of, the fact that the power bases do indeed exist. That is, members must (1) be aware that the power base exists and (2) desire to maintain or establish membership in the group in order for the power base to be effective.

10-3 REFERENCE GROUP INFLUENCE

The study of reference groups requires an understanding of group influence processes. Reference group influence generally falls into one of three categories: informational influence, utilitarian influence, and value-expressive influence. These categories of influence are discussed next.[13]

10-3a Informational Influence

The **informational influence** of groups refers to the ways in which consumers use the behaviours and attitudes of reference groups as information for making their own decisions. Reference groups often provide members with product- or issue-related information, and consumers often consider group-related information when purchasing products or services. Consumers desire to make informed decisions, and reference groups are often perceived as being effective sources of information.[14] Groups can be very influential in this way. Informational influence can be a result of explicit searching behaviour. For example, when a consumer is seeking a doctor, friends may influence the choice by saying, "This doctor is very good."

Informational influence is also present even when the consumer is *not* explicitly searching for product-related information, but rather when she is observing others' behaviours. For example, a consumer may simply see another person drinking a new soft drink and decide to try one.[15]

Informational influence helps to explain why word-of-mouth communication is so persuasive. Consumers share all kinds of information about products, services, and experiences, and this information can have a significant impact on consumer behaviour. Internet discussion groups, in particular, have rapidly become important sources of information for group members.

The informational influence of a group is particularly strong if the group is seen as being credible. Credibility is often associated with expertise. Professional groups are often perceived as being very credible, and for this reason, they can exert significant informational influence even if a consumer is not a member of the group. For example, a consumer may be persuaded by a message proclaiming that "four out of five dentists recommend brand X." This same information obtained from the Canadian Dental Association can affect a dentist's decisions as well, as informational influence is directly related to expert power.

10-3b Utilitarian Influence

The **utilitarian influence** occurs when consumers conform to group expectations to receive a reward or avoid punishment (this is sometimes referred to as "normative" influence). Compliance with group expectations often leads to valued rewards.

As discussed earlier, young consumers often think they need to buy a specific brand of shoes or clothing to fit in. By wearing apparel approved by the reference group, a child feels accepted (the reward). If the wrong clothing is selected, the child may feel shunned by the group (a punishment). When the group is perceived as being able to give rewards and punishment based on compliance, then this influence is quite strong. Importantly, rewards can be either social (the feeling of fitting in) or economic (the attainment of direct monetary value).

Utilitarian influence of groups is not limited to any age group or demographic profile. Adult consumers often perceive a great deal of utilitarian influence from reference groups. Driving the right car, living in the right neighbourhood, and belonging to the right clubs can make adults feel accepted. Here, we can see that utilitarian influence is related to reward power.

10-3c Value-Expressive Influence

Consumers often desire to seek membership in groups that hold values similar to their own. They also choose to adopt the values that are held by the desirable group. The **value-expressive influence** of groups refers to the ways in which consumers internalize a group's values or the extent to which consumers join groups to express their own closely held values and beliefs. This influence is related to referent power.

informational influence ways in which a consumer uses the behaviours and attitudes of reference groups as information for making personal decisions

utilitarian influence ways in which a consumer conforms to group expectations in order to receive a reward or avoid punishment

value-expressive influence ways in which consumers internalize a group's values or the extent to which consumers join groups to express their own closely held values and beliefs

Consumers may also use group membership as a way to project their own self-image. Importantly, the self-image of the individual is influenced by the group, and group membership helps the individual project her desired image. For example, a consumer may choose to join Mothers Against Drunk Driving because she feels strongly about the drunk driving issue. Once she has joined, she can project the values of the group as well.

10-3d Value and Reference Groups

External influences have a direct impact on the value of many activities. Reference groups and value are related in various ways.

From a utilitarian value perspective, joining a campus organization can be quite a valuable experience. The benefits associated with membership (networking, work experience, accomplishment) may be greater than the work that is put into the organization (work performed to complete a project, hours devoted to planning and meetings). In this way, utilitarian value is derived from belonging to the group, and group membership becomes a means to a valued end state.

Group membership also involves hedonic value perceptions. Value can be derived from simply enjoying group meetings and activities. Here, value is an end in itself. Attending sorority or fraternity events can be quite enjoyable beyond any utilitarian benefits that come from membership. Simply enjoying the fun is enough! Motivations and emotions are closely related topics. The motivation to belong to, or be affiliated with, a group can bring happiness and joy. Many students join sororities and fraternities not for long-term benefits but for short-term fun!

Reference group influences affect value perceptions in other ways. Because consumers learn about products and services from referent others, the information that is obtained from groups directly affects consumer expectations about product benefits such as quality and convenience. If you hear from your friends that a product is good, you'll probably believe it! These expectations, in turn, affect value perceptions and satisfaction.

10-3e Reference Group Influence on Product Selection

A number of things affect how much influence reference groups have on product selection. First, the situation in which the product is consumed must be considered.

Exhibit 10.2

Reference Group Influence on Product Selection

Product Necessity

		Necessity	Luxury
Consumption Setting	**Public**	**Public Necessity (1)** (e.g., blue jeans, automobile) *Weak group influence for product selection; strong group influence for brand selection.*	**Public Luxury (2)** (e.g., golf clubs, sailboat) *Strong group influence for product selection; strong group influence for brand selection.*
	Private	**Private Necessity (3)** (e.g., toilet, blankets) *Weak group influence for product selection; weak group influence for brand selection.*	**Private Luxury (4)** (e.g., hot tub, pool table) *Strong group influence for product selection; weak group influence for brand selection.*

Adapted from William O. Bearden and Michael J. Etzel (1982), "Reference Group Influences on Product and Brand Purchase Decisions," *Journal of Consumer Research*, 9 (2): 183–194. By permission of Oxford University Press.

"Public" products are easily seen by others (e.g., a watch). "Private" products are not (e.g., an electric blanket). Second, the extent to which the product is considered to be a necessity or a luxury affects the level of reference group influence.[16] We really do need some products (e.g., a refrigerator). Others are not necessities (e.g., a hot tub). Third, reference group influence differs depending on whether a type of product or a particular brand is being selected. Obviously, a watch is a product. Rolex is a very expensive brand of watch. These elements are presented in boxes 1–4 in Exhibit 10.2.

For necessities, reference group influence is weak for product selection (boxes 1 and 2). Reference groups rarely influence the decision to wear blue jeans. With public necessities, however, the influence of reference groups on brand selection is strong (for example, "You should get some new Aritzia jeans!"—box 1). For luxuries, reference group influence is strong for product selection (boxes 2 and 4). However, group influence on brand selection is only strong for public luxuries (box 2). Reference group members could influence the choice of product (e.g., "Don't you have a set of golf clubs?") and the brand used (e.g., Callaway). A careful look at Exhibit 10.2 reveals that group influence on brand selection is strong for all publicly viewed products!

10-3f Social Media and Group Influence

To say that social media and the Internet are radically changing consumer behaviour and group influence would be an understatement. Social media and networking now play big roles in consumer behaviour. As discussed previously, consumers get both hedonic and utilitarian value from interacting through social networking websites. Because some of these sites revolve specifically around causes, interests, and activities, they also directly affect behaviour in many different ways. Few groups ever meet physically, making most of them informal and secondary for group members. However, their importance should not be overlooked. In fact, even when other people are in close physical proximity, many consumers choose to connect with them through social media rather than face to face. One recent study even found that 20% of adults in the United States use digital tools to "talk" with neighbours![17]

SOCIAL MEDIA, SOCIAL NETWORKS, AND SOCIAL NETWORKING WEBSITES

It is important to distinguish between social media, social networking, and social networking websites as they pertain to group and interpersonal influence. **Social media** are media through which communication occurs; essentially, we mean the Internet, television, radio, and so on. **Social networks** are networks of consumers that are formed based on common interests, associations, or goals. In sociology, a social network is viewed as a group of individuals who share information and experiences. A **social networking website** (sometimes referred to as an "online social network site") is a website that facilitates online social networking. Networking has taken on a new meaning in the digital age and has almost become synonymous with social media. Interestingly, social networking has become a primarily mobile activity, as friends stay in virtual touch with others through smartphones, tablets, laptops, and other devices running specific types of software called mobile applications, or more commonly, **apps**. Statistics reveal that the majority of social media and Internet usage now originates from mobile devices instead of other types of devices.[18] Furthermore, consumers have quickly switched to apps over traditional website browsing as the preferred method of communication.

POPULARITY OF SOCIAL NETWORKING WEBSITES

Two websites in particular highlight the role that the social media play in daily life: Facebook and Twitter.

Facebook continues to be one of the most popular websites in the world, and as of mid-2015, it was surpassed only by Google in popularity.[19] Although statistics change daily, Facebook reported more than 1.49 billion active monthly users as of June 30, 2015. To put that in perspective, if Facebook were a country, it would be the third largest country in the world! The worldwide dominance of Facebook is reflected in the fact that the site is available in more than 70 languages.[20] The majority of users check Facebook frequently throughout the day and post daily as well. There's no question that Facebook has become the major player in online social networking. Facebook applies well to our discussion of groups because of all of the groups that consumers can join or "like." In Canada, Facebook is used regularly by 50.2% of the population and by 92.6% of Canadian social network users![21]

Twitter also continues to grow in popularity. Twitter's own statistics reveal that there were more than 316 million active users as of mid-2015 and 500 million tweets per day.[22] In today's information age, Twitter has become an important part of information flow, with many news stories breaking on Twitter before they are covered on network news stations. Yet, in Canada, Twitter is still well behind Facebook, as it is used regularly by 16.6% of the population and by 30.6% of Canadian social network users.[23]

There are also some interesting trends in the demographics of Canadian social media users. For example, among Canadians who are active Internet users, 33% of males use Twitter compared to only 23% of females. With Pinterest, however, this trend is reversed, with 25% of female active Internet users on Pinterest versus only 12% of males. In terms of age or generational differences, among active Internet users in Canada, Snapchat is used by 41% of those aged 16–24; the same can be said of only 3% aged 45–54. Similarly, Instagram is heavily used by Canadians aged 16–24 (40%), but much less so for those aged 45–54 (8%).[24] These numbers can change very quickly, however. For example, Myspace was once a wildly popular social network that has experienced dramatic recent declines in web rankings, falling to 1769th by mid-2015.[25]

social media media through which communication occurs

social networks consumers connecting with one another based on common interests, associations, or goals

social networking website website that facilitates online social networking

apps mobile application software that runs on devices like smartphones, tablets, and other computer-based tools

The mobile consumer is always in touch.

It is important to emphasize that the motivation to join social networking groups goes beyond a simple need to communicate. For many consumers, it's about connection, and in this way, social networking helps to fulfill the need to belong. Of course, there are countless other websites and apps that are popular, with each one attempting to satisfy a unique niche. For example, networks like LinkedIn and Tumblr can claim usage by a quarter of Canada's active Internet users. Others like YouTube, Vine, and Snapchat allow users to share visual content. Sharing images has become a very big business, as evidenced by the fact that Facebook acquired Instagram for approximately $1 billion in early 2012.[26] While this deal was huge, it pales in comparison to Facebook's $22 billion purchase of WhatsApp in 2014.[27]

SOCIAL SHOPPING AND COUPONING

Recall from an earlier discussion that consumers derive both utilitarian and hedonic value from group membership. To illustrate, consider the website Kaboodle.com, which provides both utilitarian and hedonic value by offering a social shopping community where people discover, recommend, and share products.[28] The site allows consumers to organize their shopping activities, learn about other consumers with similar styles, and enjoy discounts on popular products. Members are also able to enjoy engaging with other community members who offer suggestions for various products and services. Here, users are able to get good deals on products (a utilitarian benefit) and enjoy connections with other consumers who have similar interests (a hedonic benefit).

Another example is Stylehive.com, which offers a social shopping community where people share fashion ideas and products. The site allows consumers to organize their shopping activities, learn about other consumers with similar fashion styles, and connect with popular fashion retailers. Users are also able to learn about special deals (a utilitarian benefit) and enjoy connections with other consumers (a hedonic benefit).

Services offering electronic couponing like Groupon and Livingsocial can also have a substantial effect on consumer behaviour. Although after a great deal of initial hype these sites have recently struggled, they did demonstrate the power of combining social momentum with discounting to introduce consumers to new products and services.

New social platforms appear nearly every day, and what is most relevant for our purposes is how these sites influence group and consumer behaviour. They offer both hedonic and utilitarian value by allowing consumers to make connections with others, join groups, gather information, buy products, participate in social and political causes, and spread information by word-of-mouth. We discuss word-of-mouth in more detail in a later section.

10-3g Individual Differences in Susceptibility to Group Influence

Although group influence plays an important role in influencing consumer behaviour, not all consumers conform to group expectations equally. Individual difference variables play an important role in the extent to which consumers conform to the expectations of others and how consumers behave in the presence of others. Three important variables are susceptibility to interpersonal influence, attention to social comparison information, and separateness–connectedness.

SUSCEPTIBILITY TO INTERPERSONAL INFLUENCE

One individual difference variable, **susceptibility to interpersonal influence**, assesses the individual's need to enhance his or her image in terms of others by acquiring and using products, conforming to the

susceptibility to interpersonal influence individual difference variable that assesses a consumer's need to enhance his or her image with others by acquiring and using products, conforming to the expectations of others, and learning about products by observing others expectations of others, and learning about products by observing others.[29]

Studies reveal that consumers who are particularly susceptible to interpersonal influence are more likely to value conspicuous items (i.e., highly valued items like luxury automobiles or jewellery).[30] In the context of the value equation (value = what you get – what you give), this suggests that the benefits of quality and image are weighted heavily in some consumers' perception of what you get.

Seeking approval of others through product ownership is very important to this segment of consumers. Consumers who score highly on the susceptibility to interpersonal influence scale are also more likely to desire avoiding negative impressions in public settings.[31] For example, wearing "uncool" clothes in a shopping mall would be much more distressing to a consumer who is highly susceptible to interpersonal influence than to other consumers.

ATTENTION TO SOCIAL COMPARISON INFORMATION

Another individual difference variable that affects consumer behaviour related to group influence is **attention to social comparison information (ATSCI)**. Consumers who score highly on this measure are concerned about how other people react to their behaviour.[32] This trait is closely related to susceptibility to interpersonal influence. Sample items from this scale are presented in Exhibit 10.3.

The ATSCI trait often emerges when a consumer is shopping, as consumers with a strong degree of the trait tend to modify their purchasing behaviours when they are shopping with others. For example, a consumer who has a strong degree of ATSCI might buy an imported beer when he is shopping with others. He would buy a less expensive domestic beer when he is shopping alone. Paying attention to what others think is likely to lead consumers to conform to others' expectations, and studies have shown that consumers with a strong degree of ATSCI are more likely to conform to the expectations of others.[33]

SEPARATENESS–CONNECTEDNESS

Consumers differ in their feelings of "connectedness" to other consumers. A consumer with a **separated self-schema** perceives herself as distinct and separate from others, while a consumer with a **connected self-schema** sees himself as an integral part of a group.[34] Marketers are well aware of the differences in how people view their relationships with groups, and marketing messages are often based on "connected" or "separated" themes. One study found that consumers who feel connected respond more favourably to advertisements that promote group belonging and cohesion.[35] Another study found that consumers with a high need for connection respond quite favourably to salespeople with whom they share some degree of similarity.[36]

Culture plays an important role in how separated or connected consumers feel. For example, consumers in Eastern cultures tend to feel more connected to others, while consumers in Western cultures tend to feel more separate and distinct. Advertising themes in a collectivist culture (a culture that focuses heavily on the interdependence of citizens) therefore often promote connected themes, while advertisements in North America tend to emphasize separate themes.[37]

SOCIAL INFLUENCE AND EMBARRASSMENT

The impact of groups on consumers cannot be overstated. In fact, the mere presence of others in a specific situation can make one feel uncomfortable.[38] This is especially the case when consumers are consuming or buying personal products.

---

attention to social comparison information (ATSCI)
individual difference variable that assesses the extent to which a consumer is concerned about how other people react to his or her behaviour

separated self-schema
self-conceptualization of the extent to which a consumer perceives herself as distinct and separate from others

connected self-schema
self-conceptualization of the extent to which a consumer perceives himself as being an integral part of a group

---

Exhibit 10.3

Sample Items from Attention to Social Comparison Information Scale

It's important to me to fit into the group I'm with.

At parties I usually try to behave in a manner that makes me fit in.

I tend to pay attention to what others are wearing.

I actively avoid wearing clothes that are not in style.

My behaviour often depends on how I feel others wish me to behave.

Source: Adapted from William O. Bearden and Randall L. Ross (1990), "Attention to Social Comparison Information: An Individual Difference Factor Affecting Consumer Conformity," *Journal of Consumer Research*, 16 (March), 461–471. By permission of Oxford University Press.

Consumers with connected self-schemas respond favourably to advertisements promoting togetherness.

Consumers can feel very uneasy, or even embarrassed, by the presence of others when purchasing these items.

One study revealed that students were particularly embarrassed with the purchase of condoms when other consumers were present,[39] however, this influence was affected by the amount of experience the students had with buying condoms. Consumers who were familiar with the act of buying the product did not feel significantly higher levels of embarrassment if others were present during the purchase. As another example, many consumers are uncomfortable working out in a gym for fear of how they appear to others!

Social presence can also have positive effects. One recent study concluded that the presence of others in a service setting can make a customer feel more satisfied with a positive experience than they would be if they were alone when the positive experience occurred. Importantly, the same study concluded that consumers can be even more dissatisfied with a bad experience when other consumers are present.[40] It seems that social presence intensifies feelings of satisfaction and dissatisfaction.

10-4 WORD-OF-MOUTH

Another important concept in the study of interpersonal influence is **word-of-mouth (WOM)**—information about products, services, and experiences that is transmitted from consumer to consumer.

Two types of WOM influences can be distinguished: *organic* and *amplified*. The distinction between the concepts is highlighted by the Word of Mouth Marketing Association (WOMMA). According to WOMMA, organic WOM occurs naturally when consumers truly enjoy a product or service and they want to share their experiences with others. Amplified WOM occurs when marketers attempt to launch or accelerate WOM in existing customer circles, or when they develop entirely new forums for WOM (such as discussion boards on web pages).[41]

Consumers are heavily influenced by WOM, and its power is impressive. Consumers tell each other about products, services, and experiences all day long, so it's no wonder that word-of-mouth influences the vast majority of consumer product sales! WOM is influential because, in general, consumers tend to believe other consumers more than they believe advertisements and explicit marketing messages from companies.

10-4a Positive and Negative WOM

The more satisfied consumers are with a company or product, the more likely they are to spread positive WOM. If consumers believe strongly in a company and its products, they are more likely to talk to others about it.[42] Terms such as *brand advocate* or *brand ambassador* are beginning to emerge in marketing to describe consumers who believe strongly in a brand and tell others about it.

Consumers are also more likely to spread WOM when a product is particularly relevant to their own self-concept and when they are highly involved with the product category.[43] For example, a motorcycle enthusiast is more likely to spread WOM about motorcycle products than a consumer who doesn't even like motorcycles.

Marketers realize that negative WOM can be extremely damaging because, in general, negative word-of-mouth is more influential than is positive word-of-mouth.[44] Hearing that the food at a restaurant is terrible is much more influential than hearing that it is good! Consumers also tend to tell more people about unsatisfactory experiences than pleasing ones.

VALUE AND WORD-OF-MOUTH

As noted earlier, group influence processes are closely related to consumer perceptions of value. Similarly, WOM is affected in large part by the perceived value that consumers receive from products and services. One study, performed in a South Korean service setting, found that both utilitarian and hedonic value positively influence WOM intentions.[45] Customers who believed the restaurant allowed them to efficiently address their hunger received utilitarian value, and those who enjoyed the experience

word-of-mouth (WOM) information about products, services, and experiences that is transmitted from consumer to consumer beyond addressing hunger received hedonic value. When this value was perceived as being particularly high, consumers were motivated to encourage their families and friends to go that restaurant as well. The more value that consumers receive, the more likely they are to tell others about their experiences with products and services!

WORD-OF-MOUTH IN THE DIGITAL AGE

Not only do social networking sites and media provide value by allowing consumers to join groups and follow others, but they also represent efficient methods of spreading WOM. Consumers seek out other online users for advice on all kinds of issues, ranging from what types of products to buy to input into health, personal, and financial decisions. In fact, recent estimates reveal that 80% of Internet users have sought online advice for health issues.[46] Consumers also regularly spread WOM through text messaging. Consider that one in three teens sends more than 100 texts per day and it's easy to see how this can affect WOM.[47] And that's just teens!

Many websites encourage the spread of information from consumer to consumer. Some sites are dedicated specifically to WOM, like Yelp and BzzAgent.com, which allows consumers to spread both WOM and web content. By becoming a "BzzAgent," consumers are able to participate in a popular online WOM network.[48] Digg.com also focuses on sharing web content. Using this site, users submit content for others to see and then other users vote on what they like best.[49] The content comes in many forms, including other web pages, images, or videos. If the content gets enough votes, it is placed on the front page for millions of visitors to see. It also allows users to comment and share discussions about the content.

Many companies actively encourage WOM by including discussion boards on their own websites, which allows them to assist in the development and maintenance of brand communities. They may also hire their customers to blog about their products.

Although marketers can encourage the spread of positive WOM, they must also be mindful of the spread of negative WOM in the online world. Because negative WOM is so influential, it is important for companies to monitor the content that is posted on various websites. It is becoming quite common to see what can be called *anti-brand communities*, or communities in which members spread negative information about companies and products to other users. Marketers should pay close attention to these communities.

MEASURING ONLINE WOM

Given the importance of online WOM and how it influences consumer behaviour, it is important for consumer researchers and marketers alike to be able to gather valid information on WOM statistics. Many services

Maybe Talk Isn't Cheap

Marketers are excited about the many opportunities that are available in cyberspace. One valuable opportunity can be found in blogging (slang for "web logging"). Blogging allows consumers to voice their opinions on a number of different topics, products, and services. Blogging has become so popular that the practice is now a part of the marketing mix for many companies!

A number of websites now allow companies to hire bloggers to write about their products and services. Sites such as PayPerPost.com, SponsoredReviews.com, and LinkWorth.com have grown in popularity. Although the requirements for each site vary, the basic idea is that bloggers are given the opportunity to blog about products or companies for pay. Advertisers tell bloggers what products or services they want included in the blog, and the blogger agrees to write about it. The arrangement can be a win–win situation for both the blogger and advertiser. Of course, this practice may be considered to be unethical by some. Nevertheless, this form of Internet promotion is rapidly becoming an important component of buzz marketing, and given the popularity of the Internet blog, it is likely that this practice will continue to grow in popularity.

iStockphoto.com/Andresr

Sources: Johnson, Carolyn Y. (2007), "Blogging for Dollars," *Knight Ridder Tribune Business News*, April 16, 2007, p. 1; Fernando, Angelo (2007), "Transparency Under Attack," *Communication World*, 24 (2): 9–11; Schwartz, Matthew (2007), "Can Paid Blog Reviews Pay Off?", B to B, 92 (2): 1–3; Frazier, Mya (2006), "Want to Build Up Blog Buzz? Starting Writing Checks for $8," *Advertising Age*, 77 (44): 3–4; Armstrong, Stephen (2006), "Bloggers for Hire," *New Statesman*, 135 (4807): 26–27.

offer web traffic analytic and effectiveness services, including Quantcast, Alexa, and Comscore. Some web traffic services allow users to focus on specific topics or trends, as would be the case with WOM. Services such as Tweetreach, Whatthetrend, and of course Twitter focus specifically on tweets and trending issues. Popular trends generally include tweets about products, movies, celebrities, and news events. Search engine trends are also monitored. Google Trends, for example, monitors the popularity of search terms on its search engine. All of these services can be quite valuable for understanding popular online topics, trends, and WOM.

10-4b Buzz Marketing

One marketing tactic that continues to evolve is called **buzz marketing**—efforts that focus on generating excitement (or buzz) that is spread among market segments. Quite often, this type of marketing utilizes some form of WOM, as is found with the BzzAgent website. Successful buzz marketing can be a powerful tool for marketers, as information about products and services can spread quickly. Buzz marketing is one form of what is called **guerrilla marketing**, or the marketing of a product using unconventional means.

Although marketers have attempted to create a buzz about their products for years, buzz marketing is currently becoming popular in large part as a response to mass media fragmentation and advertising clutter. The techniques can be quite clever. For example, automobile companies can give customers automobiles simply to ride around and be seen in. This was a tactic the Ford Motor Company utilized when it gave a handful of consumers new Ford Fiesta automobiles to drive around and be seen in while performing activities assigned by the company. By having consumers see the new automobile in use and receive WOM from others, Ford was able to take advantage of the power of buzz marketing.[50]

The spreading of WOM online through social networking sites can be considered another form of buzz marketing. In fact, buzz marketing uses social media tools and websites regularly and, as we have discussed, companies sometimes hire consumers to spread such messages.

One buzz marketing tactic that relates directly to WOM is **viral marketing**, which uses online technologies to facilitate WOM by having consumers spread marketing messages through their online conversations. A great example of viral marketing can be in the signatures that mobile devices often use by default, for example, when you get an email from a friend with the signature "Sent from my iPhone." Another recent example of a very successful marketing message that quickly went viral was WestJet's "Christmas Miracle" (see the video at https://www.youtube.com/watch?v=zIEIvi2MuEk). The conversation got started when WestJet found out what a plane load of passengers wanted for Christmas and then delivered those gifts to them on the luggage carousel as they waited for their luggage. Once the video of the event was posted to YouTube, people around the country were soon talking about the WestJet brand.

Although buzz marketing may be facilitated through online message boards and networking sites, this type of marketing is not limited to online content. The term *buzz marketing* is used much more broadly than that, with messages being delivered in many different ways to create buzz.

10-4c Stealth Marketing

Another more controversial form of marketing that uses WOM is stealth marketing. A guerrilla marketing tactic that is similar to buzz marketing, in **stealth marketing** consumers are completely unaware that they are being marketed to (hence, the term *stealth*). As an example of stealth marketing, imagine a camera marketer that has employees pose as tourists. These "tourists" then ask others to take their pictures with a new camera. Of course, the picture takers don't realize that the tourists are employed by the company and that they are being targeted by a marketing message.[51] Or, imagine a person who works for a beer distributor buying a round of drinks at a bar, when other customers don't know that his company markets the beer that he is buying and promoting.

A movie entitled *The Joneses*, starring Demi Moore, presents an entertaining—albeit exaggerated—example of stealth marketing. Some consider product placements in television shows and movies to be a type of stealth marketing, because consumers generally don't realize that companies pay for these placements. Soap operas, such as *Days of Our Lives*, have recently turned to product placements as a marketing tool.[52] Research suggests

buzz marketing
marketing efforts that focus on generating excitement among consumers and that are spread from consumer to consumer

guerrilla marketing
marketing of a product using unconventional means

viral marketing
marketing method that uses online technologies to facilitate WOM by having consumers spread messages through their online conversations

stealth marketing
guerrilla marketing tactic in which consumers do not realize that they are being targeted for a marketing message

that female consumers have more positive attitudes toward product placements than do male consumers.[53] Product placements were once considered to be unique, but in today's environment they are becoming commonplace. Marketers often use the terms *branded content* or *advertainment* when using these strategies.

The use of stealth marketing techniques, though growing, is considered questionable by many marketing professional organizations, and WOMMA is opposed to the stealth tactics. In fact, WOMMA has developed several categories of what it considers "unethical" marketing practices, including the following types of marketing techniques:[54]

▸ Stealth marketing—deceiving consumers about the involvement of marketers in a communication

▸ Shilling—compensating consumers to talk about, or promote, products without disclosing that they are working for the company

▸ Infiltrating—using fake identities in online discussions to promote a product

10-4d Opinion Leaders

Buzz marketing techniques are especially effective when opinion leaders are used. An **opinion leader** is a consumer who has great influence on the behaviour of others relating to product adoption and purchase. Opinion leaders are knowledgeable about specific products or services and have a high level of involvement with those products. Characteristics of opinion leaders depend largely on the type of product under consideration, but in general, opinion leaders are socially active and self-confident.

With online social networking and media sites, it's easy to find a few key posters whom other users tend to listen to. With Twitter, you can even track the number of followers for each user. Recently, the Ford Motor Company included influential women bloggers in its "What Women Want" campaign. Popular bloggers were invited to test new Ford products and interact with company executives. Inviting the bloggers was a good way of ensuring some online buzz.[55] As with the Ford Fiesta example, it appears the company is becoming quite adept with buzz marketing campaigns.

MARKET MAVENS AND SURROGATE CONSUMERS

Opinion leaders are not the only influential consumers that have been identified. Market mavens and surrogate consumers also exert much influence on others. A **market maven** is a consumer who spreads information about all types of products and services that are available in the marketplace. The key difference between an opinion leader and a market maven is that the market maven's influence is not category specific. That is, market mavens spread information about numerous products and services.

Consumers can also be heavily influenced by what are termed *surrogate consumers*. A **surrogate consumer** is a consumer who is hired by another to provide input into a purchase decision. Interior decorators, travel consultants, and stockbrokers can all be considered surrogate consumers. Surrogate consumers can be very influential, and marketers should carefully consider the level of influence of these individuals.[56] Because of their extensive product expertise, surrogate consumers can often help others derive the maximum amount of value out of their transactions by maximizing the benefits associated with product purchase.

10-4e Diffusion Processes

One area of interest in the study of group processes is the **diffusion process**—the way in which new products are adopted and spread throughout a marketplace. Researchers have learned that different groups of consumers tend to adopt new

Twitter users can influence a lot of people.

sjscreens/Alamy

opinion leader
consumer who has a great deal of influence on the behaviour of others relating to product adoption and purchase

market maven
consumer who spreads information about all types of products and services that are available in the marketplace

surrogate consumer
consumer who is hired by another to provide input into a purchase decision

diffusion process way in which new products are adopted and spread throughout a marketplace

Exhibit 10.4

Adopter Categories

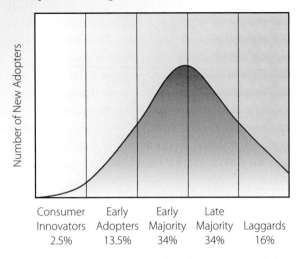

Source: Adapted from Everett M. Rogers, *Diffusion of Innovation*, 4e (New York: The Free Press), 1995.

products at different rates. One group may adopt a new product (e.g., a hybrid automobile) very early in the product's life cycle, while another group may be very slow to adopt the product, if it adopts the product at all. A product life cycle is a description of the life of a product from the time it is introduced to the time it dies off.

In all, five categories of consumers have been identified. They include innovators, early adopters, early majority, late majority, and laggards. These groups are presented in Exhibit 10.4.[57]

What makes group influence relevant to the diffusion process is that each group learns about new products not only from seeing marketing messages, but also from talking with other consumers and observing their behaviour. Group influence processes therefore apply to these categories.

Innovators and early adopter consumers tend to be influential when discussing products and services with members of other groups. As such, they tend to be opinion leaders for specific product categories. Innovators are often risk takers and financially well off. Early adopter consumers are generally young and well educated. Members of other groups, including late majority consumers and laggards, tend to be more cautious about buying new products and wait significantly longer to buy the latest innovations. These consumers also tend to be somewhat older, with lower levels of education and spending power.

10-5 HOUSEHOLD DECISION MAKING

As we discussed previously, the family unit is an important primary reference group for consumers, as family members typically have a great deal of influence over one another's attitudes, thoughts, and behaviours. Consider the many ways in which the family has an impact on consumer behaviour. **Household decision making** is the process by which household units choose between alternative courses of action. To begin with, we first discuss the various conceptualizations of the term *household*.

10-5a Traditional Family Structure

The ways in which society views the family unit have changed dramatically in recent decades. Traditionally, the **family household** has been viewed as at least two people who are related by blood or marriage and who occupy a housing unit. Other traditional family definitions include the *nuclear* family and the *extended* family.

The **nuclear family** consists of a mother, a father, and a set of siblings. The **extended family** consists of three or more generations of family members, including

Family members greatly influence one another.

household decision making process by which decisions are made in household units

family household at least two people who are related by blood or marriage who occupy a housing unit

nuclear family a mother, a father, and a set of siblings

extended family three or more generations of family members grandparents, parents, children, and grandchildren. In individualistic cultures like Canada, emphasis is placed on the nuclear family. However, in collectivist cultures, more focus is placed on the extended family, and it is not uncommon to see households of extended family members living together. With this being said, the growth in multigenerational households in Canada and the United States has been significant in recent years.[58]

EMERGING TRENDS IN FAMILY STRUCTURE

As mentioned previously, the traditional views of the family have changed over time. Today, many nontraditional household arrangements exist throughout Canada and the United States. Societal trends toward people of opposite sex sharing living quarters (shortened to the acronym *POSSLQ* or called *cohabitation*) and homosexual households have altered the way in which family households are conceptualized. For example, U.S. data indicates that 31% of households accounted for in the latest census information available are defined as nonfamily households (that is, consumers sharing the same living quarters who are not related by blood or marriage).[59] Of course, even if a household is categorized as a nonfamily household, members still exert significant influence on one another.

Divorce rates tend to be quite high in Canada, with just over 40% of marriages in Canada ending in divorce. The lowest rate of divorce is in Newfoundland and Labrador at 24%, and the highest rate is in Quebec at 52%.[60] Divorces have dramatically altered the composition of the Canadian family, and they have led to *blended families* of previously married spouses and their children from the marriages.

Many people simply decide never to marry, even when children are present. In fact, the 2006 census found that, for the first time, Canada had more unmarried people aged 15 and over than legally married couples.[61] As a result of this trend and the high divorce rate, lone-parent households have increased, representing 16.3% of all census families in 2011, higher than any other recorded census figure in the last 80 years.[62] The nature of lone-parent families has also change dramatically over time in Canada. In 1951, 66.5% of lone parents were widowed and only 1.5% had never been legally married. In 2006, 19.0% had been widowed and 29.5% of lone parents had never been legally married.[63]

Finally, we note that the meaning of the term *nonfamily* is open to debate and interpretation. One topic of current interest is same-sex marriage. Canada was the third country in the world to legalize same-sex marriage (in July 2005, after the Netherlands in 2000 and Belgium in 2003). Same-sex couples were enumerated for the first time in the 2006 census and, of the 45,300 same-sex couples in Canada, about 16.5% were legally married.[64]

Even though each of these trends offers opportunities for marketers, one clear fact remains based on the census data of households in Canada. Despite widespread attention to nontraditional households, census data reveal that the majority of Canadian families still consist of a married couple, as shown in Exhibit 10.5. The prevalence of products such as SUVs and minivans as well as family-oriented movies such as *Toy Story 3* and the *Shrek* franchise, and the profitability of retailers such as Costco, owe at least a portion of their success to the large numbers of traditional family units. Yet, for the first time in Canada, the 2011 census counted more one-person households (3,673,305) than couple households with children (3,524,915). Between 2001 and 2011, the proportion of one-person households increased from 25.7% to 27.6% of all households, continuing an upward trend that has existed for many decades.

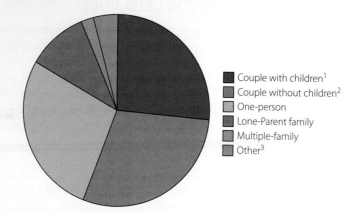

Exhibit 10.5

Family Household Type as Percentage of Canadian Households

- Couple with children[1]
- Couple without children[2]
- One-person
- Lone-Parent family
- Multiple-family
- Other[3]

Notes: 'Couple' households and 'lone-parent family' households refer to one-family households.
1. Refers to one-family households with children aged 24 and under.
2. Refers to one-family households without children aged 24 and under.
3. Refers to two or more people who share a private dwelling, but who do not constitute a census family.

Taken from Statistics Canada, censuses of population, 2001 and 2006. Found at: http://www12.statcan.ca/census-recensement/2006/as-sa/97-553/table/t1-eng.cfm.

HOUSEHOLD LIFE CYCLE

An important concept in the study of the family unit is the **household life cycle (HLC)**. The HLC represents a segmentation technique that acknowledges that changes in family composition and income alter household demand for products and services.

The traditional HLC segments families into a number of groups based on the number of adults present and the age of the head of household. This conceptualization is presented in Exhibit 10.6. Based on this conceptualization, a number of segments are present, including consumers who never marry (Bachelor 1, 2, and 3); two-adult, childless households (Young Couple, Childless Couple, and Older Couple); two adults with children (Full Nest 1, 2, and 3 and Delayed Full Nest); and one adult with children (Single Parent 1, 2, and 3).

The categorization of the household is important for consumer researchers.[65] Product expenditures vary greatly by stage in the HLC, and at each stage, consumers often try to obtain the most value that they can from their purchases. For example, Full Nest 1 consumers often face costly expenses related to raising young children, including the cost of baby clothes, furniture, and day care. These young consumers often have to search for new living accommodations in the form of larger apartments or a starter home when children are born. Single parents face the same challenges as two-adult families, but they must face these challenges alone. A great strain is therefore placed on the income of single parents. Older, childless couples have more disposable income to spend on their own needs. They are much more likely to enjoy luxuries such as vacation homes, financial investments, and upscale automobiles. Couples older than 64 often enjoy their retirement years, or choose to remain employed beyond retirement age.

The categories and assumptions in the HLC are representative of general patterns of spending behaviour. Not every consumer will fall neatly into one specific category. Rather, the categories help to explain the living situations and expenditures of many consumers. Obviously, each consumer faces his or her own situation.

MIDDLE-AGED CONSUMERS: BOOMERANG KIDS AND THE SANDWICH GENERATION

Two important groups that are currently of interest to consumer researchers are boomerang kids and members of the sandwich generation. **Boomerang kids** are young adults, aged 18–34, who graduate from postsecondary education and move back home with their parents. Quite often, the motivation is to reduce debt that has accumulated in the postsecondary years. Some

> **household life cycle (HLC)** segmentation technique that acknowledges that changes in family composition and income alter household demand for products and services
>
> **boomerang kids** young adults, aged 18–34, who move back home with their parents after they graduate from postsecondary education

Exhibit 10.6

Traditional Household Life Cycle Categories

	Under 35 Years	35–64 Years	Older than 64 Years
One-adult household	Bachelor 1	Bachelor 2	Bachelor 3
Two-adult household	Young Couple	Childless Couple	Older Couple
Two adults + children	Full Nest 1 (children < 6 years old)	Delayed Full Nest (children < 6 years old)	
	Full Nest 2 (children > 6 years old)	Full Nest 3 (children > 6 years old)	
One adult + children	Single Parent 1 (children < 6 years old)	Single Parent 3	
	Single Parent 2 (children > 6 years old)		

Source: Adapted from Gilly, Mary C. and Ben M. Enis (1982), "Recycling the Family Lifecycle: A Proposal for Redefinition," in *Advances in Consumer Research*, Vol. 9, Andrew A. Mitchell (ed.), Ann Arbor, MI: Association for Consumer Research, 271–276.

Pets Are Family Too!

It will probably come as no surprise that pets are considered to be family members for millions of consumers worldwide. Dogs, cats, fish, birds, and reptiles are all popular pets, but taking care of these pets can be costly, and the industry continues to grow. In the United States alone, consumers spend an estimated $58 billion on pet care annually, and the total is expected to increase. To put this into perspective, this is more than consumers spend on personal entertainment like watching movies, playing video games, or listening to music.

While most of the spending is attributed to food and basic medical care, one growing segment in the industry is pet services. Pet services include things like walking, boarding, and even doggie day care! Another booming segment is pet insurance. In fact, it is becoming popular for insurance policies to include coverage for pets. It seems that there is no limit to what some people will do for their pets. For most consumers, the money is well spent, considering the loyalty, comfort, and friendship that come from our furry friends.

Sources: "Pet Industry Market Size & Ownership Statistics," American Pet Products Association, http://www.americanpetproducts.org/press_industrytrends.asp (accessed April 28, 2014); Amy Silverstein, "Americans Spent Record Amount of Money Grooming Their Pets Last Year," Globalpost.com, March 3, 2012, http://www.globalpost .com/dispatches/globalpost-blogs/weird -wide-web/americans-spent-record-amount-money-grooming-their-pets (accessed April 13, 2012); "The Pet Economy: More than Movies, Music & Video Games Combined," Globalanimal.org, http://www.globalanimal.org/2010/10/20/the-pet-economy-more-than-movies-music-video-games-combined/20226/ (accessed April 12, 2012); C. Taylor, "The U.S. Pet Economy Didn't Go to the Dogs", Reuters, http://www.reuters.com/article/2013/02/08 /us-economy-spending-pets-idUSBRE9170ZP20130208 (accessed February 11, 2013).

have suggested the term *adultolescence* to describe this stage. According to Statistics Canada, the proportion of men in their 20s and 30s who are living in their parents' home has increased significantly in the last 30 years.[66] There are also regional differences, possibly tied to the strength of the local economy, in the extent to which young adults are likely to live in their parents' homes. In parts of Nova Scotia and Newfoundland and Labrador, about 60% of young adults aged 20–29 live with their parents. In contrast, in parts of Alberta, that number is below 20%.[67] This trend challenges the traditional HLC, and it greatly affects how middle-aged consumers spend their money. In fact, it has been estimated that boomerang kids cost their parents $5,000 per year in disposable income.[68] The long-term implications of this trend are yet to be seen.

Financial and emotional strains on middle-aged consumers also come from belonging to the **sandwich generation**—those consumers who must take care of both their own children and their aging parents. The number of consumers who fall into this category is expected to increase dramatically over the next decade, as millions of Baby Boomers enter their retirement years. Taking care of both children and parents obviously affects the behaviour of these consumers, as income is devoted to the needs of others. In fact, the average cost of caring for others aged 50-plus is nearly $6,000 per year. For consumers who must care for others long distance, the cost is nearly $9,000 per year.[69] Overall worker productivity is also affected. For example, it has been estimated that businesses in the United States lose as much as $34 billion per year due to sandwich generation employees missing work to take care of parents.[70]

HOUSEHOLD PURCHASE ROLES

Each member of a household plays a specific role in product purchase. Five important roles in the household purchase process can be identified:

▶ *Influencer*—the person in the household who recognizes a need and provides information about a potential purchase to others

▶ *Gatekeeper*—the person who controls information flow into the household (e.g., a mother who blocks unwanted email solicitations from her child's email account)

> **sandwich generation**
> consumers who must take care of both their own children and their aging parents

- *User*—the actual user of the product under consideration

- *Decision maker*—the person who makes the final decision regarding product purchase or nonpurchase

- *Purchaser*—the person who actually buys the product under consideration

Each role is important in product consideration and selection. The final purchase of the product is largely influenced by beliefs regarding the role of each person in the household.

GENDER ROLES AND HOUSEHOLD DECISION MAKING

Like many of the concepts pertaining to household composition, societal views on gender roles and family decision making have evolved over time. Traditionally, men were viewed as having the primary responsibility of providing for the family, while women were expected to meet everyday family needs and take care of the home.[71] However, changes in the education of women and the acceleration in the number of double-income families have challenged these conceptualizations.

sex role orientation (SRO) family's set of beliefs regarding the ways in which household decisions are reached

An important concept in gender roles and family decision making is **sex role orientation (SRO)**. A family's SRO influences the ways in which household decisions are reached. Families that have a traditional SRO believe that it is the responsibility of the male head of household to make large purchase decisions, while families with a "modern" SRO believe in a more democratic approach.[72] Given the evolving nature of the typical household in Canada, it is not surprising that SROs are changing. In particular, the role of women in household decision making is more dominant than in previous years. Indeed, studies have revealed that women are playing a bigger role in decision making in all household decision areas.[73] This, in part, reflects the fact that the percentage of women with higher education and incomes levels than their spouse has grown significantly over the last few decades.[74]

The Child's Role in CB

It is widely known that the child consumer of today is very different from the child consumer of yesteryear. Today's child is much more consumer savvy and has much more power in the marketplace. Children influence as much as $600 billion USD per year in consumer spending in North America, and have more disposable income of their own than ever before. The influence of children on household spending ranges across spending categories, from groceries to vacation destinations to automobile purchases.

Not everyone agrees that the commercialization of children is a positive development. For many, children should be off-limits to advertisers, or at least they should be targeted less frequently. Marketers often believe that parents should play a more active role in limiting commercial exposure, while parents argue that marketers should cut back on advertisements aimed at kids. Still others believe strongly in the consumer socialization concept and that consumer education should begin early in life.

What is interesting about children today is that they are active not only as influencers, but also as gatekeepers of marketing information. Because they spend more time online than ever before, children are more likely to find marketplace information and relay the information on to the actual decision maker or purchaser: their parents! Therefore not only is the power of children in the marketplace increasing from a monetary standpoint, but the roles that children play in household purchasing are evolving as well.

David Davis/Shutterstock.com

Sources: Schor, Juliet, (2008), "Understanding the Child Consumer," *Journal of the American Academy of Child and Adolescent Psychiatry*, 47 (5), 486–490; Anonymous (2006), "Business: Trillion Dollar Kids; Marketing to Children," *The Economist*, 381 (8506), 74; Tapscott, Don (2008), "Net Gen Transforms Marketing," *BusinessWeek* (online), November 17, 2008, http://www.businessweek.com/technology/content/nov2008/tc20081114_882532.htm, accessed April 10, 2009.

KID POWER

The role of children in household decision making is also evolving. Although children were once thought to have relatively little impact on purchasing decisions outside of what toy to buy, marketers are realizing that children are playing a much larger role in influencing household purchases than ever before. One recent study reveals that 36% of parents with children aged 6–11 reported that their children significantly influence their purchasing decisions.[75]

An important issue in the development of the child consumer is known as consumer socialization. **Consumer socialization** is defined as the process through which young consumers develop attitudes and learn skills that help them function in the marketplace.[76] Sometimes these skills are learned at a surprisingly young age, and children have largely begun to seek products that were once considered "too old" for their age segment. This has led to the development of a well-known marketing acronym, KGOY (Kids Growing Older, Younger).

Although many consider the issue of kid power and marketing to children controversial, it is clear that children do exert a significant influence on household decision making, and it is likely that this trend will continue.

consumer socialization
the process through which young consumers develop attitudes and learn skills that help them function in the marketplace

STUDY TOOLS 10

LOCATED AT THE BACK OF THE TEXTBOOK
☐ Rip out Chapter Review Card

LOCATED AT NELSON.COM/STUDENT
☐ Review Key Terms Flashcards (print or online)

☐ Download audio summaries to review on the go

☐ Complete practice quizzes to prepare for tests

☐ Watch video on Teenage Research Unlimited for a real company example

CASE STUDY

Case

Sharknado—Oh Hell No!

In 2012, Berger and Milkman, researchers at Wharton, published a study that examined why people share online. They found that a critical component of "virality" was the extent to which the content was arousing—that is, how excited it made the reader or viewer feel. In particular, that research indicated that the content most likely to go viral evoked either positive high-arousal states, such as awe, or negative high-arousal states, such as anger or anxiety. This suggests that although we might enjoy watching a movie that makes us sad (a negative low-arousal state) and we like to be relaxed (a positive low-arousal state), we are much less likely to tell other people about such experiences.

Maybe that helps explain the phenomenon that is *Sharknado*. If you haven't had the opportunity to watch *Sharknado* or one of its sequels, it is definitely an arousing experience. In the movie, a storm blows into a major U.S. city carrying with it many very large and very angry sharks. The sharks then attack, while the protagonists, played by Ian Ziering and Tara Reid, fight to survive and save the city. To call the *Sharknado* series B-movies might be too kind. When asked about the franchise, actor David Hasselhoff, who appears in the sequels, said, "The first one was the worst. The second one was even worse. I'm so honoured to be in *Sharknado 3*."

The Syfy channel could not be happier with *Sharknado*. When the movie first premiered, on July 11, 2013, about 1.4 million people tuned in. Although the network was likely hoping for more initial viewers, what that audience lacked in numbers they made up for in social media enthusiasm. People watching the movie produced about 5,000 tweets per minute. In fact, while *Sharknado* was playing, 17% of all tweets on Twitter were about *Sharknado*! In the days that followed, the movie was mentioned hundreds of thousands of additional times. The team at Syfy didn't expect that level of activity, but they were prepared:

Courtesy of The Global Asylum and Lantern Lane Entertainment Ltd.

"We had a war chest of bite-sized—no pun intended—shareable content, and we were able to push it out in a way that didn't feel heavy-handed or overly marketed. It felt very human and relatable and conversational. We poured fuel on the fire."

As a result, each time the movie aired the number of viewers increased dramatically, which is counter to the usual trend of declining viewership with each re-run. The second showing grabbed 1.8 million viewers, the third 2.1 million, and so on. Suddenly consumers were looking for *Sharknado* merchandise, like T-shirts and DVDs. When *Sharknado 2* (subtitled "The Second One") first aired, it drew 3.9 million viewers. With *Sharknado 3*, the network is hoping for even greater success. That movie has been subtitled "Oh Hell No!" which is likely what Syfy executives would say if asked whether such success was possible without the influence of social media.

Sources: Berger, J. and Milkman, K. L. (2012), "What Makes Online Content Viral?" *Journal of Marketing Research*: April 2012, Vol. 49, No. 2, pp. 192–205. Krieger, Daniel (2014), "Attack of the SharkTwitter!" *Fast Company*, July/August, accessed at http://www.fastcompany.com/3031370/attack-of-the-sharkwitter on June 3, 2015. Pulver, Andrew (2015), "Sharknado films 'the worst ever', says Sharknado star David Hasselhoff," *The Guardian*, March 26, accessed at http://www.theguardian.com/tv-and-radio/2015/mar/26/sharknado-star-david-hasselhoff on June 3, 2015. Tate, Ryan (2013), "B-Movie Boom: Sharknado Stirs Whirlwind of Proft," *Wired*, July 19, accessed at http://www.wired.com/2013/07/asylum-business-boom/ on June 4, 2015. Wood, Jennifer (2014), "Three Secrets That Made Sharknado 2 The Biggest TV Movie Ever," *Wired*, August 14, access at http://www.wired.com/2014/08/sharknado-2-marketing/ on June 4, 2015.

QUESTIONS

1 Why do you think the high levels of arousal are a key driver of viral marketing?

2 What type of power were viewers wielding when they took to social media to convince others to watch *Sharknado*?

3 What type of reference group influence is at play when tweets persuade people to watch *Sharknado*?

4 Have you watched *Sharknado*? If so, how did you learn about the movie? If not, are you interested in seeing it after reading this case? How susceptible are you to interpersonal influence?

5 Was the word-of-mouth about *Sharknado* organic or amplified?

11 | Consumers in Situations

Upper Cut Images/Getty Images

LEARNING OBJECTIVES

After studying this chapter, the student should be able to:

11-1 Understand how value varies with situations.

11-2 Know the different ways in which time affects consumer behaviour.

11-3 Analyze shopping as a consumer activity using the different categories of shopping activities.

11-4 Distinguish the concepts of unplanned, impulse, and compulsive consumer behaviour.

11-5 Use the concept of atmospherics to create consumer value.

11-6 Understand what is meant by antecedent conditions.

11-1 VALUE IN SITUATIONS?

For most Canadian tourists, a trip to London is not complete without spending some time at Harrods of Knightsbridge. Harrods's six storeys of upscale retailing present consumers with some of the most fabulously merchandised products to be found anywhere. Harrods spares no expense in creating a unique experience. For instance, most department stores have background music of some type, but Harrods entertains shoppers with a full-fledged orchestra on busy days. Certainly, the excitement created by live music helps frame purchase situations, and who could possibly leave Harrods without some souvenir that helps capture the experience in an enduring way?

While these Canadian tourists are on their way to London, their plane may well pass a plane full of British travellers on their way to Canada. British travellers can take off from London and fly direct to Edmonton for a one-day shopping spree at West Edmonton Mall. They leave behind Harrods and other British merchandisers such as Marks & Spencer, and spend their time, limited though it is, shopping in a different place. Certainly, after flying all the way to Edmonton, will any of these shoppers come back empty-handed? It's unlikely!

What makes these experiences different from "regular" shopping? Some of the factors involved in explaining these outcomes include:

▶ **Exchange rates**

▶ **Time of year**

▶ **Time available for shopping**

▶ **The economic situation**

▶ **Credit policies/financing**

▶ **Who is accompanying the shopper**

▶ **The purpose of the trip—fun or work?**

▶ **Airline baggage regulations**

Each of these factors and others can affect the value one experiences in exchange.

11-1a Situations and Value

This chapter focuses on precisely how the value a consumer obtains from a purchase or consumption act varies based on the context in which the act takes place. *Situational influences* is the term that captures these contextual effects, meaning effects independent of

"The social environment, referring to the other customers and employees in a service or shopping environment, cannot be ignored when explaining how 'place' affects consumer behaviour."

enduring consumer, brand, or product characteristics. As can be seen in the consumer value framework (CVF), situational influences directly affect both consumer decision making and the eventual value experienced. Situational influences are enduring characteristics of neither a particular consumer nor a product or brand. Indeed, situational influences are ephemeral, meaning they are temporary conditions in a very real sense. Contexts can affect communication, shopping, brand preference, purchase, actual consumption, and the evaluation of that consumption.

The movie theatre experience typifies situational influences. If the movie is a matinee, the consumer expects to pay a lower price than would be paid in the evening. Even though the movie hasn't changed, the number of people available to go to the movie has changed from the evening hours. Therefore, the lower demand entices the theatre to offer lower prices. In contrast, far fewer people are working in the evening and thus are more likely to be able to go to a movie.

The same consumer goes to the concession stand and pays $10 or more for a Coke and some popcorn. For some, Coke and popcorn with a movie is a highly ritualized tradition, and the entire experience is not as good without this treat. The fact that the theatre doesn't permit outside food and drink also enhances the value of the products sold at the concession stand because competition is practically eliminated. Situational influences change the desirability of consuming things and therefore change the value of these things.

Three categories of situational influences can be described based on the following influences:

▸ **Time**

▸ **Place**

▸ **Conditions**

Exhibit 11.1 provides a snapshot of examples of these influences and the way they operate. The following sections discuss each of these groups of influence in more detail with an emphasis on how value changes with each.

11-2 TIME AND CONSUMER BEHAVIOUR

Is time a consumer's most valuable resource? Time is truly scarce. In some ways, time is a consumer's only real resource because when we work, we convert time

Exhibit 11.1

Situational Influence Categories

Time can influence consumers by changing the way information is processed. A consumer shopping for a computer near the store's closing time may not deliberate and consider as much information as usual. This may shift decision making to limited problem solving when the consumer would otherwise use extended problem solving and ultimately affect brand choice.

Place can frame any purchase, consumption, or information processing situation. Think about how the theme of a restaurant as captured by the atmosphere of the place will shape the types of foods consumed there and the value they provide. Sushi, for example, may be best in an environment with an Asian influenced design.

Conditions also can influence consumption. Beverage choices are different when a consumer is cold than when a consumer is hot. Also, social settings affect choice. Consumers in crowded restaurants and bars are more likely to choose name brand beverages than when the social condition does not involve crowds.

into economic resources. In addition, time is necessary for consumption to occur. Time-related factors also affect a consumer's thoughts, feelings, and behaviour, all of which come together to create differing perceptions of value. Time can affect consumption in any of these forms:

▶ **Time pressure**

▶ **Time of year**

▶ **Time of day**

Temporal factors are situational characteristics related to time. Thus, each of the time forms listed here represents a different temporal factor.

temporal factors
situational characteristics related to time

time pressure urgency to act based on some real or self-imposed deadline

discretionary (spare) time the days, hours, or minutes that are not required for some compulsory and time-consuming activity

11-2a Time Pressure

Jeanne sits down with five co-workers for lunch. Almost immediately, the waiter comes and asks, "Are you ready to order?" All the others at the table are ready. Jeanne experiences a sense of urgency and hastily settles for a hamburger. Would Jeanne have made a different choice if she had not felt rushed to make a decision rather than make the others wait?

This situation exemplifies an intense time pressure. **Time pressure** is an urgency to act based on some real or self-imposed deadline. In the situation above, Jeanne imposes a deadline of ordering at the same time as the others at the table. Therefore, she rushes to make a decision without the due deliberation that would likely take place otherwise.

Time pressure affects consumers in several ways. First, when time is scarce, consumers process less information because time is a critical resource necessary for problem solving. Consumers who experience time pressure, for instance, are able to recall less information about product choices than are consumers in the same situation who are not under the situational influence of time pressure.[1] Second, consumers experiencing time pressure are more likely to rely on simple choice heuristics than are those in less-tense situations. Thus, rather than deciding which restaurant option is more nutritious, the consumer simply chooses the fastest option.[2] Third, consumers are more likely to shop alone than with others when they are under time pressure.[3]

Consumers who might otherwise consider many attributes in reaching a decision may simply rely on a price–quality heuristic under time pressure.[4] Time pressure shapes the value consumers perceive in products by influencing both quality and price perceptions.[5] Because consumers rely more on price–quality heuristics than they do on beliefs about financial sacrifice, brands that are positioned as relatively high quality may benefit in situations characterized by high time pressure. Consumers may simply choose the well-known and potentially higher priced brand because they don't have time to weigh different attributes against the price. Conversely, other consumers may simply choose the lowest price alternative and risk disappointment if a brand does not deliver the expected benefits.

11-2b Spare Time

Like discretionary income, **discretionary (spare) time** represents the days, hours, or minutes that are not required for some compulsory and time-consuming activity. The biggest constraint on most consumers' time is their job. Consumers who work 60 hours a week or more feel a great deal of time pressure even when going through routine consumer behaviours like dropping off dry cleaning or getting a check-up. When consumers feel like they lack spare time, personalized services that make routine activities convenient—such as getting service on the car, or house cleaning, or electronic appointments with a doctor—increase hedonic value as the feelings of relief bring about instant gratification. Conversely, consumers with a lot of spare time find little hedonic value in such things, and instead seek such services out only as a way of increasing utilitarian value.[6]

Service providers need to be able to detect whether consumers are time starved or have extra time. Consider how different consumers with varying amounts of spare time for lunch will react. A consumer with 30 minutes only needs a utilitarian experience. However, even that same consumer might wish to have a leisurely and relaxing lunch experience if she is dining on her day off.

Many consumers face chronic time pressure because so much of their time is obligated to work and family responsibilities that they have little time for leisure. Conversely, consumers today with more spare time can offer their services for hire. With little or no training, Internet-based communications allow consumers to "share" for hire. Uber, perhaps the best known ride-sharing service, provides one such opportunity. Consumers can make extra money by sharing rides with other consumers who would ordinarily be taking a cab or some other means of transportation. The service is controversial given that ride-sharing drivers often are not regulated, as a traditional taxi service would be. The consumer becomes the marketer!

11-2c Time of Year

Seasonality refers to regularly occurring conditions that vary with the time of year. The fact is that consumers' value perceptions also vary with the time of the year. A cup of hot chocolate is simply not worth as much to a consumer on a hot, sunny summer afternoon as it is on a cold, cloudy winter day.

Even though this tendency may seem as obvious as consumers' purchasing more coats and sweaters during the winter, seasonality has other effects that are perhaps not so obvious.[7] Consumers tend to shop earlier in the day during winter months, and, overall, they tend to spend more during the summer months.[8] Almost all products are susceptible to some type of seasonal influence. Fashion may lead the way with traditional spring, summer, fall, and winter fashions. However, many food items vary in demand with the season. People consume champagne predominantly during the holidays. The challenge for those who sell seasonal products like champagne is to position the product more as an everyday option.

11-2d Time of Day/Circadian Cycles

What beverage do most consumers around the world wake up to? Traditionally, Danes, Italians, and the French have been almost exclusively coffee drinkers. Consumers in the United Kingdom and in many parts of Asia wake to tea in the morning. Some Canadians drink tea in the morning, but more drink coffee. During the 1990s, American consumers turned away from coffee toward soft drinks, particularly among young consumers. Today, however, coffee sales are on the rise, and university-aged Americans have returned to drinking coffee in the morning. Coffee sales are also increasing in the United Kingdom as coffee shops, including Starbucks, can be found in all major cities.

In Canada, coffee sales continue to grow at a rapid pace. Two-thirds of adult Canadians drink coffee every day, averaging 3.2 cups per day. In 2014, retail sales grew by 19% to $2.3 billion and 81,000 tonnes. Increasingly, Canadians are drinking their coffee from single serving "pods" using machines from Keurig, Tassimo, and Nespresso. Coffee pod sales in Canada grew by 47% to $1.1 billion in 2014.[9]

Tea sales also grew in 2014 at a rate of about 5% to sales of $546 million. While Canadians are moving away from standard black tea, they are increasing consumption of specialty black teas. Loose black specialty tea grew 52% in 2014 to $8 million in sales. With the rise of retail chains like Teavana and David's Tea, younger consumers are more likely than ever to be tea drinkers and, as a result, the prospects are positive for tea sales going forward.[10]

Whether it's beverage consumption, attire, or choice of entertainment, the time of day affects the value of products and activities. Some of this influence is due to scheduled events during the day, such as one's working hours. But part is also biological. In fact, our bodies have a rhythm that varies with the time of day—a **circadian cycle rhythm**. One aspect of the circadian cycle deals with our sleeping and waking times. Consumers would prefer to sleep between the hours of midnight and 6 A.M. and from about 1 P.M to 3 P.M. Consumers who tend to shop during the "odd hours" will do so with less energy and efficiency and with depleted cognitive capacity.[11] However, they can also do so with less interference from other consumers.

Our circadian cycle is responsible for productivity in many activities. A host of products exists to try to aid consumers through the low-energy periods of the day, but

seasonality regularly occurring conditions that vary with the time of year

circadian cycle rhythm level of energy of the human body that varies with the time of day perhaps the best fix is a quick nap! Research shows that diminished capacity will affect consumers who get less than five hours of sleep each day.[12] Consumers, beware of late-night infomercials!

11-2e Advertiming

"Are you having trouble sleeping? Try Rozeram!" A popular ad campaign for a Japanese pharmaceutical product used Abraham Lincoln, a beaver, and other assorted characters to convince the consumer that this product will indeed solve sleep-related problems—primarily, the lack of sleep. Rozeram runs television ads mainly from about midnight through the early morning hours. The assumption is that consumers will be most sensitive to problems with sleeping when they should be sleeping.

Companies sometimes buy advertising with a schedule that runs the advertisement primarily at times when customers will be most receptive to the message. This practice is known as **advertiming**. Advertisers practise advertiming based on seasonal patterns and even on day-to-day changes in the weather. Swimming pool marketers realize that consumers are more receptive to their ads in the spring or summer just as they are more receptive to hot chocolate sales on a cold, cloudy day.

Social networking provides a twist on advertiming. Have you ever noticed an online ad that seemed uncanny in touching on some recent event in your life? Internet users often inadvertently allow their identity to be known through procedures related to "growth hacking." Companies are using Instagram posts to time online advertising specifically to these types of consumers. For example, people love to post Instagram photos of their new pet. Almost as soon as the posts appear, those consumers may notice a large number of ads for pet-related products. Growth hacking involves engineering mechanisms that drive up interactions between brands and consumers. Airbnb grew in large part due to growth hacking approaches that embedded it within Craigslist.

In addition, near-field communication (NFC) technologies using radio-frequency identification (RFID), Global Positioning System (GPS), or Bluetooth capabilities alert marketers when someone, or at least someone's smartphone or tablet, has entered an area. A retailer (or the retailer's computers) taking advantage of this type of technology might spot a consumer near the store, perhaps someone who has been browsing for kitchen tables online, and push out messages or coupons for kitchen tables to entice them into the store. Technologies like these can increase unplanned purchases, a topic discussed in detail later in the chapter.[13]

11-3 PLACE SHAPES SHOPPING ACTIVITIES

11-3a Introduction

The economy depends on consumers buying things. Consumers depend on purchases to receive value. Buying is the result of the shopping process. Thus, marketers understand that shopping holds the key to value creation that stimulates economies and ultimately raises standards of living.

Many of the activities involved in the CVF and consumer behaviour theory in general take place in the shopping process. What exactly is shopping? Perhaps the following questions can help put shopping in perspective:

▸ **Do consumers have to buy to shop?**

▸ **Is a store necessary for shopping?**

▸ **What motivates consumer shopping?**

Marketers naturally hope that consumers will purchase things while shopping. But not every shopping act culminates in a purchase. Sometimes a consumer goes shopping only to find out that the desired product is out of stock. Rather than buying a less desirable product, the consumer may simply pass or put off product acquisition indefinitely.

More and more, a physical store isn't necessary for shopping to take place. Consumers shop using their computers, their phones, vending machines, or more traditional "nonstore" alternatives, like catalogues. Sometimes, consumers facing an important decision like a new home or an upcoming vacation are so involved in the buying process that they can't stop thinking about their choices. In this case, they may be shopping simply from the things they hold in memory.

11-3b What Is Shopping?

Shopping can be defined as the set of value-producing consumer activities that directly increase the likelihood that something will be purchased. Thus, when a consumer surfs the Internet looking for a song for his iPod, he is shopping. When a consumer visits a car dealer after hours

advertiming ad buys that include a schedule that runs the advertisement primarily at times when customers will be most receptive to the message

shopping set of value-producing consumer activities that directly increase the likelihood that something will be purchased

Shopping Pals?

Is it better to shop with a shopping pal? Maybe, if the consumer has the time. Married consumers report that one of the main reasons for not shopping with a spouse is time pressure. Men in particular see an advantage in shopping together because of the reduced financial risk that comes from being able to make a joint decision. Thus, if there isn't enough time to shop together, the couple may spend more than they would otherwise, reducing the utilitarian value from the situation.

However, consumers also report that shopping with a family member can reduce hedonic value. Specifically, consumers appear to have more pleasure and report greater hedonic value when shopping alone or with a friend as opposed to shopping with a family member. Family members create greater anxiety about purchase decisions and can even increase the sense of time pressure as one who is enjoying an extended shopping period worries about the other family member being bored. Thus, shopping pals don't always enhance shopping value.

Sources: Lim, J. and S. E. Beatty (2010), "Factors Affecting Couples' Decisions to Jointly Shop," *Journal of Business Research*, in press. Borges, A., J.C. Chebat and B. J. Babin (2010), "Does a Companion Always Enhance the Shopping Experience?" *Journal of Retailing and Consumer Services*, 17 (July), 294–299. Grace, D. (2009), "An Examination of Consumer Embarrassment and Repatronage Intentions in the Context of Emotional Service Encounters," *Journal of Retailing and Consumer Services*, 16 (January), 1–9.

to peruse the options on new cars, she is shopping. When a consumer visits the mall as a regular weekend activity, he is shopping. Earlier, marketing was discussed as business activities that enhance the likelihood of purchase. In this sense, shopping can be looked at as the inverse of marketing. Both marketing and shopping make purchase more likely, but one involves activities of marketing people and the other involves activities of shoppers.

11-3c Virtual Shopping Situations

Shopping via the Internet brings 24-7 access to shopping environments. Many effects seen in real bricks-and-mortar shopping environments exist in the virtual shopping world too. For example, colour and sounds can work in much the same way. Images placed in the background of a website can produce active thoughts, particularly when consumer expertise or knowledge is low. A web-based furniture retailer using pictures of clouds in the background of a web page, for instance, can produce thoughts of soft and comfortable furniture. Similarly, images related to money can produce thoughts related to discounts.[14] Online retailers enhance the shopping experience by making the site visually appealing.[15] However, care should be taken, as aesthetics often take a backseat to the need for an easy-to-use site that facilitates easy transactions—especially for task-oriented shoppers that frequent the Internet. This is particularly the case for shoppers interacting through a smartphone or tablet computer, due to the smaller screen and limited functionality.

Typically, we think of shopping as a volitional activity, meaning the consumer is the active decision maker. Smart agent technology raises questions about how volitional shopping might be. **Smart agent software** is capable of learning an Internet user's preferences and automatically searching out information and distributing the information to a user's computer. Numerous vendors offer smart agent software for sale or lease. Companies that purchase software hope to leverage the information that consumers leave behind into more customized and therefore more effective sales appeals. As an illustration, even a casual virtual visit to Michael Kors will set in motion push technologies that will generate Michael Kors banner ads within the browser for days after the visit. Amazon Prime account holders leave behind browsing history, allowing Amazon to build models of what a particular consumer is going to buy. Amazon believes the models to be highly accurate; so much so that it would like to ship things to consumers before they even physically make a purchase. Technology exists to have Amazon make the "purchase" on the consumer's behalf. The added convenience of the consumer's not even having to

> **smart agent software** software capable of learning an Internet user's preferences and automatically searching out information in selected websites and then distributing it

make a decision might add utilitarian value. Amazon also has the capability of delivering those products with a fleet of GPS-directed drones that could take the item that was not purchased and drop it off right to your front lawn.[16] Are consumers shopping if Amazon makes their minds up for them? As of now, society is uncertain as to when technologies allow too much to be known about or done for us. What do you think?

11-3d Shopping Activities

Shopping activities take place in specific places, over time, and under specific conditions or contexts. Shopping thus occurs in situations that are not easily controlled by a consumer and often not by the marketer either. The consumer may be either alone or in a crowded place, rushed or relaxed, in a good mood or a bad mood. In other words, shoppers are subjected to many situational influences that affect decision making and value. Whether the shoppers are Canadian, European, or Asian, situational variables are at least as important in explaining eventual buying behaviour as are personal characteristics or product beliefs.[17] Practically all shopping activities are influenced by contextual sources.

Four different types of shopping activities exist. At least one of these types characterizes any given shopping experience, but sometimes the shopper can combine more than one type into a single shopping trip. The four types of shopping activities are:

1. **Acquisitional shopping,** involving activities oriented toward a specific, intended purchase or purchases

2. **Epistemic shopping,** involving activities oriented toward acquiring knowledge about products

3. **Experiential shopping,** involving recreationally oriented activities designed to provide interest, excitement, relaxation, fun, social interaction, or some other desired feeling

4. **Impulsive shopping,** involving spontaneous activities characterized by a diminished regard for consequences, heightened emotional involvement, and a desire for immediate self-fulfillment

ACQUISITIONAL SHOPPING

A consumer who runs out to the store on her lunch hour to buy a gift for a co-worker's baby shower is strongly oriented toward getting a gift. Thus, shopping is more like a task, and this particular activity depends on high utilitarian value as an outcome.

EPISTEMIC SHOPPING

Epistemic activities include finding information on some purchase that is imminent. Alternatively, epistemic activities include shopping simply to increase an ever-growing body of knowledge about some product category of interest. In this sense, epistemic activities can be associated with either situational involvement or enduring involvement, respectively.

EXPERIENTIAL SHOPPING

Experiential activities include things done just for the experience. Many consumers go shopping on the weekends just to do something. In other words, experiential shopping can be motivated by boredom or loneliness. On the other hand, consumers who are on vacation often take in the local shopping venues. In this way, they experience something new and possibly unique. **Outshopping** is a term used to refer to consumers who are shopping in a city or town they must travel to rather than in their own hometown. Outshopping is often motivated simply by the desire for the experience. The outshopping consumer sees this as a value opportunity and is more likely to make purchases in this less-familiar and perhaps more-intriguing place. People who live alone also go shopping to experience interacting with other people. Thus, much of the reason for shopping lies in the experience itself.

IMPULSIVE SHOPPING

Impulsive behaviours represent a unique group of shopping activities, as we will see in detail later. However, impulsive activities also illustrate how a single shopping trip can result in more than one type of activity. A shopper may go to a big box store simply to acquire a gift. However, while there, the shopper may get into the environment of the store and experience strong emotions. These may also encourage the consumer to act impulsively.

Exhibit 11.2 provides examples of each type of activity and ties the activities to the types of value they are more associated with.

acquisitional shopping activities oriented toward a specific, intended purchase or purchases

epistemic shopping activities oriented toward acquiring knowledge about products

experiential shopping recreationally oriented activities designed to provide interest, excitement, relaxation, fun, social interaction, or some other desired feeling

impulsive shopping spontaneous activities characterized by a diminished regard for consequences, spontaneity, and a desire for immediate self-fulfillment

outshopping shopping in a city or town to which consumers must travel rather than in their own hometown

Exhibit 11.2

Shopping Activities and Shopping Value

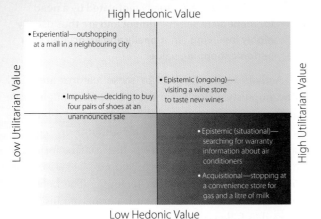

High Hedonic Value

Low Utilitarian Value ↕ High Utilitarian Value

- Experiential—outshopping at a mall in a neighbouring city
- Impulsive—deciding to buy four pairs of shoes at an unannounced sale
- Epistemic (ongoing)—visiting a wine store to taste new wines
- Epistemic (situational)—searching for warranty information about air conditioners
- Acquisitional—stopping at a convenience store for gas and a litre of milk

Low Hedonic Value

11-3e Shopping Value

All shopping activities are aimed at one key result—value. Consistent with the view of value from a previous chapter, **personal shopping value (PSV)** is the overall subjective worth of a shopping activity considering all associated costs and benefits. Like value overall, PSV can be usefully divided into two types. **Utilitarian shopping value** represents the worth obtained because some shopping task or job is completed successfully. **Hedonic shopping value** represents the worth of an activity because the time spent doing the activity itself is personally gratifying.[18]

Blend Images/Alamy

A purchase isn't needed for a consumer to get value out of shopping.

VALUE AND SHOPPING ACTIVITIES

Thus, the activities shown in Exhibit 11.2 all provide value, but they provide value in different ways to different consumers. The old term *window shopping* illustrates this point. Some consumers window shop to find information so that an upcoming shopping trip might be more successful. In this way, window shopping is a means to the end of a more successful future shopping task. Consumers may also window shop simply as a way of passing time in a gratifying way. Thus, window shopping can provide utilitarian and/or hedonic shopping value, respectively.

Situational influences may affect the type of shopping value desired by consumers. Time pressure, for example, may lead consumers to be more concerned with simple product acquisition than they might otherwise be. On the other hand, consumers who are in a bad mood may choose to change it by going shopping. The pleasant emotions can be personally gratifying and can potentially improve a shopper's mood.[19] Thus, hedonic shopping value becomes important. However, research suggests that utilitarian and hedonic shopping value relate to loyalty and that for department stores, hedonic value may build loyalty more strongly.[20]

RETAIL PERSONALITY

Retailers specializing in things like a wide selection of goods, low prices, guarantees, and knowledgeable employees can provide high proportions of utilitarian shopping value. This type of positioning emphasizes the **functional quality** of a retail store by facilitating the task of shopping.

In contrast, retailers specializing in a unique environment, an impressive decor, friendly employees, and pleasant emotions can provide relatively high hedonic shopping value. This type of positioning emphasizes the **affective quality** of a retail store. The affective quality can be managed to create an emotionally rewarding environment capable of producing high hedonic shopping value.

Together, the functional and affective qualities come together to shape retail personality. More

---

personal shopping value (PSV) overall subjective worth of a shopping activity considering all associated costs and benefits

utilitarian shopping value worth obtained because some shopping task or job is completed successfully

hedonic shopping value worth of an activity because the time spent doing the activity itself is personally gratifying

functional quality retail positioning that emphasizes tangible things like a wide selection of goods, low prices, guarantees, and knowledgeable employees

affective quality retail positioning that emphasizes a unique environment, exciting decor, friendly employees, and, in general, the feelings experienced in a retail place

Exhibit 11.3

A Retail Personality Perceptual Map

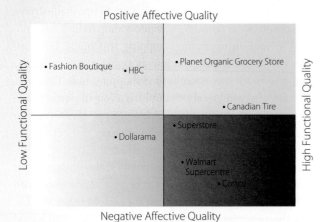

specifically, **retail personality** is the way a retail store is defined in the mind of a shopper based on the combination of functional and affective qualities.[21]

From a strategic perspective, these two retail personality dimensions are extremely useful as perceptual map dimensions (see Exhibit 11.3). Once again, a perceptual map of this type reveals which retail choices consumers view as most similar. As consumers' choices become more similar, they are more likely to compete with each other.

11-4 IMPULSIVE SHOPPING AND CONSUMPTION

Impulsive shopping activities take place every day. Some retailers and service providers survive largely as a result of consumers' compulsive activities. For instance, many behaviours associated with indulgence can be driven by impulsive motivations.

So, just what is an impulsive consumption act? As the definition implies, **impulsive consumption** is largely characterized by three components:

1. Impulsive acts are usually spontaneous and involve at least short-term feelings of liberation.

2. Impulsive acts are usually associated with a diminished regard for any costs or consequences (negative aspects) associated with the act.

3. Impulsive acts are usually motivated by a need for immediate self-fulfillment and are thus usually highly involving emotionally and associated with hedonic shopping value.

Activities characterized by these features are likely to be impulsive. For example, a consumer might have a bad morning at work and decide to cancel a business lunch to take a break shopping for self-gifts or "happies" via the Internet. This activity is likely characterized as impulsive and can be a way to suppress negative emotions and evoke more positive feelings.[22] The behaviour can be broken down to demonstrate the impulsiveness involved as follows:

1. The act involves willingly deviating from previous plans and thus shows spontaneity and no doubt feelings of liberation from the negative events of the day.

2. The act shows diminished regard for consequences either for missing the business lunch or for any expense incurred.

3. The act fulfills the need to maintain a positive outlook on the self and thus provides hedonic value.

Internet shopping, although often viewed as utilitarian in nature, can provide hedonic value in this way.[23] Additionally, consumers who feel they have restrained their spending behaviour in the past may indulge in impulsive purchases as a reward for past good behaviour.[24] Thus, when the economy turns around, consumers may let loose with a lot of impulsive purchases.

11-4a Impulsive Versus Unplanned Consumer Behaviour

Impulsive purchasing is not synonymous with unplanned purchasing behaviour. **Unplanned shopping**, buying, and consuming share some, but not all, characteristics of truly impulsive consumer behaviour. Exhibit 11.4 illustrates the relationship between impulsive and unplanned consumer activity. The right side of the exhibit shows that unplanned consumer acts are characterized by:

1. Situational memory

2. Utilitarian orientation

3. Spontaneity

retail personality way a retail store is defined in the mind of a shopper based on the combination of functional and affective qualities

impulsive consumption consumption acts characterized by spontaneity, a diminished regard for consequences, and a need for self-fulfillment

unplanned shopping shopping activity that shares some, but not all, characteristics of truly impulsive consumer behaviour, being characterized by situational memory, a utilitarian orientation, and feelings of spontaneity

Exhibit 11.4

Impulsive Versus Unplanned Shopping Behaviour

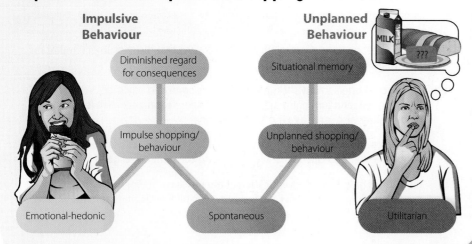

While some trips to Las Vegas may be completely spontaneous, most involve some degree of planning. But the tagline emphasizes the impulsive nature of consumer behaviour in Las Vegas. Certainly, the campaign illustrates the high hedonic value that can be obtained and encourages consumers not to worry so much about the consequences. So perhaps an impulsive consumption act, like going to Las Vegas, can even be planned. Simple unplanned purchases may lack the impulsive characteristics captured so well by this campaign.

Situational memory characterizes unplanned acts because something in the environment, such as a point-of-purchase display, usually triggers the knowledge in memory that something is needed. A consumer may enter the grocery store without Doublemint gum on her grocery list. However, the candy counter at the checkout provides a convenient reminder that her office inventory of her favourite breath freshener is depleted.

Simply put, utilitarian motivations drive many unplanned purchases. This consumer who purchases Doublemint gum is probably not very emotionally moved by the gum purchase. However, the purchase allows her to fulfill a need to replenish her supply of the product.

Unplanned acts are spontaneous and, to some extent, they share this characteristic with impulsivity. They are, by definition, unplanned and therefore done without any significant deliberation or prior decision making. The gum buyer certainly had not put a lot of thought into the decision to buy Doublemint as she planned the shopping trip.

11-4b Distinguishing Impulsive and Unplanned Consumer Behaviour

The line between impulsive and unplanned purchases is not always clear because some unplanned acts are impulsive and many impulsive acts are unplanned. Las Vegas tourism for years has used a tagline that says, "What happens in Vegas stays in Vegas."

Simple unplanned purchases usually lack any real emotional involvement or significant amounts of self-gratification. Additionally, unplanned purchases often involve only minimal negative consequences and thus fail to really qualify as having negative consequences. A pack of gum is not likely to cause severe financial problems for very many consumers.

11-4c Susceptibility to Situational Effects

Are all consumers susceptible to unplanned and impulsive behaviour? The answer is "yes," but not all consumers are equally susceptible. Individual difference characteristics can play a role. For example, **impulsivity** is a personality trait that represents how sensitive a consumer is to immediate rewards. A consumer shopping for a gift for a friend may see shoes on sale at half off and be compelled to purchase these and obtain the *reward*.[25] Naturally, consumers with high impulsivity are more prone to impulsive acts.[26]

Consumers with attention deficit disorder, for example, typically have high degrees of impulsivity, which makes them more prone to impulsive acts. One consequence is that such consumers are even less likely than others to follow step-by-step instructions for assembling or using a product.[27] Thus, they may fail to get the full value from the product because the assembly is incomplete or wrong.

Situational characteristics also influence impulse shopping.[28] For example, a consumer

> **impulsivity** personality trait that represents how sensitive a consumer is to immediate rewards

Exhibit 11.5

Retail Approaches to Encouraging Impulse Purchases

Tool	Example
1. Merchandise complementary products together.	Placing beer near the charcoal triggers memory so that the consumer remembers how well beer goes with barbecue.
2. Encourage "add-on" purchases.	Asking consumers to buy socks after they have agreed to buy shoes seems like a small request, and turning the request down risks creating negative feelings. Add-on purchases also serve as a trigger in memory.
3. Create an emotionally charged atmosphere.	Positive emotions, in particular excitement, are associated with larger purchases. Giving free samples can be one way of making consumers feel good.
4. Make things easy to buy.	Consumers have less time to think about the purchase and perhaps decide the product is not worth the price. A consumer who allows his credit card number to be automatically used by a website will be more prone to unplanned and impulse purchases.
5. Provide a discount.	Buy one watch, get a second for half price. The consequences become even easier to diminish.

shopping for a purple dress for a special occasion may encounter a black dress on the 40% off rack. The low-price cue may encourage an impulse purchase in this case. Atmospheric characteristics such as the colours, music, free samples, merchandising, and salespeople also can encourage purchase. Online retailers can facilitate the actual buying process by making the transaction a simple one-step process.[29] Exhibit 11.5 summarizes things that retailers can do to encourage unplanned and impulse purchasing.

11-4d Consumer Self-Regulation

consumer self-regulation tendency for consumers to inhibit outside, or situational, influences from interfering with shopping intentions

action-oriented consumers with a high capacity to self-regulate their behaviour

state-oriented consumers with a low capacity to self-regulate their behaviour

Another key personality trait that affects a consumer's tendency to do things that are unplanned or impulsive is self-regulatory capacity. **Consumer self-regulation**, in this sense, refers to a tendency for consumers to inhibit outside, or situational, influences from interfering with shopping intentions. Consumers with a high capacity to self-regulate their behaviour are sometimes referred to as **action-oriented**, whereas consumers with a low capacity

The emotions and timing of online auctions just may trigger impulsive actions.

to self-regulate are referred to as **state-oriented**.[30] Action-oriented consumers are affected less by emotions generated by a retail atmosphere than are state-oriented consumers. Recall the three dimensions of atmospheric emotions discussed in an earlier chapter: pleasure, arousal, and dominance. State-oriented shoppers who are emotionally aroused are far more likely to make additional purchases beyond what was planned than are action-oriented shoppers. Likewise, state-oriented shoppers' spending behaviour is strongly affected by feelings of dominance in the environment. Further, feelings of dominance among state-oriented shoppers increase hedonic shopping value and decrease utilitarian shopping value. In contrast, action-oriented shoppers' purchasing and shopping value perceptions are unaffected by dominance.

New electronics can be a tempting element in a shopping environment. Self-regulation is related to a consumer's desire, and intention, to purchase such new products. A state-oriented consumer who enters an upbeat electronics store is more likely to buy a new product than an action-oriented consumer would be under the same circumstances.[31] Retailers with a high proportion of state-oriented consumers in their target market are more likely to thrive on consumers' impulse purchases.

Exhibit 11.6 lists some questions that can distinguish consumers based on self-regulatory capacity. The exhibit shows a statement and then demonstrates the way a consumer would respond to the situation. Consumers with a high ability to self-regulate their behaviour—in other words, the action-oriented consumers—generally form rules that they stick by to limit the extent to which situational influences determine their behaviour. For example, if they know they will be tempted to overspend during a shopping trip, they may decide not to take their credit cards with them while shopping. In this way, they can resist the overspending that sometimes accompanies unplanned and impulse purchases.

Although Exhibit 11.5 lists some things retailers can do to encourage unplanned or impulse purchases, one might ask, are such actions ethical? Or, do such actions simply encourage consumers to buy things wastefully? This certainly can be the case, but unplanned purchases are often simply things consumers would indeed intend to buy if they had remembered them before they started shopping. Impulse purchases can also be a relatively harmless way that consumers control their emotions and improve their outlook on life. Impulse purchases do provide value as long as the consequences of the purchases are relatively harmless. In this way, impulse shopping can be therapeutic and emotionally uplifting. This isn't always the case, though.

11-4e Impulsive Versus Compulsive Behaviour

Impulsive and compulsive consumer behaviour share many of the same characteristics. Compulsive behaviour can be emotionally involving and certainly entails the possibility of negative consequences. Compulsive consumer behaviour can be distinguished from impulsive consumer behaviour by three distinguishing characteristics:

1. **Compulsive consumer behaviour is harmful.**
2. **Compulsive consumer behaviour seems to be uncontrollable.**
3. **Compulsive consumer behaviour is correlated with chronic depression.**

Compulsive consumer behaviour is defined and discussed in more detail in a later chapter.

Exhibit 11.6

Questions Distinguishing Low From High Self-Regulatory Capacity

Statement	Action-Oriented Consumers' Typical Response	State-Oriented Consumers' Typical Response
If I had to work at home …	I would get started right away.	I would often have problems getting started.
When I have important things to buy …	I make a shopping plan and stick to it.	I don't know how to get started.
When I have an important assignment to finish in an afternoon …	I can easily concentrate on the assignment.	It often happens that things will distract me.
When it is absolutely necessary to do some unpleasant task …	I finish it as soon as possible.	It takes a while before I can start on it.

Domino Shopping

Does shopping beget shopping? The principle of inertia applies to consumer behaviour as much as it applies in physics. Once a consumer initiates some behaviour, the tendency is to continue that behaviour. The concept of shopper's momentum is based on the idea that once a shopper makes a single purchase, an impulse to continue shopping develops, which results in even more purchases. Buying things is often emotionally rewarding. So, if one purchase creates good feelings, and perhaps hedonic shopping value, then two purchases must be even better—right?

Shoppers' momentum may also exist for nonpurchase. *Inaction inertia* is a term used to refer to the fact that once a consumer passes on buying a brand that he or she is used to buying, not buying that brand becomes easier. This becomes particularly apparent when a consumer misses an opportunity to buy an often-used brand on sale. That consumer is actually less likely to buy that brand again the next time the need becomes apparent. So, not buying can grow on a consumer just as buying can!

iStockphoto.com/Steve Corrigan

Sources: Dhar, R., J. Huber and U. Khan (2007), "The Shopping Momentum Effect," *Journal of Marketing Research*, 44 (August), 370–378; Zeelenberg, M. and Puttun, Van Marijke (2005), "The Dark Side of Discounts: An Inaction Inertia Perspective on the Post-Promotional Dip," *Psychology & Marketing*, 22 (September), 611–622.

11-5 PLACES HAVE ATMOSPHERES

All consumer behaviour takes place in some physical space, yet sometimes marketing managers forget that the physical environment can play a significant role in shaping buying behaviour and the value a consumer receives from shopping or service. Perhaps nowhere is the true impact of place more obvious than in retail and service environments.

11-5a Retail and Service Atmospherics

In consumer behaviour, **atmospherics** refers to the emotional nature of an environment or, more precisely, to the feelings created by the total aura of physical attributes that comprise the physical environment. A total list of things that make up the atmosphere would be difficult to compile; however, they can be summarized by two dimensions.[32]

atmospherics
emotional nature of an environment or the feelings created by the total aura of physical attributes that comprise a physical environment

Exhibit 11.7 provides a summary of the dimensions and what they can create.

FUNCTIONAL QUALITY

As mentioned earlier, the functional quality of an environment describes the meaning created by the total result of attributes that facilitate and make efficient the function performed there. In a shopping environment, this includes convenience in all forms: the price levels, the number and helpfulness of employees, and the breadth and depth of merchandise, along with other characteristics that facilitate the shopping task. In a service environment, the amount and expertise of service employees, the convenience of the environment, and the capability of the support staff, among other things, all contribute to the functional quality of the service environment.[33] These are often thought of as core aspects of service as some are essential for the benefits to be realized by consumers.

AFFECTIVE QUALITY

The affective quality represents the emotional meaning of an environment, which results from the sum effect of all ambient attributes that affect the way one feels

Exhibit 11.7

The Qualities of an Environment

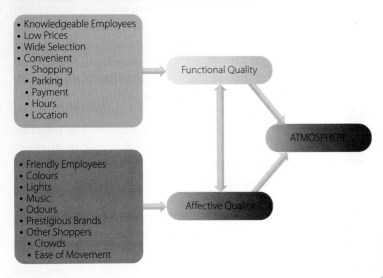

- Knowledgeable Employees
- Low Prices
- Wide Selection
- Convenient
  - Shopping
  - Parking
  - Payment
  - Hours
  - Location

Functional Quality

ATMOSPHERE

- Friendly Employees
- Colours
- Lights
- Music
- Odours
- Prestigious Brands
- Other Shoppers
  - Crowds
  - Ease of Movement

Affective Quality

in that place. A friendly service employee can make the environment more pleasant, cool colours can be relaxing, upbeat music can be exciting, and a crowded environment that restricts movement can be distressing. Although many managers focus more on core aspects, these more relational aspects also influence value and satisfaction.

Restaurants, for example, often go out of business despite having excellent food and a good location. A primary reason for their lack of competitiveness is a lack of attention to the environment. As a result, the restaurant lacks style or creates a distressing or boring affective quality. All consumers are susceptible to the effects of affective quality; however, female consumers appear much more demanding based on how they react to a place with a negative affective quality.[34]

So, does a retail environment with a distinctly high functional quality necessarily have an uninteresting or poor affective quality? Quite the contrary! If anything, the two dimensions are positively related. An environment with a favourable functional quality tends to be associated with some degree of positive affect. Adolescent girls, for example, find environments with high levels of functional qualities like accessibility and safety features also to be more pleasing places to shop.[35] Thus, retailers should keep this in mind and realize that even things they build to create shopper safety can affect both the functional and affective meaning of a particular retailer.

11-5b Atmosphere Elements

The way an atmosphere makes a consumer feel is really determined by the consumer's perception of all the elements in a given environment working together. Therefore, naming all the elements that eventually affect the retail or service atmosphere is impossible. However, a more distinct atmosphere creates a feeling that can ultimately result in a core competitive advantage based on the unique feeling. Two factors help merchandisers and retail designers create just such an atmosphere:[36]

1. **Fit** refers to how appropriate the elements of an environment are for a given environment.

2. **Congruity** refers to how consistent the elements of an environment are with each other.

Disney is well known for its ability to manage the environment in a consistent manner across a wide variety of different consumer businesses ranging from movies to theme parks and cruises to retail stores. For example, when a new *Avengers* movie opens, all of Disney's businesses consistently promote and engage consumers in the new offering. The elements of all the different environments work well together—whether it is a cruise ship gift shop or online at DisneyStore.com—to create "the happiest place on earth."

Although an atmosphere is created by a combination of elements, researchers often study elements in isolation or in combination with only one or two other attributes. In the following sections, a few of the more prominent environmental elements are singled out as being particularly effective in changing or shaping an environment's atmosphere.

ODOURS

Believe it or not, in Manchester, the United Kingdom, the Industrial Revolution museum includes a tribute to sewerage systems with a sewer museum. What should a sewer museum smell like? Well, the folks at the museum in Manchester have a sewer that smells like a sewer, and the sewer museum certainly wouldn't be authentic with the scent of roses piped in. The

fit how appropriate the elements of a given environment are

congruity how consistent the elements of an environment are with one another

Disney is well known for its ability to create a competitive advantage through fit and congruity across its consumer businesses.

market. For example, women respond more favourably to floral scents while men respond more favourably to food scents like pumpkin pie. No kidding! Perhaps the way to a man's heart, or wallet, really is through his stomach.

Retailers like the Knot Shop, a chain of specialty stores for men's fashion accessories, spend considerable amounts of time and money managing the scents in their shops. In the Knot Shop, a masculine odour reminiscent of leather and tobacco is given off to help frame the shopping environment as masculine. The smell fits and helps create the store image! Retailers can also trigger greater arousal by introducing a moderately incongruent odour into an environment. In an experimental study, wine store consumers paid more attention to label information when an incongruent and slightly less pleasant odour was present and became less risk aversive and more willing to try different wines when more pleasing and consistent odours were present.[37] Odours also seem to have a greater effect when other, more intrusive elements like crowding are not too strong.[38]

MUSIC

Fast music means fast dancing. Slow music means slow dancing. Even though consumers don't always dance through the aisles of stores, this image is fairly accurate in describing the way background music affects consumers. Both foreground and background music affect consumers, but they do so in different ways. **Foreground music** is music that becomes the focal point of attention and can have strong effects on a consumer's willingness to approach or avoid an environment. Consumers who dislike rap or country music will likely have a difficult time hanging around a place with loud rap or country music.

From a consumer behaviour standpoint, **background music**, which is music played below the

fact is, odours are prominent environmental elements that affect both a consumer's cognitive processing and affective reaction.

Olfactory is a term that refers to humans' physical and psychological processing of smells. When shoppers process ambient citrus odours, they tend to feel higher levels of pleasant emotions while shopping and to be more receptive to product information. Citrus odours produce positive responses in practically all consumers. Even more positive reactions can be obtained by matching odours with a target

olfactory refers to humans' physical and psychological processing of smells

foreground music music that becomes the focal point of attention and can have strong effects on a consumer's willingness to approach or avoid an environment

background music music played below the audible threshold that would make it the centre of attention

audible threshold that would make it the centre of attention, is perhaps more interesting than foreground music. Service providers and retailers generally provide some type of background music for customers. Muzak is one of several companies whose business is providing the appropriate background music for a particular service or retail setting. Several effects are attributable to background music:

▸ **The speed of the background music determines the speed at which consumers shop. Slower music means slower shopping. Faster music means faster shopping.**

▸ **The tempo of music affects the patience of consumers. Faster music makes consumers less patient.**

▸ **The presence of background music enhances service quality perceptions relative to an environment with no background music.**

▸ **Pop music used in the background contributes to discount store perceptions.**

▸ **Incongruent music lowers consumers' quality perceptions.**

These factors are important for retail managers interested in managing quality and value perceptions. However, background music can also affect the bottom line. In restaurants, for instance, consumers who dine with slow background music are more patient and in less of a hurry to leave. As a result, they linger longer and tend to buy more beverages than consumers dining with faster background music. Thus, gross margins can actually be increased by slowing down the background music, particularly in light of the higher margins realized on drink sales relative to food sales.[39]

COLOUR

Colour is another tool that marketing managers can use to alter consumer reactions. Some colours are more liked than other colours, but liking isn't really the key to understanding consumer reactions to colour. Blue is perhaps the most universally liked colour. Blue presents few cultural taboos. Red, white, and black, however, all present cultural barriers associated with bad omens and death in some cultures. Red is a risky colour in Japan, as is white in China and black in Western cultures. Colour, like other environmental elements, helps frame the shopping experience. Therefore, choosing the right colour depends on how consumers react in terms of both their thoughts and their feelings.

Exhibit 11.8

The Way Colour Works

$100

- High quality
- Worth $100
- Believe price is fair
- Feel pleased
- More willing to buy

$100

- Low quality/discount
- Not worth $100
- Believe price is not as fair
- Feel more distressed
- Less willing to buy

Colour, for example, affects both quality and price perceptions. Consumers who perceive a product in a predominantly blue background tend to think the product is of higher quality, and they are willing to pay more for that product.[40] In contrast, warm colours like red and orange tend to promote expectations of poor quality and low price.

Exhibit 11.8 illustrates the way these effects can play out in a retail environment. Colour changes behaviour by framing the way one thinks about a product and also by changing the way one feels. Thus, the perceived value of an object can vary with colour. Exhibit 11.8 clearly illustrates how colour can frame consumer information processing. The same product at the identical price, in this case $100, will be viewed as priced more fairly with a blue background than with an orange or red background. Consumers also express more positive feelings when presented with blue background. Not surprisingly, consumers are also more willing to buy a product presented in a blue background than in a red or orange background.

So, is blue always a good colour? Like many aspects of consumer behaviour, the story isn't quite that simple. Blue has drawbacks. For instance, blue is a cool colour. Thus, blue does not attract attention as effectively as a

Is This Going to Take Long?

Music affects consumers in many ways. As we have discussed, the tempo of music can determine the speed at which consumers shop, dine, and even browse. Tempo even affects perceptions and feelings about waiting. Fast-tempo music is generally disliked for short waits and slow tempo music is disliked for long waits. So maybe some Vivaldi would be good if the wait is short, but Green Day would be better if it's going to be a while!

Gemenacom/Shutterstock.com

Sources: Oakes, Steve (2003), "Musical Tempo and Waiting Perceptions," *Psychology & Marketing*, 29 (8), 685–713; Areni, Charles (2003), "Exploring Managers' Implicit Theories of Atmospheric Music: Comparing Academic Analysis to Industry Insight," *Journal of Services Marketing*, 17 (2/3), 161–184; Kellaris, J.J. and R.J. Kent (1992), "The Influence of Music on Consumers' Temporal Perceptions: Does Time Fly When You're Having Fun?", *Journal of Consumer Psychology*, 1, 365–376.

warm colour like red or orange does. Also, like other situational effects due to the environment, colour does not work alone. Lighting can have dramatic effects on the environment and even reverse colour's effect. For example, the effects above hold for bright lights. Change a store's lighting to soft lights and consumers' opinions regarding the product change considerably. For instance, soft lights and an orange background can eliminate the advantage for blue in that the price fairness perceptions, quality perceptions, affect, and purchase intentions are now equal to or slightly better than the combination of blue and soft lights.[41] Victoria's Secret for many years merchandised stores with predominantly warm colours; however, its soft lighting eliminated any bad effects that might be present with bright lights.

Like other elements too, a marketer must be aware of the image. If the brand is closely associated with a colour, then that association may be more important than the effects discussed here. So, if you are in a bad mood, change the colour of your space, and things may improve!

MERCHANDISING

Merchandising's point is to provide the customer with the best opportunity to purchase something. This is done by the placement of goods and store fixtures along with

Marjorie Kamys Cotera/Bob Daemmrich Photography/Alamy

Digital signage like this attracts attention.

the use of signage. The angles or racks and the visual image of the store provide a way for consumers to view and move through a store. Signs change consumers' perceptions. For example, signs that emphasize price by using large numerals create the perception of a discount store. An upscale store uses little signage. Increasingly, digital signage is delivered with electronic display boards. These seem to attract the attention of shoppers and can be used to create a specific feeling.[42] In some cases, the consumer can even interact with the display board.

SOCIAL SETTINGS

An old saying about Bishop Berkeley's forest goes:

> *If a tree falls in the forest and nobody is there to hear it, does it make any noise?*

Well, if a consumer goes to the Mink Mile in Toronto and there are no other people, is there really an atmosphere? People are a huge part of the environment, and if the people are removed the atmosphere changes entirely. Thus, the social environment—referring to the other customers and employees in a service or shopping environment—cannot be ignored when explaining how atmosphere affects consumer behaviour.

Crowding refers to the density of people and objects within a given space. A space can be crowded without any people. However, *shopper density,* meaning the number of consumers in a given space, can still exert relatively strong influences on consumer behaviour. Crowding actually exerts a **nonlinear effect** on consumers, meaning that a plot of the effect by the amount of crowding does not make a straight line.

Exhibit 11.9 illustrates the way crowding works, particularly with respect to shopper density. Generally, consumers are not particularly attracted to an environment with no other consumers. The lack of consumers might signal poor quality or, in other cases, an absence of other consumers is simply awkward. For example, a consumer who enters a restaurant alone, particularly with no other diners, may well feel quite uncomfortable. In contrast, a mild degree of crowding produces the most positive outcomes in terms of shopping affect, purchase behaviour, consumer satisfaction, and shopping value, and high degrees of crowding lower these outcomes.[43] For instance, crowding affects utilitarian shopping value less strongly than hedonic shopping value in part because of the negative affect caused by crowding.

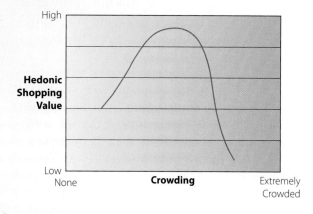

Exhibit 11.9

The Way Crowding Affects Consumers

Hypermart chains like Superstore, Carrefour, Auchan, and Walmart can unintentionally diminish the hedonic shopping value consumers experience by placing large displays on the sales floor that compound the negative affect occurring during busy shopping times. In contrast, savvy retailers can actually increase sales by decreasing the amount of merchandise on the sales floor and creating a less crowded shopping environment.

Both the number and type of salespeople can also affect shoppers. For example, the presence of more salespeople in a shopping environment can actually increase shopper purchase intentions. However, the type of salespeople can also influence shoppers' purchasing and value perceptions. In particular, salespeople and service providers should have an appropriate appearance for the type of product sold. The salespeople should simply fit the part. At Disney theme parks, employees are referred to as "cast members" in part because their appearance is tightly controlled to fit the particular environment in which they work.

Salespeople and service providers are an important source of information and influence. **Source attractiveness**

crowding density of people and objects within a given space

nonlinear effect a plot of the effect by the amount of crowding, which does not make a straight line

source attractiveness the degree to which a source's physical appearance matches a prototype for beauty and elicits a favourable or desirous response is defined as the degree to which a source's physical appearance matches a consumer's prototype (expectations) for beauty and elicits a favourable or desirous response. Intuitively, one would think that a more attractive person always is a good idea relative to a relatively less attractive person. This idea is known as the "beauty is good" hypothesis.

However, a consumer who encounters an attractive salesperson may end up making an upward social comparison. **Social comparison** is a naturally occurring mental personal comparison of the self with a target individual. Simply, it's a self–other comparison that helps give the self relative meaning. An upward comparison means the target is better and a downward comparison means the target is inferior. In the case of attractiveness, an upward comparison (the salesperson perceived as more attractive than the consumer) can cause negative feelings that reduce the likelihood of purchase.[44] The presence of other attractive customers may even cause another consumer to feel embarrassed if the upward comparison is strong. This effect is more likely for same-sex comparisons when the service is unrelated to beauty-related products. Think about how a very attractive appliance salesperson may come across.

Shopping buddies, meaning shopping companions, also cause consumers to react differently than when shopping alone. A shopping companion can be more fun and be a source of objective opinion. In this way, the companion can affect hedonic and utilitarian value. The shopping buddy can help reinforce positive feelings about products and thus encourage purchase. A simple statement like "Those jeans look great on you" can tilt the scale toward purchase. Partly as a result, consumers who shop with a companion tend to buy more than those who shop alone. Teens' behaviour is particularly affected by mall shopping companions who are members of their peer group. Research shows limits to positive effects of group shopping, however. Consumers who shop with a spouse or other family member report lower hedonic value. The family members interfere or get in the way of what could otherwise be a gratifying time alone or with a friend.[45] The presence of a shopping buddy does change things.

social comparison
a naturally occurring mental personal comparison of the self with a target individual within the environment

antecedent conditions
situational characteristics that a consumer brings to a particular information processing, purchase, or consumption environment

11-6 ANTECEDENT CONDITIONS

Antecedent conditions are situational characteristics that a consumer brings to a particular information processing, purchase, or consumption environment. Events occurring prior to this particular point in time have created a situation. Antecedent conditions include things like economic resources, orientation, mood, and other emotional perceptions such as fear. They can shape the value in a situation by framing the events that take place. The following sections elaborate.

11-6a Economic Resources

BUYING POWER

The economic resources a consumer brings to a particular purchase setting refer to the consumer's buying power. Buying power can be in the form of cash on hand, credit card spending limits, or money available by draft or debit card. Most places in Canada and the United States today accept credit cards for payment (Visa, MasterCard, Discover, American Express); however, a few businesses still insist on cash payment. Businesses not accepting "card payment" are more common in other countries. Thus, the amount of money a consumer has on hand can determine where he or she will shop or dine. For consumers short on cash, McDonald's may be a better option than The Keg.

However, other issues arise. What if consumers are near their credit limits? This can also change their shopping behaviour. Companies may put together special financing packages to deal with consumers whose credit is good enough to receive a major credit card even though they maintain high debt levels. Many consumers live paycheque to paycheque. If so, buying may increase around the day that consumers are paid. Then, the awareness that they are financially better off because of payday may stimulate increased spending. Cheque advance services take advantage of payday timing by offering to prepay consumers in return for a portion of the total paycheque. Thus, these consumer services offer utilitarian value to consumers by providing a way for them to receive their pay before the company they work for actually issues a cheque.

CONSUMER BUDGETING

In the 1990s, consumer debt ballooned to unprecedented levels. Much of this was in the form of credit card debt. The fact is, if credit card companies can charge a high interest rate (such as 18% or more), then they can afford to take a few credit risks and still maintain a profitable business. Thus, credit became easy to get. As a result, the general rule is that consumers can avoid delaying gratification and have things today. However, when consumers find themselves having difficulty making payments, their spending habits must change or they run the risk of losing their credit and worse.

A mortgage crisis in the United States rippled through financial markets around the world during the late 2000s. Many consumers had taken variable rate mortgages that offered very low rates in the first few years of the loan. However, as interest rates rose, these very same consumers sometimes found themselves in a position where their home mortgage was taking 50% or more of their total income. The higher budget allocation to make a house payment lowered their buying power. Many consumers who faced foreclosure learned the hard way about the risks of a variable rate loan.

Most consumers do not perform a formal budgeting process; however, those consumers who do budget end up with different spending habits than those who do not. Generally, budgeting is associated with frugality. As the U.S. economy continues to work toward recovery, American families continue to allocate resources cautiously and end up spending more frugally than they might otherwise. Occupancy rates, revenue, and profits fell dramatically at many U.S. resorts in Las Vegas, Atlantic City, Florida, and other locations as a result when compared with pre-2009 figures.[46] Although Canada did not experience as steep an economic downturn as the United States, many Canadians also tightened up their spending after the global recession hit in 2008.

Many consumers who do not prepare a formal budget do perform mental budgeting. **Mental budgeting** is simply a memory accounting for recent spending.[47] One result is that a consumer who has recently splurged on spending in one category will tend to make up for the exuberance through underconsumption in another category. In other words, they buy less than they typically would. Thus, the fact that the consumer has splurged recently in one area creates an antecedent condition that affects spending in another.

11-6b Orientation

Consumers enter each exchange environment. They may have natural tendencies toward one shopping orientation or another, for instance. However, some orientations may be temporary. Consumers may face a temporary orientation toward price consciousness as they seek to save money in uncertain times. Even a consumer with a tendency toward an experiential orientation may temporarily face a strong task-orientation. In these instances, the consumer may actually be distracted by things that might otherwise be pleasant. This effect is even true on the Internet, as an aesthetically pleasing website can cause lower satisfaction among consumers who are highly task-oriented.[48] Employees who sense the orientation and can adjust their approach will create higher value for the consumer. Gift shopping can dramatically shift a shopper's orientation and change the shopping experience altogether.

11-6c Mood

Mood was defined earlier as a transient affective state. While shopping and consuming can alter a consumer's mood, each consumer brings his or her current mood to the particular consumption situation. Consumers in particularly bad moods may have a tendency to binge consume. For example, a consumer in a foul mood may down a Marble Slab Creamery ice cream cone. If the mood is particularly disagreeable, perhaps eating a 1 litre take-out container is more likely to do the trick. The foul mood enhances the value of the ice cream temporarily because it provides the normal hedonic value from the good taste, but it is also therapeutic and, at least temporarily, helps restore a more favourable affective state.

Mood can also affect shopping. The mood that consumers bring to the shopping environment can exaggerate the actual experience. A consumer in a good mood may find even greater hedonic shopping value in a pleasant shopping experience than he or she may otherwise find.[49] Mood can even affect spending and consumer satisfaction. Shoppers who go shopping in a bad mood, for example, may be more likely to buy only what they absolutely need and may experience lower consumer satisfaction than consumers in good moods.

11-6d Security and Fearfulness

Consumers today live with ever-present reminders of vandalism, crime, and even terrorism. Large parking lots such as commonly found at Walmart stores or conventional

mental budgeting memory accounting for recent spending

shopping centres attract criminals who prey on seemingly defenceless consumers. Stories of abductions, muggings, assaults, carjackings, and other heinous criminal acts taking place understandably create fear among some shoppers, particularly those who view themselves as vulnerable. Shopping malls, markets, airports, and other places where large numbers of consumers gather are consistently mentioned as potential terrorist targets, providing another reason for consumers to feel less secure.

Fearfulness can affect consumers in multiple ways. A consumer who goes shopping in a fearful mood will not go about his or her shopping in the same way. A fearful consumer will tend to buy less and enjoy the experience less. Alternatively, a consumer may cope with fear of shopping by turning to nonstore outlets such as the Internet as a seemingly safer way of doing business. But even here, consumers sometimes fear providing private information often needed to complete a transaction. Thus, retailers who pay attention to making their parking and shopping environments more secure can help eliminate the feelings of fear some shoppers may have otherwise. Exhibit 11.10 lists some ways fearfulness may be reduced among consumers.

Exhibit 11.10

Enhancing Value by Making Consumers Feel Safer

Increase number and visibility of security personnel

Increase number and prominence of security cameras in parking lots

Have brightly lit parking lots

Add carry-out service for consumers—particularly for those shopping alone

Maintain an uncrowded, open entrance

Clearly mark all exits

Prevent loitering

Discourage gangs from visiting the centre

STUDY TOOLS 11

LOCATED AT THE BACK OF THE TEXTBOOK

☐ Rip out Chapter Review Card

LOCATED AT NELSON.COM/STUDENT

☐ Review Key Terms Flashcards (print or online)

☐ Download audio summaries to review on the go

☐ Complete practice quizzes to prepare for tests

☐ Watch video on Murray Cheese for a real company example

Case

Pinterest: A Collection of Consumers

Although they have not been around for very long, online social networks—such as Facebook and Twitter—have quickly become an important channel for consumer-to-consumer interactions. Recently, Pinterest has caught the attention of consumers and retailers alike.

The basic idea behind Pinterest is straightforward: The website provides an online space that people can use to "pin" and share digital images. It is sometimes referred to as a digital scrapbook that allows people to capture and share what they are thinking about, interested in, and aspiring to own. During an appearance on Conan O'Brien's late-night talk show, actor Reese Witherspoon called Pinterest "a collection of the most amazing, wonderful craftiness on the earth!" In spring 2012, Pinterest became the fastest-growing website of all time, built upon a segment of mostly female consumers who have used it to plan weddings, collect recipes, organize family photos, plan vacations, and share dreams.

Consumers can also use Pinterest as part of their pre-shopping process. For example, a consumer might want to post a photo of a couple of gowns she is considering and get the reaction of her followers before making a final decision. Alternatively, when thinking about a new car, a consumer can keep track of the leading candidates by pinning them to a "car shopping" board. Other consumers can comment on the consideration set and connect the car buyer to other information, such as reviews or quality ratings.

It is not surprising then that Pinterest has caught the attention of consumer marketers. Today, one out of three Internet users have a Pinterest account and, among affluent households (those with an income of more than $100,000), Pinterest is more popular than Twitter. More importantly, Pinterest users are actively engaged with brands and products as part of their normal use of the social network. Rather than brands popping up and interrupting the user, consumers on Pinterest are there to see and discover products that like-minded people are interested in. One study found that shoppers referred by Pinterest spend $185, which is considerably more than shoppers from other social networks like Facebook (who spend $85). The research, which compared 50,000 Pinterest shoppers to 50,000 Facebook shoppers, was conducted

© Richard Levine/Alamy

at the online jewellery and accessories retailer Boticca (boticca.com) In addition, Boticca found that its 40,000-plus Pinterest followers were using the social network to browse pins of products that they were interested in and only clicking over to the retailer's website when they were ready to buy. Beauty, food, fashion, fitness and home decorating are particular active categories on Pinterest.

Sources: Curtin, Stacy (2012), "Facebook Investors Should Be Worried by Pinterest Mania," *Daily Ticker, Yahoo Finance* (March 23), http://finance .yahoo.com/blogs/daily-ticker/facebook-investors-worried-pinterest -mania-fortune-hempel-145543971.html, accessed May 14, 2012. Hempel, Jessi (2012), "Is Pinterest the Next Facebook," *Fortune Magazine* (March). Owen, Laura Hazard (2012), "Pinterest Users Spend Way More Money than Facebook Users," *Washington Post* (May 9), http://www.washingtonpost .com/business/technology/pinterest-vs-facebook-whose-users-spend -more/2012/05/09 /glQATXkoCLLstory.html, accessed May 14, 2012. Williamson, Debra Aho, Danielle Drolet, Krista Garcia, and Corey McNair (2015), "Pinterest for Marketers: What you Need to Know," *eMarketer*, Feburary.

QUESTIONS

1 What types of shopping activities might Pinterest affect?

2 How does Pinterest influence a consumer's personal shopping value?

3 How might Pinterest encourage or discourage impulsive shopping?

4 Will Pinterest help consumers with self-control or make it more difficult? How does this compare to other popular online social networks like Facebook, Instagram, Snapchat, and Twitter?

5 How does Pinterest affect the shopping atmosphere at Boticca? Do you think other retailers would experience similar success with Pinterest? How about service and hospitality companies?

12 | Decision Making I: Need Recognition and Search

LEARNING OBJECTIVES

After studying this chapter, the student should be able to:

12-1 Understand the activities involved in the consumer decision-making process.

12-2 Describe the three major decision-making research perspectives.

12-3 Explain the three major types of decision-making approaches.

12-4 Understand the importance of the consideration set in the decision-making process.

12-5 Understand the factors that influence the amount of search performed by consumers.

12-1 CONSUMER DECISION MAKING

Consumers encounter problem situations each and every day. Most of the time, there are so many situations that it's hard to recall them all. You can run out of milk, be low on gasoline, search for a new apartment, take your car to the shop, and look for an outfit for a job interview all in the same day. In each of these situations, needs are recognized. When needs occur, decision making must take place. Where should I buy milk? Who has the cheapest gasoline? Should I buy an outfit from Joe Fresh or The Bay?

Some situations require big decisions. For example, when a student recognizes a need for a new laptop computer, a big decision usually follows. In other situations, the decisions are relatively small. For example, when you run out of milk, the decision of which brand, or even where to shop, usually doesn't take much time or effort.

You may recall the basic consumer behaviour consumption process that was presented in our opening chapter and is shown again in Exhibit 12.1. The process revolves around value-seeking activities that consumers perform as they go about satisfying needs. The consumer first realizes she has a particular need, and then moves through a series of steps that will help her find a desirable way to fill the need. Exchange then takes place, and she ultimately derives value from the process. As with other consumer behaviour concepts, we see that value is at the heart of the process.

The decision-making process has been added to Exhibit 12.1. As you can see, decision-making processes generally include five activities: (1) need recognition, (2) search for information, (3) evaluation of alternatives, (4) choice, and (5) postchoice evaluation. In this chapter, we focus on the first two stages of the process: need recognition and information search; Chapter 13 discusses evaluation of alternatives and choice.

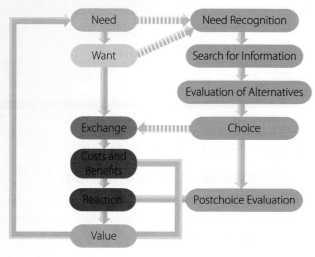

Exhibit 12.1

Basic Consumption Process and Decision Making

To better visualize this process, consider Exhibit 12.2. Here, Mike is faced with a need for a new laptop as he leaves for university. To learn about his options, he begins to read reports about laptops and he asks friends what type of laptop they think he should buy. After considering all of the information that he has gathered, he evaluates the alternatives that are realistically available. From there, he makes a choice and an exchange occurs. He then considers all the costs and benefits associated with the brand and the overall value that he has received from his purchase.

Note that the activities found in the decision-making process are not referred to as steps. The reason is that consumers do not always proceed through the activities in sequential fashion, nor do they always complete the process. Because consumers face numerous decision-making situations daily, they often decide simply to defer a decision until a later time. Consumers can also uncover additional problems or unmet needs as

Exhibit 12.2

Consumer Decision-Making Process

Process	Example
Need Recognition	Mike realizes he needs a new laptop.
Search for Information	He begins to read reports about various brands of laptops and he starts to ask his friends what type of laptop they think he should buy.
Evaluation of Alternatives	Mike compares a few brands on attributes that he considers to be important.
Choice	He makes the decision to buy a new Dell XPS.
Postchoice Evaluation	Looking back at his chioce of laptop, he considers the value that he received and thinks that he made a good overall decision.

vlad_star/Shutterstock.com

they search for information—moving them from information search to need recognition.

12-1a Decision Making and Choice

Decision-making processes lead to consumer choice. The term *choice* is important. *Choice* does not necessarily mean identifying what brand of product to buy. In fact, one of the very first choices that consumers need to make when facing a decision is whether any purchase will be made at all![1] Consumers commonly either delay the purchase of a product or forgo purchases altogether.

Decision-making processes also frequently do not involve finding a tangible product. Rather, consumers make choices about behaviours not relating directly to a purchase. For example, a consumer may be trying to decide if she should volunteer at a community theatre. Here, the decision involves whether time should be exchanged in return for greater involvement with the theatre. Thus, consumer decision making does not always focus on the purchase of a tangible product, but it does always involve choices linked to value.

DECISION MAKING AND VALUE

Both utilitarian value and hedonic value are associated with consumer decision making. As we have discussed

previously, the car-buying experience involves both value types. First, a car is in itself a means to an end. That is, owning a car enables the consumer to get from place to place. As such, an automobile delivers utilitarian value. Second, much of the car-buying (and car-owning) experience is based on hedonic value. The image associated with a particular model of car and the feelings that go with sporty handling are hedonic benefits. Many other consumption activities also provide both hedonic value and utilitarian value. For example, a $400 Coach purse may provide the same utilitarian value as an $8 purse from Walmart. However, the hedonic value of each would differ based on the feelings involved with consumption.

Value perceptions also influence the activities found in the decision-making process itself. For example, consumers generally continue searching for information about products only as long as the perceived benefits that come from searching exceed the perceived costs associated with the process.

DECISION MAKING AND MOTIVATION

As discussed in chapter 5, motivations are the inner reasons or driving forces behind human actions as consumers attempt to address needs. It isn't surprising, therefore, that decision making and motivation are closely related concepts.[2] For example, a student may

Decision Making 101

For many young consumers, selecting a university is a big decision. The educational landscape has become quite competitive, and students now regularly receive information and brochures from prospective universities while they are in their early high school years, if not sooner.

Experts in the area of postsecondary school choice suggest that students pay close attention to finding the university that fits best with their personal needs and goals. The closest university isn't always the best solution for students, even though the familiar names may be attractive. Similarly, the "top-ranked" schools may not offer the best fit for a particular student. For this reason, students are encouraged to search carefully for relevant information by visiting websites, talking with guidance counsellors, taking campus tours, and seeking out independent research sources. The information provided can go a long way toward helping them reach a final decision. Although students may spend only a handful of years on a university campus, this choice can have a profound impact on the rest of their lives.

Sources: Based on Coleman, Christina (2007), "The 'Best' School Might Not Be Best for You," *Chronicle of Higher Education*, 52 (44): p. 66. Conboy, Katie (2007), "Big-Name Schools Aren't Always Best," *Christian Science Monitor*, 99 (69): p. 9; Knight, Mimi Greenwood (2006), "The Beginner's Guide to the College Search," *Ignite Your Faith*, 65 (3): pp. 44–46.

---

notice that the ink in his printer is low and perceive a need to fix the problem (a utilitarian motivation). Or, the same student may be bored on a Saturday afternoon and decide to play paintball (a hedonic motivation). The relationship between decision making and motivation is well known and almost all consumer decisions revolve around goal-pursuit.[3]

DECISION MAKING AND EMOTION

Consumer decision making is also closely related to emotion. The decision-making process can be very emotional depending on the type of product being considered or the need that has arisen. Because the decision-making process can be draining, consumers frequently have feelings of frustration, irritation, or even anger as they attempt to satisfy needs. This is especially true when consumers must make difficult decisions, cannot find acceptable solutions to problems, or must make tradeoffs by giving up one alternative for another.[4] As a university student, you may soon face the difficult task of deciding which job offer to take. Perhaps there will be a job offer many kilometres away, or one that is closer to your family. Decisions like these can be quite emotional.

12-2 DECISION-MAKING PERSPECTIVES

Consumer researchers view the decision-making process from three perspectives: the rational decision-making perspective, the experiential decision-making perspective, and the behavioural influence decision-making perspective.[5] These perspectives are similar to the attitude hierarchies that we discussed in our attitude chapter.

It is important to remember two important aspects of these perspectives. First, each perspective serves as a theoretical framework from which decision making can be viewed. That is, the perspectives pertain to how consumer researchers view the decision-making process, and they are not consumer decision-making strategies. Second, most consumer decisions can be analyzed from a combination of these perspectives. In fact, it is unlikely that a consumer ever makes a decision entirely rationally, experientially, or behaviourally. Instead, these different influences on decision making have varying degrees of influence on consumer choice that change across contexts and people. The perspectives are presented in Exhibit 12.3.

Exhibit 12.3

Perspectives on Consumer Decision Making

Perspective	Description	Example
Rational Perspective	Consumers are rational and they carefully arrive at decisions.	Aubrey carefully considers the attributes included with various car stereos.
Experiential Perspective	Decision making is often influenced by the feelings associated with consumption.	Devin goes rock climbing simply for the fun of it.
Behavioural Influence Perspective	Decisions are responses to environmental influences.	The soothing music in the store encourages Shelby to browse longer.

12-2a Rational Decision-Making Perspective

The early study of consumer decision making centred upon what is referred to as the rational decision-making perspective. This perspective is considered by many to be the traditional approach to studying decision making. The **rational decision-making perspective** assumes that consumers diligently gather information about purchases, carefully compare various brands of products on salient attributes, and make informed decisions regarding what brand to buy. This approach centres on the assumption that human beings are rational creatures who carefully consider their decisions and that they can identify the expected value associated with a purchase. The act of selecting either cable or satellite television often follows a rational process. Consumers will tend to compare service, features, and prices carefully when making these purchases. In addition, because there are only a few options in any given region, it is relatively easy to make a more complete comparison between alternatives. The rational perspective fits very well with the concept of utilitarian value.

Even though the rational perspective makes sense, we cannot assume that consumers follow this process in all situations. In fact, consumers often make purchases and satisfy needs with very little cognitive effort or rationality. We simply don't want to think extensively about every single product choice that we make. Nor could we!

The assumption that consumers are "rational" is also debatable. Of course, what is rational to some may be irrational to others. Paying thousands of dollars for a single season ticket to a sporting event could hardly be considered rational to some, but sports fans do it every single year! Although researchers focused on the rational perspective for several years, the experiential and behavioural influence perspectives have recently gained significant attention.

12-2b Experiential Decision-Making Perspective

The **experiential decision-making perspective** assumes that consumers often make purchases and reach decisions based on the affect, or feeling, attached to the product or behaviour under consideration. Recall from the discussion in our attitude chapter that consumers sometimes follow a "feel–do–think" hierarchy. That is, behaviours are based largely on the sheer enjoyment involved with consumption rather than on extensive cognitive effort.

Experiential decision processes often focus on hedonic value. For example, although we may make a fairly rational decision when choosing our cable TV provider, choosing which TV show we watch tonight is probably better characterized as an experiential decision. Here, decisions are based on feeling—not on a drawn-out decision-making process. That is, the value comes from the experience, not from an end result.

rational decision-making perspective
assumes consumers diligently gather information about purchases, carefully compare various brands of products on salient attributes, and make informed decisions regarding what brand to buy

experiential decision-making perspective
assumes consumers often make purchases and reach decisions based on the affect, or feeling, attached to the product or behaviour under consideration

Hedonic value often results from experiential decision making.

12-2c Behavioural Influence Decision-Making Perspective

The **behavioural influence decision-making perspective** assumes that many decisions are actually learned responses to environmental influences. For example, soft music and dim lighting can have a strong influence on consumer behaviour in a restaurant. These influences generally lead consumers to slow down, stay in the restaurant for a longer time, and buy more drinks and dessert. Here, behaviour is influenced by environmental forces rather than by cognitive decision making. For example, being at home on a Sunday night in the springtime might influence you to turn on the TV to watch HBO's *Game of Thrones*.

The behavioural influence perspective also helps explain how consumers react to store layout, store design, point-of-purchase (POP) displays, and in-store samples (see the "Sampling Costco" case at the end of this chapter). Traffic flows in a grocery store greatly influence grocery shopping behaviour. In fact, consumers often buy products that are placed on display simply because they are on display! Retailers use the "brand-lift index" to measure the incremental sales that occur when a product is on display. Lift indices can be impressive. In fact, one study indicated that POP displays in convenience stores can increase product sales by nearly 10%. This is a sizable amount. Considering that incremental sales opportunities for POP materials in grocery stores can be in the billions of dollars, retailers should pay close attention to the behavioural influence perspective![6]

12-3 DECISION-MAKING APPROACHES

Consumers reach decisions in a number of different ways. The decision-making approach that is used depends heavily on the amount of involvement a consumer has with a product category or purchase and the amount of purchase risk involved with the decision. Note that involvement can be associated with the product, the purchase situation, or both. In general, as involvement and risk increase, consumers are motivated to move more carefully through the decision-making process.

You may remember from an earlier chapter that consumer involvement represents the degree of personal relevance that a consumer finds in pursuing value from a given act. **Perceived risk** refers to the perception of the negative consequences that are likely to result from a course of action and the uncertainty of which course of action is best to take. Consumers face several types of risk, including:[7]

▶ **Financial risk**, associated with the cost of the product

▶ **Social risk**, associated with how other consumers will view the purchase

▶ **Performance risk**, associated with the likelihood of a product performing as expected

▶ **Physical risk**, associated with the safety of the product and the likelihood that physical harm will result from its consumption

▶ **Time risk**, associated with the time required to search for the product and the time necessary for the product to be serviced or maintained

Risk varies across consumers and situations. For example, signing a year-long apartment lease is a financially risky process for most consumers. For the very wealthy, this may not be the case at all. Likewise, buying a new dress shirt is usually not perceived as being risky, unless one is making the purchase to wear on a first date!

Decision-making approaches can be classified into three categories: extended decision making, limited decision making, and habitual (or "routine") decision making.

behavioural influence decision-making perspective assumes many consumer decisions are actually learned responses to environmental influences

perceived risk perception of the negative consequences that are likely to result from a course of action and the uncertainty of which course of action is best to take

Exhibit 12.4

Decision-Making Approaches

Remember, these are approaches that consumers use, and they differ from the researcher perspectives discussed previously. Exhibit 12.4 presents these categories in the form of a continuum based on involvement and risk.

12-3a Extended Decision Making

When consumers engage in **extended decision making**, they tend to search diligently for information that will help them reach a satisfactory decision. This information can come from both internal sources (e.g., previous experiences) and external sources (e.g., websites). Consumers carefully assimilate the information they have gathered and evaluate each alternative based on its potential to satisfy their needs. This process is generally rather lengthy. Extended decision making occurs when involvement is high and when there is a significant amount of purchase risk involved with the decision. Expensive products such as houses, automobiles, and televisions are usually purchased only after an extended decision-making process has occurred.

12-3b Limited Decision Making

With **limited decision making**, consumers search very little for information and often reach decisions based on prior beliefs about products and their attributes. There is little comparison between brands. Given the time constraints that consumers often feel, this type of decision making occurs with great frequency. Limited decision making usually occurs when there are relatively low amounts of purchase risk and product involvement. For example, a consumer may need to buy a new roll of adhesive tape, and there may be very few attributes that are considered in the process. Perhaps the consumer will want to find a roll that is designed to be "invisible." Any brand that offers this feature would likely be selected.

12-3c Habitual Decision Making

With **habitual decision making** (sometimes referred to as "routine" decision making), consumers generally do not seek information at all when a problem is recognized. Choice is often based on habit. Here, consumers generally have a specific brand in mind that will solve the problem, and they believe that the consumption of the product will deliver value. For example, most consumers have a favourite type of soft drink that they habitually buy when they are thirsty.

Two topics are of special importance concerning habitual decision making: *brand loyalty* and *brand inertia*. **Brand loyalty** may be defined as a deeply held commitment to rebuy a product or service regardless of situational influences that could lead to switching behaviour.[8] For a consumer to be truly brand loyal, he or she must have a bond with the product and believe that the consumption activity delivers value. Companies often attempt to reward loyalty with rewards programs as found in frequent flyer miles, hotel reward points, and credit card cash-back deals. However, in order for these tactics to be successful, consumers must ultimately value both the product and the incentives offered.[9] This leads to a key difference between loyalty and what is referred to as brand inertia. **Brand inertia** is present when a consumer simply buys a product repeatedly without any real attachment. Loyalty, on the other hand, includes an attitudinal component that reflects a true affection

extended decision making assumes consumers move diligently through various problem-solving activities in search of the best information that will help them reach a decision

limited decision making consumers search very little for information and often reach decisions based largely on prior beliefs about products and their attributes

habitual decision making consumers generally do not seek information at all when a problem is recognized and select a product based on habit

brand loyalty deeply held commitment to rebuy a product or service regardless of situational influences that could lead to switching behaviour

brand inertia what occurs when a consumer simply buys a product repeatedly without any real attachment

Isn't Variety a Good Thing?

It is easy to think that a little variety is a good thing. A common problem for consumers today is that in many situations there are simply *too many alternatives* from which to choose. A simple walk down any grocery store aisle will confirm that the average consumer is bombarded with hundreds—if not thousands—of product varieties every day. Although previous generations often faced the problem of not having enough products to choose from, today there are often too many!

When should a shopper stop looking for information? Frequently, the answer comes when one finds an acceptable, rather than optimal, solution. This is what satisficing is all about. Shoppers often simply focus on finding the first alternative that meets their minimum requirements. So, instead of finding the best paper towel available, they'll simply look for the one that delivers an acceptable level of value and move on. The decision-making process becomes much easier for consumers who "satisfice."

Ragnarock/Shutterstock.com

Sources: Douglas, Kate, and Dan Jones (2007), "How to Make Better Choices," *New Scientist*, 194 (2652), 35–43. Pelusi, Nando (2007), "When to Choose Is to Lose," *Psychology Today*, 40 (5), 69–70. Moyer, Don (2007), "Satisficing," *Harvard Business Review*, (April), 144. Wright, Peter (1975), "Consumer Choices Strategies: Simplifying vs. Optimizing," *Journals of Marketing Research*, 12 (February), 60–67.

Courtesy SCENE

Reward cards can be a successful method of rewarding loyalty if consumers value both the product and the incentives offered.

for the product.[10] Strictly speaking, a consumer is not considered loyal if she simply buys the same product habitually.

Brand loyalty affects consumption value in a number of ways. First, loyalty enables consumers to reduce searching time drastically by insisting on the brand to which they are loyal. This leads to a benefit of convenience. Second, loyalty creates value for a consumer through the benefits associated with brand image. Ford trucks are well known for their ruggedness and durability, and the Ford image is one benefit of owning the product. Finally, loyalty enables consumers to enjoy the benefits that come from long-term relationships with companies.

For example, a consumer might enjoy special incentives that are offered to long-time Ford purchasers.

Brand loyalty also has an impact on the value of the brand to the firm. As branding expert David Aaker asserts, consumer brand loyalty influences the value of a product to a firm because (1) it costs much less to retain current customers than to attract new ones, and (2) highly loyal customers generate predictable revenue streams.[11] As can be seen, brand loyalty has benefits for both the consumer and the marketer. Brand loyalty is discussed in more detail in a subsequent chapter.

FINAL THOUGHT ON DECISION-MAKING APPROACHES

Consumers go through decision-making processes, but these processes do not guarantee maximum value from a consumption experience. Consumers often make mistakes or settle for alternatives that they are really unsure about. In reality, many consumer purchases are made with very little prepurchase decision effort.[12] Most purchases made on a daily basis are low-involvement purchases that do not entail significant risk. Also, consumers are not always motivated to make the "best" decision. In fact, in many situations, consumers engage in what is called **satisficing**—using decision-making shortcuts to arrive at satisfactory, rather than optimal, decisions.[13] When a consumer says to herself

satisficing using decision-making shortcuts to arrive at satisfactory, rather than optimal, decisions

"This is good enough," satisficing has occurred. Time pressures, search fatigue, and budgetary constraints often lead consumers to engage in satisficing.

12-4 NEED RECOGNITION, INTERNAL SEARCH, AND THE CONSIDERATION SET

As we have discussed, the recognition of a need leads the consumer to begin searching for information. Several important issues are relevant here.

12-4a Need Recognition

The decision-making process begins with the recognition of a need. Simply put, a need is recognized when a consumer perceives a difference between an actual state and a desired state. A consumer's **actual state** is his or her perceived current state, while the **desired state** is the perceived state for which the consumer strives. A consumer recognizes a need when there is a gap between these two. Note that either the actual state or the desired state can change, leading to a perceptual imbalance between the two. When the actual state begins to drop, for example when a consumer runs out of deodorant, a need is recognized. Obviously, needs like this are recognized on a regular basis. Importantly, however, marketers also focus on what they term *opportunity recognition*. Here, a consumer's actual state doesn't change, but his or her desired state changes in some significant way.

To illustrate how a desired state can be changed, consider how happy consumers once were with their cellphones—that is, before the iPhone was released. After the iPhone was introduced, the desired state for many consumers changed dramatically. Phones became much more than just phones. Apple then introduced the iPad and tablet devices quickly became commonplace. More recently, Apple introduced the iWatch. What will be the next consumer technology to dramatically change consumers' desired states?

Desired states can be affected by many factors, including reference group information, consumer novelty seeking, and cognitive thought processes.[14] As we discussed in our group influence chapter, reference groups are important sources of information for consumers and the information that

Will the recently introduced iWatch impact consumers' desired state?

is gathered from others directly affects what consumers think they should do and what types of products they think they should buy. Desired states are also influenced by novelty. Many times consumers desire to try a new product simply because of boredom or because of a motivation to engage in variety-seeking. Finally, consumers have the ability to cognitively plan their actions by anticipating future needs. For example, university graduates realize after graduation that they face the need for all types of insurance they may not have considered before, including life, disability, and homeowner's insurance.

Not all needs are satisfied quickly, nor does the recognition of a need always trigger the other activities found in the decision-making process. Value is again important here. If the end goal is not highly valued, consumers may simply put off a decision. For example, a consumer may realize that the leather on the seat of her bicycle has ripped, but this does not necessarily mean that she will begin to search for information on where to buy a new seat. She may simply realize that there is a problem that eventually needs to be fixed. In fact, she may have to be reminded of this need several times before she does anything about it, or, she may decide to do nothing at all about it. For instance, she may simply sell her bike and buy a new one. From this example, we are again reminded of why we don't refer to the activities found in decision making as steps. That is, the sequential ordering of the activities is not concrete.

We should once again clarify the distinction between a want and a need. Both of these terms have been discussed in a previous chapter. As you may remember,

actual state consumer's perceived current state

desired state perceived state for which a consumer strives

Luxury brands appeal to customers' desired states.

a want is the way in which a consumer goes about addressing a need. It's quite common for marketers to be criticized for attempting to turn wants into needs. For example, a consumer may want to fulfill a need for transporting personal items by buying an expensive purse from Prada or Coach, even though a much less expensive purse would suffice.

12-4b Search Behaviour

When consumers perceive a difference between an actual state (an empty gas tank) and a desired state (a full tank), the decision-making process is triggered.[15] **Consumer search behaviour** refers to the behaviours that consumers engage in as they seek information that can be used to satisfy needs. Consumers seek all types of information about potential solutions to needs, including: (1) the number of alternatives available, (2) the price of various alternatives, (3) the relevant attributes that should be considered and their importance, and (4) the performance of each alternative on the attributes.[16] Consumer search behaviours can be categorized in a number of ways, including ongoing search, prepurchase search, internal search, and external search.

ONGOING AND PREPURCHASE SEARCH

A consumer performs an **ongoing search** when she seeks information simply because she is interested in a particular topic (such as a product or an organization). Here, the search effort is not necessarily focused on an upcoming purchase or decision; rather the effort is focused on simply staying up to date on a topic of interest. Consumers who perform ongoing searches are usually highly involved with the product category and seek information simply for enjoyment. They also tend to spend more in the relevant product category than do consumers who do not regularly search for information.[17]

Prepurchase search activities are focused on locating information that will enable the consumer to reach a decision for a specific problem. These searches are purchase-specific. A prepurchase search can also be exhibited in browsing behaviour. When consumers browse, they are simply gathering information that can be used in decisions that involve a longer time frame. Note that browsing and ongoing searches are similar. The difference between ongoing searches and browsing behaviour is that an ongoing search is performed when consumers have an enduring interest in or involvement with the product, not simply when information is being gathered for a specific purchase.

The concept of information search has changed dramatically in recent years due to the mass adoption of the Internet as well as the proliferation of mobile information technologies like smartphones and tablets. In today's environment, finding information generally isn't a problem. The problem is that there is simply too much information out there[18] and consumers are suffering from **information overload**—being presented with so much information that they cannot assimilate it all. One way that consumers can try to minimize information overload in the online environment is by joining a

consumer search behaviour behaviours that consumers engage in as they seek information that can be used to resolve a problem

ongoing search search effort that is not necessarily focused on an upcoming purchase or decision but rather on staying up to date on the topic

prepurchase search search effort aimed at finding information to solve an immediate problem

information overload situation in which consumers are presented with so much information that they cannot assimilate it all specific group for a product or brand on a site like Facebook. By focusing specifically on a group or fan page, consumers are able to look for relevant information in one place and can gain a sense of whom they can and cannot trust for information. Information search on social network sites can be either ongoing or prepurchase.

12-4c The Consideration Set

Internal search includes the retrieval of knowledge about products, services, and experiences that is stored in memory. This type of knowledge is related directly to consumers' experiences with products and services. When confronted with a need, consumers begin to scan their memories for available solutions to the problem that can aid in decision making. As such, consumers most often perform internal searches before any other type of search begins.

Marketers find it valuable to understand the **consideration set** of their customers in order to learn about the total number of brands, or alternatives, that are considered in consumer decision making.[19] The conceptualization of a consideration set is presented in Exhibit 12.5.

The total collection of all possible solutions to a recognized need (e.g., the total number of brands of deodorant available on the market) is referred to as the **universal set** of alternatives. Although the universal set may be quite large, consumers generally do not realize how many solutions are potentially available when a need arises. In fact, decision making is limited by what is referred to as the **awareness set** which is, quite simply, the set of brands or alternatives of which a consumer is aware. Alternatives that have been

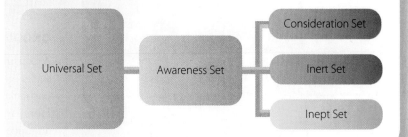

Exhibit 12.5
Consideration Set

previously selected are included in this set,[20] and the size of the awareness set increases as external search proceeds.

Within the awareness set, three categories of alternatives are found. The first is the consideration set (or the "evoked set"), which includes the brands, or alternatives, that are considered acceptable for further consideration in decision making. There are also alternatives in the awareness set that are deemed to be unacceptable for further consideration; these alternatives make up the **inept set**. The **inert set** includes those alternatives to which consumers are indifferent, or for which strong feelings are not held.

Exhibit 12.5 demonstrates how the size of both the awareness set and the consideration set is smaller than the universal set. This is because, for most decisions, these sets are much smaller than the universal set. Research confirms that consumers generally consider only a small fraction of the actual number of problem solutions that are available.[21] Note that although the consideration set is held internally in a consumer's memory, alternatives that are found in external search can be added to the set as the decision-making process continues. Of course, good marketers ensure that their brands are placed in consumers' consideration sets.

12-5 EXTERNAL SEARCH

Frequently, consumers do not have stored in their memories enough information that will lead to adequate problem solving. For this reason, external search efforts are often necessary. **External search** includes the gathering of information from sources external to the consumer, including friends, family, salespeople,

internal search retrieval of knowledge stored in memory about products, services, and experiences

consideration set alternatives that are considered acceptable for further consideration in decision making

universal set total collection of all possible solutions to a consumer problem

awareness set set of alternatives of which a consumer is aware

inept set alternatives in the awareness set that are deemed to be unacceptable for further consideration

inert set alternatives in the awareness set about which consumers are indifferent or do not hold strong feelings

external search gathering of information from sources external to the consumer such as friends, family, salespeople, advertising, independent research reports, and the Internet advertising, independent research reports (such as *Consumer Reports*), or the Internet. In selecting the best information source, consumers consider factors such as:

▶ **The ease of obtaining information from the source**

▶ **The objectivity of the source**

▶ **The trustworthiness of the source**

▶ **The speed with which the information can be obtained**

In general, consumers find that information from family and friends is dependable but that information from commercial sources (like advertising or salespeople) is less credible for input into decision making.[22]

12-5a The Role of Price and Quality in the Search Process

The term *evaluative criteria* is used to refer to the attributes of a product that consumers consider when reviewing possible solutions to a problem. Many things can become evaluative criteria. However, two evaluative criteria are used across almost all consumer decisions: price and quality. Consumers tend to seek out information about these concepts early in the search process, and they play important roles in external search.

Price represents an important type of information that consumers generally seek. Specifically, **price** is information signalling how much potential value may be derived from consuming something.

Generally, we think of a high price as being a bad thing. In other words, a higher price means greater sacrifice to obtain some product. This view of price is referred to as the negative role of price. From this view, needless to say, a lower price is more desirable. Some consumers are very sensitive to the negative role of price. They tend to be very bargain conscious and do things like collect and redeem coupons.

However, a positive role of price also exists. In this sense, price signals how desirable a product is

and how much prestige may be associated with owning the product. Some consumers are more sensitive to the positive role of price and tend to desire things with high prices as a way of signalling prestige and desirability to others.[23] You may remember from an earlier discussion that a backward-sloping demand curve is not necessarily rare.

Consider a consumer shopping for a new outfit to wear "out on the town." She may find a cute outfit at Target, but this outfit may not offer enough value given that it will be worn in a socially sensitive situation. Therefore, she may opt for a higher-priced outfit that may be somewhat similar. The higher price will signal more prestige. Thus, she may feel more comfortable shopping at Banana Republic or some other more prestigious fashion retailer.

Consumers also commonly search for information about a product's quality as an important evaluative criterion. Although quality can mean many things to many people, from a consumer perspective, **quality** represents the perceived overall goodness or badness of some product. In other words, consumers generally use the word *quality* as a synonym for relative goodness. A high-quality hotel room is a good hotel room and a low-quality hotel room is a bad hotel room.

Quality perceptions take place both before and after purchase. However, consumers do not always seek high quality because many times, consumers do not need the "best" product available. Although a Motel 6 may not offer as high quality of an experience as does a Four Seasons hotel, it does adequately address the need for a place to sleep on a cross-country drive.

Consumers almost always use price and quality when making decisions. Indeed, price and quality perceptions are related as consumers generally assume that higher prices mean higher quality. This issue is discussed in more detail in our next chapter.

Terri Miller/ E-Visual Communications, Inc.

Price and quality perceptions are related, as consumers generally assume that higher prices mean higher quality.

price information that signals the amount of potential value contained in a product

quality perceived overall goodness or badness of some product

12-5b External Search and the Internet

As discussed previously, in today's fast-paced, information-rich environment, a tremendous amount of information is at our fingertips. There's no denying that the Internet has quickly become a popular consumer search tool.[24] Due to the popularity of various search engines like Google and Bing as well as social networking sites like Facebook, consumers can find solutions to all sorts of problems online. Of course, this has simplified search processes to a large extent.

The Internet improves consumer search activities in several ways. First, the Internet can lower the costs associated with search and can also make the process more productive.[25] Second, the search process itself can be enjoyable and deliver hedonic value to the consumer.[26] Third, consumers have the ability to control information flow much more efficiently than if they are viewing product information on a television commercial or hearing about a product from radio ads. In general, the ability to control information flow increases the value of information and increases the consumers' ability to remember information that is gathered.[27] Of course, consumers may also buy products directly from companies that place sponsored advertisements on search engines and social media sites. This greatly affects the ease of consumer online shopping behaviour.

Studies have indicated that Internet search behaviour depends heavily on website construction. For example, one recent study found that consumers spend more time searching in three-dimensional, interactive web environments than in two-dimensional web spaces. However, the study also revealed that the number of brands examined was actually higher for two-dimensional web pages than for three-dimensional sites.[28] Of course, website design is very important! We can expect consumers to use the Internet for search activities even more as computer availability becomes more widespread and as mobile technologies continue to be embraced.

12-5c Amount of Search

The amount of search that a consumer performs related to decision making can be measured in a number of ways, including the number of stores visited, the number of Internet sites visited, the number of personal sources (friends, family, salespeople) used, the number of alternatives considered, and the number of advertisements studied.

Many factors influence information search effort, including previous experience with a product,

involvement, perceived risk, value of search effort, time availability, attitudes toward shopping, personal factors, and situational influencers.[29]

PRODUCT EXPERIENCE

Prior experience with a product has been shown to influence how much a consumer searches. A number of researchers have examined this issue, sometimes with conflicting results. As a general statement, evidence shows that moderately experienced consumers search for purchase-related information more than do either experienced or inexperienced consumers, as shown in Exhibit 12.6.[30]

One explanation for the finding that moderately experienced consumers search more than other consumers is that individuals with little experience are unable to make fine distinctions between product differences and will likely see product alternatives as being similar. As such, they find little value in extensive information search. Highly experienced consumers can make fine distinctions between products and may know so much about products that they do not need to search at all. Moderately experienced consumers, on the other hand, perceive some differences among brands and are more likely to value information about these distinctions.[31]

Involvement. As noted earlier, purchase involvement is positively associated with search activities, especially for ongoing searches. Because involvement represents a level of arousal and interest in a product,

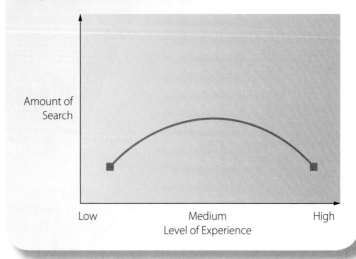

Exhibit 12.6

Experience and External Search

search tends to increase when a consumer possesses a high level of purchase involvement.[32]

Perceived Risk. As perceived risk increases, search effort increases.[33] As discussed earlier in the chapter, a number of risks can be associated with the consumption act, including financial, social, performance, physical, and time risks. Consumers are usually motivated to reduce these risks as much as possible and will therefore expend considerable time and effort in searching for information.

Value of Search Effort. Value can be obtained from the search process itself. When the benefits received from searching exceed the associated costs, consumers derive value. When searching costs are greater than the benefits of the search process, consumers no longer value the activity and search stops.[34] Costs associated with search can be either monetary (e.g., the cost of driving around town looking for a new bedroom dresser) or nonmonetary (e.g., psychological or physical exhaustion or stress). Even online searching brings about certain mental costs.[35]

Time Availability. All other things being equal, more time to spend on search usually results in increased search activity.[36] Because time is valued so highly by most consumers, search will decrease when time constraints are present.

Attitude Toward Shopping. Consumers who value shopping and who possess positive attitudes toward shopping generally spend more time searching for product information.[37]

Personal Factors. Search tends to increase as a consumer's level of education and income increases. Search also tends to decrease as consumers become older.[38]

Situational Influencers. Situational factors also influence the amount of search that takes place. Perceived urgency, financial pressure, and mood can all affect search behaviour. The purchase occasion can also affect the search. Consumers sometimes have such an urgent need for a product that they will select the first option they come across. When a product is being purchased as a gift, the amount of search will depend on the relationship between the giver and the receiver and on the amount of time before the occasion.

EXTERNAL SEARCH OFTEN MINIMIZED

While many factors influence the amount of search that takes place, consumers tend to search surprisingly little

Pay to Play

One controversial method for introducing new products to consumers requires marketers to pay retailers what are known as "slotting allowances" or "slotting fees." Slotting allowances are sums of money that are paid by a vendor to a retailer for specific locations or shelf placement in a store. These fees are often required for new products and can play a big role in the success of these products.

One advantage of slotting allowances is that they help balance the risk of new products between both vendors and retailers. They also signal how valuable a new product is for a vendor. Vendors often have better information about the likely success of a new product than do retailers. Accordingly, the amount paid by a vendor can be a signal of the attractiveness of the product.

Critics often charge that these allowances represent a type of extortion on the part of retailers. Retailers, on the other hand, recognize the value of prime retail location in supporting product success. Regardless of the views of vendors or retailers, consumers are often unaware that slotting fees have often been paid in an effort to introduce new products. New products enter the consumer's consideration set at a cost!

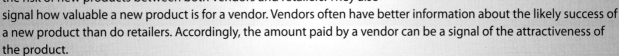

Adapted from: Sudhir, K. and Vithala Rao (2006), "Do Slotting Allowances Enhance Efficiency or Hinder Competition?", *Journal of Marketing Research*, 43 (May): 137–155; Davis, Ronald W. (2001), "Slotting Allowances and Antitrust," *Antitrust*, 15 (2), Spring, pp. 69–76; Anonymous (2005), "Slotting Allowances—A Good Thing," *Chain Store Age*, (May), p. 43.

for most products.[39] This is true for both high- and low-involvement products. Consumers may already have a stored rule in memory for low-involvement products and may engage in extensive ongoing search activities and have acceptable alternative solutions in mind for high-involvement categories.[40]

12-5d Search Regret

As we have discussed, emotions and decision making are closely related topics. The search process can lead directly to emotional responses for consumers as well. The term **search regret** refers to the negative emotions that come from failed search processes. Many times, consumers are simply not able to find an acceptable solution to their problems. As a result, the decision-making process stops. In these situations, consumers may feel as if the entire search process was a waste of time, and they will start to feel search regret. Regret is related to the amount of search effort,

search regret negative emotions that come from failed search processes

the emotions felt during the process, and the use of unfamiliar search techniques.[41]

Many issues relate to the topics of need recognition and search. Our next chapter discusses evaluation of alternatives and choice.

STUDY TOOLS 12

LOCATED AT THE BACK OF THE TEXTBOOK

☐ Rip out Chapter Review Card

LOCATED AT NELSON.COM/STUDENT

☐ Review Key Terms Flashcards (print or online)

☐ Download audio summaries to review on the go

☐ Complete practice quizzes to prepare for tests

☐ Watch video on Scholfield Honda for a real company example

Case

Sampling Costco

With annual sales of just over $100 billion, Costco is the second largest retailer in North America (behind Walmart) and the fourth largest in the world. The company's Canadian same-store sales have been growing rapidly and it continues to open new stores across the country.

Yet, Costco is a very unusual retailer. In contrast to conventional wisdom, which urges specialization, the company carries products in an incredibly diverse array of categories ranging from grocery to tires to jewellery. For example, to the surprise of many observers, Costco recently surpassed Whole Foods as North America's largest organic grocer with sales in that category of more than $3.6 billion! It could also be considered one of the largest fast food restaurants in North America, with in-store pizzerias and sales of almost 100 million hot dogs per year.

Another unique aspect of the company's business model is its membership fee. More than 10 million Canadians pay $55 or more per year for the privilege of shopping at Costco and more than 90% of customers renew that membership every year. In fact, those membership fees generate the majority of the company's pretax profits!

As a retailer, the company focuses on getting products into stores and out to consumers at very low prices, often in large sizes for bulk buying. This approach can mean that the products and brands that Costco is selling one day will be unavailable a few weeks later. Many items are temporary and, the next time the customer visits Costco, they may well be out of stock. Yet, even with the sporadic nature of the company's large and diverse inventory, loyalty is not a problem for Costco. It might be an advantage as customers talk to each other and come to the store to see what deals they can get this week. Unlike traditional grocery or general merchandise chains—such as Walmart, Loblaws, Target, or Canadian Tire—Costco does very little advertising and instead relies heavily on consumer word-of-mouth.

When customers do visit a store, they tend to have only a general idea of what they will buy. Instead, they plan to look at what the store has to offer before finalizing their decisions. This creates a perfect opportunity

to use product samples to increase sales and enhance the shopping experience. Research indicates that three-quarters of people who are offered a free sample take one and that once people take a sample they are substantially more likely to buy the product. For example, *The Atlantic* magazine reported on a study of yogurt and found that almost 60% of samplers purchased the product, compared to only 15% of nonsamplers. For frozen pizza and bagels, more than 20% of shoppers who sampled the items made a purchase, while those who did not sample the food did not purchase those products. In extreme cases, samples have been shown to boost sales by 2,000%!

Overall, Costco's business model makes it different from other retailers, but those differences have created a loyal customer base that enjoys sampling the unique shopping environment.

Adapted from: Sudhir, K. and Vithala Rao (2006), "Do Slotting Allowances Enhance Efficiency or Hinder Competition?", *Journal of Marketing Research*, 43 (May): 137–155; Davis, Ronald W. (2001), "Slotting Allowances and Antitrust," *Antitrust*, 15 (2), Spring, pps. 69–76; Anonymous (2005), "Slotting Allowances—A Good Thing," *Chain Store Age*, (May), p. 43.

QUESTIONS

1 How do utilitarian and hedonic values influence the choices that consumers make when shopping at Costco?

2 Would you consider a Costco shopper to be a habitual decision maker? Are Costco shoppers likely to be loyal based on brand inertia?

3 How do Costco's samples influence consumers' learned responses to the environment?

4 What consumer risks does Costco alleviate? Does it create risks that wouldn't exist in a more traditional retail shopping environment?

5 How does Costco influence consumer search and the creation of a consideration set?

6 What is the likely impact of in-store samples on search regret?

MindTap®

MindTap empowers students.
Personalized content in an easy-to-use interface
helps you achieve better grades.

The new **MindTap Mobile App** allows for learning anytime, anywhere with flashcards, quizzes and notifications.

The **MindTap Reader** lets you highlight and take notes online, right within the pages, and easily reference them later.

www.nelson.com/mindtap

13 | Decision Making II: Alternative Evaluation and Choice

LEARNING OBJECTIVES

After studying this chapter, the student should be able to:

13-1 Understand the difference between evaluative criteria and determinant criteria.

13-2 Comprehend how value affects the evaluation of alternatives.

13-3 Explain the importance of product categorization in the evaluation of alternatives process.

13-4 Distinguish between compensatory and noncompensatory rules that guide consumer choice.

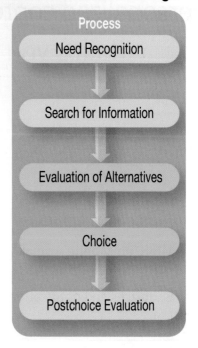

Paper Boat Creative/Getty Images

INTRODUCTION

Selecting a new apartment is obviously a big decision with many issues to consider. Which location is best? How much rent will I have to pay? Is this apartment complex safe? Are utilities included in the rent? What kind of lease do I have to sign? Making a final decision can be draining. Thankfully, not every decision we face is this difficult.

As you will remember from our first decision-making chapter, the decision-making process includes need recognition, search for information, alternative evaluation, choice, and postchoice evaluation. The decision-making model is shown once again in Exhibit 13.1.

In the current chapter, we focus on evaluation of alternatives and choice.

13-1 EVALUATION OF ALTERNATIVES: CRITERIA

A very important part of decision making is evaluating alternative solutions to problems. As we have discussed throughout this text, consumers are bombarded daily by

Exhibit 13.1

Consumer Decision-Making Process

Process

Need Recognition

↓

Search for Information

↓

Evaluation of Alternatives

↓

Choice

↓

Postchoice Evaluation

a blistering array of product varieties, brands, and experiences from which to choose. For example, consumers can select from hundreds of varieties of breakfast cereals, snack foods, and athletic shoes. Musical choices are no different. A quick look at a popular music site like iTunes reveals thousands of songs to download! Trying to make sense out of all the alternatives can be very difficult. Fortunately, consumer researchers have learned much about how consumers evaluate alternatives. The first thing to understand is how consumers select criteria that can be used in differentiating one alternative from another.

13-1a Evaluative Criteria

After a need is recognized and a search process has taken place, consumers begin to examine the criteria that will be used for making a choice. **Evaluative criteria** are the attributes, features, or potential benefits that consumers consider when reviewing possible solutions to a problem. A **feature** is a performance characteristic of an object. Remember from our attitude chapter that features are often referred to as attributes. A **benefit** is a perceived favourable result that is derived from the presence of a particular feature.[1] A timer button on a coffee maker is a

feature. A benefit of the button is that it keeps consumers from having to wait for hot coffee in the morning.

Benefits play an important role in the value equation. Consumers don't really buy a coffee maker because of a timer button. What they really want is hot coffee as soon as possible! If there was some other way to deliver this benefit without the button, consumers would be quick to buy this other solution. You may remember that benefits represent "what you get" in the value equation.

$$\text{Value} = \underset{\text{(Benefits)}}{\text{What you get}} - \underset{\text{(Costs)}}{\text{What you give}}$$

13-1b Determinant Criteria

Not all evaluative criteria are equally important. **Determinant criteria** (sometimes called determinant attributes) are the evaluative criteria that are related to the actual choice that is made.[2]

evaluative criteria attributes that consumers consider when reviewing alternative solutions to a problem

feature performance characteristic of an object

benefit perceived favourable result derived from a particular feature

Screen size is an important feature for a phablet.

Consumers don't always reveal, or may not even know, the criteria that truly are determinant. This is true even when several attributes are considered to be important. For example, airline safety is definitely an important feature of an airline, and consumers would quickly voice this opinion. Since consumers do not perceive a difference in safety among major airlines, safety does not actually determine the airline that is eventually selected. For this reason, statistical tools are often needed to establish which criteria are determinant.

The situation in which the product is consumed affects which criteria are determinant. For example, a consumer might consider gas mileage as a determinant criterion when buying a car for himself. However, the safety of a car would likely be a determinant factor if he is buying a car for his daughter. Marketers therefore position products on the determinant criteria that apply to a specific situation.

determinant criteria criteria that are most carefully considered and directly related to the actual choice that is made

13-2 VALUE AND ALTERNATIVE EVALUATION

To understand how alternatives are evaluated and how final choices are made, we must again highlight the key role that value plays in decision making. The value that consumers believe they will receive from a product has a direct impact on their evaluation of that product. In fact, the word *evaluate* literally means "to set a value or worth to an object." Remember that benefits are at the heart of the value equation, and value is a function of both benefits and costs.

13-2a Hedonic and Utilitarian Value

It should be clear that consumers seek both hedonic and utilitarian value. The criteria that consumers use when evaluating a product can also often be classified as either hedonic or utilitarian.[3] *Hedonic criteria* include emotional, symbolic, and subjective attributes or benefits that are associated with an alternative. For example, the prestige that one associates with owning a BMW is a hedonic criterion. These criteria are largely experiential. *Utilitarian criteria* pertain to functional or economic aspects associated with an alternative. For example, safety of a BMW is a utilitarian criterion.

Marketers often promote both the utilitarian and the hedonic potential of a product. Consumers often use

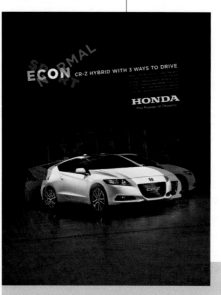

Utilitarian Ad - Honda

Hedonic Ad - Porsche

both categories of criteria when evaluating alternatives and making a final choice.

RATIONALITY, EFFORT, AND VARIETY

As discussed previously, consumers are not always rational when they are evaluating and choosing from possible solutions to a problem. What's more, consumers often have limited ability to process all the information that's available in the environment. The term **bounded rationality** describes the idea that perfectly rational decisions are not always feasible due to constraints or limits of human information processing.

Even when consumers have the ability to consider all possible solutions to a problem, they do not always do so. Quite simply, sometimes the task just isn't worth it. In fact, consumers often minimize the effort that they put into alternative evaluation and choice. As we discussed in our need recognition and information search chapter, consumers often settle for a solution that is simply good enough to solve a problem. Realistically, there are just too many choices out there. In fact, even though variety is a good thing, studies indicate that too much variety actually contributes to feelings of discontent and unhappiness![4]

13-2b Affect-Based and Attribute-Based Evaluations

We can distinguish between two major types of evaluation processes: affect-based and attribute-based. With **affect-based evaluation**, consumers evaluate products based on the overall feeling that is evoked by the alternative.[5] When consumers say something like, "I'm not even sure why I bought this sweater; I just liked it," an affect-based process is reflected. Emotions play a big role in affect-based evaluation, as do mood states.[6]

In general, positive mood states lead to positive evaluations, while negative mood states lead to negative evaluations. Mood is also influential when limited information is found about an alternative.[7] For example, when you are in a good mood, you may evaluate a product positively even if there is not a lot of information given about the product.

Strong feelings also motivate consumers to seek variety as a means of escaping boredom. Beverage marketers like Coca-Cola and Pepsi-Cola frequently update their offerings in order to combat consumer boredom. Snacks are also updated frequently in an attempt to keep things new and exciting. It's common to see new flavours of Doritos or Pringles on the grocery store shelf.

With **attribute-based evaluation**, alternatives are evaluated across a set of attributes that are considered relevant to the purchase situation. As we have noted, the rational decision-making process assumes that consumers carefully integrate information about product attributes and make careful comparisons between products. This process illustrates attribute-based evaluation.

13-3 PRODUCT CATEGORIZATION AND CRITERIA SELECTION

One of the first things that a consumer does when she receives information from the environment is attempt to make sense of the information by placing it in the context of a familiar category. Existing schemas, as discussed in our comprehension chapter, allow consumers to provide meaning to objects. Within these schemas, both product categories and brand categories are found.

Product categories are mental representations of stored knowledge about groups of products. When considering a new product, consumers rely on the knowledge that they have regarding the relevant product category. Knowledge about the existing category is then transferred to the novel item. For example, when consumers drive an electric car for the first time, they start to compare it with existing automobile categories and draw from their knowledge of cars. Even if a product is very different from products that are currently available—for example, an iWatch compared to a traditional mechanical watch—consumers still draw on existing category knowledge to guide their expectations and attitudes toward the new product.[8]

13-3a Category Levels

Consumers possess different levels of product categories. The number of levels and details within each level is influenced by familiarity and expertise with products.[9]

bounded rationality idea that consumers attempt to act rationally within their information-processing constraints

affect-based evaluation evaluative process wherein consumers evaluate products based on the overall feeling that is evoked by the alternative

attribute-based evaluation evaluative process wherein alternatives are evaluated across a set of attributes that are considered relevant to the purchase situation

product categories mental representations of stored knowledge about groups of products

May I Help You?

A fundamental challenge for consumers when they shop online is that they can't always reach their final choice without some help. Because more information is now available online than ever before, many websites have incorporated the use of interactive decision aids. Decision aids allow consumers to make more informed decisions and, online companies hope, to be more satisfied with the outcome.

Consumers can, of course, decide whether they want to use the online aids. One study found that those consumers who decide not to seek online help tend to have less complex search behaviours than those who do. As such, they end up viewing fewer options and visit web pages less frequently. They instead rely on themselves rather than relying on others.

Of course, it is often to the company's advantage to have consumers browse in more depth. By doing so, consumers are able to consider options that they would not have otherwise. Many times, these products are more profitable for the company than the ones that the consumer would have originally sought to purchase. The consumers benefit because they are able to make better decisions while expending much less effort. From the company's perspective, the decision aids can also influence the choices that consumers make. As a result, such tools have been called "double agents" because they have the potential to help both the company and the consumer.

Sources: Bechwati, Nada Nasr, and Lan Xia (2003), "Do Computers Sweat? The Impact of Perceived Effort of Online Decision Aids on Consumers' Satisfaction with the Decision Process," *Journal of Consumer Psychology*, 13 (1–2): pp. 139–148; Senecal, Sylvain, Pawel J. Kalczynski, and Jacques Nantel (2005), "Consumer's Decision-Making Process and Their Online Shopping Behavior: A Clickstream Analysis," *Journal of Business Research*, 58: 1599–1608; Haubl, Gerald and Valerie Trifts (2000), "Consumer Decision Making in Online Shopping Environments: The Effects of Interactive Decision Aids," *Marketing Science*, 19 (1): pp. 4–21.

For example, consumers know the differences between snacks, breakfast, and dinner. Further distinctions can be made within any of these categories. For example, within the "snack" category, distinctions can be made between salty snacks, sweet snacks, fruits, and vegetables. Even finer distinctions can be made at yet a third level. Salty snacks may be broken down into crackers, chips, snack mix, and so on. Therefore, distinctions at basic levels are generally made across product categories (e.g., snacks, breakfast foods, dinner foods). Distinctions at subsequent levels increase in specificity, ultimately to the brand and attribute level.[10] Expertise and familiarity play important roles in this process.

SUPERORDINATE AND SUBORDINATE CATEGORIES

The different levels of product categories are referred to as being either superordinate or subordinate.[11] *Superordinate categories* are abstract in nature and represent the highest level of categorization. An example of a superordinate category would be "beverages." *Subordinate categories* are more detailed. Here, the consumer examines the knowledge that he has stored about various options.

For example, a consumer would proceed through the beverage superordinate category to the subordinate categories of "colas," "sports drinks," and "juices." As a hypothetical example, assume that a consumer visited the web pages for sports drinks and found the information listed in Exhibit 13.2.

We should note that evaluations are generally more relevant and meaningful at subordinate levels.[12] For example, assume that the consumer who is looking at the information in Exhibit 13.2 notices specific differences in the brands at the subordinate level. Hypothetically, he may notice that G-O2 has fewer calories than the other products. Or he may notice that All-Sport has less sodium than the competitors. Or he may notice that Powerade ION4 has less potassium than the others. This information would then guide his final decision for which sports drink to buy.

Recall from our memory chapter that exemplars are first thought of within any category. An exemplar for sports drinks may be G. New alternatives will be compared to exemplars first and then to other brands that are found in the brand category. For example, when our consumer sees an advertisement for a new brand of sports

Exhibit 13.2

Superordinate and Subordinate Categorization

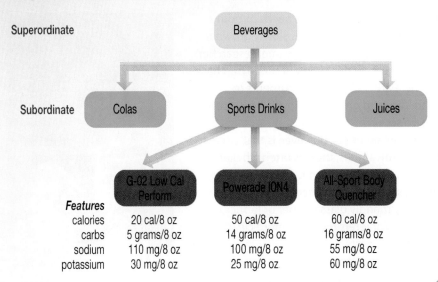

Features			
calories	20 cal/8 oz	50 cal/8 oz	60 cal/8 oz
carbs	5 grams/8 oz	14 grams/8 oz	16 grams/8 oz
sodium	110 mg/8 oz	100 mg/8 oz	55 mg/8 oz
potassium	30 mg/8 oz	25 mg/8 oz	60 mg/8 oz

drink, he will quickly move through the beverage and sports drinks categories and arrive at G. G will then be used as the first benchmark. Other brand comparisons will then occur.

PERCEPTUAL AND UNDERLYING ATTRIBUTES

When evaluating products, consumers also distinguish between perceptual and underlying attributes. **Perceptual attributes** are visually apparent and easily recognizable. Size, shape, colour, and price are perceptual attributes. These attributes are sometimes referred to as search qualities because they can easily be evaluated prior to actual purchase.

Underlying attributes are not readily apparent and can only be learned through experience with the product. These attributes are sometimes referred to as experience qualities because they are often perceived only during consumption. An example of an underlying attribute is product quality.

The distinction between the two types is important because consumers most often infer the existence of underlying attributes through perceptual attributes. As we discussed in our search chapter, the price of a product often tells the consumer something about its quality. In this way, price is used as a signal of quality. A **signal** is a characteristic that allows a consumer to diagnose something distinctive about an alternative. When retailers offer a price-matching guarantee, meaning that they will match any competitor's advertised price, they give a

signal that consumers will enjoy low prices when they shop at this particular store.

Signals such as brand name, price, appearance, and retailer reputation often imply information about product quality. This is particularly so in the following situations:

▸ **When the consumer is trying to reduce risk**

▸ **When purchase involvement is low**

▸ **When the consumer lacks product expertise**[13]

Interestingly, young and inexperienced consumers rely more heavily on perceptual attributes than do older consumers.[14]

13-3b Criteria Selection

WHAT DETERMINES THE TYPE OF EVALUATIVE CRITERIA THAT CONSUMERS USE?

A number of factors influence the type of criteria that consumers use when evaluating alternatives. Situational influences, product knowledge, expert opinions, social influences, online sources, and marketing communications all influence the type of criteria that are used.

Situational Influences. As discussed earlier in this chapter, the criteria that are considered depend heavily on situational influences. If a product is being purchased as a gift, the buyer may pay close attention to hedonic attributes such as the image of the product and its reputation. For example, when buying perfume for a loved one, brand name and imagery can be very important. These criteria would therefore be weighted heavily in the evaluation process. Perhaps a consumer buying perfume for personal use may rely more heavily on other criteria such as price and convenience.

Product Knowledge. As a consumer's level of knowledge

perceptual attributes attributes that are visually apparent and easily recognizable

underlying attributes attributes that are not readily apparent and can be learned only through experience or contact with the product

signal attribute that consumers use to infer something about another attribute

Seeing Green

Green marketing focuses on offering products that satisfy the needs of both consumers and society in a sustainable way. The practice has slowly grown to become a major movement in the marketing world. Early on, consumer researchers focused their efforts on the "green" segment and how this segment made purchase decisions. Today, however, it is clear that there are really several segments to consider, ranging from consumers who are die-hard greens to those who buy only when it is economically advantageous to do so.

One barrier to green marketing reaching its potential, however, is that when it comes to decision making for the majority of consumers, there is often a belief that green products are actually inferior to their mainstream alternatives. The attribute correlation between "green" and "effective" is therefore often negative. For example, consumers may think that an environmentally friendly glass cleaner or fabric softener just isn't as good as a traditional one. Marketers must therefore clearly communicate the effectiveness of their green products. For many consumers, it is not enough for a product to be green; it still has to do the job!

Sources: Peattie, K. and M. Charter (1997), "Green Marketing". In P. McDonaugh and A. Prothero (eds.) *Green Management*. New York: The Dryden Press, pp. 388–412; Banikarim, Maryam (2010), "Seeing Shades in Green Consumers," *AdWeek*, 51 (16), p. 18; Pickett-Baker, Josephine, and Ritsuko Ozaki (2008), "Pro-Environmental Products: Marketing Influence on Consumer Purchase Decision," *Journal of Consumer Marketing*, 25 (5): pp. 281–293.

increases, he or she is able to focus on criteria that are most important in making a selection and to discount irrelevant information.[15] As such, an expert would be expected to be able to discern quickly what information is important and what is not.

Expert Opinions. Because brand experts have well developed knowledge banks for products, they can be used to help others determine what types of information to pay attention to when evaluating products. For example, a computer science professor would be able to guide students in selecting the most important criteria to consider when buying a new computer.

Social Influences. Friends, family members, and reference groups also have an impact on the criteria that are used for decision making. This is especially true for socially visible products like automobiles or clothing.[16] Friends and families are considered to be trustworthy sources of information, and their guidance about attributes to consider is usually closely followed.

Online Sources. Numerous websites can assist consumers with information on product attributes and brand differences. ConsumerReports.org explains what types of criteria to consider when buying products. Popular retail sites like BestBuy.ca also explain what attributes consumers should consider.

Marketing Communications. Marketing communications also assist consumers in deciding what features to consider when buying a particular product. Marketers generally promote the attributes that their products excel on and attempt to convince consumers that these are the most important. For example, Papa John's Pizza is well known for advertising "Better Ingredients, Better Pizza." While the company claims that its pizza contains better ingredients than that of its competitors, it also attempts to convince consumers that ingredients are important criteria to consider when buying pizza.

ARE CONSUMERS ACCURATE IN THEIR ASSESSMENT OF EVALUATIVE CRITERIA?

The accuracy of consumers' evaluations depends heavily on the quality of judgments that they make. **Judgments** are mental assessments of the presence of attributes and the benefits associated with those attributes. Consumer judgments are affected by the amount of knowledge or experience a consumer has with a particular object.

judgments
mental assessments of the presence of attributes and the consequences associated with those attributes

During the evaluation process, consumers make judgments about the following:

▸ **Presence of features—"Does this refrigerator make ice?"**

▸ **Feature levels—"Does it make cubes and crushed ice?"**

▸ **Benefits associated with features—"It provides easy access to ice for cool drinks on warm days."**

▸ **Value associated with the benefit—"That would be nice."**

▸ **How objects differ from each other—"The other one doesn't have this."**

Several issues affect consumer judgments; here, we will review the just noticeable difference, attribute correlation, quality perceptions, and brand name associations.

Just Noticeable Difference.

The ability of a consumer to make accurate judgments when evaluating alternatives is influenced by his or her ability to perceive differences in levels of stimuli between two options. As was discussed in our perception chapter, the just noticeable difference (JND) represents how much stronger one stimulus must be compared to another if someone is to notice that the two are not the same. For example, when judging sound quality, a consumer may not be able to discern the difference between speakers that have a frequency range between 47 Hz and 20 kHz and those that have a range between 50 Hz and 20 kHz. If consumers cannot tell the difference, then their judgments about the products may not be accurate.

Sometimes, the same manufacturer offers different brands or models that are very similar to each other. The term *branded variants* is used to describe the practice of offering essentially identical products with different model numbers or names.[17] Even if differences are perceived, the differences might not be very meaningful. As we discussed earlier, the JND concept is also important.

The impact of the JND on consumer judgments applies to how consumers react to counterfeit products. Some counterfeits are so much like the original that consumers simply can't perceive the difference between them. This is, of course, a bad situation for marketers of the original.

Attribute Correlation.

Consumers often make judgments about features based on their perceived relationship with other features. For example, earlier we stated that price is often used as a signal for quality. Here, consumers rely on **attribute correlation** to describe the perceived relationship between attributes

Waiting time can be correlated with perceptions of quality.

of products.[18] Recall from our consumer search chapter that price and quality are often assumed to be positively correlated. That is, when a product has a high price, consumers often assume it will be high quality.

Attributes can also be negatively correlated. For example, if a consumer's wait time at a bank is long, he or she might think that the bank offers poor service. Here, the consumer assumes that as wait time goes up, service quality goes down (hence, a negative correlation). This can be a faulty assumption because a long wait time may simply mean that consumers get individualized attention and really good service. Some things are worth waiting for!

Quality Perceptions.

Marketers have long realized that consumer perception is critical to marketing success. As we have discussed, perceptions are not always in line with reality. One issue that pertains to consumer judgments is the difference between objective quality and perceived quality. *Objective quality* refers to the actual quality of a product that can be assessed through industry specification or expert rating. For example, a mobile phone provider may advertise that its service has been proven to have the fewest dropped calls in the industry. *Perceived quality* is based on consumer perceptions. Even if the mobile phone has objectively been shown to have the best coverage in the industry, consumers may still perceive poor quality if the coverage in their immediate area is not good.

Companies spend a great deal of time and money on improving the objective quality of their products. These efforts are limited, however,

attribute correlation
perceived relationship between product features

What can a brand name tell you about a product?

by consumer perceptions of quality. In fact, a recent study revealed that improvements in objective quality may take as many as six years to be fully recognized by consumers![19] You may remember from our discussion in the comprehension chapter that consumers act on declarative knowledge even if the knowledge is incorrect. So if a company invests in improving the quality of its products, consumers may still act on the assumption that the product's quality is not good.

Brand Name Associations. Brand names also have an impact on consumer judgments. Much like price, brand names can be used as signals of quality. In fact, studies have found that brand names are even stronger signals of quality than is price.[20] For example, Energizer batteries are assumed to last a long time and Gillette razors are believed to be "the best a man can get."

Unusual product names also influence consumer judgments. One technique that marketers have used for several years is to come up with unexpected, even humorous, names for products. This is especially true in the snack food industry. Hot sauce brands are known for their funny names, such as "Arizona Gunslinger" and "Java Hot Sauce." Research indicates that unexpected names can lead to increased product preference and choice.[21]

HOW MANY CRITERIA ARE NECESSARY TO EVALUATE ALTERNATIVES EFFECTIVELY?

As we have discussed, too many alternatives can be draining for consumers. However, research suggests that consumers can handle a surprisingly high number of comparisons before overload sets in. One study revealed that consumers can evaluate as many as 10 product alternatives and 15 attributes before overload occurs.[22] Even though consumers can handle this much information, they rarely like to do so. And they generally do not consider this many alternatives. In fact, consumers are often able to make good choices when considering only a single attribute.[23]

WHAT IF INFORMATION IS MISSING?

Consumers may have a good understanding of the types of attributes that they would like to use for alternative evaluation, but sometimes attribute information is not available. This actually happens quite frequently in the marketplace. For example, consider the information given in Exhibit 13.3, collected by a consumer from print advertisements about two televisions. Assume that both televisions cost roughly the same amount—say, $1,000. As you can see, the information for television A lacks the details for picture quality, while the information given for television B lacks the details regarding the product's warranty. Consumer satisfaction ratings are available for both products.

To help solve this dilemma, consumers tend to weigh the criteria that are common to both alternatives quite heavily in the evaluation. They also tend to discount information that is missing for the option that performs better on the common criteria. For example, satisfaction ratings are given for both sets in this exhibit. Consumers would likely discount the missing warranty information for television B because this alternative performs better on the common criterion of consumer satisfaction ratings.[24]

HOW DO MARKETERS DETERMINE WHICH CRITERIA CONSUMERS USE?

Marketers can use several techniques to determine the criteria that consumers use when judging products. They

Exhibit 13.3

Missing Information

Features	Television A	Television B
Consumer satisfaction ratings	Good	Excellent
Warranty	2 years parts and labour	Not given
Picture quality	Not given	Good

Source: Adapted from Kivetz, Ran, and Itamar Simonson (2000), "The Effects of Incomplete Information on Consumer Choice," *Journal of Marketing Research*, 37 (4): 427–448.

"Real" Estate Downsize

It's well known that the housing market played a major role in the world-wide economic tailspin of the last few years. Lenders lent money to risky borrowers and the subprime mortgage business boomed. Housing prices escalated to unrealistic levels and adjustable rate mortgage payments eventually began to climb. The market finally burst as many consumers began to default on their mortgages. Obviously, severe economic ramifications resulted.

One of the direct results of the housing market collapse, especially in the United States, is that many consumers today are intentionally "downsizing" their home purchases. Granted, mortgages are harder to come by than in previous years, but for those home buyers who can qualify for mortgages, many are deciding to buy well below their means. This has actually put an increased demand on smaller rather than larger homes. However, a very large home with all the upgrades and luxuries has long been considered a status symbol, many consumers are readjusting their ways of thinking and this is dramatically affecting decision making.

Sources: Gopal, Prashant (2009), "Even Once-Strong Housing Markets Stumble," *Business Week* (online), January 28, 2009; Gardner, Dave (2008), "The Incredible Shrinking House," *Northeast Pennsylvania Business Journal*, 23 (10), p. 77; Farrell, Christopher (1998), "Choosing Where to Grow Old," *Business Week*, July 14, 2008 (4092), 44; Gandel, Stephen (2008), "Real Estate's Next Evolution," *Money*, June, 38 (6), 98; Evans, Kelly (2007), "Size of New Homes Starts Shrinking as Builders Battle Housing Slump," *The Wall Street Journal*, September 12, 2007, A1.

can directly ask consumers through surveys. They can also gather information from warranty registrations that ask consumers to indicate the specific criteria that were used in arriving at a purchase decision. Marketers also use techniques such as perceptual mapping and conjoint analysis to assess choice.

Perceptual mapping was discussed in a previous chapter. **Conjoint analysis** is used to understand the attributes that guide preferences by having consumers compare products across levels of evaluative criteria and the expected utility associated with the alternatives.[25]

13-4 CONSUMER CHOICE: DECISION RULES

Once consumers have evaluated alternative solutions to a problem, they begin to make a choice. *Choice* does not mean that a particular alternative will be chosen. Rather, consumers may simply choose to delay a choice until a future date or to forgo a selection indefinitely.

There are two major types of rules that consumers use when selecting products: compensatory rules and noncompensatory rules. A **compensatory rule** allows consumers to select products that may perform poorly on one attribute by compensating for the poor performance by good performance on another attribute. A consumer using a compensatory rule might say something like, "It's okay that this car isn't very stylish; it gets good gas mileage. I'll buy it."

Noncompensatory models do not allow for this process to take place. Rather, when a **noncompensatory rule** is used, strict guidelines are set prior to selection, and any option that does not meet the specifications is eliminated from consideration. For example, a consumer might say, "I'll only choose a car that gets good gas mileage. I am not budging on that."

13-4a Compensatory Models

The attitude-toward-the-object model (Fishbein model) that was presented in Chapter 7

conjoint analysis technique used to develop an understanding of the attributes that guide consumer preferences by having consumers compare product preferences across varying levels of evaluative criteria and expected utility

compensatory rule decision-making rule that allows consumers to select products that may perform poorly on one criterion by compensating for the poor performance on one attribute by good performance on another

noncompensatory rule decision-making rule in which strict guidelines are set prior to selection and any option that does not meet the guidelines is eliminated from consideration

Exhibit 13.4

A Compensatory Approach

Attribute	e	City Pointe		Crown View		Kings Landing	
		b	(b)(e)	b	(b)(e)	b	(b)(e)
Location	3	7	21	9	27	6	18
High rent/fees	−2	8	−16	9	−18	7	−14
Security	3	7	21	8	24	6	18
Fitness center	1	5	5	7	7	10	10
Pet friendliness	−3	5	−15	2	−6	9	−27
A_o			16		34		5

Note: e = evaluative ratings. These ratings are generally scaled from −3 to +3, with −3 being very negative and +3 being very positive. b = strength of belief that the object possesses the attribute in question. Beliefs are generally scaled from 1 to 10, with 1 meaning "highly unlikely" and 10 meaning "highly likely." $(b)(e)$ is the product term that is derived by multiplying the evaluative ratings (e) by belief strength (b). A_o is the overall attitude toward the object. This is determined by adding the $(b)(e)$ product terms for each object.
Adapted from: Kivetz, Ran and Itamar Simonson (2000), "The Effects of Incomplete Information on Consumer Choice," *Journal of Marketing Research*, 37 (4): pp. 427–448.

conjunctive rule
noncompensatory decision rule where the option selected must surpass a minimum cutoff across all relevant attributes

disjunctive rule
noncompensatory decision rule where the option selected surpasses a relatively high cutoff point on any attribute

lexicographic rule
noncompensatory decision rule where the option selected is thought to perform best on the most important attribute

elimination-by-aspects (EBA) rule noncompensatory decision rule where the consumer begins evaluating options by first looking at the most important attribute and eliminating any option that does not meet a minimum cutoff point for that attribute and where subsequent evaluations proceed in order of importance until only one option remains

represents a compensatory approach. The formula $[A_o + \Sigma(b_i)(e_i)]$ allows for poor scores on one attribute to be compensated for by good scores on another. Our example from Chapter 7 is shown again in Exhibit 13.4. This example revealed that Crown View was the apartment complex to which Jamal held the most positive attitude, even though it scored highest on the attribute that Jamal rated very poorly: high rent/fees. The high ratings on other attributes compensated for his belief that the complex has high fees.

13-4b Noncompensatory Models

Consumer researchers have identified four major categories of noncompensatory rules.[26] They include the conjunctive rule, the disjunctive rule, the lexicographic rule, and the elimination-by-aspects (EBA) rule.

1. Following the **conjunctive rule**, the consumer sets a minimum mental cutoff point for various features and rejects any product that fails to meet or exceed this cutoff point across all features.

2. Following the **disjunctive rule**, the consumer sets a minimum mental cutoff for various features. This is similar to the conjunctive rule. However, with the disjunctive rule, the cutoff point is usually high. The product that meets or exceeds this cutoff on any feature is selected.

3. Following the **lexicographic rule**, the consumer selects the product that he or she believes performs best on the most important feature.

4. Following the **elimination-by-aspects (EBA) rule**, the consumer sets minimum cutoff points for the attributes. Beginning with the most important feature, he or she then eliminates options that don't meet or surpass the cutoff point on this important feature. The consumer then moves on to the next most important feature and repeats the process and does this until only one option remains and a choice is made.

To illustrate these rules, consider the information that is presented in Exhibit 13.5. Here, the consumer is evaluating different makes and models of cars.

The process involved with each decision rule would be as follows:

1. **Conjunctive Rule.** Assume that all features must meet or surpass a mental cutoff of 5 in order for the car to be selected. Looking across the

Exhibit 13.5

Noncompensatory Decision Approaches

Attribute	Importance	Chevy Cruz Belief Ratings	Ford Fiesta Belief Ratings	Honda Fit Belief Ratings	Hyundai Accent Belief Ratings
Gas mileage	10	5	7	9	8
Low price	9	8	6	7	10
Styling	8	9	8	4	4
Warranty	5	4	8	9	8
Service	6	5	6	7	3
Handling	7	6	5	3	3

Note: Belief ratings are performance judgments scaled from 1 = very poor to 10 = very good. Importance ratings are scaled so that 10 = most important, 9 = next most important, and so on.
Source: Wright, Peter (1975), "Consumer Choice Strategies: Simplifying vs Optimizing," *Journal of Marketing Research*, 12 (1): 60–67.

various features for the cars, we see that only the Ford Focus has performance ratings at or above 5 on all features. Using this rule, the Ford Focus would therefore be selected. Its performance ratings are, respectively, 7, 6, 8, 8, 6, 5. Notice that at least one of the performance ratings for the attributes of the other cars falls below the cutoff of 5.

2. **Disjunctive Rule.** Assume that the consumer wants a car that excels at any of the features. Here, he would set a high cutoff of, say, 10. The only car that offers a performance rating of 10 on any attribute is the Hyundai Accent. The "low price" criterion is particularly strong for this car, and the consumer rates this feature as a 10. Using the disjunctive rule, the Hyundai Accent would be selected. He is considering performance ratings, and not the importance of the attributes.

3. **Lexicographic Rule.** Here, the product that is thought to perform best on the most important attribute is selected. In this example, the Honda Fit would be selected because it scores highest (9) on the most important attribute, gas mileage.

4. **EBA Rule.** Assuming a minimum cutoff point of 5 once again, the consumer begins with the most important attribute, gas mileage. Any product that does not meet or surpass the cutoff of 5 on this attribute would be eliminated. All options meet or surpass 5 on the gas mileage attribute and no products are eliminated. Next, the consumer looks at the next most important attribute, low price. Again, all options meet the 5 criterion and no options are eliminated.

Choosing a car is a highly involving decision and probably involves both compensatory and noncompensatory rules.

On the next most important attribute, styling, two options are eliminated because they don't reach the 5 cutoff—the Honda Fit and the Hyundai Accent. The consumer continues on with the next most important attribute, handling. Both the Cruz and the Focus surpass the 5 cutoff on this attribute. The same is true for the next most important attribute, service. Finally, on the final attribute, warranty, the Cruz is eliminated from consideration because it does not reach the cutoff and the Ford Focus is ultimately selected. Notice that the conjunctive and EBA rules can result in the same decision. This will occur if the same cutoff points are used for both rules.

13-4c Use of Decision Rules

Noncompensatory rules are often used in low-involvement situations because these rules allow consumers to simplify their thought processes. However, these rules are also used in high-involvement purchase situations. The decision of what car to buy is certainly a high-involvement decision for most people.

Consumers can combine decision rules in order to arrive at a final solution. For example, a consumer might begin with a conjunctive rule to narrow down the choices and then use a compensatory approach to finalize the decision.

You may be wondering what type of rule consumers use most often. Studies have revealed that the lexicographic rule is very common. This is because consumers usually know what features are most important, and they simply select the product that offers the best performance on that feature.

You may also wonder how often consumers use these rules. Actually, the rules are used quite frequently. We should emphasize, however, that the processes are indeed mental. That is, the comparisons are almost always made mentally, without the strict use of a mathematical formula. Nevertheless, by considering issues such as cutoff points, researchers are able to gain a better understanding of the processes behind consumer choice.

STUDY TOOLS 13

LOCATED AT THE BACK OF THE TEXTBOOK
☐ Rip out Chapter Review Card

LOCATED AT NELSON.COM/STUDENT
☐ Review Key Terms Flashcards (print or online)
☐ Download audio summaries to review on the go
☐ Complete practice quizzes to prepare for tests
☐ Watch video on Ford Motor Company for a real company example

CASE STUDY

Case 1

Consumer Decision Making With Compensatory, Noncompensatory Models

Written by: Lindsey M. Hudson, Rhode Island College graduate (Lindsey was a student of Dr. Stephen P. Ramocki, a professor of marketing at Rhode Island College when this case was written.)

Palm trees, soft sand, sun-soaked women in bikinis sipping on exotic drinks portrays a typical scenario for alcohol advertising. On the flip side, alcohol can take on prestigious roles with certain target markets. Alcohol advertising relies heavily on peripheral cues to get consumers to take an interest in their products. Every customer views his or her decision as rational, but realistically there are implications of status that can play a role in the process. In many situations, friends' social influences can also play a significant role in a consumer's decision-making process. Recently, four vodka brands launched advertising campaigns and three friends viewed the ads as part of a class assignment. The brands were Grey Goose, Smirnoff, Belvedere, and Absolut.

The advertisers of these brands employ brand personality to differentiate themselves from other brands in addition to claiming that their brands each have desirable and distinguishing attributes. Grey Goose reflects the personality of a reliable and dependable alcohol brand. This brand is viewed as stately and has a certain status quality associated with it to attract affluent and successful consumers. Smirnoff casts the image of being both daring and spirited. The positioning is toward a more experiential and youthful target market. Belvedere's personality revolves around luxury and glamour in addition to quality. The brand image is geared toward those who live extravagantly and have discretionary purchasing power. Absolut is represented as honest and genuine. It is viewed as high-quality vodka with an indisputable taste.

The three university students see the ads in different ways based on their personal lifestyles and personalities. Thus, both hedonic and utilitarian factors influence their decision-making processes. Greg is aspiring to be a CPA after graduating from university. His personality is relatively meticulous and directed with rational considerations. He relentlessly looks for quality in all the purchases he makes to preserve his image of practical opulence.

Angelina is a logical shopper who is going to be hosting a dinner party at her house this weekend with friends. She is rational with many of her higher-involvement purchases and considers a number of attributes in her decisions. However, she really wants to impress her guests, so perceived quality becomes the most important attribute. She generally follows a compensatory approach.

Bella is getting ready to go on vacation in Miami with her roommates. Her relationship with her friends is a huge part of her life and she relies on them for decision-making inputs. Significant portions of her life are spent developing strong social ties and establishing more acquaintances. She is not illogical by any means, as she does have her own preferences and considers multiple attributes when making purchase decisions. She is drawn to many advertisements by peripheral cues and she remains quite susceptible to influence from the social sphere captured by these cues. Even though she may be fully aware that her friends don't consider the attributes at all or in the same way she might, she accommodates their suggestions.

Bella is aware of all the ads for Grey Goose, Belvedere, Smirnoff, and Absolut. Although she doesn't really care too much about vodka, her beliefs and evaluations regarding these attributes are well established. However, she is influenced significantly by her friends' opinions. She has a relatively clear idea of the attributes and their advantages; however, when she gets to the store she begins to reflect on previous conversations and the attitudes of her peers. As she approaches the vodka display in the store, she takes into consideration the full array of evaluative characteristics shown in Table C.

As the above discussion implies, for purchases of this nature, consumers may or may not have distinct assessments of various attributes and the beliefs that these attributes are contained in the products they buy. What is fascinating, and at the same time challenging for marketers, concerning such purchases is that what may begin as a totally rational process may not exactly pan out that way. As the text clearly states, for purchases of this nature various consumers are apt to use compensatory or

CASE STUDY

noncompensatory models, or even combinations of the two. What can be frustrating in understanding decision-making approaches is that consumers may be inclined to start with one model and then switch to another or even blend different approaches. In this situation, both Greg's and Angelina's decision models are intended to be relatively straightforward. Greg is prone to applying the lexicographic model, while Angelina will likely use the compensatory model. Bella's choice revolves highly around brand personality and social influence, but she simply seeks a brand that is good enough because she doesn't really care too much about vodka.

Advertisers obviously have to consider the approaches that they are taking in terms of the elaborative likelihood model discussed in the text. They need to consider the directness of the advertising in terms of attributes versus the more peripheral approach that draws people in by focusing on personality and lifestyle. For a product such as vodka, companies want consumers to consider taste and utilitarian attributes. However, they also realize that brand personalities can play significant roles in the final decision process and in establishing brand loyalty.

As each of these purchasers is settling on the actual purchase decisions, they will be employing different cognitive and affective strategies. Although the questions below suggest an answer or an outcome in each of these three students' buying situations, there still is reasonable room for discussion concerning why different choices may result. Each of these college students is led to select

Table A: Lexicographic Model

Attributes	Importance	Grey Goose Belief Ratings	Smirnoff Belief Ratings	Belvedere Belief Ratings	Absolut Belief Ratings
Perceived quality	9	8	5	9	6
Price	8	6	8	7	8
Quantity	1	8	4	9	8
Bottle design	1	5	4	7	5

Note: Belief ratings are measured on a 1–10 scale with 1 = very unlikely and 10 = very likely. The importance ratings are based on a scale from 1 = not at all important to 10 = very important.

Table B: Compensatory Model

Attributes	e	Grey Goose		Smirnoff		Belvedere		Absolut	
		b	(b)(e)	b	(b)(e)	b	(b)(e)	b	(b)(e)
Perceived quality	3	8	24	1	3	7	21	2	6
Price	−3	4	−12	8	−24	5	−15	8	−24
Quantity	2	7	14	7	14	6	12	7	14
Bottle design	−1	2	−2	2	−2	6	−6	3	−3
A_o			24		−9		12		−7

Note: Belief ratings (belief that the attribute is present) are measured on a 1–10 scale with 1 = very unlikely and 10 as very likely. Attribute evaluations (e) are based on a −3 to +3 scale with 3 = good and −3 = bad.

Table C: Conjunctive Approach

Attributes	e	Grey Goose		Smirnoff		Belvedere		Absolut	
		b	*(b)(e)*	*b*	*(b)(e)*	*b*	*(b)(e)*	*b*	*(b)(e)*
Imagery	3	4	12	6	18	5	15	9	27
Attractiveness of spokesperson	1	4	4	4	4	6	6	9	9
Brand personality	3	3	9	6	18	2	6	7	21
Friends' opinions/ subjective norm	3	1	3	7	21	1	3	5	3
A_o			28		61		30		60

Note: Belief ratings are measured on a 1–10 scale with 1 = very unlikely and 10 = very likely. Attribute evaluations are based on a −3 to +3 scale with 3 = good and −3 = bad. Conjunctive approach method is used with 5 as the cutoff.

a different brand of vodka based on his or her individual decision-making preferences. Your task is to assess each student's decision-making approach along with the likely brand of choice.

Source: *Consumer Decision Making with Compensatory, Non-Compensatory, and Behavior Intentions Models.* Written by Lindsey M. Hudson, graduate of Rhode Island College. Reproduced by permission of the author.

QUESTIONS

1 Do you believe brand personality plays a major part in decision making? Explain.

2 After evaluating Table A, which alcohol brand will Greg be most likely to purchase?

3 Using Table B and taking Angelina's shopping habits into consideration, which brand of alcohol will she buy?

4 Looking at Table C and considering what you know about Bella's decision-making style, which brand is she likely to purchase?

5 How might the decision-making processes for each consumer change if shopping for the product at a warehouse store like Costco as opposed to an upscale wine shop in Florida?

Case 2

Redefining Good Cleaning Products

Written by Nancy Artz, Ph.D., University of Southern Maine and Dudley Greeley, USM Sustainability Coordinator. Reprinted by permission of the authors.

Jill thinks all dishwashing soaps are alike, so she buys the cheapest brand. Jack buys the brand of laundry detergent his mom always bought. Consumers typically have low involvement with the decision to buy household cleaning products, and make quick choices. But Elena researches nontoxic cleaning supplies in detail before her baby is born.

The market for green cleaning products was pioneered by small firms like Seventh Generation Inc., which, in 1988, started selling environmentally friendly household products in health food stores and specialty stores. Two decades later, in 2007, green cleaners still accounted for less than 1% of cleaning product sales,[1] even though surveys found that 60% of consumers were "concerned about the impact cleaning products have on the environment."[2] Only truly committed green consumers will make an extra trip to a specialty store to pay more for utilitarian-looking products that are perceived

CASE STUDY

to be less effective because they are environmentally safer.

Even though mainstream consumers aren't willing to sacrifice price, convenience, quality, and other product benefits for the sake of greener products, they will use green features to break a tie between otherwise comparable brands. Marketers have used this knowledge to introduce a host of new green cleaners.

Two young entrepreneurs launched Method, an environmentally friendly line of cleaning products that differentiates itself from other brands—green and non-green alike—by innovative, stylish packaging. For example, Method's Le Scrub bathroom cleaner has a built-in sponge holder. Method is sold at specialty stores and mass-market retailers like Target, at about twice the price of traditional brands. The co-founders believe that style "creates mass market relevance for a green product"[3] and that consumers discover Method because of its trendy designer look, find that they love the fragrance, and then "discover it's good for you—it's that third piece that drives loyalty."[4] Perhaps that explains the company's sales growth from about $90,000 in 2001 to $77 million in 2006.[5]

The market for green cleaners took off in 2008, when the Clorox Company launched its Green Works line of cleaners. Green Works became the market leader the next year, with $200 million in sales (42% share of the green cleaner market).[6] Interestingly, Green Works's success didn't come at the expense of Seventh Generation and Method—sales of those products didn't drop—Green Works attracted consumers from mass market brands. This is consistent with Green Works's strategy to target chemical-avoiding naturalists, who want a greener cleaner but view existing options as not working well, not coming from brands they know or trust, and not generally available where they shop.[7]

The Green Works line launched with five products: an all-purpose cleaner, a glass cleaner, a toilet bowl cleaner, a dilutable cleaner, and a bathroom cleaner. The line was quickly expanded to include dishwashing liquid, laundry products, and biodegradable wipes. The products were priced 20% higher than typical cleaners, considerably less than Seventh Generation or Method's

100% higher price.[8] As a large company, Clorox was able to launch Green Works with a substantial advertising campaign (e.g., 30-second television spots and use of social media) and broad retail distribution (e.g., Walmart agreed to provide prominent shelf space and other forms of in-store promotion).

Green Works cleaners are green-tinted liquids sold in recyclable bottles with a prominent yellow flower on the label. The products have been promoted as made from natural, plant-based ingredients with no harsh chemical fumes or residues. One claim, for example, was that "clothes washed in Green Works are gentle on skin."[9] Consumers who read the label or the website find the product is made from ingredients such as coconuts and lemon oil and is biodegradable, nonallergenic, and not tested on animals. The products are formulated to have a pleasant fragrance rather than a strong "cleaner" odour.

Rather than downplaying the connection between Green Works and Clorox, the company emphasized the link to promote the new brand as dependable and effective. Likewise, the Green Works brand name was chosen to counter consumer beliefs that natural cleaners don't work.[10] Green Works was initially promoted in ads and on the package as working just as well as traditional cleaners. A competitor complained to the National Advertising Division (NAD) of the Council of Better Business Bureaus. NAD determined that Green Works was not as effective as traditional cleaners in grease removal and that consumers might incorrectly assume the product to be a disinfectant. Green Works agreed to stop claiming "works as well" as other cleaners.[11]

Because Clorox is known for bleach and "chemical" cleaners, Green Works has used third-party endorsements to reassure consumers about the legitimacy of its environmental and health features:

From its inception, Green Works packaging has displayed the Design for Environment (DfE) logo. DfE certification means a product only contains ingredients that pose the least concern among chemicals in their class. Few consumers recognize or understand the DfE criteria, but the logo indicates that DfE is sponsored by the well-respected U.S. Environmental Protection Agency.

Four months after product launch, packaging displayed the Sierra Club logo. This well-known nonprofit agreed to the use of its logo to help "move" the market to offer more environmentally preferred products and, in return for a percentage of sales ($470,000 in 2008).[12] Although not widely known among mainstream consumers, this arrangement was criticized by some as a conflict of interest and inappropriate because the Sierra Club's expertise is public policy, not consumer-product chemistry.

Almost two years after product launch, Green Works added Good Housekeeping's new green label to its bathroom cleaner. This "green" certification is not particularly rigorous, but the Good Housekeeping seal is widely recognized.[13]

Green Works is not the only firm pursuing third-party endorsements. Method now carries significant sustainability certifications such as Cradle-to-Cradle, DfE, and B-Corp. Do ecolabels add value for the consumer? Credible labels relating to the product's most important ecological and social attributes can help consumers distinguish truly green products from products engaged in greenwashing. Unfortunately, a proliferation of new ecolabels—including in-house labels without independent verification—has caused consumer doubt about the relevance, rigor, and credibility of labels.

Green Works's success demonstrates that environmentally preferred products appeal to mainstream consumers—in one year, Green Works doubled sales in the green cleaner market. Sales in this market are expected to grow rapidly as other established firms introduce their own green lines and the price premium for green drops. Mintel, a prominent research firm, predicts the green share of the cleaning market will grow from 3% in 2008 to 30% by 2013.[14] The green cleaner market contributes to a paradigm shift that is redefining what it means for a product to provide good value. Price, efficacy, and availability are still desired attributes—but a good product today is increasingly one that is also safe for people and the planet. How much longer will Jill continue to view all cleaners as alike?

Source: *Redefining Good Cleaning Products*. Written by Nancy Artz, Ph.D., University of Southern Maine and Dudley Greeley, USM Sustainability Coordinator. Reprinted by permission of the authors.

1 http://www.npr.org/templates/story/story.php?storyId=18751684

2 http://www.usatoday.com/money/advertising/adtrack/2007-11-25-green-mop_N.htm

3 http://www.grist.org/article/fighting-dirty/

4 http://www.sfgate.com/cgi-bin/article.cgi?f=/c/a/2006/10/08/BUGRM-LJPJB1.DTL

5 http://www.usatoday.com/money/advertising/adtrack/2007-11-25-green-mop_N.htm

6 http://www.environmentalleader.com/2010/03/10/method-green-household-cleaners-try-to-take-market-share-from-clorox/

7 http://makower.typepad.com/joel_makower/2008/01/clorox-aims-to.html

8 http://www.bnet.com/2403-13241_23-253321.html

9 http://www.youtube.com/watch?v=N-gGAe8Ltsw&feature=related

10 http://www.npr.org/templates/transcript/transcript.php?storyId=18751684

11 http://www.greenbiz.com/news/2008/08/19/clorox-told-modify-green-works-claims#ixzz0nNemoTRa

12 http://www.greenbiz.com/news/2009/01/19/clorox-expands-green-works-line-gives-470k-sierra-club#ixzz0nMI0Y9eq

13 http://www.greenbiz.com/news/2009/09/25/aveeno-green-works-natures-source-products-get-green-good-housekeeping-seal#ixzz0nMJHj4Rv

14 http://www.environmentalleader.com/2010/03/10/method-green-house-hold-cleaners-try-to-take-market-share-from-clorox/

QUESTIONS

1 What temporary situations, or changes in life circumstances, might influence a consumer to recognize a need for a cleaning product in general, or a green cleaner in particular? How might a marketer leverage this knowledge?

2 What types of purchase decisions were made by Jack, Jill, and Elena: (a) extended decision making, (b) limited decision making, or (c) habitual decision making: brand inertia versus brand loyalty? Explain.

3 How do perceptual attributes and packaging characteristics of the brands in this case study signal product quality in terms of the underlying environmental and health benefits?

	Whole Foods	Walmart
Consideration set		
Determinant criteria		
(Non-)compensatory rule		

14 | Consumption to Satisfaction

YAY Media A... my

LEARNING OBJECTIVES

After studying this chapter, the student should be able to:

14-1 Gain an appreciation of the link from consumption to value to satisfaction.

14-2 Discuss the relative importance of satisfaction and value in consumer behaviour.

14-3 Know that emotions other than satisfaction can affect postconsumption behaviour.

14-4 Use expectancy/disconfirmation, equity, and attribution theory approaches to explain consumers' postconsumption reactions.

14-5 Understand problems with commonly applied satisfaction measures.

14-6 Describe some ways in which consumers dispose of refuse.

14-1 CONSUMPTION, VALUE, AND SATISFACTION

Consumption is at the heart of all consumer behaviour. Obviously, a consumer *consumes*! In fact, one might say that all human activity focuses on some form of consumption. Even when we work, we consume time so that we can earn money to consume other things! In the **consumption process**, consumers use the product, service, or experience that has been selected. Ultimately, consumers consume products and receive value in return.

consumption process process in which consumers use the product, service, or experience that has been selected

durable goods goods that are usually consumed over a long period of time

nondurable goods goods that are usually consumed quickly

consumption frequency number of times a product is consumed

14-1a Consumption Leads to Value

The important role of consumption becomes apparent when one considers that without

consumption, there is no value. Accordingly, consumer value is directly derived from product consumption.[1] Earlier, we defined consumption as the process that converts time, goods, ideas, or service into value. Consumption experiences potentially produce utilitarian and/or hedonic value.

The basic consumption process that is at the heart of the consumer value framework (CVF) is shown again in Exhibit 14.1.

14-1b Consumption and Product Classification

Many issues go along with the consumption of goods, services, and experiences. Important differences exist for the consumption of durable and nondurable goods. **Durable goods** are consumed over long periods of time. A dishwasher is a durable good. **Nondurable goods** are consumed quickly. Soft drinks are nondurable goods.

For nondurable goods especially, marketers try to increase consumption frequency as much as possible. **Consumption frequency** refers to the number of times a product or service is consumed in a given time

"Marketers can be extremely successful by focusing on value. In fact, Walmart's success is more about value than satisfaction."

Exhibit 14.1

Basic Consumption Process

- Need
- Want
- Exchange
- Costs and Benefits
- Reaction
- Value

Consumption, postchoice evaluation, loyalty, repeat purchase behaviour, disposal.

period. Credit card companies have made it easier and easier for consumers to use their cards on routine shopping trips. Visa and MasterCard were once thought of as inappropriate for routine purchases like groceries. Today, however, consumers often use these for all manner of everyday purchases.

Marketers may also attempt to increase the amount of product consumed per occasion. For example, soft drink marketers gradually increased the average size of soft drinks over time. Many students may be surprised to find out that the traditional Coke bottle was much smaller than today—weighing in at a mere 6.5 ounces (192 millilitres). Pepsi's selling point was a 10-ounce (295-millilitre) bottle at the same price. Today consumers often consume 20-ounce (590-millilitre) or even 34-ounce (1-litre) bottles a number of times per day! The soft drink industry has slowly facilitated an increase in the average soft drink serving size. At the same time, these companies have introduced new, smaller 7.4-ounce (220-millilitre) cans that are closer in size to the original bottles. This packaging offers consumers a reduced serving size, with correspondingly fewer calories, which appeals to a health-conscious segment that still wants to enjoy an occasional soft drink.

The original Pepsi strategy encouraged a larger serving size at the same price as Coke's 6.5-ounce (192-mililitre) bottle.

Services and experiences are usually classified as "nondurable" by default. However, some services are more clearly consumed over extended time periods. For example, we consume insurance daily even though consumers may pay premiums only periodically. Experiences are complete when consumption stops. However, marketers of these products encourage repeat consumption of their products by offering season tickets, club memberships, and special invitations to events. By encouraging increased consumption, these marketers are able to foster customer relationships.

14-1c Situations and Consumer Reactions

As discussed previously, consumption situations and settings have a significant impact on the consumer experience. The temporal factors, antecedent conditions, and physical environment are particularly influential on the consumption experience. How, what, and when we consume is largely dependent upon the environment that we are in.

authenticity being real and genuine and having a history or tradition

meaning transference process through which cultural meaning is transferred to a product and on to the consumer

For example, many Canadians enjoy barbecuing. However, the food and drink that consumers expect as part of a summer barbecue might range from lobster on the East Coast to beef in Alberta to salmon on the West Coast. Similarly, beer preferences might range from Alexander Keith's to Big Rock to Granville Island. Some Canadians swear by charcoal, while others prefer a gas-fuelled grill. These products can become artefacts as part of the summer barbecue ritual. Without these, the experience is less than authentic. **Authenticity** means something is real and genuine and has a history or tradition.[2] The consumption of authentic things adds value over the consumption of synthetic experiences, particularly when the consumption environment contains high degrees of symbolism or consumers are highly involved in some activity. The very same products, like charcoal, offer less value when they are not contributing to an authentic consumer experience.

The environment plays a large role in influencing consumption and consumer satisfaction. When golfers play a crowded golf course, other golfers determine how fast one can play. Although proper etiquette is to allow faster players to pass slower golfers on the course, the interference with one's usual pace of play distracts from the enjoyment of the experience. Some courses have employees who will even require a group that is playing too slowly to skip a hole. Environmental factors like this influence how much value consumers receive and how satisfied they are with the experience.

14-1d Consumption, Meaning, and Transference

Consumers' lives are very much intertwined with consumption. Value depends on a process called **meaning transference**, through which cultural meaning is transferred to a product and on to the consumer. From a utilitarian standpoint, the meaning of consumption is straightforward. For example, consumers buy shoe polish to polish their shoes; that's easy. What is not as straightforward is the hedonic component of consumption. Here, inner meanings, including cultural meaning, must be considered.

Meaning transference begins with culture. Value is affected largely by the meaning of goods, services, and experiences. Marketers work to transfer important cultural ideals or values into products via advertising and word-of-mouth that occurs between consumers. If they can attach a freedom theme to a product—for example, a motorcycle—then a consumer consumes not only the motorcycle itself, but also the meaning attached to the bike. Ultimately, the

For Better, For Worse

Few material items are as symbolic as the diamond wedding ring. The diamond is a well-known symbol of love and commitment, and diamond rings bring about feelings of love, fulfillment, and excitement for the bride-to-be.

Consumer researchers carefully observed diamond ring sales during the recent economic downturn. What they found was that although the demand for diamonds did fall, the symbolism of the diamond ring ensured that wedding rings would still sell. Of course, people continue to marry whether the economy is good or bad. Many consumers simply turned away from high-end diamonds to less-pricey alternatives.

The demand for diamond rings highlights the importance of product symbolism and the strong impact that emotions have on consumption even during economic hard times. Economic conditions can sour, but diamonds still hold their symbolic meaning. When it comes to marriage, diamonds are still a girl's best friend!

iStockphoto.com/Tomasz Pietryszek

Sources: Barbee, Jeffrey (2009), "Diamonds Are Forever?", *GlobalPost*, May 13, 2009, online content found at www.globalpost.com/dispatch/aftrica/090512/diamonds-are-forever.htm; Mortished, Carl (2009), "Now Cheaper, Are Diamonds Still a Girl's Best Friend", *The Times*, April 11, 2009, p. 49; Greene, Jay (2008), "Blue Nile: A Guy's Best Friend," *Business Week*, June 09, 2008, p. 39.

meaning of the product becomes an important part of the consumption experience.[3] The transfer of meaning in the consumption process is illustrated in Exhibit 14.2.

14-1e Consumption Outcomes and Emotion

Consumers choose products, services, and experiences that they believe will deliver value by addressing their wants and needs. They anticipate good outcomes from their choices or else they would have made another choice. In previous chapters, we've stressed how

Canadian Breast Cancer Foundation CIBC Run for the Cure

Cause-related efforts like CIBC's Run for the Cure rely on feelings of hope. In this case, it is the hope that someday soon breast cancer can be cured.

emotions play key roles before and during consumption. Fantasies, fun, and feelings all are associated with consumption, and these elements of consumption are closely tied to perceived value.[4]

In this portion of the CVF, we stress how consumer emotions end up influencing consumption outcomes. This process begins with anticipation. **Hope**, for example, is a

hope a fundamental emotion evoked by positive, anticipatory appraisals

Exhibit 14.2

Transfer of Meaning in Consumption

Culturally defined meaning

↓

Product, service, experience

↓

Consumer

Adapted from: McCracken, Grant (1986), "Culture and Consumption: A Theoretical Account of the Structure and Movement of the Cultural Meaning of Consumer Goods," *Journal of Consumer Research*, 13 (1): 71–84.

fundamental emotion evoked by positive, anticipatory appraisals. The consumer anticipates an outcome that could bring about a better situation in some way, and he or she feels the emotion hope in return. In this way, hope is the opposite of fear, which involves anticipation of a negative outcome.[5] Feelings like hope are linked with expectations, and in this way they play a role in creating consumption outcomes.

Consumption, value, and satisfaction are tied closely together. Not surprisingly, consumers tend to be more satisfied with exchanges they find valuable, as value is at the heart of marketing transactions. Value perceptions, therefore, directly influence consumer satisfaction.[6] However, the link between value and satisfaction is nowhere near perfect, as will be seen later.

14-2 VALUE AND SATISFACTION

Many companies try hard to satisfy customers. However, is satisfaction the key outcome variable for marketers and consumers? Consider Exhibit 14.3. This chart plots scores for major retailers from the American

Exhibit 14.3

The ACSI Scores for U.S. Retailers

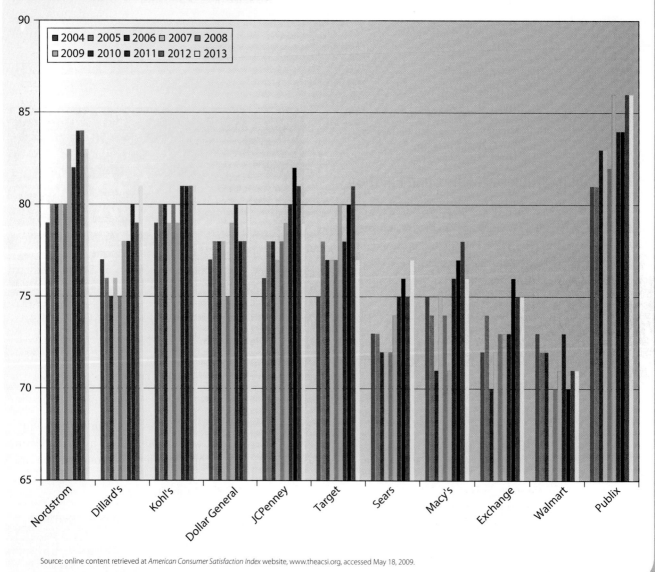

Source: online content retrieved at *American Consumer Satisfaction Index* website, www.theacsi.org, accessed May 18, 2009.

Consumer Satisfaction Index (ACSI).[7] This index provides satisfaction scores for many major companies across many industries and even some governmental organizations (we use the example of U.S. companies here because equivalent data is not tracked on the same scale for Canadian businesses). Notice that Publix (a large supermarket chain operating in the southeastern United States) has the highest customer satisfaction rating over the entire period, with Nordstrom, which recently entered the Canadian market, also scoring higher on the ACSI than practically all other retailers. JCPenney, Dillard's, Target, Dollar General, and Sears all have higher satisfaction ratings than Walmart. What does this mean? Has any retailer in recent history enjoyed more success than Walmart?

Yet, as the ACSI shows, Walmart is hardly the satisfaction leader. In fact, Walmart's satisfaction ratings are the lowest of all retailers listed, according to the ACSI. What can explain this? The answer lies in value. Even if Walmart does not provide high customer satisfaction, it does provide value leadership, particularly the perception that high utilitarian value results from shopping there. Thus, the track record says Walmart should continue to prioritize value over satisfaction.

Indications are that Walmart executives have learned what drives customers to Walmart. Walmart briefly launched campaigns to increase customer satisfaction and spawn positive perceptions about the brand. These included initiatives to make the store atmosphere more comfortable through reduced crowding of aisles and floor space, increased availability of higher quality brands, and an increased emphasis on sustainability. In each case, Walmart found the results unsustainable and quickly shifted back to an emphasis on large assortments at low prices.[8]

Managers acknowledge that initiatives that increase customer satisfaction do not always improve sales growth. The importance of value in the consumption experience cannot be overstated. In fact, one can argue that the reason a firm exists at all is to create value.[9] Value and satisfaction relate to one another to some degree, but value is the heart of consumer behaviour (CB) and is what consumers seek from consumption experiences.

If marketers ever face the decision of providing value or satisfaction, value should be prioritized because, as illustrated by the ACSI, firms can do well even when they do not enjoy the highest industry satisfaction scores. However, as Target found out with its brief tenure in Canada (see "Target Misses the Mark in Canada" case at the end of Chapter 3), a firm that does not provide satisfaction or value in some form cannot succeed for long.

14-2a What Is Consumer Satisfaction?

Customer satisfaction has received much attention from consumer researchers and marketing managers. However, different people define satisfaction differently and, as a result, it is often confused with numerous closely related concepts like quality or general happiness. However, satisfaction is distinct from these concepts. **Consumer satisfaction** is a mild, positive emotional state resulting from a favourable appraisal of a consumption outcome. Several points distinguish consumer satisfaction from other important consumer behaviour concepts:

▸ Consumer satisfaction is a postconsumption phenomenon because it is a reaction to an outcome.

▸ Like other emotions, satisfaction results from a cognitive appraisal. Some refer to this appraisal as the satisfaction judgment.

▸ Satisfaction is a relatively mild emotion that does not create strong behavioural reactions.

consumer satisfaction
mild, positive emotion resulting from a favourable appraisal of a consumption outcome

Limited-Service Restaurants

	Base-line	95	96	97	98	99	00	01	02	03	04	05	06	07	08	09	10	11	12	13	14	Previous Year % Change	First Year % Change
All Others	73	74	75	73	74	74	72	73	74	75		78	80	79	80	83	76	81	82	82	84	2.4	15.1
Burger King	66	65	67	68	64	66	67	65	68	68		71	70	69	71	69	74	75	75	76	76	0.0	15.2
Domino's Pizza	67	70	68	68	70	67	69	73	75	75		71	75	75	75	77	77	77	77	81	80	−1.2	19.4
Dunkin' Donuts	NM	NM	NM	NM	NM	NM	NM	NM	NM	NM		NM	NM	NM	NM	NM	NM	NM	79	80	75	−6.3	−5.1
KFC (Yum! Brands)	67	68	69	67	64	64	65	63	69	71		69	70	71	70	69	75	75	75	81	74	−8.6	10.4
Limited-Service Restaurants	69	70	66	68	69	69	70	71	71	74	NM**	76	77	77	78	78	75	79	80	80	80	0.0	15.9
Little Caesar	72	69	69	73	71	NM	69	70	75	75		74	77	75	75	75	78	80	82	82	80	−2.4	11.1
McDonald's	63	63	60	60	61	61	59	62	61	64		62	63	64	69	70	67	72	73	73	71	−2.7	12.7
Papa John's	NM	NM	NM	NM	NM	76	77	78	76	76		78	79	77	76	75	80	79	83	82	82	0.0	7.9
Pizza Hut (Yum! Brands)	69	66	63	71	71	68	70	71	70	75		71	76	72	76	74	78	81	78	80	82	2.5	18.8
Starbucks	NM	NM	NM	NM	NM	NM	NM	NM	NM	NM		NM	77	78	77	76	78	80	76	80	76	−5.0	−1.3
Subway	NM	NM	NM	NM	NM	NM	NM	NM	NM	NM		NM	NM	NM	NM	NM	NM	NM	82	83	78	−6.0	−4.9
Taco Bell (Yum! Brands)	66	66	66	67	64	64	63	66	67	68		72	70	69	70	73	74	76	77	74	72	−2.7	9.1
Wendy's	72	73	71	69	73	71	70	72	74	74		75	76	78	73	76	77	77	78	79	78	−1.3	8.3

From this ACSI excerpt for fast-food restaurants, how do success and satisfaction relate? Do you agree with these scores?

Other key consumer variables like expectations, quality, or attitude are generally more relevant before consumption or even before the purchase in explaining consumer behaviour.[10] Nevertheless, managers consider consumer satisfaction to be important because consumers' word-of-mouth, repeat purchases, and ultimately, consumer loyalty correlate with consumer satisfaction scores. These relationships are discussed in detail in the next chapter.

14-2b What Is Consumer Dissatisfaction?

Recall from the material on consumer information processing (CIP) that consumers react quite differently when responding to losses than when responding to gains. Additionally, some debate exists over whether low satisfaction necessarily means a consumer has high dissatisfaction. For reasons like these, consumer behaviour theory distinguishes consumer dissatisfaction from consumer satisfaction. Therefore, **consumer dissatisfaction** can be defined as a mild, negative affective reaction resulting from an unfavourable appraisal of a consumption outcome.[11] Even though, conceptually, dissatisfaction is an opposite concept to satisfaction, the fact that consumers react differently to negative contexts means that dissatisfaction will explain behaviours that satisfaction cannot.

consumer dissatisfaction mild, negative affective reaction resulting from an unfavourable appraisal of a consumption outcome

14-3 OTHER POSTCONSUMPTION REACTIONS

Although people often use *satisfaction* as a colloquialism for everything that happens after a consumer buys something, many other things, including other emotions, may also occur postconsumption. This view can cause other important postconsumption reactions to be overlooked. Among these are specific emotions, including delight, disgust, surprise, exhilaration, and even anger. These particular emotions are often much more strongly linked to behaviour because, although they are also emotional reactions to appraisals, they are often much stronger.

An angry consumer exhibits much more noticeable and persistent behaviour than does a consumer with low satisfaction. The angry consumer likely complains and

I Hope It's Real, Really!

Marketers often claim to offer an authentic experience as a way of creating more value. That means the experience has to be the real thing! A restaurant that promises an authentic Parisian café experience needs to offer a menu and decor that are true to the promise. The consumer enters this experience hoping to experience something special—not a warmed-over (no pun intended) roadside dinner house. Pâté, Tavel (a French rosé wine), and crusty bread may just fulfill the hope and replace it with delight. In contrast, many Internet companies offer "authentic" designer products from Gucci, Prada, Louis Vuitton, Rolex, and so on. Evidence suggests, however, that a large portion of designer products sold through the Internet are actually counterfeit. Imagine the postpurchase reactions from a consumer who recently got a good deal on a Louis Vuitton backpack for his fiancée—claimed to be 60% off! He can fill the bag with expectations. Before he gives it to her, a friend jokes, "Hey, is that thing real?" After a few seconds of silence, he adds in a comforting tone, "Don't worry, it still works even if it isn't real!" Will the hope turn to anxiety or fear? How will his satisfaction be affected by the thought that it just might not be authentic?

Eric Gaillard/Reuters/Landov

Sources: Boss, D.L. (2008), "Providing Authentic Customer Experiences Yields Real Results," *Nation's Restaurant News*, (February 25), 40; Stumpf, S.A. and P. Chaudry (2010), "Country Matters: Executives Weigh In on the Causes and Counter Measures of Counterfeit Trade," *Business Horizons*, 53, pp. 305–314.

sometimes shouts and, in extreme cases, begins boycott initiatives against a company that is the target of anger. A consumer with low satisfaction would not likely exhibit any visible signs of irritation. The particular emotion experienced by consumers will do much to determine the behavioural reaction, as we will see in the following chapter when we discuss complaining in more detail. We will see more on this in the next chapter, but any model of what happens after purchase would be remiss not to include possibilities beyond satisfaction.

Exhibit 14.4

Basic Disconfirmation Process

Performance > Expectations = +Disconfirmation ➡ Satisfaction
Expectations < Performance = −Disconfirmation ➡ Dissatisfaction

14-4 THEORIES OF POSTCONSUMPTION REACTIONS

14-4a Expectancy/Disconfirmation

The most commonly accepted theory of consumer satisfaction is the **expectancy/disconfirmation theory**. The basic disconfirmation model proposes that consumers enter into a consumption experience with predetermined cognitive expectations of a product's performance. These expectations are used as a type of benchmark against which actual performance perceptions are judged.

Disconfirmation becomes central in explaining consumer satisfaction. When performance perceptions are more positive than what was expected, **positive disconfirmation** occurs and leads to consumer satisfaction. When performance perceptions do not meet expectations, meaning performance is less than expected, **negative disconfirmation** occurs and leads to dissatisfaction. Finally, if performance perceptions exactly match what was expected, confirmation (sometimes simply referred to as *neutral disconfirmation*) is said to occur.

The expectancy disconfirmation approach is shown in Exhibit 14.4. Taken together, disconfirmation represents the cognitive appraisal that produces postconsumption emotions like consumer satisfaction. Using different terminology, disconfirmation is the satisfaction judgment. The blue boxes represent cognitive postconsumption reactions, whereas the green box represents an affective or emotional postconsumption reaction. The relationships between the concepts are explained in the section that follows.

EXPECTATIONS

Expectations may be thought of as preconsumption beliefs of what will occur during an exchange and/ or consumption of a product. Consumer expectations have two components: (1) the probability that something will occur, and (2) an evaluation of that potential occurrence.[12] Exhibit 14.4 reveals that expectations also can have a direct impact on satisfaction (by the dotted line), independent of their role in the disconfirmation process.[13] This can occur when the consumer has very little involvement. In these cases, little effort is put into either expectation or performance appraisal, and satisfaction formation is largely affected by consumer expectations alone. In other words, with low involvement, high expectations will be associated directly with increased satisfaction and low expectations will be associated directly with increased dissatisfaction.

The same can be found with very high involvement. In these cases, balance theory kicks in and consumers may adjust their reactions automatically as a way of protecting themselves from the realization that they may have made a poor choice. When consumers go on spring break, they may anticipate the event so highly that they block out some of the bad things that happen so that their satisfaction reaction adjusts to their preconsumption expectations. Thus,

expectancy/ disconfirmation theory proposes that consumers use expectations as a benchmark against which performance perceptions are judged and this comparison is a primary basis for satisfaction/ dissatisfaction

positive disconfirmation according to the expectancy/ disconfirmation approach, a perceived state wherein performance perceptions exceed expectations

negative disconfirmation according to the expectancy/ disconfirmation approach, a perceived state wherein performance perceptions fall short of expectations

How will expectations influence the spring break experience?

Andres Rodriguez/Alamy

under conditions of very low or very high involvement, expectations can influence satisfaction directly.

TYPES OF EXPECTATIONS

Consumers bring different types of expectations into a consumption situation:

▸ *Predictive expectations* that form about what a consumer thinks will actually occur during an experience

▸ *Normative expectations* of what a consumer thinks should happen given past experiences with a product or service

▸ *Ideal expectations* about what a consumer really wants to happen during an experience if everything were ideal

▸ *Equitable expectations* that a consumer forms regarding what he or she thinks should happen given the level of work that he or she has put into the experience

SOURCE OF EXPECTATIONS

How do consumers form expectations? In other words, what are the sources of information that allow consumers to form expectations? In reality, consumers form expectations based on a number of different sources.[14] Word-of-mouth communication from other consumers is an important source of information and has increased in importance with the rise of social media and online review sites. Amazon and TripAdvisor have been leaders in facilitating word-of-mouth communication in the form of online reviews that appear to have a substantial effect on consumer behaviour.

Word-of-mouth is even more powerful when it comes from people whom you trust and who are socially close to you. For example, when your best friend posts to Facebook raving about a new television show, that information is likely to generate an expectation in your mind that you too will enjoy watching that show. Similarly, when a favourite relative tells you about the fantastic meal they had at a local restaurant, you are likely to expect an above average experience when you book your own reservation. Word-of-mouth plays a critical role in consumer behaviour and is discussed in more detail in the next chapter, on consumer relationships.

A consumer's experience also influences expectations. If you've gone to a dentist who was caring and respectful of your feelings on the first visit, then you would expect the same kind of treatment during the next visit. Explicit promises such as advertisements and promotions create consumer expectations as well. If a company promises that it will deliver a package within two days, a two-day delivery is what you probably expect! Personal factors also influence expectations. Some people simply expect more out of products and services than do others. Perhaps you know people who expect restaurant meals to be perfect or flights to arrive on time in any conditions. Here, personal factors influence the expectations that consumers have about the service.

EXPECTATION CONFIDENCE AND PERFORMANCE PERCEPTIONS

The disconfirmation approach seems to be relatively straightforward; however, the processes behind the approach can be complex. This is especially true given the roles of performance perceptions, expectation confidence, and the "confirmatory bias."

Performance Perceptions. Recall that perception plays a very important role in consumer behaviour: "Perception *is* reality!" Marketers are well aware of this. Perception directly influences how a consumer interacts with the world.

Perception is also very important for the consumption and postconsumption processes. As is the case with expectations, performance perceptions can also directly influence consumer satisfaction formation independent of the disconfirmation process (dotted line in Exhibit 14.4). This is particularly the case when expectations are low. For example, if a consumer buys a brand of product that he or she knows will be bad, expectations are likely to be low. Even if these low expectations are met by performance perceptions, the consumer is likely to be dissatisfied. Also, if a consumer has no previous experience or expectation regarding a product (e.g., a new product), then perception can directly influence satisfaction.[15]

Marketers may think twice about setting expectations too firmly among consumers. For example, Domino's Pizza once emphasized a 30-minute delivery guarantee for its pizzas. Consumers then began to expect this performance so strongly that they became very dissatisfied when the expectation was not met, so much so that the drivers became hazards on the road in an effort to meet the 30-minute deadline. In the end, Domino's had to back off the guarantee to avoid legal liability for accidents incurred by drivers who could easily be accused of driving recklessly in an effort to meet the 30-minute promise.

Confidence in Expectations and the Confirmatory Bias.

Another issue that is important in satisfaction theory is the degree to which consumers are confident in their expectations. For example, if a complete stranger tells a consumer that a movie is good, the consumer may not be very confident in his or her expectations. However, if a family member tells the consumer that a movie is good, then the consumer might feel much more confident in expecting the movie to be good. Research has indicated that when expectations are held with a strong degree of confidence, both disconfirmation and performance perceptions affect satisfaction. However, when expectations lack a strong degree of confidence, perceived performance more strongly influences satisfaction.[16]

Expectations not only play a key role in satisfaction formation, but also can affect how consumers see things. That is, expectations can affect performance perceptions.[17] Imagine a student who goes into a class thinking, "This class is going to be really bad!" There is a tendency for an expectation like this to actually alter the student's perception of the class experience. If the student thinks it's going to be bad, he or she may very well look for evidence to support this expectation! The term to explain this phenomenon is **confirmatory bias**. The confirmatory bias works in conjunction with self-perception theory. **Self-perception theory** states that consumers are motivated to act in accordance with their attitudes and behaviours. Here, consumers are motivated to perceive their environment through the lens of their expectations. The confirmatory influence of expectations on perceptions is especially strong when consumers are quite confident in what to expect.

Expectations and Service Quality.

Service quality can be thought of as the overall goodness or badness of a service provided. Service

confirmatory bias tendency for expectations to guide performance perceptions

self-perception theory theory that consumers are motivated to act in accordance with their attitudes and behaviours

service quality overall goodness or badness of a service experience, which is often measured by SERVQUAL

Outcomes Are Cocreated

Consumption is a partnership. Consumer researchers often express that idea by emphasizing the fact that consumers *coproduce* or *cocreate* outcomes.

The consumer's role in cocreating the outcome from a frozen entrée seems very simple. However, nearly 40% of frozen dinner consumers admit to ignoring instructions such as those stating that the food should be stirred halfway through the microwave cooking time. The nonstirred result is a meal scorched on the outside yet still frozen in the middle. As a result, average customer satisfaction with frozen meals is surprisingly low. Thus, even when the company gets everything right, the consumer is still a partner in creating the value, and sometimes the consumer does not make a good partner! Some brands, such as Whole Foods, are turning away from microwave ovens as the recommended way of creating the meals and encouraging partners to use a skillet.

iStockphoto.com/Spauln

Sources: A. M. Chaker, "Frozen Entrees Give Microwaves a Cold Shower," *The Wall Street Journal*, March 27, 2013, D3. G. Cairins, "Evolutions in Food Marketing, Quantifying the Impact and Policy Implications," *Appetite* 62 (March 2013): 194–197.

quality is often discussed as the difference between consumer expectations of different service aspects and the actual service that is delivered. When a gap exists—for example, when a dental hygienist is not as empathetic as a consumer expected—then quality perceptions are diminished. In fact, the **SERVQUAL** scale, a commonly applied instrument for measuring service quality, takes this approach. From this perspective, service quality is really a disconfirmation approach.[18] Perhaps it goes without saying, but service quality then becomes a key driver of consumer satisfaction or dissatisfaction.

DESIRES AND SATISFACTION

Although expectations play a major role in satisfaction formation, consumer desires are also very important. **Desires** are the level of a particular benefit that will lead to a valued end state. Studies have shown that desires directly affect satisfaction, beyond the influence of disconfirmation alone.[19] What consumers truly desire rather than expect from a product, service, or experience is therefore very important.

EMOTIONS, MEANING, AND SATISFACTION

As discussed earlier, emotions and meaning play important roles in consumption. These elements are also an important part of satisfaction formation. An experience producing positive emotions is logically likely to be satisfying as well. Conversely, if a consumer is in a bad mood when he or she goes to a restaurant, overall satisfaction with the experience will likely be affected in a mood-congruent direction. In other words, a bad mood tends to create dissatisfaction. Furthermore, the meaning behind the meal contributes to satisfaction as well. For example, perhaps that meal is with a loved one, or a business meal that will be used to seal an important business agreement. Here, the meaning of the consumption experience affects the overall satisfaction with the meal independently of prior expectations or perceptions. A study of river-rafting consumers revealed that the emotions that consumers felt while consuming the experience related strongly to the value they experienced during the trip.[20]

SERVQUAL instrument for measuring service quality that captures consumers' disconfirmation of service expectations

desires level of a particular benefit that will lead to a valued end state

equity theory theory that people compare their own level of inputs and outcomes to those of another party in an exchange

How are the emotions of river-rafting consumers related to the value they experience during the trip?

14-4b Equity Theory and Consumer Satisfaction

Perceptions of fairness can also have an impact on consumer satisfaction. **Equity theory** proposes that consumers cognitively compare their own level of inputs and outcomes to those of another party in an exchange.[21] Equitable exchanges occur when these ratios are equal. In equation form:

$$\frac{\text{outcomes}_A}{\text{inputs}_A} \approx \frac{\text{outcomes}_B}{\text{inputs}_B}$$

The equation states that as long as comparisons of outcomes to inputs for a consumer are approximately the same as the same ratio for another party (e.g., a company or another consumer), then satisfaction will be positively affected. So, an inequitable exchange can occur when a consumer believes that he or she has been taken advantage of by a company or when another customer has been treated more favourably.

When a consumer sets out to buy a computer, she will put quite a bit of effort into finding just the right one. She will take time to visit a store such as Best Buy, talk with friends about what brand to buy, visit websites such as Dell.ca, and try to figure out the best way to finance the computer. She considers all these inputs before conducting the transaction. What will the consumer get when she buys the computer? Of course, she will get a computer, but she will also get a warranty, service contract, and maybe even in-home installation. These things represent her outcomes.

The computer salesperson should take time to understand the consumer's desires and the way she will use the computer, and then try to match these with a good arrangement of product features. Perhaps the salesperson will show effort by listening and physically searching store inventory for the most appropriate product. These are inputs for the salesperson. Salesperson outcomes include a salary and any commission tied directly to the sale. When consumers put a lot into an important purchase, they don't like to be shortchanged by an apathetic employee. That wouldn't be fair, and the output-to-input ratios would reflect this. Fairness perceptions affect satisfaction in addition to any influence of disconfirmation. In fact, consumers sometimes feel overrewarded—for example, in a service recovery effort—and these consumers pay the business back with very high satisfaction.[22]

INEQUITABLE TREATMENT

Perhaps more often, equity perceptions involve inequitable treatment of customers. A single customer enters a restaurant for lunch and puts in an order. A few minutes later, a couple enters and sits beside the first customer at the next table. They place their order. After 10 minutes, the couple receives their food and the original customer is still waiting. To the original customer, this may seem unfair and be a source of dissatisfaction. Thus, service providers need to be keenly aware of how customers are treated in public to maintain perceptions that all customers are treated in much the same way—or at least treated in a fair way.

INEQUITABLE CONSUMERS

Some consumers will try to take advantage of situations. Even though treatment is inequitable, if the inequity is in the consumers' favour, these particular customers may be very satisfied. For example, some consumers may take a minor mishap and complain so fiercely that managers feel compelled to offer something overly generous as a way of calming the consumer down. Other consumers may realize that a cashier has made a significant error and given them significantly too much change and not correct the mistake. These consumers may be satisfied because the equity balance favours them. However, their actions can sometimes disadvantage other consumers.

14-4c Attribution Theory and Consumer Satisfaction

Another approach to satisfaction can be found in **attribution theory**, which focuses on explaining

why a certain event has occurred. When consumers select and consume products, they are motivated to make attributions as to why good or bad things happen. Humans are innately curious. There are three key elements to the attribution theory approach: locus, control, and stability.[23]

Locus refers to judgments of who is responsible for an event. Consumers can assign the locus to themselves or to an external entity like a service provider. A self-ascribed event occurs when a consumer blames himself or herself for a bad event. For example, a consumer might say to himself, "I took way too long between oil changes; it's no wonder that my engine blew up!" Self-ascribed causes are referred to as internal attributions. If an event is attributed to a product or company, an external attribution is made. For example, a consumer might say, "I changed my oil regularly! It's not my fault that the engine blew up! Chrysler is still turning out junk!" This type of attribution of blame toward a marketing entity increases consumer dissatisfaction.

Control refers to the extent to which an outcome was controllable or not. Here, consumers ask themselves, "Should this company have been able to control this event?" Two consumers are stranded in the airport in Frankfurt, Germany, overnight because their destination airport, Toronto, is iced over. One consumer is irate (beyond dissatisfaction) with the airline because he believes the airline should have equipment to clear the ice off the runway and safely land the plane. Another consumer who is booked on the same flight is not happy about the situation but does not blame the airline because she understands that weather events are uncontrollable. Therefore, the situation does not significantly affect her satisfaction process.

Stability refers to the likelihood that an event will occur again in the future. Here, consumers ask themselves, "If I buy this product again, is another bad outcome likely to happen?" Let's briefly return to the Frankfurt airport example. If a customer has recently been stranded because of weather problems in Toronto on occasions other than the recent ice storm, he naturally comes to believe that this is a stable situation and his satisfaction with the airline will be diminished. On the other hand, if the other consumer has never before been stranded due to problems at the Toronto airport, her satisfaction with the airline is not likely to be affected by the current situation.

attribution theory
theory that consumers look for the cause of particular consumption experiences when arriving at satisfaction judgments

Dissonance has also been responsible for more than a few cold feet in the days before a wedding.

14-4d Cognitive Dissonance

Consumers also can experience what is known as cognitive dissonance following a purchase or a big decision. As was discussed with the balance theory approach, consumers prefer consistency among their beliefs. When faced with the knowledge that a bad decision may have been made, consumers experience dissonance (literally meaning "lack of agreement") between the thought that they are a good decision maker and that they made a bad decision. **Cognitive dissonance** refers to lingering doubts about a decision that has already been made.[24] Dissonance is sometimes known as buyer's regret. For example, a consumer may reach a decision to buy one house and then experience discomfort due to doubt that creeps in when the consumer realizes there were many other attractive houses available in addition to the one purchased.

Cognitive dissonance does not occur for all decisions. For high-ticket items like automobiles or homes, though, dissonance is a real possibility if not a probability. Dissonance has also been responsible for more than a few cold feet in the days before a wedding. These are situations that naturally lend themselves to the experience of dissonance. A consumer is more likely to experience true dissonance after making a purchase when the following conditions exist:

1. **The consumer is aware that there are many attractive alternatives that may offer comparable value relative to the product/brand purchased.**

2. **The decision is difficult to reverse.**

3. **The decision is important and involves risk.**

4. **The consumer has low self-confidence.**

The dissonance among consumers' beliefs following a consumption experience can be very discomforting and be a source of negative postconsumption emotions. Consumers may therefore be motivated to lessen this discomfort. Furthermore, effective marketing can target consumers after purchase to take steps to reinforce their

cognitive dissonance
an uncomfortable feeling that occurs when a consumer has lingering doubts about a decision that has occurred

> ### Exhibit 14.5
> ## Dissonance Reduction Strategies
>
> Return the product if possible.
>
> Complain about the experience.
>
> Seek positive information about the alternative selected.
>
> Seek negative information about the alternatives not selected.
>
> Minimize the perceived importance of the decision.

customers' decisions to select a brand. Many universities automatically send graduates university-sponsored magazines in order to maintain relationships and to reinforce the idea that choosing the school was indeed a good idea.

To lessen feelings of discomfort following purchase, consumers may engage in any, or all, of the activities listed in Exhibit 14.5.

COGNITIVE DISSONANCE AND SATISFACTION

Satisfaction and cognitive dissonance are closely related topics. The major difference between the two concepts is that satisfaction is generally felt *after* a consumption experience, but dissonance may be experienced even *before* consumption begins. For example, after a decision has been made, a consumer might immediately think, "I should have bought the other one!" The uncertainty of events that might occur provides the basis for dissonance.[25]

14-5 CONSUMER SATISFACTION/ DISSATISFACTION MEASUREMENT ISSUES

There are many ways in which marketers can measure consumer satisfaction. Three popular ways are through direct global measures, attribute-specific ratings, and disconfirmation.

Direct Global Measures. Simply ask consumers to assess their satisfaction on a scale such as:

How do you rate your overall satisfaction with your television?

completely dissatisfied	dissatisfied	satisfied	completely satisfied
☐	☐	☐	☐

Attribute-Specific Ratings. Assess a consumer's satisfaction with various components, or attributes, of a product, service, or experience, such as:

How satisfied are you with the following attribute of your television?

Picture Quality

completely dissatisfied				completely satisfied
1	2	3	4	5

Disconfirmation. Compare the difference between expectations and performance perceptions. This measure can be taken in a direct, subjective fashion, such as:[26]

Compared to my expectations, this television performs …

much worse than I expected				much better than I expected
1	2	3	4	5

14-5a Improving Satisfaction Measures

Satisfaction is one of the most commonly measured concepts in consumer behaviour but is also one of the most difficult to measure accurately. For example, the typical four-choice satisfaction approach as shown in the direct global measure example actually proves quite problematic in practice. The problems can be severe and limit the ability to use satisfaction ratings to explain or predict other outcomes, including whether the consumer will return.

Consider that marketers measure satisfaction among existing customers most frequently. These customers have already decided to patronize a business. So, a web pop-up for Amazon.ca may ask a consumer to rate satisfaction with a simple measure of this type. This consumer should already be favourable because he or she has purposefully decided to visit Amazon.ca and shop using this site. Thus, he or she already feels favourable toward Amazon.ca. Therefore, we would expect even without knowing what happened during the visit that the customer would report some degree of satisfaction. In fact, typical consumer responses to this type of measure show that the vast majority of consumers, 80% or more, choose "satisfied" or "completely satisfied." Statistically speaking, these data are **left skewed**, in this instance meaning that the bulk of consumers have indicated that they are satisfied or completely satisfied with the product or service.

Does this reflect reality, or is the scale simply inadequate in truly differentiating consumers experiencing different levels of satisfaction? The truth is that both possibilities are likely true to some extent. From a measurement perspective, giving consumers more response choices may increase the amount of variance displayed in the satisfaction measure and thereby increase its usefulness in trying to use satisfaction to predict and explain other behaviours. An alternative would be to have consumers score their satisfaction on a 0 (no satisfaction) to 100 (complete satisfaction) point scale. The results will still typically show an average satisfaction score above 50 points; however, the statistical properties are much improved, making for a more useful measure. Even better, a researcher might have a respondent rate his or her satisfaction with multiple scale items.

Exhibit 14.6 displays an improved way of measuring consumer satisfaction using multiple scale items.[27] The scale mitigates problems with skewness and/or bias by providing scales with more response points and by using different response formats for each response item. The scale also focuses only on satisfaction. Although a marketer may choose to measure only satisfaction, this scale suggests that dissatisfaction should be measured with its own scale. A dissatisfaction scale can be formed by substituting the word *dissatisfaction* for *satisfaction* in each of the four items. Even if a total of eight items are used (four satisfaction and four dissatisfaction items), a consumer can typically respond to these items in less than one minute. The question of whether dissatisfaction is more than just low satisfaction can be sorted out statistically. That topic is left for another course.

left skewed when a disproportionate number of observations cluster toward the right end of a scale, as when most people report satisfied or very satisfied

Exhibit 14.6

A Multi-Item Satisfaction Scale[28]

Please rate your satisfaction with your experience in the Air Canada's Executive Lounge using the following items. It will take you no longer than 1 minute to complete this survey.

Please an X in the box that describes the way you feel about your stay in the Air Canada's Executive Lounge.

Not satisfied at all	Somewhat satisfied	Satisfied	Very satisfied	Completly satisfied
☐	☐	☐	☐	☐

Indicate the percent to which you feel satisfied with your stay in the Air Canada's Executive Lounge using a 100 point scale where 0 = no satisfaction at all and 100 = total satisfaction.

_____ %

Indicate the extent to which you experienced the feeling of satisfaction with your visit to the Air Canada's Executive Lounge. Place an X in the box that matches the way you feel.

Did not feel at all	Felt only slightly	Felt a little	Felt Somewhat	Felt moderatly	Felt very much	Felt extremely
☐	☐	☐	☐	☐	☐	☐

To what extent do you agree with the following statement?
I feel completely satisfied with my experience with the Air Canada's Executive Lounge.

Strongly disagree	Disagree	Slightly disagree	Slightly agree	Agree	Strongly agree
☐	☐	☐	☐	☐	☐

14-6 DISPOSING OF REFUSE

14-6a Disposal Decisions

A final step in consumption is disposal of any consumer refuse. **Consumer refuse** is any packaging that is no longer necessary for consumption to take place or, in some cases, the actual good that is no longer providing value to the consumer. Many consumers have old computers that they no longer use but have not yet disposed of because of various concerns, including security issues. At first, this may seem like a straightforward process wherein the consumer simply throws away their trash. However, a number of disposal alternatives are available. These include trashing, recycling, converting to another use, trading, donating, or reselling.[29]

consumer refuse any packaging that is no longer necessary for consumption to take place or, in some cases, the actual good that is no longer providing value to the consumer

Trashing. One alternative that a consumer has is simply to throw away waste material, including unused products, packaging, and by-products. Of course, there are environmental concerns with this alternative. According to the Conference Board of Canada, the amount of municipal waste generated by Canadians has increased substantially over the past 30 years. In 1980, the average waste generated per Canadian was 510 kilograms per year. In 2007, that number had climbed to 894 kilograms.[30] In response to growing concerns about the amount of garbage going into landfills, marketers have turned to so-called green marketing initiatives, which aim to use packaging materials that cut down on the environmental impact of waste. Early evidence suggests some success as the disposal of residential waste decreased by 1% and the disposal of nonresidential waste fell by 6% between 2008 and 2010. In addition, recycling increased by 5% overall and by 60% for electronic products.[31]

Recycling. Another alternative for consumers is to recycle used products or packaging. Recycling cuts down on garbage while providing raw materials for other new products. Consumers can then buy new products made of recycled materials.

Converting to Another Use. Consumers can convert products, or product packaging, into new products in a number of creative ways. For example, consumers often use old T-shirts and socks as car-wash rags.

Trading. Another alternative for consumers is to trade old products for new products. The automotive industry has encouraged this practice for years. Consumers can often get thousands of dollars off of a new automobile purchase by trading-in an old model. Even a car that doesn't run has some value in the form of spare parts.

Buy, Sell, and Trade the Online Way

From eBay.ca to Craigslist.ca to Kijiji.ca, online buying, selling, and trading has become a huge business. Although consumers once had only a few options if they wanted to buy, sell, or trade used items, the Internet has made the process much easier.

Of course, the Internet phenomenon eBay has long been the benchmark in the online trading world. The Internet giant that is well known for allowing consumers to auction off their belongings in an online marketplace has been wildly successful for several years. Rival Craigslist, which focuses on online classified advertising, has also experienced rapid growth, and the site currently accounts for more than 90% of online classified listing traffic. Not to be outdone, eBay's Kijiji, which also focuses on online classified advertising, is a major player in the growing industry.

Thanks to sites such as these, consumers can now auction their products, place classified ads online, or simply browse local pages for good deals. The ease and availability of these sites are rapidly changing how consumers buy and sell goods and, ultimately, how consumers interact with one another.

Sources: Fowler, Geoffrey A. (2009), "Auctions Fade in eBay's Bid for Growth," *The Wall Street Journal* (online), May 26, 2009, p. A1, accessed June 15, 2009; MacMillan, Douglas (2009), "Craiglist Fuels Online Classified-Ad Surge," *Business Week* (online), New York: May 25, 2009, accessed June 15, 2009; Dell, Kristina (2008)," eBay Bids for Revitalization," *Time* (online), 172 (25), December 22, 2008, p. G1, accessed June 15, 2009.

Donating. Consumers also have the ability to donate used products to various causes. Eyeglasses, clothing, and (surprisingly) automobiles are often donated in order to help other consumers who may not be able to afford new products.

Reselling. One of the most popular methods for permanently disposing of used products is simply to sell them. Garage sales and swap meets are popular means of disposing of products in this way. Of course, online methods such as eBay and Craigslist are also quite popular with consumers.

14-6b Disposal, Emotions, and Product Symbolism

As discussed in an earlier chapter, possessions can help express a consumer's self-concept, and so consumers often develop emotional bonds with their possessions. The decision to part with belongings can therefore be very emotional, especially for older consumers who place much symbolic value on products[32] they are strongly attached to, especially those considered to be family heirlooms. Selling, giving away, or donating these goods can lead consumers to feel as if they have lost a part of themselves. In other situations, consumers can be quite ready to dispose of products that bring back bad memories or that lead the consumers to have uneasy feelings about themselves or their past.[33]

Some consumers are very reluctant to part with their possessions. The terms *packrat* and *hoarder* are used to describe a person who keeps possessions that fulfill no utilitarian or hedonic need and who has a difficult time disposing of products. Packrats are likely to visit garage sales, swap meets, and flea markets to purchase products that serve no immediate need.[34] Even though the term *packrat* is often used loosely, hoarder behaviour can be associated with various psychological conditions, including obsessive-compulsive disorder.

STUDY TOOLS 14

LOCATED AT THE BACK OF THE TEXTBOOK

☐ Rip out Chapter Review Card

LOCATED AT NELSON.COM/STUDENT

☐ Review Key Terms Flashcards (print or online)

☐ Download audio summaries to review on the go

☐ Complete practice quizzes to prepare for tests

☐ Watch video on Sephora for a real company example

Case

The Cult of Apple

Apple recently became the world's most valuable company. Not to be confused with the company that produces the greatest revenue—that would be Walmart—Apple *is* the company that has the highest stock market valuation. Although Walmart has more than three times the sales of Apple, it is worth only about one-quarter of Apple's value. While Apple's satisfaction ratings regularly rank at or near the top of consumer-focused companies, Walmart's ACSI scores are generally among the lowest of large retail companies (see Exhibit 14.3). As Claus Fornell, founder of the ACSI, says, "Companies with weak customer satisfaction often have weak stock performance."

With the launch of the iPhone 4S, Apple opened up a major gap between its customer satisfaction scores and those of its competitors, like Nokia, LG, or Canadian-based BlackBerry devices. In spring 2012, the Apple iPhone's ACSI score was 83 (on a 100-point scale), which is eight points better than its nearest competitors (HTC, LG, and Nokia, which all scored 75 points) and 14 points better than BlackBerry, at the bottom of the list with a 69 rating. That high level of satisfaction among Apple's customers, combined with their willingness to stand in line overnight for the privilege of paying the iPhone's premium prices, has led some observers to refer to the extremely strong relationship between Apple and its consumers as a "cult."

The biggest problem for competitors is that Apple is perceived by consumers to be offering superior value, even at premium prices. When Apple launches a new laptop, tablet, phone, or other device, it is able to charge a substantial premium over its competitors. Take the first iWatch as an example. A number of other companies, including Pebble and Samsung, were in the smart watch market well before Apple entered, but Apple quickly gained a dominant market share. In fact, the iWatch sold more units in its first three months than either the first iPad or the first iPhone. When the $20,000 Apple Watch Edition went on sale in China, it sold out in less than an hour!

In fact, even when products fail to meet expectations, it does not seem to significantly affect how most consumers feel about Apple. The Apple iPhone 4 was introduced with an antenna that resulted in dropped calls. Apple responded by telling customers to get a case for the phone that would solve the problem. The iPhone 4S was launched with a massive advertising campaign that introduced the world to Siri, a voice-activated virtual assistant. The ads made it appear that you could talk to Siri and ask the assistant to complete a variety of tasks with relative ease. In practice, many consumers found Siri's ability to be more limited than they expected and some have even sued Apple for misleading them. Apple's response: If you don't like the phone, take it back and get a refund. More recently, consumers have had trouble using the lightning connector to charge their iPhones.

Yet, Apple continues to surge forward. The company has launched new services that charge a subscription fee to store photos and stream music. Once again, these products are expected to be significant players in the consumer market for cloud-based services at a price premium to the competition. To fuel this growth, Apple is relying on the value it has created in the very strong relationships it has with its very satisfied consumers.

Sources: Barrie, Joshua (2015), "The $20,000 gold Apple Watch Edition sold out in China in less than an hour," *Business Insider*, April 10, http://www .businessinsider.com/apple-watch-edition-sold-out-in-china-2015 -4#ixzz3eBwC3C7z accessed on June 26, 2015. Cassidy, John (2012), "How Long Will the Cult of Apple Endure?" *The New Yorker*, Online Daily (March 20), http://www.newyorker.com/online/blogs/johncassidy/2012/03/how -long-will-the-cult-of-apple-last-for.html, accessed May 23, 2012. Cline, Seth (2012), "Don't Like It? Get a Refund, Apple Says of Siri Lawsuits," *US News & World Report* (May 18), http://www.usnews.com/news/ articles/2012/05/18/dont-like-it-get-a-refund-apple-says-of-siri-lawsuits, accessed May 23, 2012. Reed, Brad (2012), "Apple Dominates Other Smartphone Vendors in Customer Satisfaction," *Network World US* (May 15), http://www.pcadvisor.co.uk/news/mobile-phone /3357579/

apple-dominates-other-smartphone-vendors-in-consumer-satisfaction, accessed May 23, 2012. Villapez, Luke (2015), "Apple Watch US Sales Outpacing iPad Debut, According To New Estimate ," *IBI Times*, June 4, http://www.ibtimes.com/apple-watch-us-sales-outpacing-ipad-debut-according-new-estimate-1950917 accessed June 26, 2015.

QUESTIONS

1 What meaning is being transferred from Apple to its customers?

2 Are Apple customers satisfied, or are they feeling a different, more powerful emotion as part of the iPhone consumption experience? If so, what might that emotion be?

3 How has the iPhone changed what consumers expect from a smart phone? How might this change in expectations affect consumer satisfaction with competing products?

4 Why have the dropped calls of the Apple 4, the underperformance of Siri, and other product issues not had a more negative impact on satisfaction with the iPhone? Are Apple's customers suffering from a confirmatory bias? Are they attributing the failure to something other than Apple itself?

5 How can other companies compete with Apple's powerful "cult" of customers?

15 | Consumer Relationships

LEARNING OBJECTIVES

After studying this chapter, the student should be able to:

15-1 List and define the behavioural outcomes of consumption.

15-2 Know why consumers complain and the ramifications of complaining behaviour for a marketing firm.

15-3 Use the concept of switching costs to understand why consumers do or do not repeat purchase behaviour.

15-4 Describe each component of true consumer loyalty.

15-5 Understand the role that value plays in shaping loyalty and building consumer relationships.

15-1 OUTCOMES OF CONSUMPTION

The previous chapter focused significantly on customer satisfaction/dissatisfaction. Many companies have satisfaction guarantees: *100% Satisfaction or Your Money Back!* Assuming that marketers' motivations for such guarantees are well intentioned, are companies really interested in satisfaction? If consumers could not return to do business again, the pursuit of satisfaction would be relegated to a purely altruistic exercise. Many firms might lose interest in serving customers well if this were the case. However, firms are interested in what happens after a consumer is satisfied or dissatisfied because they would like customers to return to do business again. Thus, this chapter picks up where the previous chapter left off. Here, the focus is squarely on postconsumption reactions—the things that happen after a consumer has received most consumption benefits.

Exhibit 15.1 expands the disconfirmation framework traditionally used to explain consumer satisfaction. This particular chart divides up the different concepts into three groups. The green-colour variables represent things that are predominantly cognitive. These include the actual disconfirmation formation process that results from comparing experienced performance with expected performance. Additionally, consumers' attribution and equity cognitions are also included among cognitions. Perceptions of justice are included within the equity cognitions. **Procedural justice**, in particular, refers to the extent that consumers believe the processes involved in processing a transaction and handling any complaints are fair.

Postconsumption cognitions lead to an affective reaction most conventionally represented by consumer satisfaction/dissatisfaction (CS/D). This particular model recognizes that the evaluation process could lead to any number of varying affective outcomes, many of which have stronger behavioural reactions than CS/D. The blue sections in Exhibit 15.1 show the affective variables.

Finally, the exhibit shows behavioural outcomes of the postconsumption process in red boxes. Indeed, this is why marketers are interested in pursuing satisfaction. The behaviours that complete this process do

procedural justice
the extent that consumers believe the processes involved in processing a transaction and handling any complaints are fair

Truly loyal customers are like gold to a company.

Exhibit 15.1

A More Detailed Look at Postconsumption Reactions

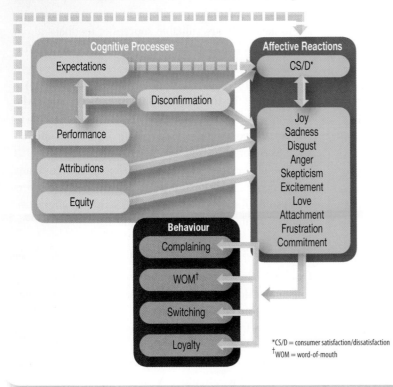

Cognitive Processes
- Expectations
- Disconfirmation
- Performance
- Attributions
- Equity

Affective Reactions
- CS/D*
- Joy
- Sadness
- Disgust
- Anger
- Skepticism
- Excitement
- Love
- Attachment
- Frustration
- Commitment

Behaviour
- Complaining
- WOM†
- Switching
- Loyalty

*CS/D = consumer satisfaction/dissatisfaction
†WOM = word-of-mouth

much to determine the success or failure of competitive enterprises. Never has this been truer than in today's relationship marketing era. While the negative behaviours like complaining perhaps receive more attention as reactions to consumption, positive outcomes, including positive word-of-mouth behaviour and ultimately the development of a strong relationship, are essential elements to success.

We begin this chapter by looking at some common behaviours that follow consumption. Exhibit 15.1 lists the behaviours, and although all but the last, loyalty, may seem negative, if properly managed the firm can turn these negative behaviours into positive value experiences. When this is done, customers are more likely to become loyal, and loyalty is the positive outcome that relationship-oriented firms seek.

CHAPTER 15: Consumer Relationships **285**

15-2 COMPLAINING AND SPREADING WOM

15-2a Complaining Behaviour

Complaining behaviour occurs when a consumer actively seeks out someone to share an opinion with regarding a negative consumption event. The person may be a service provider, a supervisor, or someone designated by a company to take complaints. Think about this question:

How long should a consumer have to wait for service before complaining?

The answer to this may depend on several factors, including the type of service involved. A 30-minute wait may be unacceptable and evoke negative disconfirmation, a negative affective consequence, and an active complaint if a consumer is waiting to be served for lunch. However, a consumer waiting to see a doctor for 30 minutes may not experience the same reaction because the expectation is that one will wait for 30 minutes or more. Even if one waits longer than expected to see a doctor, the consumer still may not complain for other reasons.

COMPLAINERS

Generally, we think of dissatisfied customers as complainers. Not all customers reporting dissatisfaction complain. In fact, far less than half of customers experiencing some dissatisfaction complain to management. Only 17% of health care consumers complain upon experiencing some problem with the service or care they are receiving, and a recent survey among restaurant consumers suggests that no more than 5% of consumers with a problem complain.[1] What makes a *complainer* different? Consumers who do complain experience different emotions than do those who do not complain. In contrast to consumers who are merely dissatisfied, angry consumers are very likely to complain, and at times, the anger becomes very strong and reaches the stage of rage.[2]

A potentially worse outcome for a business occurs when a consumer has a negative experience, realizes this, and then reacts more with disgust than anger. Compared with the angry customer, a disgusted or hopeless consumer is not likely to complain.[3] Consumers'

Actively listening to the complaints of annoyed customers can lead to greatly improved service.

behavioural reactions can be understood by considering whether the emotions they experience evoke approach or avoidance reactions. Negative approach emotions like anger are most likely to precede complaining behaviour. Complaining is a relatively mild way of coping with anger.

The consumer who reacts with disgust is unlikely to complain. Disgust evokes an avoidance response, and as a result, a disgusted consumer avoids a potential confrontation and simply goes away; thus, the information about what caused the problem in the first place also goes away. Complainers, although sometimes unpleasant to deal with, are valuable sources of feedback about potential problems in service quality, product performance, or system malfunction.

When a consumer complains, the marketer has a chance to rectify the negative situation. A consumer who sulks away takes the valuable information with him or her. A truly consumer-oriented company should encourage customers to complain when things go wrong. If "100% satisfaction" is not just a slogan, the company must encourage its customers to act like whistleblowers when something goes wrong. In this sense, an angry customer is a valuable asset for a business!

THE RESULT OF COMPLAINING

Exhibit 15.2 provides a summary of what happens when consumers do or do not complain. The fact of the matter is that for consumers as well as marketers, complaining pays off. When consumers complain, more often than not, some corrective action is taken that culminates with the consumer feeling satisfied when he or she re-evaluates the situation. A consumer who complains

complaining behaviour action that occurs when a consumer actively seeks out someone to share an opinion with regarding a negative consumption event

Exhibit 15.2

The Complainer Versus the Noncomplainer and Negative Word-of-Mouth

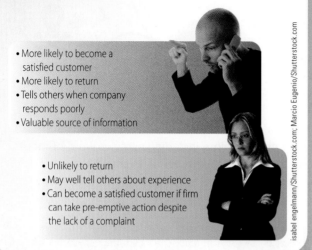

- More likely to become a satisfied customer
- More likely to return
- Tells others when company responds poorly
- Valuable source of information

- Unlikely to return
- May well tell others about experience
- Can become a satisfied customer if firm can take pre-emptive action despite the lack of a complaint

isabel engelmann/Shutterstock.com; Marcio Eugenio/Shutterstock.com

about a noisy hotel room gets moved to another room, perhaps a suite! In such a case, the customer is likely to believe that he or she was treated fairly after complaining, and these thoughts evoke a more positive outcome. This positive outcome can represent a win–win situation.

Earlier, we mentioned that only about 5% of restaurant customers with a service problem actually complained to management. However, among those who complained, 95% were likely to remain customers of the restaurant when their complaint was handled quickly and responsively. Service providers can handle consumer complaints effectively if they:[4]

1. **Thank the guest for providing the information.**
2. **Ask questions to clarify the issue.**
3. **Apologize sincerely.**
4. **Show empathy for the customer's situation.**
5. **Explain the corrective action that will take place.**
6. **Act quickly.**
7. **Follow up with the customer after the corrective action.**

Today, it's easier than ever for consumers to complain publicly. Several websites—including www.consumer.ca, http://esupport.fcc.gov/complaints.htm, and http://www.bbb.org/canada—allow consumers to lodge formal complaints, make their complaints public, and get advice on the proper steps to follow should the consumer need to take further official action.

THE RESULT OF NOT COMPLAINING

So, what happens when the consumer does not complain? Let's return to the noisy hotel room. A customer may simply put up with the inconvenience and end up leaving miserable after a poor night's sleep. Is this the end of the story? Not really! The consumer may well remember this incident and be less likely to do business with this hotel again. He or she may also complain to others about the episode, or may use social media—such as TripAdvisor, Facebook, or Twitter—to disseminate the complaint publicly. Interestingly, though, when marketers can take action to address a negative situation before a consumer complains, a very positive outcome can result. So, imagine that a bell clerk reports the noise in one of the halls of the hotel to management. Management then takes action by calling the adjacent rooms to suggest that they move to a better room. These customers are likely to be very appreciative and become more likely to return again.[5]

REVENGE

On occasion, consumers' verbal complaints to the marketing company do not eliminate the negative emotions they are experiencing. In these instances, consumers may retaliate in the form of revenge-oriented behaviours. These could be as simple as trying to prevent others from using the business by spreading the word about how bad the business is, but the behaviours can become more aggressive. **Rancorous revenge** occurs when a consumer yells, insults, and/or makes a public scene in an effort to harm the business.[6] However, in extreme cases, the furious consumer can become violent or try to vandalize the business; **retaliatory revenge** is a term that captures these extreme types of behaviour.

15-2b Word-of-Mouth

Just because a consumer doesn't complain to the offending company doesn't mean he or she just keeps the episode inside. **Negative word-of-mouth (negative WOM)** takes place when consumers pass on negative information about a company from one to another.

rancorous revenge when a consumer yells, insults, and/or makes a public scene in an effort to harm the business in response to an unsatisfactory experience

retaliatory revenge when a consumer becomes violent with employees and/or tries to vandalize a business in response to an unsatisfactory experience

negative word-of-mouth (negative WOM) action that takes place when consumers pass on negative information about a company from one to another

Payback Can Be Swell!

All too often, the news contains stories of customers gone wild. For example, an angry McDonald's customer tried to run over two customers with her car in a parking lot in a situation that started with a long line to place the order. Another woman, enraged because McDonald's was out of Chicken McNuggets, went berserk and attacked the person working at the drive-through window.

Sometimes, complaining behaviour becomes extreme and takes the form of revenge. Every consumer has a critical boiling point, and once this is reached, the likelihood of retaliatory actions becomes real. One key trigger is procedural justice, or the lack thereof. Consumers think they have been treated unfairly and that the business is responsible. When this happens, they become prone to all manner of complaints, including negative word-of-mouth and potentially unethical or even illegal action such as vandalism or battery. These types of revenge behaviours help consumers cope with their feelings and create an opportunity for them to reduce or eliminate their own negative mood state. In that way, revenge is swell.

Sources: Rio-Lanza, A. B., R. Vazquez-Casielles and A. M. Diaz-Martin (2009), "Satisfaction with Service Recovery: Perceived Justice and Emotional Responses," *Journal of Business Research*, 62, 775–781; Zourrig, H., J.C. Chebat and R. Tofoli (2009), "Consumer Revenge Behavior: A Cross-Cultural Perspective," *Journal of Business Research*, 62, 995–1001. Kalamas, M., M. Laroche and L. Makdessian (2008), "Reaching the Boiling Point: Consumers' Negative Affective Reactions to Firm-Attributed Service Failures," *Journal of Business Research*, 61, 813–824. www.breitbart.com/article.php?id=08JGINJG18show_article=1, accessed August 10, 2010.

As can be seen from Exhibit 15.2, both the complainer and the noncomplainer may well participate in this kind of potentially destructive behaviour. Some estimates suggest that a consumer who fails to achieve a valuable consumption experience is likely to tell his or her story to more than 10 other consumers.[7] Recall that, as a source of information, WOM is powerful because of relatively high source credibility. The fact that most consumers who participate in WOM do so to multiple consumers makes the matter all the more important.

WOM is not always negative. In fact, **positive word-of-mouth (positive WOM)** occurs when consumers spread information from one to another about positive consumption experiences with companies. Conventionally, negative WOM is seen as more common than positive WOM. However, in the television industry, consumers appear more likely to spread the word about shows they find valuable rather than those they do not.[8] Whether positive or negative, WOM exerts very strong influences on other consumers. As we will see later, a consumer spreading positive WOM is likely to be an asset to a business.

NEGATIVE PUBLIC PUBLICITY

When negative WOM spreads to a relatively large scale, it can result in **negative public publicity**. Negative public publicity could even involve media coverage. Thus, most large companies have employees whose job it is to try to quell or respond to negative public publicity. In the United States, a Delta Air Lines customer had a camera stolen from a checked bag. After personally investigating the situation, he was able to track down the culprit, a Delta baggage handler. Eventually, the media picked up the story, at which point a Delta Air Lines official contacted the customer and refunded him the price of the original flight.[9] In this case, the negative publicity paid off for the customer.

Today, consumers can easily make their complaints public using the World Wide Web and the numerous websites that facilitate just this sort of behaviour. On one such site, ConsumerAffairs.com, consumers who are considering a purchase can search for complaints on brands and products that are being considered.

Negative publicity can do considerable harm to a brand. In chapter 4, we discussed how Toyota received a

positive word-of-mouth (positive WOM) action that occurs when consumers spread information from one to another about positive consumption experiences with companies

negative public publicity action that occurs when negative WOM spreads on a relatively large scale, possibly even involving media coverage lot of negative publicity about "unintended acceleration." Interestingly, in the 1980s, Audi's U.S. market share was virtually wiped out within a short period after the news show *60 Minutes* ran a segment claiming that Audis were susceptible to sudden acceleration syndrome. In reality, *60 Minutes* producers had rigged an Audi sedan to appear to be driving in circles with no driver in the car as a way of trying to convince viewers that Audis were indeed dangerous.[10] After more than a decade of study, the Federal Transit Administration (FTA) actually cleared Audi of this charge, with the cases being attributed to driver error—hitting the accelerator when meaning to press the brake. While the negative publicity hit Audi hard, the impact on Toyota seems to be much less.

How should a firm handle negative public publicity? Here are some alternative courses of action:

1. Do nothing; the news will eventually go away.

2. Deny responsibility for any negative event.

3. Take responsibility for any negative events and be visible in the public eye.

4. Release information, allowing the public to draw its own conclusion.

What is the best approach?

DOING NOTHING OR DENYING RESPONSIBILITY

Doing nothing is neither the best nor the worst option. Taking action seems to be a responsible thing to do, but the action can backfire. Even when the basis for the negative publicity is simply rumour, denying any responsibility can be a very bad idea.

Online forums and social networking sites have expanded the potential power of positive and negative WOM.

Common sense should suggest that McDonald's would never substitute worms for ground beef simply on the basis of cost alone (worms would have to be more expensive than ground beef). Enough consumers believed this rumour at one point that McDonald's market share suffered. McDonald's reacted with a 100% beef ad campaign, and even Ray Kroc, the founder of McDonald's, did interviews suggesting the idea had no basis in common sense or reality.[11] In essence, this was a denial response. Claiming the burgers were 100% beef was much the same as saying they are 0% worm! Denying a ridiculous claim only gives it credibility and results in negative effects for the brand.

TAKING RESPONSIBILITY

One might easily see that attribution theory plays a role in dealing with negative publicity. If consumers blame the company for the event garnering the negative publicity, then the potential repercussions appear serious. However, public action to deal with any consequences of a negative event can alleviate any negative effects.

One of the most famous negative publicity cases of all time involves Tylenol pain medicine. In the fall of 1982, seven consumer deaths in the Chicago area were attributed to cyanide in Tylenol capsules. Tylenol executives considered their options, including plausible deniability, and decided to take action by having all Tylenol removed from shelves all around the country immediately. In addition, they agreed to take steps to make sure they discovered what had happened and to make sure it could not happen again. The dramatic action helped convince consumers that Tylenol truly cared about the welfare of customers and wanted to prevent any reoccurrence. Even though the executives were quite certain the company had no culpability in what appeared to be senseless murder, they acted in a way that led to a huge short-term financial loss for the business. However, this action saved Tylenol's reputation. In fact, many younger consumers may wonder how we came to have tamper-proof packaging for over-the-counter medications and now practically all food products. While today government mandates require such packaging in many instances, the beginning of tamper-proof packaging goes back to Tylenol's response to this potentially damaging negative publicity associated with these murders.

RELEASING INFORMATION

Sometimes a company may be able to release some counter-information to media that allows consumers to make up their own minds about the potential source of any negative reports. If this is done properly, the company does not publicly deny any allegation about the event and instead insists that actions are being taken to get to the bottom of the event.

In the mid-1990s, a consumer made the news by claiming that he was simply drinking a Pepsi when a hypodermic needle began to flow out of the can and stuck his lip. Within two days of this story going public, dozens of consumers from all around the country made the same claim. Pepsi, rather than denying any responsibility, opened the doors of canning operations around North America. Film crews were allowed to record footage of cans streaming down an assembly line at high speed. Pepsi released information about the number of canning plants that exist and how they are spread around the country. This action worked to prevent any negative fallout for Pepsi, as the media coverage allowed consumers to draw their own conclusions. Obviously, if needles were to get into some Pepsi cans, the chances that this would happen at multiple canning plants all around the country seemed very remote. Thus, how could this be happening all over? Also, watching the canning operations made clear that nobody could possibly slip a needle into a can at the assembly line's very high operating speeds. This entire incident was over in just a couple of weeks, and all of the alleged needle victims confessed to making up the stories with the hope of getting some part of any settlement that Pepsi might be forced to pay.

PARTICIPATING IN NEGATIVE WOM

One of the factors that helps determine negative word-of-mouth returns to the issue of equity. Consumers who believe they have not been treated with fairness or justice become particularly likely to tell others and, in some cases, report the incident to the media.[12]

Consumers can be angry when they believe they have been wronged, and these actions are a small way of trying to get revenge. Consumers who spread negative WOM without complaining to the company itself are particularly likely not ever to do business with that company again.[13] This tendency provides all the more reason for companies to make consumers feel comfortable about complaining and to create the impression of genuine concern for the consumer's situation.

IMPLICATIONS OF NEGATIVE WOM

One reason consumers share negative WOM is as a way of preventing other consumers from falling victim to a company; thus, negative WOM can

The media are a vehicle for both spreading negative publicity and managing the implications of negative publicity.

hurt sales. However, this is not the only potential negative effect: Negative WOM can also damage the image of the firm. When a consumer hears the negative WOM from a credible source, that information is very likely to become strongly attached to the schema for that brand. Thus, not only is the consumer's attitude toward the brand lowered but the consumer will also find the firm's advertising harder to believe.[14]

In extreme cases, the negative WOM attached to one company can have effects that spill over to an entire industry. For instance, news attributing accidents at one amusement park to a lack of maintenance will certainly damage the image of that particular amusement park. However, a consumer hearing this news may end up not feeling very comfortable about any similar amusement park. Thus, firms must be wary of negative WOM not just for their own brand, but for the industry as well.[15]

Negative WOM does not affect all consumers in the same way. Consumers who have very strong, positive feelings about a brand may have a difficult time accepting negative WOM. Once again, this can be due to balance theory as consumers try to maintain their existing belief systems. If the relationship with the brand is strong, accepting negative information also diminishes the consumer's self-concept. Thus, a consumer who holds strong convictions about a brand is less likely to be affected by negative WOM or negative publicity. Brands whose images are strongly linked to positive emotions such that the emotions help provide meaning can also insulate themselves from negative WOM to some degree.[16]

15-3 SWITCHING BEHAVIOUR

Exhibit 15.1 suggests that a consumer evaluates a consumption experience, reacts emotionally, and then, perhaps, practises switching behaviour. **Switching** in a

switching times when a consumer chooses a competing choice, rather than the previously purchased choice, on the next purchase occasion consumer behaviour context refers to the times when a consumer chooses a competing choice rather than the previously purchased choice on the next purchase occasion. If a consumer visited Tim Hortons for breakfast last Tuesday and chooses Cora on Saturday the next time she goes out for breakfast, the consumer has practised switching behaviour. This could be due to any number of reasons, but perhaps the last experience at Tim Hortons was less than satisfying.

All things considered, consumers prefer the status quo. Change can mean costs that diminish the value of an experience. If the consumer has been a regular Tim Hortons customer, she now has to learn the new assortment of breakfast options available at Cora, may lose the opportunity to "RRRoll Up the Rim to Win," and cannot refill her Tim Hortons insulated coffee mug.

Thus, the consumer will incur some **switching costs**, or the costs associated with changing from one choice (brand/retailer/service provider) to another. Switching costs are one reason why a consumer may be dissatisfied with a service provider but will continue to do business with them. Switching costs can be divided into three categories:[17]

1. **Procedural**
2. **Financial**
3. **Relational**

15-3a Procedural Switching Costs

Procedural switching costs involve lost time and effort. Although Apple computers have a stellar reputation for being easy to use, most computer users stick with PC models. Why? Even if an Apple is easy to use, a consumer familiar with a PC-based Windows operating platform would have to forgo this knowledge to learn how to use an Apple. Thus, the effort that went into learning the PC system is lost and replaced by effort that would be needed to learn how to use an Apple. Most consumers would not want to invest the time and effort needed to learn a new system that would in their minds produce similar benefits. Thus, when consumers master a technologically complex product, they become very resistant to switching.[18] As a countermeasure to procedural switching costs, when Microsoft introduced Windows 8, with near instant start-up times, it made sure the old Windows desktop view was easily accessible to reduce the costs of adopting a new version of the familiar product.

15-3b Financial Switching Costs

Financial switching costs consist of the total economic resources that must be spent or invested as a

consumer learns how to obtain value from a new product choice. A consumer in Rivel, France, plans a summer vacation to the Mexican Riviera. A few weeks later, the consumer hears friends discussing their upcoming vacation in Florida and suffers cognitive dissonance. Even though the Florida vacation now seems better, he has already purchased airfare for his family and the airline would impose a €50 penalty on each ticket. This financial cost of switching does much to influence the final decision to go to Mexico. On some occasions, consumers receive services with bundled prices (cable, Internet, and phone in one bill). The consumer could potentially perceive, and may actually realize, an increased price if only one of the services in the bundle is replaced.[19] A financial switching cost would be incurred in this situation.

15-3c Relational Switching Costs

The **relational switching cost** refers to the emotional and psychological consequences of changing from one brand/retailer/service provider to another. Imagine a consumer who has used the same hairstylist for five years. When she moves away from home to attend university, however, she finds another hair salon that is more convenient. She is greeted by a stylist named Karla just after entering the salon. Although Karla seems nice, the consumer is very uneasy during the entire salon visit. In fact, she even feels a bit guilty for letting Karla do her hair. This uneasiness is an example of a typical relational switching cost.

15-3d Understanding Switching Costs

Exhibit 15.3 demonstrates conventional consumer behaviour theory that explains switching costs. Consumers become dissatisfied for any number of reasons, and these reasons and dissatisfaction together determine how likely a consumer is to return on the next purchase occasion.[20] Equity judgments—in particular, perceptions of unfair treatment—are especially prone to leading consumers to switch. Perceptions of unfair prices may make

switching costs costs associated with changing from one choice (brand/retailer/service provider) to another

procedural switching costs lost time and extended effort spent in learning ways of using some product offering

financial switching costs total economic resources that must be spent or invested as a consumer learns how to obtain value from a new product choice

relational switching cost emotional and psychological consequences of changing from one brand/retailer/service provider to another

Exhibit 15.3

Factors Contributing to Switching Costs

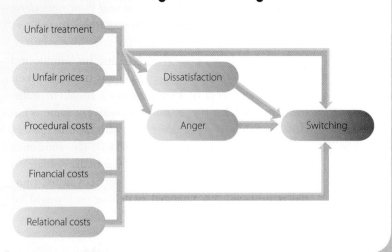

consumers temporarily angry, but they also create lasting memories. When coastal building centres raise plywood prices immediately before a hurricane's landfall, they may enjoy a short-term profit, but consumers will probably remember this and switch to a different retailer the next time they need a building centre. Retailers like Home Depot make a point of advertising policies that they maintain prices during weather crises such as hurricanes.

Furthermore, even though all types of functional costs can prevent switching, evidence suggests that relational barriers may be the most resistant to influence. Retailers who build up procedural switching costs, particularly through the use of loyalty cards and other similar programs, may gain temporary repeat purchase behaviour, but they fail to establish the connection with the customer that wins them true loyalty.[21] Additionally, the inability of web-based retailers to build in anything other than procedural loyalty may be responsible for the low levels of loyalty observed for some pure play (Internet only) retailers.[22]

competitive intensity
number of firms competing for business within a specific category

15-3e Satisfaction and Switching

The intermingling of consumer satisfaction/dissatisfaction and switching costs has received considerable attention. In fact, in addition to the measurement difficulties associated with CS/D, switching costs are another important reason why CS/D results often fail to predict future purchasing behaviour. Exhibit 15.4 summarizes how vulnerable a company is to consumer defections based on the interaction between switching costs, competitive intensity, and consumer satisfaction.

As can be seen in Exhibit 15.4, dissatisfaction does not always mean that the consumer is going to switch. Before reaching a conclusion on vulnerability to losing a customer, one also has to take into account at least two other factors. For instance, the amount of competition and the competitive intensity also play a role in determining who switches. **Competitive intensity** refers to the number of firms competing for business within a specific category. For example, until 1994, the Alberta Liquor Control Board (ALCB) operated the province's retail liquor stores and regulated the sale of alcohol. Competition did not exist in the market, as one entity controlled liquor sales. Today, Albertans can choose from hundreds of private liquor stores in a competitive market environment.

When competitive intensity is high and switching costs are low, a company is vulnerable to consumers who will switch providers even when customers are satisfied. The consumer has many companies vying

Exhibit 15.4

Vulnerability to Defections Based on CS/D

Customers Are Relatively:	High Competitive Intensity		Low Competitive Intensity	
	Switching Costs		Switching Costs	
	Low	High	Low	High
Satisfied	Vulnerable	Low vulnerability	Low vulnerability	No vulnerability
Dissatisfied	High vulnerabilty	Vulnerable	Vulnerable	Low vulnerability

for the business and changing presents little barrier. Today, a consumer has many choices for getting a car's oil changed, and the switching costs are virtually negligible. Even if a consumer is satisfied with the corner Jiffy Lube, he or she may try Mr. Lube the next time if the location is slightly more convenient.

In contrast, Exhibit 15.4 suggests that even when consumers are dissatisfied, consumers may not switch. Consider the case when competitive intensity is low, meaning there are few alternatives for the consumer and switching costs are high. In this case, even dissatisfied consumers may return time and time again. This is often the case with national airlines, like Air Canada, that are the only choice on many routes within and outside the country. A customer who is unhappy with the service from Edmonton's International Airport to London's Heathrow Airport would have to give up the direct flight and make one or more stops if he were to change carriers. Thus, although consumers may experience dissatisfaction, the fact that there are few alternatives and that switching costs might involve adding many hours to the trip makes Air Canada less vulnerable to defections due to low consumer satisfaction.

 15-4 ## CONSUMER LOYALTY

15-4a Customer Share

Marketing managers have come to accept the fact that getting business from a customer who has already transacted with the company before is easier and less expensive than getting a new customer. This basic belief motivates much of relationship marketing. The rubrics that determine marketing success then switch from pure sales and margin toward indicators that take into account marketing efficiencies. One important concept is **customer share**, which is the portion of resources allocated to one brand from the set of competing brands. Here, *brand* is used loosely to capture any type of consumer alternative, including a retailer, service provider, or actual product brand. Some managers use the term **share of wallet** to refer to customer share.

Exhibit 15.5 illustrates customer share by showing the choices made by two consumers for their daily coffee shop visits. On July 1, Bill goes to Starbucks (SB) and spends $5 and Erin does the same thing. On July 2, Bill returns to Starbucks and spends $10. Erin, however, goes to Tim Hortons (TH) and spends $15. In ten days, Bill chooses Starbucks eight out of ten times and spends $60 out of the $80 total at Starbucks. Erin chooses Starbucks only three times out of ten visits and spends $20 out of the $70 total at Starbucks. Thus, Starbucks gets considerably greater customer share from Bill than from Erin. The tenet of relationship marketing is that a company's marketing is much more efficient when most of the business comes from repeat customers. In this sense, Bill is a more valuable consumer to Starbucks than Erin, because Starbucks gets a greater share of Bill's coffee business than it does out of Erin.

Customer share represents a behavioural component that is indicative of customer loyalty. Behaviourally, Bill is more loyal than Erin. When customers don't switch, they repeat their purchase behaviour over again. At times, they repeat the behaviour over and over and over again. We examine the question of whether a consumer is truly

> **customer share** portion of resources allocated to one brand from the set of competing brands
>
> **share of wallet** customer share

Exhibit 15.5

Customer Share Information for Two Coffee Shop Customers

	Date of Visit										Total Spent
	7/1	7/2	7/3	7/4	7/5	7/6	7/7	7/8	7/9	7/10	
Bill's Choice	SB	SB	TH	SB	SB	TH	SB	SB	SB	SB	
$ Spent	5	10	10	5	15	10	5	5	10	5	$80
Erin's Choice	SB	TH	M	M	SB	M	TH	SB	TH	M	
$ Spent	5	15	5	5	5	5	10	10	5	5	$70

Resistance to change is one of the biggest reasons why new products fail in the marketplace.

loyal by examining why a consumer is repeating behaviour. This brings us to the concept of consumer inertia.

CONSUMER INERTIA

In physics, inertia refers to the fact that a mass that is in motion (or at rest) will stay in motion (or at rest) unless the mass is acted upon by a greater force. The concept of consumer inertia presents an analogy. **Consumer inertia** means that a consumer will tend to continue a pattern of behaviour until some stronger force motivates him or her to change. In fact, resistance to change is one of the biggest reasons why new products fail in the marketplace.[23] Change often means consumers must give something up. For example, many grocers try to take advantage of technology to increase the utilitarian value of getting groceries. The latest approach involves a regular grocery purchase for which the customer simply drives up, pays using a credit card, and drives away within a matter of minutes. This seems like a great value-added service. However, it comes at the price of the value that a customer gets by actually entering the store and getting to see, touch, and smell the products beforehand. Remember that losses loom larger than gains and a potential loss motivates consumers more to continue with their current consumer behaviour.

LOYALTY PROGRAMS

Many marketers have experimented with loyalty cards or programs as a way of increasing customer share. Loyalty cards also allow marketers to learn more about customer groups' demographics and shopping patterns. A **loyalty card/program** is a device that keeps track of the amount of purchasing a consumer has had with a given marketer (as well as a list of actual items purchased by the consumer), and once some level is reached, a reward is offered, usually in terms of future purchase incentives. Loyalty programs differ somewhat based on the firms offering them. Today, Canadian and European firms typically offer the standard reward in terms of a future purchase incentive, but in the United States, loyalty programs often work by offering on-the-spot discounts on selected items. One result is a two-tiered pricing system where there is one price for customers who comply with the card program and a higher price for those who do not use the card on those selected items.

However, the results are mixed with respect to the effectiveness of loyalty cards. In fact, they can sometimes even backfire by appealing too strongly to consumers who are bargain shoppers. Consumers with a strong economic orientation display lower customer share with all competitors, instead choosing to shop in the place with the current best offer.[24]

While these programs are referred to as "loyalty" programs, the question occurs as to exactly what constitutes loyalty. Customer share reflects a behavioural component of loyalty by reflecting repeated behaviour. In Exhibit 15.5, Bill repeats similar behaviour over again and appears to be loyal to Starbucks, but is he really? This question is the focus of the next section.

15-4b Customer Commitment

Bill does appear at least partially loyal to Starbucks. However, repeated behaviour alone cannot answer the loyalty question. True consumer loyalty consists of both a pattern of repeated behaviour as evidenced by high customer share and a strong feeling of attachment, dedication, and sense of identification with a brand. **Customer commitment** captures this sense of attachment, dedication, and identification. Exhibit 15.6 depicts the components of loyalty. Customer share is behavioural, and commitment is an affective component of loyalty.

Highly committed customers are true assets to a company. They are willing to sacrifice to continue doing business with the brand and serve as a source of promotion by spreading positive WOM. If we look at a consumer with a pattern of consistent behaviour such as Bill in Exhibit 15.5, the question becomes whether the

consumer inertia
situation in which a consumer tends to continue a pattern of behaviour until some stronger force motivates him or her to change

loyalty card/program
device that keeps track of the amount of purchasing a consumer has had with a given marketer

customer commitment sense of attachment, dedication, and identification

Exhibit 15.6

True Loyalty Requires Customer Commitment

Customer share

⇕

Customer commitment

Good airline customers get to wait in a comfortable area and enjoy a snack and a glass of wine on the house—but this area is not for just anybody!

behaviour is simply inertia or is motivated by true commitment. Perhaps this particular customer just happens to live next door to a Starbucks and thus getting coffee there is merely the easiest thing to do. If Second Cup were to take over the current Starbucks location, the customer would then buy his coffee there. However, if Bill were truly committed, he would seek out another Starbucks location even if the one next to his place were to close or get leased to a different coffee competitor. This

distinguishes inertia from a truly loyal customer. Even if Starbucks is not convenient or the least-expensive alternative, the truly loyal consumer will still seek out Starbucks!

The customer lifetime value (CLV) equation concept (from Chapter 2) demonstrates why high customer

Breaking Up Is Hard to Do!

Breaking up a relationship nearly always causes some pain. But as painful as breaking up is for individual consumers, breaking up can be devastating for an entire company when a business switches service providers. At times, businesses may even try to build switching costs into their products as a way of making it more difficult for competitors to compete successfully for business.

Think about all the computer systems necessary to manage a large organization. SAP is a provider of software for businesses, including customer relationship management (CRM) software programs and even more generalized systems known as enterprise suites. Many firms that implement CRM programs are dissatisfied with their decision. However, even though they are dissatisfied, they often stick with the software systems because changing would mean significant procedural and financial switching costs as well as facing the trauma that goes along with sunk costs incurred from implementing the system. As a result, their employees, who are consumers of the software, must cope with the consequences. Thus, breaking up the relationship—in this case, between a firm and a software systems provider—really is hard to do.

In much the same way, many consumers who are less than satisfied with things like digital entertainment and communication services also hang in there and try to reconcile because of the financial costs involved with breaking a service contract and the procedural costs involved in learning a new system.

Sources: Porter, M.E. (2008), "The Five Competitive Forces that Shape Strategy," *Harvard Business Review, 86* (January), 78–93; Whitten, D. and K. W. Green, Jr. (2005), "The Effect of Switching Costs on Intent to Switch: An Application in IS Service Provision Markets," *International Journal of Mobile Communication, 3* (4), 1.

NEL

CHAPTER 15: Consumer Relationships **295**

commitment is so beneficial to a company. The certainty of a lengthy stream of revenues is much less for a customer acting only on inertia. In addition, the customer acting on inertia alone is likely not contributing on the equity side of the equation as is the truly committed customer. A firm that concentrates on repeated behaviour alone, perhaps by always being convenient, can do well but remains more vulnerable to competitors. The reason for the vulnerability is that competitors easily duplicate tangible assets like convenience; but the intangible assets, like the feel associated with a choice or place, like the feelings consumers have for visiting Starbucks or drinking a Coke, are very hard to duplicate.

15-4c Anti-Loyalty

Loyalty is almost always discussed from a positive perspective. However, at times consumers act in an antiloyal way. **Anti-loyal consumers** are those who will do everything possible to avoid doing business with a particular marketer. These consumers generally are driven by a severe dislike of this particular company and by the negative emotions that go along with the aversion. Antiloyalty is often motivated by a bad experience between a consumer and the marketer in which the marketer could not redress the problem.

Attributes a marketer builds into a product to create procedural switching costs are one source of frustration. These attributes include parts that are incompatible with widely available replacements, or a mobile phone contract that locks a consumer into a specific service set for a lengthy time period. Consumers may wonder if their mobile phone number is transferable. In fact, many consumers may be frustrated with their mobile phone carrier but feel locked in, particularly if the phone number is not transferable or difficult to transfer.[25]

Anti-loyal customers are often consumers who have switched and treat the former marketing partner as a jilted partner. They obviously have no net positive lifetime value for the target firm. Moreover, these anti-loyal consumers who are former customers become perhaps the most frequent source for negative word-of-mouth.[26] Thus, anti-loyal consumers can be a major force to reckon with. See, for example, Jeremy Dorosin's crusade against Starbucks at www.starbucked.com.

anti-loyal consumers consumers who will do everything possible to avoid doing business with a particular marketer

15-4d Value and Switching

Exhibit 15.7 reproduces the centre portion of the CVF. The

Exhibit 15.7

Value and Relationship Outcomes

Consumption Process
- Needs
- Wants
- Costs and Benefits
- Exchange
- Reactions

Value
- Utilitarian
- Hedonic

Relationship Quality
- CS/D
- Switching Behaviour
- Customer Share
- Customer Commitment

exhibit clearly shows that value plays a role in the postconsumption process. During an exchange, the consumer goes through the consumption process, and the result produces some amount and type of value. The value, in turn, shapes what happens next. Thus, the CVF makes up for a shortcoming of the disconfirmation theory approach (as displayed in Exhibit 15.1) by explicitly accounting for value.

For a host of reasons, consumers may end up maintaining a relationship even if they experience dissatisfaction. However, consumers do not maintain relationships in which they find no value. Even if consumers do not enjoy shopping at Walmart, they tend to repeat the behaviour because of high utilitarian value. Also, even though a consumer may be able to bank at a more convenient location, he might continue doing business with his original bank because he enjoys the personal relationships he has developed with bank personnel. Thus, both utilitarian and hedonic value can be a key in preventing consumers from switching to a competitor and in creating true loyalty among consumers.

Is one type of value more important in preventing switching behaviour? The answer to this question depends on the nature of the goods or services being consumed. For functional types of services, such as banking, utilitarian value is more strongly related to customer share (and therefore preventing switching) than is hedonic value.[27] However, for more experiential types of services, such as mall shopping, hedonic value is more strongly related to customer share.[28]

Value also is linked to the affective side of loyalty, customer commitment. Again, both value dimensions relate positively to commitment, but hedonic value plays a larger role in creating commitment. In particular, customers who have switched service providers are more likely to become loyal customers when they experience increased hedonic value compared with the previous service provider.

VALUE, RELATIONSHIPS, AND CONSUMERS

15-5a Relationships and the Marketing Firm

Marketers have come to realize that the exchange between a business and a consumer comprises a relationship. Two factors help make this clear:

1. **Customers have a lifetime value to the firm.**

2. **True loyalty involves both a continuing series of interactions and feelings of attachment between the customer and the firm.**

In return, many firms that truly adopt a relationship marketing approach with customers enjoy improved

Universities hope a high-value experience leads graduates to continue a lifelong relationship with the school.

performance.[29] This is particularly the case as the relationship between customer and seller becomes very personal and involves trust.

Taken together, CS/D, complaining behaviour, switching, customer share, and commitment all indicate relationship quality, or the degree of connectedness between a consumer and a retailer. Healthy relationships are likely to continue. When consumers are truly loyal

Loyalty's in the Bag

What does it mean to be in a relationship? A relationship implies sacrifice and a willingness to overlook some inconveniences. Few products say more about a person than her handbag. After all, the bag takes care of your stuff. Like picking a spouse, picking a designer handbag is work. A designer bag should last for decades, so the comparison between choosing bags and husbands isn't so crazy. How many marriages will last two decades? Like husbands, a bag has to be loved even if it's not perfect. A rugged, yet soft, Louis Vuitton Sofia Coppola Duffle goes for nearly $5,000. The Yves Saint Laurent Classic 12 Duffle, about $2,500, is sleek and functional—the bag must balance function and style. A Legacy Coach Duffle goes for under $500 and gives a retro look.

The fact that you will be in a long-term relationship means you shouldn't get tired of looking at the object. Something too trendy is not likely to fit the criteria for a long-term relationship. Therefore, women looking for a long-term relationship in their bags prefer neutral colors, natural fabrics, and a look that will last. The bag may not fit perfectly with every outfit—but it clashes with none. A person can learn a lot from the way a smart consumer buys a handbag!

Sources: Rachel Dodes, "Shopping for a Handbag," The Wall Street Journal, February 9–10, 2013, D1–D2. "Bag Style: Set the Tone for Your Look," Harper's Bazaar.com, n.d., http://www.harpersbazaar .com/fashion/fashion-articles/handbag-style-0210#slide-1, accessed March 31, 2013.

and this loyalty is returned by the marketer, relationship quality is high and the prospects are good for a continued series of mutually valuable exchanges.

15-5b Value and Relationship Quality

A healthy relationship between a consumer and a marketer enhances value for both the consumer and the marketer.[30] For the consumer, decision making becomes simpler, enhancing utilitarian value, and relational exchanges often involve pleasant relational and experiential elements, enhancing hedonic value. For the marketer, the regular consumer does not have to be resold and thus much of the selling effort required to convert a new customer is not necessary.

In fact, when relationship quality is very strong in business-to-business contexts, the marketer and the customer act as partners. When something bad happens to one, the other is affected as well. However, relationship quality can be very important in business-to-consumer contexts too. When a parent sends a child off to university, chances are that a strong relationship exists or will soon exist between the family and the university. The family will don school colours on game day and become a prime target for fundraising campaigns. The strong relationship quality means that the family and the university share many common goals.

Exhibit 15.8 displays some of the characteristics of a very healthy marketing relationship. Consider this example: A consumer uses the same travel agent for practically all travel. When the consumer calls the agent, the agent does not have to ask the customer for preferences or personal information, not even a credit card number, because she has all the information about the customer. She knows the customer is an Aeroplan member so she books on Air Canada whenever possible. She knows the customer doesn't like close connections (under an hour), so she always tries to allow at least an hour and a half between connecting flights. Whenever the customer flies, the agent monitors the flight status. If there is a delay, she phones the customer to exchange information and begins rebooking any connecting flights, hotel reservations, or car rentals in case the delay disrupts the original plans. In this case, we can see that many of the characteristics

Exhibit 15.8

The Characteristics of Relationship Quality

Competence. The consumer views the company and service providers as knowledgeable and capable.

Communication. The consumer and the firm understand each other and "speak the same language."

Trust. The buyer and seller can depend on each other.

Equity. Both the buyer and the seller see equity in the exchange and are able to resolve conflicts equitably.

Personalization. The buyer treats the customer as an individual with unique desires and requirements.

Customer Orientation. Strong relationships are more likely to develop when a firm practises a marketing orientation, and this filters down to service providers and salespeople.

displayed in Exhibit 15.8 are illustrated. This agent is customer oriented, has a personal relationship with the customer, communicates well, and is competent; the relationship is characterized by trust. Chances are that this customer will be loyal for quite some time.

STUDY TOOLS 15

LOCATED AT THE BACK OF THE TEXTBOOK
☐ Rip out Chapter Review Card

LOCATED AT NELSON.COM/STUDENT
☐ Review Key Terms Flashcards (print or online)

☐ Download audio summaries to review on the go

☐ Complete practice quizzes to prepare for tests

☐ Watch video on Harley-Davidson for a real company example

Case

Abercrombie & Fitch Wants to Be Cool Again

It surprises many people to learn that Abercrombie & Fitch (A&F) is more than a century old. It built its early reputation as a sporting goods outfitter for adventurers and the American elite, and Teddy Roosevelt, Charles Lindbergh, and Ernest Hemingway all shopped there. A lot has changed for the company since those early days, however. The modern store is focused on casual teen fashion, and by 1992, 100 years after the first store had opened in Manhattan, the company was struggling. To turn things around, A&F hired a new CEO: Michael Jeffries.

The company thrived under Jeffries's early guidance. For the next 10 years, profits increased annually and the company grew to 600 stores. The brand became a fashion icon, re-establishing the popularity of an "all-American" jeans and T-shirt look. Abercrombie & Fitch raised its prices and its customers gladly paid the premium. A&F made plans for overseas expansion and other retailers began copying its styles.

As 2002 came to an end, Jeffries was asked about the retailer's product choices, including tight shirts and very low-rise jeans. He responded, "Does it exclude people? Absolutely. We are the cool brand." In fact, Abercrombie & Fitch built its business on being the cool brand and being exclusionary, but with mass market appeal. In a 2006 interview with *Salon*, Jeffries was quoted as saying "In every school there are the cool and popular kids, and then there are the not-so-cool kids. Candidly, we go after the cool kids. We go after the attractive all-American kid with a great attitude and a lot of friends. A lot of people don't belong [in our clothes], and they can't belong. Are we exclusionary? Absolutely. Those companies that are in trouble are trying to target everybody: young, old, fat, skinny. But then you become totally vanilla. You don't alienate anybody, but you don't excite anybody, either."

In 2013, retail analyst Robin Lewis pointed out that this attitude was the reason the company did not carry large sizes, sparking a viral campaign that spoofed A&F ads, protested its standards, and led to an online

AP Photo/Gary Gardiner

petition for bigger sizes. The company's profits, which were already under pressure, plunged 77% in 2013 and the stock price fell nearly 20%. By the end of 2014, Mike Jeffries was gone as CEO and chairman of the company. Although A&F committed to expand its product line to include plus sizes, the move was not enough to stem the tide of negative consumer sentiment. As of mid-2015 the stock price is still languishing well below its highs and competition for teen apparel sales remains intense. Companies like H&M, Zara, and Uniqlo appear to be meeting the needs of consumers, while Aéropostale, Gap, and American Eagle struggle. All of this has retail observers asking: Is Abercrombie & Fitch cool enough to survive?

CASE STUDY

Sources: Berfield, Susan and Lindsey Rupp (2015), "The Aging of Abercrombie and Fitch," *Bloomberg Business*, January 22, http://www .bloomberg.com/news/features/2015-01-22/the-aging-of-abercrombie -fitch-i58ltcqx accessed June 29, 2015. Denizet-Lewis, Benoit (2006), "The man behind Abercrombie & Fitch," *Salon*, January 24, http://www.salon .com/2006/01/24/jeffries/ accessed June 29, 2015. Lutz, Ashley (2013), "Abercrombie & Fitch Refuses to Make Clothes for Large Women," *Business Insider*, May 3, http://www.businessinsider.com/abercrombie-wants -thin-customers-2013-5 accessed June 29, 2015. McGregor, Jena (2014), "Abercrombie & Fitch CEO Mike Jeffries Steps Down," the *Washington Post*, December 9, http://www.washingtonpost.com/blogs/on-leadership/ wp/2014/12/09/abercrombie-fitch-ceo-mike-jeffries-steps-down/ accessed June 29, 2015.

QUESTIONS

1 Jeffries had been quoted confirming the company's focus on "cool kids" and its willingness to exclude others for more than a decade. Why did it take so long for the negative WOM to catch fire?

2 Was there an element of consumer revenge in the social media campaign?

3 How did A&F handle the negative publicity? Which of the four alternative courses of action did the company undertake? Why was the response not more effective?

4 What are the switching costs for a consumer who stops shopping at A&F and begins shopping at Zara or H&M?

5 How loyal are today's Abercrombie & Fitch customers? Is loyalty to A&F driven by consumer inertia or a deeper customer commitment?

MindTap®

MindTap empowers students.
Personalized content in an easy-to-use interface
helps you achieve better grades.

The new **MindTap Mobile App** allows for learning anytime, anywhere with flashcards, quizzes and notifications.

The **MindTap Reader** lets you highlight and take notes online, right within the pages, and easily reference them later.

www.nelson.com/mindtap

16 | Marketing Ethics and Consumer Misbehaviour

LEARNING OBJECTIVES

After studying this chapter, the student should be able to:

16-1 Understand the consumer misbehaviour phenomenon and how it affects the exchange process.

16-2 Distinguish between consumer misbehaviour and consumer problem behaviour.

16-3 Discuss the interplay between marketing ethics and consumerism within the marketing concept.

16-4 Comprehend the role of corporate social responsibility as it relates to consumer behaviour (CB).

16-5 Understand consumer protection, privacy, and the regulation of marketing activities.

16-6 Comprehend the major areas of criticism to which marketers are subjected.

INTRODUCTION

Most of the behaviours that we have discussed so far are generally considered "acceptable" or "normal" by societal standards. A number of important topics, however, fall outside of what would be considered acceptable. In this chapter, we focus on what is referred to as consumer and marketer misbehaviour. The term *misbehaviour* is used cautiously because opinions regarding what is acceptable or normal depend on our ethical beliefs, ideologies, and even culture. For consumers, examples include shoplifting, downloading music illegally, drinking and driving, and engaging in fraud. Marketers sometimes engage in unethical activities as well. For example, they mislead consumers through deceptive advertising, state that regular prices are "sale" prices, and artificially limit the availability of products in order to increase prices.

There are times when consumers misbehave and act in an unethical manner, and there are times when marketers misbehave and act in an unethical manner. An efficient and effective marketplace depends on each party in an exchange acting fairly and with due respect for each other. Thus, consumers, marketing entities, and government officials who regulate business activity must all act with integrity. Whenever anyone acts unethically, inefficiencies result and chances are that somebody will suffer.

First of all, there is no denying that some companies' actions are at best questionable and at times immoral or even illegal. News headlines frequently highlight stories of accounting scandals, manipulative marketing practices, and deceptive advertising. Unscrupulous actions of companies directly affect the marketplace because they upset the value equation associated with a given exchange. When a company misrepresents a product, consumers are led to expect more than is actually delivered. Unfair exchanges result. A fair value exchange exists when marketers and consumers act with good faith, complete disclosure, and trust. When trust is violated, value perceptions are harmed.

The issue of marketer misbehaviour is complicated by the fact that not everyone will agree on what behaviours really should be considered "unethical." The term *ethics* has been used in many ways, and ethical issues permeate our everyday lives. The term refers to standards or moral codes of conduct to which a person,

group, or organization adheres. Marketing ethics consist of societal and professional standards of right and fair practices that are expected of managers as they develop and implement marketing strategies. More simply, ethics determine how much tolerance one has for actions that take advantage of others.

Many organizations have explicitly stated rules and codes of conduct for their employees. Most professional organizations do as well. Exhibit 16.1 presents the Overarching Ethical Principles from the Canadian Marketing Association (CMA) Code of Ethics and Standards of Practice.

Ultimately, firms that misbehave risk the wrath of the consumer. Today, the marketplace is extremely competitive and consumers have a great deal of choice in the products they buy and the stores they visit. Firms that misbehave tend to quickly lose the trust of their customers. Those poorly treated consumers not only change their own buying behaviour, but they also tell their friends and family and influence the consumption decisions of other people. In the modern economy, consumers have enormous power and when they vote with their wallet they determine whether a company will succeed or fail.

16-1 CONSUMER MISBEHAVIOUR AND EXCHANGE

Consumer misbehaviour may be viewed as a subset of the *human deviance* topic, which has a long history of research in the fields of sociology and social psychology. We consider misbehaviour a subset in part because the term covers only negative or destructive deviance and does not consider positive deviance.

Although it can be defined in numerous ways, we define **consumer misbehaviour** as behaviours that are in some way unethical and that potentially harm the self or others.[1] Misbehaviour violates norms and also disrupts the flow of consumption activities. For example, a consumer screaming at a waiter because his order is wrong makes other consumers feel uncomfortable. His actions disrupt others' meals and may ruin the entire evening. Chances are that a waiter who endures such scolding will perform poorly during the rest of the evening as well.

consumer misbehaviour behaviours that are in some way unethical and that potentially harm the self or others

This single consumer's actions potentially affect all the other customers in the restaurant.

Consumer misbehaviour is sometimes called the "dark side" of consumer behaviour, and words such as *aberrant, illicit, dysfunctional,* and *deviant* have been used to describe it. Some behaviours are clearly illegal, while others are simply immoral. There's a difference. For example, shoplifting is illegal and almost always considered immoral. Speeding, however, is illegal but not necessarily immoral. Not returning excess change that is mistakenly given at a store is immoral but not illegal.[2] A consumer might purchase a product one day, use it, and then return it for a refund. This may be immoral but not illegal. This practice is called *retail borrowing* and it costs the retail sector billions of dollars annually.

In order for exchanges to occur in an orderly fashion, the expectations of the consumer, the marketer, and even other consumers must coincide with one another.[3] When we see consumers becoming abusive, cutting in line at a movie theatre, or making other people uncomfortable, the exchange process is disrupted. Consumers who shoplift disrupt the exchange process and increase costs for all consumers. Consumers who make fraudulent insurance claims increase insurance costs. Belligerent sports fans turn otherwise joyous occasions into annoying events for everybody. All sorts of misbehaviours affect exchange.

16-1a The Focus of Misbehaviour: Value

As we have discussed throughout this text, a central component for understanding consumer behaviour is value. It shouldn't be surprising then that the focal motivation for consumer misbehaviour is value.[4] However, *how* consumers obtain value is the key issue. Rowdy sports fans think that the best way to obtain value is to be obnoxious. Identity thieves believe that the best way to obtain value is to steal from others. In each instance, consumers seek to maximize the benefits they receive from an action while minimizing, or eliminating, their own costs. Ultimately, others' costs increase. In this way, consumer misbehaviour is, quite simply, selfish!

16-1b Consumer Misbehaviour and Ethics

Moral beliefs and evaluations influence decisions pertaining to marketplace behaviours.[5]

MORAL BELIEFS

Moral beliefs, or beliefs about the perceived ethicality or morality of behaviours, play a very important role. The effect of moral beliefs on ethical decision making and consumer misbehaviour is shown in Exhibit 16.2.

Notice that a consumer's moral beliefs comprise three components: moral equity, contractualism, and relativism.[6]

moral beliefs beliefs about the perceived ethicality or morality of behaviours

Exhibit 16.2

Moral Beliefs, Ethical Evaluations, and Behaviour

Moral Beliefs
- Moral equity
- Contractualism
- Relativism

→

Ethical Evaluations
- Deontology
- Teleology

→

Consumer Behaviour/
Misbehaviour

Moral equity represents beliefs regarding an act's fairness or justness. Do I consider this action to be fair? Is it fair for me to shoplift this item?

Contractualism refers to beliefs about the violation of written (or unwritten) laws. Does this action break a law? Does it break an unwritten promise of how I should act? Is shoplifting illegal?

Relativism represents beliefs about the social acceptability of an act. Is this action culturally acceptable? Is shoplifting acceptable in this culture?

ETHICAL EVALUATIONS

Consumers bring their moral beliefs into all decision-making settings. Once a consumer enters into a situation that calls for an ethical decision (*Should I steal these sunglasses?*), he or she considers the various alternative courses of action. Here, two sets of ethical evaluations occur: deontological evaluations and teleological evaluations.[7]

Deontological evaluations focus on specific *actions*. Is this action "right"? As such, deontology focuses on *how* people accomplish their goals. The deontological perspective is, in large part, attributed to the work of Immanuel Kant. Kant's *categorical imperative* suggests that one should act in a way that would be considered a universal law for all people facing the same situation.

Teleological evaluations focus on the *consequences* of the behaviours and the individual's assessment of those consequences. How much "good" will result from this decision? With teleological evaluations, consumers consider the perceived consequences of the actions for various stakeholders, the probability that the consequences will occur, the desirability of the consequences for the stakeholders, and the importance of the stakeholder groups to the consumer.[8]

16-1c Motivations of Misbehaviour

Moral beliefs and behavioural evaluations indeed play important roles in consumer misbehaviour. However, the question remains: Why do consumers misbehave? This is not an easy question to answer and there are a large variety of possible motivations for misbehaviour, ranging from the internal states (e.g., consumers' mood) to individual traits (e.g., thrill seekers) to social and situational factors (peer pressure). One perspective on consumers underlying motivations is offered by researchers Ronald Fullerton and Girish Punj.[9] When reviewing the motivations they have identified, ask yourself: Is this list comprehensive? What else might cause me to misbehave as a consumer?

Unfulfilled Aspirations. Many consumers have unfulfilled aspirations that influence their misbehaviour. An important concept here is *anomie*. Anomie has been conceptualized as both a response to rapid cultural change and an explanation for deviance. To understand anomie as an explanation for deviance, consider the goals that are generally accepted in a culture. Canadian culture places a great deal of emphasis on attaining material possessions and "getting ahead." However, not all members of the society have the necessary resources to be able to get ahead and enjoy the things that society deems important. As a result, some consumers turn to deviant actions, or actions deemed inappropriate by society, in order to acquire these things. It's when societal goals are out of reach given the accepted means of achieving them that deviance occurs.[10]

Thrill-Seeking. The thrill arising from the action or risky behaviour may lead consumers to misbehave. For example, breaking the speed limit can be exciting for some consumers, while shoplifting may be exciting for others.

Lack of Moral Constraints. Some consumers simply don't have a set of moral beliefs that are in agreement with society's expectations and see no problem with their behaviour. For example, some consumers who scare others by driving aggressively or cutting into lines don't see a problem with the behaviour.

Differential Association. Differential association explains why groups of people replace one set of acceptable norms with another set that others view as unacceptable. By acting

moral equity beliefs regarding an act's fairness or justness

contractualism beliefs about the violation of written (or unwritten) laws

relativism beliefs about the social acceptability of an act in a culture

deontological evaluations evaluations regarding the inherent rightness or wrongness of specific actions

teleological evaluations consumers' assessment of the goodness or badness of the consequences of actions in opposition to acceptable standards, group members forge their own identities and strengthen group cohesion.[11] For example, gangs often accept behaviours that society finds unacceptable.

Pathological Socialization. Consumers may view misbehaviour as a way of getting revenge against companies. Stealing from large corporations may seem less severe than stealing from a family-owned retailer, and consumers may believe that big companies "deserve it."

Provocative Situational Factors. Factors like crowding, wait times, excessive heat, and noise can contribute to consumer misbehaviour. A well-mannered, quiet person may erupt and misbehave after waiting in line for 20 minutes at a drive-through restaurant.

Opportunism. Misbehaviour can also be the outcome of a deliberate decision-making process that weighs the risks and rewards of the behaviour. For example, consumers may believe that the rewards associated with stealing outweigh the risks of getting caught.

Exhibit 16.3

Consumer Misbehaviour and Problem Behaviour

Consumer Misbehaviour	Consumer Problem Behaviour
Shoplifting	Compulsive buying
Computer-mediated behaviours: illicit sharing of software and music, computer attacks, cyberbullying	Compulsive shopping
Fraud	Eating disorders
Abusive consumer behaviour	Binge drinking
Dysfunctional sports behaviours	Problem gambling
Illegitimate complaining	Drug abuse
Product misuse: aggressive driving, drunk driving, cell phone use while driving	

16-2 DISTINGUISH CONSUMER MISBEHAVIOUR AND PROBLEM BEHAVIOUR

Consumer misbehaviour can be distinguished from what we refer to as consumer "problem behaviour." *Misbehaviour* is used to describe behaviour deliberately harmful to the self or another party during an exchange. **Consumer problem behaviour** refers to behaviours that are seemingly outside of a consumer's control. For example, some people compulsively shop. Some people are addicted to drugs or alcohol. In cases like these, consumers may express a desire to stop the behaviours but simply find quitting too difficult.

Although the line between consumer misbehaviour and problem behaviour can be blurred, we distinguish between the two areas by considering the issue of self-control. Exhibit 16.3 presents examples of consumer behaviour and problem behaviours, but again the line is blurry. Drug addiction is listed as a problem behaviour, but when someone drives under the influence of drugs, the individual risks injuring or killing someone else. Shoplifting could also be considered either a problem behaviour or misbehaviour, as the behaviour can sometimes be clinically diagnosed as *kleptomania*.

16-2a Consumer Misbehaviour

Many of the behaviours listed in Exhibit 16.3 are discussed frequently in the popular press. For example, you may have heard stories in the news media about the devastating effects of binge drinking or problem gambling. Although there are many different types of consumer misbehaviour, we limit our discussion to behaviours that have gathered significant attention.

SHOPLIFTING

Canadian retailers lose about $3.5 billion per year to shoplifting—that is, an average of $9.5 million per day.[12] How could this number be so high? Consumers' motivations for shoplifting are similar to motivations for other forms of misbehaviour. Specifically, consumers shoplift because the temptation can be very strong, they believe that retailers can afford the monetary loss, they believe they probably won't get caught, they seek acceptance into a group, and the act can be exciting.[13]

consumer problem behaviour consumer behaviour that is deemed to be unacceptable but that is seemingly beyond the control of the consumer

As we have mentioned, shoplifting can sometimes be diagnosed as kleptomania. Although there are many differences between the behaviour and the illness, as a general statement the shoplifting behaviour is usually premeditated, whereas kleptomania is generally triggered by compulsion with little or no rationale for the items that are stolen.

Emotions and Shoplifting. Emotions play a large role in shoplifting. Fear of being caught plays a role in predicting shoplifting intentions, especially among young consumers. Interestingly, the shoplifting intentions of adolescents appear to be more heavily influenced by emotions than by moral beliefs. The opposite occurs in older consumers. Research also shows that consumers who shoplift are sometimes motivated by repressed feelings of stress and anger.[14]

Age and Shoplifting. Shoplifting behaviour appears to peak during the adolescent years. This may be because adolescents are not fully mature and often find themselves in the stressful transition from childhood to adulthood. Adolescents also tend to consider shoplifting as being more ethical than do adult shoppers.[15]

COMPUTER-MEDIATED BEHAVIOURS: ILLEGAL SHARING OF SOFTWARE AND MUSIC

Due to improvements in technology, consumers often have the ability to download electronic material illicitly from a number of sources. Major problems here include the pirating of computer software, video games, and music.

The software industry loses billions of dollars annually due to illegal copying. In fact, the Business Software Alliance estimates that as much as 41% of software loaded on PCs worldwide is obtained illegally and that $53 billion is lost globally due to the illegal use of software products.[16] The music industry has also been hit hard by these actions. Although there are numerous legal download services, consumers continue to share music in other ways.

Interestingly, research reveals that how consumers view illegal downloading depends on the motivation for the behaviour. For example, if the motivation is primarily based on utilitarian value (i.e., for personal gain), then the act is viewed as less morally ethical and socially acceptable than if the behaviour occurs based on hedonic value (i.e., for "fun").[17]

COMPUTER-MEDIATED BEHAVIOURS: ATTACKS

Computers present other opportunities for misbehaviour. It has been estimated that spam and other malware that clogs up computers and slows Internet connectivity results in productivity losses that cost businesses billions of dollars per year.[18] Computer viruses are another major problem. Today, thousands of computer viruses are being circulated from computer to computer, and the effects range from mildly annoying to devastating. In fact, it has been estimated that, in the United States, viruses cost businesses more than $55 billion annually.[19]

Another form of computer misbehaviour is *cyberbullying*, the attack of innocent people on the Internet. It is especially a problem for young consumers. Current research indicates that girls tend to be targeted by, and instigate, cyberattacks more often than boys.[20] However, cyberbullying is a serious issue for both genders. Recent statistics reveal that as many as 32% of online teens have been victims of some type of cyberbullying.[21]

CONSUMER FRAUD

There are many types of consumer fraud. For instance, consumers fraudulently obtain credit cards, open bank accounts, and make insurance claims. Although it is difficult to know exactly how much consumer fraud ends up costing consumers, estimates place the annual cost in the tens of billions of dollars.[22]

Identity theft is another major public concern. In the United States, the Federal Trade Commission estimates that as many as 9 million consumers have their identities stolen each year, and this number appears to be growing.[23] The increased reliance on computer technology for transactions has contributed to the spread of identity theft. It is no wonder that information privacy and security concerns are becoming hot topics for consumers.

ABUSIVE CONSUMER BEHAVIOUR

As we have discussed, abusive consumers can be a real problem. Consumers who are aggressive or rude to employees and other consumers are considered to be abusive.[24] One early study in the area of problem customers suggested that four categories of customers can be identified: verbally or physically abusive customers, uncooperative customers, drunken customers, and customers who break company policy.[25] Needless to say, employees don't like to deal with customers who act this way, and abusive behaviours can have negative effects on other consumers as well.[26]

One area of abusive behaviour that has gained attention is *dysfunctional fan behaviour,* or abnormal functioning relating to sporting event consumption. Riots have occurred in several cities after local sports teams have suffered big losses or even when they have won big games. Unfortunately, riots can get out of hand quickly. While there are many explanations for such behaviour, some have speculated that dysfunctional fan behaviour is simply a result of an increasingly violent society.[27]

Another controversial issue today is *culture jamming*—attempts to disrupt marketing campaigns by altering the messages in some meaningful way. For example, billboards are often altered in a way that delivers messages that conflict with those originally intended. Also, websites that attempt to disrupt marketing efforts are often created. Of course, calling culture jamming an abusive behaviour depends on your own perspective. Proponents believe that their behaviours are good for society.

ILLEGITIMATE COMPLAINING

Consumers sometimes complain about products and services when there really isn't a problem. To date, the research on illegitimate complaining remains relatively scarce. However, one study did find that illegitimate complaining is motivated by a desire for monetary gain, a desire to evade personal responsibility for product misuse, a desire to enhance the consumer's ego and look good to others, or a desire to harm a service provider or company.[28]

PRODUCT MISUSE

Consumers also sometimes use products in ways that were clearly not intended. For example, some consumers will sniff glue or household cleaners to get "high." Marketers therefore work hard to ensure that consumers understand the ways in which products should be used. However, even when warnings and instructions are provided, consumers still misuse products. Injuries that result can be very costly. For example, statistics from the Consumer Product Safety Commission reveal that deaths and injuries resulting from product consumption cost the United States more than $800 billion annually.[29]

Why do consumers use products in unsafe ways? A number of explanations have been offered. Consumers may simply not pay attention to what they are doing, may feel as though they generally get away with risky behaviours, may have a tendency to be error prone, or may focus more on the thrill of misuse rather than the actual risk of the behaviour.[30] Here, we discuss three major issues regarding the misuse of a highly visible product: the automobile.

Aggressive Driving. Aggressive driving may range from mild displays of anger to seriously violent acts while driving. Although aggressive driving is often thought of as an act by a solitary consumer, aggressive driving problems often involve multiple drivers, as victims often retaliate with their own aggression.[31] Younger, less-educated males have been shown to be more likely to engage in aggressive driving behaviour.[32] Situational factors, such as intense traffic congestion and driver stress, and personality traits also play a part. Traits like instability and competitiveness have been found among aggressive drivers.[33]

Drunk Driving. Mothers Against Drunk Driving (MADD) Canada estimates that there are between 1,350 and 1,600 impaired car crash fatalities in Canada each year. This works out to an average of 3.7 to 4.4 deaths per day! MADD also estimates the social cost of car crashes that result from impaired driving—including deaths, injuries, and property damage—at more than $20 billion per year.[34]

Use of Mobile Devices While Driving. As we have stated previously, there are currently nearly 6 billion cellphones worldwide,[35] and approximately 83% of Canadian households have a mobile phone.[36] A growing area of public concern involves the use of mobile devices while driving. Like drinking and driving, neither behaviour in isolation is considered to be a problem, but the use of the two products at the same time is a problem. Studies reveal that consumers who use cellphones while driving are four times as likely to get into serious accidents, and the problem is particularly serious for teens. One study found that 26% of surveyed 16- and 17-year-olds have texted while driving and 43% have talked on a handheld phone while driving.[37] Many of Canada's provinces have taken a hard line on texting, cellphone use, and general distracted driving. The use of mobile technology while

Texting while driving is extremely dangerous.

driving has become a global problem, and 40 countries worldwide currently restrict or ban the use of cellphones while driving.[38]

16-2b Consumer Problem Behaviour

Consumer problem behaviours include other acts that do not necessarily break any specific laws or societal norms. For example, consumers shop too much, rack up large amounts of debt, and sometimes harm their own bodies in desperate attempts to look thin. Psychological problems can cause or influence these behaviours.

COMPULSIVE CONSUMPTION

Compulsive consumption refers to repetitive, excessive, and purposeful consumer behaviours that are performed as a response to tension, anxiety, or obtrusive thoughts.[39] The term *compulsive consumption* is often used broadly and consists of a number of specific behaviours related to the purchase and use of consumer products and services.[40] Compulsive consumption should not be confused with **addictive consumption**, which is a physiological dependency on the consumption of a product. The word *dependency* is important, and in the strictest sense, addictions are characterized by the physical inability to discontinue a behaviour, or a physical reliance.

A person who is addicted to a product physically needs it. Compulsive consumption often takes two forms: *compulsive buying* and *compulsive shopping*.

Compulsive Buying. Compulsive buying may be defined as chronic, repetitive *purchasing* behaviours that are a response to negative events or feelings.[41] This behaviour can have harmful results, including the accumulation of debt, domestic problems, and feelings of frustration. Influencers of this form of buying include feelings of low self-esteem, obsessive–compulsive tendencies, fantasy-seeking motivations, and materialism,[42] as well as a focus on the short term rather than the long term.[43] Among adolescents, the behaviour can be a response to family problems such as divorce.[44] The same negative feelings that influence compulsive buying can also result from the behaviour itself, so that a consumer who buys compulsively as a reaction to negative feelings often experiences even more negative feelings after going on buying binges.[45] In this way, compulsive buying can be a vicious circle.

Compulsive Shopping. Compulsive shopping refers to repetitive *shopping* behaviours. The word

Exhibit 16.4

Binge Eating Disorder

Binge eating disorder consists of:

▶ Frequent eating episodes that include large quantities of food in short time periods.

▶ A felt loss of control over eating behaviour.

▶ Feelings of shame, guilt, and/or disgust about the amount of food consumed.

▶ The consumption of food when one is not hungry.

▶ The consumption of food in secret.

Source: Based on National Eating Disorders Association, www.nationaleatingdisorders.org.

oniomania is sometimes used to describe this behaviour. Compulsive shoppers often feel preoccupied with shopping, exhibit uncontrollable shopping tendencies, and experience guilt from their behaviours.[46] The key difference between compulsive shopping and buying is the buying process itself. Compulsive shoppers tend to focus on the mental highs associated with "the hunt,"[47] whereas compulsive buyers feel the need to buy. Although early research on this issue revealed that compulsive shopping was predominantly a problem for women, more recent evidence suggests that both women and men engage in compulsive shopping. One study confirmed that equal proportions of men and women are compulsive shoppers (6% of women, and 5.5% of men).[48]

EATING DISORDERS

Binge eating refers to the consumption of large amounts of food while feeling a general loss of control over intake. Binge eating may result in medical complications, including high cholesterol, high blood pressure, and heart disease. Exhibit 16.4 presents a description of the binge eating disorder.

compulsive consumption repetitive, excessive, and purposeful consumer behaviours that are performed as a response to tension, anxiety, or obtrusive thoughts

addictive consumption physiological dependency on the consumption of a consumer product

compulsive buying chronic, repetitive purchasing that is a response to negative events or feelings

compulsive shopping repetitive shopping behaviours that are a response to negative events or feelings

binge eating consumption of large amounts of food while feeling a general loss of control over food intake

"Too Much Is Too Much"

Some consumer behaviour texts have suggested that overconsumption in and of itself is a form of misbehaviour. When is too much simply too much?

The advertising world sends all kinds of messages wrapped around promises to make consumers younger looking, sexier, more popular, better loved, and more successful. As a result, consumers often buy many more products and services than are really necessary. What's more, the value that the advertising world attempts to place on possessions, money, physical appearance, and success actually leads to overconsumption, which can lead to unhappiness, anxiety, financial problems, or even mental disorders.

Some consumers have actually fought back on the temptation to overconsume by voluntarily simplifying their lives. This has been noted by consumer researchers during the current turbulent economic times. Many consumers have adjusted their perspectives by moving their focus away from overconsumption to "voluntary simplicity." Attitudes toward buying, credit, and saving have changed for many consumers.

Even though attitudes toward overconsumption appear to have changed for some, the issue remains important. The impact of overconsumption on personal finance, pollution, and personal happiness continues to be noted. Sometimes, enough is simply enough!

© iStockphoto.com/Nikola Hristovski

Sources: Ives, Nat (2009), "Marketers Fear Frugality May Just Be Here to Stay," *Advertising Age*, June 1, 2009, 80 (21), pp. 1-2; Evans, Kelly (2009), "The Outlook: Frugality Forged in Today's Recession Has Potential to Outlast it," *The Wall Street Journal*, April 6, 2009, p. A2; James, Oliver (2008), "It's More than Enough to Make You Sick," *Marketing*, January 23, 2008, pp. 26–28.

Binge eating has been shown to be associated with compulsive buying. This is particularly the case for obese consumers. In fact, obese consumers who engage in binge eating are likely to have other psychiatric disorders that require treatment.[49] Unfortunately, many consumers who binge eat fail to seek treatment. Binge eating is also often associated with *bulimia*, a disorder that includes binge eating episodes followed by self-induced vomiting. *Anorexia*, or the starving of one's body in the pursuit of thinness, is another consumer eating disorder.

BINGE DRINKING

Binge drinking is defined as the consumption of five or more drinks in a single drinking session for men and four or more drinks for women,[50] and the behaviour is particularly prevalent among full-time university students. In fact, estimates reveal that binge drinking rates among full-time university students are more than 45%, compared to 38% for students who are not enrolled full-time.[51] Binge drinking occurs globally. In fact, one study revealed that students in the United Kingdom binge drink for the sole purpose of getting drunk and feel that getting drunk is a key part of university life.[52]

Binge drinking has been linked to suicide attempts, unsafe sexual practices, legal problems, academic disruptions, and even death.[53] Students who have higher self-actualization values generally have lower attitudes toward binge drinking, whereas students who value social affiliation tend to have more positive attitudes toward the behaviour.[54]

PROBLEM GAMBLING

Problem gambling is another serious issue. This behaviour may be described as an obsession with gambling and the loss of control over gambling behaviour and its consequences.[55] Consumers who are problem gamblers frequently gamble longer than planned, borrow money to finance their gambling, and feel major depression due to their gambling behaviours. Although casino and online gambling receives much research

binge drinking
consumption of five or more drinks in a single drinking session for men and four or more drinks for women

problem gambling
obsession over the thought of gambling and the loss of control over gambling behaviour and its consequences

attention, lottery-ticket and scratch-ticket purchases can also be considered problem gambling behaviours.[56]

Estimates reveal that in North America as many as 2 million consumers meet the criteria of pathological gambling and another 4–6 million could be considered problem gamblers.[57] Problem gamblers exhibit at least some of the criteria for pathological gambling. Although problem gambling is often thought of as being primarily an issue for middle-aged consumers, approximately 8% of university students gamble problematically.[58] What's more, a recent study revealed that nearly 70% of seniors older than 65 had gambled at least once in the previous year and nearly 11% were considered "at risk" for problem gambling.[59] Research indicates that problem gambling is often associated with compulsive buying and drug abuse.[60]

DRUG ABUSE

Both illegal and legal drugs (such as over-the-counter medications) can become problematic for consumers. A recent U.S. study revealed that nearly one in five teenagers report using prescription drugs to get high, and nearly one in ten report abusing cough medicine. Even more troubling is the finding that nearly 40% of teenagers sampled believe that abusing prescription drugs is safer than abusing illegal drugs.[61]

The abuse of illegal drugs (including marijuana, cocaine, and hallucinogens) has been a major problem for years and is particularly serious for young consumers. One study in 2013 revealed that nearly 23% of high school students in the United States were current marijuana users, and 6.5% used marijuana daily. More than 46% of students will have tried marijuana by the time they graduate high school.[62]

We've discussed only a handful of behaviours that may be considered consumer problem areas here. Space prohibits a complete discussion of several other consumer problem areas.

16-3 ETHICS, CONSUMERS, AND THE MARKETING CONCEPT

Marketing ethics consist of societal and professional standards of right and fair practices that are expected of managers as they develop and implement marketing strategies. A fair marketplace depends on each party in an exchange acting ethically.

Like consumer misbehaviour, marketer misbehaviour can be viewed as a subset of *deviance*. For a marketer to misbehave, he or she must be aware that an action will be considered unethical and act with deviance to cover intent. Sometimes, marketers don't intend to misbehave but mistakes are made in marketing execution. As in a court of law, proving intent is rarely an easy thing to do.

16-3a Consumerism

The **marketing concept** proposes that all the functions of the organization should work together in satisfying its customers' wants and needs. This is important for any business. When businesses begin taking advantage of consumers, consumers lose, businesses lose, and society as a whole eventually loses. In fact, it can be said that the ethical treatment of consumers is a cornerstone of a fair marketplace.[63]

Much of the pressure that has been placed on marketers comes directly from consumer groups. **Consumerism** is used to describe the activities of various groups to protect basic consumer rights. Many years ago, the voice of the consumer simply didn't garner much attention. In the early days of mass production, much of the focus was on production efficiencies rather than on the consumer. This changed gradually throughout the 20th century as the marketplace became more competitive. The voice of the consumer grew steadily. Today, the consumer has an unprecedented ability to broadcast concerns and express dissatisfaction through social media platforms like Facebook and Twitter. Consumers are beginning to harness this power to effect change in how businesses operate.

16-3b The Marketing Concept

The marketing concept developed greatly in the 1960s, and it was early in this time period that Theodore Levitt published the article "Marketing Myopia." Among other things, Levitt's work brought about a new perspective that businesses should define themselves in terms of the consumer needs that they satisfy rather than in terms of the products they make. He argued that a firm's long-term health depends on its ability to exist as a consumer-satisfying entity rather than a goods-producing entity.

marketing ethics societal and professional standards of right and fair practices that are expected of marketing managers as they develop and implement marketing strategies

marketing concept statement that a firm should focus on consumer needs as a means of achieving long-term success

consumerism activities of various groups to voice concern for, and to protect, basic consumer rights

Exhibit 16.5

The Marketing Mix and Business Ethics

Tool	Common Use	Unethical Use
Product	The development of a good, service, or experience that will satisfy consumers' needs.	Failure to disclose that product won't function properly without necessary component parts.
Place	The distribution of a marketing offer through various channels of delivery.	Limiting product availability in certain markets as a means of raising prices.
Price	The marketer's statement of value received from an offering, which may be monetary or nonmonetary.	Stating that a regular price is really a "sale" price. This practice is prohibited by law.
Promotion	Communicating an offering's value through techniques such as advertising, sales promotion, and word-of-mouth.	Promoting one item as being on sale and then informing the customer that the product is out of stock and that a more expensive item should be bought. This practice, known as "bait and switch," is illegal.

As we have discussed in this text, companies should focus on the *total value concept* and remember that products provide value in multiple ways.

While many companies today adhere to the marketing concept, numerous questions arise regarding actual marketing practice. For example, companies often come under criticism for marketing products that some consider harmful. In particular, the fast-food, cereal, tobacco, and alcohol industries are often under fire from various groups. Even though freedom of choice is a central tenet of the Canadian economic system, these products are among many that society often considers harmful.

THE MARKETING MIX AND THE CONSUMER

Marketers should use the tools found in the marketing mix carefully as they target consumers. When consumers question the way in which they are treated, they are likely to spread negative information through word-of-mouth and seek some form of remedy.

One of the most visible elements of the marketing mix is pricing. When consumers believe that a firm's prices are unfair, they are likely to leave the firm and spread negative information about it.[64] Consumers also complain that

marketing efforts lead to overall higher prices. Marketers counter by explaining that marketing expenditures allow for increased economies of scale that contribute to lower overall production costs. Pricing issues are certainly debatable. Exhibit 16.5 presents the four P's of marketing as well as their ethical and unethical uses.

The product portion of the marketing mix also commonly comes under fire. Consumers question the extent to which products are actually harmful to them or society in the long run. Many products can lead to short-term satisfaction, but they can also lead to long-term consumer and/or societal problems. Consider the following categories of products originally discussed by Philip Kotler:[65]

▸ **Deficient products** are products that have little to no potential to create value of any type (e.g., faulty appliances).

▸ **Salutary products** are products that are good for both consumers and society in the long run (e.g., air bags). These products offer high utilitarian value but do not provide hedonic value.

▸ **Pleasing products** are products that provide hedonic value to consumers but may be harmful in the long run (e.g., cigarettes).

▸ **Desirable products** are products that deliver high utilitarian and hedonic value and that benefit both consumers and society in the long run (e.g., personal computers).

Marketers clearly want to avoid offering *deficient* products. The difficult issue comes with the marketing of *pleasing* products. Many consumers know that the products they enjoy are harmful, but they buy them anyway! Needless to say, the tobacco industry has been under criticism for years for marketing products that many think are unsafe. Individual responsibility and freedom are important factors in consumer decisions to use these products.

The promotion and place elements of the marketing mix can also be questioned. Consumers often believe that products are promoted in ways that are simply too good to be true. Consumers also question distribution tactics used by marketers. For example, they complain about tickets to major events being made available in only a few very select channels. As a result, consumers often feel like they are being treated unfairly. In 2009, Bruce Springsteen fans were enraged when they tried to buy tickets to his New Jersey concerts through Ticketmaster.com. After logging in at the appropriate time, fans were given a website error message and redirected to the Ticketmaster-owned site TicketsNow.com, where ticket prices were much higher than face value. Springsteen condemned the practice and Ticketmaster later apologized.[66]

Restricting tickets to popular events can ultimately harm consumers.

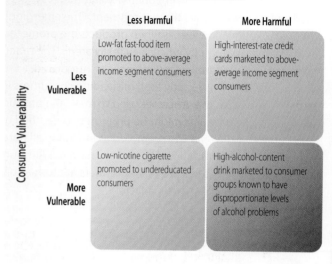

Exhibit 16.6

Product Harmfulness and Consumer Vulnerability

Source: Smith, N. Craig and Elizabeth Cooper-Martin (1997), "Ethics and Target Marketing: The Role of Product Harm and Consumer Vulnerability," *Journal of Marketing*, 61 (3): 1–20.

CONSUMER VULNERABILITY AND PRODUCT HARMFULNESS

Two important issues to consider when discussing marketing ethics are product harmfulness and consumer vulnerability.[67] A classification of product harmfulness/consumer vulnerability applied to marketing decision making is presented in Exhibit 16.6. Public criticism of marketing strategies tends to be most intense when a marketer targets vulnerable consumer groups with harmful products, as is the case when a marketer targets high-alcohol-content beverages to segments that have a large proportion of alcohol problems.

Of course, what constitutes a "harmful" product is a question of interpretation, as is the definition of a "vulnerable" consumer. What is a harmful product? What is a vulnerable consumer? One issue that is currently a hot topic is the growth of obesity in North America. Both media attention and public pressure have led fast-food marketers to rethink their menu offerings.

EMPLOYEE BEHAVIOUR

Individual employees play an important part in the execution of marketing programs. Although consumers hope that a firm's employees are acting in good faith, this is not always the case. When a used car salesperson sets the odometer back on automobiles, the salesperson

"All Shades of Green"

The growth in consumer demand for "green," environmentally friendly products has produced all kinds of opportunities for marketers. Green products continue to gain in popularity and there is much money to be made while helping save the environment. One emerging problem with green marketing, however, is when products are promoted as being green or environmentally friendly when they really aren't. The practice has become so common that the term *greenwashing* was introduced.

Greenwashing is exactly that: misleading consumers into believing that either a product or the processes used to make the product are green. For example, some products might be promoted as certified green when they really aren't, or they may be promoted as including all natural ingredients when the natural ingredients are actually harmful. Although research in this area is scarce, it is safe to say that consumers are turned off by the practice and this is a form of marketer misbehaviour.

iStockphoto.com/Irina Chirkova

Sources: Brent, Paul (2008), "Greenwashing: It's a Sin", *Marketing*, April 28, 2008, 7 (27), p. 1; Schaefer, Paul (2007), "The Six Sins of Greenwashing—Misleading Claims Found in Many Products," online content retrieved at *Environmental News Network* website, http://www.enn.com/green_building/article/26388, accessed July 1, 2010; online content retrieved at *Organic Consumers* website, "Whole Foods Market Imposes One-Year Deadline on Brands to Drop Bogus Organic Label Claims and Calls for Federal Regulation of Personal Care Products, http://www.organicconsumers.org/bodycare/index.cfm, accessed July 1, 2010.

should know that the act is unethical and illegal. Some situations, however, are not as straightforward. Consider a salesperson facing the temptation to use bribery as a means of obtaining a sale. In some cultures, this practice is commonplace and acceptable; however, the practice is prohibited in Canada. But what if the salesperson is dealing with a customer who is living in Canada but is from a country where bribes are commonplace?

Individual behaviour is guided largely by **morals**—personal standards and beliefs that are used to guide individual action. Certainly, each individual must answer to his or her own belief system.

16-4 CORPORATE SOCIAL RESPONSIBILITY

morals personal standards and beliefs used to guide individual action

corporate social responsibility an organization's activities and status related to its societal obligations

Corporate social responsibility may be defined as an organization's activities and status related to its societal obligations.[68] Due to increased pressure from consumer groups, companies are finding that they must be socially responsible. In fact, a popular catchphrase for socially responsible businesses is "doing well by doing good."

There are many ways in which companies can be responsible. Activities such as making donations to causes, supporting minority programs, ensuring responsible manufacturing processes and environmental protectionism, acting quickly when product defects are detected, focusing on employee safety, and encouraging employees to volunteer for local causes are some of the many ways in which companies can demonstrate their social responsibility.[69] Basically, the actions described fall into one of three categories:

1. *Ethical duties* include acting within expected ethical boundaries.

2. *Altruistic duties* include giving back to communities through philanthropic activities.

3. *Strategic initiatives* include strategically engaging in socially responsible activities in order to increase the value of the firm.[70]

Although comprehensive coverage of corporate responsibility is beyond the scope of this text, it is worth nothing that socially responsible marketing is associated with important CB metrics—including favourable consumer evaluations, increased customer satisfaction, and the likelihood of increased sales. This is especially the case when an individual consumer

Exhibit 16.7

Prescriptions for Improved Marketing Ethics

▶ Marketers must put people first and consider the effects of their actions on all stakeholders.

▶ Actions must be based on standards that go beyond laws and regulations.

▶ Marketers must be held responsible for the means they use to achieve their desired ends. Focusing on profit motivations is not enough.

▶ Marketing organizations should focus on training employees in ethical decision making.

▶ Marketing organizations should embrace and disseminate a core set of ethical principles.

▶ Decision makers must adopt a stakeholder orientation that leads to an appreciation of how marketing decisions affect all relevant parties.

▶ Marketing organizations should specify ethical decision-making protocols.

Source: Based on Laczniak, Gene R. and Patrick E. Murphy (2006), "Normative Perspectives for Ethical and Socially Responsible Marketing," *Journal of Macromarketing*, 26 (2): 154–177.

identifies with the company and the causes to which it contributes.[71]

16-4a The Societal Marketing Concept

Part of being socially responsible is adopting the **societal marketing concept**. This concept considers the needs of society along with the wants and needs of individual consumers.[72] All firms have many stakeholders, and the effects of marketing actions on all these stakeholder groups should be considered. Some argue that if a product promotion achieves profitability at the expense of the general good, then the effort should not be undertaken. All of the stakeholders of a firm should be considered when marketing programs are initiated. Exhibit 16.7 presents prescriptions for improved marketing ethics.

⬤16-5 REGULATION OF MARKETING ACTIVITIES: CONSUMER PROTECTION AND PRIVACY

Many federal, provincial, and municipal laws, by-laws, and regulations have been enacted to protect consumers from unsafe products and marketer misbehaviour. At the federal level, these include Health Canada, Industry Canada, Transport Canada, the Competition Bureau of Canada, the Canadian Radio-television and Telecommunications Commission (CRTC), the Privacy Commissioner of Canada, and the Canadian Food Inspection Agency. Other groups such as the Better Business Bureau, Canadian Association of Broadcasters, Concerned Children's Advertisers, the Public Interest Advocacy Centre, Canadian Marketing Association, and the Association of Canadian Advertisers also play an important role in monitoring and enforcing the country's laws and regulations. Although these organizations work diligently to ensure a fair and safe marketplace for consumers across a variety of different industries, it is ultimately the responsibility of managers to act ethically and in accordance with the law. Of course, that does not always happen. As a result, government plays a critical role in protecting consumers and their privacy.

16-5a Consumer Privacy

The Department of Justice, Industry Canada, and federal and provincial privacy commissioners play an important role in protecting and promoting the privacy rights of individual Canadian consumers. In particular, the Privacy Commissioner of Canada is an advocate for Canadians' privacy rights. This role includes investigating complaints, publicly reporting information-handling practices in the public and private sector, researching privacy issues, and promoting public awareness of privacy issues. A basic principle underlying national and provincial privacy regulations is the notion that consumer trust and confidence in Canada's system of commerce is fundamental to a well-functioning economy.

> **societal marketing concept** marketing concept that marketers should consider not only the wants and needs of consumers but also the needs of society

Canada's federal *Personal Information Protection and Electronic Documents Act* (PIPEDA) received royal assent in the House of Commons in 2000 and was last updated and amended in 2011. At the heart of the Act is the notion that to collect, use, or disclose personal information about people, you need their consent. In addition, the Act allows businesses to use or disclose individuals' personal information only for the purpose for which they gave consent. Even with consent, firms have to limit collection, use, and disclosure to purposes that a reasonable person would consider appropriate under the circumstances. The Act also provides individuals with the right to request and see the personal information that a business holds about them and to correct any inaccuracies in that information. Oversight for this Act lies with the Privacy Commissioner of Canada, who is charged with ensuring that the law is respected. However, the ability of the Privacy Commissioner to enforce the Act has been criticized because remedies under PIPEDA require taking the matter to federal court. The lack of strong penalties for violations may explain why many companies are still not in compliance with PIPEDA, as illustrated by the results of a recent study[73] from the Office of the Privacy Commissioner of Canada summarized in Exhibit 16.8.

16-5b Canada's Anti-Spam Law (CASL)

Recently introduced by the federal government to protect Canadians against spam and malicious software, Canada's Anti-Spam Law (CASL) came into effect on July 1, 2014, and was followed by the prohibition against malware on January 15, 2015. In essence, this law requires that any organization sending a commercial electronic message must have the recipient's **express consent**. Businesses are also required to be truthful in the content of the message, clearly identify themselves, and offer recipients of the message an opportunity to unsubscribe from the mail list. The CRTC enforces this law using tools that range from warnings to steep financial penalties. Individuals who violate CASL can be fined up to $1 million per incident, and

express consent
unequivocal opt-in consent from the recipient for a stated communication purpose, which does not require any inference on the part of the organization

negative consent the organization assumes it has consent unless the individual takes action to opt out or deny consent

implied consent consent that may be reasonably inferred from the action or inaction of the individual

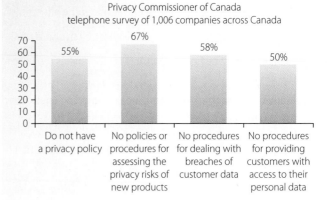

Exhibit 16.8

How Are Canadian Companies Doing?

Privacy Commissioner of Canada telephone survey of 1,006 companies across Canada

Source: Based on statistics found on government blog, *Mind the Gap*, http://blog.priv.gc.ca/index.php/2014/06/19/mind-the-gap-poll-finds-many-canadian-businesses-believe-privacy-is-important-but-not-taking-basic-steps-to-protect-customer-information, accessed September 21, 2015. Used with permission of the Office of the Privacy Commissioner of Canada.

businesses up to $10 million per incident. Moreover, after July 1, 2017, private parties will be able to sue for breaches of CASL. An organization could be liable to a penalty of up to $1 million per day per occurrence in addition to actual damages.

A key to successfully navigating electronic marketing to avoid being penalized under CASL is understanding what is meant by express consent. Any organization or individual sending out an electronic message needs to be sure that they have clear consent from the recipient of the message and that the consent relates to the purpose of the message. This means, for example, that a car dealership that receives consent from a consumer for service reminders does not have express consent for marketing messages about its new car sales. Express consent must also be positive or opt-in consent. In other words, consumers must make some effort to agree to provide such consent. This is distinct from opt-out or **negative consent** that is assumed unless the individual takes some action to deny the organization consent.

Another important term under CASL is implied consent. **Implied consent** arises when consent may be reasonably inferred from the action or inaction of the individual consumer. For example, if you were to sign up to connect to an Internet service provider such as Telus or Rogers, the company might rely on implied consent to provide service support. This might include identifying and correcting delivery problems or service failures. If an organization receives a business card from a potential customer at a trade show, it might also have implied consent to contact that individual. An organization that has implied consent must ask that individual for express consent within 24 months. After that time, implied consent expires.

As part of the introduction of CASL, businesses have been given until 2017 to transition individuals' implied consent into express consent. CASL also explicitly includes a number of exemptions. For example, messages sent to consumers who request information (such as a complaint or product inquiry), messages sent to enforce a legal right (e.g., debt collection or enforcing contractual obligations), and messages sent from outside of Canada are exempt from CASL regulations. Similarly business-to-business communications within organizations or between organizations with an ongoing relationship are exempt. For example, messages are exempt when sent between employees, from a company to a franchisee, or from a firm to its marketing agency. Marketing and consumer behaviour students who work in Canada should be familiar with CASL and it is worth spending some time reviewing the details of the law, including tips for compliance, at www.fightspam.gc.ca.

16-5c Consumer Product Safety

Health Canada is the main federal body responsible for consumer product safety, and it works to protect Canadians through research, assessment, and collaboration to manage health and safety risks.

On June 20, 2011, the Canada Consumer Product Safety Act (CCPSA) came into force. This law applies to a wide variety of consumer products, including toys, sporting goods, and household products; however, it excludes motor vehicles, food, and drugs (which are covered by separate acts, as described below). The Act requires industry to report concerns over safety and product defects that could harm Canadians. The CCPSA also prohibits the manufacture, importation, sale, or advertisement of consumer products that pose a danger to Canadians. In addition, the Act prohibits packaging, labelling, or advertising a consumer product in a false, misleading, or deceptive manner with respect to its safety.[74]

Health Canada is responsible for food and drug safety and nutritional quality under the authority of the Food and Drug Act and the Food and Drug Regulations. This involves collecting, analyzing, and disseminating information about nutrition, including *Canada's Food Guide*. The Canadian Food Inspection Agency is responsible for enforcement, as well as for the administration of related regulations concerning food packaging, labelling, and advertising. With respect to drug products, Health Canada reviews prescription and nonprescription pharmaceuticals and disinfectants to assess their safety, efficacy, and quality before they are authorized for sale.

Transportation safety—whether by air, water, rail, or road—falls primarily under the auspices of Transport Canada. When it comes to consumer road safety, Transport Canada works with other levels of government and private-sector partners to support Canada's Road Safety Strategy 2015.[75]

16-6 PUBLIC CRITICISM OF MARKETING

Unethical marketers intend to do harm in some way, act negligently, and/or manipulate consumers. As we have stated, however, marketers can simply make innocent mistakes. For example, a company may not discover a product defect until it has been released for public consumption; it would then issue a product recall. At issue is the *intent* and *knowledge* of the firm. Consumer perception is also important, as bad events can mean disaster for the firm in terms of lost business, customer boycotts, and bad publicity. We could discuss any number of different issues regarding public criticism of marketing; however, we focus on only a handful of issues here.

16-6a Deceptive Advertising

Deceptive advertising (sometimes called false or misleading advertising) is an important issue for marketers. **Deceptive advertising** is advertising that (1) contains or omits information that is important in influencing a consumer's buying behaviour and (2) is likely to mislead consumers who are acting "reasonably."[76] The extent to which advertisers *intentionally* misrepresent their products is crucial. In practice, deception can be difficult to prove.

Although regulatory mechanisms and government agencies are in place to protect consumers from deceptive advertising, most businesses prefer forms of self-regulation over governmental regulation. For this reason, the advertising industry created the

deceptive advertising message that omits information that is important in influencing a consumer's buying behaviour and is likely to mislead consumers acting "reasonably"

Canadian Code of Advertising Standards in 1963. The code is regularly updated to match changes in consumer products and marketing, as well as changes in societal standards and expectations. The code contains 14 clauses that require advertising to be truthful, fair, and accurate.[77]

16-6b Marketing to Children

Children typify a vulnerable group because they often lack the knowledge of how to behave as responsible consumers. Two important issues arise with marketing to children. First, there is the question of whether children can understand that some marketing messages do not offer literal interpretations of the real world. For example, many toys are shown in unrealistic settings. Second, the quantity of marketing messages to which children are exposed can be called into question. It has been estimated that the average North American child sees more than 40,000 television commercials per year—or an average of over 100 commercials per day.[78] A number of organizations play a role in monitoring advertising to children, including the CRTC, Canadian Association of Broadcasters (CAB), Concerned Children's Advertisers, and Better Business Bureau.

The CRTC requires advertisements to adhere to the Broadcast Code for Advertising to Children published by the CAB in cooperation with Advertising Standards Canada. In Quebec, commercial advertising to children under the age of 13 is generally prohibited and is the responsibility of the Office de la protection du consommateur.[79]

Internet marketing aimed at children is another important issue. In 2008, two important resolutions were passed with respect to online privacy for children in Canada. The first was drafted by Canada's Privacy Commissioner in June 2008 and is referred to as the Regina Resolution. The second, known as the Strasbourg Resolution, was drafted in October 2008 at the International Conference of Data Protection and Privacy Commissioners. Both resolutions call for an education-based approach to online privacy for children. The Strasbourg Resolution states that "children and young people have the right to a safe and positive online experience in which they know and understand the intent of those they interact with."[80] Discussion papers following up on these resolutions recommend legal reforms that limit or prohibit the online collection of children's data and enshrine the right to privacy for children.

Marketing to children is a controversial issue.

16-6c Pollution

The process of marketing a product often leads to pollution, and marketers are often criticized for harming the environment. Of course, consumption also leads to pollution.[81] Ultimately, both marketers and consumers play important roles in environmental protection.

16-6d Planned Obsolescence

Marketers are also criticized for intentionally phasing out products before their usefulness expires. For example, video game manufacturers are criticized for releasing new and seemingly "improved" gaming consoles even when older models haven't been on the market very long. The practice of managing and intentionally setting discontinue dates for products is known as **planned obsolescence**. Critics charge that it is both wasteful and greedy for marketers to engage in planned obsolescence. Marketers counter that by continually offering improved products they allow consumers to enjoy improved standards of living and innovation.

16-6e Artificial Needs

Marketers are also criticized for imposing what might be called "artificial" needs on consumers. You may recall that a want represents the way in which a consumer goes about addressing a need. A consumer might have a need for food and sustenance but have the want to fulfill that

planned obsolescence act of planning the premature obsolescence of product models that perform adequately need with an expensive steak dinner. Do consumers really need an 80-inch 4K 3D Smart LED TV? Do consumers really need whiter teeth or luxury cars? Wants and needs can easily become confused, and some argue that marketers only fuel the fire. By confusing wants and needs, consumers often give in to overconsumption.

Consumers also complain that advertisers create unrealistic expectations in their advertisements. For example, marketers of weight-loss products often promote lofty expectations. Advertisers include disclaimers such as "results vary" or "results are not typical" in their advertisements, but consumers rarely notice them.

16-6f Manipulative Sales Tactics

High-pressure and manipulative sales pitches are often the cause of consumer dissatisfaction. For example, a realtor might tell a client that several other people have looked at a particular house when they actually haven't. Or a salesperson might tell a customer that a product is in short supply when it really isn't.

Salespeople who adhere to a sales orientation are often guilty of these types of high-pressure tactics. To have a **sales orientation** means that the salesperson is more focused on the immediate sale and short-term results than on long-term customer satisfaction and relationship development. A more appropriate way to approach a sale is to adhere to what is referred to as a **customer orientation**, where the salesperson focuses on customer needs. Several studies have shown that having a customer orientation leads to favourable results for salespeople.

Ingratiation tactics are sometimes used by salespeople in order to get a sale. These techniques are often viewed as being manipulative.[82] Techniques such as the foot-in-the-door technique, the door-in-the-face technique, the even-a-penny-will-help technique, and the "I'm working for you!" technique can be called into question. These methods are considered unethical to the extent to which they are used for manipulation.

A salesperson using the **foot-in-the-door technique** focuses on simply getting a "foot in the door." When consumers realize that they have opened themselves up to a sales pitch, they are more likely to listen to the pitch and they are also more likely to buy a product. The salesperson first makes a small request, such as "May I have a few minutes of your time?" and follows with a larger request, such as "May I show you how this works?" and finally by the largest request of "May I have your order?" The foot-in-the-door technique is based on *self-perception theory*, which proposes that

consumers use perceptions of their own actions when forming attitudes. The consumer realizes that he has "let the salesperson in" and has given in to a small request; therefore, he must be the type of person who would give in to larger requests and ultimately buy the product. Of course, salespeople could argue that this is simply good salesmanship.

With the **door-in-the-face technique**, a salesperson begins by making a really large request, such as "Can I get you to buy this car today?" Realizing that very few, if any, customers would say, "Yes!" the salesperson prepares for the dreaded "No!" Showing that her feelings are hurt, she follows with a guilt-ridden statement like, "Well, can I show you its features?" Many consumers would feel bad about responding negatively to the first request and would allow the salesperson to explain the car's features. This tactic relies on the *reciprocity norm*, which states that individuals are motivated to give back to those who have given them something. By feeling that he just rejected a salesperson, the customer feels that he at least owes the salesperson the courtesy of listening.

Using the **even-a-penny-will-help technique**, cause-related marketers suggest to potential donors that even the smallest donation will go a long way toward reaching the desired goal, such as ending child abuse, feeding the hungry, or sheltering the homeless.[83] The idea is to make the donor feel ashamed to give such a small amount. Instead of giving the penny, they may give a dollar. This technique is considered unethical to the extent that it relies on feelings of guilt.

Using the **"I'm working for you!" technique**, salespeople attempt to lead customers into believing that

sales orientation
practice of using sales techniques that are aimed at satisfying the salesperson's own needs and motives for short-term sales success

customer orientation
practice of using sales techniques that focus on customer needs

foot-in-the-door technique ingratiation technique used in personal selling in which a salesperson begins with a small request and slowly leads up to one major request

door-in-the-face technique ingratiation technique used in personal selling in which a salesperson begins with a major request and then follows with a series of smaller requests

even-a-penny-will-help technique
ingratiation technique in which a marketing message suggests that even the smallest donation, such as a penny or a dollar, will help a cause

"I'm working for you!" technique
technique used by salespeople to create the perception that they are working as hard as possible to close a sale when they really are not doing so

Hill Street Studios/Blend Images/Jupiterimages

Salespeople can manipulate consumers in many ways.

16-6g Stealth Marketing

One area of marketing that is currently receiving increased attention is the use of stealth marketing. Is it ethical for businesses to market products to consumers when the consumers do not realize that they are being targeted by marketing messages? With *stealth marketing*, consumers are completely unaware that they are being marketed to (hence, the term *stealth*). Again, WOMMA (Word of Mouth Marketing Association) is opposed to such tactics and considers their use to be unethical.[84]

they are working as hard as possible to give them the best deal when in reality they are following a script or routine. A salesperson walks away from his office during a negotiation to "go check with the manager" when he is really going to get coffee. The salesperson returns and says something like "I'm really working for you and here's a good deal!" This technique relies on *equity theory*. Here, the consumer would think that the salesperson is working hard, thereby raising the denominator in the equity theory comparison equation and leading to higher levels of satisfaction, and potentially purchase likelihood. Of course, salespeople often do consult with managers and work as hard as possible to give their customers the best deal.

Case

Canada's CASL Protects Against Spam

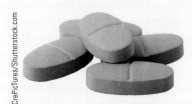

CrePicTures/Shutterstock.com

Can I sell you some "Vl@gra"? Or maybe you would prefer a hot stock tip? Every day, many unwanted and unsolicited emails flow into Canadians' inboxes. From medication to pornography to shady business deals, the low cost of sending an email has made this approach to reaching potential customers seemingly irresistible to some marketers. While most consumers relegate these messages to the trash without a second thought, such emails, texts, and other electronic communications continue to be sent. In fact, although estimates vary, best guesses put the amount of spam at something like 70% to 90% of all email.

Technology has made substantial advances in filtering out the vast majority of these messages before we ever see them, dramatically reducing the probability that we will receive an offer for "V!@gra" in our inbox. Yet, many Canadians do still receive unsolicited messages from retailers, training companies, vacation promoters, and others.

Designed to address this problem, the federal government's Canadian Anti-Spam Legislation (CASL) came into effect on July 1, 2014, and aims to encourage organizations to behave better, while punishing those that do not. Enforcing CASL is the responsibility of the Canadian Radio-television and Telecommunications Commission (CRTC). Quebec-based Compu-Finder, the first company to be fined by the CRTC, was hit with a $1.1 million penalty for what the CRTC called flagrant violations of the basic principles of the law. According to the CRTC, Compu-Finder sent commercial electronic messages about its training courses, without consent and on multiple occasions, after CASL came into effect. In fact, estimates suggest that the company accounted for 26% of the spam complaints submitted for this industry sector.

Manon Bombardier, chief compliance and enforcement officer at the CRTC, said, "By issuing this Notice of Violation, my goal is to encourage a change of behaviour on the part of Compu-Finder such that it adapts its business practices to the modern reality of electronic commerce and the requirements of the anti-spam law." Although more than 245,000 complaints over spam have been registered with the CRTC and only one penalty handed down so far, many are hoping this first fine sends a strong message to spammers that the Government of Canada and the CRTC are serious about enforcement.

Overall, CASL seems to be having an effect. According to *Infosecurity* magazine, research from mail security firm Cloudmark indicates that spam originating in Canada has dropped 37% since CASL went into effect. CASL is even being touted as a potential model for other governments around the world that are also interested in deterring spam and reducing unwanted electronic communications.

Sources: Canadian Radio-television and Telecommunications Commission (2015), "CRTC Chief Compliance and Enforcement Officer issues $1.1 million penalty to Compu-Finder for spamming Canadians," http://news.gc.ca/web/article-en.do?nid=944159, accessed May 11, 2015. Tara Seals (2015), "Spam plummets 37% in Canada," *Infosecurity Magazine*, May 1, accessed May 11, 2015. Nicole Bogart (2015), "CRTC issues $1.1M penalty to Compu-Finder, first fine under anti-spam law," *Global News*, March 5, http://globalnews.ca/news/1866029/crtc-issues-1-1m-penalty-to-compu-finder-first-fine-under-anti-spam-law/ accessed May 11, 2015. Jennifer Brown (2015), "Quebec company hit with $1.1 million penalty under CASL," *Canadian Lawyer Magazine*, March 9, http://www.canadianlawyermag.com/5499/Quebec-company-hit-with-$1.1-million-penalty-under-CASL.html accessed May 11, 2015.

QUESTIONS

1 Prior to CASL being enacted, spam was annoying but not clearly illegal in Canada. Even then many argued that organizations had a moral obligation to restrict communications to recipients who would find the message relevant. Do you agree?

2 If the majority of spam today is caught by email filters, why do organizations continue to send it out? Are emails for "V!@gra" effective?

3 Do you agree with the government that regulation and stiff fines were required to curb spam in Canada?

4 CASL also deals with the installation of software on someone else's computer without their express consent. You may be able to imagine nefarious reasons why someone might want to install a program on your computer without your knowing, but why would a marketer want to do that?

5 Are there other types of misleading or unwanted communications that companies in Canada use in an attempt to reach potential customers? Should the government intervene in those areas as well?

INTEGRATIVE CASE STUDY

Axe, Dove, and the Old Spice Man: Soap and Self-Esteem

At the heart of marketing soap and deodorant is an interesting insight: The majority of college-aged males consider themselves to be more attractive than the average guy, but only one-quarter of females believe that they are more attractive than the average girl.[1] This difference can be seen very clearly in the marketing campaigns run by Axe and Dove. The basic value proposition for Axe is that "it helps guys be attractive to women."[2] Consistent with this message, advertisements for Axe suggest that using the brand's body wash or spray will make you irresistible to women. The successful campaign features women getting a sniff of a man wearing Axe and then being overcome by desire. Women chase men down the street, tackle them, and tear off their clothes. In one commercial, the scent of Axe is so powerful it causes angels to fall from the sky and discard their halos in pursuit of a man wearing the body spray.[3] Another popular and controversial commercial was Axe's "Clean Your Balls"[4]—a three-minute video that resembled a Shopping Channel infomercial and featured actresses washing soccer and golf balls and promoting the importance of keeping one's "equipment" clean. Whether cause or effect, the rapid rise in sales of Axe products has coincided with a significant increase in the willingness of men to spend money on personal care products.[5]

In contrast, Dove aims "to inspire women to reconsider and recognize the choices they make every day and encourage them to realize that feeling beautiful is a choice they can make every day."[6] The brand's ads aim to build confidence and celebrate women. "Real Beauty Sketches," for example, was a campaign pointing out that other people tend to see women as more beautiful than they see themselves.[7] The "Dove Evolution" video has more than 18 million views on YouTube and makes a strong argument that society has a distorted view of female beauty because of its unrealistic depiction in advertising.[8]

While understanding the differences between demographic segments is important in many consumer markets, in Canada's billion-dollar soap, shower, and deodorant business it is absolutely critical. Unilever Canada Inc., which owns both the Axe and Dove brands, is the national market leader and controls a market share of just over 18% of the approximately $1.3 billion in total annual sales for this category.[9]

Canadians clearly see value in using soap and deodorant. There is a utilitarian benefit to being clean and smelling nice, but the real value that separates competitors in the market and determines consumers' choices at the shelf is in the hedonic domain. Successful brands, like Axe and Dove, use strong visceral emotional appeals to create associations between the product and the fulfillment of basic human emotions. Both are related to self-esteem, but they differ in the way that they connect to their target consumers. Axe takes a peripheral approach with a very low need for cognition that appeals to men's view of themselves as attractive. Angels falling from the sky, women running in bikinis down beaches, and a body spray making you irresistible appeal to the key segment. It is not, however, an idea that will stand up very well to serious scrutiny of the message's realism. Dove takes a different approach, asking its target consumers to think more about beauty and its role in their lives and society. Dove wants to associate "real beauty" and positive self-esteem with the brand.

These two appeals reflect very different beauty cultures for men and women in western society. They are focused on the psychographic insight that men tend to see themselves as more attractive than average, while women tend to see themselves as less attractive than average. Dove has carved out a successful business focusing on women of all ages, actively reaching out to young girls as well as their mothers and grandmothers. At the same time, Axe revolutionized the personal grooming category for young men with its focus on making them more attractive to women.

But that left another key demographic segment underserved. Men over 35 who were married and had children of their own were less receptive to the Axe message. The over-the-top sexual advertising was entertaining, but spoke less directly to their day-to-day lives, values, and goals. In fact, this segment was much less influenced by the brand of deodorant or soap they used and was more focused on the utilitarian benefits of being clean and smelling good. Axe was doing well with the segment, but something was missing in the fit between brands and consumer behaviour in the over-35 male market.

Procter & Gamble (P&G)—Unilever's top competitor with 15.6% of the soap, shower, and deodorant market in Canada—was looking for a way to compete with Axe. Historically, its Old Spice brand had been a top player in the market. In years past, men tended to give little thought to the product category and they were fairly habitual buyers, often choosing to buy what they were familiar with or had seen their father use. Axe's aggressive campaign so effectively offered consumers what they really wanted from personal grooming products that Old Spice and other brands were struggling to maintain their market share. What P&G realized was that there is a critical behavioural difference between the younger and older markets for men's grooming products. While young men were shopping for a product that would make them more attractive to women, the behaviour of older consumers was quite different. In fact, in many households the consumers of the product were not the ones who made the purchase. Instead, it was the wives who were often making the buying decision. Armed with this understanding, P&G launched a marketing campaign with a message that was distinct from both Axe and Dove. Old Spice began selling "The Man Your Man Could Smell Like."

Intended to be a humorous appeal that worked for both the male consumer and the female buyer, Old Spice used a behavioural rather than psychographic insight to uncover a market segment that was looking for a different value proposition. Like Axe and Dove, the Old Spice story was told in a very visceral way. While Axe was hypersexual and Dove focused on self-esteem, Old Spice got attention by being funny. All three brands were able to generate a great deal of word-of-mouth around their campaigns. In doing so, they were able to turn dull utilitarian products like soap and deodorant into a topic of casual conversation.

From a consumer behaviour perspective, one of the most interesting things about the evolution of this market is how these very utilitarian products evolved into a more hedonic shopping experience. Rather than compete for a rational shopper focused on price and product benefits, Unilever and P&G built large groups of loyal experiential consumers, many of whom have strong emotional connections to their brands. This is important in a market where the product is purchased on a regular basis and the switching costs are very low.

Some observers have argued that, based on expectancy/disconfirmation theory, Axe customers should be dissatisfied with their product experience. After all, does a body spray really make you more attractive to women? The answer to this question might lie in the original insight—that is, the majority of young guys already think they are more attractive than average and using Axe does not disconfirm this expectation.

A more substantial problem for Unilever has been the backlash against the company based on the two very different messages it is selling to consumers.[10] The premise for this consumer complaint is that the company cannot possibly be authentic in its promotion of Dove's "Real Beauty" for women if it is simultaneously promoting women as powerless against Axe's body spray. Nevertheless, from a business perspective, Unilever's marketing has been very effective. Over the last decade, the company has moved from being in a distant third place in the category to being the market leader.[11]

QUESTIONS

1 How have Axe, Dove and Old Spice created value?

2 Which variables are playing key roles in segmenting Canada's soap, shower, and deodorant market?

3 How has each brand been able to turn a utilitarian product into a hedonic experience?

4 How did each brand gain attention for itself in the marketplace?

5 What associations, positive and negative, are connected to each of these brands?

6 What basic human motivations are Axe and Dove tapping into? How about Old Spice?

7 What role might need for cognition play in the response of individual consumers to the differentiated messages of Axe, Dove, and Old Spice?

8 What role does a consumer's self-concept play in his response to Axe versus Old Spice?

INTEGRATIVE CASE STUDY

9 How would you apply the elaboration likelihood model to better understand the messages of each of these three brands?

10 What is the impact of Canada's beauty culture on consumer behaviour in the soap, shower, and deodorant market?

11 What role does word-of-mouth play in the success of Axe, Dove, and Old Spice? How does each of these brands facilitate consumers' talking about the products?

12 How has this product category evolved from rational to experiential? To what extent is behavioural shopping also playing a role? What other product categories have evolved in a similar way?

13 Why are customers of each of these brands satisfied?

14 What drives loyalty for Axe, Dove, and Old Spice? Are there differences in the nature of the loyalty consumers have to each of these brands?

15 Do you think Dove's message of "Real Beauty" that celebrates women and builds confidence is damaged by Unilever's ownership of the Axe brand? Is Dove's message authentic? Why are some consumers complaining?

ENDNOTES

1 Feifer, Jason (2012), "How Axe Built a Highly Scientific, Totally Irresistible Marketing Machine Built on Lust," *Fast Company*, September, http://www .fastcocreate.com/1681417/how-axe-built-a-highly-scientific-totally -irresistible-marketing-machine-built-on-lust, accessed July 22, 2014.

2 Ibid.

3 Axe Excite new ad, "Even Angels Will Fall," https://www.youtube.com/ watch?v=EqGQCM_JlUc

4 Axe, "Clean Your Balls," https://www.youtube.com/watch?v=mPwhMoQBg_8

5 Kane, Courtney (2002), "Personal-Grooming Marketers Decide That American Men Are Ready for Body Sprays," *The New York Times* (September 4), http:// www.nytimes.com/2002/09/04/business/media-business-advertising -personal-grooming-marketers-decide-that-american-men.html, accessed July 22, 2014.

6 Mackenzie, Emma (2015), "Dove Wants to Prove Beauty Is a Choice in New Campaign," April 8, http://www.bandt.com.au/marketing/dove -wants-to-proves-beauty-is-a-choice-in-new-campaign, accessed July 22, 2014.

7 Dove "Real Beauty Sketches," https://www.youtube.com/watch?v=litXW91UauE

8 Dove, "Evolution," https://www.youtube.com/watch?v=iYhCn0jf46U

9 Euromonitor International: Passport (2015), "Deodorants in Canada," *May*; and Euromonitor International: Passport (2015), "Bath and Shower in Canada," *May*.

10 Stamler, Laura (2013), "Why People Hate Dove's 'Real Beauty Sketches' Video," April 22, http://www.businessinsider.com/why-people-hate-doves -real-beauty-ad-2013-4, access July 22, 2014.

11 Howard, Theresa (2006), "Success Can Be a Matter of Degree," *USA Today* (November 12), http://www.usatoday.com/money/advertising/ adtrack/2006-11-12-degree_x.htm, accessed July 2, 2015.

ENDNOTES

1

1. See Walters, C. Glenn, and Gordon W. Paul (1970), *Consumer Behavior: An Integrated Approach*, 3rd ed. Irwin, Homewood, IL; Howard, John L., and Jagdish Sheth (1969), *The Theory of Buyer Behavior*, New York: Wiley

2. MacInnis, Deborah J., and Valerie S. Folkes, "The Disciplinary Status of Consumer Behavior: A Sociology of Science Perspective on Key Controversies," *Journal of Consumer Research*, 36 (April 2010): 899–914.

3. MacInnis and Folkes, "Disciplinary Status."

4. See http://dictionary.laborlawtalk.com/Economics for different perspectives on economics; accessed January 8, 2007.

5. Pan, Suwen, Cheng Fang, and Jaime Malaga (2006), "Alcoholic Beverage Consumption in China: A Censored Demand System Approach," *Applied Economics Letters* 13 (12/15), 975–979.

6. Christie, Jennifer, Dan Fisher, John C. Kozup, Scott Smith, Scott Burton, and Elizabeth H. Creyer (2001), "The Effects of Bar-Sponsored Alcohol Beverage Promotions Across Binge and Nonbinge Drinkers," *Journal of Public Policy & Marketing* 20 (Fall), 240–253.

7. Mullainathan, Sendhil, and Richard H. Thaler (2000), "Behavioral Economics," *National Bureau of Economic Research*, No. w7948. http://www.nber.org/papers/w7948.

8. Tyler, Leona E. (1981), "More Stately Mansions—Psychology Extends Its Boundaries," *Annual Review of Psychology* 32, 1–20.

9. Yoon, Carolyn, Gilles Laurent, Helen H. Fung, Richard Gonzales, Angela H. Gutchess, Trey Hedden, Raphaelle Lambert-Pandraud, Mara Mather, Denise C. Park, Ellen Peters, and Ian Skurnik (2005), "Cognition, Persuasion and Decision Making in Older Consumers," *Marketing Letters* 16 (3), 429–441.

10. Moore, David J. "Is Anticipation Delicious? Visceral Factors as Mediators of the Effect of Olfactory Cues on Purchase Intentions," *Journal of Business Research*, 67, no. 9 (September 2014), http://dx.doi.org/10.1016/j.jbusres.2013.10.005.

11. Darroch, Jenny, Morgan P. Miles, Andrew Jardine, and Ernest F. Cooke (2004), "The 2004 AMA Definition of Marketing and Its Relationship to a Market Orientation: An Extension of Cooke, Rayburn, & Abercrombie (1992)," *Journal of Marketing Theory & Practice* 12 (Fall), 29–38.

12. Mittelstaedt, Robert A. (1990), "Economics, Psychology, and the Literature of the Subdiscipline of Consumer Behavior," *Journal of the Academy of Marketing Science* 18 (4), 303–311.

13. Zinkhan, George M., Martin S. Roth, and Mary Jane Saxton (1992), "Knowledge Development and Scientific Status in Consumer-Behavior Research: A Social Exchange Perspective," *Journal of Consumer Research* 19 (September), 282–291.

14. Zinkhan, Roth, and Saxton (1992).

15. Henry, G. T., and Theodore Poister (1994), "Citizen Ratings of Public and Private Service Quality: A Comparative Perspective," *Public Administration Review* 54, 11a. Winkler, C. (2003), "When Yanking the Mainframe Isn't an Option," *Computerworld*, 37, 35–36.

16. Competition Bureau (2014), "Bell Aliant to Lease Part of Ontera Network in Response to Competition Bureau Concerns," http://www.competitionbureau.gc.ca/eic/site/cb-bc.nsf/eng/03822.html, accessed May 6, 2015.

17. Narver, J. C., and S. F. Slater (1990), "The Effect of a Market Orientation on Business Profitability," *Journal of Marketing* 54 (October), 20–35. Narver, J. C., S. Slater, and B. Tietje (1998), "Creating a Market Orientation," *Journal of Market-Focused Management 2* (3), 241–55.

18. Voss, G. B., and Z. G. Voss (2000), "Strategic Orientation and Firm Performance in an Artistic Environment," *Journal of Marketing* 64, 67–83. Auh, Seigyoung, and B. Menguc (2006), "Diversity at the Executive Suite: A Resource-Based Approach to the Customer Orientation–Organizational Performance Relationship," *Journal of Business Research* 59, 564–572.

19. Skogland, I., and J. A. Siguaw (2004), "Are Your Satisfied Customers Loyal?" *Cornell Hotel and Restaurant Administration Quarterly* 45, 221–234. Berger, P. D., N Eechambadi, G. Morris, D. R. Lehmann, R. Rizley, and R. Venkatesan (2006), "From Customer Lifetime Value to Shareholder Value: Theory, Empirical Evidence and Issues for Future Research," *Journal of Services Research* 9, 156–167.

20. Neslin, S. A., D. Grewal, R. Leghorn, V. Shankar, M. L. Teerling, J. S. Thomas, and P. C. Verhoef (2006), "Challenges and Opportunities in Multichannel Customer Management," *Journal of Services Research* 9, 95–112.

21. Mah, Bill (2015), "Target's Closure Leaves Malls Scrambling, Shoppers Shrugging," *Edmonton Journal*, January 16.

22. All dates taken from company websites. Samsung was originally founded in 1938 but as a Korean food exporter. In 1969, Samsung Electronics was created.

23. Christenson, C. M., S. Cook, and T. Hall (2005), "Marketing Malpractice: The Cause and the Cure," *Harvard Business Review* 83, 74–83.

24. Statistics Canada (2014), "Percentage of Households by Type of Telephone Service, by Province," *The Daily*, June 23, http://www.statcan.gc.ca/daily-quotidien/140623/t140623a001-eng.htm, accessed May 6, 2015.

25. Wang, Y. "More People Have Cell Phones Than Toilets, U.N. Study Shows," TIME.com, March 25, 2013, http://newsfeed.time.com/2013/03/25/more-people-have-cell-phones-than-toilets-u-n-study-shows/#ixzz2tWBD7ZRW, accessed February 16, 2014.

26. Oliveira, Michael (2014), "25% of Grade 4 Students Have Cellphone: Canadian Survey," *Toronto Star*, January 22, http://www.thestar.com/news/canada/2014/01/22/25_of_grade_4_students_have_cellphone_canadian_survey.html, accessed May 6, 2015.

27. Statistics Canada (2015), "Study: Changes in Debt and Assets of Canadian families, 1999 to 2012," *The Daily*, April 29, http://www.statcan.gc.ca/daily-quotidien/150429/dq150429b-eng.htm, accessed May 6, 2015.

28. BMO Financial Group (2015), "BMO Poll: Nearly Half of Canadian Credit Card Holders Currently Hold Credit Card Debt," http://newsroom.bmo.com/press-releases/bmo-poll-nearly-half-of-canadian-credit-card-hold-tsx-bmo-201502100991483001, accessed May 6, 2015.

29. Statistics Canada (2011), "Debt and Family Type in Canada," http://www.statcan.gc.ca/pub/11-008-x/2011001/article/11430-eng.htm, accessed August 13, 2012.

30. U.S. Federal Reserve Statistics, http://www.federalreserve.gov, accessed June 19, 2010.

31. *Market Europe* (2006), "UK Consumers Carry a Heavy Load of Debt," 17 (October), 3.

32. Pinto, M. B., P. M. Mansfield, and D. H. Parente (2004), "Relationship of Credit Attitude and Debt to Self-Esteem, and Locus of Control in College-Age Consumers," *Psychological Reports 94*, 1405–1418.

33. Zikmund, W. G., and B. J. Babin (2010), *Exploring Marketing Research*, Cengage/Southwestern, Mason, OH.

34. Bode, Mathias (2006), "Now That's What I Call Music! An Interpretive Approach to Music in Advertising," *Advances in Consumer Research* 33, 580–585.

35. Tadajewski, M. (2006), "Remembering Motivation Research: Toward an Alternative Genealogy of Interpretive Consumer Research," *Marketing Theory 6*, 429–466.

36. Zikmund and Babin (2007), *Exploring Marketing Research*, 9th edition, Cengage/Southwesterdn, Mason, OH.

37. Peterson, Hayley (2014), "How Uniqlo—The Japanese Clothing Giant That May Buy J. Crew—Is Taking Over the World," *Business Insider* (March 3), http://www.businessinsider.com/uniqlo-taking-over-the-world-2014-2?op=1, accessed May 6, 2015.

38. Starbucks company profile, http://assets.starbucks.com/assets/company-profile-feb10.pdf, accessed June 19, 2010.

39. http://academic.emporia.edu/smithwil/00spmg456/eja/pieschl.html#Sears.

40. Smith, L., "Email Preferred Communication Method: Commands More Clicks & ROI," Litmus, February 20, 2013, https://litmus.com/blog/email-preferred-more-clicks-conversions-roi, accessed February 16, 2014. S. Olenski, "Consumers Choose Email to Communicate with Favorite Brands," *Social Media Today*, January 3, 2012, https://litmus.com/blog/email-preferred-more-clicks-conversions-roi, accessed May 6, 2015.

41. "Top Sites," http://www.alexa.com/topsites, accessed May 6, 2015.

42. Karlgaard, R. "Big Data's Promise: Messy, Like Us," *Forbes*, 191, no. 11 (2013), 36.

43. Rohwedder, C. (2009), "U.K. Grocers in Price Fight, and It's Drawing Customers," *The Wall Street Journal* (August 10), A1. Benning, T. (2009), "Slump Strains Church Finances as Need Grows," *The Wall Street Journal* (August 11), A13.

2

1. Sorokanich, Robert (2014), "Matthew McConaughey Ads Deliver Huge Sales Bump for Lincoln," *Car and Driver Blog*, November 4, accessed at http://blog.caranddriver.com/matthew-mcconaughey-ads-deliver-huge-sales-bump-for-lincoln/ on May 7, 2015.

2. Grégoire, Yany, T. M. Tripp, and R. Legoux (2009), "When Customer Love Turns Into Lasting Hate: The Effects of Relationship Strength and Time on Customer Revenge and Avoidance," *Journal of Marketing* 73 (November), 18–32. Grégoire, Yany, and Robert Fisher (2006), "The Effects of Relationship Quality on Customer Retaliation," *Marketing Letters* 17 (1), 31–6. Kressmann, Frank, M. Joseph Sirgy, Andreas Herrmann, Frank Huber, Stephanie Huber, and Dong-Jin Lee (2006), "Direct and Indirect Effects of Self-Image Congruence on Brand Loyalty," *Journal of Business Research* 59 (September), 955–964.

3. Babin, B. J., W. R. Darden, and M. Griffin (1994), "Work and/or Fun: Measuring Hedonic and Utilitarian Shopping Value," *Journal of Consumer Research* 20 (March), 644–656.

4. Levitt, T. (1960), "Marketing Myopia," *Harvard Business Review* 38 (July–August), 57–66.

5. "Coca-Cola Gains Market Share Over Pepsi; Soft Drink Industry Shows Modest Growth," *Food and Drink Weekly* (March 3, 2003), http://www.findarticles.com/p/articles/mi_m0EUY/is_8_9/ai_98594588, accessed June 30, 2010.

6. Ferrari website, www.ferrari.com, accessed May 7, 2015.

7. Halliday, Jean (2005), "Total Value Promise a Total Mess for GM Sales," *Advertising Age* 76, 3.

8. Adner, R. (2006), "Match Your Innovation Strategy to Your Innovation Ecosystem," *Harvard Business Review* 84 (April), 98–108.

9. Vargo, S. L., and R. F. Lusch (2008), "Service-Dominant Logic: Continuing the Evolution," *Journal of the Academy of Marketing Science* 36 (March), 1–10.

10. Dickson, P. R., and J. L. Ginter (1987), "Market Segmentation, Product Differentiation and Marketing Strategy," *Journal of Marketing* 51, 1–10.

11. More precisely, in economics, price elasticity represents the proportionate change in demand associated with a proportionate change in price. The slope coefficient represents the parameter of the line showing how demand responds to price. The slope of the line is constant over the range while the elasticity changes at any point on the line. To calculate the actual total quantity demanded, the total size of the population would have to be included in the equation. For simplicity of illustration, this is omitted here.

12. Orth, U. R., M. McDaniel, T. Shellhamer, and K. Lopetcharat (2004), "Promoting Brand Benefits: The Role of Consumer Psychographics and Lifestyle," *Journal of Consumer Marketing* 21, 97–108.

13. Swinyard, William R., and Scott M. Smith (2003), "Why People (Don't) Shop Online: A Lifestyle Study of the Internet Consumer," *Psychology & Marketing* 20, 567–597. Martin, C. (2009), "Consumption Motivation and Perceptions of Malls: A Comparison of Mothers and Daughters," *Journal of Marketing, Theory and Practice* 17 (Winter), 49–61.

14. See Kim, W. C., and R. Mauborgne, "Blue Ocean Strategy," *Harvard Business Review* (October 2004): 2–10. From a creative thinking view, blue ocean strategies are built around the key words of "Reduce," "Eliminate," "Raise," and "Create." Blue ocean strategists often refer to perceptual maps as a strategy canvas.

15. For similar perceptual map illustrations: Kuo, R. T., K. Aksana, and B. Subrota, "Application of Particle Swarm Optimization and Perceptual Map to Tourist Market Segmentation," *Expert Systems with Applications*, 39 (August 2012): 5726–8735. Xiang, L., F. Meng, M. Uysal, and B. Milhalik, "Understanding China's Long-Haul Outbound Travel Market: An Overlapped Segmentation Approach," *Journal of Business Research*, 66, no. 6 (June 2013): 786–793.

16. Sciulli, L. M., and C. Bebko, "Positioning Strategies for Social Cause Organizations: A Multivariate Analysis of Dimensions and Ideals," *Journal of Nonprofit and Public Sector Marketing*, 23, no. 2 (2012): 99–133.

17. Sunil, G., D. Hanssens, B. Hardie, W. Kahn, V. Kumar, L. Nathaniel, and N. R. Sriram (2006), "Modeling Customer Lifetime Value," *Journal of Service Research* 9 (November), 139–155.

18. Kumar, V., D. Shah, and R. Venkatesan (2006), "Managing Retailer Profitability—One Customer at a Time!" *Journal of Retailing* 82, 277–294.

19. Kumar et al. (2006)

3

1. Levinsky, D. L., and T. Youm (2004), "The More Food Young Adults Are Served, the More They Overeat," *Journal of Nutrition*, 134, 2546–2549. Rolls, B. J., L. S. Roe, and J. S. Meengs (2006), "Reductions in Portion Size and Energy Density of Foods Are Addictive and Lead to Sustained Decreases in Energy Intake," *American Journal of Clinical Nutrition* 83, 11–17.

2. Antonides, G., P. C. Verhoef, and M. van Aalst (2002), "Consumer Perception and Evaluation of Waiting Time: A Field Experiment," *Journal of Consumer Psychology* 12 (3), 193–202.

3. Argo, J. J., M. Popa, and M. C. Smith (2010), "The Sound of Brands," *Journal of Marketing* 74 (July), 97–109.

4. Raghunathan, Rajagopal, and Julie R. Irwin (2010), "Walking the Hedonic Product Tread-Mill: Default Contrast and Mood-Based Assimilation in Judgments of Predicted Happiness with a Target Product," *Journal of Consumer Research* 28, 355–368.

5. Meyers-Levy, Joan, and Alice M. Tybout (1989), "Schema Congruity as a Basis for Product Evaluation," *Journal of Consumer Research* 16 (1), 39–54.

6. Sylvie, M., L. Dubé, and J. C. Chebat (2007), "The Role of Pleasant Music in Service-Scapes: A Test of the Dual Model of Environmental Perception," *Journal of Retailing* 83, 115–130.

7. Kim, J., A. M. Flore, and H. H. Lee (2006), "Influences of Online Store Perception, Shopping Enjoyment, and Shopping Involvement on Consumer Patronage Behavior Towards an Online Retailer," *Journal of Retailing and Consumer Services* 14, 95–107.

8. Aggarwal, P., and A. L. McGill, "Is That Car Smiling at Me? Schema Congruity as a Basis for Evaluating Anthropomorphized Products," *Journal of Consumer Research*, 14 (December 2007): 468–479.

9. Waytz, A., J. Heafner, and N. Epley, "The Mind in the Machine: Anthropomorphism Increases Trust in Autonomous Vehicle," *Journal of Experimental Social Psychology*, 52 (2014): 113–117.

10. Merkile, P. M. (2000), "Subliminal Perception," *Encyclopedia of Psychology* 7, 497–499.

11. Gable, M., H. Wilkens, L. Harris, and R. Feinbert (1987), "An Evaluation of Subliminally Embedded Sexual Stimuli in Graphics," *Journal of Advertising* 16, 26–31.

12. Broyles, S.J. (2006), "Misplaced Paranoia over Subliminal Advertising: What's the Big Uproar?" *Journal of Consumer Marketing* 23, 312–313.

13. Lantos, G. (1996), "Ice Cube Sex: The Truth about Subliminal Advertising: Book Review," *Journal of Consumer Marketing* 13, 62–64.

14. Broyles, S. J. (2006), "Subliminal Advertising and the Perceptual Popularity of Playing to People's Paranoia," *Journal of Consumer Affairs* 40, 392–406.

15. Key, W. B. (1974), *Subliminal Seduction: Ad Media's Manipulation of a Not so Innocent America*, New York: Signet. Packard, V. (1957), *The Hidden Persuaders*, New York: D. McKay Co.

16. Cook, W. A. (1993), "Looking Behind Ice Cubes," *Journal of Advertising Research* 33 (March/April), 7–8.

17. Garfield, Bob (2000), "Subliminal Seduction and Other Urban Myths," *Advertising Age* 71 (September 18), 104–105.

18. Vroomen, J., and M. Keetels (2006), "The Spatial Constraint in Intersensory Pairing: No Role in Temporal Ventriloquism," *Journal of Experimental Psychology* 32, 1063–1071.

19. Miller, Richard L. (1962), "Dr. Weber and the Consumer," *Journal of Marketing*, 57–67.

20. Hoffman, K. D., L. W. Turley, and S. W. Kelley (2002), "Pricing Retail Services," *Journal of Business Research* 55 (December), 1015–1023.

21. Kalyanam, K., and T. S. Shively (1998), "Estimating Irregular Pricing Effects: A Stochastic Spline Regression Approach," *Journal of Marketing Research* 35, 16–29.

22. Miller (1962).

23. Friend, David (2014), "Tim Hortons to hike coffee, breakfast sandwich prices next Wednesday," *National Post*, November 19, accessed at http://business.financialpost.com/news/retail-marketing/tim-hortons-to-hike-coffee-breakfast-sandwich-prices-next-wednesday on May 12, 2015.

24. Heinrich, S. (2003), "Mercedes Recasts Brand as Affordable: New Ad Campaign," *National Post*, (May 22), FP6.

25. Yoo, C. Y. (2008), "Unconscious Processing of Web Advertising: Effects on Implicit Memory, Attitude toward the Brand and Consideration Set," *Journal of Interactive Marketing* 22 (Spring), 2–18.

26. Janiszewski, Chris (1993), "Preattentive Mere Exposure Effects," *Journal of Consumer Research* 20 (3), 376–392.

27. Smith, Gene F. (1982), "Further Evidence of the Mediating Effect of Learning in the 'Mere Exposure' Phenomenon," *Journal of General Psychology* 197, 175–178. Stang, D. J. (1975), "Effects of 'Mere Exposure' on Learning and Affect," *Journal of Personality and Social Psychology* 31, 7–12.

28. Gustav, K., and Z. Dienes (2005), "Implicit Learning of Nonlocal Musical Rules: Implicitly Learning More than Chucks," *Journal of Experimental Psychology/Learning, Memory & Cognition* 31 (November), 1417–1432; Chakraborty, G., V. Lala, and D. Warran (2003), "What Do Customers Consider Important in B2B Websites?" *Journal of Advertising Research* (March), 50.

29. Bulik, B. S. (2007), "Media Morph: People Search," *Advertising Age* 78 (March 28), 18. Ballenson, J. N., S. Iyengar, N. Yee, and N. A. Collins

(2008), "Facial Similarity between Voters and Candidates Causes Influence," *Public Opinion Quarterly* 72 (5), 935–961.

30. Yang, M., D. Roskos-Ewoldson, L. Dinu, and L. M. Arpan (2006), "The Effectiveness of 'In-Game' Advertising," *Journal of Advertising* 35 (Winter), 143–152.

31. Auty, S., and C. Lewis (2004), "Exploring Children's Choice: The Reminder Effect of Product Placement," *Psychology & Marketing* 21 (9), 697–713.

32. Ang, S. H., S. M. Leong, and W. Yeo (1999), "When Silence Is Golden: Effects of Silence on Consumer Ad Responses," *Advances in Consumer Research* 26, 295–299.

33. David, B., and D. W. Wooten (2006), "From Labeling Possessions to Possessing Labels: Ridicule and Socialization Among Adolescents," *Journal of Consumer Research* 33, 188–198.

34. Skinner, B. F. (1989), "The Origins of Cognitive Thought," *American Psychologist* 44 (1), 13–18.

35. Skinner (1989).

36. Malone, John C., Jr., and Natalie M. Cruchon (2001), "Radical Behaviorism and the Rest of the Psychology: A Review/Precis of Skinner's About Behaviorism," *Behavior and Philosophy* 29, 31–57.

37. http://www.simplypsychology.pwp.blueyonder .co.uk/behaviourism.html, accessed July 9, 2010.

4

1. Lepkowska-White, E., and A. Parsons (2001), "Comprehension of Warnings and Resulting Attitudes," *Journal of Consumer Affairs* 35, 278–294. Cox, A. D., D. Cox, and S. Powell Mantel (2010), "Consumer Response to Drug Risk Information: The Role of Positive Affect," *Journal of Marketing* 74 (July), 31–44.

2. Argo, J. J., and K. J. Main (2004), "Meta-Analysis of the Effectiveness of Warning Labels," *Journal of Public Policy and Marketing*, 23 (Fall), 193–208.

3. Borges, A. (2009), "Price Matching Guarantees: The Effect of Refund Size and the Moderating Role of Retail Price Strategy," *Recherche et Applications en Marketing* 24 (1), 29–39. Kukar-Kinney, M., and R. G. Walters (2007), "Comparison of Consumers to PMGs in Internet and Bricks-and-Mortar Retail Environments," *Journal of the Academy of Marketing Science* 35 (Summer), 197–207.

4. Bix, L., S. Wontae, and R. P. Sundar, "The Effect of Colour Contrast on Consumers' Attentive Behaviours and Perception of Fresh Produce," *Packaging Technology & Science*, 26 (March 2013): 96–104.

5. Doyle, J. R., and P. A. Bottemly (2006), "Dressed for the Occasion: Font–Product Congruity in the Perception of Logotype," *Journal of Consumer Psychology* 16 (2), 112–123.

6. Noel, H., and B. Vallen (2009), "The Spacing Effect in Marketing: A Review of Extant Findings and Directions for Future Research," *Psychology & Marketing* 26 (November), 951–969.

7. Madhubalan, V., and M. Hastak (2002), "The Role of Summary Information in Facilitating Consumers' Comprehension of Nutrition Information," *Journal of Public Policy & Marketing* 21, 305–318.

8. Rice, D. H., K. Kelting, and R. J. Lutz, "Multiple Endorsers and Multiple Endorsements: The Influence of Message Repetition, Source Congruence and Involvement on Brand Attitudes," *Journal of Consumer Psychology*, 22 (2012): 249–259.

9. Burke, R. R., and T. K. Srull (1988), "Competitive Interference and Consumer Memory for Advertisements," *Journal of Consumer Research* 15 (June), 55–68.

10. See Kellaris, J. J., A. D. Cox, and D. Cox (1993), "The Effects of Background Music on Ad Processing: A Contingency Explanation," *Journal of Marketing* 57, 114–125.

11. Dholokia, R. R., and B. Sternthal (1997), "Highly Credible Sources Persuasive Facilitator or Persuasive Liabilities?" *Journal of Consumer Research* 3, 223–232.

12. GoingLikeSixty, March 23, 2010, "Boomer Favorite Icons: M & M's Are Most Beloved Characters in the Whole Universe," http://goinglikesixty .com/2010/03/boomer-favorite-icons-m-ms-are -most-beloved-characters-in-the-whole-universe/, accessed July 7, 2010. LeBel, J. L., and N. Cooke (2008), "Branded Food Spokescharacters: Consumers' Contributions to the Narrative of Commerce," *Journal of Product & Brand Management* 17(3), 143–153.

13. Taylor, V. A., and A. B. Bower (2004), "Improving Product Instruction Compliance: If You Tell Me Why, I Might Comply," *Psychology & Marketing* 21, 229–245.

14. Block, L., and T. Kramer (2009), "The Effect of Superstitious Beliefs on Performance Expectations," *Journal of the Academy of Marketing Science* 37, 161–169.

15. Celsi, Richard L., and Jerry C. Olson (1988), "The Role of Involvement in Attention and Comprehension Processes," *Journal of Consumer Research* 15 (2), 210–224.

16. Menon, S., and D. Soman (2004) "Managing the Power of Curiosity for Effective Web Advertising Strategies," *Journal of Advertising* 31, 1–14.

17. Redden, J. P. (2008), "Reducing Satiation: The Role of Categorization Level," *Journal of Consumer Research* 34 (February), 624–634. Nordhielm, C. L. (2002), "The Influence of Levels of Processing on Advertising Repetition Levels," *Journal of Consumer Research* 29 (December), 371–382.

18. Griffin, M., B. J. Babin, and D. Modianos (2000), "Shopping Values of Russian Consumers: The Impact of Habituation in a Developing Economy," *Journal of Retailing* 76, 33–52.

19. Allison, Ralph I., and Kenneth P. Uhl (1964), "Influence of Beer Brand Identification on Taste Perception," *Journal of Marketing Research* 1 (August), 36–39.

20. Kaufman-Scarborough, C. (2000), "Seeing through the Eyes of the Color-Deficient Shopper: Consumer Issues for Public Policy," *Journal of Consumer Policy* 23, 461–492.

21. Bapna, Ravi, P. Goes, A. Gupta, and G. Karuga (2002), "Optimal Design of the Online Auction Channel: Empirical and Computational Insights," *Decision Sciences* 33, 557–577.

22. Cox, A. D., D. Cox, and G. Zimet (2006), "Understanding Consumer Responses to Product Risk Information," *Journal of Marketing* 70 (January), 79–91.

23. Tversky, A., and D. Kahneman (1981), "The Framing of Decisions and the Psychology of Choice," *Science* 211, 453–458.

24. Rick, S. (2011), "Losses, Gains, and Brains: Neuroeconomics Can Help to Answer Open Questions about Loss Aversion," *Journal of Consumer Psychology* 21 (4), 453–463.

25. Fitzsimons, G. M., T. L. Chartrand, and G. J. Fitzsimons (2008), "Automatic Effects of Brand Exposure on Motivated Behavior: How Apple Makes You Think Different," *Journal of Consumer Research* 35 (1), 21–35.

26. Saini, R., R. S. Rao, and A. Monga (2010), "Is That Deal Worth My Time? The Interactive Effect of Relative and Referent Thinking on Willingness to Seek a Bargain," *Journal of Marketing* 74 (January), 34–48.

27. Luna, D., and H. M. Kim (2009), "How Much Was Your Shopping Basket? Working Memory Processes in Total Basket Price Estimation," *Journal of Consumer Psychology* 19, 346–355.

28. Vanhuele, M., and X. Drèze (2002), "Measuring the Price Knowledge Consumers Bring to the Store," *Journal of Marketing* 66, 72–85.

29. Krishna, A., M. Q. Lwin, and M. Morrin (2010), "Product Scent and Memory," *Journal of Consumer Research* 37 (June), 57–67.

30. Dawson, B. (2005), "Jingles' Best Days May Be Behind Them," *Minneapolis Star Tribune*, April 13, http://www.ocregister.com/ocr/sections/life/ lf_trends/article_478162.php, accessed April 4, 2007.

31. Vanhuele, M., G. Laurent, and X. Drèze (2006), "Consumers, Immediate Memory for Prices," *Journal of Consumer Research* 33, 153–172.

32. Cline, T. W., and J. J. Kellaris (2007), "The Influence of Humor Strength and Humor-Message Relatedness and Ad Memorability," *Journal of Advertising* 36, 55–67.

33. Chan, J. C. K., K. B. McDermott, J. M. Watson, and D. A. Gallo (2005), "The Importance of Material-Processing Interactions in Inducing False Memories," *Memory & Cognition* 33, 389–395.

34. Winkler, R., "Google Deal with Luxottica Will Bring Glass to Ray-Ban, Oakley," *The Wall Street Journal*, March 24, 2014, D1.

35. Fennis, B. M., L. Janssen, and K. D. Vohs, "Acts of Benevolence: A Limited-Resource Account of Compliance with Charitable Requests," *Journal of Consumer Research*, 35 (April 2009): 906–924.

36. Lee, A. Y., and B. Sternthal (1999), "The Effects of Positive Mood on Memory," *Journal of Consumer Research* 26,115–127.

37. McFerran, B., D. W. Dahl, G. J. Fitzsimons, and A. C. Morales (2010), "Might an Overweight Waitress Make You Eat More? How the Body Type of Others Is Sufficient to Alter Our Food Consumption," *Journal of Consumer Psychology* 20, 146–151.

38. Peterson, Kim, "Wealthy Prius Drivers Can Be Huge Jerks," MSN Money, August 13, 2013, http:// money.msn.com/now/wealthy-prius-drivers-can-be -huge-jerks, accessed August 13, 2013.

39. Fisher, R. J., and L. Dubé (2005), "Gender Differences in Responses to Emotional Advertising: A Social Desirability Perspective," *Journal of Consumer Research* 31, 850–858.

40. Chaplin, L. N., and T. M. Lowrey (2009), "The Development of Consumer-Based Consumption Constellations in Children," *Journal of Consumer Research* 36 (February), 757–777.

41. Moore, R. S. (2005), "The Sociological Impact of Attitudes Toward Smoking: Secondary Effects of the Demarketing of Smoking," *The Journal of Social Psychology* 145, 703–718.

42. Celsi and Olson (1988).

43. Saegert, J. (1979), "A Demonstration of Levels of Processing Theory in Memory for Advertisements," *Advances in Consumer Research* 6, 82–84.

5

1. Childers, T. L., C. L. Carr, J. Peck, and S. Carson (2001), "Hedonic and Utilitarian Motivations for Online Retail Shopping Behavior," *Journal of Retailing* 77 (Winter), 511–535.

2. Laurent, G., and J. N. Kapferer (1985), "Measuring Consumer Involvement Profiles," *Journal of Marketing Research* 22 (February), 41–53.

3. Howard, D. J., and R. A. Kerin (2006), "Broadening the Scope of Reference Price Advertising Research: A Field Study of Shopping Involvement," *Journal of Marketing* 70 (October), 185–204.

4. Kim, H., K. Park, and N. Schwarz (2010), "Will This Trip Be Exciting? The Role of Incidental Emotions in Product Evaluations," *Journal of Consumer Research* 36 (April), 983–991.

5. Plutchik, R. (2003), *Emotions and Life: Perspectives from Psychology, Biology and Evolution*, Washington, DC: American Psychological Association.

6. Fonberg, E. (1986), "Amygdala: Emotions, Motivation, and Depressive States," in *Emotion: Theory, Research, and Experience*, R. Plutchik and H. Kellerman, eds., New York: Kluwer Press, 302.

7. Babin, B. J., W. R. Darden, and L. A. Babin (1998), "Negative Emotions in Marketing Research: Affect or Artifact?" *Journal of Business Research* 42, 271–285. Russell, J. A., and J. Snodgrass (1987), "Emotion and the Environment," in *Environment and Psychology*, D. Stokols and I. Altman, eds., New York: John Wiley and Sons, 245–280.

8. Saini, R., and S. C. Thota (2010), "The Psychological Underpinnings of Relative Thinking in Price Comparisons," *Journal of Consumer Psychology* 20, 185–192.

9. Watson, L., and M. Spencer (2007), "Causes and Consequences of Emotions on Consumer Behaviour: A Review and Integrative Cognitive Appraisal Theory," *European Journal of Marketing* 41, 487–511. Stephens, N., and K. Gwinner (1998), "Why Don't Some People Complain: A Cognitive-Emotive Process Model of Consumer Behavior," *Journal of the Academy of Marketing Science* 26, 172–189.

10. Brennan, L., and W. Binney (2010), "Fear, Guilt and Shame Appeals in Social Marketing," *Journal of Business Research* 62, 140–146.

11. Zourrig, H., J. C. Chebat, and R. Toffoli (2009), "Consumer Revenge Behavior: A Cross-Cultural Perspective," *Journal of Business Research* 62, 995–1001.

12. Babin, B. J., and W. R. Darden (1996), "Good and Bad Shopping Vibes: Spending and Patronage Satisfaction," *Journal of Business Research* 35, 201–206.

13. Pucinelli, N. M. (2006), "Putting Your Best Foot Forward: The Impact of Customer Mood on Salesperson Evaluation," *Journal of Consumer Psychology* 16, 156–162.

14. Raghunathan, R., and J. R. Irwin (2001), "Walking the Hedonic Product Treadmill: Default Contrast and Mood-Based Assimilation in Judgments of Predicted Happiness with a Target Product," *Journal of Consumer Research* 28 (December), 355–368.

15. Cialdini, R. B., and D. T Kenrick (1976), "Altruism as Hedonism: A Social Development Perspective on the Relationship of Negative Mood State and Helping," *Journal of Personality and Social Psychology* 34, 907–914.

16. Raghubir, P. (2006)"An Information Processing View of the Subjective Value of Money and Prices," *Journal of Business Research* 59, 1053–1062.

17. See Karolein, P., and S. Dewitte (2006), "How to Capture the Heart? Twenty Years of Emotion Measurement in Advertisement," *Journal of Advertising* 46, 18–37.

18. For an overview, see Drake, R. A., and L. R. Myers (2006), "Visual Attention, Emotion, and Action Tendency: Feeling Active or Passive," *Cognition and Emotion* 20, 608–622.

19. Russell, J. A., and G. Pratt (1979), "Affect Space Is Bipolar," *Journal of Personality and Social Psychology* 37, 1161–1178. Babin et al. (1998).

20. Havlena, W. J., and M. B. Holbrook (1986), "The Varieties of Consumption Experience: Comparing Two Typologies of Emotion in Consumer Behavior," *Journal of Consumer Research* 13, 97–112. Kottasz, R. (2006), "Understanding the Influences of Atmospheric Cues on the Emotional Responses and Behaviours of Museum Visitors," *Journal of Nonprofit & Public Sector Marketing* 16, 95–121.

21. White, C., and Y. Yi-Ting (2005), "Satisfaction Emotions and Consumer Behavioral Intentions," *Journal of Services Marketing* 19, 411–420. Chebat, J. C., and W. Sluszrczyk (2005), "How Emotions Mediate the Effects of Perceived Justice on Loyalty in Service Recovery Situation: An Empirical Study," *Journal of Business Research* 56, 664–673.

22. Moorradian, T. A., and J. M. Oliver (1997), "I Can't Get No Satisfaction: The Impact of Personality and Emotion on Postpurchase Processes," *Psychology & Marketing* 14, 379–393.

23. Mascarenhas, O., R. Kesavan, and M. Bernacchi (2006), "Lasting Customer Loyalty: A Total Customer Experience Approach," *Journal of Consumer Marketing* 23, 397–405.

24. Hiam, A. (2000), "Match Premiums to Marketing Strategies," *Marketing News,* 34 (20), 12.

25. Hoffman, D. L., and T. P. Novak (2009), "Flow Online: Lessons Learned and Future Prospects," *Journal of Interactive Marketing* 23, 23–24.

26. Chou, T. J., and C. C. Ting (2003), "The Role of *Flow* Experience in Cyber-Game Addiction," *Cyber Psychology & Behavior* 6, 663–675.

27. Cohen, E. (2009), "Five Clues That You Are Addicted to Facebook," cnnhealth.com, http://www.cnn.com/2009/HEALTH/04/23/ep.facebook.addict/index.html, accessed July 28, 2010.

28. Sénécal, Sylvain, J. E. Gharbi, and J. Nantel (2002), "The Influence of Flow on Utilitarian and Hedonic Shopping Values," *Advances in Consumer Research* 29, 483–484.

29. Smith, Donnavieve N., and K. Sivakumar (2004), "Flow and Internet Shopping Behavior," *Journal of Business Research* 57, 1199–1208.

30. Dailey, L. (2004), "Navigational Web Atmospherics: Explaining the Influence of Restrictive Navigation Cues," *Journal of Business Research* 57, 795–803.

31. Gottman J. M., and R. W. Leveson (1992), "Emotional Suppression: Physiology, Self-Report, and Expressive Behavior," *Journal of Personality and Social Psychology* 64 (April), 970–986.

32. Gross, J. J., and O. P. John (1997), "Revealing Feelings: Facets of Emotional Expressivity in Self-Reports, Peer Ratings, and Behavior," *Journal of Personality and Social Psychology* 72 (February), 435–448.

33. Particularly when the emotions are consistent with the sex-role expectations of the female social schema. Social schemata are discussed in a later chapter.

34. Taute, H. A., B. A. Huhmann, and R. Thakur (2010), "Emotional Information Management: Concept Development and Measurement in Public Service Announcements," *Psychology & Marketing* 27 (May), 417–444.

35. Rozell, E. J., C. E. Pettijohn, and R. S. Parker (2006), "Emotional Intelligence and Dispositional Affectivity as Predictors of Performance in Salespeople," *Journal of Marketing Theory and Practice* 14, 113–124.

36. Chang, J. (2003), "Born to Sell?" *Sales & Marketing Management* 155, 34–39.

37. Ferré, P. (2003), "Effects of Level of Processing on Memory for Affectively Valenced Words," *Cognition and Emotion* 17, 859–880, quotation taken from p. 859.

38. Baird, Thomas R., R. G. Wahlers, and C. K. Cooper (2007), "Non-Recognition of Print Advertising: Emotion Arousal and Gender Effects," *Journal of Marketing Communications* 13, 39–57.

39. White, K., and C. McFarland (2009), "When Are Moods Likely to Influence Consumers' Product Preferences? The Role of Mood Focus and Perceived Relevance of Moods," *Journal of Consumer Psychology* 19, 526–536. Merchanta, A., J. B. Ford, and G. Rose (2011), "How Personal Nostalgia Influences Giving to Charity," *Journal of Business Research* 64 (6), 610–616.

40. Forgas, J. P., and J. Ciarrochi (2001), "On Being Happy and Possessive: The Interactive Effects on Mood and Personality on Consumer Judgments," *Psychology & Marketing* 18 (3) 239–260.

41. Sierra, J. J., and S. McQuitty (2007), "Attitudes and Emotions as Determinants of Nostalgic Purchases: An Application of Social Identity Theory, *Journal of Marketing Theory and Practice* 15, 99–112.

42. Schema adapted from Babin, B. J., J. S. Boles, and W. R. Darden (1995), "Salesperson Stereotypes, Consumer Emotions, and Their Impact on Information Processing," *Journal of the Academy of Marketing Science* 23, 94–105.

43. Proyer, R. T., T. Platt, and W. Ruch (2010), "Self-Conscious Emotions and Ridicule: Shameful Gelotophobes and Guilt Free Katagelasticists," *Personality and Individual Differences* 49, 54–58. Brennan and Binney (2010); Lau-Gesk, L., and A. Drolet (2008), "The Publicly Self-Conscious Consumer: Prepared to Be Embarrassed," *Journal of Consumer Psychology* 18, 127–136.

1. For a discussion of individual difference variables in consumer research and marketing practice, see Mowen, John C. (2000), *The 3M Model of Motivation and Personality: Theory and Empirical Applications to Consumer Behavior*, Boston: Kluwer Academic Publishers.

2. This definition is based on a number of different sources in personality psychology literature, including Allport, G. W. (1961), *Pattern and Growth in Personality*, New York: Holt, Rinehart, and Winston. Pervin, L. A., and O. P. John (1977), *Personality Theory and Research*, New York: John Wiley & Sons. Brody, Nathan, and Howard Ehrlichman (1998), *Personality Psychology: The Science of Individuality*, Upper Saddle River, NJ: Prentice Hall. Mowen (2000).

3. Angleitner, Alois (1991), "Personality Psychology: Trends and Developments," *European Journal of Personality* 5, 185–197.

4. A discussion of the debate regarding personality and behavioural consistency across situations may be found in Mischel, W., and P. K. Peake (1983), "Some Facets of Consistency: Replies to Epstein, Funder, and Bem," *Psychological Review* 89, 394–402. Epstein, S. (1983), "The Stability of Confusion: A Reply to Mischel and Peake," *Psychological Review* 90, 179–194. Buss, David (1989), "Personality as Traits," *American Psychologist* 44, 1378–1388.

5. For a discussion of psychoanalytical theory and applications to marketing, see Kassarjian, Harold H. (1971), "Personality and Consumer Behavior: A Review," *Journal of Marketing Research* 8 (November), 409–418. Also see Kassarjian, Harold

H., and Mary Jane Sheffet (1991), "Personality and Consumer Behavior: An Update," in *Perspectives in Consumer Behavior,* 4th ed., Harold H. Kassarjian and Thomas S. Robertson eds., Upper Saddle River, NJ: Prentice Hall, 81–303. For a general description of the psychoanalytical approach in psychology, see Brody and Ehrlichman (1998).

6. Interesting examples of the early use of these motivational techniques can be found in Gustafson, Philip (1958), "You Can Gauge Customers' Wants," *Nation's Business* 49 (April), 76–84.

7. Kassarjian, Harold H. (1971), "Personality and Consumer Behavior: A Review," *Journal of Marketing Research* 8 (November), 409–418.

8. Brody and Ehrlichman (1998).

9. Buss (1989).

10. Allport, G. W., and H. S. Odbert (1936), "Trait Names," *Psychological Monographs* 47 (211), 1–37.

11. Lichtenstein, Donald R., Richard G. Netemeyer, and Scot Burton (1990), "Distinguishing Coupon Proneness from Value Consciousness: An Acquisition-Transaction Utility Theory Perspective," *Journal of Marketing* 54 (3), 54–67.

12. Belk, Russell W. (1985), "Materialism: Trait Aspects of Living in the Material World," *Journal of Consumer Research,* 12 (3) (December), 265–280.

13. Richins, Marsha L. (1994), "Special Possessions and the Expression of Material Values," *Journal of Consumer Research,* 21 (3) (December), 522–533; Belk (1985).

14. Rindfleisch, Aric, James E. Burroughs, and Nancy Wong (2009), "The Safety of Objects: Materialism, Existential Insecurity, and Brand Connection," *Journal of Consumer Research* 36 (June), 1–16.

15. Tian, Kelly, and Russell W. Belk (2005), "Extended Self and Possessions in the Workplace," *Journal of Consumer Research* 32 (2) (September), 297–310.

16. Wallendorf, Melanie, and Eric J. Arnould (1988), "My Favorite Things: A Cross-Cultural Inquiry into Object Attachment, Possessiveness, and Social Linkage," *Journal of Consumer Research* 14 (4) (March), 531–547.

17. Belk (1985).

18. Graham, Judy F. (1999), "Materialism and Consumer Behavior: Toward a Clearer Understanding," *Journal of Social Behavior & Personality* 14 (2) (June), 241–259. Loftus, Mary (2004), "Till Debt Do Us Part," *Psychology Today* 37 (6) (November/December), 42–50.

19. This definition is based on the works of Midgley, David F., and Grahame R. Dowling (1978), "Innovativeness: The Concept and Its Measurement," *Journal of Consumer Research,* 229–242. Rogers, Everett M., and Floyd F. Shoemaker (1971), *Communication of Innovations,* New York: The Free Press.

20. Hartman, Jonathan B., Kenneth C. Gerht, and Kittichai Watchravesringkan (2004), "Re-Examination of the Concept of Innovativeness in the Context of the Adolescent Segment: Development of a Measurement Scale," *Journal of Targeting, Measurement and Analysis for Marketing* 12, 353–366. Wood, Stacy L., and Joffre Swait (2002), "Psychological Indicators of Innovation Adoption: Cross-Classification Based on Need for Cognition and Need for Change," *Journal of Consumer Psychology* 12, 1–13. Goldsmith, Ronald E., and Charles E. Hofacker (1991), "Measuring Consumer Innovativeness," *Journal of the Academy of Marketing Science* 19, 209–221. Venkatraman, Meera A. (1991), "The Impact of Innovativeness and Innovation Type on Product Adoption," *Journal of Retailing* 67, 51–67.

21. Hirunyawipada, Tanawat, and Audhesh K. Paswan (2006), "Consumer Innovativeness and Perceived Risk: Implications for High Technology Product Adoption," *Journal of Consumer Marketing* 23/24,182–198. Hirschman, Elizabeth C. (1980), "Innovativeness, Novelty Seeking, and Consumer Creativity," *Journal of Consumer Research* 7, 283–295. Manning, Kenneth C, William O. Bearden, and Thomas J. Madden (1995), "Consumer Innovativeness and the Adoption Process," *Journal of Consumer Psychology* 4, 329–345. Citrin, A. V., D. E. Sprott, S. N Silverman, and D. E. Stem (2000), "Adoption of Internet Shopping: The Role of Consumer Innovativeness," *Industrial Management & Data Systems* 100, 294–300.

22. Cacioppo, John, and Richard Petty (1982), "The Need for Cognition," *Journal of Personality and Social Psychology* 42 (January), 116–131.

23. Haugtvedt, Curt, Richard Petty, John Cacioppo, and Theresa Steidley (1988), "Personality and Ad Effectiveness: Exploring the Utility of Need for Cognition," in *Advances in Consumer Research,* Vol. 15, Michael Houston, ed., Provo, UT: Association for Consumer Research, 209–212.

24. Zhang, Yong (1996), "Responses to Humorous Advertising: The Moderating Effect of Need for Cognition," *Journal of Advertising* 25 (1), 15–31.

25. Putrevu, Sanjay (2008), "Consumer Responses Toward Sexual and Nonsexual Appeals: The Influence of Involvement, Need for Cognition, and Gender," *Journal of Advertising* 37 (2), 57–70.

26. Mowen, John C. (2004), "Exploring the Trait of Competitiveness and Its Consumer Behavior Consequences," *Journal of Consumer Psychology* 14, 52–63.

27. Cialdini, Robert B., Richard J. Borden, Avril Thorne, Marcus R. Walker, Stephen Freeman, and Lloyd R. Sloan (1976), "Basking in Reflected Glory: Three (Football) Field Studies," *Journal of Personality and Social Psychology* 34 (3), 366–375.

28. Pons, Frank, and Mehdi Mourali (2006), "Consumer Orientation Toward Sporting Events," *Journal of Service Research* 8 (3) (February), 276–287.

29. A number of researchers have contributed to the development of the Five-Factor Model. For example, see Costa, P. T., and R. R. McCrae (1985), *The NEO Personality Inventory Manual,* Odessa, FL, Psychological Assessment Resources; Goldberg, L.R. (1992), "The Development of Matters for the Big-Five Factor Structure," *Psychological Assessment* 4, 26–42; and Wiggins, J. S. (1996), *The Five-Factor Model of Personality,* New York: Guilford Press.

30. Harris, Eric G., and John C. Mowen (2001), "The Influence of Cardinal, Central-, and Surface-Level Personality Traits on Consumers' Bargaining and Complaining Behaviors," *Psychology & Marketing* 18 (11) (November), 1150–1185. Harris, Eric G., and David E. Fleming (2005), "Assessing the Human Element in Service Personality Formation: Personality Congruency and the Five Factor Model," *Journal of Services Marketing* 19 (4), 187–198. Mowen, John C, and Nancy Spears (1999), "Understanding Compulsive Buying Among College Students," *Journal of Consumer Psychology* 8 (4), 407–430. Finn, Seth (1997), "Origins of Media Exposure: Linking Personality Traits to TV, Radio, Print, and Film Use," *Communication Research* 24 (5) (October), 507–530. Fraj, Elena, and Eva Martinez (2006), "Influence of Personality on Ecological Consumer Behaviour," *Journal of Consumer Behaviour* 5, 167–181.

31. Notable works in this area include Eysenck, H. J. (1947), *Dimensions of Personality,* London: Routledge & Kegan Paul; Allport, G. W. (1961),

Pattern and Growth in Personality, New York: Holt, Rinehart, and Winston; Paunonen, S. V (1998), "Hierarchical Organization of Personality and Prediction of Behavior," *Journal of Personality and Social Psychology* 74, 538–556; and Mowen (2000).

32. This section is based on a number of sources that have discussed problems with the trait approach in consumer behavior, including Kassarjian, Harold H. (1971), "Personality and Consumer Behavior: A Review," *Journal of Marketing Research* 8 (November), 409–418; Kassarjian and Sheffet (1991); Lastovicka, John L., and Eric A. Joachimsthaler (1988), "Improving the Detection of Personality-Behavior Relationships," *Journal of Consumer Research* 14 (4) (March), 583–587; and Mowen (2000).

33. Aaker, Jennifer (1997), "Dimensions of Brand Personality," *Journal of Marketing Research* 34 (3) (August), 347–356.

34. Gwinner, K. P., and J. Eaton (1999), "Building Brand Image Through Event Sponsorship: The Role of Image Transfer" *Journal of Advertising* 38, 47–57.

35. Swaminathan, Vanitha, Karen M. Stilley, and Rohini Ahluwalia (2009), "When Brand Personality Matters: The Moderating Role of Attachment Styles," *Journal of Consumer Research* 35 (April), 985–1002.

36. Aaker, David A. (1996), *Building Strong Brands,* New York: Free Press; online content retrieved at http://www.gsb.standford.edu/news/research/mktg_good-brands.shtml, accessed May 24, 2010.

37. This section based on Aaker (1996).

38. Fournier, Susan (1998), "Consumers and Their Brands: Developing Relationship Theory in Consumer Research," *Journal of Consumer Research* (March), 343–373. Aaker, Jennifer, Susan Fournier, and S. Adam Brasel (2004), "When Good Brands Do Bad," *Journal of Consumer Research* (June), 1–16.

39. Fournier (1998).

40. Harris, Eric G., and David E. Fleming (2005), "Assessing the Human Element in Services Personality Formation: Personality Congruency and the Five-Factor Model," *Journal of Services Marketing* 19, 187–198.

41. This information from www.harleydavidson.com, accessed February 25, 2008.

42. Aaker, Fournier, and Brasel (2004).

43. Darden, W. R., and D. Ashton (1974), "Psychographics Profiles of Patronage Preference Groups," *Journal of Retailing* 50 (Winter), 99–112.

44. Lazer, W. (1963), "Lifestyle Concepts and Marketing," in *Towards Scientific Marketing,* S. Greyer, ed., Chicago: American Marketing Association.

45. Lawson, Rob, and Sarah Todd (2002), "Consumer Lifestyles: A Social Stratification Perspective," *Marketing Theory* 2, 295–307.

46. Gonzalez, Ana M., and Laurentino Bello (2002), "The Construct 'Lifestyle' in Market Segmentation: The Behaviour of Tourist Consumers," *European Journal of Marketing* 36, 51–85.

47. Benezra, Karen (1998), "The Fragging of the American Mind," *Brandweek* (June), S12–S19.

48. Johnson, Trent, and Johan Bruwer (2003), "An Empirical Confirmation of Win-Related Lifestyle Segments in the Australian Wine Market," *International Journal of Wine Marketing* 15, 5–33.

49. Taylor, A. (1995), "Porsche Slices Up Its Buyers," *Fortune* (January 16), 24.

50. Online content retrieved at Natural Marketing Institute website, www.nmisolutions.com/lohasd_segment.html, accessed May 24, 2010.

51. This section based on information obtained on the SBI International website, http://www.strategic businessinsights.com/vals/presurvey.shtml, accessed May 25, 2010.

52. This information based on materials found at http://enus.nielsen.com/tab/product_families/ nielsen_claritas/prizm, accessed May 25, 2010.

53. DePoe, Jack (2015), "Do You Know the REAL Canada? PRIZM5 From Environics Analytics Now Identifies 68 Distinct Lifestyles" *EA News Archive* (March 30), accessed at http://www .environicsanalytics.ca/footer/news/2015/03/30/do -you-know-the-real-canada-prizm5-from-environics -analytics-now-identifies-68-distinct-lifestyles on June 1, 2015.

54. Ridgeway, Cecilia L., and Henry A. Walker (1995), "Status Structures," in *Sociological Perspectives on Social Psychology*, Karen S. Cook, Gary A. Fine, and James S. House, eds., Boston: Allyn and Bacon, 281–310.

55. Mead, George H. (1934), *Mind, Self and Society*, Chicago: University of Chicago Press. Mick, David Glen (1986), "Consumer Research and Semiotics: Exploring the Morphology of Signs, Symbols, and Significance," *Journal of Consumer Research* 13 (2) (September), 196–213. Holbrook, Morris B. (2001), "The Millennial Consumer in the Texts of Our Times: Exhibitionism," *Journal of Macromarketing* 21, 81–95. Chaudhuri, Himadri Roy, and Sitanath Majumdar (2006), "Of Diamonds and Desires: Understanding Conspicuous Consumption from a Contemporary Marketing Perspective," *Academy of Marketing Science Review* (2006), 1.

56. See also Schau, Hope Jensen, and Mary Gilly (2003), "We Are What We Post? Self-Presentation in Personal Web Space," *Journal of Consumer Research* 30 (3) (December), 385–404; and Trammell, Kaye D., and Ana Keshelashvili (2005), "Examining the New Influencers: A Self-Presentation Study of A-List Blogs," *Journalism and Mass Communication Quarterly* 82 (4) (Winter), 968–983.

57. Aaker, Jennifer (1999), "The Malleable Self: The Role of Self-Expression in Persuasion," *Journal of Marketing Research* 36 (1) (February), 45–57.

58. These concepts based on Sirgy, M. Joseph (1982), "Self-Concept in Consumer Behavior: A Critical Review," *Journal of Consumer Research* 9 (3) (December), 287–300; and Belk, Russell (1988), "Possessions and the Extended Self," *Journal of Consumer Research* 15 (2) (September), 139–168.

59. Ahuvia, Aaron C. (2005), "Beyond the Extended Self: Loved Objects and Consumers' Identity Narratives," *Journal of Consumer Research* 32 (1) (June), 171–184. Escalas, Jennifer, and James R. Bettman (2005), "Self-Construal, Reference Groups, and Brand Meaning," *Journal of Consumer Research* 32 (3) (December), 378–389.

60. Chaplin, Lon Nguyen, and Debrah Roedder John (2005), "The Development of Self–Brand Connections in Children and Adolescents," *Journal of Consumer Research* 32 (1) (June), 119–130.

61. Smeesters, Dirk, and Naomi Mandel (2006), "Positive and Negative Media Image Effects on the Self," *Journal of Consumer Research* 32 (4) (March), 576–582. Richins, Marsha (1991), "Social Comparison and the Idealized Images of Advertising," *Journal of Consumer Research* 18 (1) (June), 71–83. Grogan, Sarah (1999), *Understanding Body Dissatisfaction in Men, Women, and Children*, London, Routledge.

62. Tan, Cheryl Lu-Lien (2007), "Fashion Group Sets Guides to Rein in Ultra-Thin Models," *The Wall Street Journal* (January 8), B4.

63. Keim, Brandon (2006), "Media Messes with Men's Minds Too," *Psychology Today* 39 (5) (September/October), 26.

64. Hafner, Michael (2004), "How Dissimilar Others May Still Resemble the Self: Assimilation and Contrast After Social Comparison," *Journal of Consumer Psychology* 14, 187–196.

65. Medicard Finance Inc. and Plastic Surgery Statistics Canada (PLSS) (2007), "Canadians Say They're Doing Research Before Cosmetic Surgery," Canada Newswire (November 20), http://www .newswire.ca/en/story/84865/canadians-say-they-re -doing-research-before-cosmetic-surgery, accessed July 5, 2012. The American Society for Aesthetic Plastic Surgery website, http://www.surgery.org/ media/news-releases/despite-recession-overall -plastic-surgery-demand-drops-only-2-percent -from-last-year, accessed May 25, 2010.

66. Bui, Eric, Rachel Rodgers, Lionel Cailhol, Phillippe Birmes, Henri Chabrol, and Laurent Schmitt (2010), "Body Piercing and Psycho-pathology: A Review of the Literature," *Psychotherapy and Psychosomatics* 79,125–129.

67. Brumberg, Joan Jacobs (2006), "Are We Facing an Epidemic of Self-Injury?" *Chronicle of Higher Education* 53, B6–B8.

68. Braithwaite, R., A. Robillard, T. Woodring, T. Stephens, and K. J. Arriola (2001), "Tattooing and Body Piercing Among Adolescent Detainees: Relationship to Alcohol and Other Drug Use," *Journal of Substance Abuse* 13, 5–16. Grief, J., and W. Hewitt (1998), "The Living Canvas: Health Issues in Tattooing, Body Piercing, and Branding," *Advances for Nurse Practitioners* 12, 26–31. Roberti, Jonathon W., and Eric A. Storch (2005), "Psychosocial Adjustment of College Students with Tattoos and Piercings," *Journal of College Counseling* 8 (1) (Spring), 14–19.

69. Totten, Jeff W., Thomas J. Lipscomb, and Michael A. Jones (2009), "Attitudes Toward and Stereotypes of Persons with Body Art: Implications for Marketing Management," *Academy of Marketing Studies Journal* 13 (2), 77–96.

70. Sirgy, M. Joseph, Dhruv Grewal, Tamara Mangleburg, and Jae-ok Park (1997), "Assessing the Predictive Validity of Two Methods of Measuring Self-Image Congruence," *Journal of the Academy of Marketing Science* 25 (3) (Summer), 229–241.

71. Sirgy, M. Joseph, and A. Coskun Samli (1985), "A Path Analytic Model of Store Loyalty Involving Self-Concept, Store Image, Geographic Loyalty, and Socioeconomic Status," *Journal of the Academy of Marketing Science* 13 (3) (Summer), 265–291.

72. Aaker (1999), 47.

73. Landon, E. Laird (1974), "Self Concept, Ideal Self Concept, and Consumer Purchase Intentions," *Journal of Consumer Research* 1 (2) (September), 44–51.

7

1. This definition is based on a summary of several works in the social psychology and consumer behaviour literatures, including Eagly, Alice, and Shelly Chaiken (1993), *The Psychology of Attitudes*, New York: Harcourt Brace; Cacioppo, John, Stephen Harkins, and Richard Petty (1981), "The Nature of Attitudes and Cognitive Responses and Their Relations to Behavior," in *Cognitive Responses in Persuasion*, Richard Petty, Thomas Ostrom, and Timothy C. Brock, eds., Hillsdale, NJ: Lawrence Erlbaum; and Thurstone L.L. (1931), "The Measurement of Social Attitudes," in *Readings in Attitude Theory and Measurement*, M. Fishbein ed., New York: Wiley

2. The information in this section is based on Katz, Daniel (1960), "The Functional Approach to the Study of Attitudes," *Public Opinion Quarterly* 24 (2), 163–204.

3. Gibson, Heather, Cynthia Willming, and Andrew Holdnak (2003), "We're Gators … Not Just Gator Fans: Serious Leisure and University of Florida Football," *Journal of Leisure Research* 34 (4), 397–425.

4. Ray, Michael (1973), "Marketing Communications and the Hierarchy-of-Effects," in *New Models for Mass Communications*, P. Clarke, ed., Beverly Hills, CA: Sage, 147–176.

5. Krugman, Herbert (1965), "The Impact of Television Advertising: Learning Without Involvement," *Public Opinion Quarterly* 29 (Fall), 349–356.

6. A recent example of the experiential nature of consumption may be found in Belk, Russell, Guliz Ger, and Soren Askegaard (2003), "The Fire of Desire: A Multisited Inquiry into Consumer Passion," *Journal of Consumer Research* 30 (3), 326–351.

7. Fishbein, Martin, and Icek Ajzen (1975), *Belief, Attitude, Intention, and Behavior: An Introduction to Theory and Research*, Reading, MA: Addison-Wesley.

8. A number of researchers have addressed this issue, including Alwitt, Linda F., and Ida E. Berger (1992), "Understanding the Link Between Environmental Attitudes and Consumer Product Usage: Measuring the Moderating Role of Attitude Strength," in *Advances in Consumer Research*, vol. 20, Leigh McAlister and Michael Rothschild, ed., Provo, UT: Association for Consumer Research, 189–194; and Wicker, Allan (1969), "Attitudes versus Actions: The Relationship of Verbal and Overt Behavioral Responses to Attitude Objects," *Journal of Social Issues* 25 (Autumn), 41–78.

9. Ajzen, Icek, and Martin Fishbein (1977), "Attitude–Behavior Relations: A Theoretical Analysis and Review of Empirical Research," *Psychological Bulletin* 84 (5) (September), 888–918.

10. Ryan, Michael J., and E. H. Bonfeld (1980), "Fishbein's Intentions Model: A Test of External and Pragmatic Validity," *Journal of Marketing* 44 (2), 82–95.

11. More on this model may be found in Notani, Art Sahni (1998), "Moderators of Perceived Behavioral Control's Predictiveness in the Theory of Reasoned Action," *Journal of Consumer Psychology* 7 (3), 247–71. Also, an interesting presentation of the planned behaviour model applied to food choice may be found in Conner, Mark T. (1993), "Understanding Determinants of Food Choice: Contributions from Attitude Research," *British Food Journal* 9 5 (9), 27–32.

12. Mitchell, Andrew A., and Jerry Olson (1981), "Are Product Attribute Beliefs the Only Mediator of Advertising Effects on Brand Attitude?" *Journal of Marketing Research* 18, 318–332.

13. Several studies have approached this issue, including MacKenzie, Scott, and Richard Lutz (1989), "An Empirical Examination of the Structural Antecedents of Attitude towards the Ad in an Advertising Pretesting Context," *Journal of Marketing* 53 (April), 48–65; and Burton, Scot, and Donald Lichtenstein (1988), "The Effect of Ad Claims and Ad Context on Attitude towards the Advertisement," *Journal of Advertising* 17 (1), 3–11.

14. Brown, Tom J., and Peter A. Dacin (1997), "The Company and the Product: Corporate Associations and Consumer Product Responses," *Journal of Marketing* 61 (January), 68–84.

15. Sen, Sankar, and C. B. Bhattacharya (2001), "Does Doing Good Always Lead to Doing Better?

Consumer Reactions to Corporate Social Responsibility," *Journal of Marketing Research* 38 (May), 225–243.

16. Petty, Richard E., John T. Cacioppo, and David Schuman (1983), "Central and Peripheral Routes to Advertising Effectiveness: The Moderating Role of Involvement," *Journal of Consumer Research* 10 (2), 135–146.

17. Celsi, Richard L., and Jerry C. Olson (1988), "The Role of Involvement in Attention and Comprehension Processes," *Journal of Consumer Research* 15 (2) (September), 210–224. MacInnis, Deborah J., and C. Whan Park (1991), "The Differential Role of Characteristics of Music on High- and Low-Involvement Consumers' Processing of Ads," *Journal of Consumer Research* 18 (2) (September), 161–173.

18. Heider, Fritz (1958), *The Psychology of Interpersonal Relations,* New York: John Wiley.

19. Russell, Cristel, and Barbara B. Stern (2006), "Consumers, Characters, and Products: A Balance Model of Sitcom Product Placement Effects," *Journal of Advertising* 35 (1), 7–21.

20. Woodside, Arch (2004), "Advancing Means–End Chains by Incorporating Heider's Balance Theory and Fournier's Consumer-Brand Relationship Typology," *Psychology & Marketing* 21 (4), 279–294.

21. Escalas, Jennifer Edson, and James R. Bettman (2005), "Self-Construal, Reference Groups, and Brand Meaning," *Journal of Consumer Research* 32 (3), 378–389.

22. Sherif, Muzafer, and Carl Hovland (1961), *Social Judgment: Assimilation and Contrast Effects in Communication and Attitude Change,* New Haven, CT: Yale University Press.

23. Hoffman, Donna L., and Thomas P. Novak (1996), "Marketing in Hypermedia Computer-Mediated Environments: Conceptual Foundations," *Journal of Marketing* 60 (3), 50–68.

24. This estimate based on data from "Key ICT indicators for developed and developing countries and the world (totals and penetration rates)," International Telecommunications Unions (ITU), Geneva, February 27, 2013, http://www.itu.int/en/ITU-D/Statistics/Documents/statistics/2012/ITU_Key_2006-2013_ICT_data.xls, accessed July 14, 2014.

25. Hoffman and Novak, "Marketing in Hypermedia Computer-Mediated Environments."

26. O'Cass, A., and J. Carlson, "An Empirical Assessment of Consumers' Evaluations of Web Site Service Quality: Conceptualizing and Testing a Formative Model," *Journal of Services Marketing* 26, no. 6 (2012): 419–434.

27. Dudley, Sid C. (1999), "Consumer Attitudes Toward Nudity in Advertising," *Journal of Marketing Theory and Practice* 7 (4), 89–96.

28. LaTour, Michael S. (1990), "Female Nudity in Print Advertising: An Analysis of Gender Differences in Arousal and Ad Response," *Psychology & Marketing* 7 (1), 65–81.

29. Simpson, Penny M., Steve Horton, and Gene Brown (1996), "Male Nudity in Advertisements: A Modified Replication and Extension of Gender and Product Effects," *Journal of the Academy of Marketing Science* 24 (3), 257–262.

30. Huang, Ming-Hui (2004), "Romantic Love and Sex: Their Relationship and Impacts on Ad Attitudes," *Psychology & Marketing* 21 (1), 53–73.

31. Eisend, Martin (2009), "A Meta-Analysis of Humor in Advertising," *Journal of the Academy of Marketing Science* 37 (Summer), 191–203.

32. Krishnan, H. S., and D. Chakravarti (2003), "A Process Analysis of the Effects of Humorous

Advertising Executions on Brand Claims Memory," *Journal of Consumer Psychology* 13 (3), 230–245.

33. Zhang, Yong (1996), "The Effect of Humor in Advertising: An Individual-Difference Perspective," *Psychology & Marketing* 13 (6), 531–545.

34. Cline, Thomas W., Moses B. Altsech, and James J. Kellaris (2003), "When Does Humor Enhance or Inhibit Ad Responses?" *Journal of Advertising* 32 (3), 31–46.

35. Chattopadhyay, Amitava (1990), "Humor in Advertising: The Moderating Role of Prior Brand Evaluations," *Journal of Marketing Research* 29 (November), 466–476.

36. Smith, Stephen M. (1993), "Does Humor in Advertising Enhance Systematic Processing?" in *Advances in Consumer Research,* vol. 20, L. McAlister and M. Rothschild, eds., Provo, UT: Association of Consumer Research, 155–158.

37. LaTour, Michael S., and Herbert J. Rotfeld (1997), "There Are Threats and (Maybe) Fear-Caused Arousal: Theory and Confusions of Appeals to Fear and Fear Arousal Itself," *Journal of Advertising* 3 (Fall), 45–59.

38. Keller, Punam Anand, and Lauren Goldberg Block (1996), "Increasing the Persuasiveness of Fear Appeals: The Effect of Arousal and Elaboration," *Journal of Consumer Research* 22 (4), 448–459.

39. Mowen, John C., Eric G. Harris, and Sterling A. Bone (2004), "Personality Traits and Fear Response to Print Advertisements: Theory and an Empirical Study," *Psychology & Marketing* 21 (11), 927–943.

40. Potter, Robert F., Michael S. LaTour, Kathryn A. Braun-LaTour, and Tom Reichert (2006), "The Impact of Program Context on Motivational System Activation and Subsequent Effects on Processing a Fear Appeal," *Journal of Advertising* 35 (3), 67–80.

41. Tanner, John F., James B. Hunt, and David R. Eppright (1991), "The Protection Motivation Model: A Normative Model of Fear Appeals," *Journal of Marketing* 55 (3), 36–45.

42. Duke, Charles R., Gregory M. Pickett, Les Carlson, and Stephen J. Grove (1993), "A Method for Evaluating the Ethics of Fear Appeals," *Journal of Public Policy & Marketing* 1 (Spring), 120–130.

43. Brocato, E. Deanne, Douglas A. Gentile, Russell N. Laczniak, Julia A. Maier, and Mindy Ji-Song, "Television Commercial Violence: Potential Effects on Children," *Journal of Advertising,* 39, no. 4 (2010): 95–107.

44. Capella, Michael L., Ronald Paul Hill, Justine M. Rapp, and Jeremy Kees, "The Impact of Violence Against Women in Advertisements," *Journal of Advertising,* 39, no. 4 (2010): 37–51.

45. Blackford, Benjamin J., James Gentry, Robert L. Harrison, and Les Carlson, "The Prevalence and Influence of the Combination of Humor and Violence in Super Bowl Commercials," *Journal of Advertising,* 49, no. 4 (2011): 123–133.

46. Sawyer, Alan G., and Daniel J. Howard (1991), "Effects of Omitting Conclusions in Advertisements to Involved and Uninvolved Audiences," *Journal of Marketing Research* 28 (November), 467–474.

47. Wilkie, William L., and Paul W. Ferris (1973), "Comparison Advertising: Problems and Potential," *Journal of Marketing* 39 (October), 7–15.

48. Miniard, Paul W., Michael J. Barone, Randall L. Rose, and Kenneth C. Manning (2006), "A Further Assessment of Indirect Advertising Claims of Superiority Overall All Competitors," *Journal of Advertising* 35 (4), 53–64.

49. Stewart, Dennis D., Cheryl B. Stewart, Clare Tyson, Vinci Gail, and Tom Fioti (2004), "Serial

Position Effects and the Picture-Superiority Effect in the Group Recall of Unshared Information," *Group Dynamics: Theory, Research, and Practice* 8 (3), 166–181.

50. Haugtvedt, Curtis P., and Duance T. Wegener (1994), "Message Order Effects in Persuasion: An Attitude Strength Perspective," *Journal of Consumer Research* 21 (June), 205–218.

51. Unnava, H. Rao, Robert E. Burnkrant, and Sunil Erevelles (1994), "Effects of Presentation Order and Communication Modality on Recall and Attitude," *Journal of Consumer Research* 21 (December), 481–490.

52. Li, Cong (2009), "Primacy Effect or Recency Effect? A Long-Term Memory Test of Super Bowl Commercials," *Journal of Consumer Behaviour* 9 (October), 32–44.

53. Jain, S. P., and S. S. Posavac (2001), "Prepurchase Attribute Verifiability, Source Credibility, and Persuasion," *Journal of Consumer Psychology* 11 (3), 169–180.

54. Homer, Pamela M., and Lynn R. Kahle (1990), "Source Expertise, Time of Source Identification, and Involvement in Persuasion," *Journal of Advertising* 19 (1), 30–39.

55. Nan, Xiaoli (2009), "The Influence of Source Credibility on Attitude Certainty: Exploring the Moderating Effects of Time of Source Identification and Individual Need for Cognition," *Psychology & Marketing* 26 (4), 321–332.

56. Wilson, Elizabeth, and Daniel L. Sherrell (1993), "Source Effects in Communication and Persuasion Research: A Meta-Analysis of Effect Size," *Journal of the Academy of Marketing Science* 21 (2), 101–112.

57. Wiener, Josh, and John C. Mowen (1985), "The Impact of Product Recalls on Consumer Perceptions," *Journal of the Society of Consumer Affairs Professionals in Business* (Spring), 18–21.

58. Lafferty, Barbara A., Ronald E. Goldsmith, and Stephen J. Newell (2002), "The Dual Credibility Model: The Influence of Corporate and Endorser Credibility on Attitudes and Purchase Intention," *Journal of Marketing Theory & Practice* 10 (3), 1–12.

59. Till, Brian D., and Michael Busler (2000), "The Match-Up Hypothesis: Physical Attractiveness, Expertise, and the Role of Fit on Brand Attitude, Purchase Intent, and Brand Beliefs," *Journal of Advertising* 3 (Fall), 1–13. Chaiken, Shelly (1979), "Communicator Physical Attractiveness and Persuasion," *Journal of Personality and Social Psychology* 37 (August), 1387–1397.

60. Baker, Michael, and Gilbert Churchill (1977), "The Impact of Physically Attractive Models on Advertising Effectiveness," *Journal of Marketing Research* 14 (November), 538–555.

61. Kang, Yoon-Soon, and Paul M. Herr (2006), "Beauty and the Beholder: Toward an Integrative Model of Communication Source Effects," *Journal of Consumer Research* 33 (1), 123–130.

62. Information gathered from Marketing Evaluations, Inc. website accessed at http://www.qscores.com on May 28, 2010.

63. Reinhard, Marc-Andre, and Matthias Messner (2009), "The Effects of Source Likeability and Need for Cognition on Advertising Effectiveness Under Explicit Persuasion," *Journal of Consumer Behaviour* 8 (4), 179–191.

64. Lynch, James, and Drue Schuler (1994), "The Matchup Effect of Spokesperson and Product Congruency: A Schema Theory Interpretation," *Psychology & Marketing* 11 (September-October), 417–445. Kamins, Michael A. (1990), "An Investigation into the 'Match-Up' Hypothesis in Celebrity

Advertising: When Beauty May Be Only Skin Deep," *Journal of Advertising* 19 (1), 4–13.

65. Rogers, Simon (2012), "London 2012 Olympics sponsors list: Who are they and what have they paid?" *The Guardian* (July 19), accessed at http://www.theguardian.com/sport/datablog/2012/jul/19/london-2012-olympic-sponsors-list on April 30, 2015.

66. Hall, James (2011), "London 2012 Olympics: Adidas aims to beat Nike into second place at Games," *The Telegraph* (2011), accessed at http://www.telegraph.co.uk/finance/london-olympics-business/8545104/London-2012-Olympics-Adidas-aims-to-beat-Nike-into-second-place-at-Games.html on April 30, 2015.

67. BoxUK (2013), "Analysis: Nike #findyourgreatness," BoxUK.com (April 5), accessed at http://www.boxuk.com/blog/analysis-nike-findyourgreatness/ on April 30, 2015.

8

1. McCracken, G. (1986), "Culture and Consumption: A Theoretical Account of the Structure and Movement of the Cultural Meaning of Consumer Goods," *Journal of Consumer Research* 13, 71–84.

2. Lenartowicz, T., and K. Roth (1999), "A Framework for Culture Assessment," *Journal of International Business Studies* 30, 781–798. Lenartowicz, T., and K. Roth (2001), "Culture Assessment Revisited: The Selection of Key Informants in IB Cross-Cultural Studies," 2001 Annual Meeting of the Academy of International Business.

3. Overby, J.W., R.B. Woodruff, and S.F. Gardial (2005), "The Influence of Culture on Consumers' Desired Value Perceptions: A Research Agenda," *Marketing Theory* 5 (June), 139–163.

4. For an overview, Hofstede, Geert (2010), accessed at http://www.geert-hofstede.com/geert_hof-stede_resources.shtml on August 3, 2010.

5. For a concise review of Hofstede's value dimensions, see Soares, A.M., M. Farhangmehr, and A. Shoham (2007), "Hofstede's Dimensions of Culture in International Marketing Studies," *Journal of Business Research* 60, 277–284.

6. Hirschman, E.C. (2003), "Men, Dogs, Guns and Cars," *Journal of Advertising* 32 (Spring), 9–22.

7. Petrova, P. K., R. B. Cialdini, and S.J. Sills (2007), "Consistency-Based Compliance Across Cultures," *Journal of Experimental and Cosial Psychology* 43, 104–111.

8. Hofstede (2010).

9. Jung, J.M., and J.J. Kellaris (2006), "Responsiveness to Authority Appeals Among Young French and American Consumers," *Journal of Business Research* 59 (June), 735–744.

10. Jung, J.M., and J.J. Kellaris (2004), "Cross-National Difference in Proneness to Scarcity Effects: The Moderating Roles of Familiarity, Uncertainty Avoidance and Need for Cognitive Closure," *Psychology & Marketing* 21 (September), 739–753.

11. Erevelles, S., R. Abhik, and L. Yip (2001), "The Universality of the Signal Theory for Products and Services," *Journal of Business Research* 52 (May), 175–187.

12. Martin, D. (2010), "Uncovering Unconscious Memories and Myths for Understanding International Tourism Behavior," *Journal of Business Research* 63, 372–383. Mowen, J.C., X. Fang, and K. Scott (2009), "A Hierarchical Model Approach for Identifying the Trait Antecedents of General Gambling Propensity and of Four Gambling-Related Genres," *Journal of Business Research* 62, 1262–1268.

13. Hofstede, G. (2001), *Culture's Consequences*, Thousand Oaks, CA: Sage Publications.

14. Keysuk, K., and C. Oh (2002), "On Distributor Commitment in Marketing Channels for Industrial Products: Contrast Between the United States and Japan," *Journal of International Marketing* 10, 72–107. Ryu, S., S. Kabadavi, and C. Chung (2007), "The Relationship Between Unilateral and Bilateral Control Mechanisms: The Contextual Effect of Long-Term Orientation," *Journal of Business Research* 60 (July), 681–689.

15. Hofstede (2001).

16. Wang, C.L. (2007), "Guanxi vs. Relationship Marketing: Exploring Underlying Differences," *Industrial Marketing Management* 36, 81–86.

17. Worthington, S. (2005), "Entering the Market for Financial Services in Transitional Economies," *International Journal of Bank Marketing* 23, 381–396.

18. Ren, X., S. Oh, and J. Noh (2010), "Managing Supplier–Retailer Relationships: From Institutional and Task Environment Perspectives," *Industrial Marketing Management* 39, 593–604.

19. Byrne, P.M. (2007), "Thinking Beyond BRIC," *Logistics Management* 46, 24–26.

20. For example, see Muller, T.E. (2000), "Targeting the CANZUS Baby-Boomer Explorer and Adventurer Market," *Journal of Vacation Marketing* 6, 154–169.

21. Laroche, M., Z. Yang, C. Kim, and M.O. Richard (2007), "How Culture Matters in Children's Purchase Influence: A Multi-Level Investigation," *Journal of the Academy of Marketing Science* 35 (Winter), 113–126.

22. Bokale, J. (2008), "Supermarkets Bolster Focus on Children's Ranges," *Marketing* (February 6), 1.

23. Chankon, K., M. Laroche, and M. Tomiuk (2004), "The Chinese in Canada: A Study of Ethnic Change with Emphasis on Gender Roles," *Journal of Social Psychology* 144 (February), 5–27.

24. Laroche, M., K. Chankon, M. Tomiuk, and D. Belisle (2005), "Similarities in Italian and Greek Multidimensional Ethnic Identity: Some Implications for Food Consumption," *Canadian Journal of Administrative Science* 22, 143–167.

25. Bristol, T., and T.F. Mangleburg (2005), "Not Telling the Whole Story: Teen Deception in Purchasing," *Journal of the Academy of Marketing Science* 33 (Winter), 79–95.

26. Bakir, A., G.M. Rose, and A. Shoham (2005), "Consumption Communication and Parental Control of Children's Viewing: A Multi-Rater Approach," *Journal of Marketing Theory and Practice* 13 (Spring), 47–58. Carlson, L., and S. Grossbart (1988), "Parental Style and Consumer Socialization in Children," *Journal of Consumer Research* 15 (June), 77–94.

27. Miller, C., F. Bram, J. Reardon, and I. Vida (2006), "Teenagers' Response to Self- and Other-Directed Anti-Smoking Messages," *International Journal of Market Research* 49, 515–533.

28. Clark, A.E., and Y. Loheac (2007), "It Wasn't Me, It Was Them! Social Influence in Risky Behavior by Adolescents," *Journal of Health Economics* 26, 763–784. Kelly, K.J., M.D. Slater, and D. Karan (2002), "Image Advertisements' Influence on Adolescents' Perceptions of the Desirability of Beer and Cigarettes," *Journal of Public Policy & Marketing* 21 (Fall), 295–304.

29. Neeleman, S.E. (2010), "Firm Toots Horn Via Search," *The Wall Street Journal* (July 1), B1.

30. Mourali, M., M. Laroche, and F. Pons (2005), "Individual Orientation and Consumer Susceptibility to Interpersonal Influence," *Journal of Services Marketing* 19, 164–173.

31. Matilla, A.S., and P.G. Patterson (2004), "The Impact of Culture on Consumers' Perceptions of Service Recovery Efforts," *Journal of Retailing* 80, 196–207.

32. See Griffin, M., B.J. Babin, and D. Modianos (2000), "Shopping Values of Russian Consumers: The Impact of Habituation in a Developing Economy," *Journal of Retailing* 76, 33–52.

33. Dallimore, K.S., B.A. Sparks, and K. Butcher (2007), "The Influence of Angry Customer Outbursts on Service Providers' Facial Displays and Affective States," *Journal of Services Marketing* 10 (August), 78–92.

34. Wang, L.A., J. Baker, J.A. Wagner, and K. Wakefield (2007), "Can a Retail Website Be *Social?*" *Journal of Marketing* 71 (July), 143–157. Qiu, L., and I. Bernbasat (2005), "Online Consumer Trust and Live Help Interfaces: The Effects of Text-to-Speech Voice and Three-Dimensional Avatars," *Journal of Human-Computer Interaction* 19, 75–94.

35. Kramer, T., S. Spolter-Weisfeld, and M. Thakker (2007), "The Effect of Cultural Orientation on Consumer Responses to Personalization," *Marketing Science* 26 (March/April), 246–258.

36. Pigliasco, G.C. (2005), "Lost in Translation: From Omiyage to Souvenir: Beyond Aesthetics of the Japanese Ladies' Gaze in Hawaii," *Journal of Material Culture* 10 (July), 177–196.

37. See www.transparency.org for an overview of culture and corruption around the world.

9

1. Beverland, M. B., F. Farrelly, and P. G. Quester (2010), "Authentic Subcultural Membership: Antecedents and Consequences of Authenticating Acts and Authoritative Performances," *Psychology & Marketing* 27 (July), 608–716.

2. Berger, J., and C. Heath (2008), "Who Drives Divergence? Identity Signaling, Out-group Similarity, and the Abandonment of Cultural Tastes," *Journal of Personality and Social Psychology* 95, 593–607.

3. Guimond, S., S. Brunot, A. Chatard, D. M. Garcia, D. Martinot, N. R. Branscombe, M. Desert, S. Haque, and V. Yzerbyt (2007), "Culture, Gender, and the Self: Variations and Impact of Social Comparison Processes," *Journal of Personality and Social Psychology* 92 (June), 1118–1134.

4. Sung, Y., and S. F. Tinkham (2005), "Brand Personality Structures in the United States and Korea: Common and Culture-Specific Factors," *Journal of Consumer Psychology* 15 (4), 334–350.

5. Williams, C. (2010), "Women in Canada: A Gender-Based Statistical Report," Statistics Canada, December, http://www.statcan.gc.ca/pub/89-503-x/2010001/article/11388-eng.htm, accessed May 28, 2012.

6. Crompton, S., and L. Geran (1995), "Women as Main Wage-Earners," Statistics Canada, Perspectives, Winter, http://www.statcan.gc.ca/studies-etudes/75-001/archive/e-pdf/2457-eng.pdf, accessed May 28, 2012.

7. Mendleson, R. (2010), "Head of the Household," *Maclean's* (March 15), http://www2.macleans.ca/2010/03/15/head-of-the-household/, accessed May 28, 2012.

8. Rosin, H. (2011), "She Makes More Money Than He Does. So?" *Slate* (February 16), http://www.slate.com/articles/double_x/doublex/2011/02/she_makes_more_money_than_he_does_so.html, accessed May 28, 2012.

9. Hinsliff, G. (2011), "Young Women Are Now Earning More Than Men—That's Not Sexist, Just

Fair," *The Guardian* (November 27), http://www
.guardian.co.uk/commentisfree/2011/nov/27/young
-women-earning-more-men, accessed May 28, 2012.

10. Bustillo, M., and M. E. Lloyd (2010), "Best Buy
Seeks Female Shoppers," *The Wall Street Journal*
(June 16), B5.

11. Smith, R. A. (2010), "Wanted: Guy Shoppes for
Fashion Sites," *The Wall Street Journal* (July 22), B1.

12. Statistics Canada. "Table 051-0001—Estimates
of Population, by Age Group and Sex for July 1,
Canada, Provinces and Territories, Annual (persons
unless otherwise noted)," CANSIM (database).

13. Lueg, J. E., and R. Z. Finney (2007), "Interpersonal Communication in the Consumer Socialization Process: Scale Development and Validation,"
Journal of Marketing Theory and Practice 15
(Winter), 25–39.

14. Business Wire (1999), "International Survey
Shows That Coca-Cola and McDonald's Are
Teenagers' Favorite Brands" (February 8), www
.encyclopedia.com/printable.aspx?id=1G1:53724844,
accessed August 18, 2007.

15. Devaney, P. (2007), "Coca-Cola to Launch
on Virtual World Second Life," *Marketing Week*
(February 19), 6.

16. Muk, A., and B. J. Babin (2006), "U.S.
Consumers' Adoption–Non-Adoption of Mobile
SMS Advertising," *Journal of Mobile Marketing*
1 (June), 21–29.

17. "Global Teen Culture—Does It Exist?" *Brand
Strategy* 167 (January 2003), 37–38.

18. Parker, R. S., A. D. Schaefer, and C. M.
Hermans (2006), "An Investigation Into Teens'
Attitudes Towards Fast-Food Brands in General:
A Cross-Culture Analysis," *Journal of Foodservice
Business Research* 9 (4), 25–40.

19. The birth years for the three generations were
taken from: The Conference Board of Canada
(2009), "Winning the 'Generational Wars': Making
the Most of Generational Differences and Similarities in the Workplace," November.

20. Marshall, K. (2001), "Generational Change in
Paid and Unpaid Work," *Canadian Social Trends*,
Winter 2011, no. 92, Statistics Canada Catalogue
no. 11-008-X, http://www.statcan.gc.ca/pub/75-001
-x/2012001/article/11612-eng.htm, accessed
May 28, 2012.

21. Neuborne, E., and K. Kerwin (1999), "Genera-
tion Y: Today's Teens—the Biggest Bulge Since the
Boomers—May Force Marketers to Toss Their Old
Tricks," *Bloomberg Business Week* (February 15).

22. Statistics Canada (2002), "Religions in Canada,"
2001 Census: Analysis Series (May 13), http://
www12.statcan.gc.ca/english/census01/products/an
alytic/companion/rel/pdf/96F0030XIE2001015.pdf,
accessed May 28, 2012.

23. Boski, P. (2006), "Humanism–Materialism:
Centuries-Long Polish Cultural Origins and 20
Years of Research" in U. Kim, K. S. Yang, and K.-K.
Hwang, eds., *Indigenous and Cultural Psychol-
ogy: Understanding People in Context*, New York:
Springer, 373–402.

24. Taylor, V. A., D. Halstead, and P. J. Haynes
(2010), "Consumer Advertising to Christian Religious Symbols in Advertising," *Journal of Advertising* 39 (2), 79–92.

25. Sandikci, O., and G. Ger (2010), "Veiling in
Style: How Does a Stigmatized Practice Become
Fashionable?" *Journal of Consumer Research* 37
(June), 15–36.

26. Online content retrieved at BBC News online
edition, "French MPs Vote to Ban Islamic Full
Veil in Public," *BBC News Online*, http://www.bbc
.co.uk/news/10611398, accessed August 9, 2010.

27. CBC News (2015), "Hijab-wearing woman
should be allowed to testify, Harper spokesman
says," (February 27), http://www.cbc.ca/news/
canada/montreal/hijab-wearing-woman-should-be
-allowed-to-testify-harper-spokesman-says-1.2975582
accessed on April 27, 2015.

28. Government of Canada, Immigration and
Citizenship website, http://www.cic.gc.ca/english/
multiculturalism/citizenship.asp, accessed
May 30, 2012.

29. The immigration statistics in this paragraph
were taken from Statistics Canada (2008), "Some
Facts About the Demographic and Ethnocultural
Composition of the Population," *Canadian
Demographics at a Glance* (January 25), http://www
.statcan.gc.ca/pub/91-003-x/2007001/4129904-eng
.htm, accessed May 30, 2012.

30. O'Neal, Brian (1995), "Distinct Society:
Origins, Interpretations, Implications," *Library of
Parliament* (December), http://www.parl.gc.ca/
Content/LOP/Research-Publications/bp408-e.htm#B,
accessed May 30, 2012.

31. The immigration statistics in this paragraph
were taken from Statistics Canada (2008), "The
Proportion of Francophones in Canada Declined
in the Second Half of the Twentieth Century,"
Canadian Demographics at a Glance (January 25),
http://www.statcan.gc.ca/pub/91-003-x/2007001/
4129904-eng.htm, accessed May 30, 2012.

32. The statistics on Canada's Aboriginal population in this paragraph are from Statistics Canada
(2008), "Population Growth," *Aboriginal Peoples,
2006 Census* (July 29), http://www5.statcan.gc.ca/
bsolc/olc-cel/olc-cel?lang=eng&catno=97-558-X,
accessed May 30, 2012.

33. The statistics reported in this section come from
two sources: Statistics Canada (2010), *Aboriginal
Statistics at a Glance* (June 21), http://www.statcan
.gc.ca/pub/89-645-x/89-645-x2010001-eng.htm, and
Statistics Canada (2006), "Family, Community and
Child Care," *Aboriginal Children's Survey 2006*,
http://www.statcan.gc.ca/pub/89-634-x/89-634
-x2008001-eng.htm, both accessed May 30, 2012.

34. This definition based on Ritzer, George
(1996), *Sociological Theory*, 4th ed. New York:
McGraw-Hill.

35. Schaninger, Charles M. (1981), "Social Class
Versus Income Revisited: An Empirical Investigation," *Journal of Marketing Research* (May),
192–208.

36. Warner, Lloyd W., and Paul S. Hunt, eds.
(1941), *The Social Life of a Modern Community*,
New Haven: CT: Yale University Press.

37. Schwartz, C. R., and R. D. Mare (2005),
"Trends in Educational Assortative Marriage from
1940 to 2003," *Demography* 42 (4), 621–646. Sny-
der, E. C. (1964), "Attitudes: A Study of Homogamy
and Marital Selectivity," *Journal of Marriage and
Family* 26 (3), 332–336.

38. This definition based on Eller, Jack (2009),
Cultural Anthropology: Global Forces, Local Lives,
New York: Routledge; and Jonathon H. Turner
(1981), *Sociology: Studying the Human System*,
Santa Monica, CA: Goodyear Publishing.

39. Ling, Lisa, and Katie Hinman, "Under Las
Vegas: Tunnels Stretch for Miles," ABC News,
September 23, 2009, http://abcnews.go.com/
Nightline/las-vegas-strip-home-homeless/story?id
=8652139, accessed August 11, 2010. Powers,
Ashley, "A Life Saved from the Shadows," *Los
Angeles Times*, December 22, 2009, http://articles
.latimes.com/2009/dec/22/nation/la-na-tunnel22
-2009dec22, accessed August 11, 2010.

40. Hodgson, An (2007), "China's Middle Class
Reaches 80 Million," *Euromonitor* online (July 25),

http://www.euromonitor.com/Chinas_middle_class
_reaches_80_million, accessed August 11, 2010.

41. This section based on Fernando, Vincent
(2010), "Faber: India's Middle Class Will Soon
Be Larger than America's," *Business Insider*, http://
www.businessinsider.com/faber-dont-ignore-india
-2010-2, accessed August 11, 2010; also Beinhocker,
Eric, Diana Ferrell, and Adil Zainulbhai (2007),
"Tracking the Growth of India's Middle Class,"
McKinsey Quarterly online, http://www.mckinsey
quarterly.com/Tracking_the_growth_of_Indias
_middle_class_2032, accessed August 11, 2010.

42. Goulding, C., and M. Saren (2009), "Performing Identity: An Analysis of Gender Expressions at
the Whitby Goth Festival," *Consumption Markets
& Culture* 12 (March), 27–46.

43. Martin, Bob (2007), "Wife Shortage Looms
in China," *Culture Briefings*, http://www.culture
briefngs.com/articles/chwifesh.html, accessed
August 12, 2010; also "Study: China Faces 24M
Bride Shortage by 2020," *CNN* online (2010),
http://www.cnn.com/2010/WORLD/asiapcf/01/
11/china.bride.shortage/index.html, accessed
August 12, 2010.

44. "Asian Youth Trends," *American Demographics*
26 (8) (2004), 14.

10

1. Park, C. Whan, and V. Parker Lessig (1977),
"Students and Housewives: Differences in Suscep-
tibility to Reference Group Influence," *Journal of
Consumer Research* 4 (September), 102–110.

2. Michener, H. Andrew, and Michelle P. Wasser-
man (1995), "Group Decision Making," in *Sociological Perspectives on Social Psychology*, Karen
S. Cook, Gary Alan Fine, and James S. House, eds.,
Boston: Allyn and Bacon, 336–361.

3. Webley, Paul, and Ellen K. Nyhus (2006), "Parents' Influence on Children's Future Orientation
and Saving," *Journal of Economic Psychology* 27
(1), 140–149.

4. Muniz, Albert M., Jr., and Thomas C. O'Guinn
(2001), "Brand Community," *Journal of Consumer
Research* 27 (4), 412–432.

5. Alexander, James H., John W. Schouten, and
Harold F. Koening (2002), "Building Brand Community," *Journal of Marketing* 66 (1), 38–54.

6. Lascu, Dana-Nicoleta, and George Zinkhan
(1999), "Consumer Conformity: Review and Applications for Marketing Theory and Practice," *Journal
of Marketing Theory and Practice* 7 (3), 1–12.

7. Ross, Jill, and Ross Harradine (2004), "I'm Not
Wearing That! Branding and Young Children,"
Journal of Fashion Marketing and Management 8
(1), 11–26.

8. Online content retrieved at Suite101 website,
http://public-healthcare-issues.suite101.com/article
.cfm/tobacco-company-undermines-global-treaty
-on-facebook, accessed June 17, 2010.

9. Smith, Karen H., and Mary Ann Stutts (2006),
"The Influence of Individual Factors on the
Effectiveness of Message Content in Antismoking
Advertisements Aimed at Adolescents," *Journal
of Consumer Affairs* 40 (2), 261–293. Rosenberg,
Merri (2002), "Anti-Smoking Ads Aimed at Peers,"
The Wall Street Journal (February 17), http://query
.nytimes.com/gst/fullpage.html?sec=health&res=9D
0Canadian Edition5D8163FF934A25751C0A9649
C8B63.

10. Albers-Miller, Nancy (1999), "Consumer
Misbehavior: Why People Buy Illicit Goods,"
The Journal of Consumer Marketing 16 (3),
273–287.

11. Gergen, Kenneth J., and Mary Gergen (1981), *Social Psychology*, New York: Harcourt Brace Jovanovich.

12. French, J. R. P., and B. Raven (1959), "The Bases of Social Power," in D. Cartwright, ed., *Studies in Social Power*, Ann Arbor, MI: Institute for Social Research.

13. Park and Lessig (1977).

14. Bearden, William O., and Michael J. Etzel (1982), "Reference Group Influence on Product and Brand Purchase Decisions," *Journal of Consumer Research* 9 (2), 183–194.

15. Park and Lessig (1977).

16. Bearden and Etzel (1982).

17. Online content retrieved at Pew Research Center website, "Neighbors Online," http://pewresearch.org/pubs/1620/neighbors-online-using-digital-tools-to-communicate-monitor-community-developments, accessed June 11, 2010.

18. Perez, Sarah (2010), "Social Networking Now More Popular on Mobile than Desktop," ReadWriteWeb, February 18, 2010, www.readwriteweb.com/archives/social_networking_now_more_popular_on_mobile_than_desktop.php, accessed July 17, 2012.

19. "Top Sites," Alexa, http://www.alexa.com/topsites, accessed June 3, 2015.

20. Statistics obtained from http://newsroom.fb.com/company-info/, accessed September 30, 2015.

21. eMarketer (2015), "Facebook Users and Penetration in Canada, 2013–2019," *eMarketer.com* (April 2015).

22. Statistics obtained from https://about.twitter.com/company, accessed September 30, 2015.

23. eMarketer (2015), "Twitter Users and Penetration in Canada, 2013–2019," *eMarketer.com* (April 2015).

24. eMarketer (2015), "Demographic Profile of Social Media Users in Canada by Platform, Nov 2014," *eMarketer.com* (February 2015).

25. Alexa.com, http://www.alexa.com/topsites, accessed June 3, 2015.

26. "Facebook to Acquire Instagram," Facebook, April 9, 2012, http://newsroom.fb.com/news/2012/04/facebook-to-acquire-instagram/, accessed June 3, 2015.

27. Frier, Sarah (2014), "Facebook $22 Billion WhatsApp Deal Buys $10 Million in Sales," *Bloomberg Business* (October 28), accessed at http://www.bloomberg.com/news/articles/2014-10-28/facebook-s-22-billion-whatsapp-deal-buys-10-million-in-sales on June 3, 2015.

28. Online content retrieved at Kaboodle website, http://www.kaboodle.com/zm/about, accessed June 10, 2010.

29. Bearden, William O., Richard G. Netemeyer, and Jesse E. Teel (1989), "Measurement of Consumer Susceptibility to Interpersonal Influence," *Journal of Consumer Research* 15 (4), 473–481.

30. Batra, Rajeev, Pamela M. Homer, and Lynn R. Kahle (2001), "Values, Susceptibility to Normative Influence, and Attribute Importance Weights: A Nomological Perspective," *Journal of Consumer Research* 11 (2), 115–128.

31. Wooten, David B., and Americus Reed II (2004), "Playing It Safe: Susceptibility to Normative Influence and Protective Self-Presentation," *Journal of Consumer Research* 31 (3), 551–556.

32. Wooten, David B., and Randall L. Rose (1990), "Attention to Social Comparison Information: An Individual Difference Variable Affecting Consumer Conformity," *Journal of Consumer Research* 16 (4), 461–471.

33. Clark, Ronald A., and Ronald E. Goldsmith (2006), "Global Innovativeness and Consumer Susceptibility to Interpersonal Influence," *Journal of Marketing Theory and Practice* 14 (4), 275–285.

34. Wang, Cheng Lu, and Allan K. K. Chan (2001), "A Content Analysis of Connectedness vs. Separateness Themes Used in U.S. and PR.C. Print Advertisements," *International Marketing Review* 18 (2), 145–157. Wang, Cheng Lu, and John C. Mowen (1997), "The Separateness–Connectedness Self-Schema: Scale Development and Application to Message Construction," *Psychology & Marketing* 14 (March), 185–207.

35. Wang and Mowen (1997).

36. Lan, Jiang, Joandrea Hoegg, Darren W. Dahl, and Amitava Chattopadhyay (2010), "The Persuasive Role of Incidental Similarity on Attitudes and Purchase Intentions in a Sales Context," *Journal of Consumer Research* 36 (5), 778–791.

37. Wang and Chan (2001).

38. Argo, Jennifer J., Darren W. Dahl, and Rajesh V. Manchanda (2005), "The Influence of a Mere Social Presence in a Retail Context," *Journal of Consumer Research* 32 (2), 207–212.

39. Dahl, Darren W., Rajesh V. Manchanda, and Jennifer J. Argo (2001), "Embarrassment in Consumer Purchase: The Roles of Social Presence and Purchase Familiarity," *Journal of Consumer Research* 28 (3), 473–481.

40. He Yi, Qimei Chen, and Dana L. Alden, "Consumption in the Public Eye: The Influence of Social Presence on Service Experience," *Journal of Business Research*, 65 (2012): 302–310.

41. Online content retrieved at Word of Mouth Marketing Association (WOMMA) website, http://www.womma.org/wom101/04/.

42. Brown, Tom J., Thomas E. Berry, Peter A. Dacin, and Richard F. Gunst (2005), "Spreading the Word: Investigating Antecedents of Consumers' Positive Word-of-Mouth Intentions and Behaviors in a Retailing Context," *Journal of the Academy of Marketing Science* 33 (2), 123–138.

43. Chung, Cindy M. Y. (2006), "The Consumer as Advocate: Self-Relevance, Culture, and Word-of-Mouth," *Marketing Letters* 17 (4), 269–284. Wangenheim, Florian V. (2005), "Postswitching Negative Word-of-Mouth," *Journal of Service Research* 8 (1), 67–78.

44. Bone, Paula (1995), "Word-of-Mouth Effects on Short-Term and Long-Term Product Judgments," *Journal of Business Research* 32 (3), 213–223.

45. Babin, Barry J., Yong-Ki Lee, Eun-Ju Kim, and Mitch Griffin (2005), "Modeling Consumer Satisfaction and Word-of-Mouth: Restaurant Patronage in Korea," *Journal of Services Marketing* 19 (3), 133–139.

46. Online content retrieved at Pew Internet Net and American Life Project website, http://www.pewinternet.org/topics/Health.aspx, accessed June 11, 2010.

47. Online content retrieved at Pew Research Center website, "Teens and Mobile Phones," http://www.pewinternet.org/Reports/2010/Teens-and-Mobile-Phones.aspx?r=1, accessed June 12, 2010.

48. Online content retrieved at BzzAgent.com website, www.bzzagent.com, accessed June 17, 2010.

49. Online content retrieved at Digg website, www.digg.com, accessed June 10, 2010.

50. Online content retrieved at *BusinessWeek* website, "How Ford Got Social Marketing Right," http://www.business-week.com/managing/content/jan2010/ca2010018_445530.htm, accessed June 12, 2010.

51. Kaikati, Andrew M., and Jack G. Kaikati (2004), "Stealth Marketing: How to Reach Consumers Surreptitiously," *California Management Review* 46 (4), 6–22.

52. "*Days of Our Lives* Botches Product Placements," Fox News, November 16, 2010, http://www.foxnews.com/entertainment/2010/11/16/days-lives-product-placements-cheerios-chex/, accessed June 3, 2015.

53. de Gregorio, Federico, and Yongjun Sung, "Understanding Attitudes Toward and Behaviors in Response to Product Placement: A Consumer Socialization Framework," *Journal of Advertising*, 39, no. 1 (2010): 83–96.

54. Online content retrieved at Word of Mouth Marketing Association (WOMMA), "Unethical Word-of-Mouth Marketing Strategies," http://www.womma.org/wom101/06/.

55. "Ford Gets Women Involved in 'What Women Want' for Instant Buzz," Market Autopsy Blog, http://www.marketing-autopsyblog.com/customer-facing/ford-bloggers-involved-women-instant-buzz/, accessed April 14, 2012.

56. Solomon, Michael (1986), "The Missing Link: Surrogate Consumers in the Marketing Chain," *Journal of Marketing* 50 (October), 208–218.

57. Rogers, Everett M. (1995), *Diffusion of Innovations*, 4th ed., New York: The Free Press.

58. Online content retrieved at Pew Research Center website, "The Return of the Multi-Generational Household," http://pewre-search.org/pubs/1528/multi-generational-family-household, accessed June 11, 2010.

59. Data retrieved from U.S. Census Bureau website, www.factfinder.census.gov, June 12, 2010.

60. Statistics Canada, "Table 101-6511, 30 and 50 Year Total Divorce Rates per 100 Marriages, Canada, Provinces and Territories," CANSIM (database).

61. Statistics Canada (2006), "Family Portrait: Continuity and Change in Canadian Families and Households in 2006; National Portrait: Individuals," 2006 Census, http://www12.statcan.ca/census-recensement/2006/as-sa/97-553/p10-eng.cfm, accessed May 4, 2012.

62. Statistics Canada (2011), " Census Families in Private Households by Family Structure and Presence of Children, by Province and Territory," *Statistics Canada, 2011 Census of Population and Statistics Canada catalogue no. 98-312-XCB*, accessed June 3, 2015.

63. Statistics Canada (2006), "Family Portrait: Continuity and Change in Canadian Families and Households in 2006," 2006 Census, http://www12.statcan.ca/census-recensement/2006/as-sa/97-553/index-eng.cfm, accessed May 4, 2012.

64. Statistics Canada (2006), "Family Portrait: Continuity and Change in Canadian Families and Households in 2006," 2006 Census, http://www12.statcan.ca/census-recensement/2006/as-sa/97-553/p4-eng.cfm, accessed May 4, 2012.

65. Wilkes, Robert E. (1995), "Household Life-Cycle Stages, Transitions, and Product Expenditures," *Journal of Consumer Research*, 22 (1), 27–41.

66. Statistics Canada, "Home Ownership Over the Life Course of Canadians," http://www.statcan.gc.ca/daily-quotidien/100607/dq100607a-eng.htm, accessed May 4, 2012.

67. Statistics Canada (2006), "Family Portrait: Continuity and Change in Canadian Families and Households in 2006," 2006 Census, http://www12.statcan.ca/census-recensement/2006/as-sa/97-553/p44-eng.cfm, accessed May 4, 2012.

68. John Chatzky, "Your Adult Kids Are Back. Now What?" *Money*, 36, no. 1 (2007): 32–35.

69. "Valuing the Invaluable: The Economic Value of Family Caregiving, 2008 Update," AARP Public Policy Institute, online content retrieved at http://assets.aarp.org/rgcenter/il/i13_caregiving.pdf, accessed April 3, 2009.

70. Online content retrieved at New Jersey Newsroom website, "The Sandwich Generation: Modern Dilemma of Elder Care," http://www.newjerseynewsroom.com/healthquest/the-sandwich-generation-the-modern-dilemma-of-elder-care, accessed June 11, 2010.

71. Gentry, James W., Suraj Commuri, and Sunkyu Jun (2003), "Review of Literature on Gender in the Family," *Academy of Marketing Science Review*, 1–18

72. Lee, Christina K. C., and Sharon E. Beatty (2002), "Family Structure and Influence in Family Decision Making," *Journal of Consumer Marketing* 19 (1), 24–41.

73. Belch, Michael A., and Laura A. Willis (2002), "Family Decisions at the Turn of the Century: Has the Changing Structure of Households Impacted the Family Decision-Making Process?" *Journal of Consumer Behaviour* 2 (2), 111–125.

74. Online content retrieved at Pew Research Center website, http://pewresearch.org/pubs/1466/economics-marriage-rise-of-wives?src=prc-latest&proj=peoplepress, accessed June 11, 2010.

75. "Kid Power," *Chain Store Age*, 83 (3) (2007), 20.

76. This definition based on Scott Ward (1980), "Consumer Socialization," in *Perspectives in Consumer Behavior*, Harold H. Kassarjian and Thomas S. Robertson, eds., Glenview, IL: Scott, Foresman, 380.

11

1. Dhar, R., and S. M. Nowlis (1999), "The Effect of Time Pressure on Consumer Choice Deferral," *Journal of Consumer Research* 25 (March), 369–384.

2. Bublitz, M. G., L. A. Peracchio, and L. G. Block (2010), "Why Did I Eat That? Perspectives on Food Decision Making and Dietary Restraint," *Journal of Consumer Psychology* 20 (3), 239–258.

3. Lim, J., and S. E. Beatty (2010), "Factors Affecting Couples' Decisions to Jointly Shop," *Journal of Business Research* 64 (7), 774–781.

4. Nowlis, S. M. (1995), "The Effect of Time Pressure on the Choice Between Brands that Differ in Quality, Price and Product Features," *Marketing Letters* 6 (October), 287–296.

5. Suri, R., and K. B. Monroe (2003), "The Effects of Time Constraints on Consumers' Judgments of Prices and Products," *Journal of Consumer Research* 30 (June), 92–104.

6. Lloyd, Alison Elizabeth, Ricky Y. K. Chan, Leslie S. C. Yip, and Andrew Chan, "Time Buying and Time Saving: Effects on Service Convenience and the Shopping Experience at the Mall," *Journal of Services Marketing*, 28 (2014): 36–49.

7. Wagner, J., and M. Mokhtari (2000), "The Moderating Effect on Household Apparel Expenditure," *Journal of Consumer Affairs* 34 (2), 22–78.

8. Roslow, S., T. Li, and J. A. F. Nicholls (2000), "Impact of Situational Variables and Demographic Attributes in Two Seasons on Purchase Behavior," *European Journal of Marketing* 34 (9), 1167–1180.

9. Euromonitor (2015), "Coffee in Canada," *Passport: Euromonitor International.*

10. Euromonitor (2015), "Tea in Canada," *Passport: Euromonitor International.*

11. Yoon, C., C. Cole, and M. P. Lee (2009), "Consumer Decision Making and Aging: Current Knowledge and Future Decisions," *Journal of Consumer Psychology* 19, 2–16; Bublitz et al. (2010).

12. Okamura, H., A. Tsuda, J. Yajima, H. Mark, S. Horiuchi, N. Troyoshima, and T. Matsuishi (2010), "Short Sleeping Time and Psychological Responses to Acute Stress," *International Journal of Psychophysiology*, doi 10.1016/j.ijpsycho. 2010.0/.010.

13. Hui, S. K., J. Inman, H. Yanliu, and J. Suher, "The Effect of In-Store Travel Distance on Unplanned Spending: Applications to Mobile Promotion Strategies," *Journal of Marketing*, 77, no. 2 (2013): 1–16.

14. Mandel, N., and E. J. Johnson, "When Web Pages Influence Choice: Effects of Visual Primes on Experts and Novices," *Journal of Consumer Research*, 20 (September 2002): 235–245.

15. Wang, Y. J., M. S. Minor, and J. Wei, "Aesthetics and the Online Shopping Environment: Understanding Consumer Responses," *Journal of Retailing*, 87 (2011): 46–58.

16. Bensinger, G., "Amazon Wants to Ship Your Package Before You Buy It," *The Wall Street Journal*, January 21, 2014, B1. "Amazon Files Patent for 'Anticipatory' Shipping," CBS News, www.cbsnews.com/news/amazon-files-patent-for-anticipatory-shipping/, accessed January 21, 2014. Manjoo, F., "Why Bezos's Drone Is More Than a Joke," *The Wall Street Journal*, December 5, 2013, B1–B7.

17. Zhuang, G., A. S. Tsang, N. Zhou, F. Li, and J. A. Nicholls (2006), "Impacts of Situational Factors on Buying Decisions in Shopping Malls," *European Journal of Marketing* 40, 17–43.

18. Babin, B. J., W. R. Darden, and M. Griffin (1994), "Work and/or Fun: Measuring Hedonic and Utilitarian Shopping Value," *Journal of Consumer Research* 20 (4), 644–656.

19. Babin et al. (1994).

20. Babin, B. J., and J. S. Attaway (2000), "Atmospheric Affect as a Tool for Creating Value and Gaining Share of Customer," *Journal of Business Research* 49, 91–99.

21. Darden, W. R., and B. J. Babin (1994), "Exploring the Concept of Affective Quality: Expanding the Concept of Retail Personality," *Journal of Business Research* 29 (February), 101–109.

22. Ramanathan, S., and P. Williams (2007), "Immediate and Delayed Emotional Consequences of Indulgence: The Moderating Influence of Personality Type on Mixed Emotions," *Journal of Consumer Research* 34, 212–223.

23. Childers, T. L., C. L. Carr, J. Peck, and S. Carson (2001), "Hedonic and Utilitarian Motivations for Online Shopping Behavior," *Journal of Retailing* 77, 511–535.

24. Mukhopadhyay, A., and G. V. Johar (2009), "Indulgence as Self-Reward for Prior Shopping Restraint: A Justification-Based Mechanism," *Journal of Consumer Psychology* 19 (July), 334–345.

25. Franken, I. H. A., and P. Muris (2006), "Gray's Impulsivity Dimension: A Distinction Between Reward Sensitivity and Rash Impulsiveness," *Personality & Individual Differences* 40 (July), 1337–1347. Ramanathan and Williams (2007).

26. Dholakia, U. M. (2000), "Temptation and Resistance: An Integrated Model of Consumption Impulse Formation and Enactment," *Psychology & Marketing* 17 (November), 955–982.

27. Kaufman-Scarborough, C., and J. Cohen (2004), "Unfolding Consumer Impulsivity: An Existential–Phenomenological Study of Consumers with Attention Deficit Disorder," *Psychology & Marketing* 21 (August), 637–669.

28. Beatty, S. E., and E. M. Ferrell (1998), "Impulse Buying: Modeling Its Precursors," *Journal of Retailing* 74, 161–191.

29. Zhang, X., V. R. Prybutok, and D. Strutton (2007), "Modeling Influences on Impulse Purchasing Behaviors During Online Marketing Transactions," *Journal of Marketing Theory and Practice* 15 (Winter), 79–89.

30. Babin, B. J., and W. R. Darden (1995), "Consumer Self-Regulation in a Retail Environment," *Journal of Retailing* 71 (1) (Spring), 47–70.

31. Herzenstein, M., S. S. Posavac, and J. J. Brakus (2007), "Adoption of New and Really New Products: The Effects of Self-Regulation Systems and Risk Salience," *Journal of Marketing Research* 44 (May), 251–260.

32. Darden and Babin (1994); Russell, J. A., and G. Pratt (1980), "A Description of the Affective Quality Attributable to Environments," *Journal of Personality and Social Psychology* 38, 311–322.

33. Brady, M. K., C. M. Voorhees, J. J. Cronin, and B. L. Boudreau (2006), "The Good Guys Don't Always Win: The Effect of Valence on Service Perceptions and Consequences," *Journal of Services Marketing* 20, 83–91.

34. Williams, G. (2004), "It's a Style Thing," *Entrepreneur* 32 (March), 34. Iacobucci, D., and A. Ostrom (1993), "Gender Differences in the Impact of Core and Relational Aspects of Services on the Evaluation of Service Encounters," *Journal of Consumer Psychology* 2, 257–286.

35. Haytko, D. L., and J. Baker (2004), "It's All at the Mall: Exploring Adolescent Girls' Experiences," *Journal of Retailing* 80 (Spring), 67–83.

36. Babin, B. J., and J. C. Chebat (2004), "Perceived Appropriateness and Its Effect on Quality, Affect and Behavior," *Journal of Retailing and Consumer Services* 11 (September), 287–298. Michon, R., J. C. Chebat, and L. W. Turley (2005), "Mall Atmospherics: The Interaction Effects of the Mall Environment on Shopping Behavior," *Journal of Business Research* 58 (May), 576–583.

37. Orth, O. R., and A. Bourrain (2005), "Ambient Scent and Consumer Exploratory Behavior: A Causal Analysis," *Journal of Wine Research* 16, 137–150.

38. Michon et al. (2005).

39. Turley, L. W., and J. C. Chebat (2002), "Linking Retail Strategy, Atmospheric Design and Shopping Behavior," *Journal of Marketing Management* 18, 125–144. Milliman, R. E. (1986), "The Influence of Background Music on the Behavior of Restaurant Patrons," *Journal of Consumer Research* 13 (September), 286–289. Babin and Chebat (2004).

40. Crowley, A. E. (1993), "The Two-Dimensional Impact of Color on Shopping," *Marketing Letters* 4, 59–69. Bellizi, J., and R. E. Hite (1992), "Environmental Color, Consumer Feelings and Purchase Likelihood," *Psychology & Marketing* 59 (Spring), 347–363. Babin, B. J., D. M. Hardesty, and T. A. Suter (2003), "Color and Shopping Intentions: The Intervening Effect of Price Fairness and Affect," *Journal of Business Research* 56, 541–551.

41. Babin, Hardesty, and Suter (2003).

42. Dennis, C., A. Newman, R. Michon, J. J. Brakus, and L. T. Wright (2010), "The Mediating Effects of Perception and Emotion: Digital Signage in Mall Atmospherics," *Journal of Consumer and Retail Services* 17, 205–215.

43. Cottet, P., M. C. Lichtlé, and V. Plichon (2006), "The Role of Value in Services: A Study in a Retail Environment" *Journal of Consumer Marketing*, 23, 219–227. Eroglu, S. A., K. Machleit, and T. F. Barr (2005), "Perceived Retail Crowding and Shopper

Satisfaction: The Role of Shopping Values," *Journal of Business Research* 58 (August), 1146–1153.

44. Price, B., and D. Murray (2010), "Match-Up Revisited: The Effect of Staff Attractiveness on Purchase Intentions in Younger Adult Females: Social Comparative and Product Relevance Effects," *Journal of International Business and Economics* 9, 55–76. Koering, S. K., and A. L. Page (2002), "What if Your Dentist Looked Like Tom Cruise? Applying the Match-Up Hypothesis to a Service Encounter," *Psychology & Marketing* 19 (January), 91–110. Grace, D. (2009), "An Examination of Consumer Embarrassment and Repatronage Intentions in the Context of Emotional Service Encounters," *Journal of Retailing and Consumer Services* 16 (January), 1–9.

45. Borges, A., J. C. Chebat, and B. J. Babin (2010), "Does a Companion Always Enhance the Shopping Experience?" *Journal of Retailing and Consumer Services* 17 (July), 294–299. Lim, J., and S. E. Beatty (2010), "Factors Affecting Couples' Decisions to Jointly Shop," *Journal of Business Research* 64 (7), 774–781.

46. Associated Press, "Atlantic City Casinos Struggle Against Tough Economy," http://www.nj.com/news/index.ssf/2010/04/atlantic_city_casinos_struggli.html, accessed October 1, 2015.

47. Heath, C., and J. B. Soll (1996), "Mental Budgeting and Consumer Decisions," *Journal of Consumer Research* 23 (June), 40–52.

48. Wang, Y. J., M. D. Hernandez, and M. S. Minor (2010), "Web Aesthetics Effects on Perceived Online Service Quality and Satisfaction in an e-tail Environment: The Moderating Role of Purchase Task," *Journal of Business Research* 53, 935–942.

49. Michon, R., H. Yu, D. Smith, and J. C. Chebat (2007), "The Shopping Experience of Female Fashion Leaders," *International Journal of Retail and Distribution Management* 35 (6), 488–501. Swinyard, W. R. (1992), "The Effects of Mood, Involvement, and Quality of Store Experience on Shopping Intentions," *Journal of Consumer Research* 20 (September), 271–280.

12

1. Xu, Alison Jing, and Robert W. Wyer, Jr. (2008), "The Effect of Mind-Sets on Consumer Decision Strategies," *Journal of Consumer Research* 34 (4), 556–566.

2. Bagozzi, Richard P., and Utpal Dholakia (1999), "Goal Setting and Goal Striving in Consumer Behavior," *Journal of Marketing* 63 (Special Issue), 19–32.

3. Lawson, Robert (1997), "Consumer Decision Making Within a Goal-Driven Framework," *Psychology & Marketing* 14 (5), 427–449.

4. Luce, Mary Frances, James R. Bettman, and John W. Payne (2001), "Tradeoff Difficulty: Determinants and Consequences for Consumer Decisions," *Monographs of the Journal of Consumer Research Series* 1 (Spring). Menon, Kalyani, and Laurette Dube (2000), "Ensuring Satisfaction by Engineering Salesperson Response to Customer Emotions," *Journal of Retailing* 76 (3), 285–307.

5. Mowen, John C. (1988), "Beyond Consumer Decision Making," *Journal of Consumer Marketing* 5 (1), 15–25.

6. Anonymous (2003), "POP Sharpens Its Focus," *Brandweek* 44 (24), 31–36.

7. Prasad, V. Kanti (1975), "Socioeconomic Product Risk and Patronage Preferences of Retail Shoppers," *Journal of Marketing* 39 (July), 42–47. Dowling, Grahame R., and Richard Staelin (1994),

"A Model of Perceived Risk and Intended Risk-Handling Activity," *Journal of Consumer Research* 21 (1), 119–134.

8. This definition is based on Oliver, Richard (1997), *Satisfaction: A Behavioral Perspective on the Consumer,* New York: McGraw-Hill.

9. O'Brien, Louise, and Charles Jones (1995), "Do Rewards Really Create Loyalty?" *Harvard Business Review* 73 (May/June), 75–82.

10. Keller, Kevin Lane (1998), *Strategic Brand Management: Building, Measuring, and Managing Brand Equity.* Upper Saddle River, NJ: Prentice Hall.

11. Aaker, David A. (1997), *Building Strong Brands,* New York: The Free Press, 21.

12. Olshavsky, Richard W., and Donald H. Granbois (1979), "Consumer Decision Making—Fact or Fiction?" *Journal of Consumer Research* 6 (2), 93–100.

13. Moyer, Don (2007), "Satisficing," *Harvard Business Review* 85 (4), 144. Schwartz, Barry, Andrew Ward, John Monterosso, Sonja Lyubomirsky, Katherine White, and Darrin R. Lehman (2002), "Maximizing versus Satisficing: Happiness Is a Matter of Choice," *Journal of Personality and Social Psychology* 83 (5), 1178–1197.

14. Bruner, Gordon C., III, and Richard J. Pomazal (1988), "Problem Recognition: The Crucial First Stage of the Consumer Decision Process," *Journal of Consumer Marketing* 5 (1), 51–63.

15. Sirgy, Joseph M. (1983), *Social Cognition and Consumer Behavior,* New York: Praeger.

16. Beatty, Sharon, and Scott M. Smith (1987), "External Search Effort: An Investigation Across Several Product Categories," *Journal of Consumer Research* 14 (1), 83–95.

17. Bloch, Peter H., Daniel L. Sherrell, and Nancy M. Ridgway (1986), "Consumer Search: An Extended Framework," *Journal of Consumer Research* 13 (1), 119–126.

18. Lurie, Nicholas H. (2004), "Decision Making in Information-Rich Environments: The Role of Information Structure," *Journal of Consumer Research* 30 (4), 473–487.

19. Punj, Girish, and Richard Brookes (2004), "Decision Constraints and Consideration Set Formation in Consumer Durables," *Psychology & Marketing* 18 (8), 843–864. Shocker, Allan D., Moshe Ben-Akiva, Bruno Boccara, and Prakash Nedungadi (1991), "Consideration Set Influences on Consumer Decision Making and Choice: Issues, Models, and Suggestions," *Marketing Letters* 2 (3), 181–197.

20. Donkers, Bas (2002), "Modeling Consideration Sets Across Time: The Relevance of Past Consideration," in *American Marketing Association Conference Proceedings,* vol. 13, Chicago: American Marketing Association, 322.

21. Hauser, John R., and Birger Wernerfelt (1990), "An Evaluation Cost Model of Consideration Sets," *Journal of Consumer Research* 16 (4), 393–408.

22. Jarvis, Cheryl Burke (1998), "An Exploratory Investigation of Consumers' Evaluations of External Information Sources in Prepurchase Search," in *Advances in Consumer Research,* vol. 25, Joseph W. Alba and J. Wesley Hutchinson, eds, Provo, UT: Association for Consumer Research.

23. Lichtenstein, D. R., N. M. Ridgway, and R. P. Netemeyer (1993), "Price Perceptions and Consumer Shopping Behavior," *Journal of Marketing Research* 30, 234–245.

24. Bickart, Barbara, and Robert M. Schindler (2001), "Internet Forums as Influential Sources of Consumer Information," *Journal of Interactive Marketing* 15 (3), 31–40.

25. Ratchford, Brian T., Myung-Soo Lee, and Debabrata Talukdar (2003), "The Impact of the Internet on Information Search for Automobiles," *Journal of Marketing Research* 40 (2), 193–209.

26. Mathwick, Charla, and Edward Rigdon (2004), "Play, Flow, and the Online Search Experience," *Journal of Consumer Research* 31 (2), 324–332.

27. Ariely, Dan (2000), "Controlling the Information Flow: Effects on Consumers' Decision Making and Preferences," *Journal of Consumer Research* 27 (2), 233–248.

28. Mazursky, David, and Gideon Vinitzky (2005), "Modifying Consumer Search Processes in Enhanced On-Line Interfaces," *Journal of Business Research* 58 (10), 1299–1309.

29. Beatty and Smith (1987).

30. Srinivasan, Narasimhan, and Brian T. Ratchford (1991), "An Empirical Test of a Model of External Search for Automobiles," *Journal of Consumer Research* 18, 233–242. Johnson, Eric J., and Edward J. Russo (1984), "Product Familiarity and Learning New Information," *Journal of Consumer Research* 11, 542–550. Moore, William L., and Donald R. Lehmann (1980), "Individual Differences in Search Behavior for a Nondurable," *Journal of Consumer Research* 7, 296–307.

31. Moorthy, Sridhar, Brian T. Ratchford, and Debabrata Talukdar (1997), "Consumer Information Search Revisited: Theory and Empirical Analysis," *Journal of Consumer Research* 23 (4), 263–277; also see Alba, Joseph W., and J. Wesley Hutchinson (1987), "Dimensions of Consumer Expertise," *Journal of Consumer Research* 13 (4), 411–454.

32. Beatty and Smith (1987).

33. Dowling, G. R., and R. Staelin (1994), "A Model of Perceived Risk and Intended Risk-Handling Activity," *Journal of Consumer Research* 21 (1), 119–134. Dedler, Konrad, I. Gottschalk, and K. G. Grunert (1981), "Perceived Risk as a Hint for Better Information and Better Products," in *Advances in Consumer Research,* vol. 8, Kent Monroe, ed., Ann Arbor, MI: Association for Consumer Research, 391–397.

34. Mehta, Nitin, Surendra Rajiv, and Kannan Srinivasan (2003), "Price Uncertainty and Consumer Search: A Structural Model of Consideration Set Formation," *Marketing Science* 22 (1), 58–84.

35. Hofacker, Charles F., and Jamie Murphy (2009), "Consumer Web Page Search, Clicking Behavior, and Reaction Time," *Direct Marketing: An International Journal* 3 (2), 88–96.

36. Beatty and Smith (1987).

37. Beatty and Smith (1987).

38. Capon, Noel, and Mariane Burke (1980), "Individual, Product Class, and Task-Related Factors in Consumer Information Processing," *Journal of Consumer Research* 7 (3), 314–326. Newman, Joseph, and Richard Staelin (1972), "Prepurchase Information Seeking for New Cars and Major Household Appliances," *Journal of Marketing Research* 7 (August), 249–257.

39. Cobb, Cathy J., and Wayne D. Hoyer (1988), "Direct Observation of Search Behavior in the Purchase of Two Nondurable Products," *Psychology & Marketing* 2 (3), 161–179. Newman and Staelin (1972).

40. Punj, Girish (1987), "Presearch Decision Making in Consumer Durable Purchases," *Journal of Consumer Marketing* 4 (1), 71–83.

41. Reynolds, Kristy E., Judith Anne Garretson Folse, and Michael A. Jones (2006), "Search Regret: Antecedents and Consequences," *Journal of Retailing* 82 (4), 339–348.

13

1. Futrell, Charles M. (2003), *ABCs of Relationship Selling*, 7th ed., Boston: McGraw-Hill.

2. Myers, James H., and Mark Alpert (1968), "Determinant Buying Attitudes: Meaning and Measurement," *Journal of Marketing* 32 (4) (October), 13–20.

3. Williams, Terrell G. (2002), "Social Class Influences on Purchase Evaluation Criteria," *Journal of Consumer Marketing* 19 (2/3), 249–276. Dhar, Ravi, and Klaus Wertenbroch (2000), "Consumer Choice Between Hedonic and Utilitarian Goods," *Journal of Marketing Research* 37 (February), 60–71. Hirschman, Elizabeth C., and S. Krishnan (1981), "Subjective and Objective Criteria in Consumer Choice: An Examination of Retail Store Choice," *Journal of Consumer Affairs* 15 (1), 115–127.

4. Schwartz, Barry (2004), "The Tyranny of Choice," *Scientific American* 290 (4), 70–75.

5. Pham, Michel T., Joel B. Cohen, John W. Pracejus, and G. David Hughes (2001), "Affect Monitoring and the Primacy of Feelings in Judgment," *Journal of Consumer Research* 28 (2), 167–188.

6. Gorn, Gerald J., Marvin E. Goldberg, and Kunal Basu (1993), "Mood, Awareness, and Product Evaluation," *Journal of Consumer Psychology* 2 (3), 237–256.

7. Bakamitsos, Georgios A. (2006), "A Cue Alone or a Probe to Think? The Dual Role of Affect in Product Evaluations," *Journal of Consumer Research* 33 (December), 403–412.

8. Moreau, C. Page, Arthur B. Markman, and Donald R. Lehmann (2001), "What Is It? Categorization Flexibility and Consumers' Responses to Really New Products," *Journal of Consumer Research* 27 (4), 489–498.

9. This discussion based on Alba, Joseph W., and J. Wesley Hutchinson (1987), "Dimensions of Consumer Expertise," *Journal of Consumer Research* 13 (4), 411–454.

10. Johnson, Michael D., and Claes Fornell (1987), "The Nature and Methodological Implications of the Cognitive Representation of Products," *Journal of Consumer Research* 14 (2), 214–228.

11. Viswanathan, Madhubalan, and Terry L. Childers (1999), "Understanding How Product Attributes Influence Product Categorization: Development and Validation of Fuzzy Set-Based Measures of Gradeness in Product Categories," *Journal of Marketing Research* 36 (1), 75–94.

12. Sujan, Mita, and Christine Dekleva (1987), "Product Categorization and Inference Making: Some Implications for Comparative Advertising," *Journal of Consumer Research* 14 (3), 372–378.

13. Dawar, Niraj, and Philip Parker (1994), "Marketing Universals: Consumers' Use of Brand Name, Price, Physical Appearance, and Retailer Reputation as Signals of Product Quality," *Journal of Marketing* 58 (2), 81–95.

14. John, Deborah Roedder, and Mita Sujan (1990), "Age Differences in Product Categorization," *Journal of Consumer Research* 16 (4), 452–460.

15. Alba and Hutchinson (1987).

16. Williams (2002).

17. Bergen, Mark, Shantanu Dutta, and Steven M. Shugan (1996), "Branded Variants: A Retail Perspective," *Journal of Marketing Research* 33 (1), 9–19.

18. Fasolo, Barbara, Gary H. McClelland, and Peter M. Todd (2007), "Escaping the Tyranny of Choice: When Fewer Attributes Make Choice Easier," *Marketing Theory* 7 (1), 13–26.

19. Mitra, Debanjan, and Peter N. Golder (2006), "How Does Objective Quality Affect Perceived Quality?" *Marketing Science* 25 (3), 230–247.

20. Dawar and Parker (1994).

21. Miller, Elizabeth G., and Barbara E. Kahn (2006), "Shades of Meaning: The Effect of Color and Flavor Names on Consumer Choice," *Journal of Consumer Research* 32 (1), 86–92.

22. Jacoby, J., D. E. Speller, and C. A. Kohn (1974), "Brand Choice Behavior as a Function of Information Load: Replication and Extension," *Journal of Consumer Research* 1, 33–41. Malhotra, Naresh K. (1982), "Information Load and Consumer Decision Making," *Journal of Consumer Research* 8, 419–430.

23. Fasolo et al. (2007).

24. Kivetz, Ran, and Itamar Simonson (2000), "The Effects of Incomplete Information on Consumer Choice," *Journal of Marketing Research* 37 (4), 427–448.

25. Hair, Joseph F., Jr., Rolph Anderson, Ronald L. Tatham, and William C. Black, *Multivariate Data Analysis*, 5th ed., Upper Saddle River, NJ: Prentice Hall.

26. Wright, Peter (1975), "Consumer Choice Strategies: Simplifying vs. Optimizing," *Journal of Marketing Research* 12 (February), 60–67.

14

1. Woodruff, Robert B. (1997), "Customer Value: The Next source for Competitive Advantage," *Journal of the Academy of Marketing Science* 25 (2), 139–153.

2. Beverland, M.B., and F. Farrelly (2010), "The Quest for Authenticity in Consumption: Consumers' Purposive Choice of Authentic Cues to Shape Experienced Outcomes," *Journal of Consumer Research* 36 (February), 838–856.

3. McCracken, Grant (1986), "Culture and Consumption: A Theoretical Account of the Structure and Movement of the Cultural Meaning of Consumer Goods," *Journal of Consumer Research* 13 (1), 71–84.

4. Holbrook, Morris B. (2006), "Consumption Experience, Customer Value, and Subjective Personal Introspection: An Illustrative Photographic Essay," *Journal of Business Research* 59, 714–725. Hirschman, Elizabeth C., and Morris B. Holbrook (1983), "Hedonic Consumption: Emerging Concepts, Methods, and Propositions," *Journal of Marketing* 46, 92–101.

5. MacInnis, D., and G.E. deMello (2005), "The Concept of Hope and Its Relevance to Product Evaluations and Choice," *Journal of Marketing* 69 (January), 1–14.

6. Patterson, Paul G., and Richard G. Spreng (1997), "Modeling the Relationship Between Perceived Value, Satisfaction, and Repurchase Intentions in a Business-to-Business, Services Context: An Empirical Investigation," *International Journal of Industry Management* 8 (5), 414–434.

7. The American Consumer Satisfaction Index, www.theacsi.org, accessed July 5, 2014.

8. Jack Neff, "What Scandal? Walmart Rides Low Prices to Regain Mojo," *Advertising Age*, June 4, 2012, 1–19.

9. Stanley Slater, "Developing a Customer Value-Based Theory of the Firm," *Journal of the Academy of Marketing Science*, 25, no. 2 (1997): 162–167.

10. This definition based in part on Westbrook, Robert A., and Richard L. Oliver (1991), "The Dimensionality of Consumption Emotion Patterns and Consumer Satisfaction," *Journal of Consumer Research* 18 (1), 84–91.

11. Babin, Barry J., and Mitch Griffin (1998), "The Nature of Satisfaction: An Updated Examination and Analysis," *Journal of Business Research* 41, 127–136.

12. Oliver, Richard L. (1983), "Measurement and Evaluation of Satisfaction Processes in Retail Settings," *Journal of Retailing* 57 (Fall), 25–48.

13. Churchill, Gilbert A., and Carol J. Surprenant (1982), "An Investigation Into the Determinants of Consumer Satisfaction," *Journal of Marketing Research* 19 (4), 491–504.

14. Zeithaml, Valarie A., Leonard L. Berry, and A. Parasuraman (1993), "The Nature and Determinants of Customer Expectations of Service," *Journal of the Academy of Marketing Science* 21 (1), 1–12.

15. Tse, David K., and Peter C. Wilton (1988), "Models of Consumer Satisfaction Formation: An Extension," *Journal of Marketing Research* 24 (2), 204–212. LaTour, Stephen A., and Nancy C. Peat (1979), "Conceptual and Methodological Issues in Consumer Satisfaction Research," in *Advances in Consumer Research*, vol. 6, William L. Wilkie, ed., Ann Arbor, MI: Association of Consumer Research.

16. Spreng, Richard A., and Thomas J. Page, Jr. (2001), "The Impact of Confidence in Expectations on Consumer Satisfaction," *Psychology & Marketing* 18 (11), 1187–1204.

17. Hoch, Stephen J., and John Deighton (1989), "Managing What Consumers Learn from Experience," *Journal of Marketing* 53 (2), 1–20.

18. For a discussion of this topic, see Carrilat, F. A., J. Fernando, and J. P. Mulki (2007), "The Validity of the SERVQUAL and SERVPREF Scales," *International Journal of Service Industry Management* 18 (May), 472–490. Also see Bebko, C., L. M. Sciulli, and R. K. Garg (2006), "Consumers' Level of Expectations for Services and the Role of Implicit Service Promises," *Services Marketing Quarterly* 28, 1–23.

19. Spreng, Richard A., Scott B. MacKenzie, and Richard W. Olshavsky (1996), "A Reexamination of the Determinants of Consumer Satisfaction," *Journal of Marketing* 60 (3), 15–32.

20. Price, Linda L., Eric J. Arnould, and Patrick Tierney (1995), "Going to Extremes: Managing Service Encounters and Assessing Provider Performance," *Journal of Marketing* 59 (April), 83–97.

21. Adams, J. Stacey (1965), "Inequity in Social Exchange," in *Advances in Experimental Social Psychology*, vol. 2, Richard Berkowitz, ed., New York: Academic Press, 267–299.

22. Barnes, D. C., M. B. Beauchamp, and C. Webster (2010), "To Delight, or Not to Delight? This Is the Question Service Firms Must Address," *Journal of Marketing Theory and Practice* 18 (Summer), 275–283.

23. Wiener, Bernard (2000), "Attributional Thoughts About Consumer Behavior," *Journal of Consumer Research* 27 (3), 382–387.

24. Festinger, L. (1957), *A Theory of Cognitive Dissonance*, Stanford, CA: Stanford University Press.

25. Sweeney, Jillian C., Douglas Hausknecht, and Geoffrey N. Soutar (2000), "Cognitive Dissonance After Purchase: A Multidimensional Scale," *Psychology & Marketing* 17 (5), 369–387.

26. Peter, J. Paul, Gilbert A. Churchill, Jr., and Tom J. Brown (1993), "Caution in the Use of Difference Scores in Consumer Research," *Journal of Consumer Research* 19 (4), 655–662.

27. Babin and Griffin (1998).

28. Adapted from Babin and Griffin (1998).

29. Jacoby, Jacob, Carol K. Berning, and Thomas F. Dietvorst (1977), "What About Disposition?" *Journal of Marketing* 41 (2), 22–28.

30. "What Can Canada Learn From Other Countries to Improve Its Environment Report Card?" material retrieved from Conference Board of Canada website, http://www.conferenceboard.ca/hcp/hot-topics/environment.aspx, accessed May 21, 2012.

31. Statistics Canada (2013), "Waste Management Industry Survey: Business and Government Sectors 2010," *Environment Accounts and Statistics Division, Environmental Protection Accounts and Surveys*, http://www.statcan.gc.ca/pub/16f0023x/16f0023x2013001-eng.pdf, accessed June 26, 2015.

32. Price, Linda L., Eric J. Arnould, and Carolyn Folkman Curasi (2000), "Older Consumers' Disposition of Special Possessions," *Journal of Consumer Research* 27 (2), 179–182.

33. Lastovicka, John L., and Karen V Fernandez (2005), "Three Paths to Disposition: The Movement of Meaningful Possessions to Strangers," *Journal of Consumer Research* 31 (4), 813–823.

34. Coulter, Robin A., and Mark Ligas (2003), "To Retain or to Relinquish: Exploring the Disposition Practices of Packrats and Purgers," *Advances in Consumer Research* 30, 38–43.

15

1. Consumer Policy (2007), "Complain? Why Bother, It's the NHS," *Consumer Policy Review* 17 (September/October), 221. Simos, P. (2005), "Seven Steps to Handle Complaints," *Restaurant Hospitality* 89 (August), 36. Blodgett, J. G., D. H. Granbois, and R.G. Walters (1993), "The Effects of Perceived Justice on Complainants' Negative Word-of-Mouth Behavior and Repatronage Intentions," *Journal of Retailing* 69 (Winter), 399–428.

2. Kalamas, M., M. Laroche, and L. Makdessian (2008), "Reaching the Boiling Point: Consumers' Negative Affective Reactions to Firm-Attributed Service Failures," *Journal of Business Research* 61, 813–824.

3. Voorhees, C. M., M. K. Brady, and D. M. Horowitz (2006), "A Voice From the Silent Masses: An Exploratory and Comparative Analysis of Non-Complaining," *Journal of the Academy of Marketing Science* 34 (September), 513–527.

4. Simos (2005).

5. Voorhees et al. (2006).

6. McColl-Kennedy, J. R., P. G. Patterson, A. K. Smith, and M. K. Brady (2009), "Customer Rage Episodes: Emotions, Expressions and Behaviors," *Journal of Retailing* 85, 222–237.

7. Hart, C. A., J. L. Heskett, and E. W. Sasser (1990), "The Profitable Art of Service Recovery," *Harvard Business Review* 68 (4), 148–156.

8. Romaniuk, J. (2007), "Word of Mouth and the Viewing of Television Programs," *Journal of Advertising Research* 47 (December), 462–470.

9. Morran, Chris (2011), "Complaints Against Airlines Continue to Soar," *Consumerist*, July 7, www.consumerist.com/consumer/complaints, accessed October 5, 2015.

10. Crain, K. (2004), "At CBS, Shades of Audi Debate," *Automotive News* 79 (9/20), 12; Flint, J. (1988), "Hot Seat," *Forbes* 142 (June), 199.

11. See http://www.snopes.com/horrors/food/wormburger.asp for more on this story, accessed October 5, 2015.

12. Blodgett, J. G., D. H. Granbois, and R. G. Walters (1993), "The Effects of Perceived Justice on Complainants' Negative Word-of-Mouth Behavior and Repatronage Intentions," *Journal of Retailing* 69 (Winter), 399–428.

13. Nyer, P. M., and M. Gopinath (2005), "Effects of Complaining Versus Negative WOM on Subsequent Changes in Satisfaction: The Role of Public Commitment," *Psychology & Marketing* 22 (December), 937–953.

14. Lange, F., and M. Dahlen (2006), "Too Much Bad PR Can Make Ads Ineffective," *Journal of Advertising Research* 46 (December), 528–542. Aaker, J., S. Fournier, and B. S. Adam (2004), "When Good Brands Go Bad," *Journal of Consumer Research* 31 (June), 1–16.

15. Lange and Dahlen (2006).

16. Pullig, C., R. C. Netemeyer, and A. Biswas (2006), "Attitude Basis Certainty and Challenge Alignment: A Case of Negative Publicity," *Journal of the Academy of Marketing Science* 34 (Fall), 528–542.

17. Burnham, T. A., J. K. Frels, and V. Mahajan (2003), "Consumer Switching Costs: A Typology, Antecedents and Consequences," *Journal of the Academy of Marketing Science* 31 (Spring), 109–126.

18. Murray, K. B., & Häubl, G. (2007), "Explaining Cognitive Lock-in: The Role of Skill-Based Habits of Use in Consumer Choice," *Journal of Consumer Research* 34 (1), 77–88.

19. Andrews, M. L., R. L. Benedicktus, and M. K. Brady (2010), "The Effect of Incentives on Customer Evaluations of Service Bundles," *Journal of Business Research* 63, 71–76.

20. Antón, C., C. Camarero, and M. Carrero (2007), "The Mediating Effect of Satisfaction on Consumers' Switching Intention," *Psychology & Marketing* 24 (June), 511–538.

21. Jones, M. A., K. E. Reynolds, D. L. Mothersbaugh, and S. E. Beatty (2007), "The Positive and Negative Effects of Switching Costs on Relational Outcomes," *Journal of Services Research* 9 (May), 335–355.

22. Balabanis, G., N. Reynolds, and A. Simintiras (2006), "Base of E-Store Loyalty: Perceived Switching Barriers and Satisfaction," *Journal of Business Research* 59 (February), 214–224.

23. Gourville, J. T. (2006), "Eager Sellers and Stony Buyers: Understanding the Psychology of New-Product Adoption," *Harvard Business Review* 84 (June), 99–106.

24. Magi, A. W. (2003), "Share of Wallet in Retailing: The Effects of Consumer Satisfaction, Loyalty Cards and Shopper Characteristics," *Journal of Retailing* 79 (Summer), 97–106.

25. Shin, Dong H., and Won Y. Kim (2007), "Mobile Number Portability on Customer Switching Behavior: In the Case of the Korean Mobile Market," *Info* 9, 38–54.

26. Wangenheim, F. V. (2005), "Postswitching Negative Word of Mouth," *Journal of Services Research* 8, 67–78.

27. Chiu, H. C., Y. C. Hsieh, Y. C. Li, and L. Monle (2005), "Relationship Marketing and Consumer Switching Behavior," *Journal of Business Research* 58 (December), 1681–1689.

28. Babin, B. J., and J. P. Attaway (2000), "Atmospheric Affect as a Tool for Creating Value and Gaining Share of Customer," *Journal of Business Research* 49 (August), 91–99.

29. Palmatier, R. W., R. P. Dant, D. Grewal, and K. R. Evans (2006), "Factors Influencing the Effectiveness of Relationship Marketing: A Meta-Analysis," *Journal of Marketing* 70 (October), 136–153.

30. Palmatier, R. W., L. K. Scheer, M. B. Houston, K. R. Evans, and S. Gopalakrishna (2007), "Use of Relationship Marketing Programs in Building Customer–Salesperson and Customer–Firm Relationships: Differential Influences on Financial Outcomes," *International Journal of Research in Marketing* 24, 210–223.

16

1. Fullerton, R. A., and G. Punj (2004), "Repercussions of Promoting an Ideology of Consumption: Consumer Misbehavior," *Journal of Business Research* (57), 1239–1249.

2. Fowler, Aubry R., III, Barry J. Babin, and Amy K. Este (2005), "Burning for Fun or Money: Illicit Consumer Behavior in a Contemporary Context," paper presented at the Academy of Marketing Science Annual Conference, May 27, 2005, Tampa, FL.

3. Fullerton and Punj (2004).

4. Fowler et al. (2005).

5. Vitell, Scott J. (2003), "Consumer Ethics Research: Review, Synthesis and Suggestions for the Future," *Journal of Business Ethics* 43 (1/2) (March), 33–47.

6. Babin, Barry J., and Laurie A. Babin (1996), "Effects of Moral Cognitions and Consumer Emotions on Shoplifting Intentions," *Psychology & Marketing* 13 (December), 785–802.

7. Vitell (2003).

8. Hunt, Shelby, and Scott Vitell (1986), "A General Theory of Marketing Ethics," *Journal of Macromarketing* 6 (1) (Spring), 5–16.

9. This section is based on Fullerton and Punj (2004).

10. Merton, Robert (1968), *Social Theory and Social Structure*. New York: Free Press.

11. Hamilton, V. Lee, and David Rauma (1995), "Social Psychology of Deviance and Law," in *Sociological Perspectives on Social Psychology*, Karen S. Cook, Gary A. Fine, and James S. House, eds., Boston: Allyn and Bacon, 524–547.

12. Price Waterhouse Coopers (2007), "Canadian Retail Security Survey 2007," Retail Council of Canada, http://www.pwc.com/en_CA/ca/retail-consumer/publications/canadian-retail-security-survey-2008-en.pdf, accessed May 21, 2012.

13. Cox, Dena, Anthony D. Cox, and George P. Moschis (1990), "When Consumer Behavior Goes Bad: An Investigation of Adolescent Shoplifting," *Journal of Consumer Research* 17 (2) (September), 149–159.

14. Babin and Babin (1996); Webster, Cynthia (2000), "Exploring the Psychodynamics of Consumer Shoplifting Behavior," *American Marketing Association Conference Proceedings* (11), 360–365.

15. Babin, Barry J., and Mitch Griffin (1995), "A Closer Look at the Influence of Age on Consumer Ethics," *Advances in Consumer Research* (22), 668–673.

16. Information obtained from Business Software Alliance website, http://global.bsa.org/internetreport2009/2009internetpiracyreport.pdf, accessed June 30, 2010.

17. Fowler et al. (2005).

18. Shropshire, Corilyn (2007), "Spam Floods Inboxes" *Knight Ridder Tribune Business News* (January 23), 1; Anonymous (2007), "U.S. Branded 'Biggest Spam and Virus Host," *Precision Marketing* (January 26), 9.

19. Online content by Mark Smail (2010), "Are We Risking Our Digital Lives?" Technewsworld.com, http://www.technewsworld.com/story/69145.html, accessed June 30, 2010.

20. Herskovits, Beth (2006), "APA Shows Public How Psychology Fits Into Their Lives," *PR Week* (January 2), 19.

21. Lenhart, Amanda (2010), online presentation "Cyberbullying: What the Research Is Telling Us…" Pew Internet & American Life Project, online content retrieved at http://www.pewinternet.org/Presentations/2010/May/Cyberbullying-2010.aspx, accessed June 30, 2010.

22. Information obtained from Coalition Against Insurance Fraud website, http://www.insurancefraud.org, accessed June 9, 2009.

23. Information obtained from http://www.ftc.gov/bcp/edu/microsites/idtheft/consumers/about-identity-theft.html, accessed June 30, 2010.

24. Dupre, Kathryne, Tim Jones, and Shirley Taylor (2001), "Dealing With the Difficult: Understanding Difficult Behaviors in a Service Encounter," *American Marketing Association Proceedings*, 173–180.

25. Bitner, Mary J., Bernard H. Booms, and Lois Mohr (1994), "Critical Service Encounters: The Employee's Viewpoint," *Journal of Marketing* 58 (4), 95–106.

26. Harris, Lloyd, and Kate L. Reynolds (2003), "The Consequences of Dysfunctional Customer Behavior," *Journal of Service Research* 6 (2) (November), 144–161.

27. Based on Thorne, Scott (2006), "An Exploratory Investigation of the Characteristics of Consumer Fanaticism," *Qualitative Market Research* 9, 51–72. Pimentel, Robert W., and Kristy E. Reynolds (2004), "A Model for Consumer Devotion: Affective Commitment with Proactive Sustaining Behaviors," *Academy of Marketing Science Review* (5) 1–45. Wakefield, Kirk L., and Daniel L. Wann (2006), "An Examination of Dysfunctional Sports Fans: Method of Classification and Relationships with Problem Behaviors," *Journal of Leisure Research* 38, 168–186. Hunt, Kenneth A., Terry Bristol, and R. Edward Bashaw (1999), "A Conceptual Approach to Classifying Sports Fans," *Journal of Services Marketing* 13, 439–449. Saporito, Bill (2004), "Why Fans and Players Are Playing So Rough," *Time* (December 6), 30–35.

28. Reynolds, Kate L., and Lloyd C. Harris (2005), "When Service Failure Is Not Service Failure: An Exploration of the Forms and Motives of 'Illegitimate' Customer Complaining," *Journal of Services Marketing* 19, 321–335.

29. Information obtained from Consumer Products Safety Commission website, http://www.cpsc.gov, accessed March 17, 2008.

30. Stoltman, Jeffrey, and Fed Morgan (1993), "Psychological Dimensions of Unsafe Product Usage," in Rajan Varadarajan and Bernard Jaworski, eds., *Marketing Theory and Applications,* 4th ed., Chicago: American Marketing Association.

31. National Safety Commission (2006), "Road Rage Leads to More Road Rage" (December 6), http://www.nationalsafetycommisson.com, accessed March 17, 2008.

32. Crimmins, Jim, and Chris Callahan (2003), "Reducing Road Rage: The Role of Target Insight in Advertising for Social Change," *Journal of Advertising Research,* (December), 381–390.

33. Bone, Sterling A., and John C. Mowen (2006), "Identifying the Traits of Aggressive and Distracted Drivers: A Hierarchical Trait Model Approach," *Journal of Consumer Behaviour* 5 (5) (September–October), 454–465; also Hennessy, D. A., and

D. L. Wiesenthal (1997), "The Relationship Between Traffic Congestion, Driver Stress, and Direct versus Indirect Coping Behaviors," *Ergonomics* 40, 348–361.

34. Mothers Against Drunk Driving (2008), "The Magnitude of the Alcohol/Drug-Related Crash Problem in Canada: Overview," http://www.madd.ca/english/research/Magnitude%202011(2008%20Stats).pdf, accessed May 21, 2012.

35. Y. Wang, "More People Have Cell Phones Than Toilets, U.N. Study Shows," *TIME.com*, March 25, 2013, http://newsfeed.time.com/2013/03/25/more-people-have-cell-phones-than-toilets-u-n-study-shows/#ixzz2tWBD7ZRW, accessed February 16, 2014.

36. Statistics Canada (2014), "Percentage of Households by Type of Telephone Service, by Province," *The Daily*, June 23, accessed at http://www.statcan.gc.ca/daily-quotidien/140623/t140623a001-eng.htm on May 6, 2015.

37. Statistics in this section are based on online content retrieved at Insurance Institute website, http://www.iii.org/media/hottopics/insurance/cellphones/, accessed July 1, 2010.

38. This information based on online content retrieved at http://www.iihs.org/laws/cellphonelaws.aspx, accessed June 30, 2010.

39. This definition based on O'Guinn, Thomas C., and Ronald J. Faber (1989), "Compulsive Buying: A Phenomenological Exploration," *Journal of Consumer Research* 16 (2) (September), 147–157.

40. Nataraajan, Rajan, and Brent G. Goff (1992), "Manifestations of Compulsiveness in the Consumer–Marketplace Domain," *Psychology & Marketing* 9, 31–44.

41. This definition based on Faber, Ronald, and Thomas O'Guinn (1992), "A Clinical Screener for Compulsive Buying," *Journal of Consumer Research* 19 (3) (December), 459–469.

42. Hirschman, Elizabeth C. (1992), "The Consciousness of Addiction: Toward a General Theory of Compulsive Consumption," *Journal of Consumer Research*, (September), 155–179. O'Guinn and Faber (1989). Dittmar, Helga (2005), "A New Look at Compulsive Buying: Self-Discrepancies and Materialistic Values as Predictors of Compulsive Buying Tendencies," *Journal of Social and Clinical Psychology* (September), 832–859.

43. Joireman, Jeff, Jeremy Kees, and David Sprott (2010), "Concern with Immediate Consequences Magnifies the Impact of Compulsive Buying Tendencies on College Students' Credit Card Debt," *Journal of Consumer Affairs* 44 (1), 155–178.

44. Roberts, James A., Chris Manolis, and John F. Tanner, Jr. (2006), "Adolescent Autonomy and the Impact of Family Structure on Materialism and Compulsive Buying," *Journal of Marketing Theory and Practice* 14 (4) (Fall), 301–314.

45. Roberts, James A. (1998), "Compulsive Buying Among College Students: An Investigation of Its Antecedents, Consequences, and Implications for Public Policy," *Journal of Consumer Affairs* 32 (2) (Winter), 295–319. O'Guinn and Faber (1989).

46. Black, D. W. (2000). "Assessment of compulsive buying," In *I Shop, Therefore I Am: Compulsive Buying and the Search for Self*, A. L. Benson, ed., Northvale, NJ: Jason Aronson, 191–216.

47. Parker-Pope, Jessica (2005), "This Is Your Brain at the Mall: Why Shopping Makes You Feel So Good," *The Wall Street Journal* (December 6), D1.

48. Koran, Lorrin M., Ronald J. Faber, Elias Aboujaoude, Michael D. Large, and Richard T. Serpe (2006), "Estimated Prevalence of Compulsive Buying Behavior in the United States," *The American Journal of Psychiatry* (October), 1806–1812.

49. Yanovski, Susan, and Billinda K. Dubbert (1993), "Association of Binge Eating Disorder and Psychiatric Comorbidity in Obese Subjects," *The American Journal of Psychiatry* (October), 1472–1479.

50. National Institute for Alcohol Abuse and Alcoholism website, http://www.niaaa.nih.gov, accessed March 17, 2008.

51. Information obtained from Mothers Against Drunk Drivers website, http://www.madd.org/Under-21/College/Statistics/AllStats.aspx#STAT_1800, accessed July 2, 2010.

52. Piacentini, Maira G., and Emma N. Banister (2006), "Getting Hammered? … Students Coping with Alcohol," *Journal of Consumer Behaviour* 5 (2) (March–April), 145–156.

53. Wechsler H., J. E. Lee, M. Kuo, M. Seibring, T. F. Nelson, and H. P. Lee (2002), "Trends in College Binge Drinking During a Period of Increased Prevention Efforts: Findings from Four Harvard School of Public Health Study Surveys," *Journal of American College Health* 50, 203–217. Presley, C. A., M. A. Leichliter, and P. W. Meilman (1998), *Alcohol and Drugs on American College Campuses: A Report to College Presidents: Third in a Series, 1995, 1996, 1997,* Carbondale, IL: Core Institute, Southern Illinois University.

54. Shim, Soyeon, and Jennifer Maggs (2005), "A Cognitive and Behavioral Hierarchical Decision-Making Model of College Students' Alcohol Consumption," *Psychology & Marketing* 22 (8) (August), 649 668.

55. This definition based on Netemeyer, Richard G., Scot Burton, Leslie K. Cole, Donald A. Williamson, Nancy Zucker, Lisa Bertman, and Gretchen Diefenbach (1998), "Characteristics and Beliefs Associated with Probable Pathological Gambling: A Pilot Study with Implications for the National Gambling Impact and Policy Commission," *Journal of Public Policy & Marketing* 17 (2) (Fall), 147–160.

56. Balabanis, George (2002), "The Relationship Between Lottery-Ticket and Scratch-Card Buying Behaviour, Personality and Other Compulsive Behaviors," *Journal of Consumer Behaviour* 2 (1) (September), 7–22.

57. Statistics based on information found at National Council on Problem Gambling, http://www.ncpgambling.org/i4a/pages/Index.cfm?pageID=3315#widespread, accessed June 30, 2010.

58. McComb, J. L., and Hanson W. E. (2009), "Problem Gambling on College Campuses," *NASPA Journal* 46 (1), 1–29.

59. Levens, Suzi, Anne-Marie Dyer, Cynthia Zubritsky, Kathryn Knott, and David W. Oslin (2005), "Gambling Among Older, Primary Care Patients," *American Journal of Geriatric Psychiatry* 13, 69–76. Loroz, Peggy Sue (2004), "Golden-Age Gambling: Psychological Benefits and Self-Concept Dynamics in Aging Consumers' Consumption Experiences," *Psychology & Marketing* 25 (1) (May), 323–350.

60. Kwak, Hyokjin, George M. Zinkhan, and Elizabeth P. Lester Roushanzamir (2004), "Compulsive Comorbidity and Its Psychological Antecedents: A Cross-Cultural Comparison Between the U.S. and South Korea," *The Journal of Consumer Marketing* 21, 418–434. Netemeyer, Richard G., Scot Burton, Leslie K. Cole, Donald A. Williamson, Nancy Zucker, Lisa Bertman, and Gretchen Diefenbach (1998), "Characteristics and Beliefs Associated with Probable Pathological Gambling: A Pilot Study with Implications for the National Gambling Impact and Policy Commission," *Journal of Public Policy & Marketing* 17 (2) Fall, 147–160.

61. Partnership for a Drug Free America (2006), "Generation Rx: National Study Confirms Abuse of Prescription and Over-the-Counter Drugs," Partnership for a Drug Free America website, http://www.drugfree.org, accessed March 17, 2008.

62. Online content retrieved at http://www.drugabuse.gov/publications/marijuana-facts-parents-need-to-know/letter-to-parents, accessed October 5, 2015.

63. Karpatkin, Rhoda H. (1999), "Toward a Fair and Just Marketplace for All Consumers: The Responsibilities of Marketing Professionals," Journal of Public Policy & Marketing 18 (1), 118–122.

64. Xia, Lan, Kent B. Monroe, and Jennifer L. Cox (2004), "The Price Is Unfair! A Conceptual Framework of Price Fairness Perceptions," Journal of Marketing 68 (October), 1–15. Campbell, Margaret C. (1999), "Perceptions of Price Fairness: Antecedents and Consequences," Journal of Marketing Research 36 (May), 187–199.

65. Kotler, Philip (1972), "What Consumerism Means for Marketers," Harvard Business Review 50 (May-June), 48–57.

66. McShane, Larry (2009), "Bruce Springsteen Slams Tickmaster Over Working on a Dream Ticket Sales," New York Daily News (online), online content retrieved at http://www.nydailynews.com/gossip/2009/02/04/2009-02-04_bruce_springsteen_slams_ticketmaster_ove.html, accessed June19, 2009.

67. Smith, N. Craig, and Elizabeth Cooper-Martin (1997), "Ethics and Target Marketing: The Role of Product Harm and Consumer Vulnerability," Journal of Marketing 61 (3), 1–20.

68. This definition based on Brown, Tom J., and Peter A. Dacin (1997), "The Company and the Product: Corporate Associations and Consumer Product Responses," Journal of Marketing 61 (1), 68–84.

69. Sen, Sankar, and C. B. Bhattacharya (2001), "Does Doing Good Always Lead to Doing Better? Consumer Reactions to Corporate Social Responsibility," Journal of Marketing Research 38 (2), 225–243.

70. Lantos, Geoffrey P. (2001), "The Boundaries of Strategic Corporate Social Responsibility," Journal of Consumer Marketing 18 (7), 595–630.

71. These assertions are based on several works, including Luo, Xueming, and C. B. Bhattacharya (2006), "Corporate Social Responsibility, Customer Satisfaction, and Market Value," Journal of Marketing 70 (4), 1–18; Lichenstein, Donald R., Minette E. Drumwright, and Bridgette M. Braig (2004), "The Effect of Corporate Social Responsibility on Customer Donations to Corporate-Supported Nonprofits," Journal of Marketing 68 (4), 16–32; Sen and Bhattacharya (2001); Brown, Tom J., and Peter A. Dacin (1997), "The Company and the Product: Corporate Associations and Consumer Product Responses," Journal of Marketing 61 (1), 68–84.

72. Kotler (1972).

73. Ormerod, Heather (2014), "Mind the Gap: Poll Finds Many Canadian Businesses Believe Privacy Is Important but Not Taking Basic Steps to Protect Customer Information," Office of the Privacy Commissioner of Canada, http://blog.priv.gc.ca/index.php/2014/06/19/mind-the-gap-poll-finds-many-canadian-businesses-believe-privacy-is-important-but-not-taking-basic-steps-to-protect-customer-information/, accessed on May 11, 2015.

74. Material from Health Canada's website, http://www.hc-sc.gc.ca/cps-spc/legislation/acts-lois/ccpsa-lcspc/index-eng.php, accessed May 24, 2012.

75. Material from Canadian Council of Motor Transport Administrators website, http://www.ccmta.ca/crss-2015/index.php?lang=en_CA, accessed May 24, 2012.

76. Federal Trade Commission website, http://www.ftc.gov/bcp/conline/pubs/buspubs/ad-faqs.shtm, accessed March 17, 2008.

77. Advertising Standards Canada, http://www.adstandards.com/en/standards/canCodeOfAd Standards.asp, accessed September 5, 2012.

78. American Psychological Association (2004), "Television Advertising Leads to Unhealthy Habits in Children; Says APA Task Force" (February 23), http://www.apa.org/releases/childrenads.html, accessed August 2007.

79. Advertising Standards Canada (2010), "The Broadcast Code for Advertising to Children," http://www.adstandards.com/en/clearance/childrens/broadcastCode-ForAdvertisingToChildren.pdf, accessed May 21, 2012.

80. Privacy Commissioner of Canada (2008), "Draft Resolution on Children's Online Privacy," 30th International Conference on Data Protection and Privacy Commissioners, Strasbourg (October 17), http://www.privacyconference2011.org/htmls/adoptedResolutions/2008_Strasbourg/2008_E4.pdf, accessed May 21, 2012.

81. Fry, Marie-Louis, and Michael Jay Polonsky (2004), "Examining the Unintended Consequences of Marketing," Journal of Business Research 57, 1303–1306.

82. Tybout, Alice M., Brian Sternthal, and Bobby J. Calder (1988), "Information Availability as a Determinant of Multiple-Request Effectiveness," Journal of Marketing Research 20 (August), 280–290. Mowen, John C., and Robert Cialdini (1980), "On Implementing the Door-in-the-Face Compliance Strategy in a Marketing Context," Journal of Marketing Research 17 (May), 253–258. Freedman, Jonathon L., and Scott C. Fraher (1966), "Compliance Without Pressure: The Foot-in-the-Door Technique," Journal of Personality and Social Psychology 4 (August), 195–202.

83. Cialdini, Robert, and David Schroeder (1976), "Increasing Compliance by Legitimizing Paltry Contributions: When Even a Penny Helps," Journal of Personality and Social Psychology 34 (October), 599–604.

84. WOMMA, "Unethical Word-of-Mouth Marketing Strategies," http://www.womma.org/wom101/06/, accessed March 17, 2008.

GLOSSARY

A

ABC approach to attitudes approach that suggests that attitudes encompass one's affect, behaviour, and cognitions toward an object (p. 119)

absolute threshold minimum strength of a stimulus that can be perceived (p. 47)

accommodation state that results when a stimulus shares some but not all of the characteristics that would lead it to fit neatly in an existing category, and consumers must process exceptions to rules about the category (p. 45)

acculturation process by which consumers come to learn a culture other than their natural, native culture (p. 152)

acquisitional shopping activities oriented toward a specific, intended purchase or purchases (p. 214)

action-oriented consumers with a high capacity to self-regulate their behaviour (p. 218)

actual state consumer's perceived current state (p. 238)

adaptation level level of a stimulus to which a consumer has become accustomed (p. 65)

addictive consumption physiological dependency on the consumption of a consumer product (p. 309)

advertiming ad buys that include a schedule which runs the advertisement primarily at times when customers will be most receptive to the message (p. 212)

aesthetic labour effort put forth by employees in carefully managing their appearance as a requisite for performing their job well (p. 95)

affect feelings associated with objects or experienced during events (p. 25)

affect-based evaluation evaluative process wherein consumers evaluate products based on the overall feeling that is evoked by the alternative (p. 251)

affective quality retail positioning that emphasizes a unique environment, exciting decor, friendly employees, and, in general, the feelings experienced in a retail place (p. 215)

age-based microculture people of the same age end up sharing many of the same values and develop similar consumer preferences (p. 168)

aggregation approach approach to studying personality in which behaviour is assessed at a number of points in time (p. 99)

AIO statements activity, interest, and opinion statements that are used in lifestyle studies (p. 109)

antecedent conditions situational characteristics that a consumer brings to a particular information-processing, purchase, or consumption environment (p. 226)

anthropology study in which researchers interpret relationships between consumers and the things they purchase, the products they own, and the activities in which they participate (p. 7)

anthropomorphism giving humanlike characteristics to inanimate objects (p. 46)

anti-loyal consumers consumers who will do everything possible to avoid doing business with a particular marketer (p. 296)

apps mobile application software that runs on devices like smartphones, tablets, and other computer-based tools (p. 193)

aspirational group group of which a consumer desires to become a member (p. 188)

assimilation state that results when a stimulus has characteristics such that consumers readily recognize it as belonging to some specific category (p. 45)

associative network network of mental pathways linking all knowledge within memory; sometimes referred to as a semantic network (p. 73)

atmospherics emotional nature of an environment or the feelings created by the total aura of physical attributes that comprise a physical environment (p. 220)

attention purposeful allocation of information processing capacity toward developing an understanding of some stimulus (p. 42)

attention to social comparison information (ATSCI) individual difference variable that assesses the extent to which a consumer is concerned about how other people react to his or her behaviour (p. 195)

attitude-behaviour consistency extent to which a strong relationship exists between attitudes and actual behaviour (p. 125)

attitude-toward-the-object (ATO) model attitude model that considers three key elements, including beliefs consumers have about salient attributes, the strength of the belief that an object possesses the attribute, and evaluation of the particular attribute (p. 123)

attitude tracking effort of a marketer or researcher to track changes in consumer attitudes over time (p. 128)

attitudes relatively enduring overall evaluations of objects, products, services, issues, or people (p. 118)

attributes product features that deliver a desired consumer benefit (p. 10)

attribute-based evaluation evaluative process wherein alternatives are evaluated across a set of attributes that are considered relevant to the purchase situation (p. 251)

attribute correlation perceived relationship between product features (p. 255)

attribution theory theory that consumers look for the cause of particular consumption experiences when arriving at satisfaction judgments (p. 277)

authenticity being real and genuine and having a history or tradition (p. 268)

autobiographical memories cognitive representation of meaningful events in one's life (p. 94)

autonomic measures responses that are automatically recorded based on either automatic visceral reactions or neurological brain activity (p. 88)

awareness set set of alternatives of which a consumer is aware (p. 240)

B

background music music played below the audible threshold that would make it the centre of attention (p. 222)

balance theory theory that states that consumers are motivated to maintain perceived consistency in the relations found in a system (p. 131)

behavioural economics study of what happens in markets with decision makers who display human limitations and complications (p. 6)

behavioural influence decision-making perspective assumes many consumer decisions are actually learned responses to environmental influences (p. 235)

behavioural intentions model model, developed to improve on the ATO model, that focuses on behavioural intentions, subjective norms, and attitude toward a particular behaviour (p. 126)

behaviourist approach to learning theory of learning that focuses on changes in behaviour due to association, without great concern for the cognitive mechanics of the learning process (p. 53)

benefit perceived favourable result derived from a particular feature (p. 249)

benefits positive results of consumption (p. 4)

big data massive amounts of data available to companies, which can be used to predict customer behaviours (p. 19)

binge drinking consumption of five or more drinks in a single drinking session for men and four or more drinks for women (p. 310)

binge eating consumption of large amounts of food while feeling a general loss of control over food intake (p. 309)

bipolar situation wherein if one feels joy he or she cannot also experience sadness (p. 89)

blue ocean strategy positioning a firm far away from competitors' positions so that it creates an industry of its own and, at least for a time, isolates itself from competitors (p. 34)

body language nonverbal communication cues signalled by somatic responses (p. 159)

boomerang kids young adults, aged 18–34, who move back home with their parents after they graduate from postsecondary education (p. 202)

bounded rationality idea that consumers attempt to act rationally within their information-processing constraints (p. 251)

brand community group of consumers who develop relationships based on shared interests or product usage (p. 188)

brand inertia what occurs when a consumer simply buys a product repeatedly without any real attachment (p. 236)

brand loyalty deeply held commitment to rebuy a product or service regardless of situational influences that could lead to switching behaviour (p. 236)

brand personality collection of human characteristics that can be associated with a brand (p. 106)

BRIC acronym that refers to the collective economies of Brazil, Russia, India, and China (p. 150)

buzz marketing marketing efforts that focus on generating excitement among consumers and that are spread from consumer to consumer (p. 198)

C

CANZUS acronym that refers to the close similarity in values between Canada, Australia, New Zealand, and the United States (p. 152)

central cues information presented in a message about the product itself, its attributes, or the consequences of its use (p. 130)

central route to persuasion path to persuasion found in ELM where the consumer has high involvement, motivation, and/or ability to process a message (p. 130)

chunking process of grouping stimuli by meaning so that multiple stimuli can become one memory unit (p. 72)

circadian cycle rhythm level of energy of the human body that varies with the time of day (p. 211)

classical conditioning change in behaviour that occurs simply through associating some stimulus with another stimulus that naturally causes some reaction; a type of unintentional learning (p. 54)

cognition thinking or mental processes that go on as we process and store things that can become knowledge (p. 25)

cognitive appraisal theory theory proposing that specific types of appraisal thoughts can be linked to specific types of emotions (p. 86)

cognitive dissonance an uncomfortable feeling that occurs when a consumer has lingering doubts about a decision that has occurred (p. 278)

cognitive interference notion that everything else that the consumer is exposed to while trying to remember something is also vying for processing capacity, and thus interfering with memory and comprehension (p. 71)

cognitive organization process by which the human brain assembles sensory evidence into something recognizable (p. 44)

cognitive psychology study of the intricacies of mental reactions involved in information processing (p. 6)

cohort a group of people who have lived the same major experiences in their life (p. 170)

collectivism extent to which an individual's life is intertwined with a large cohesive group (p. 147)

compensatory model attitudinal model wherein low ratings for one attribute are compensated for by higher ratings on another (p. 125)

compensatory rule decision-making rule that allows consumers to select products that may perform poorly on one criterion by compensating for the poor performance on one attribute by good performance on another (p. 257)

competitive intensity number of firms competing for business within a specific category (p. 292)

competitiveness enduring tendency to strive to be better than others (p. 103)

complaining behaviour action that occurs when a consumer actively seeks out someone to share an opinion with regarding a negative consumption event (p. 286)

comprehension the way people cognitively assign meaning to (i.e., understand) things they encounter (p. 59)

compulsive buying chronic, repetitive purchasing that is a response to negative events or feelings (p. 309)

compulsive consumption repetitive, excessive, and purposeful consumer behaviours that are performed as a response to tension, anxiety, or obtrusive thoughts (p. 309)

compulsive shopping repetitive shopping behaviours that are a response to negative events or feelings (p. 309)

conditioned response response that results from exposure to a conditioned stimulus that was originally associated with the unconditioned stimulus (p. 54)

conditioned stimulus object or event that does not cause the desired response naturally but that can be conditioned to do so by pairing with an unconditioned stimulus (p. 54)

confirmatory bias tendency for expectations to guide performance perceptions (p. 275)

conformity result of group influence in which an individual yields to the attitudes and behaviours of others (p. 189)

congruity how consistent the elements of an environment are with one another (p. 221)

conjoint analysis technique used to develop an understanding of the attributes that guide consumer preferences by having consumers compare product preferences across varying levels of evaluative criteria and expected utility (p. 257)

conjunctive rule noncompensatory decision rule where the option selected must surpass a minimum cutoff across all relevant attributes (p. 258)

connected self-schema self-conceptualization of the extent to which a consumer perceives

himself as being an integral part of a group (p. 195)

consideration set alternatives that are considered acceptable for further consideration in decision making (p. 240)

consistency principle principle that states that human beings prefer consistency among their beliefs, attitudes, and behaviours (p. 132)

consumer affect feelings a consumer has about a particular product or activity (p. 87)

consumer behaviour set of value-seeking activities that take place as people go about addressing needs (p. 3)

consumer behaviour as a field of study study of consumers as they go about the consumption process; the science of studying how consumers seek value in an effort to address needs (p. 4)

consumer culture commonly held societal beliefs that define what is socially gratifying (p. 142)

consumer (customer) orientation way of doing business in which the actions and decision making of the institution prioritize consumer value and satisfaction above all other concerns (p. 8)

consumer dissatisfaction mild, negative affective reaction resulting from an unfavourable appraisal of a consumption outcome (p. 272)

consumer ethnocentrism belief among consumers that their ethnic group is superior to others and that the products that come from their native land are superior to other products (p. 153)

consumer inertia situation in which a consumer tends to continue a pattern of behaviour until some stronger force motivates him or her to change (p. 294)

consumer involvement degree of personal relevance a consumer finds in pursuing value from a particular category of consumption (p. 83)

consumer misbehaviour behaviours that are in some way unethical and that potentially harm the self or others (p. 303)

consumer problem behaviour consumer behaviour that is deemed to be unacceptable but that is seemingly beyond the control of the consumer (p. 306)

consumer refuse any packaging that is no longer necessary for consumption to take place or, in some cases, the actual good that is no longer providing value to the consumer (p. 280)

consumer satisfaction mild, positive emotion resulting from a favourable appraisal of a consumption outcome (p. 271)

consumer search behaviour behaviours that consumers engage in as they seek information that can be used to resolve a problem (p. 239)

consumer self-regulation tendency for consumers to inhibit outside, or situational, influences from interfering with shopping intentions (p. 218)

consumer socialization the process through which young consumers develop attitudes and learn skills that help them function in the marketplace (p. 205)

consumer value framework (CVF) consumer behaviour theory that illustrates factors that shape consumption-related behaviours and ultimately determine the value associated with consumption (p. 24)

consumerism activities of various groups to voice concern for, and to protect, basic consumer rights (p. 311)

consumption process by which goods, services, or ideas are used and transformed into value (p. 4)

consumption frequency number of times a product is consumed (p. 266)

consumption process process in which consumers use the product, service, or experience that has been selected (p. 266)

contractualism beliefs about the violation of written (or unwritten) laws (p. 305)

contrast state that results when a stimulus does not share enough in common with existing categories to allow categorization (p. 45)

core societal values (CSV) or cultural values commonly agreed-upon consensus about the most preferable ways of living within a society (p. 147)

corporate social responsibility an organization's activities and status related to its societal obligations (p. 314)

corporate strategy way a firm is defined and its general goals (p. 30)

costs negative results of consumption (p. 4)

counterarguments thoughts that contradict a message (p. 63)

credibility extent to which a source is considered to be both an expert in a given area and trustworthy (p. 63)

crowding density of people and objects within a given space (p. 225)

cultural distance representation of how disparate one nation is from another in terms of their CSVs (p. 151)

cultural norm rule that specifies the appropriate consumer behaviour in a given situation within a specific culture (p. 144)

cultural sanction penalty associated with performing a nongratifying or culturally inconsistent behaviour (p. 144)

customer commitment sense of attachment, dedication, and identification (p. 294)

customer lifetime value (CLV) approximate worth of a customer to a company in economic terms; overall profitability of an individual consumer (p. 37)

customer orientation practice of using sales techniques that focus on customer needs (p. 319)

customer relationship management (CRM) systematic management information system that collects, maintains, and reports detailed information about customers to enable a more customer-oriented managerial approach (p. 24)

customer share portion of resources allocated to one brand from among the set of competing brands (p. 293)

D

deceptive advertising message that omits information that is important in influencing a consumer's buying behaviour and is likely to mislead consumers acting "reasonably" (p. 317)

declarative knowledge cognitive components that represent facts (p. 74)

deficient products products that have little or no potential to create value of any type (p. 312)

demographic analysis a profile of a consumer group based on their demographics (p. 180)

demographics observable, statistical aspects of populations such as age, gender, or income (p. 109)

demographics relatively tangible human characteristics that describe consumers (p. 180)

deontological evaluations evaluations regarding the inherent rightness or wrongness of specific actions (p. 305)

desirable products products that deliver high utilitarian and hedonic value and that benefit both consumers and society in the long run (p. 312)

desired state perceived state for which a consumer strives (p. 238)

desires level of a particular benefit that will lead to a valued end state (p. 276)

determinant criteria criteria that are most carefully considered and directly related to the actual choice that is made (p. 250)

dialects variations of a common language (p. 156)

differentiated marketers firms that serve multiple market segments, each with a unique product offering (p. 12)

diffusion process way in which new products are adopted and spread throughout a marketplace (p. 199)

discretionary (spare) time the days, hours, or minutes that are not required for some compulsory and time-consuming activity (p. 210)

discriminative stimuli stimuli that occur solely in the presence of a reinforcer (p. 55)

disjunctive rule noncompensatory decision rule where the option selected surpasses a relatively high cutoff point on any attribute (p. 258)

dissociative group group to which a consumer does not want to belong (p. 189)

divergence situation in which consumers choose membership in microcultures in an effort to stand out or define themselves from the crowd (p. 166)

door-in-the-face technique ingratiation technique used in personal selling in which a salesperson begins with a major request and then follows with a series of smaller requests (p. 319)

dual coding coding that occurs when two different sensory traces are available to remember something (p. 71)

durable goods goods that are usually consumed over a long period of time (p. 266)

E

ecological factors physical characteristics that describe the physical environment and habitat of a particular place (p. 146)

economics study of production and consumption (p. 5)

ego component in psychoanalytic theory that attempts to balance the struggle between the superego and the id (p. 100)

ego-defensive function of attitudes function of attitudes whereby attitudes work as a defence mechanism for consumers (p. 121)

elaboration extent to which a consumer continues processing a message even after an initial understanding is achieved (p. 77)

elaboration likelihood model attitudinal change model that shows attitudes are changed based on differing levels of consumer involvement through either central or peripheral processing (p. 130)

elasticity reflects how sensitive a consumer is to changes in some product characteristic (p. 33)

elimination-by-aspects (EBA) rule noncompensatory decision rule where the consumer begins evaluating options by first looking at the most important attribute and eliminating any option that does not meet a minimum cutoff point for that attribute and where subsequent evaluations proceed in order of importance until only one option remains (p. 258)

emotional effect on memory relatively superior recall for information presented with mild affective content compared with similar information presented in an affectively neutral way (p. 93)

emotional expressiveness extent to which a consumer shows outward behavioural signs and otherwise reacts obviously to emotional experiences (p. 92)

emotional intelligence awareness of the emotions experienced in a given situation and the ability to control reactions to these emotions (p. 92)

emotional involvement type of deep personal interest that evokes strongly felt feelings simply from the thoughts or behaviour associated with some object or activity (p. 85)

emotions specific psychobiological reactions to human appraisals (p. 85)

encoding process by which information is transferred from working memory to long-term memory for permanent storage (p. 70)

enculturation way a person learns his or her native culture (p. 152)

enduring involvement ongoing interest in some product or opportunity (p. 85)

episodic memory memory for past events in one's life (p. 76)

epistemic shopping activities oriented toward acquiring knowledge about products (p. 214)

equity theory theory that people compare their own level of inputs and outcomes to those of another party in an exchange (p. 276)

ethnic identification degree to which consumers feel a sense of belonging to the culture of their ethnic origins (p. 153)

ethnography qualitative approach to studying consumers that relies on interpretation of artifacts to draw conclusions about consumption (p. 16)

etiquette customary mannerisms consumers use in common social situations (p. 160)

evaluative criteria attributes that consumers consider when reviewing alternative solutions to a problem (p. 249)

even-a-penny-will-help technique ingratiation technique in which a marketing message suggests that even the smallest donation, such as a penny or a dollar, will help a cause (p. 319)

exchange acting out of the decision to give something up in return for something of greater value (p. 4)

exemplar concept within a schema that is the single best representative of some category; schema for something that really exists (p. 75)

expectancy/disconfirmation theory proposes that consumers use expectations as a benchmark against which performance perceptions are judged and this comparison is a primary basis for satisfaction/dissatisfaction (p. 273)

expectations beliefs of what will happen in some future situation (p. 66)

experiential decision-making perspective assumes consumers often make purchases and reach decisions based on the affect, or feeling, attached to the product or behaviour under consideration (p. 234)

experiential shopping recreationally oriented activities designed to provide interest, excitement, relaxation, fun, social interaction, or some other desired feeling (p. 214)

experimental methodology a quantitative approach to research that examines cause-and-effect relationships by measuring changes in one or more key variables, while systematically manipulating and controlling other variables (p. 17)

expertise amount of knowledge that a source is perceived to have about a subject (p. 63)

explicit memory memory that develops when a person is exposed to, attends, and tries to remember information (p. 50)

exposure process of bringing some stimulus within proximity of a consumer so that the consumer can sense it with one of the five human senses (p. 42)

express consent unequivocal opt-in consent from the recipient for a stated communication purpose, which does not require any inference on the part of the organization (p. 316)

extended decision making assumes consumers move diligently through various problem-solving activities in search of the best information that will help them reach a decision (p. 236)

extended family three or more generations of family members (p. 200)

external influences social and cultural aspects of life as a consumer (p. 26)

external search gathering of information from sources external to the consumer such as friends, family, salespeople, advertising, independent research reports, and the Internet (p. 240)

extinction process through which behaviours cease because of lack of reinforcement (p. 56)

F

family household at least two people who are related by blood or marriage who occupy a housing unit (p. 200)

feature performance characteristic of an object (p. 249)

femininity sex role distinction within a group that emphasizes the prioritization of relational variables such as caring, conciliation, and community; core societal value opposite of masculinity (p. 148)

figure object that is intended to capture a person's attention; the focal part of any message (p. 63)

figure–ground distinction notion that each message can be separated into the focal point (figure) and the background (ground) (p. 63)

financial switching costs total economic resources that must be spent or invested as a consumer learns how to obtain value from a new product choice (p. 291)

fit how appropriate the elements of a given environment are (p. 221)

five-factor model multiple-trait perspective that proposes that the human personality consists of five traits: agreeableness, extroversion, openness to experience (or creativity), conscientiousness, and neuroticism (or stability) (p. 105)

flow extremely high emotional involvement in which a consumer is engrossed in an activity (p. 91)

foot-in-the-door technique ingratiation technique used in personal selling in which a salesperson begins with a small request and slowly leads up to one major request (p. 319)

foreground music music that becomes the focal point of attention and can have strong effects on a consumer's willingness to approach or avoid an environment (p. 222)

formal group group in which a consumer officially becomes a member (p. 188)

framing a phenomenon in which the meaning of something is influenced (perceived differently) by the information environment (p. 67)

functional quality retail positioning that emphasizes tangible things like a wide selection of goods, low prices, guarantees, and knowledgeable employees (p. 215)

functional theory of attitudes theory that attitudes perform four basic functions (p. 119)

G

geodemographic techniques techniques that combine data on consumer expenditures and socioeconomic variables with geographic information in order to identify commonalities in consumption patterns of households in various regions (p. 111)

geodemographics study of people based on the fact that people with similar demographics tend to live close to one another (p. 180)

ground background in a message (p. 63)

group influence ways in which group members influence attitudes, behaviours, and opinions of others within the group (p. 186)

guanxi (pronounced *gawn-shi*) Chinese term for a way of doing business in which parties must first invest time and resources in getting to know one another and becoming comfortable with one another before consummating any important deal (p. 150)

guerrilla marketing marketing of a product using unconventional means (p. 198)

H

habitual decision making consumers generally do not seek information at all when a problem is recognized and select a product based on habit (p. 236)

habituation process by which continuous exposure to a stimulus affects the comprehension of, and response to, the stimulus (p. 65)

habitus mental and cognitive structures through which individuals perceive the world based largely on their standing in a social class (p. 177)

hedonic motivation drive to experience something emotionally gratifying (p. 83)

hedonic shopping value worth of an activity because the time spent doing the activity itself is personally gratifying (p. 215)

hedonic value value derived from the immediate gratification that comes from some activity (p. 28)

hierarchical approaches to personality approaches to personality inquiry that assume that personality traits exist at varying levels of abstraction (p. 105)

hierarchy of effects attitude approach that suggests that affect, behaviour, and cognitions form in a sequential order (p. 121)

homeostasis state of equilibrium wherein the body naturally reacts in a way so as to maintain a constant, normal bloodstream (p. 80)

homogamy the finding that most marriages comprise people from similar classes (p. 177)

hope a fundamental emotion evoked by positive, anticipatory appraisals (p. 269)

household decision making process by which decisions are made in household units (p. 200)

household life cycle (HLC) segmentation technique that acknowledges that changes in family composition and income alter household demand for products and services (p. 202)

I

id the personality component in psychoanalytic theory that focuses on pleasure-seeking motives and immediate gratification (p. 100)

ideal point combination of product characteristics that provides the most value to an individual consumer or market segment (p. 34)

idiographic perspective approach to personality that focuses on understanding the complexity of each individual consumer (p. 101)

implicit memory memory for things that a person did not try to remember (p. 50)

implied consent consent that may be reasonably inferred from the action or inaction of the individual (p. 316)

impulsive consumption consumption acts characterized by spontaneity, a diminished regard for consequences, and a need for self-fulfillment (p. 216)

impulsive shopping spontaneous activities characterized by a diminished regard for consequences, spontaneity, and a desire for immediate self-fulfillment (p. 214)

impulsivity personality trait that represents how sensitive a consumer is to immediate rewards (p. 217)

"I'm working for you!" technique technique used by salespeople to create the perception that they are working as hard as possible to close a sale when they really are not doing so (p. 319)

individual difference variables descriptions of how individual consumers differ according to specific traits or patterns of behaviour (p. 98)

individual differences characteristic traits of individuals, including personality and lifestyle (p. 25)

individualism extent to which people are expected to take care of themselves and their immediate families (p. 147)

inept set alternatives in the awareness set that are deemed to be unacceptable for further consideration (p. 240)

inert set alternatives in the awareness set about which consumers are indifferent or do not hold strong feelings (p. 240)

informal group group that has no membership or application requirements and that may have no code of conduct (p. 188)

information intensity amount of information available for a consumer to process within a given environment (p. 67)

information overload situation in which consumers are presented with so much information that they cannot assimilate it all (p. 239)

information processing (or cognitive) perspective approach that focuses on changes in thought and knowledge and how these precipitate behavioural changes (p. 54)

informational influence ways in which a consumer uses the behaviours and attitudes of reference groups as information for making personal decisions (p. 191)

innovativeness degree to which an individual is open to new ideas and tends to be relatively early in adopting new products, services, or experiences (p. 103)

instrumental conditioning type of learning in which a behavioural response can be conditioned through reinforcement— either punishment or rewards associated with undesirable or desirable behaviour (p. 55)

intentional learning process by which consumers set out specifically to learn information devoted to a certain subject (p. 53)

internal influences things that go on inside of the mind and heart of the consumer (p. 25)

internal search retrieval of knowledge stored in memory about products, services, and experiences (p. 240)

interpretive research approach that seeks to explain the inner meanings and motivations associated with specific consumption experiences (p. 15)

involuntary attention attention that is beyond the conscious control of a consumer (p. 52)

involvement the personal relevance toward, or interest in, a particular product (p. 52)

J

just meaningful difference (JMD) smallest amount of change in a stimulus that would influence consumer consumption and choice (p. 49)

just noticeable difference (JND) condition in which one stimulus is sufficiently stronger than another so that someone can actually notice that the two are not the same (p. 48)

judgments mental assessments of the presence of attributes and the consequences associated with those attributes (p. 254)

K

knowledge function of attitudes function of attitudes whereby attitudes allow consumers to simplify decision-making processes (p. 120)

L

learning change in behaviour resulting from some interaction between a person and a stimulus (p. 40)

left skewed when a disproportionate number of observations cluster toward the right end of a scale, as when most people report satisfied or very satisfied (p. 279)

lexicographic rule noncompensatory decision rule where the option selected is thought to perform best on the most important attribute (p. 258)

lifestyles distinctive modes of living, including how people spend their time and money (p. 108)

limited decision making consumers search very little for information and often reach decisions based largely on prior beliefs about products and their attributes (p. 236)

long-term memory repository for all information that a person has encountered (p. 72)

long-term orientation values consistent with Confucian philosophy and a prioritization of future rewards over short-term benefits (p. 149)

loyalty card/program device that keeps track of the amount of purchasing a consumer has had with a given marketer (p. 294)

M

market maven consumer who spreads information about all types of products and services that are available in the marketplace (p. 199)

market orientation organizational culture that embodies the importance of creating value for customers among all employees (p. 8)

market segmentation separation of a market into groups based on the different demand curves associated with each group (p. 32)

marketing multitude of value-producing seller activities that facilitate exchanges between buyers and sellers (p. 6)

marketing concept statement that a firm should focus on consumer needs as a means of achieving long-term success (p. 311)

marketing ethics societal and professional standards of right and fair practices that are expected of marketing managers as they develop and implement marketing strategies (p. 311)

marketing mix combination of product, pricing, promotion, and distribution strategies used to implement a marketing strategy (p. 32)

marketing myopia a common condition in which a company views itself in a product business rather than in a value, or benefits producing, business; in this way, it is short sighted (p. 29)

marketing strategy way a company goes about creating value for customers (p. 29)

marketing tactics ways marketing management is implemented; involves price, promotion, product, and distribution decisions (p. 30)

masculinity role distinction within a group that values assertiveness and control; core societal value opposite of femininity (p. 148)

Maslow's hierarchy of needs a theory of human motivation that describes consumers as addressing a finite set of prioritized needs (p. 82)

matchup hypothesis hypothesis that states that a source feature is most effective when it is matched with relevant products (p. 139)

materialism extent to which material goods have importance in a consumer's life (p. 102)

meaning transference process through which cultural meaning is transferred to a product and on to the consumer (p. 268)

meaningful encoding coding that occurs when information from long-term memory is placed in the working memory and attached to the information in the working memory in a way that the information can be recalled and used later (p. 71)

memory psychological process by which knowledge is recorded (p. 69)

memory trace mental path by which some thought becomes active (p. 73)

mental budgeting memory accounting for recent spending (p. 227)

mere exposure effect that which leads consumers to prefer a stimulus to which they've previously been exposed (p. 50)

message congruity extent to which a message is internally consistent and fits surrounding information (p. 62)

message effects how the appeal of a message and its construction affects persuasiveness (p. 134)

metric equivalence statistical tests used to validate the way people use numbers to represent quantities across cultures (p. 157)

microculture a group of people who share similar values and tastes that are subsumed within a larger culture (p. 164)

modelling process of imitating others' behaviour; a form of observational learning (p. 154)

moderating variable variable that changes the nature of the relationship between two other variables (p. 83)

mood transient and general affective state (p. 87)

mood-congruent judgments evaluations in which the value of a target is influenced in a consistent way by one's mood (p. 87)

mood-congruent recall consumers will remember information better when the mood they are currently in matches the mood they were in when originally exposed to the information (p. 94)

moral beliefs beliefs about the perceived ethicality or morality of behaviours (p. 304)

moral equity beliefs regarding an act's fairness or justness (p. 305)

morals personal standards and beliefs used to guide individual action (p. 314)

motivational research era era in consumer research that focused heavily on psychoanalytic approaches (p. 100)

motivations inner reasons or driving forces behind human actions as consumers are driven to address real needs (p. 80)

multiple store theory of memory theory that explains memory as utilizing three different storage areas within the human brain: sensory, working, and long-term (p. 69)

multiple-trait approach approach in trait research wherein the focus remains on combinations of traits (p. 101)

N

need for cognition refers to the degree to which consumers enjoy engaging in effortful cognitive information processing (p. 103)

negative consent the organization assumes it has consent unless the individual takes action to opt out or deny consent (p. 316)

negative disconfirmation according to the expectancy/disconfirmation approach, a perceived state wherein performance perceptions fall short of expectations (p. 273)

negative public publicity action that occurs when negative WOM spreads on a relatively large scale, possibly even involving media coverage (p. 288)

negative reinforcement removal of harmful stimuli as a way of encouraging behaviour (p. 56)

negative word-of-mouth (negative WOM) action that takes place when consumers pass on negative information about a company from one to another (p. 287)

neuroscience study of the central nervous system including brain mechanisms associated with thoughts, emotion, and behaviour (p. 6)

niche marketing plan wherein a firm specializes in serving one market segment with particularly unique demand characteristics (p. 12)

nodes concepts found in an associative network (p. 74)

nomothetic perspective variable-centred approach to personality that focuses on particular traits that exist across a number of people (p. 101)

noncompensatory rule decision-making rule in which strict guidelines are set prior to selection and any option that does not meet the guidelines is eliminated from consideration (p. 257)

nondurable goods goods that are usually consumed quickly (p. 266)

nonlinear effect a plot of the effect by the amount of crowding, which does not make a straight line (p. 225)

nonverbal communication information passed through some nonverbal act (p. 157)

nostalgia a mental yearning to relive the past associated with emotions related to longing (p. 73)

nuclear family a mother, a father, and a set of siblings (p. 200)

O

olfactory refers to humans' physical and psychological processing of smells (p. 222)

one-to-one marketing plan wherein a different product is offered for each individual customer so that each customer is treated as a segment of one (p. 12)

ongoing search search effort that is not necessarily focused on an upcoming purchase or decision but rather on staying up to date on the topic (p. 239)

opinion leader consumer who has a great deal of influence on the behaviour of others relating to product adoption and purchase (p. 199)

orientation reflex natural reflex that occurs as a response to something threatening (p. 52)

outshopping shopping in a city or town to which consumers must travel rather than in their own hometown (p. 214)

P

paths representations of the association between nodes in an associative network (p. 74)

peer pressure extent to which group members feel pressure to behave in accordance with group expectations (p. 189)

perceived risk perception of the negative consequences that are likely to result from a course of action and the uncertainty of which course of action is best to take (p. 235)

perception consumer's awareness and interpretation of reality (p. 40)

perceptual attributes attributes that are visually apparent and easily recognizable (p. 253)

perceptual map tool used to depict graphically the positioning of competing products (p. 34)

peripheral cues non-product related information presented in a message (p. 131)

peripheral route to persuasion path to persuasion found in ELM where the consumer has low involvement, motivation, and/or ability to process a message (p. 131)

personal elaboration process by which a person imagines himself or herself somehow associating with a stimulus that is being processed (p. 77)

personal shopping value (PSV) overall subjective worth of a shopping activity considering all associated costs and benefits (p. 215)

personality totality of thoughts, emotions, intentions, and behaviours that a person exhibits consistently as he or she adapts to the environment (p. 98)

persuasion attempt to change attitudes (p. 128)

phenomenology qualitative approach to studying consumers that relies on interpretation of the lived experience associated with some aspect of consumption (p. 16)

physical characteristics tangible elements or the parts of a message that can be sensed (p. 61)

planned obsolescence act of planning the premature obsolescence of product models that perform adequately (p. 318)

pleasing products products that provide hedonic value for consumers but may be harmful in the long run (p. 312)

pleasure–arousal–dominance (PAD) scale self-report measure that asks respondents to rate feelings using semantic differential items; acronym stands for pleasure–arousal–dominance (p. 89)

pleasure principle principle found in psychoanalytic theory that describes the factor that motivates pleasure-seeking behaviour within the id (p. 100)

positive-affect–negative-affect scale (PANAS) self-report measure that asks respondents to rate the extent to which they feel one of twenty emotional adjectives (p. 88)

positive disconfirmation according to the expectancy/disconfirmation approach, a perceived state wherein performance perceptions exceed expectations (p. 273)

positive reinforcers reinforcers that take the form of a reward (p. 55)

positive word-of-mouth (positive WOM) action that occurs when consumers spread information from one to another about positive consumption experiences with companies (p. 288)

power distance extent to which authority and privileges are divided among different groups within society and the extent to which these facts of life are accepted by the people within the society (p. 148)

pre-attentive effects learning that occurs without attention (p. 50)

prepurchase search search effort aimed at finding information to solve an immediate problem (p. 239)

price information that signals the amount of potential value contained in a product (p. 241)

primacy effect occurs when the information placed early in a message has the most impact (p. 137)

primary group group that includes members who have frequent, direct contact with one another (p. 187)

priming cognitive process in which context or environment activates concepts and frames thoughts and therefore affects both value and meaning (p. 67)

PRIZM5 popular geodemographic segmentation system developed by Environics Analytics (p. 111)

problem gambling obsession over the thought of gambling and the loss of control over gambling behaviour and its consequences (p. 310)

procedural justice the extent that consumers believe the processes involved in processing a transaction and handling any complaints are fair (p. 284)

procedural switching costs lost time and extended effort spent in learning ways of using some product offering (p. 291)

product potentially valuable bundle of benefits (p. 10)

product categories mental representations of stored knowledge about groups of products (p. 251)

product differentiation marketplace condition in which consumers do not view all competing products as identical to one another (p. 33)

product enthusiasts consumers with very high involvement in some product category (p. 84)

product involvement the personal relevance of a particular product category (p. 84)

product placements products that have been placed conspicuously in movies or television shows (p. 52)

product positioning way a product is perceived by a consumer (p. 34)

production orientation approach where innovation is geared primarily toward making the production process as efficient and economic as possible (p. 12)

productivity orientation represents the tendency for consumers to focus on being productive, making progress, and accomplishing more in less time (p. 103)

prospect theory theory that suggests that a decision, or argument, can be framed in different ways and that the framing affects risk assessments consumers make (p. 67)

prototype schema that is the best representative of some category but that is not represented by an existing entity; conglomeration of the most associated characteristics of a category (p. 75)

psychoanalytic approach to personality approach to personality research, advocated by Sigmund Freud, that suggests personality results from a struggle between inner motives and societal pressures to follow rules and expectations (p. 100)

psychobiological a response involving both psychological and physical human responses (p. 85)

psychographics quantitative investigation of consumer lifestyles (p. 109)

psychology study of human reactions to environments, including behaviour and mental processes (p. 6)

punishers stimuli that decrease the likelihood that a behaviour will persist (p. 56)

purchasing power parity (PPP) total size of the consumer market in each country in terms of total buying power (p. 161)

Q

qualitative research tools means for gathering data in a relatively unstructured way, including case analysis, clinical interviews, and focus group interviews (p. 16)

quality perceived overall goodness or badness of some product (p. 241)

quantitative research approach that addresses questions about consumer behaviour using numerical measurement and analysis tools (p. 16)

quartet of institutions four groups responsible for communicating the CSV through both formal and informal processes from one generation to another: family, school, church, and media (p. 153)

R

rancorous revenge when a consumer yells, insults, and/or makes a public scene in an effort to harm the business in response to an unsatisfactory experience (p. 287)

rational decision-making perspective assumes consumers diligently gather information about purchases, carefully compare various brands of products on salient attributes, and make informed decisions regarding what brand to buy (p. 234)

reality principle the principle in psychoanalytic theory under which the ego attempts to satisfy the id within societal constraints (p. 100)

recency effect occurs when the information placed late in a message has the most impact (p. 137)

reference group individuals who have significant relevance for a consumer and who have an impact on the consumer's evaluations, aspirations, and behaviour (p. 186)

regulatory focus theory consumers orient their behaviour through either a prevention or a promotion focus (p. 81)

relational switching cost emotional and psychological consequences of changing from one brand/retailer/service provider to another (p. 291)

relationship marketing activities based on the belief that the firm's performance is enhanced through repeat business (p. 8)

relationship quality degree of connectedness between a consumer and a retailer, brand, or service provider (p. 25)

relativism beliefs about the social acceptability of an act in a culture (p. 305)

renqing the idea that favours given to another are reciprocal and must be returned (p. 150)

repetition simple mechanism in which a thought is kept alive in short-term memory by mentally repeating the thought (p. 71)

retail personality way a retail store is defined in the mind of a shopper based on the combination of functional and affective qualities (p. 216)

retaliatory revenge when a consumer becomes violent with employees and/or tries to vandalize a business in response to an unsatisfactory experience (p. 287)

retrieval process by which information is transferred back into working memory for additional processing when needed (p. 70)

role conflict a situation involving conflicting expectations based on cultural role expectations (p. 165)

role expectations the specific expectations that are associated with each type of person within a culture or society (p. 145)

S

sales orientation practice of using sales techniques that are aimed at satisfying the salesperson's own needs and motives for short-term sales success (p. 319)

salutary products products that are good for both consumers and society in the long run and that provide high utilitarian value, but no hedonic value (p. 312)

sandwich generation consumers who must take care of both their own children and their aging parents (p. 203)

satisficing using decision-making shortcuts to arrive at satisfactory, rather than optimal, decisions (p. 237)

schema cognitive representation of a phenomenon that provides meaning to that entity (p. 74)

schema-based affect emotions that become stored as part of the meaning for a category (a schema) (p. 94)

script schema representing an event (p. 76)

search regret negative emotions that come from failed search processes (p. 244)

seasonality regularly occurring conditions that vary with the time of year (p. 211)

secondary group group whose members have less frequent contact than that found in a primary group (p. 188)

selective attention process of paying attention to only certain stimuli (p. 46)

selective distortion process by which consumers interpret information in ways that are biased by their previously held beliefs (p. 46)

selective exposure process of screening out certain stimuli and purposely exposing oneself to other stimuli (p. 46)

self-concept totality of thoughts and feelings that an individual has about himself or herself (p. 112)

self-congruency theory theory that proposes that much of consumer behaviour can be explained by the congruence of a consumer's self-concept with the image of typical users of a focal product (p. 114)

self-conscious emotions specific emotions that result from some evaluation or reflection of one's own behaviour, including pride, shame, guilt, and embarrassment (p. 96)

self-esteem positivity of the self-concept that one holds (p. 113)

self-improvement motivation motivation aimed at changing the current state to a level that is more ideal, not at simply maintaining the current state (p. 81)

self-perception theory theory that consumers are motivated to act in accordance with their attitudes and behaviours (p. 275)

semiotics study of symbols and their meanings (p. 112)

sensation consumer's immediate response to a stimulus (p. 42)

sensory memory area in memory where a consumer stores things exposed to one of the five senses (p. 69)

separated self-schema self-conceptualization of the extent to which a consumer perceives herself as distinct and separate from others (p. 195)

serial position effect occurs when the placement of information in a message affects recall of the information (p. 137)

service quality overall goodness or badness of a service experience, which is often measured by SERVQUAL (p. 275)

SERVQUAL instrument for measuring service quality that captures consumers' disconfirmation of service expectations (p. 276)

sex role orientation (SRO) family's set of beliefs regarding the ways in which household decisions are reached (p. 204)

sex roles societal expectations for men and women among members of a cultural group (p. 166)

shaping process through which a desired behaviour is altered over time, in small increments (p. 55)

share of wallet customer share (p. 293)

shopping set of value-producing consumer activities that directly increase the likelihood that something will be purchased (p. 212)

shopping involvement personal relevance of shopping activities (p. 84)

signal attribute that consumer uses to infer something about another attribute (p. 253)

signal theory explains ways in which communications convey meaning beyond the explicit or obvious interpretation (p. 60)

single-trait approach approach in trait research wherein the focus is on one particular trait (p. 101)

situational influences things unique to a time or place that can affect consumer decision making and the value received from consumption (p. 27)

situational involvement temporary interest in some imminent purchase situation (p. 85)

smart agent software software capable of learning an Internet user's preferences and automatically searching out information in selected websites and then distributing it (p. 213)

social class a culturally defined group to which a consumer belongs based on resources like prestige, income, occupation, and education (p. 177)

social comparison a naturally occurring mental personal comparison of the self with a target individual within the environment (p. 226)

social environment elements that specifically deal with the way other people influence consumer decision making and value (p. 26)

social judgment theory theory that proposes that consumers compare incoming information to their existing attitudes about a particular object or issue and that attitude change depends upon how consistent the information is with the initial attitude (p. 133)

social media media through which communication occurs (p. 193)

social networks consumers connecting with each other based on interests, associations, or goals (p. 193)

social networking website website that facilitates online social networking (p. 193)

social power ability of an individual or a group to alter the actions of others (p. 189)

social psychology study that focuses on the thoughts, feelings, and behaviours that people have as they interact with other people (p. 6)

social schema cognitive representation that gives a specific type of person meaning (p. 76)

social stratification the division of society into classes that have unequal access to scarce and valuable resources (p. 178)

socialization learning through observation of and the active processing of information about lived, everyday experience (p. 152)

societal marketing concept marketing concept that marketers should consider not only the wants and needs of consumers but also the needs of society (p. 315)

sociology the study of groups of people within a society, with relevance for consumer behaviour because a great deal of consumption takes place within group settings or is affected by group behaviour (p. 7)

source attractiveness the degree to which a source's physical appearance matches a prototype for beauty and elicits a favourable or desirous response (p. 225)

source effects characteristics of a source that affect the persuasiveness of a message (p. 134)

spreading activation way cognitive activation spreads from one concept (or node) to another (p. 73)

state-oriented consumers with a low capacity to self-regulate their behaviour (p. 218)

status symbols products or objects that are used to signal one's place in society (p. 178)

stealth marketing guerrilla marketing tactic in which consumers do not realize that they are being targeted for a marketing message (p. 198)

stigmatization a situation in which a consumer is marked in some way that indicates their place in society (p. 173)

strategy a planned way of doing something to accomplish a goal (p. 29)

subliminal persuasion behaviour change induced by subliminal processing (p. 47)

subliminal processing way that the human brain deals with very low-strength stimuli, so low that the person has no conscious awareness (p. 47)

superego component in psychoanalytic theory that works against the id by motivating behaviour that matches the expectations and norms of society (p. 100)

support arguments thoughts that further support a message (p. 64)

surrogate consumer consumer who is hired by another to provide input into a purchase decision (p. 199)

susceptibility to interpersonal influence individual difference variable that assesses a consumer's

need to enhance his or her image with others by acquiring and using products, conforming to the expectations of others, and learning about products by observing others (p. 194)

switching times when a consumer chooses a competing choice, rather than the previously purchased choice, on the next purchase occasion (p. 290)

switching costs costs associated with changing from one choice (brand/retailer/service provider) to another (p. 291)

symbolic interactionism perspective that proposes that consumers live in a symbolic environment and interpret the myriad of symbols around them, and that members of a society agree on the meanings of symbols (p. 112)

T

tag small piece of coded information that helps with the retrieval of knowledge (p. 73)

target market identified segment or segments of a market that a company serves (p. 32)

teleological evaluations consumers' assessment of the goodness or badness of the consequences of actions (p. 305)

temporal factors situational characteristics related to time (p. 210)

theory of planned action attitudinal measurement approach that expands upon the behavioural intentions model by including a perceived control component (p. 127)

time pressure urgency to act based on some real or self-imposed deadline (p. 210)

total value concept business practice wherein companies operate with the understanding that products provide value in multiple ways (p. 31)

touchpoints direct contacts between the firm and a customer (p. 9)

tradition customs and accepted ways of everyday behaviour in a given culture (p. 146)

trait distinguishable characteristic that describes one's tendency to act in a relatively consistent manner (p. 101)

trait approach to personality approaches in personality research that focus on specific consumer traits as motivators of various consumer behaviours (p. 101)

translational equivalence two phrases share the same precise meaning in two different cultures (p. 156)

trustworthiness how honest and unbiased the source is perceived to be (p. 63)

U

uncertainty avoidance extent to which a culture is uncomfortable with things that are ambiguous or unknown (p. 149)

unconditioned response response that occurs naturally as a result of exposure to an unconditioned stimulus (p. 54)

unconditioned stimulus stimulus with which a behavioural response is already associated (p. 54)

underlying attributes attributes that are not readily apparent and can be learned only through experience or contact with the product (p. 253)

undifferentiated marketing plan wherein the same basic product is offered to all customers (p. 12)

unintentional learning learning that occurs when behaviour is modified through a consumer–stimulus interaction without any effortful allocation of cognitive processing capacity toward that stimulus (p. 53)

universal set total collection of all possible solutions to a consumer problem (p. 240)

unplanned shopping shopping activity that shares some, but not all, characteristics of truly impulsive consumer behaviour, being characterized by situational memory, a utilitarian orientation, and feelings of spontaneity (p. 216)

utilitarian function of attitudes function of attitudes in which consumers use attitudes as ways to maximize rewards and minimize punishment (p. 120)

utilitarian influence ways in which a consumer conforms to group expectations in order to receive a reward or avoid punishment (p. 191)

utilitarian motivation drive to acquire products that can be used to accomplish something (p. 83)

utilitarian shopping value worth obtained because some shopping task or job is completed successfully (p. 215)

utilitarian value value derived from a product that helps the consumer with some task (p. 27)

V

VALS popular psychographic method in consumer research that divides consumers into groups based on resources and psychological consumer behaviour motivations (p. 109)

value a personal assessment of the net worth obtained from an activity (p. 27)

value co-creation the realization that a consumer is necessary and must play a part in order to produce value (p. 32)

value consciousness the extent to which consumers tend to maximize what they receive from a transaction as compared to what they give (p. 102)

value-expressive function of attitudes function of attitudes whereby attitudes allow consumers to express their core values, self-concept, and beliefs to others (p. 120)

value-expressive influence ways in which consumers internalize a group's values or the extent to which consumers join groups in order to express their own closely held values and beliefs (p. 191)

verbal communication transfer of information through either the literal spoken or written word (p. 156)

viral marketing marketing method that uses online technologies to facilitate WOM by having consumers spread messages through their online conversations (p. 198)

visceral responses certain feeling states that are tied to physical reactions/behaviour in a very direct way (p. 85)

W

want way a consumer goes about addressing a recognized need (p. 4)

Weber's Law law stating that a consumer's ability to detect differences between two levels of the stimulus decreases as the intensity of the initial stimulus increases (p. 48)

word-of-mouth (WOM) information about products, services, and experiences that is transmitted from consumer to consumer (p. 196)

working memory storage area in the memory system where information is stored while it is being processed and encoded for later recall (p. 70)

world teen culture speculation that teenagers around the world are more similar to each other than to people from other generations in the same culture (p. 168)

INDEX

NOTE: Entries in **boldface** are key terms.

G

Gambling, 310–311
Geico, 63
Gender
    acculturation and, 153
    advertising and, 136
    affective quality and, 221
    at car dealerships, 95
    compulsive shopping and, 309
    culture and, 148
    cyberbullying and, 307
    emotional expressiveness and, 92
    household roles, 204
    imbalance in China, 181
    microcultures and, 166–168
    product placements and, 199
    religion and, 173
    scents and, 222
    self-image, 113, 114
    soap and self-esteem case study, 322–323
    social media usage, 193
General Motors (GM), 31–32
Generation microcultures, 170–172
Generation X, 170
Generation Y, 171
Geodemographic techniques, 111
Geodemographics, 180
Germany, 153, 157, 179
Gilt Groupe, 168
Glass, Google, 76, 79
Globalization, 17–18
GM (General Motors), 31–32
Good Housekeeping seal, 265
Google, 19, 155
Google Glass, 79
Google Trends, 198
Gosling, Ryan, 126
Gothic microculture, 179
Green Works, 264–265
Greenwashing, 314
Greetings, 160
Grey Goose, 261–263
Ground, 62–63
Group influence
    categories, 191–192
    defined, 186–187
    differences in susceptibility, 194–196
    household decision making, 200–205
    on product selection, 192
    social power, 189–191
    word-of-mouth, 196–200
Groupon, 194
Growth hacking, 212
Guanxi, 150
Guerilla marketing, 198
Guess, 106
Gupshup, 18

H

Habitual decision making, 236–237
Habituation, 65–66
Habitus, 177
Halal, 173
Hallmark, 106
Harley-Davidson, 107, 109, 188
Harmfulness, product, 313
Harrods of Knightsbridge, 208

Hasselhoff, David, 206
Hayward, Tony, 64
HBC (Hudson's Bay Company), 9–10, 21, 73
Health Canada, 317
Hedonic motivation, 83
Hedonic shopping value, 215, 216–217, 219
Hedonic value
    alternative evaluation and, 250–251
    main discussion, 28–29
    reference groups and, 192, 194
    in South Korea, 196–197
    switching and, 296–297
    See also **Value**
Heider, Fritz, 131
Hemispheric lateralization, 67
**Hierarchical approaches to
    personality**, 105–106
Hierarchy of effects, 121–123
High-involvement hierarchy, 121
Hip-hop microculture, 179
HLC (Household life cycle), 202
Hoarders, 281
Hockey, 97, 166
Hofstede, Geert, 147, 150
Home Alone, 52
Homeostasis, 80–81
Homogamy, 177
Hope, 269–270
Household decision making, 200–205
Household life cycle (HLC), 202
Housing market, 257
Hudson's Bay Company (HBC), 9–10, 21, 73
Human behaviour, consumer behaviour as, 3–4
Humour
    in advertising, 103, 130, 136, 137
    as memory aid, 72
    violence and, 137

I

Id, 100–101
Ideal expectations, 274
Ideal point, 34–35
Ideal self, 113, 188
Ideal social self, 113
Identity theft, 307
Idiographic perspective, 101
IKEA, 37–38
Illegal downloading, 307
Illegal vs. immoral behaviour, 304
Illegitimate complaining, 308
"I'm working for you!" technique,
    319–320
Images as memory aid, 71
Immigrants in Canada, 173–176
Immoral vs. illegal behaviour, 304
Implicit memory, 49–52
Implied consent, 316–317
Impulse purchases, 122
Impulsive consumption, 216
Impulsive shopping, 214, 216–220
Impulsiveness, 104
Impulsivity, 217
Inaction inertia, 220
Income, as demographic variable, 108
Income microcultures, 176–179
India
    immigrants from, 168
    market potential of, 150, 161
    social classes in, 179, 181

Individual differences, defined, 25
Individualism, 147–148, 156
Industrial Revolution museum, 221
Inept set, 240
Inequity, 277
Inert set, 240
Inertia
    brand, 236
    consumer, 294
    inaction, 220
Infiltrating, 199
Informal groups, 188
Information intensity, 67
Information overload, 239–400
Information processing components, 58, 60
**Information processing (or cognitive)
    perspective**, 54
Informational influence, 191
Infosecurity magazine, 321
Ingratiation tactics, 319
Innovations, characteristics of, 11
Innovativeness, 103
Innovators, 200
Instagram, 193, 212
Instrumental conditioning, 54–55
Integrated marketing communications, 72
Intelligence, 64
Intensity
    attention and, 52
    comprehension and, 61, 67
Intentional learning, 53–54
Intentions, 126–127
Internal influences, 25
Internal search, 240
Internationalization, 17–18
Internet
    attacks on, 307
    censorship, 155
    communication via, 134
    counterfeit products on, 272
    filing complaints on, 287, 288
    help with criteria selection on, 254
    impact on consumer behaviour, 18–19
    memes, 126
    piracy, 16, 307
    privacy for children, 318
    product differentiation, 33
    searching on, 242
    shopping on, 83, 213–214, 252, 281
    word-of-mouth on, 197–198
    See also **Social networking websites**
Interpersonal influence. *See* **Group
    influence**
Interpretive research, 15–17
Inuit, 176
Involuntary attention, 52
Involvement
    attention and, 52
    comprehension and, 64
    defined, 52
    hierarchy of effects, 121–122
    memory and, 70
    motivation and, 83–85
    search process and, 242–243
    types of, 84–85
iPad, 238, 282
iPhone, 30–31, 282
Islam, 172, 173, 179, 182
Italy, 168
iWatch, 76, 79, 282

Twitter
  opinion leaders on, 199
  Sharknado movie, 206–207
  statistics, 193
  use of cookies by, 18
Tylenol, 289

U

Uber, 211
UFC (Ultimate Fighting Championship, 184–185
The Ultimate Fighter, 184
Ultimate Fighting Championship (UFC), 184–185
Uncertainty avoidance, 149
Unconditioned response, 54
Unconditioned stimulus, 54
Underlying attributes, 253
Undifferentiated marketing, 12
Unfulfilled aspirations, 305
Unilever, 113, 322–323
Unintentional learning, 53–56
Uniqlo, 17
Unit relations, 132
United Kingdom, 182, 310
United States, 147, 178
Universal set, 240
University selection, 233
Unplanned shopping, 216–217
Utilitarian function of attitudes, 120
Utilitarian influence, 191
Utilitarian motivation, 83
Utilitarian shopping value, 215, 216–217, 219
Utilitarian value
  alternative evaluation and, 250–251
  main discussion, 27–29
  reference groups and, 192, 194
  in South Korea, 196–197
  switching and, 296–297
  See also **Value**

V

VALS, 109–110
Value
  alternative evaluation and, 250–251
  associations and, 77

attitude and, 118–119
consumer behaviour and, 2–3, 4
consumer misbehaviour and, 304
consumer relationships and, 297–298
consumer value framework, 24–27
consumption and, 4, 266–270
cultural, 147–152
customer lifetime value, 35–38
decision making and, 232
defined, 27
emotions and, 85–88
equation, 27, 28
marketing strategy and, 29–32
price vs., 25, 27
reference groups and, 192
satisfaction and, 270–272
from search process, 243
shopping and, 215–216
situations and, 208–209
switching and, 296–297
total value concept, 30–32
types, 27–29
word-of-mouth and, 196–197
Value co-creation, 32
Value consciousness, 102
Value-expressive function of attitudes, 120–121
Value-expressive influence, 191–192
Variety, 251
Verbal communication, 156–157
Vespa, 168
Vicary experiment, 47
Victoria's Secret, 224
Violence appeals, 137
Viral marketing, 198, 206–207
Virtual shopping, 213–214
Viruses, 307
Visceral responses, 85, 86
Vodka case study, 261–263
von Furstenberg, Diane, 113
Vulnerability, consumer, 313
Vuvuzelas, 155

W

Walmart
  Apple vs., 282
  CLV data, 37
  HBC and, 21
  production orientation by, 12

satisfaction rating, 271
value delivered by, 27, 271
wedding promotion by, 64
Wants
  defined, 4
  needs vs., 238–239, 318–319
Waste disposal, 280
Watches, smiling, 44, 46
Wearables, 76, 79
Weber's Law, 48
Webvan, 40
West 49, 185–186
Western Europe, immigrants from, 174
WestJet, 49, 198
White-Bright, 82
Wilson, Chip, 17, 116
Window shopping, 215
Witherspoon, Reese, 229
Word of Mouth Marketing Association (WOMMA), 196, 199, 320
Word-of-mouth (WOM)
  consumer relationship and, 287–290
  interpersonal influence by, 196–200
  as source of expectations, 274
Working memory, 69–70, 72
World teen culture, 168–170, 182–183
Wrangler, 106

Y

Yanai, Tadashi, 17
Yelp, 197
Youppi, 64, 65
YouTube, viral video on, 198

Z

Zeitgest, 65
Zellers Inc., 9–10, 57

KEY CONCEPTS

1-1

Understand the meaning of *consumption* and *consumer behaviour*. Consumption represents the process by which goods, services, or ideas are used and transformed into value. The basic consumer behaviour process includes steps that begin with consumer needs and finish with value. Consumer behaviour—or CB, as it is sometimes called—can be viewed either from the standpoint of human behaviour or as a field of study. In terms of human behaviour, consumer behaviour is the set of value-seeking activities that take place as people go about addressing realized needs. Thus, consumer behaviour captures the things that we do as we try to seek out, purchase, and use goods, products, services, and ideas. Consumer behaviour as a field of study represents the study of consumers as they go about the consumption process. Thus, textbooks, trade literature, and research journals all direct their subject matter toward the behaviour of consumers in an effort to develop consumer behaviour theory.

1-2

Describe how consumers get treated differently in various types of exchange environments. Two market characteristics help explain how customers are treated: competitiveness and dependence. In a competitive market, consumers do not have to put up with poor treatment because some other business will gladly provide a better alternative. Thus, competitive markets drive organizations toward a consumer orientation as a way of surviving in the marketplace. Similarly, an organization that depends on repeat business also must emphasize the creation of valuable exchange relationships with its customers; otherwise, customers will simply go elsewhere the next time they desire that particular good or service.

1-3

Explain the role of consumer behaviour in business and society. Consumer behaviour is clearly an important input to business/marketing strategy. The firm can build value only with an understanding of what exactly leads to a high-value experience. In addition, consumer behaviour knowledge is necessary in understanding how customers view competing firms within a market. Consumer behaviour also is important because it is a force that shapes society. In fact, consumer behaviour helps form society in many ways. Trends (such as the decreasing acceptability of smoking, and the increasing acceptability of using mobile phones in social situations) as well as changes in general marketplace etiquette are all caused by consumers. Finally, knowledge of consumer behaviour is important in making responsible decisions as a consumer. An educated consumer is a more effective consumer.

1-4

Be familiar with basic approaches to studying consumer behaviour. Many people with varied backgrounds study consumer behaviour, bringing many different perspectives involving many different research tools. An

KEY TERMS

anthropology (p. 7) study in which researchers interpret relationships between consumers and the things they purchase, the products they own, and the activities in which they participate

attributes (p. 10) product features that deliver a desired consumer benefit

behavioural economics (p. 6) study of what happens in markets with decision makers who display human limitations and complications

benefits (p. 4) positive results of consumption

big data (p. 19) massive amounts of data available to companies, which can be used to predict customer behaviours

cognitive psychology (p. 6) study of the intricacies of mental reactions involved in information processing

consumer behaviour (p. 3) set of value-seeking activities that take place as people go about addressing needs

consumer behaviour as a field of study (p. 4) study of consumers as they go about the consumption process; the science of studying how consumers seek value in an effort to address needs

consumer (customer) orientation (p. 8) way of doing business in which the actions and decision making of the institution prioritize consumer value and satisfaction above all other concerns

consumption (p. 4) process by which goods, services, or ideas are used and transformed into value

costs (p. 4) negative results of consumption

CHAPTER REVIEW 1

differentiated marketers (p. 12) firms that serve multiple market segments, each with a unique product offering

economics (p. 5) study of production and consumption

ethnography (p. 16) qualitative approach to studying consumers that relies on interpretation of artifacts to draw conclusions about consumption

exchange (p. 4) acting out of the decision to give something up in return for something of greater value

experimental methodology (p. 17) a quantitative approach to research that examines cause-and-effect relationships by measuring changes in one or more key variables, while systematically manipulating and controlling other variables

interpretive research (p. 15) approach that seeks to explain the inner meanings and motivations associated with specific consumption experiences

market orientation (p. 8) organizational culture that embodies the importance of creating value for customers among all employees

marketing (p. 6) multitude of value-producing seller activities that facilitate exchanges between buyers and sellers

neuroscience (p. 6) study of the central nervous system including brain mechanisms associated with thoughts, emotion, and behaviour

niche marketing (p. 12) plan wherein a firm specializes in serving one market segment with particularly unique demand characteristics

one-to-one marketing (p. 12) plan wherein a different product is offered for each individual customer so that each customer is treated as a segment of one

interpretive approach seeks to explain the inner meanings and motivations associated with specific consumption experiences. Interpretive research usually involves qualitative research tools such as case analyses, clinical interviews, focus group interviews, and others where data are gathered in a relatively unstructured way. Quantitative research addresses questions about consumer behaviour using numerical measurement and analysis tools. The measurement is usually structured, meaning the consumer simply chooses a response from among alternatives supplied by the researcher.

1-5

Describe why consumer behaviour is so dynamic and how recent trends affect consumers. Consumer behaviour is ever changing. Several trends are shaping today's consumer climate, including increasing internationalization of the marketplace, the rate of technological innovation, changing communications, big data, and changes in demographics that affect buying power and quality of life. Consumer research continues to evolve along with these changes.

phenomenology (p. 16) qualitative approach to studying consumers that relies on interpretation of the lived experience associated with some aspect of consumption

product (p. 10) potentially valuable bundle of benefits

production orientation (p. 12) approach where innovation is geared primarily toward making the production process as efficient and economic as possible

psychology (p. 6) study of human reactions to environments, including behaviour and mental processes

qualitative research tools (p. 16) means for gathering data in a relatively unstructured way, including case analysis, clinical interviews, and focus group interviews

quantitative research (p. 16) approach that addresses questions about consumer behaviour using numerical measurement and analysis tools

relationship marketing (p. 8) activities based on the belief that the firm's performance is enhanced through repeat business

social psychology (p. 6) study that focuses on the thoughts, feelings, and behaviours that people have as they interact with other people

sociology (p. 7) the study of groups of people within a society with relevance for consumer behaviour because a great deal of consumption takes place within group settings or is affected by group behaviour

touchpoints (p. 9) direct contacts between the firm and a customer

undifferentiated marketing (p. 12) plan wherein the same basic product is offered to all customers

want (p. 4) way a consumer goes about addressing a recognized need

KEY CONCEPTS

2-1

Describe the consumer value framework, including its basic components. The consumer value framework (CVF) represents consumer behaviour theory, illustrating factors that shape consumption-related behaviours and that ultimately determine the value associated with consumption. Value lies at the heart of the CVF. Value results from the consumption process, which represents the decision-making process of consumers seeking value. This process is influenced directly and indirectly by external and internal influences such as culture and psychology, respectively. When high value results, consumers may become loyal and build relationships. The CVF is useful for organizing consumer behaviour knowledge both in theory and in practice.

2-2

Define consumer value and compare and contrast two key types of value. Value is a personal assessment of the net worth—that is, benefits minus the costs—obtained from an activity. Value is what consumers ultimately pursue because valuable actions address motivations that manifest themselves in needs and desires. In this sense, value captures how much gratification a consumer receives from consumption. Activities and objects that lead to high utilitarian value do so because they help the consumer accomplish some task. Utilitarian value is how the consumer solves jobs that come along with being a consumer. The second type of value is hedonic value, which is the net worth obtained from the experience itself and the emotions associated with consumption. Hedonic value represents the immediate gratification that comes from some activity or experience. Hedonic value is very emotional and subjective in contrast to utilitarian value. However, the best consumption experiences offer some levels of both types of value.

Value = What you get — What you give

2-3

Apply the concepts of marketing strategy and marketing tactics to describe the way firms go about creating value for consumers. A marketing strategy is the way a company goes about creating value for customers. Thus, strategy and value go hand in hand. Marketing strategy is most effective when a firm adopts the total value concept. The total value concept is practised when companies operate with the understanding that products provide value in multiple ways. Many products and brands, for instance, provide benefits that produce utilitarian value and some that provide hedonic value.

KEY TERMS

affect (p. 25) feelings associated with objects or experienced during events

blue ocean strategy (p. 34) positioning a firm far away from competitors' positions so that it creates an industry of its own and, at least for a time, isolates itself from competitors

cognition (p. 25) thinking or mental processes that go on as we process and store things that can become knowledge

consumer value framework (CVF) (p. 24) consumer behaviour theory that illustrates factors that shape consumption-related behaviours and ultimately determine the value associated with consumption

corporate strategy (p. 30) way a firm is defined, and its general goals

customer lifetime value (CLV) (p. 37) approximate worth of a customer to a company in economic terms; overall profitability of an individual consumer

customer relationship management (CRM) (p. 24) systematic management information system that collects, maintains, and reports detailed information about customers to enable a more customer-oriented managerial approach

elasticity (p. 33) reflects how sensitive a consumer is to changes in some product characteristic

external influences (p. 26) social and cultural aspects of life as a consumer

hedonic value (p. 28) value derived from the immediate gratification that comes from some activity

ideal point (p. 34) combination of product characteristics that provides the most value to an individual consumer or market segment

individual differences (p. 25) characteristic traits of individuals, including personality and lifestyle

internal influences (p. 25) things that go on inside of the mind and heart of the consumer

market segmentation (p. 32) separation of a market into groups based on the different demand curves associated with each group

marketing mix (p. 32) combination of product, pricing, promotion, and distribution strategies used to implement a marketing strategy

marketing myopia (p. 29) a common condition in which a company views itself in a product business rather than in a value, or benefits producing, business; in this way, it is short sighted

marketing strategy (p. 29) way a company goes about creating value for customers

marketing tactics (p. 30) ways marketing management is implemented; involves price, promotion, product, and distribution decisions

perceptual map (p. 34) tool used to depict graphically the positioning of competing products

product differentiation (p. 33) marketplace condition in which consumers do not view all competing products as identical to one another

product positioning (p. 34) way a product is perceived by a consumer

relationship quality (p. 25) degree of connectedness between a consumer and a retailer, brand, or service provider

situational influences (p. 27) things unique to a time or place that can affect consumer decision making and the value received from consumption

2-4

Explain the way market characteristics such as market segmentation and product differentiation affect marketing strategy.
Market segmentation is the separation of a market into groups based on the different demand curves associated with each group. Product differentiation is a marketplace condition in which consumers do not view all competing products as identical to one another. Thus, if multiple segments are offered a unique product that closely matches their particular desires, all segments can receive high value. These characteristics affect the value consumers take from consumption. Individual market segments represent groups of consumers with similar tastes and thus receive value in much the same way as the other.

2-5

Analyze consumer markets using elementary perceptual maps.
Positioning refers to the way a product is perceived by a consumer. This can be represented by the amount and types of characteristics perceived. A perceptual map is a standard marketing tool that can be used to depict the positioning of competing products graphically. Consumer ideal points also can be located on a perceptual map. Perceptual mapping can help marketers identify competitors, analyze the potential effect associated with changing the marketing mix, and spot opportunities in the marketplace.

2-6

Justify consumers' lifetime value as an effective focus for long-term business success.
Customer lifetime value (CLV) represents the approximate worth of a customer to a company in economic terms. Put another way, CLV is the overall profitability of an individual consumer. Thus, marketers can maximize the value they receive from exchange by concentrating their marketing efforts on consumers with high CLVs. From a business standpoint, firms that adopt the CLV as an important outcome are consumer oriented in the long term.

social environment (p. 26) elements that specifically deal with the way other people influence consumer decision making and value

strategy (p. 29) a planned way of doing something to accomplish a goal

target market (p. 32) identified segment or segments of a market that a company serves

total value concept (p. 31) business practice wherein companies operate with the understanding that products provide value in multiple ways

utilitarian value (p. 27) value derived from a product that helps the consumer with some task

value (p. 27) a personal assessment of the net worth obtained from an activity

value co-creation (p. 32) the realization that a consumer is necessary and must play a part in order to produce value

KEY CONCEPTS

3-1

Define learning and perception and how the two are connected. Perception can be thought of as a consumer's awareness and interpretation of reality. Perception essentially represents one's subjective reality. During the perceptual process, consumers are exposed to stimuli, devote attention to stimuli, and attempt to comprehend the stimuli. Exposure refers to the process of bringing some stimulus within the proximity of a consumer so that it can be sensed by one of the five human senses. Attention is the purposeful allocation of information processing capacity toward developing an understanding of some stimulus. Comprehension occurs when the consumer attempts to derive meaning from information that is received.

3-2

List and define phases of the consumer perception process. Consumers develop perceptions through the perceptual process. The perceptual process consists of three stages: sensing some stimuli by seeing, hearing, smelling, tasting, or touching; organizing the input from these human senses; and reacting as a result of this organization. This perceptual process allows consumers to interpret stimuli.

3-3

Apply the concept of the just noticeable difference (JND). The just noticeable difference (JND) represents how much stronger one stimulus is relative to another so that someone can actually notice the two are not the same. The key to using the JND concept is to realize that when some positive change is made to a stimulus, the best strategy is usually to make the change in a big enough increment that consumers notice something has changed. When some negative change must be made, marketers may consider small incremental changes that are less likely to be noticed.

3-4

Contrast the concepts of implicit and explicit memory. Implicit memory is memory for things that a person did not try to remember. Thus, when someone learns something after only a simple exposure to a stimulus, implicit memory is the explanation. Pre-attentive processes like mere exposure can produce implicit memory. Information processing and cognitive learning result in explicit memory, whereby a consumer actively tries to remember the stimuli to which he or she has been exposed.

3-5

Know ways to help get a consumer's attention. Attention is the purposeful allocation of information processing capacity toward developing an understanding of some stimulus. Consumer attention can be enhanced in a number of ways. These include the use of stronger stimuli, contrast, movement, and surprise.

KEY TERMS

absolute threshold (p. 47) minimum strength of a stimulus that can be perceived

accommodation (p. 45) state that results when a stimulus shares some but not all of the characteristics that would lead it to fit neatly in an existing category, and consumers must process exceptions to rules about the category

anthropomorphism (p. 46) giving humanlike characteristics to inanimate objects

assimilation (p. 45) state that results when a stimulus has characteristics such that consumers readily recognize it as belonging to some specific category

attention (p. 42) purposeful allocation of information processing capacity toward developing an understanding of some stimulus

behaviourist approach to learning (p. 53) theory of learning that focuses on changes in behaviour due to association, without great concern for the cognitive mechanics of the learning process

classical conditioning (p. 54) change in behaviour that occurs simply through associating some stimulus with another stimulus that naturally causes some reaction; a type of unintentional learning

cognitive organization (p. 44) process by which the human brain assembles sensory evidence into something recognizable

conditioned response (p. 54) response that results from exposure to a conditioned stimulus that was originally associated with the unconditioned stimulus

conditioned stimulus (p. 54) object or event that does not cause the desired response naturally but that can be conditioned to do so by pairing with an unconditioned stimulus

contrast (p. 45) state that results when a stimulus does not share enough in common with existing categories to allow categorization

discriminative stimuli (p. 55) stimuli that occur solely in the presence of a reinforcer

explicit memory (p. 50) memory that develops when a person is exposed to, attends, and tries to remember information

exposure (p. 42) process of bringing some stimulus within proximity of a consumer so that the consumer can sense it with one of the five human senses

extinction (p. 56) process through which behaviours cease because of lack of reinforcement

implicit memory (p. 50) memory for things that a person did not try to remember

information processing (or cognitive) perspective (p. 54) perspective that focuses on changes in thought and knowledge and how these precipitate behavioural changes

instrumental conditioning (p. 55) type of learning in which a behavioural response can be conditioned through reinforcement—either punishment or rewards associated with undesirable or desirable behaviour

intentional learning (p. 53) process by which consumers set out specifically to learn information devoted to a certain subject

involuntary attention (p. 52) attention that is beyond the conscious control of a consumer

involvement (p. 52) the personal relevance toward, or interest in, a particular product

3-6

Understand key differences between intentional and unintentional learning. Learning is a change in behaviour. Learning takes place in one of two ways. Either consumers learn things without trying to do so, or they actively expend some effort. The first approach corresponds more to a behavioural theory of learning, while the second approach corresponds more closely to an information processing, or cognitive learning, perspective. Learning without trying only requires that a consumer be exposed to a stimulus. In contrast, the information processing perspective requires active learning and the ability to pay attention to information.

just meaningful difference (JMD) (p. 49) smallest amount of change in a stimulus that would influence consumer consumption and choice

just noticeable difference (JND) (p. 48) condition in which one stimulus is sufficiently stronger than another so that someone can actually notice that the two are not the same

learning (p. 40) change in behaviour resulting from some interaction between a person and a stimulus

mere exposure effect (p. 50) that which leads consumers to prefer a stimulus to which they've previously been exposed

negative reinforcement (p. 56) removal of harmful stimuli as a way of encouraging behaviour

orientation reflex (p. 52) natural reflex that occurs as a response to something threatening

perception (p. 40) consumer's awareness and interpretation of reality

positive reinforcers (p. 55) reinforcers that take the form of a reward

pre-attentive effects (p. 50) learning that occurs without attention

product placements (p. 52) products that have been placed conspicuously in movies or television shows

punishers (p. 56) stimuli that decrease the likelihood that a behaviour will persist

selective attention (p. 46) process of paying attention to only certain stimuli

selective distortion (p. 46) process by which consumers interpret information in ways that are biased by their previously held beliefs

selective exposure (p. 46) process of screening out certain stimuli and purposely exposing oneself to other stimuli

sensation (p. 42) consumer's immediate response to a stimulus

shaping (p. 55) process through which a desired behaviour is altered over time, in small increments

subliminal persuasion (p. 47) behaviour change induced by subliminal processing

subliminal processing (p. 47) way that the human brain deals with very low-strength stimuli, so low that the person has no conscious awareness

unconditioned response (p. 54) response that occurs naturally as a result of exposure to an unconditioned stimulus

unconditioned stimulus (p. 54) stimulus with which a behavioural response is already associated

unintentional learning (p. 53) learning that occurs when behaviour is modified through a consumer–stimulus interaction without any effortful allocation of cognitive processing capacity toward that stimulus

Weber's law (p. 48) law stating that a consumer's ability to detect differences between two levels of the stimulus decreases as the intensity of the initial stimulus increases

CHAPTER REVIEW

4

Comprehension, Memory, and Cognitive Learning

KEY CONCEPTS

4-1

Identify factors that influence consumer comprehension.
Comprehension refers to the interpretation or understanding that a consumer develops about some attended stimulus. From an information processing perspective, comprehension results after a consumer is exposed to and attends to some information. Several factors influence comprehension, including characteristics of the message, characteristics of the receiver, and characteristics of the environment. Multiple aspects of each of these factors come together to shape what things mean in the mind of the consumer.

4-2

Explain how knowledge, meaning, and value are inseparable using the multiple store memory theory. The multiple store theory of memory explains how processing information involves three sensory, working (short-term), and long-term memory. Everything sensed is recorded by sensory memory, but the record lasts too short a time to develop meaning. A small portion of this information is passed to the working memory, where already known concepts are retrieved from long-term memory and attached to new stimuli in a process known as meaningful encoding. All meaning is stored in an associative network residing in long-term memory. This network of knowledge links together concepts in a way that explains why things have value. Thus, value is rooted in meaning.

4-3

Understand how the mental associations that consumers develop are a key to learning. Chunking is a way that multiple stimuli can become one memory unit. Chunking is related to meaningful encoding in that meaning can be used to facilitate this process. A group of randomly arranged letters is likely to be difficult to chunk. In this case, seven letters are seven memory units. Arranged into a word, however, such as *meaning*, the seven become one memory unit. Marketers who aid chunking are better able to convey information to consumers. The things that become associated with a brand are the things that will shape the brand's value and meaning.

4-4

Use the concept of associative networks to map relevant consumer knowledge. An associative network, sometimes referred to as a semantic network, is the network of mental pathways linking all knowledge within memory. Associative networks can be drawn similarly to the way a road map would be constructed. All nodes are linked to all other nodes through a series of paths. Nodes with high strength tend to become conscious together based on their high strength of association.

KEY TERMS

adaptation level (p. 65) level of a stimulus to which a consumer has become accustomed

associative network (p. 73) network of mental pathways linking all knowledge within memory; sometimes referred to as a semantic network

chunking (p. 72) process of grouping stimuli by meaning so that multiple stimuli can become one memory unit

cognitive interference (p. 71) notion that everything else that the consumer is exposed to while trying to remember something is also vying for processing capacity and thus interfering with memory and comprehension

comprehension (p. 59) the way people cognitively assign meaning to (i.e., understand) things they encounter

counterarguments (p. 63) thoughts that contradict a message

credibility (p. 63) extent to which a source is considered to be both an expert in a given area and trustworthy

declarative knowledge (p. 74) cognitive components that represent facts

dual coding (p. 71) coding that occurs when two different sensory traces are available to remember something

elaboration (p. 77) extent to which a consumer continues processing a message even after an initial understanding is achieved

encoding (p. 70) process by which information is transferred from working memory to long-term memory for permanent storage

episodic memory (p. 76) memory for past events in one's life

CHAPTER REVIEW 4

exemplar (p. 75) concept within a schema that is the single best representative of some category; schema for something that really exists

expectations (p. 66) beliefs of what will happen in some future situation

expertise (p. 63) amount of knowledge that a source is perceived to have about a subject

figure (p. 63) object that is intended to capture a person's attention; the focal part of any message

figure-ground distinction (p. 63) notion that each message can be separated into the focal point (figure) and the background (ground)

framing (p. 67) a phenomenon in which the meaning of something is influenced (perceived differently) by the information environment

ground (p. 63) background in a message

habituation (p. 65) process by which continuous exposure to a stimulus affects the comprehension of, and response to, the stimulus

information intensity (p. 67) amount of information available for a consumer to process within a given environment

long-term memory (p. 72) repository for all information that a person has encountered

meaningful encoding (p. 71) coding that occurs when information from long-term memory is placed in the working memory and attached to the information in the working memory in a way that the information can be recalled and used later

memory (p. 69) psychological process by which knowledge is recorded

memory trace (p. 73) mental path by which some thought becomes active

message congruity (p. 62) extent to which a message is internally consistent and fits surrounding information

4-5

Apply the cognitive schema concept in understanding how consumers react to products, brands, and marketing agents. A schema is the cognitive representation of a phenomenon that provides meaning to that entity. Thus, products and brands have schemas. To the extent that a new product or brand can share the same "nodes" or characteristics with an existing brand, consumers will more easily understand what the product does. Category exemplars and prototypes often provide the comparison standard for new brands. In addition, consumers react initially to service providers based on how much they match the expected social schema for that particular category of person.

multiple store theory of memory (p. 69) theory that explains memory as utilizing three different storage areas within the human brain: sensory, working, and long-term

nodes (p. 74) concepts found in an associative network

nostalgia (p. 73) a mental yearning to relive the past associated with emotions related to longing

paths (p. 74) representations of the association between nodes in an associative network

personal elaboration (p. 77) process by which a person imagines himself or herself somehow associating with a stimulus that is being processed

physical characteristics (p. 61) tangible elements or the parts of a message that can be sensed

priming (p. 67) cognitive process in which context or environment activates concepts and frames thoughts and therefore affects both value and meaning

prospect theory (p. 67) theory that suggests that a decision, or argument, can be framed in different ways and that the framing affects risk assessments consumers make

prototype (p. 75) schema that is the best representative of some category but that is not represented by an existing entity; conglomeration of the most associated characteristics of a category

repetition (p. 71) simple mechanism in which a thought is kept alive in short-term memory by mentally repeating the thought

retrieval (p. 70) process by which information is transferred back into working memory for additional processing when needed

schema (p. 74) cognitive representation of a phenomenon that provides meaning to that entity

script (p. 76) schema representing an event

sensory memory (p. 69) area in memory where a consumer stores things encountered by one of the five senses

signal theory (p. 60) explains ways in which communications convey meaning beyond the explicit or obvious interpretation

social schema (p. 76) cognitive representation that gives a specific type of person meaning

spreading activation (p. 73) way cognitive activation spreads from one concept (or node) to another

support arguments (p. 64) thoughts that further support a message

tag (p. 73) small piece of coded information that helps with the retrieval of knowledge

trustworthiness (p. 63) how honest and unbiased the source is perceived to be

working memory (p. 70) storage area in the memory system where information is stored while it is being processed and encoded for later recall

KEY CONCEPTS

5-1

Understand what initiates human behaviour. Human behaviour, meaning the actions of a consumer, is initiated by the realization that something is needed either to maintain one's current status or to improve one's life status. The concept of homeostasis captures this phenomenon. Consumer motivations are the inner reasons or driving forces behind human actions as consumers are driven to address real needs. Needs are the first stage in the consumption process, which is in the centre of the customer value framework.

5-2

Classify basic consumer motivations. Consumer motivations can be classified a number of ways. Maslow's hierarchy of needs provides a classification mechanism by which consumer needs are prioritized. The most basic needs are physical, followed by needs for safety, belongingness, esteem and status, and self-actualization, respectively. Additionally, consumer motivations can be usefully divided into two groups: utilitarian motivations drive the pursuit of utilitarian value, and hedonic motivations drive the pursuit of hedonic value.

5-3

Describe consumer emotions and demonstrate how they help shape value. Emotions are psychobiological reactions to human appraisals. Emotions are considered psychobiological because they involve psychological processing and physical responses. Emotions result from cognitive appraisals, and each emotion creates visceral responses so that they are tied to behaviour in a very direct way. The close link between emotion and behaviour means that marketing success is determined by the emotions that consumption creates because consumers value positive emotional experiences. Emotions are particularly closely linked to hedonic value.

5-4

Apply different approaches to measuring consumer emotions. Several different approaches for measuring emotion exist. Because of the visceral nature of emotion, autonomic measures can capture emotional experience by sensing changes in the body chemistry, such as sweating or neurological activity. Unfortunately, such measures are usually obtrusive and interfere with the natural experience of emotion. Therefore, self-report approaches such as the positive-affect–negative-affect scale (PANAS) and pleasure–arousal–dominance (PAD) scale are popular for assessing consumer emotion. The PANAS assumes that positive and negative emotion can be experienced separately to some extent, while the PAD scale assumes that emotions such as pleasure and displeasure are bipolar opposites.

5-5

Understand how different consumers express emotions in different ways. Several individual difference characteristics influence

KEY TERMS

aesthetic labour (p. 95) effort put forth by employees in carefully managing their appearance as a requisite for performing their job well

autobiographical memories (p. 94) cognitive representation of meaningful events in one's life

autonomic measures (p. 88) responses that are automatically recorded based on either automatic visceral reactions or neurological brain activity

bipolar (p. 89) situation wherein if one feels joy he or she cannot also experience sadness

cognitive appraisal theory (p. 86) theory proposing that specific types of appraisal thoughts can be linked to specific types of emotions

consumer affect (p. 87) feelings a consumer has about a particular product or activity

consumer involvement (p. 83) degree of personal relevance a consumer finds in pursuing value from a particular category of consumption

emotional effect on memory (p. 93) relatively superior recall for information presented with mild affective content compared with similar information presented in an affectively neutral way

emotional expressiveness (p. 92) extent to which a consumer shows outward behavioural signs and otherwise reacts obviously to emotional experiences

emotional intelligence (p. 92) awareness of the emotions experienced in a given situation and the ability to control reactions to these emotions

emotional involvement (p. 85) type of deep personal interest that evokes strongly felt feelings simply from the thoughts or behaviour associated with some object or activity

emotions (p. 85) specific psychobiological reactions to human appraisals

enduring involvement (p. 85) ongoing interest in some product or opportunity

flow (p. 91) extremely high emotional involvement in which a consumer is engrossed in an activity

hedonic motivation (p. 83) drive to experience something emotionally gratifying

homeostasis (p. 80) state of equilibrium wherein the body naturally reacts in a way so as to maintain a constant, normal bloodstream

Maslow's hierarchy of needs (p. 82) a theory of human motivation that describes consumers as addressing a finite set of prioritized needs

moderating variable (p. 83) variable that changes the nature of the relationship between two other variables

mood (p. 87) transient and general affective state

mood-congruent judgments (p. 87) evaluations in which the value of a target is influenced in a consistent way by one's mood

mood-congruent recall (p. 94) consumers will remember information better when the mood they are currently in matches the mood they were in when originally exposed to the information

motivations (p. 80) inner reasons or driving forces behind human actions as consumers are driven to address real needs

pleasure–arousal–dominance (PAD) scale (p. 89) self-report measure that asks respondents to rate feelings using semantic differential items

the way consumers react emotionally and react to emotions in consumption situations. For example, high levels of the personality trait neuroticism tend to lead to consumers experiencing relatively high levels of negative emotion. Additionally, in any given consumption situation, consumers are likely to vary in emotional involvement. Consumers with high emotional involvement can experience intense emotions during consumption and can even reach the level of a flow experience. Furthermore, consumers have different levels of emotional expressiveness. Although men and women tend to experience the same amounts of emotion, women tend to be more emotionally expressive. Very highly involved consumers can obtain flow experiences. These experiences create a great deal of value. Computer activities like gaming and Facebook typify these flow experiences.

5-6

Define and apply the concepts of schema-based affect and emotional contagion.
Perhaps no concept better illustrates how emotion and cognition are "wired" together than schema-based affect. Schema-based affect represents the fact that emotions become stored as part of the meaning for any category or thing. The feelings associated with a category are activated along with the activation of the schema. When a brand schema becomes associated with high levels of positive affect, the brand has high brand equity. Similarly, a brand that is associated with high levels of negative schema-based affect is probably in trouble. Negative self-conscious emotions such as embarrassment, guilt, shame, and regret can be particularly important in motivating consumer behaviour.

positive-affect–negative-affect scale (PANAS) (p. 88) self-report measure that asks respondents to rate the extent to which they feel one of 20 emotional adjectives

product enthusiasts (p. 84) consumers with very high involvement in some product category

product involvement (p. 84) the personal relevance of a particular product category

psychobiological (p. 85) a response involving both psychological and physical human responses

regulatory focus theory (p. 81) consumers orient their behaviour through either a prevention or a promotion focus

schema-based affect (p. 94) emotions that become stored as part of the meaning for a category (a schema)

self-conscious emotions (p. 96) specific emotions that result

from some evaluation or reflection of one's own behaviour, including pride, shame, guilt, and embarrassment

self-improvement motivation (p. 81) motivation aimed at changing the current state to a level that is more ideal, not at simply maintaining the current state

shopping involvement (p. 84) personal relevance of shopping activities

situational involvement (p. 85) temporary interest in some imminent purchase situation

utilitarian motivation (p. 83) drive to acquire products that can be used to accomplish something

visceral responses (p. 85) certain feeling states that are tied to physical reactions/behaviour in a very direct way

CHAPTER REVIEW

Personality, Lifestyles, and the Self-Concept

KEY CONCEPTS

6-1

Define personality and know how various approaches to studying personality can be applied to consumer behaviour. Personality can be defined as "the totality of thoughts, emotions, intentions, and behaviours that people exhibit consistently as they adapt to their environment." There are several different ways to study the human personality. Freud's psychoanalytic approach received considerable attention in the early days of consumer research. Trait theory, wherein researchers examine specific traits that relate to consumption, has also received much research attention. With this approach, consumer researchers have focused on both single- and multiple-trait perspectives. The five-factor model is a popular multiple-trait model. The personology approach combines both motivational theory and personality.

6-2

Discuss major traits that have been examined in consumer research. Value consciousness refers to the tendency of consumers to be highly focused on receiving value in their purchases. Materialism refers to the extent to which material goods have importance in a consumer's life. Consumers who are relatively materialistic view possessions as a means to achieving happiness and symbols of success. Innovativeness refers to the degree to which an individual is open to new ideas and tends to be relatively early in adopting new products, services, or experiences. Innovativeness has been shown to relate to a number of consumer behaviours, including new product adoption, novelty seeking, information seeking, and online shopping. Need for cognition refers to the degree to which consumers enjoy engaging in effortful cognitive information processing. Consumers who have a high degree of need for cognition think carefully about products, problems, and advertisements. They also tend to pay close attention to the quality of arguments in ads. Competitiveness refers to the extent to which consumers strive to be better than others.

6-3

Understand why lifestyles and psychographics are important to the study of consumer behaviour. Given that lifestyle concepts give marketers much valuable information about consumers, lifestyle studies have been popular with consumer researchers for many years. Purchase patterns are often influenced heavily by consumer lifestyles, and for this reason marketers often target consumers based on lifestyles. Psychographics, the quantitative investigation of consumer lifestyles, is well suited to help marketers in this process. Both VALS and PRIZM5 represent important psychographic techniques. The great advantage of lifestyles and psychographics is the ability to capture information in a specific, relevant consumer context.

KEY TERMS

aggregation approach (p. 99) approach to studying personality in which behaviour is assessed at a number of points in time

AIO statements (p. 109) activity, interest, and opinion statements that are used in lifestyle studies

brand personality (p. 106) collection of human characteristics that can be associated with a brand

competitiveness (p. 103) enduring tendency to strive to be better than others

demographics (p. 109) observable, statistical aspects of populations such as age, gender, or income

ego (p. 100) component in psychoanalytic theory that attempts to balance the struggle between the superego and the id

five-factor model (p. 105) multiple-trait perspective that proposes that the human personality consists of five traits: agreeableness, extroversion, openness to experience (or creativity), conscientiousness, and neuroticism (or stability)

geodemographic techniques (p. 111) techniques that combine data on consumer expenditures and socioeconomic variables with geographic information in order to identify commonalities in consumption patterns of households in various regions

hierarchical approaches to personality (p. 105) approaches to personality inquiry that assume that personality traits exist at varying levels of abstraction

id (p. 100) the personality component in psychoanalytic theory that focuses on pleasure-seeking motives and immediate gratification

idiographic perspective (p. 101) approach to personality that focuses on understanding the complexity of each individual consumer

individual difference variables (p. 98) descriptions of how individual consumers differ according to specific traits or patterns of behaviour

innovativeness (p. 103) degree to which an individual is open to new ideas and tends to be relatively early in adopting new products, services, or experiences

lifestyles (p. 108) distinctive modes of living, including how people spend their time and money

materialism (p. 102) extent to which material goods have importance in a consumer's life

motivational research era (p. 100) era in consumer research that focused heavily on psychoanalytic approaches

multiple-trait approach (p. 101) approach in trait research wherein the focus remains on combinations of traits

need for cognition (p. 103) the degree to which consumers enjoy engaging in effortful cognitive information processing

nomothetic perspective (p. 101) variable-centred approach to personality that focuses on particular traits that exist across a number of people

personality (p. 98) totality of thoughts, emotions, intentions, and behaviours that a person exhibits consistently as he or she adapts to the environment

pleasure principle (p. 100) principle found in psychoanalytic theory that describes the factor that motivates pleasure-seeking behaviour within the id

PRIZM5 (p. 111) popular geodemographic segmentation system developed by Environics Analytics

6-4

Comprehend the role of the self-concept in consumer behaviour. The self-concept, defined as "the totality of thoughts and feelings that an individual has about himself or herself," is another important topic in consumer behaviour research. Consumers are motivated to act in accordance with their self-concepts, and for this reason, several product choices can be related to the self-concept. A consumer can hold a number of different concepts about the self, including the actual self, the ideal self, the social self, the ideal social self, the possible self, and the extended self.

6-5

Understand the concept of self-congruency and how it applies to consumer behaviour issues. Self-congruency theory helps explain why a consumer is motivated to purchase products that match his or her self-concept. Consumers often desire to buy products that match their own self-concepts, and marketers segment markets based on the match between consumer self-concept and product attributes.

productivity orientation (p. 103) represents the tendency for consumers to focus on being productive, making progress, and accomplishing more in less time

psychoanalytic approach to personality (p. 100) approach to personality research, advocated by Sigmund Freud, that suggests personality results from a struggle between inner motives and societal pressures to follow rules and expectations

psychographics (p. 109) quantitative investigation of consumer lifestyles

reality principle (p. 100) the principle in psychoanalytic theory under which the ego attempts to satisfy the id within societal constraints

self-concept (p. 112) totality of thoughts and feelings that an individual has about himself or herself

self-congruency theory (p. 114) theory that proposes that much of consumer behaviour can be explained by the congruence of a consumer's self-concept with the image of typical users of a focal product

self-esteem (p. 113) positivity of the self-concept that one holds

semiotics (p. 112) study of symbols and their meanings

single-trait approach (p. 101) approach in trait research wherein the focus is on one particular trait

superego (p. 100) component in psychoanalytic theory that works against the id by motivating behaviour that matches the expectations and norms of society

symbolic interactionism (p. 112) perspective that proposes that consumers live in a symbolic environment and interpret the myriad of symbols around them, and that members of a society agree on the meanings of symbols

trait (p. 101) distinguishable characteristic that describes one's tendency to act in a relatively consistent manner

trait approach to personality (p. 101) approaches in personality research that focus on specific consumer traits as motivators of various consumer behaviours

VALS (p. 109) popular psychographic method in consumer research that divides consumers into groups based on resources and consumer behaviour motivations

value consciousness (p. 102) the extent to which consumers tend to maximize what they receive from a transaction as compared to what they give

KEY CONCEPTS

7-1

Define attitudes and describe attitude components. Consumer attitudes are relatively enduring evaluations of objects, products, services, issues, or people. Attitudes have three components. (1) A cognitive component consists of the beliefs that consumers have about products and their features. (2) The affective component consists of the feelings that consumers have about the product and its features. (3) A behavioural component describes how consumers act toward the object in question.

7-2

Describe the functions of attitudes. Several functions of attitudes have been presented, including the utilitarian, ego-defensive, value-expressive, and knowledge functions. The utilitarian function refers to the use of attitudes to gain something that is valued. The ego-defensive function refers to the use of attitudes to protect oneself from harm. The value-expressive function refers to the use of attitudes to express a consumer's core beliefs and self-image. The knowledge function refers to the use of attitudes to simplify consumer decision making.

7-3

Understand how the hierarchy of effects concept applies to attitude theory. The hierarchy of effects approach explains the process through which beliefs, affect, and behaviour occur. These hierarchies depend upon the consumer's buying situation. In a high-involvement context, consumer beliefs are formed, followed by affect, and finally by behaviour. Low-involvement, experiential, and behavioural influence hierarchies are also quite frequent in consumer behaviour.

7-4

Comprehend the major consumer attitude models. Two major approaches to measuring consumer attitudes were presented in this chapter: the attitude-toward-the-object (ATO) and behavioural intentions models. The ATO model includes three key elements: salient beliefs, strength of beliefs, and evaluation of attributes. The behavioural intentions model includes two key elements: attitude toward a behaviour and subjective norms. These models are commonly used by consumer researchers who focus on understanding the elements that comprise consumer attitudes. The approaches are also useful for marketing managers who develop marketing campaigns.

7-5

Describe attitude change theories and their role in persuasion. A number of major approaches to changing attitudes were presented in this chapter. The first approach focuses on the ATO model. According to this approach, attitudes can be changed by changing the strength of beliefs

KEY TERMS

ABC approach to attitudes (p. 119) approach that suggests that attitudes encompass one's affect, behaviour, and cognitions (or "beliefs") toward an object

attitude-behaviour consistency (p. 125) extent to which a strong relationship exists between attitudes and actual behaviour

attitude-toward-the-object (ATO) model (p. 123) attitude model that considers three key elements, including beliefs consumers have about salient attributes, the strength of the belief that an object possesses the attribute, and evaluation of the particular attribute

attitude tracking (p. 128) effort of a marketer or researcher to track changes in consumer attitudes over time

attitudes (p. 118) relatively enduring overall evaluations of objects, products, services, issues, or people

balance theory (p. 131) theory that states that consumers are motivated to maintain perceived consistency in the relations found in a system

behavioural intentions model (p. 126) model, developed to improve on the ATO model, that focuses on behavioural intentions, subjective norms, and attitude toward a particular behaviour

central cues (p. 130) information presented in a message about the product itself, its attributes, or the consequences of its use

central route to persuasion (p. 130) path to persuasion found in elaboration likelihood model (ELM) where the consumer has high involvement, motivation, and/or ability to process a message

compensatory model (p. 125) attitudinal model wherein low ratings for one attribute are compensated for by higher ratings on another

consistency principle (p. 132) principle that states that human beings prefer consistency among their beliefs, attitudes, and behaviours

ego-defensive function of attitudes (p. 121) function of attitudes whereby attitudes work as defence mechanisms for consumers

elaboration likelihood model (p. 130) attitudinal change model that shows attitudes are changed based on differing levels of consumer involvement through either central or peripheral processing

functional theory of attitudes (p. 119) theory that attitudes perform four basic functions

hierarchy of effects (p. 121) attitude approach that suggests that affect, behaviour, and cognitions form in a sequential order

knowledge function of attitudes (p. 120) function of attitudes whereby attitudes allow consumers to simplify decision-making processes

matchup hypothesis (p. 139) hypothesis that states that a source feature is most effective when it is matched with relevant products

message effects (p. 134) how the appeal of a message and its construction affects persuasiveness

peripheral cues (p. 131) non-product related information presented in a message

peripheral route to persuasion (p. 131) path to persuasion found in ELM where the consumer has low involvement, motivation, and/or ability to process a message

persuasion (p. 128) attempt to change attitudes

about attributes, by adding new beliefs to the attitude equation, by changing the evaluation of attributes, or by altering the schema-based affect for the brand/object. The second approach was the behavioural influence approach, which focuses on changing behaviours directly. The third approach was the schema-based affect approach, which focuses on changing affect found in product schemas. The fourth approach was the balance theory approach, which suggests that consumers seek consistency in systems that comprise three elements: the observer, another person, and an object. Attitudes toward an object are affected by the perceived relations found with the system. The fifth approach was the elaboration likelihood model (ELM), which suggests that persuasion occurs as the result of processing within one of two routes: a central route and a peripheral route. In high-involvement situations, the central route is activated, and in low-involvement situations, the peripheral route is activated. Attitude change is usually longer lasting when persuasion occurs in the central route. The sixth and final approach to attitude change was the social judgment theory approach, which suggests that an incoming message is compared to an initial attitudinal position and an assimilation or contrast effect occurs depending on the perceived closeness of the incoming message to the original attitude.

7-6

Understand how message and source effects influence persuasion. Both source and message effects play important roles in persuasion. Message effects include issues related to the overall content and construction of the message. Sex appeals, humorous appeals, fear appeals, and violence appeals are all used frequently by marketers. Source effects, or effects that are attributed to the spokesperson or company, are also important. Source effects include source credibility, source likeability, source attractiveness, and source meaningfulness.

primacy effect (p. 137) occurs when the information placed early in a message has the most impact

recency effect (p. 137) occurs when the information placed late in a message has the most impact

serial position effect (p. 137) occurs when the placement of information in a message affects recall of the information

social judgment theory (p. 133) theory that proposes that consumers compare incoming information to their existing attitudes about a particular object or issue and that attitude change depends upon how consistent the information is with the initial attitude

source effects (p. 134) characteristics of a source that affect the persuasiveness of a message

theory of planned action (p. 127) attitudinal measurement approach that expands upon the behavioural intentions model by including a perceived control component

utilitarian function of attitudes (p. 120) function of attitudes in which consumers use attitudes as ways to maximize rewards and minimize punishment

value-expressive function of attitudes (p. 120) function of attitudes whereby attitudes allow consumers to express their core values, self-concept, and beliefs to others

KEY CONCEPTS

8-1
Understand how culture provides the true meaning of objects and activities. Culture is the set of commonly held societal beliefs that define what behaviours are socially gratifying among a societal group. These societal beliefs are sometimes referred to as core societal values (CSVs), or cultural values. These beliefs frame everyday life and provide a reference point with which to judge behaviours. Acceptable behaviours become norms of the society, and when consumers act inconsistently with these norms, they face negative repercussions in the form of cultural sanctions. Culturally consistent behaviours are rewarded and are thus associated with greater value than culturally inconsistent behaviours.

8-2
Use the key dimensions of core societal values to apply the concept of cultural distance. Five key CSV dimensions are discussed in the chapter: individualism–collectivism, power distance, masculinity–femininity, uncertainty avoidance, and long-term orientation. Societies that share similar CSV profiles, like the CANZUS nations, tend to have low cultural distance. In contrast, societies with very different profiles, such as the CANZUS nations compared to most Arab nations, have high cultural distance. Chances are that high cultural distance means consumers in those different cultures find value in significantly different behaviours. Therefore, cultural distance may be at least as important as geographic distance when a company is facing a decision about serving a foreign market. Cultural difference can be computed using a simple distance formula described in the

Inputs and Outputs of Culture

chapter. Consumer markets that are close culturally should find value in the same sorts of products and brands.

8-3
Define acculturation and enculturation. Acculturation and enculturation are two important consumer socialization processes. Acculturation is the process by which consumers come to learn a culture other than their natural, native culture. Enculturation is the process by which consumers learn their native culture. In both cases, the learning takes place through both formal and informal methods. Much of this learning occurs through the process of modelling. Modelling means that consumers try to mimic the behaviour of others within the societal group.

KEY TERMS

acculturation (p. 152) process by which consumers come to learn a culture other than their natural, native culture

body language (p. 159) nonverbal communication cues signalled by somatic responses

BRIC (p 150) acronym that refers to the collective economies of Brazil, Russia, India, and China

CANZUS (p. 152) acronym that refers to the close similarity in values between Canada, Australia, New Zealand, and the United States

collectivism (p. 147) extent to which an individual's life is intertwined with a large cohesive group

consumer culture (p. 142) commonly held societal beliefs that define what is socially gratifying

consumer ethnocentrism (p. 153) belief among consumers that their ethnic group is superior to others and that the products that come from their native land are superior to other products

core societal values (CSV) or cultural values (p. 147) commonly agreed-upon consensus about the most preferable ways of living within a society

cultural distance (p. 151) representation of how disparate one nation is from another in terms of their CSVs

cultural norm (p. 144) rule that specifies the appropriate consumer behaviour in a given situation within a specific culture

cultural sanction (p. 144) penalty associated with performing a nongratifying or culturally inconsistent behaviour

dialects (p. 156) variations of a common language

ecological factors (p. 146) physical characteristics that describe the physical environment and habitat of a particular place

enculturation (p. 152) way a person learns his or her native culture

ethnic identification (p. 153) degree to which consumers feel a sense of belonging to the culture of their ethnic origins

etiquette (p. 160) customary mannerisms consumers use in common social situations

femininity (p. 148) sex role distinction within a group that emphasizes the prioritization of relational variables such as caring, conciliation, and community; core societal value opposite of masculinity

guanxi (p. 150) (pronounced *gawn-shi*) Chinese term for a way of doing business in which parties must first invest time and resources in getting to know one another and becoming comfortable with one another before consummating any important deal

individualism (p. 147) extent to which people are expected to take care of themselves and their immediate families

long-term orientation (p. 149) values consistent with Confucian philosophy and a prioritization of future rewards over short-term benefits

masculinity (p. 148) role distinction within a group that values assertiveness and control; core societal value opposite of femininity

metric equivalence (p. 157) statistical tests used to validate the way people use numbers to represent quantities across cultures

modelling (p. 154) process of imitating others' behaviour; a form of observational learning

nonverbal communication (p. 157) information passed through some nonverbal act

power distance (p. 148) extent to which authority and privileges are divided among different groups within society and the extent to which these facts of life are accepted by the people within the society

When the behaviour is consistent with cultural norms, the rewards the consumer receives helps shape his or her overall pattern of behaviour.

8-4

List and describe the fundamental elements of verbal and nonverbal communication. Verbal communication refers to the transfer of information

Nonverbal Communication Affects the Message Comprehended

through the literal spoken or written word. One of the key elements of verbal communication is comprehension across languages. When communicating with consumers in a different language, the process of translation–back translation is important to make sure the intended message is really being communicated. Nonverbal communication refers to elements such as body language, etiquette, symbols, and the meaning of time and space, as well as the way a consumer signals agreement. High-context cultures depend heavily on nonverbal communication.

8-5

Discuss current emerging consumer markets and scan for opportunities. New consumer markets have emerged over the previous few years. The fall of communism, advances in technology, and the desire for firms to obtain low-cost labour have enabled consumers in places like China and Russia to participate more fully in the free-market economy. In fact, the acronym BRIC refers to the combined market power of consumers in Brazil, Russia, India, and China. Firms can have success marketing to these emerging consumer markets, but they must first understand each culture's CSV profile and the most effective way to communicate with consumers in those markets.

purchasing power parity (PPP) (p. 161) total size of the consumer market in each country in terms of total buying power

quartet of institutions (p. 153) four groups responsible for communicating the CSV through both formal and informal processes from one generation to another: family, school, church, and media

renquing (p. 150) the idea that favours given to another are reciprocal and must be returned

role expectations (p. 145) the specific expectations that are associated with each type of person within a culture or society

socialization (p. 152) learning through observation of and the active processing of information about lived, everyday experience

tradition (p. 146) customs and accepted ways of everyday behaviour in a given culture

translational equivalence (p. 156) two phrases share the same precise meaning in two different cultures

uncertainty avoidance (p. 149) extent to which a culture is uncomfortable with things that are ambiguous or unknown

verbal communication (p. 156) transfer of information through either the literal spoken or written word

KEY CONCEPTS

9-1

Apply the concept of microculture as it influences consumer behaviour. A microculture is a group of people who share similar values and tastes that are subsumed within a larger culture. Both culture and microculture are important influencers of consumer behaviour. Ultimately, they explain the habits and idiosyncrasies of all groups of consumers. Consumers move in and out of microcultures and their behaviour is strongly influenced by membership. Microcultures bring sets of role expectations for their members that provide signals as to the behaviours that one should perform to belong to the group. Microculture membership changes the value of things. What is valued by one microculture may not be valued at all by another.

The Hierarchical Nature of Culture and Microculture

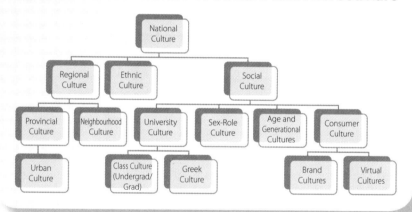

9-2

Know the major Canadian microcultural groups. There are many microcultural groups in Canada. Marketers can divide Canada into consumer groups along a number of these dimensions as market segmentation strategies. This chapter discusses the following microcultures that are found in the Canadian culture: regional, sex role, age-based, generation, religious, ethnic, income/social class, and street microcultures.

9-3

Realize that microculture is not a uniquely Canadian phenomenon. Although Canada's multicultural approach to ethnic diversity differentiates it from many other countries in the world, it is clear that microcultures are not only a Canadian phenomenon. Rather, they exist throughout the world. Countries worldwide have many bases around which

KEY TERMS

age-based microculture (p. 168) people of the same age end up sharing many of the same values and develop similar consumer preferences

cohort (p. 170) a group of people who have lived the same major experiences in their life

demographic analysis (p. 180) a profile of a consumer group based on their demographics

demographics (p. 180) relatively tangible human characteristics that describe consumers

divergence (p. 166) situation in which consumers choose membership in microcultures in an effort to stand out or define themselves from the crowd

geodemographics (p. 180) study of people based on the fact that people with similar demographics tend to live close to one another

habitus (p. 177) mental and cognitive structures through which individuals perceive the world based largely on their standing in a social class

homogamy (p. 177) the finding that most marriages comprise people from similar classes

microculture (p. 164) a group of people who share similar values and tastes that are subsumed within a larger culture

role conflict (p. 165) a situation involving conflicting expectations based on cultural role expectations

sex roles (p. 166) societal expectations for men and women among members of a cultural group

social class (p. 177) a culturally defined group to which a consumer belongs based on resources like prestige, income, occupation, and education

social stratification (p. 178) the division of society into classes that have unequal access to scarce and valuable resources

status symbols (p. 178) products or objects that are used to signal one's place in society

stigmatization (p. 173) a situation in which a consumer is marked in some way that indicates their place in society

world teen culture (p. 168) speculation that teenagers around the world are more similar to each other than to people from other generations in the same culture

microcultures are formed, and nearly all countries exhibit at least some degree of diversity. Religious, age-based, generational, ethnic, income, and street microcultures exist in nearly all nations.

Similarities and Differences Among Teen Consumers

Favourite Brands	Similar Activities	Less Similar Choices
Coca-Cola	Listening to Music	Religious Ideas/Activities
McDonald's	Using Mobile Phone	Cosmetic Brands
Nike	Surfing the Internet	Political Ideas
Disney	Video Games	Equality of Sexes
Cadbury	Smoking	
Apple		

9-4

Perform a demographic analysis. Demographics refer to relatively tangible human characteristics that describe consumers. Demographics include characteristics such as age, ethnicity, sex, occupation, income, region, religion, and gender. Demographic variables are closely related to microcultures, and demographic analyses assist the researcher in gaining a better understanding of microcultures. The information obtained becomes even more valuable when it is combined with geodemographic information. One very important source for performing a demographic analysis is the Statistics Canada website.

9-5

Identify major cultural and demographic trends. Two of the biggest trends in Western countries are declining birth rates and increasing life expectancies. As a general statement, consumer affluence is growing in many parts of the world, particularly in North America, India, and China. At the same time, poverty remains a significant problem in many countries around the world.

Cultural and microcultural trends vary widely throughout the world. Growing cultural diversity has been witnessed throughout Europe, particularly with the growth of Islam. Cultural diversity has also increased in Canada, where one in five Canadians is expected to be foreign born by 2017—a higher proportion of the population than has been seen since the period between 1911 and 1931. These trends are important to our understanding of consumer behaviour and they do attract a great deal of attention from marketers.

CHAPTER REVIEW 10
Group and Interpersonal Influence

KEY CONCEPTS

10-1
Understand the different types of reference groups that influence consumers and how reference groups influence value perceptions. A number of different types of reference groups influence consumers. A primary group includes members who have frequent, direct contact. A secondary group has much less contact than a primary group, but these groups still influence consumer behaviour. A formal group is a group in which consumers officially become members. An informal group has no membership or application requirements and codes of conduct may be nonexistent. Most online social networking groups are informal and secondary. An aspirational group is a group in which a consumer desires to become a member. A dissociative group is a group that a consumer wants to avoid being perceived as belonging to. Belonging to groups can be quite valuable for consumers. The benefits associated with membership often outweigh the costs associated with membership. Also, hedonic value is derived from belonging to groups and from participating in group activities. Group members receive economic, or utilitarian, value from membership as well.

10-2
Describe the various types of social power that reference groups exert on members. Social power refers to the ability of an individual or a group to alter the actions of others. Social power is divided into specific categories that include referent power, legitimate power, expert power, reward power, and coercive power. Referent power exists when a consumer wishes to model his or her behaviours after a group or another person. Here, the consumer imitates the behaviours and attitudes of the referent others because of liking or admiration for that person or group of people. Legitimate power is exerted when one's position in a group determines the level of social power that can be held over group members. Expert power refers to the ability of a group or individual to influence a consumer due to knowledge of, or experience with, a specific subject matter. Reward power exists when groups are able to reward members for compliance with expectations. Finally, coercive power exists when groups have the ability to sanction or punish members for noncompliance with group expectations.

10-3
Comprehend the difference between informational, utilitarian, and value-expressive reference group influence. The informational influence of groups refers to the ways in which consumers use the behaviours and attitudes of reference groups as information for making their own decisions. The utilitarian influence of groups refers to the ways in which consumers conform to group expectations in order to receive a reward or avoid punishment. The value-expressive influence of groups refers to the ways in which consumers internalize a group's values or the extent to which consumers join groups in order to express their own closely held values and beliefs.

KEY TERMS

apps (p. 193) mobile application software that runs on devices like smartphones, tablets, and other computer-based tools

aspirational group (p. 188) group of which a consumer desires to become a member

attention to social comparison information (ATSCI) (p. 195) individual difference variable that assesses the extent to which a consumer is concerned about how other people react to his or her behaviour

boomerang kids (p. 202) young adults, aged 18–34, who move back home with their parents after they graduate from postsecondary education

brand community (p. 188) group of consumers who develop relationships based on shared interests or product usage

buzz marketing (p. 198) marketing efforts that focus on generating excitement among consumers and that are spread from consumer to consumer

conformity (p. 189) result of group influence in which an individual yields to the attitudes and behaviours of others

connected self-schema (p. 195) self-conceptualization of the extent to which a consumer perceives himself as being an integral part of a group

consumer socialization (p. 205) the process through which young consumers develop attitudes and learn skills that help them function in the marketplace

diffusion process (p. 199) way in which new products are adopted and spread throughout a marketplace

dissociative group (p. 189) group to which a consumer does not want to belong

extended family (p. 200) three or more generations of family members

family household (p. 200) at least two people who are related by

NEL

WWW.NELSON.COM/STUDENT

CHAPTER REVIEW 10

blood or marriage who occupy a housing unit

formal group (p. 188) group in which a consumer officially becomes a member

group influence (p. 186) ways in which group members influence attitudes, behaviours, and opinions of others within the group

guerrilla marketing (p. 198) marketing of a product using unconventional means

household decision making (p. 200) process by which decisions are made in household units

household life cycle (HLC) (p. 202) segmentation technique that acknowledges that changes in family composition and income alter household demand for products and services

informal group (p. 188) group that has no membership or application requirements and that may have no code of conduct

informational influence (p. 191) ways in which a consumer uses the behaviours and attitudes of reference groups as information for making personal decisions

market maven (p. 199) consumer who spreads information about all types of products and services that are available in the marketplace

nuclear family (p. 200) a mother, a father, and a set of siblings

opinion leader (p. 199) consumer who has a great deal of influence on the behaviour of others relating to product adoption and purchase

peer pressure (p. 189) extent to which group members feel pressure to behave in accordance with group expectations

primary group (p. 187) group that includes members who have frequent, direct contact with one another

reference group (p. 186) individuals who have significant relevance for a consumer and who have an impact on the consumer's evaluations, aspirations, and behaviour

10-4

Understand the importance of word-of-mouth communications in consumer behaviour. Word-of-mouth (WOM) refers to information about products, services, and experiences that is transmitted from consumer to consumer. WOM is influential because consumers tend to believe other consumers more than they believe advertisements and explicit marketing messages from companies. Consumers tend to place more emphasis on negative WOM than on positive WOM. It is also important because, in today's information age, WOM can be spread to millions of consumers very easily on the Internet via social networking websites or emailing, or even through texting.

10-5

Comprehend the role of household influence in consumer behaviour. The family unit is a very important primary reference group for consumers. Family members typically have a great deal of influence over one another's attitudes, thoughts, and behaviours. This is also true of "nonfamily" households. Because household members often have frequent, close contact with one another, they have a great deal of influence on the behaviour of one another. The role that each household member plays in the household decision-making process depends on the beliefs and sex orientation of each individual household.

sandwich generation (p. 203) consumers who must take care of both their own children and their aging parents

secondary group (p. 188) group whose members have less frequent contact than that found in a primary group

separated self-schema (p. 195) self-conceptualization of the extent to which a consumer perceives herself as distinct and separate from others

sex role orientation (SRO) (p. 204) family's set of beliefs regarding the ways in which household decisions are reached

social media (p. 193) media through which communication occurs

social networks (p. 193) consumers connecting with each other based on interests, associations, or goals

social networking website (p. 193) website that facilitates online social networking

social power (p. 189) ability of an individual or a group to alter the actions of others

stealth marketing (p. 198) guerrilla marketing tactic in which consumers do not realize that they are being targeted for a marketing message

surrogate consumer (p. 199) consumer who is hired by another to provide input into a purchase decision

susceptibility to interpersonal influence (p. 194) individual difference variable that assesses a consumer's need to enhance his or her image with others by acquiring and using products, conforming to the expectations of others, and learning about products by observing others

utilitarian influence (p. 191) ways in which a consumer conforms to group expectations in order to receive a reward or avoid punishment

value-expressive influence (p. 191) ways in which consumers internalize a group's values or the extent to which consumers join groups to express their own closely held values and beliefs

viral marketing (p. 198) marketing method that uses online technologies to facilitate WOM by having consumers spread messages through their online conversations

word-of-mouth (WOM) (p. 196) information about products, services, and experiences that is transmitted from consumer to consumer

NEL

KEY CONCEPTS

11-1

Understand how value varies with situations. The value a consumer obtains from a purchase or consumption act varies based on the context in which the act takes place. These contextual effects are known as situational influences, meaning effects independent of enduring consumer, brand, or product characteristics. Contextual effects can involve things related to time, place, or antecedent conditions. They also can affect consumer information processing, shopping, including purchase situations, and actual consumption. Situational influences change the desirability of consuming things and therefore change the value of these things. Situational influences can also override consumer brand preferences in many product categories.

11-2

Know the different ways in which time affects consumer behaviour. The term *temporal factors* refers to situational characteristics related to time. Time can affect consumer behaviour by creating time pressure. A consumer facing time pressure may not be able to process information related to making the best choice. The time of year can affect consumer behaviour through seasonality. Cyclical patterns of consumption exist for many products, such as champagne, that are predominantly sold during the holiday times. The time of day can also influence consumption. Time of day affects the consumption context significantly. For instance, most consumers do not want gumbo for breakfast. But for lunch or dinner, gumbo is great! The circadian rhythm concept explains how a person's body reacts to time-of-day effects.

11-3

Analyze shopping as a consumer activity using the different categories of shopping activities. Shopping can be defined as the set of value-producing consumer activities that directly increase the likelihood that something will be purchased. Shopping activities are very strongly shaped by the sense of place and therefore they are highly relevant to understanding how situations influence consumption. Shopping activities can be divided into four categories: acquisitional, epistemic, experiential, and impulsive. Each category is associated with a different orientation toward buying things and receiving shopping value.

11-4

Distinguish the concepts of unplanned, impulse, and compulsive consumer behaviour. The line between unplanned and impulse is not always clear because some unplanned acts are impulsive and many impulsive acts are unplanned. Simple unplanned purchases usually lack any real emotional involvement or significant amounts of self-gratification. Additionally, unplanned purchases often involve only minimal negative consequences and thus fail to really qualify as having negative consequences at all. Compulsive acts are distinguished from impulsive acts by the relative degree of harmfulness

KEY TERMS

acquisitional shopping (p. 214) activities oriented toward a specific, intended purchase or purchases

action-oriented (p. 218) consumers with a high capacity to self-regulate their behaviour

advertiming (p 212) ad buys that include a schedule that runs the advertisement primarily at times when customers will be most receptive to the message

affective quality (p. 215) retail positioning that emphasizes a unique environment, exciting decor, friendly employees, and, in general, the feelings experienced in a retail place

antecedent conditions (p. 226) situational characteristics that a consumer brings to a particular information processing, purchase, or consumption environment

atmospherics (p. 220) emotional nature of an environment or the feelings created by the total aura of physical attributes that comprise a physical environment

background music (p. 222) music played below the audible threshold that would make it the centre of attention

circadian cycle rhythm (p. 211) level of energy of the human body that varies with the time of day

congruity (p. 221) how consistent the elements of an environment are with one another

consumer self-regulation (p. 218) tendency for consumers to inhibit outside, or situational, influences from interfering with shopping intentions

crowding (p. 225) density of people and objects within a given space

discretionary (spare) time (p. 210) the days, hours, or minutes that are not required for some compulsory and time-consuming activity

epistemic shopping (p. 214) activities oriented toward acquiring knowledge about products

experiential shopping (p. 214) recreationally oriented activities designed to provide interest, excitement, relaxation, fun, social interaction, or some other desired feeling

fit (p. 221) how appropriate the elements of a given environment are

foreground music (p. 222) music that becomes the focal point of attention and can have strong effects on a consumer's willingness to approach or avoid an environment

functional quality (p. 215) retail positioning that emphasizes tangible things like a wide selection of goods, low prices, guarantees, and knowledgeable employees

hedonic shopping value (p. 215) worth of an activity because the time spent doing the activity itself is personally gratifying

impulsive consumption (p. 216) consumption acts characterized by spontaneity, a diminished regard for consequences, and a need for self-fulfillment

impulsive shopping (p. 214) spontaneous activities characterized by a diminished regard for consequences, spontaneity, and a desire for immediate self-fulfillment

impulsivity (p. 217) personality trait that represents how sensitive a consumer is to immediate rewards

mental budgeting (p. 227) memory accounting for recent spending

nonlinear effect (p. 225) a plot of the effect by the amount of crowding, which does not make a straight line

olfactory (p. 222) refers to humans' physical and psychological processing of smells

associated with them. Impulsive acts are relatively harmless and in fact can have significant positive outcomes in terms of a consumer's emotional well-being. Compulsive acts, however, are associated with a consumer whose behaviour is either self-detrimental or truly harmful to another consumer.

11-5

Use the concept of atmospherics to create value. A store's atmosphere can create value through facilitating either the task of shopping or the gratification of the shopping experience itself. Each retail or service place is characterized by a particular atmosphere. An atmosphere can be designed that greatly facilitates the shopping task. Convenience stores have redesigned their sales floors and taken out substantial numbers of product offerings. The result is that the consumer can complete the task of getting a needed product in less time. An atmosphere can also simply be more emotionally pleasant and therefore gratifying to be in. People make up a big part of the atmosphere and create social factors. One result is social comparison. Shopping companions influence shopping outcomes.

11-6

Understand what is meant by antecedent conditions. Antecedent conditions refer to situational characteristics that a consumer brings to a particular information processing, purchase, or consumption environment. Antecedent conditions include things like economic resources, orientation, mood, and other emotional perceptions such as fear. They can shape the value in a situation by framing the events that take place. A consumer in a good mood, for example, tends to look at things more favourably than a consumer in a bad mood.

outshopping (p. 214) shopping in a city or town to which consumers must travel rather than in their own hometown

personal shopping value (PSV) (p. 215) overall subjective worth of a shopping activity considering all associated costs and benefits

retail personality (p. 216) way a retail store is defined in the mind of a shopper based on the combination of functional and affective qualities

seasonality (p. 211) regularly occurring conditions that vary with the time of year

shopping (p. 212) set of value-producing consumer activities that directly increase the likelihood that something will be purchased

smart agent software (p. 213) software capable of learning an Internet user's preferences and automatically searching out information in selected websites and then distributing it

social comparison (p. 226) a naturally occurring mental personal comparison of the self with a target individual within the environment

source attractiveness (p. 225) the degree to which a source's physical appearance matches a prototype for beauty and elicits a favourable or desirous response

state-oriented (p. 218) consumers with a low capacity to self-regulate their behaviour

temporal factors (p. 210) situational characteristics related to time

time pressure (p. 210) urgency to act based on some real or self-imposed deadline

unplanned shopping (p. 216) shopping activity that shares some, but not all, characteristics of truly impulsive consumer behaviour, being characterized by situational memory, a utilitarian orientation, and feelings of spontaneity

utilitarian shopping value (p. 215) worth obtained because some shopping task or job is completed successfully

KEY CONCEPTS

12-1

Understand the activities involved in the consumer decision-making process. The consumer decision-making process consists of five activities: (1) need recognition, (2) search for information, (3) evaluation of alternatives, (4) choice, and (5) postchoice evaluation. Consumers recognize needs when discrepancies are noted between actual and desired states. Consumers search for information from both internal and external sources. With internal search, consumers search their memories for appropriate solutions to problems. External searches consist of information-gathering activities that focus on friends, family, salespeople, advertising, and Internet-based information. Consumers evaluate alternatives based on the information that has been gathered and eventually make a decision.

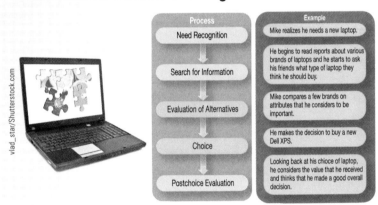

Consumer Decision-Making Process

Process	Example
Need Recognition	Mike realizes he needs a new laptop.
Search for Information	He begins to read reports about various brands of laptops and he starts to ask his friends what type of laptop they think he should buy.
Evaluation of Alternatives	Mike compares a few brands on attributes that he considers to be important.
Choice	He makes the decision to buy a new Dell XPS.
Postchoice Evaluation	Looking back at his choice of laptop, he considers the value that he received and thinks that he made a good overall decision.

vlad_star/Shutterstock.com

12-2

Describe the three major decision-making research perspectives. The three major decision-making research perspectives are the rational decision-making perspective, the experiential decision-making perspective, and the behavioural influence decision-making perspective. The rational perspective assumes that consumers diligently gather information about purchases, carefully compare various brands of products on salient attributes, and make informed decisions regarding what brand to buy. This approach centres around the assumption that human beings are rational creatures who are careful with their decision making and behaviour. The experiential decision-making perspective assumes that consumers often make purchases and reach decisions based on the affect, or feeling, attached to the product or behaviour under consideration. The behavioural influence-making perspective assumes that consumer decisions are learned responses to environmental influences.

KEY TERMS

actual state (p. 238) consumer's perceived current state

awareness set (p. 240) set of alternatives of which a consumer is aware

behavioural influence decision-making perspective (p. 235) assumes many consumer decisions are actually learned responses to environmental influences

brand inertia (p. 236) what occurs when a consumer simply buys a product repeatedly without any real attachment

brand loyalty (p. 236) deeply held commitment to rebuy a product or service regardless of situational influences that could lead to switching behaviour

consideration set (p. 240) alternatives that are considered acceptable for further consideration in decision making

consumer search behaviour (p. 239) behaviours that consumers engage in as they seek information that can be used to resolve a problem

desired state (p. 238) perceived state for which a consumer strives

experiential decision-making perspective (p. 234) assumes consumers often make purchases and reach decisions based on the affect, or feeling, attached to the product or behaviour under consideration

extended decision making (p. 236) consumers move diligently through various problem-solving activities in search of the best information that will help them reach a decision

external search (p. 240) gathering of information from sources external to the consumer such as friends, family, salespeople, advertising, independent research reports, and the Internet

habitual decision making (p. 236) consumers generally do not seek information at all when a problem is recognized and select a product based on habit

inept set (p. 240) alternatives in the awareness set that are deemed to be unacceptable for further consideration

inert set (p. 240) alternatives in the awareness set about which consumers are indifferent or do not hold strong feelings

information overload (p. 239) situation in which consumers are presented with so much information that they cannot assimilate it all

internal search (p. 240) retrieval of knowledge stored in memory about products, services, and experiences

limited decision making (p. 236) consumers search very little for information and often reach decisions based largely on prior beliefs about products and their attributes

ongoing search (p. 239) search effort that is not necessarily focused on an upcoming purchase or decision but rather on staying up to date on the topic

perceived risk (p. 235) perception of the negative consequences that are likely to result from a course of action and the uncertainty of which course of action is best to take

prepurchase search (p. 239) search effort aimed at finding information to solve an immediate problem

price (p. 241) information that signals the amount of potential value contained in a product

quality (p. 241) perceived overall goodness or badness of some product

rational decision-making perspective (p. 234) assumes consumers diligently gather information about purchases, carefully compare various brands of products on salient attributes, and make informed decisions regarding what brand to buy

satisficing (p. 237) using decision-making shortcuts to arrive at satisfactory, rather than optimal, decisions

Perspectives on Consumer Decision Making

Perspective	Description	Example
Rational Perspective	Consumers are rational and they carefully arrive at decisions.	Aubrey carefully considers the attributes included with various car stereos.
Experiential Perspective	Decision making is often influenced by the feelings associated with consumption.	Devin goes rock climbing simply for the fun of it.
Behavioural Influence Perspective	Decisions are responses to environmental influences.	The soothing music in the store encourages Shelby to browse longer.

12-3

Explain the three major types of decision-making approaches.
Decision-making approaches can be classified into extended decision making, limited decision making, and habitual (or "routine") decision-making categories. With extended decision making, consumers search diligently for the best information that will help them reach a decision. They then assimilate the information that they have gathered and evaluate each alternative based on its potential to solve their problem. This process is usually lengthy and generally occurs when involvement is high and when there is a significant amount of purchase risk involved with the decision. With limited decision making, consumers spend little time searching for information and often reach decisions based largely on prior beliefs about products and their attributes. There is also little comparison between brands. Choice strategies are often based on simple decision rules that consumers develop. With habitual decision making, practically no information search takes place, and decisions are reached via habit.

12-4

Understand the importance of the consideration set in the decision-making process. The consideration set is valuable because brands are placed in the set as consumers proceed through the decision-making process. For this reason, marketers find it valuable to understand the consideration set of their customers. Although the total universe of alternatives available for potentially satisfying a need may be quite large, only a small fraction of these options are generally included in the consideration set.

Consideration Set

Universal Set → Awareness Set → Consideration Set / Inert Set / Inept Set

12-5

Understand the factors that influence the amount of search performed by consumers. Several factors influence the amount of search that consumers actually perform. Factors such as previous experience with a product, purchase involvement, perceived risk, time availability, attitudes toward shopping, personal factors, and situational pressures all have an impact on the information search effort.

search regret (p. 244) negative emotions that come from failed search processes

universal set (p. 240) total collection of all possible solutions to a consumer problem

KEY CONCEPTS

13-1

Understand the difference between evaluative criteria and determinant criteria. The attributes that consumers consider when evaluating alternative solutions to a problem are evaluative criteria. These criteria include features or benefits associated with a potential solution. Determinant criteria are the factors that have the biggest impact on actual consumer choice. Both evaluative and determinant criteria influence decision making.

13-2

Comprehend how value affects the evaluation of alternatives. Value is at the heart of the alternative evaluation process. Consumers seek benefits that are associated with a potential solution to a problem. Benefits come from the features or characteristics of the alternatives under consideration. From the value perspective, consumers seek solutions that will deliver benefits while minimizing associated costs.

13-3

Explain the importance of product categorization in the evaluation of alternatives process. Categorization is important because product categories provide the framework from which consumers evaluate alternative solutions to a problem. When new information about a viable alternative is presented, this information is compared to information that is stored as knowledge in a consumer's perceived product category. This information allows the consumer to make better inferences about the alternative solution.

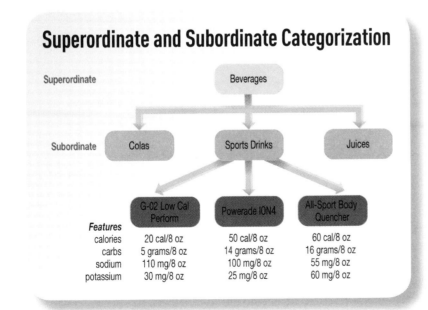

Superordinate and Subordinate Categorization

KEY TERMS

affect-based evaluation (p. 251) evaluative process wherein consumers evaluate products based on the overall feeling that is evoked by the alternative

attribute-based evaluation (p. 251) evaluative process wherein alternatives are evaluated across a set of attributes that are considered relevant to the purchase situation

attribute correlation (p. 255) perceived relationship between product features

benefit (p. 249) perceived favourable result derived from a particular feature

bounded rationality (p. 251) idea that consumers attempt to act rationally within their information-processing constraints

compensatory rule (p. 257) decision-making rule that allows consumers to select products that may perform poorly on one criterion by compensating for the poor performance on one attribute by good performance on another

conjoint analysis (p. 257) technique used to develop an understanding of the attributes that guide consumer preferences by having consumers compare product preferences across varying levels of evaluative criteria and expected utility

conjunctive rule (p. 258) noncompensatory decision rule where the option selected must surpass a minimum cutoff across all relevant attributes

determinant criteria (p. 250) criteria that are most carefully considered and directly related to the actual choice that is made

disjunctive rule (p. 258) noncompensatory decision rule where the option selected surpasses a relatively high cutoff point on any attribute

elimination-by-aspects (EBA) rule (p. 258) noncompensatory decision rule where the consumer begins evaluating options by first looking at the most important attribute and eliminating any option that does not meet a minimum cutoff point for that attribute and where subsequent evaluations proceed in order of importance until only one option remains

evaluative criteria (p. 249) attributes that consumers consider when reviewing alternative solutions to a problem

feature (p. 249) performance characteristic of an object

judgments (p. 254) mental assessments of the presence of attributes and the consequences associated with those attributes

lexicographic rule (p. 258) noncompensatory decision rule where the option selected is thought to perform best on the most important attribute

noncompensatory rule (p. 257) decision-making rule in which strict guidelines are set prior to selection and any option that does not meet the guidelines is eliminated from consideration

perceptual attributes (p. 253) attributes that are visually apparent and easily recognizable

product categories (p. 251) mental representations of stored knowledge about groups of products

signal (p. 253) attribute that consumers use to infer something about another attribute

underlying attributes (p. 253) attributes that are not readily apparent and can be learned only through experience or contact with the product

13-4

Distinguish between compensatory and noncompensatory rules that guide consumer choice. The attitude-toward-the-object model is a compensatory model. This type of model allows an alternative to be selected even if it performs poorly on a specific attribute. Noncompensatory models focus on strict guidelines that are set before alternative evaluation. The major noncompensatory rules are the conjunctive, disjunctive, lexicographic, and elimination-by-aspects rules. With the conjunctive rule, an option that is selected must surpass a minimum cutoff across all relevant attributes. The disjunctive rule is used when an option that surpasses a relatively high cutoff point on any attribute is selected. The lexicographic rule leads the consumer to select the option that performs best on the most important attribute. The elimination-by-aspects rule is used when the consumer begins evaluating options by first looking at the most important attribute and eliminating any option that does not meet a minimum cutoff point for that attribute. The process continues as the consumer considers the next most important attribute and so on, until only one option is left to be chosen.

Noncompensatory Decision Approaches

Attribute	Importance	Chevy Cruz Belief Ratings	Ford Fiesta Belief Ratings	Honda Fit Belief Ratings	Hyundai Accent Belief Ratings
Gas mileage	10	5	7	9	8
Low price	9	8	6	7	10
Styling	8	9	8	4	4
Warranty	5	4	8	9	8
Service	6	5	6	7	3
Handling	7	6	5	3	3

Note: Belief ratings are performance judgments scaled from 1 = very poor to 9 = very good. Importance ratings are scaled so that 10 = most important, 9 = next most important, and so on.

Source: Wright, Peter (1975), "Consumer Choice Strategies: Simplifying vs. Optimizing," *Journal of Marketing Research*, 12 (1): 60–67.

KEY CONCEPTS

14-1

Gain an appreciation of the link from consumption to value to satisfaction. Consumers receive value from marketing efforts through consumption. Consumers consume products, services, and experiences and receive value in return. The value that they receive helps create overall satisfaction, as consumers tend to be more satisfied with exchanges they find valuable. Meaning plays a key role in consumption and the meaning of products, which can change over different situations, transfers itself into the experience and adds value.

Consumption, Value, and Satisfaction

Satisfaction → Value → Loyalty

14-2

Discuss the relative importance of satisfaction and value in consumer behaviour. Many companies go out of their way to emphasize how hard they work to create customer satisfaction. Consumer satisfaction itself is a mild, positive emotional state resulting from a favourable appraisal of a consumption outcome—that is, a favourable satisfaction judgment. Satisfaction, in turn, correlates with a number of postconsumption behaviours such as word-of-mouth intentions, loyalty, and repeat purchase behaviour. Satisfaction and value relate to one another, but not perfectly. In fact, some marketers provide customers with low satisfaction but still do remarkably well in the marketplace because they provide high value. Walmart is perhaps one of the best companies to illustrate this phenomenon. For this reason, while satisfaction is important, value remains even more important as the key outcome for consumer behaviour.

14-3

Know that emotions other than satisfaction can affect postconsumption behaviour. Emotions other than satisfaction result from appraisals of consumption outcomes. Some, like anger, are both negative and much stronger in motivating behaviour following consumption. Others, like warmth, are controlling and can help build relationships. While satisfaction receives considerable attention, a fuller range of emotion is needed to fully account for consumption outcomes.

KEY TERMS

attribution theory (p. 277) theory that consumers look for the cause of particular consumption experiences when arriving at satisfaction judgments

authenticity (p. 268) being real and genuine and having a history or tradition

cognitive dissonance (p. 278) an uncomfortable feeling that occurs when a consumer has lingering doubts about a decision that has occurred

confirmatory bias (p. 275) tendency for expectations to guide performance perceptions

consumer dissatisfaction (p. 272) mild, negative affective reaction resulting from an unfavourable appraisal of a consumption outcome

consumer refuse (p. 280) any packaging that is no longer necessary for consumption to take place or, in some cases, the actual good that is no longer providing value to the consumer

consumer satisfaction (p. 271) mild, positive emotion resulting from a favourable appraisal of a consumption outcome

consumption frequency (p. 266) number of times a product is consumed

consumption process (p. 266) process in which consumers use the product, service, or experience that has been selected

desires (p. 276) level of a particular benefit that will lead to a valued end state

durable goods (p. 266) goods that are usually consumed over a long period of time

equity theory (p. 276) theory that people compare their own level of inputs and outcomes to those of another party in an exchange

expectancy/disconfirmation theory (p. 273) proposes that consumers use expectations as a benchmark against which performance perceptions are judged and this comparison is a primary basis for satisfaction/dissatisfaction

hope (p. 269) a fundamental emotion evoked by positive, anticipatory appraisals

left skewed (p. 279) when a disproportionate number of observations cluster toward the right end of a scale as when most people report satisfied or very satisfied

meaning transference (p. 268) process through which cultural meaning is transferred to a product and on to the consumer

negative disconfirmation (p. 273) according to the expectancy/disconfirmation approach, a perceived state wherein performance perceptions fall short of expectations

nondurable goods (p. 266) goods that are usually consumed quickly

positive disconfirmation (p. 273) according to the expectancy/disconfirmation approach, a perceived state wherein performance perceptions exceed expectations

self-perception theory (p. 275) theory that consumers are motivated to act in accordance with their attitudes and behaviours

service quality (p. 275) overall goodness or badness of a service experience, which is often measured by SERVQUAL

SERVQUAL (p. 276) instrument for measuring service quality that captures consumers' disconfirmation of service expectations

14-4

Use the expectancy/disconfirmation, equity, and attribution theory approaches to explain consumers' postconsumption reactions. The expectancy/disconfirmation model proposes that consumers use expectations as benchmarks against which performance perceptions are judged. When performance perceptions are more positive than what was expected, *positive disconfirmation* is said to occur. When performance perceptions fall below expectations, *negative disconfirmation* occurs. The expectancy disconfirmation approach remains the dominant theory of viewing satisfaction processes today.

Equity theory proposes that consumers consider the fairness of transactions by comparing their own outcomes and inputs to the outcomes and inputs of another party in the transaction. As long as the ratios of outcomes to inputs of each party are approximately equal or favour the consumer, satisfaction is likely to result. Attribution theory proposes that consumers consider the cause of events when making satisfaction judgments. When consumers make external attributions, they tend to be more dissatisfied with unpleasant experiences than when they make internal attributions. Taken together, disconfirmation, attributions, and equity judgments make up the primary cognitive bases for consumer satisfaction/dissatisfaction.

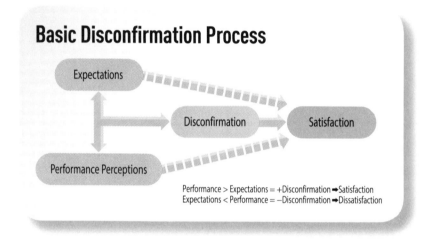

Basic Disconfirmation Process

Performance > Expectations = +Disconfirmation ➡ Satisfaction
Expectations < Performance = −Disconfirmation ➡ Dissatisfaction

14-5

Understand problems with commonly applied satisfaction measures. Marketers often express frustration with measuring satisfaction because the results may not be as useful or diagnostic as they may have hoped. One problem is that the typical ways of measuring, such as a four-item check box, end up providing very little information because consumers overwhelmingly report satisfaction. The result is left-skewed data, in this instance meaning that the bulk of consumers have indicated that they are satisfied or very satisfied. A better way of measuring satisfaction is to ask the question several different ways with at least some of those ways providing a wider range of possible responses.

14-6

Describe some ways in which consumers dispose of refuse. Disposal represents the final process in consumption. In this stage of the consumption process, consumers either permanently or temporarily get rid of products. There are many alternatives available to consumers to do this, including trashing, recycling, trading, donating, or reselling.

KEY CONCEPTS

15-1
List and define the behavioural outcomes of consumption.
Complaining behaviour occurs when a consumer actively seeks out someone to share an opinion with regarding a negative consumption event. WOM (word-of-mouth) behaviour occurs when a consumer decides to complain or state an opinion publicly to other consumers about something that happened during a consumption experience with a specific company. When negative WOM reaches a large scale, such as when public media get involved, negative WOM becomes negative publicity. Switching behaviour refers to times when a consumer chooses a competing choice, rather than repeating the previous purchase behaviour in a given product category. Consumers can also exhibit loyalty-related behaviours. Loyal consumers tend to repeat consumption behaviour.

15-2
Know why consumers complain and the ramifications of complaining behaviour for a marketing firm. Emotions influence whether a consumer complains. Negative approach emotions (such as anger) are more likely to precede complaining behaviour than are avoidance emotions (such as disgust) or even milder negative emotions (such as dissatisfaction). Complaining should actually be encouraged because when a customer complains, the firm has a chance to recover and convert the complaining customer into a satisfied customer. Aside from this, complaints are an extremely valuable source of feedback for improving the product offering. In the extreme, though, complaining can go beyond verbal behaviour to revenge-oriented behaviours.

The Complainer Versus the Noncomplainer and Negative Word-of-Mouth

- More likely to become a satisfied customer
- More likely to return
- Tells others when company responds poorly
- Valuable source of information

- Unlikely to return
- May well tell others about experience
- Can become a satisfied customer if firm can take pre-emptive action despite the lack of a complaint

isabel engelmann/Shutterstock.com; Marcio Eugenio/Shutterstock.com

KEY TERMS

anti-loyal consumers (p. 296) consumers who will do everything possible to avoid doing business with a particular marketer

competitive intensity (p. 292) number of firms competing for business within a specific category

complaining behaviour (p. 286) action that occurs when a consumer actively seeks out someone to share an opinion with regarding a negative consumption event

consumer inertia (p. 294) situation in which a consumer tends to continue a pattern of behaviour until some stronger force motivates him or her to change

customer commitment (p. 294) sense of attachment, dedication, and identification

customer share (p. 293) portion of resources allocated to one brand from the set of competing brands

financial switching costs (p. 291) total economic resources that must be spent or invested as a consumer learns how to obtain value from a new product choice

loyalty card/program (p. 294) device that keeps track of the amount of purchasing a consumer has had with a given marketer

negative public publicity (p. 288) action that occurs when negative WOM spreads on a relatively large scale, possibly even involving media coverage

negative word-of-mouth (negative WOM) (p. 287) action that takes place when consumers pass on negative information about a company from one to another

CHAPTER REVIEW 15

positive word-of-mouth (positive WOM) (p. 288) action that occurs when consumers spread information from one to another about positive consumption experiences with companies

procedural justice (p. 284) the extent that consumers believe the processes involved in processing a transaction and handling any complaints are fair

procedural switching costs (p. 291) lost time and extended effort spent in learning ways of using some product offering

rancorous revenge (p. 287) when a consumer yells, insults and/ or makes a public scene in an effort to harm the business in response to an unsatisfactory experience

relational switching cost (p. 291) emotional and psychological consequences of changing from one brand/retailer/service provider to another

retaliatory revenge (p. 287) when a consumer becomes violent with employees and/or tries to vandalize a business in response to an unsatisfactory experience

share of wallet (p. 293) customer share

switching (p. 290) times when a consumer chooses a competing choice, rather than the previously purchased choice, on the next purchase occasion

switching costs (p. 291) costs associated with changing from one choice (brand/retailer/service provider) to another

15-3

Use the concept of switching costs to understand why consumers do or do not repeat purchase behaviour. Switching costs involve the cost of changing from one brand/retailer/service provider to another. Switching costs can be procedural, financial, or relational, and any of these can motivate a consumer to continue making the same purchase decisions as in the past. This can occur even if the consumer is dissatisfied with this behaviour. When switching costs are high and few competitors are available to a consumer, he or she can end up feeling captive and feel forced to continue to do business with a company even when he or she believes service is bad and feels dissatisfied. Some types of procedural switching costs in particular, such as loyalty cards or incompatible features, can alienate consumers.

Vulnerability to Defections Based on CS/D

Customers Are Relatively:	High Competitive Intensity		Low Competitive Intensity	
	Switching Costs		Switching Costs	
	Low	High	Low	High
Satisfied	Vulnerable	Low vulnerability	Low vulnerability	No vulnerability
Dissatisfied	High vulnerabilty	Vulnerable	Vulnerable	Low vulnerability

15-4

Describe each component of true consumer loyalty. True consumer loyalty is more than just repeated behaviour. Consumer loyalty can be described behaviourally by the concept of customer share, sometimes known as share of wallet. This is the percent of resources allocated to one marketer from a set of competitors. Over time, consumers may also begin to identify strongly with a brand and develop customer commitment. A committed customer will go out of his or her way and even pay more to continue doing business with a preferred brand, retailer, or service provider.

15-5

Understand the role that value plays in shaping loyalty and building consumer relationships. Value is the result of consumption, and as such plays a key role in determining how the consumer behaves following consumption. For functional goods and services, such as banking or auto repair, utilitarian value is particularly important in bringing consumers back and creating loyalty. For experiential goods and services, such as fine dining, hedonic value is relatively important in bringing consumers back and creating loyalty.

KEY CONCEPTS

16-1

Understand the consumer misbehaviour phenomenon and how it affects the exchange process. Consumer misbehaviour does indeed affect the exchange process. For fair exchanges to occur, the consumer, the marketer, and other consumers must trust each another. Abusive or threatening consumers can harm employees, other consumers, and even themselves. Consumers who misbehave also cause monetary harm to the entire marketing system. Insurance costs escalate, prices of consumer products soar, employees must be counselled, and new technologies must be added to retail outlets, all because of consumer misbehaviour. Computer-mediated misbehaviour also causes disruptions in electronic commerce.

16-2

Distinguish between consumer misbehaviour and consumer problem behaviour. Consumer misbehaviour can be distinguished from consumer problem behaviour in terms of self-control. In most situations, a consumer can control misbehaviour; however, a consumer will experience great difficulty controlling problem behaviour. This is particularly the case for addictive consumer behaviour when a consumer becomes physically dependent on the consumption of a product.

16-3

Discuss the interplay between marketing ethics and consumerism within the marketing concept. Marketing ethics are societal and professional standards of right and fair practices that are expected of marketing managers. Marketing programs must be planned in ways that adhere to marketing ethics. Most firms have explicitly stated rules and codes of conduct for their employees and their activities in the marketplace. Most professional organizations also have these codes. These ethics provide a framework from which marketing decisions can be made.

16-4

Comprehend the role of corporate social responsibility as it relates to CB. It is important for businesses today to focus on "doing well by doing good." Being socially responsible is one way in which businesses attempt to do well by doing the right things. Corporate social responsibility refers to an organization's activities and status related to its societal obligations. Due to increased pressure from various consumer and media groups, companies are finding that they must be socially responsible with their marketing programs.

16-5

Understand consumer protection, privacy, and the regulation of marketing activities. Many federal, provincial, and municipal laws, by-laws, and regulations have been enacted to protect consumers from unsafe products and marketer misbehaviour. At the federal level, the relevant agencies

KEY TERMS

addictive consumption (p. 309) physiological dependency on the consumption of a consumer product

binge drinking (p. 310) consumption of five or more drinks in a single drinking session for men and four or more drinks for women

binge eating (p. 309) consumption of large amounts of food while feeling a general loss of control over food intake

compulsive buying (p. 309) chronic, repetitive purchasing that is a response to negative events or feelings

compulsive consumption (p. 309) repetitive, excessive, and purposeful consumer behaviours that are performed as a response to tension, anxiety, or obtrusive thoughts

compulsive shopping (p. 309) repetitive shopping behaviours that are a response to negative events or feelings

consumer misbehaviour (p. 303) behaviours that are in some way unethical and that potentially harm the self or others.

consumer problem behaviour (p. 306) consumer behaviour that is deemed to be unacceptable but that is seemingly beyond the control of the consumer

consumerism (p. 311) activities of various groups to voice concern for, and to protect, basic consumer rights

contractualism (p. 305) beliefs about the violation of written (or unwritten) laws

corporate social responsibility (p. 314) an organization's activities and status related to its societal obligations

customer orientation (p. 319) practice of using sales techniques that focus on customer needs

deceptive advertising (p. 317) message that omits information that is important in influencing a consumer's buying behaviour and is likely to mislead consumers acting "reasonably"

deficient products (p. 312) products that have little or no potential to create value of any type

deontological evaluations (p. 305) evaluations regarding the inherent rightness or wrongness of specific actions

desirable products (p. 312) products that deliver high utilitarian and hedonic value and that benefit both consumers and society in the long run

door-in-the-face technique (p. 319) ingratiation technique used in personal selling in which a salesperson begins with a major request and then follows with a series of smaller requests

even-a-penny-will-help technique (p. 319) ingratiation technique in which a marketing message suggests that even the smallest donation, such as a penny or a dollar, will help a cause

express consent (p. 316) unequivocal opt-in consent from the recipient for a stated communication purpose, which does not require any inference on the part of the organization

foot-in-the-door technique (p. 319) ingratiation technique used in personal selling in which a salesperson begins with a small request and slowly leads up to one major request

"I'm working for you!" technique (p. 319) technique used by salespeople to create the perception that they are working as hard as possible to close a sale when they really are not doing so

implied consent (p. 316) consent that may be reasonably inferred from the action or inaction of the individual

include Health Canada, Industry Canada, Transport Canada, the Competition Bureau of Canada, Canadian Radio-television and Telecommunications Commission, the Privacy Commissioner of Canada, and the Canadian Food Inspection Agency. Other groups such as the Better Business Bureau, Canadian Association of Broadcasters, Concerned Children's Advertisers, the Public Interest Advocacy Centre, Canadian Marketing Association, and the Association of Canadian Advertisers also play an important role in monitoring and enforcing the country's laws and regulations. Although these organizations work diligently to ensure a fair and safe marketplace for consumers across a variety of different industries, it is ultimately the responsibility of managers to act ethically and in accordance with the law. Of course, that does not always happen. As a result, government plays a critical role in protecting consumers and their privacy.

16-6

Comprehend the major areas of criticism to which marketers are subjected. Several issues in marketing receive criticism from various groups. Issues such as deceptive advertising, marketing to children, marketing unsafe products, planning the obsolescence of current products, using manipulative sales tactics, and stealth marketing campaigns are all considered questionable by various groups.

marketing concept (p. 311) statement that a firm should focus on consumer needs as a means of achieving long-term success

marketing ethics (p. 311) societal and professional standards of right and fair practices that are expected of marketing managers as they develop and implement marketing strategies

moral beliefs (p. 304) beliefs about the perceived ethicality or morality of behaviours

moral equity (p. 305) beliefs regarding an act's fairness or justness

morals (p. 314) personal standards and beliefs used to guide individual action

negative consent (p. 316) the organization assumes it has consent unless the individual takes action to opt out or deny consent

planned obsolescence (p. 318) act of planning the premature obsolescence of product models that perform adequately

pleasing products (p. 312) products that provide hedonic value for consumers but may be harmful in the long run

problem gambling (p. 310) obsession over the thought of gambling and the loss of control over gambling behaviour and its consequences

relativism (p. 305) beliefs about the social acceptability of an act in a culture

sales orientation (p. 319) practice of using sales techniques that are aimed at satisfying the salesperson's own needs and motives for short-term sales success

salutary products (p. 312) products that are good for both consumers and society in the long run and that provide high utilitarian value, but no hedonic value

societal marketing concept (p. 315) marketing concept that marketers should consider not only the wants and needs of consumers but also the needs of society

teleological evaluations (p. 305) consumers' assessment of the goodness or badness of the consequences of actions